W9-ARU-059

WEBSTER'S II
New Riverside
Desk Quotations

by
James B Simpson

Houghton Mifflin Company
Boston   New York   London

Library of Congress Cataloging-in-Publication Data

Simpson, James Beasley.
 Webster's II new Riverside desk quotations / [compiled] by James
B. Simpson.
  p. cm.
 Includes index.
 ISBN 0-395-62024-4. — ISBN 0-395-62025-2 (deluxe)
 1. Quotations, English. I. Title. II. Title: Webster's 2 new
Riverside desk quotations.
PN6081.S475 1992
082—dc20   91-43811
                                                                         CIP

Manufactured in the United States of America

To the quotable spokespersons of our times,
especially Russell Baker, Dan Boorstin, Jimmy Breslin,
Francis X Clines, Alistair Cooke, William Manchester,
V S Pritchett, Roger Rosenblatt, and William Safire

Contents

Preface

Webster's II New Riverside Desk Quotations is the first compilation of its kind to be devoted exclusively to memorable utterances made during the years since 1950. Over 6,000 quotations have been specially chosen to enable you to inject into your written and spoken communications an element of flair that might not be easily achievable without this handy reference.

As the educator Clara Park once said, "Creative thinking of any kind requires more than just knowing where to look things up; you have to know that they're there before you know you need them." So browse through this volume and you will find a lively collection of bons mots, witticisms, epigrams, and profundities from nearly 4,000 people—the famous and the infamous, the renowned and the obscure. In *Webster's II New Riverside Desk Quotations* you will find the articulate, often rambunctious voices of people who speak for our time, such as Ted Turner, Lee Iacocca, Malcolm Forbes, H L Hunt, Bill Paley, T Boone Pickens, Charles Revson, Donald Trump, An Wang, Edgar Bronfman, Woody Allen, Russell Baker, Mark Russell, Coretta Scott King, Tallulah Bankhead, Sandra Day O'Connor, Bette Midler, Margaret Atwood, Margaret Thatcher, Helen Gurley Brown, and many others.

If you have ever looked for an effective line or two for use in a speech, report, memorandum, or other presentation, consider these examples and consult *Webster's II New Riverside Desk Quotations* in order to find out Who Said What:

The conventional definition of management is getting work done through people, but real management is developing people through work.

To turn $100 into $110 is work. To turn $100 million into $110 million is inevitable.

Problems are only opportunities in work clothes.

It is much more difficult to measure nonperformance than performance.

The quotations in *Webster's II New Riverside Desk Quotations* are presented in alphabetical order by source, divided into three major sections, 25 subsections, and 54 subcategories, all clearly listed in the Contents. Full references and attributions are given in order to place the quotations in a meaningful context. Everything you might need is here—words from business, law and government; words from sports, the media, and medicine; and much more. Two indexes, one by sources, the other by subjects and key lines, afford you easy and quick access to just the quotations you seek.

Sander A. Flaum, President and Chief Executive Officer of Robert A. Becker, Inc., has said that " 'big ideas' are going to push America ahead in business and help us to outdistance the competition from abroad. ... Our inventiveness and foresightedness are going to be called on as never before." May this book be of assistance to you in wording, conveying, and defending your own big ideas and inventive proposals, and in engaging the interests of your audiences.

James B Simpson†

Explanatory Notes

The quotations in this book are divided into three major sections, 25 subsections, and 54 subcategories. This is an ideal arrangement for discovering quotations about a specific topic or for browsing in pleasurable search of an apt phrase. The Contents and the headings at the top of each page will direct you to the section you are seeking.

Author & Source Names

In each section and subsection, author and source names appear in alphabetical order before the quoted selections. Authors and sources frequently appear in more than one section. The Index by Sources lists each author and source in this book.

Brief identifications of authors are included where required. The identification usually reflects the status of the author at the time the words were written or spoken.

Order of Entries

Multiple quotations from an individual author or source within a particular section are in chronological order, with the earliest appearing first. If more than one quotation comes from a particular year, quotations from books precede those from monthly magazines and both precede quotations from weekly magazines.

Attributions

Attributions give the fullest possible information to help you pinpoint the quotation in its appropriate context or discover more in the original source. Judicial opinions and major speeches include, where possible, the date of the opinion or speech. Quotations recalled in obituaries include the actual date of death.

In attributions all months and years appear in shortened form. Day, month and year are given in inverted order; for example, 8 Jun 87.

The abbreviation *ib*, short for *ibidem*, "in the same place," is used when a quotation has the same author and attribution as the preceding one. It is also used when the author and publication are the same as in the preceding quotation, even though the date of publication is different.

Abbreviations

Standard abbreviations are used in identifications and attributions for military ranks (such as Adm for Admiral), for professional titles (such as Dr for Doctor), and for state names (such as CA for California). Months of the year and radio and television networks have also been abbreviated.

Indexes

Since this book is organized by categories, many quotations will be found by simply looking up the section you want in the list of Contents. To aid you further in searching out just the right quotation, there are two completely separate Indexes at the end of the book.

In the Index by Sources (starting on page 353) you will find an alphabetical list of the authors and sources of quotations. Page references will guide you to just the right places to find all the quotes from, for example, Ronald Reagan or "that elusive fellow," Anonymous.

In addition, a listing of particularly interesting topics will be found in the Index by Subjects and Key Lines (starting on page 379). In this Index references include both a page number and a quotation number.

Quotation numbers—beginning with 1 for the first complete quotation on each page—appear to the left of individual quotations.

A particularly helpful feature of the Index by Subjects and Key Lines is the inclusion of hundreds of well-known and not-so-well known phrases and lines from public officials, noted commentators, and humble folk. Many of these Key Lines will be instantly recognizable. In both Indexes *see* and *see also* cross-references have been included where needed.

The World

POLITICS & GOVERNMENT

Heads of State

IDI AMIN, President of Uganda

1 I am the hero of Africa.
Newsweek 12 Mar 73

CORAZON C AQUINO, President of the Philippines

2 They came out in the millions to show their
dogged support for the woman the dictatorship claimed it had defeated in the election.
As victor in election ending Ferdinand E Marcos's 20-year regime, NY *Times* 27 Feb 86

3 The nation was awakened by that deafening
shot.
Dedicating a marker at Manila Airport where
her husband Benigno was assassinated on August 21, 1983, *US News & World Report* 1 Sep 86

4 It is not I who have been consigned to the bedroom of history.
Alluding to remark by Ferdinand E Marcos that
a woman's place was in the bedroom, NY *Times*
1 Dec 86

CLEMENT ATTLEE, Prime Minister of Great Britain

5 Few thought he was even a starter.
There were many who thought themselves
smarter.
But he ended PM, CH and OM,
An earl and a Knight of the Garter.
On his political career, news summaries 8 Apr 56

VINCENT AURIOL, President of France

6 The work was killing me; they called me out of
bed at all hours of the night to receive resigna-
tions of prime ministers.
On leaving office, news summaries 1 Feb 54

BENJAMIN NNAMDI AZIKIWE, President of Nigeria

7 It is better we disintegrate in peace and not in
pieces.
Newsweek 8 Aug 66

BEATRIX, Queen of the Netherlands

8 I realize that much will be asked of me, yet I
am resolved to accept it as a great and splendid task.
On succeeding to the throne, NY *Times* 1 May
80

9 Nature is under control but not disturbed.
On opening a new Dutch sea barrier, *ib* 5 Oct 86

MENACHEM BEGIN, Prime Minister of Israel

10 Israel is still the only country in the world
against which there is a written document to
the effect that it must disappear.
On PLO charter, statement to the press, Washington DC, 22 Mar 78

DAVID BEN GURION, Prime Minister of Israel

11 In Israel, in order to be a realist you must believe in miracles.
CBS TV 5 Oct 56

12 The trebling of the population in this small
and impoverished country, flowing with milk
and honey but not with sufficient water, rich in
rocks and sand dunes but poor in natural resources and vital raw materials, has been no
easy task: Indeed, practical men, with their
eyes fixed upon things as they are, regarded it
as an empty and insubstantial utopian dream.
NY *Herald Tribune* 28 Apr 63

13 Israel has created a new image of the Jew in
the world—the image of a working and an intellectual people, of a people that can fight
with heroism.
Time 9 Jun 67

14 Ours is a country built more on people than on
territory. The Jews will come from everywhere: from France, from Russia, from America, from Yemen. ... Their faith is their
passport.
Recalled by Shimon Peres on 100th anniversary
of Ben Gurion's birth, NY *Times* 5 Oct 86

ZULFIKAR ALI BHUTTO, President of Pakistan

15 Pakistan was once called the most allied ally of
the United States. We are now the most nonallied.
NY *Times* 6 Jul 73

P W BOTHA, President of South Africa

1 Not only will we survive [sanctions], we will emerge stronger on the other side.
NY *Times* 28 Sep 86

LEONID I BREZHNEV, Soviet Premier

2 God will not forgive us if we fail.
To President Jimmy Carter at June 1979 summit meeting, recalled when Mikhail S Gorbachev also invoked the deity, NY *Times* 2 Sep 85

KOFI BUSIA, Prime Minister of Ghana

3 I don't like hypocrisy—even in international relations.
Interview 2 Feb 70

4 Diplomacy . . . means the art of nearly deceiving all your friends, but not quite deceiving all your enemies.
ib

JIMMY CARTER, 39th US President

5 You have given me a great responsibility: to stay close to you, to be worthy of you and to exemplify what you are.
Inaugural address 20 Jan 77

6 I personally think that he did violate the law, that he committed impeachable offenses. But I don't think that he thinks he did.
On former President Richard M Nixon, to reporters after press conference 12 May 77

7 The experience of democracy is like the experience of life itself—always changing, infinite in its variety, sometimes turbulent and all the more valuable for having been tested by adversity.
To Indian Parliament 2 Jan 78

8 If you fear making anyone mad, then you ultimately probe for the lowest common denominator of human achievement.
To Future Farmers of America, Kansas City, 9 Nov 78

9 Human rights is the soul of our foreign policy, because human rights is the very soul of our sense of nationhood.
At White House ceremony commemorating 30th anniversary of UN Declaration of Human Rights 6 Dec 78

10 For the first time in the history of our country the majority of our people believe that the next five years will be worse than the past five years.
Address to the nation 15 Jul 79

11 An act of terrorism totally outside the bounds of international law and diplomatic tradition. . . . a crisis [that] calls for firmness and restraint.
On embassy personnel taken hostage in Iran, 15 Nov 79

12 Aggression unopposed becomes a contagious disease.
On Soviet intervention in Afghanistan, address to the nation 4 Jan 80

13 America did not invent human rights. In a very real sense . . . human rights invented America.
Farewell address 14 Jan 81

14 For this generation, ours, life is nuclear survival, liberty is human rights, the pursuit of happiness is a planet whose resources are devoted to the physical and spiritual nourishment of its inhabitants.
ib

FIDEL CASTRO, President of Cuba

15 I began revolution with 82 men. If I had [to] do it again, I do it with 10 or 15 and absolute faith. It does not matter how small you are if you have faith and plan of action.
NY *Times* 22 Apr 59

KONSTANTIN U CHERNENKO, Soviet Premier

16 Those who try to give us advice on matters of human rights do nothing but provoke an ironic smile among us. We will not permit anyone to interfere in our affairs.
Time 2 Jul 84

WINSTON CHURCHILL, Prime Minister of Great Britain

17 One does not leave a convivial party before closing time.
Responding to queries on when he would retire as prime minister, news summaries 22 Mar 54

18 To jaw-jaw is better than to war-war.
On visit to Washington DC 26 Jun 54

19 I have never accepted what many people have kindly said—namely that I inspired the nation. Their will was resolute and remorseless, and as it proved, unconquerable. It fell to me to express it.
On World War II, 80th birthday address to Parliament 30 Nov 54

20 It was the nation and the race dwelling all round the globe that had the lion's heart. I had the luck to be called upon to give the roar.
ib

1 I also hope that I sometimes suggested to the lion the right place to use his claws.
ib

2 It may be that we shall by a process of sublime irony have reached a stage in this story where safety will be the sturdy child of terror, and survival the twin brother of annihilation.
On the hydrogen bomb, news summaries 3 Mar 55

3 It is a remarkable comment on our affairs that the former prime minister of a great sovereign state should thus be received as an honorary citizen of another.
On receiving honorary US citizenship, NY *Times* 10 Apr 63

4 Meeting Franklin Roosevelt was like opening your first bottle of champagne; knowing him was like drinking it.
Recalled on Churchill's death 24 Jan 65

5 If the Almighty were to rebuild the world and asked me for advice, I would have English Channels round every country. And the atmosphere would be such that anything which attempted to fly would be set on fire.
1952 comment quoted by Lord Moran *Churchill: Taken from the Diaries of Lord Moran* Houghton Mifflin 66

6 I always seem to get inspiration and renewed vitality by contact with this great novel land of yours which sticks up out of the Atlantic.
To Vice President Richard M Nixon during 1954 dinner in Washington DC, quoted in *RN: Memoirs of Richard Nixon* Grosset & Dunlap 78

7 In wartime, truth is so precious that she should always be attended by a bodyguard of lies.
Quoted by Thomas Griffith "Ducking the Truth" *Time* 24 Dec 84

8 "No comment" is a splendid expression. I am using it again and again.
ib

9 [Their] insatiable lust for power is only equaled by their incurable impotence in exercising it.
On opposition government after World War II, quoted by John Colville *The Fringes of Power* Norton 85

10 No lover ever studied every whim of his mistress as I did those of President Roosevelt.
Recalling 1942 Anglo-American disputes over a second front, *ib*

11 The Russians will try all the rooms in a house, enter those that are not locked, and when they come to one that cannot be broken into, they will withdraw and invite you to dine genially that same evening.
On postwar negotiations with the Soviets, quoted by Walter Isaacson and Evan Thomas *The Wise Men* Simon & Schuster 86

CHARLES DE GAULLE, President of France

12 I was France.
On leadership of Free France resistance during World War II, *The Complete War Memoirs of Charles de Gaulle*, translated by Jonathan Griffin, Simon & Schuster 55

13 France cannot be France without greatness.
ib

14 Now I shall return to my village and there will remain at the disposition of the nation.
Press conference 19 May 58

15 The national task that had been incumbent upon me for 18 years is hereby confirmed.
On election as president of the Fifth Republic 28 Dec 58

16 The great leaders have always stage-managed their effects.
The Edge of the Sword Criterion Books 60

17 My dear and old country, here we are once again together faced with a heavy trial.
On uprising in Algeria, NY *Times* 30 Jan 60

18 Once upon a time there was an old country, wrapped up in habit and caution. . . . We have to transform our old France into a new country and marry it to its time.
ib 15 Jun 60

19 You start out giving your hat, then you give your coat, then your shirt, then your skin and finally your soul.
On dealing with the Soviets, NY *Herald Tribune* 22 Sep 61

20 Diplomats are useful only in fair weather. As soon as it rains they drown in every drop.
Quoted by former aide Constantin Melnick, *Newsweek* 1 Oct 62

21 Treaties are like roses and young girls. They last while they last.
On Franco-German treaty talks, *Time* 12 Jul 63

22 A great country worthy of the name does not have any friends.
ib 28 May 65

23 To govern is always to choose among disadvantages.
NY *Times* 14 Nov 65

1 When I want to know what France thinks, I ask myself.

Time 17 Dec 65

2 I have heard your views. They do not harmonize with mine. The decision is taken unanimously.

Quoted by Jean Raymond Tournoux De Gaulle and Pétain: Sons of France Viking 66

3 The better I get to know men, the more I find myself loving dogs.

Quoted in Time 8 Dec 67

4 I have tried to lift France out of the mud. But she will return to her errors and vomitings. I cannot prevent the French from being French.

ib

5 You may be sure that the Americans will commit all the stupidities they can think of, plus some that are beyond imagination.

ib

6 I respect only those who resist me, but I cannot tolerate them.

NY Times 12 May 68

7 I have against me the bourgeois, the military and the diplomats, and for me, only the people who take the Métro.

ib

8 Patriotism is when love of your own people comes first; nationalism, when hate for people other than your own comes first.

Recalled on leaving the presidency, Life 9 May 69

9 I predict you will sink step by step into a bottomless quagmire, however much you spend in men and money.

On Vietnam War, 1961 statement to President John F Kennedy, quoted in Memories of Hope Press Ltd 76

10 [He is] a lion with a lion's countenance.

After 1960 meeting with Israeli Prime Minister David Ben Gurion, quoted by Shimon Peres NY Times 5 Oct 86

DENG XIAOPING, Chinese Premier

11 By following the concept of "one country, two systems," you don't swallow me up nor I you.

On policy adopted for Hong Kong, quoted in NY Times 2 Jan 85

12 It doesn't matter if a cat is black or white, so long as it catches mice.

On liberalization of Communist Party rules, quoted in Time 6 Jan 86

13 Young leading cadres have risen up by helicopter. They should really rise step by step.

On influential proponents of the Cultural Revolution in the 1960s, ib

ALEC DOUGLAS-HOME, Prime Minister of Great Britain

14 There are two problems in my life. The political ones are insoluble and the economic ones are incomprehensible.

NY Times 9 Jan 64

FRANÇOIS ("PAPA DOC") DUVALIER, President of Haiti

15 I know the Haitian people because I am the Haitian people.

Recalled on his death 21 Apr 71

JEAN CLAUDE ("BABY DOC") DUVALIER, President of Haiti

16 People of Haiti, I am the heir to the political philosophy, the doctrine and the revolution which my late father incarnated as president-for-life [and] I have decided to continue his work with the same fierce energy and the same intransigence.

On assuming presidency after his father's death, radio address 21 Apr 71

17 It is the destiny of the people of Haiti to suffer.

Quoted by V S Naipaul The Return of Eva Perón Knopf 80

ANTHONY EDEN, Prime Minister of Great Britain

18 If you've broken the eggs, you should make the omelette.

Letter to his brother during Suez Crisis, quoted by Elizabeth Longford The Queen: The Life of Elizabeth II Knopf 83

DWIGHT D EISENHOWER, 34th US President

19 Whatever America hopes to bring to pass in the world must first come to pass in the heart of America.

Inaugural address 20 Jan 53

20 Every gun that is made, every warship launched, every rocket fired, signifies in the final sense a theft from those who hunger and are not fed, those who are cold and are not clothed.

To Amer Society of Newspaper Editors 16 Apr 53

21 From behind the Iron Curtain, there are signs that tyranny is in trouble and reminders that its structure is as brittle as its surface is hard.

State of the Union address 7 Jan 54

22 I have one yardstick by which I test every major problem—and that yardstick is: Is it good for America?

On farm bill veto, address to the nation 16 Apr 56

1 Farming looks mighty easy when your plow is a pencil and you're a thousand miles from the corn field.

> Address at Peoria IL 25 Sep 56

2 I could have spoken from Rhode Island where I have been staying . . . But I felt that, in speaking from the house of Lincoln, of Jackson, and of Wilson, my words would better convey both the sadness I feel in the action I was compelled today to make and the firmness with which I intend to pursue this course until the orders of the federal court at Little Rock can be executed without unlawful interference.

> On sending troops to enforce integration in Little Rock AR High School, address to the nation broadcast from White House 24 Sep 57

3 This desk of mine is one at which a man may die, but from which he cannot resign.

> Quoted by a friend, *Parade* 2 Feb 58

4 Oh, that lovely title, ex-president.

> NY *Post* 26 Oct 59

5 I feel like the fellow in jail who is watching his scaffold being built.

> On construction of reviewing stands for inauguration of his successor John F Kennedy, NY *Times* 6 Dec 60

6 Unlike presidential administrations, problems rarely have terminal dates.

> State of the Union address 12 Jan 61

7 No one should ever sit in this office over 70 years old, and that I know.

> On leaving office in 1961 at age 70, quoted in *Newsweek* 2 Mar 87

Elizabeth II, Queen of England

8 I declare before you all that my whole life, whether it be long or short, shall be devoted to your service and the service of our great imperial family to which we all belong.

> Twenty-first birthday address, recalled five years later on her succession to the throne 6 Feb 52

9 The upward course of a nation's history is due in the long run to the soundness of heart of its average men and women.

> Christmas address 25 Dec 54

10 I cannot lead you into battle. I do not give you laws or administer justice but I can do something else—I can give my heart and my devotion to these old islands and to all the peoples of our brotherhood of nations.

> First televised Christmas address 25 Dec 57

11 It is as queen of Canada that I am here. Queen of Canada and all Canadians, not just one or two ancestral strains.

> Recognizing dissent of French-Canadians, address 9 Jul 73

12 We lost the American colonies because we lacked the statesmanship to know the right time and the manner of yielding what is impossible to keep.

> In Philadelphia on six-day Bicentennial visit, *Newsweek* 19 Jul 76

13 It is easy enough to define what the Commonwealth is not. Indeed this is quite a popular pastime.

> Silver Jubilee address 7 Jun 77

14 I myself prefer my New Zealand eggs for breakfast.

> After she was pelted with eggs during a walkabout on New Zealand visit, new summaries 26 Feb 86

Gerald R Ford, 38th US President

15 My fellow Americans, our long national nightmare is over.

> On succeeding Richard M Nixon as president 9 Aug 74

16 Our constitution works. Our great republic is a government of laws, not of men.

> *ib*

17 I am acutely aware that you have not elected me as your president by your ballots, so I ask you to confirm me with your prayers.

> *ib*

18 A government big enough to give you everything you want is a government big enough to take from you everything you have.

> Address to Congress 12 Aug 74

19 As I rejected amnesty, so I reject revenge. I ask all Americans who ever asked for goodness and mercy in their lives, who ever sought forgiveness for their trespasses, to join in rehabilitating all the casualties of the tragic conflict of the past.

> On Americans who avoided conscription during the Vietnam War, to Veterans of Foreign Wars, Chicago, 19 Aug 74

20 An American tragedy in which we all have played a part.

> On Watergate, announcing pardon of former President Richard M Nixon 8 Sep 74

21 It can go on and on, or someone must write "The End" to it. I have concluded that only I can do that. And if I can, I must.

> *ib*

INDIRA GANDHI, Prime Minister of India

1 All my games were political games; I was, like Joan of Arc, perpetually being burned at the stake.

On her childhood, NY *Times* 5 Nov 71

2 You cannot shake hands with a clenched fist.

Quoted in *Christian Science Monitor* 17 May 82

3 If I die a violent death, as some fear and a few are plotting, I know that the violence will be in the thought and the action of the assassins, not in my dying.

Handwritten statement found in her residence and later used on plaque in the garden where she was assassinated on October 31, 1984, opened to the public 27 May 85

RAJIV GANDHI, Prime Minister of India

4 She was mother not only to me but to the whole nation. She served the Indian people to the last drop of her blood.

On succeeding his mother as prime minister 31 Oct 84

5 For some days, people thought that India was shaking. But there are always tremors when a great tree falls.

Address three weeks after his mother's assassination, NY *Times* 20 Nov 84

MIKHAIL S GORBACHEV, Soviet Premier

6 Surely, God on high has not refused to give us enough wisdom to find ways to bring us an improvement . . . in relations between the two great nations on earth.

Time 9 Sep 85

7 Certain people in the United States are driving nails into this structure of our relationship, then cutting off the heads. So the Soviets must use their teeth to pull them out.

ib

8 Sometimes . . . when you stand face to face with someone, you cannot see his face.

Following summit meeting with Ronald Reagan in Iceland, press conference 12 Oct 86

9 Without glasnost there is not, and there cannot be, democratism, the political creativity of the masses and their participation in management.

February 1986 address to Party Congress on new policy of openness, NY *Times* 9 Nov 86

10 What we need is Star Peace and not Star Wars.

To Indian Parliament, New Delhi, *ib* 28 Nov 86

11 Our enemy sees us clearly. . . . They will not start a war. They're worried about one thing: If democracy develops here, if we succeed, we will win.

On relations with the US, *Time* 5 Jan 87

YAKUBU GOWON, President of Nigeria

12 The trouble with military rule is that every colonel or general is soon full of ambition. The navy takes over today and the army tomorrow.

Chicago *Daily News* 29 Aug 70

EDWARD HEATH, Prime Minister of Great Britain

13 Abhorrence of apartheid is a moral attitude, not a policy.

At Lord Mayor's banquet, London, 16 Nov 70

CHAIM HERZOG, President of Israel

14 I do not bring forgiveness with me, nor forgetfulness. The only ones who can forgive are dead; the living have no right to forget.

On first visit of an Israeli head of state to Bergen-Belsen, West Germany, where 50,000 persons died in Nazi concentration camp, NY *Times* 12 Apr 87

HIROHITO, Emperor of Japan

15 That most unfortunate war, which I deeply deplore.

1975 comment on World War II, quoted in NY *Times* 12 Jul 84

HERBERT HOOVER, 31st US President

16 When there is a lack of honor in government, the morals of the whole people are poisoned.

Recalled on eve of his 90th birthday, NY *Times* 9 Aug 64

17 Many years ago, I concluded that a few hair shirts were part of the mental wardrobe of every man. The president differs from other men in that he has a more extensive wardrobe.

Quoted by Brooks Atkinson *ib* 17 Oct 64

18 I outlived the bastards.

When asked about those who blamed him for the Depression, quoted by William O Douglas *The Court Years 1939-75* Random House 80

19 I'm the only person of distinction who's ever had a depression named for him.

Quoted by Richard Norton Smith *An Uncommon Man* Simon & Schuster 84

HUSSEIN, King of Jordan

20 It is my firm belief that I have a link with the past and a responsibility to the future. I cannot

give up. I cannot despair. There's a whole future, generations to come. I have to keep trying.

> Quoted by Curtis Wilkie "The Durable Monarch" Boston *Globe* 28 Jun 87

LYNDON B JOHNSON, 36th US President

1 I will do my best. That is all I can do. I ask for your help—and God's.

> On arriving in Washington DC on the evening of John F Kennedy's assassination, 22 Nov 63

2 I'd rather give my life than be afraid to give it.

> On decision to walk in Kennedy's funeral procession 25 Nov 63

3 We have talked long enough in this country about equal rights. . . . It is time now to write the next chapter—and to write it in the books of law.

> To Congress 27 Nov 63

4 This administration here and now declares unconditional war on poverty.

> State of the Union address 8 Jan 64

5 I want to make a policy statement. I am unabashedly in favor of women.

> On appointing 10 women to top government positions as part of his pledge to end a "stag government," 4 Mar 64

6 To conclude that women are unfitted to the task of our historic society seems to me the equivalent of closing male eyes to female facts.

> At White House swearing-in ceremony of women appointees 13 Apr 64

7 We have the opportunity to move not only toward the rich society and the powerful society, but upward to the Great Society.

> Address at University of Michigan 22 May 64

8 We Americans know—although others appear to forget—the risk of spreading conflict. We still seek no wider war.

> On ordering retaliatory action against North Vietnam Communist forces after renewed attacks on US destroyers in Gulf of Tonkin, address to the nation 4 Aug 64

9 They call upon us to supply American boys to do the job that Asian boys should do.

> Urging a policy of restraint in Vietnam, 12 Aug 64

10 When I was a boy . . . we didn't wake up with Vietnam and have Cyprus for lunch and the Congo for dinner.

> To Conference on Educational Legislation 1 Mar 65

11 A rioter with a Molotov cocktail in his hands is not fighting for civil rights any more than a Klansman with a sheet on his back and mask on his face. They are both more or less what the law declares them: lawbreakers, destroyers of constitutional rights and liberties and ultimately destroyers of a free America.

> To White House Conference on Equal Employment Opportunity held during rioting in Watts section of Los Angeles, 20 Aug 65

12 Our purpose in Vietnam is to prevent the success of aggression. It is not conquest, it is not empire, it is not foreign bases, it is not domination. It is, simply put, just to prevent the forceful conquest of South Vietnam by North Vietnam.

> Accepting Freedom House Award, *Time* 4 Mar 66

13 Our numbers have increased in Vietnam because the aggression of others has increased in Vietnam. There is not, and there will not be, a mindless escalation.

> *ib*

14 It is the common failing of totalitarian regimes that they cannot really understand the nature of our democracy. They mistake dissent for disloyalty. They mistake restlessness for a rejection of policy. They mistake a few committees for a country. They misjudge individual speeches for public policy.

> Answering North Vietnamese charge that US could not endure a long, inconclusive war, address at San Antonio 29 Sep 67

15 I report to you that our country is challenged at home and abroad: that it is our will that is being tried and not our strength; our sense of purpose and not our ability to achieve a better America.

> State of the Union address 17 Jan 68

16 What we won when all of our people united . . . must not be lost in suspicion and distrust and selfishness and politics. . . . Accordingly, I shall not seek, and I will not accept, the nomination of my party for another term as president.

> Address to the nation 31 Mar 68

17 The presidency has made every man who occupied it, no matter how small, bigger than he was; and no matter how big, not big enough for its demands.

> NY *Times* 26 Mar 72

18 Being president is like being a jackass in a hailstorm. There's nothing to do but stand there and take it.

> Recalled on his death 22 Jan 73

1 The Russians feared Ike. They didn't fear me.
> On Korean War in contrast to Vietnam War, quoted by Richard M Nixon *Time* 29 Jul 85

2 If you let a bully come in your front yard, he'll be on your porch the next day and the day after that he'll rape your wife in your own bed.
> On appeasement, quoted by Walter Isaacson and Evan Thomas *The Wise Men* Simon & Schuster 86

3 I don't believe I'll ever get credit for anything I do in foreign affairs, no matter how successful it is, because I didn't go to Harvard.
> To Hugh Sidey, quoted by *ib*

KENNETH KAUNDA, President of Zambia

4 The power which establishes a state is violence; the power which maintains it is violence; the power which eventually overthrows it is violence.
> Quoted in Colin M Morris ed *Kaunda on Violence* Collins 80

JOHN F KENNEDY, 35th US President

5 When at some future date the high court of history sits in judgment on each one of us—recording whether in our brief span of service we fulfilled our responsibilities to the state—our success or failure, in whatever office we may hold, will be measured by the answers to four questions—were we truly men of courage ... were we truly men of judgment ... were we truly men of integrity ... were we truly men of dedication?
> As president-elect, to Massachusetts legislature, NY *Times* 10 Jan 61

6 Let the word go forth from this time and place, to friend and foe alike, that the torch has been passed to a new generation of Americans—born in this century, tempered by war, disciplined by a hard and bitter peace, proud of our ancient heritage and unwilling to witness or permit the slow undoing of those human rights to which this nation has always been committed and to which we are committed today at home and around the world.
> Inaugural address 20 Jan 61

7 Let every nation know, whether it wishes us well or ill, that we shall pay any price, bear any burden, meet any hardship, support any friend, oppose any foe to assure the survival and the success of liberty.
> *ib*

8 Let us never negotiate out of fear. But let us never fear to negotiate.
> *ib*

9 In the long history of the world, only a few generations have been granted the role of defending freedom in its hour of maximum danger. I do not shrink from this responsibility—I welcome it.
> *ib*

10 And so, my fellow Americans: Ask not what your country can do for you—ask what you can do for your country.
> *ib*

11 All this will not be finished in the first hundred days. Nor will it be finished in the first thousand days, nor in the life of this administration, nor even perhaps in our lifetime on this planet. But let us begin.
> *ib*

12 To state the facts frankly is not to despair the future nor indict the past. The prudent heir takes careful inventory of his legacies and gives a faithful accounting to those whom he owes an obligation of trust.
> On outgoing administration, State of the Union address 30 Jan 61

13 Geography has made us neighbors. History has made us friends. Economics has made us partners, and necessity has made us allies. Those whom God has so joined together, let no man put asunder.
> To Canadian Parliament 17 May 61

14 Tell him, if he doesn't mind, we'll shake hands.
> On meeting Soviet Premier Nikita S Khrushchev in Vienna 4 Jun 61

15 I hear it said that West Berlin is militarily untenable—and so was Bastogne, and so, in fact, was Stalingrad. Any danger spot is tenable if men—brave men—will make it so.
> Address to the nation 25 Jul 61

16 The freedom of the city is not negotiable. We cannot negotiate with those who say, "What's mine is mine and what's yours is negotiable."
> *ib*

17 Khrushchev reminds me of the tiger hunter who has picked a place on the wall to hang the tiger's skin long before he has caught the tiger. This tiger has other ideas.
> NY *Times* 24 Dec 61

18 My father always told me that all businessmen were sons of bitches, but I never believed it till now.
> On steel industry executives who increased prices, to staff members 11 Apr 62

1 The path we have chosen for the present is full of hazards, as all paths are.... The cost of freedom is always high, but Americans have always paid it. And one path we shall never choose, and that is the path of surrender, or submission.
> Announcing blockade of Cuba to stop delivery of Soviet missiles, address to the nation 22 Oct 62

2 There are many people in the world who really don't understand—or say they don't—what is the great issue between the free world and the Communist world. ... Let them come to Berlin!
> At West Berlin City Hall 26 Jun 63

3 All free men, wherever they may live, are citizens of Berlin. And therefore, as a free man, I take pride in the words *"Ich bin ein Berliner!"*
> *ib*

4 I don't think the intelligence reports are all that hot. Some days I get more out of the New York *Times*.
> Recalled on his death 22 Nov 63

5 If anyone is crazy enough to want to kill a president of the United States, he can do it. All he must be prepared to do is give his life for the president's.
> Quoted by Pierre Salinger *With Kennedy* Doubleday 66

6 [Like] dealing with Dad—all give and no take.
> On negotiating with Soviet Premier Nikita S Khrushchev, quoted by Peter Collier and David Horowitz *The Kennedys* Summit 84

7 You never know what's hit you. A gunshot is the perfect way.
> When asked how he would choose to die, *ib*

MOHAMMED DAUD KHAN, President of Afghanistan

8 I feel the happiest when I can light my American cigarettes with Soviet matches.
> *Newsweek* 30 Jul 73

AYATOLLAH RUHOLLA KHOMEINI, spiritual leader of Iran

9 One thing I congratulate everyone on is the great explosion which has occurred in Washington's Black House and the very important scandal which has gripped leaders of America.
> On disclosure of US arms sales to Iran, NY *Times* 21 Nov 86

10 [Americans] are the great Satan, the wounded snake.
> On Americans, NBC TV 8 Dec 86

NIKITA S KHRUSHCHEV, Soviet Premier

11 Whether you like it or not, history is on our side. We will bury you!
> To Western ambassadors at reception in Moscow 17 Nov 56

12 Revolutions are the locomotives of history.
> To Supreme Soviet, *Pravda* 8 May 57

13 If you live among dogs, keep a stick. After all, this is what a hound has teeth for—to bite when he feels like it!
> On military preparedness, interview in Japanese newspaper 9 Jul 57

14 Support by United States rulers is rather in the nature of the support that the rope gives to a hanged man.
> Interview in Egyptian newspaper 25 Nov 57

15 We say the name of God, but that is only habit.
> *Time* 6 Jan 58

16 Don't you have a machine that puts food into the mouth and pushes it down?
> To Vice President Richard M Nixon during "kitchen debate" in model home at Amer National Exhibition, Moscow, news summaries 25 Jul 59

17 Bombs do not choose. They will hit everything.
> At Moscow rally, NY *Herald Tribune* 12 Aug 61

18 I once said, "We will bury you," and I got into trouble with it. Of course we will not bury you with a shovel. Your own working class will bury you.
> To Westerners, address at Split, Yugoslavia, 24 Aug 63

19 If you start throwing hedgehogs under me, I shall throw a couple of porcupines under you.
> On US criticism of Berlin Wall, NY *Times* 7 Nov 63

20 I want to talk to these people because they stay in power and you change all the time.
> Asking to meet with Italian businessmen instead of government officials, *Life* 24 Nov 67

21 There are still some people who think that we have Stalin to thank for all our progress, who quake before Stalin's dirty underdrawers, who stand at attention and salute them.
> *Khrushchev Remembers*, translated and edited by Strobe Talbott, Little, Brown 70

22 I'll step on your corns any time I want.
> On East Berlin and failed US invasion of Cuba, to President John F Kennedy at 1961 Vienna summit meeting, quoted by Ralph G Martin *A Hero for Our Time* Macmillan 83

HELMUT KOHL, Chancellor of West Germany

1 I have been underestimated for decades. I've done very well that way.
  On eve of victory for his coalition, NY *Times* 25 Jan 87

ADOLFO LÓPEZ MATEOS, President of Mexico

2 A woman is a citizen who works for Mexico. We must not treat her differently from a man, except to honor her more.
  On emancipation of women, *Time* 12 Oct 59

DIOSDADO MACAPAGAL, President of the Philippines

3 I have sat at the sumptuous tables of power, but I have not run away with the silverware.
  On his political career, *Time* 24 Nov 61

HAROLD MACMILLAN, Prime Minister of Great Britain

4 There might be 1 finger on the trigger, but there will be 15 fingers on the safety catch.
  On breakdown of summit conference on nuclear disarmament, to House of Commons 31 May 60

5 A strange, a perverted creed that has a queer attraction both for the most primitive and for the most sophisticated societies.
  On Communism, NY *Herald Tribune* 15 Oct 61

6 Once the bear's hug has got you, it is apt to be for keeps.
  On Soviet domination, *ib*

7 It is the duty of Her Majesty's government . . . neither to flap nor to falter.
  London *Observer* 19 Nov 61

8 I was determined that no British government should be brought down by the action of two tarts.
  On Profumo Affair, news summaries 13 Jun 63

9 Britain's most useful role is somewhere between bee and dinosaur.
  On mixing strength with efficiency, recalled on his death 29 Dec 86

10 [It was] not at all like an experience in the modern world. More like meeting George III at Brighton.
  On 1953 meeting with President Dwight D Eisenhower in Bermuda to discuss the Middle East, *ib*

11 It's no use crying over spilt summits.
  On Soviet cancellation of summit conference after 1960 downing of US spy plane, *ib*

12 Sixty-three years ago . . . the unemployment figure was 29 percent. Last November [it] was 28 percent. A rather sad end to one's life.
  On his home borough Stockton-on-Tees, quoted in *Newsweek* 12 Jan 87

13 I was a sort of son to Ike, and it was the other way round with Kennedy.
  On relationship with Presidents Dwight D Eisenhower and John F Kennedy, quoted in *Time* 12 Jan 87

MAO ZEDONG, Chinese premier

14 Passivity is fatal to us. Our goal is to make the enemy passive.
  Time 18 Dec 50

15 Communism is not love. Communism is a hammer which we use to crush the enemy.
  ib

16 Revolution is not a dinner party, not an essay, nor a painting, nor a piece of embroidery; it cannot be advanced softly, gradually, carefully, considerately, respectfully, politely, plainly and modestly.
  ib

17 Let a hundred flowers bloom.
  Address acknowledging contradictions within Communist society 27 Feb 57

18 All reactionaries are paper tigers.
  News summaries 31 Aug 60

19 Despise the enemy strategically, but take him seriously tactically.
  In handbook for revolutionaries, quoted in *Time* 22 Mar 63

20 I voted for you during your last election.
  To President Richard M Nixon, quoted in *RN: Memoirs of Richard Nixon* Grosset & Dunlap 78

FERDINAND E MARCOS, former President of the Philippines

21 It is not a choice of life, it is a choice of death. If this is life, I'd rather die.
  On exile in Hawaii, NBC TV 9 Dec 86

GOLDA MEIR, Prime Minister of Israel

22 We have always said that in our war with the Arabs we had a secret weapon—no alternative.
  Life 3 Oct 69

23 The Egyptians could run to Egypt, the Syrians into Syria. The only place we could run was into the sea, and before we did that we might as well fight.
  ib

1 It is true we have won all our wars, but we have paid for them. We don't want victories anymore.
ib

2 [The Soviet government] is the most realistic regime in the world—no ideals.
Interview 7 Oct 69

3 Arab sovereignty in Jerusalem just cannot be. This city will not be divided—not half and half, not 60-40, not 75-25, nothing.
Time 19 Feb 73

4 It's no accident many accuse me of conducting public affairs with my heart instead of my head. Well, what if I do? . . . Those who don't know how to weep with their whole heart don't know how to laugh either.
Ms Apr 73

5 Let me tell you something that we Israelis have against Moses. He took us 40 years through the desert in order to bring us to the one spot in the Middle East that has no oil!
At dinner honoring West German Chancellor Willy Brandt, NY *Times* 10 Jun 73

6 To be or not to be is not a question of compromise. Either you be or you don't be.
When asked during a White House visit about the question of Israel's future, *ib* 12 Dec 74

7 I don't know why you use a fancy French word like *détente* when there's a good English phrase for it—cold war.
Newsweek 19 Jan 76

8 What do you gain, Soviet Union, from this miserable policy? Where is your decency? Would it be a disgrace for you to give up this battle?
On suppression of freedom for Jews in the USSR, to World Conference on Soviet Jewry, Brussels, NY *Times* 20 Feb 76

9 I never did anything alone. Whatever was accomplished in this country was accomplished collectively.
To Egyptian President Anwar el-Sadat during his unprecedented visit to Israel, news summaries 21 Nov 77

10 Above all, this country is our own. Nobody has to get up in the morning and worry what his neighbors think of him. Being a Jew is no problem here.
On 30th anniversary of founding of Israel, *International Herald Tribune* 11 May 78

11 We do not rejoice in victories. We rejoice when a new kind of cotton is grown and when strawberries bloom in Israel.
Recalled on her death 8 Dec 78

ISKANDER MIRZA, President of Pakistan

12 Democracy is hypocrisy without limitation.
Time 20 Oct 58

FRANÇOIS MITTERRAND, President of France

13 A man loses contact with reality if he is not surrounded by his books.
On why he continued to live in Rue de Bièvre, using the Elysée Palace only for official functions, London *Times* 10 May 82

14 France is delighted at this new opportunity to show the world . . . that when one has the will one can succeed in joining peoples who have been brought close by history.
Announcing plans for joint British-French railroad tunnel under English Channel, NY *Times* 21 Jan 86

JOSEPH MOBUTO, President of Zaire

15 I no longer have a borrowed soul. I no longer have borrowed thoughts or ideas. I no longer speak in a borrowed language.
On changing his country's name from Democratic Republic of the Congo to Zaire, quoted in San Francisco *Examiner & Chronicle* 25 Jun 72

BRIAN MULRONEY, Prime Minister of Canada

16 The biggest trading partner of the United States is not West Germany or Japan, it's right here.
Demand that Reagan administration make greater efforts to honor commitments on trade and acid rain, NY *Times* 22 Jan 87

GAMAL ABDEL NASSER, President of Egypt

17 We're a sentimental people. We like a few kind words better than millions of dollars given in a humiliating way.
Refusing economic aid from the West, *Réalités* Jan 58

18 People do not want words—they want the sound of battle . . . the battle of destiny.
To National Assembly 20 Jan 69

JAWAHARLAL NEHRU, Prime Minister of India

19 The only alternative to coexistence is codestruction.
London *Observer* 29 Aug 54

20 Democracy is good. I say this because other systems are worse.
NY *Times* 25 Jan 61

21 I have become a queer mixture of the East and the West, out of place everywhere, at home nowhere.
On influence of his British education, recalled on his death 27 May 64

RICHARD M NIXON, 37th US President

1 Certainly in the next 50 years we shall see a woman president, perhaps sooner than you think. A woman can and should be able to do any political job that a man can do.
> To League of Women Voters, Washington DC, 16 Apr 69

2 My concern today is not with the length of a person's hair but with his conduct.
> On campus radicals, at General Beadle State College, Madison SD, 3 Jun 69

3 This is the greatest week in the history of the world since the Creation.
> Saluting crew of the Apollo 11 four days after the first manned landing on the moon, aboard USS *Hornet* 24 Jul 69

4 If we take the route of the permanent handout, the American character will itself be impoverished.
> Proposal to reform welfare programs, address to the nation 8 Aug 69

5 Tonight—to you, the great silent majority of my fellow Americans—I ask for your support.
> On his Vietnam War policy, address to the nation 3 Nov 69

6 You see these bums, you know, blowing up campuses ... storming around about this issue.
> On student protesters against Vietnam War, remark on leaving Pentagon meeting 1 May 70

7 There are some people, you know, they think the way to be a big man is to shout and stomp and raise hell—and then nothing ever really happens. I'm not like that ... I never shoot blanks.
> *Look* 19 Oct 71

8 My strong point is not rhetoric, it isn't showmanship, it isn't big promises—those things that create the glamour and the excitement that people call charisma and warmth.
> CBS TV 2 Jan 72

9 My strong point, if I have a strong point, is performance. I always do more than I say. I always produce more than I promise.
> *ib*

10 The presidency has many problems, but boredom is the least of them.
> 60th birthday interview 9 Jan 73

11 I believe in the battle—whether it's the battle of a campaign or the battle of this office, which is a continuing battle.
> Interview two days after his second inauguration, 22 Jan 73

12 As this long and difficult war ends, I would like to address a few special words to ... the American people: Your steadfastness in supporting our insistence on peace with honor has made peace with honor possible.
> On the Vietnam War, address to the nation 23 Jan 73

13 Under the doctrine of separation of powers, the manner in which the president personally exercises his assigned executive powers is not subject to questioning by another branch of government.
> Statement issued from the White House 12 Mar 73

14 I want you to stonewall it.
> To staff on news of break-in at Watergate headquarters of Democratic Party, taped conversation 22 Mar 73

15 There will be no whitewash in the White House.
> On Watergate investigation, press conference 17 Apr 73

16 I doubt if any of them would even intentionally double-park.
> On suspects in Watergate break-in, LA *Times* 1 May 73

17 If I were to make public these tapes, containing blunt and candid remarks on many different subjects, the confidentiality of the office of the president would always be suspect.
> Address to the nation 15 Aug 73

18 People have got to know whether or not their president is a crook. Well, I'm not a crook. I earned everything I've got.
> To Associated Press Managing Editors Assn, Disneyland, 17 Nov 73

19 There is a time to be timid. There is a time to be conciliatory. There is a time, even, to fly and there is a time to fight. And I'm going to fight like hell.
> On Congressional moves toward impeachment, press conference 27 Jan 74

20 Unless a president can protect the privacy of the advice he gets, he cannot get the advice he needs.
> *ib*

21 The 1976 Bicentennial is not going to be invented in Washington, printed in triplicate by the Government Printing Office [and] mailed to you by the United States Postal Service.
> Calling for citizens to supersede government in preparing observance of nation's 200th birthday, address to the nation 10 Mar 74

1 My own view is that taping of conversations for historical purposes was a bad decision on the part of all the presidents. I don't think Kennedy should have done it. I don't think Johnson should have done it, and I don't think we should have done it.

To Executives Club, Chicago, NY *Times* 16 Mar 74

2 I have never been a quitter. To leave office before my term is completed is opposed to every instinct in my body. But as president I must put the interests of America first ... Therefore, I shall resign the presidency effective at noon tomorrow.

Address to the nation 8 Aug 74

3 This [is] a burden I shall bear for every day of the life that is left to me.

On Watergate, statement to the press 8 Sep 74

4 I brought myself down. I impeached myself by resigning.

Television interview with David Frost 4 May 77

5 I let the American people down.

ib

6 When the president does it, that means that it is not illegal.

Arguing for extenuating circumstances, *ib*

7 I had never expected that the China initiative would come to fruition in the form of a Ping-Pong team.

On first friendly overture by People's Republic of China in March 1972, *RN: Memoirs of Richard Nixon* Grosset & Dunlap 78

8 My telephone calls and meetings and decisions were now parts of a prescribed ritual aimed at making peace with the past; his calls, his meetings and his decisions were already the ones that would shape America's future.

On transfer of power to his successor Gerald R Ford after Nixon's decision to resign, *ib*

9 I took a look around the office. ... I walked out and closed the door behind me. I knew that I would not be back there again.

On leaving the Executive Office Building on August 8, 1974, *ib*

10 "Good luck, Mr President," I said to him. "As I told you when I named you, I know the country is going to be in good hands with you in the Oval Office."

Farewell to Gerald R Ford on August 9, 1974, *ib*

11 The memory of that scene for me is like a frame of film forever frozen at that moment: the red carpet, the green lawn, the white house, the leaden sky. ... The new president and his first lady.

ib

12 I turned into the helicopter ... the red carpet was rolled up. ... The White House was behind us now.

ib

13 What starts the process, really, are laughs and slights and snubs when you are a kid. ... If your anger is deep enough and strong enough, you learn that you can change those attitudes by excellence, personal gut performance.

Quoted by Ken W Clawson Washington *Post* 9 Aug 79

14 It's a piece of cake until you get to the top. You find you can't stop playing the game the way you've always played it.

ib

15 So you are lean and mean and resourceful and you continue to walk on the edge of the precipice because over the years you have become fascinated by how close you can walk without losing your balance.

ib

16 Get a good night's sleep and don't bug anybody without asking me.

To re-election campaign manager Clark MacGregor, recorded on tape later made public, *Christian Science Monitor* 14 Aug 80

17 No event in American history is more misunderstood than the Vietnam War. It was misreported then, and it is misremembered now.

No More Vietnams Arbor House 85, quoted in NY *Times* 28 Mar 85

18 Rarely have so many people been so wrong about so much.

ib

19 People see me and they think, "He's risen from the dead."

Newsweek 19 May 86

20 They say, "Gee, you look great." That means they thought you looked like hell before.

ib

21 When I retire I'm going to spend my evenings by the fireplace going through those boxes. There are things in there that ought to be burned.

1971 statement recalled by John Ehrlichman, *Parade* 30 Nov 86

JULIUS K NYERERE, Prime Minister of Tanganyika/Tanzania

22 Small nations are like indecently dressed women. They tempt the evil-minded.

Reporter 9 Apr 64

MOHAMMED REZA PAHLAVI, Shah of Iran

1 *Shah* is a kind of magic word with the Persian people.
> NY *Times* 25 Sep 67

2 Let me tell you quite bluntly that this king business has given me personally nothing but headaches.
> *ib* 27 Oct 67

3 My advisers built a wall between myself and my people. I didn't realize what was happening. When I woke up, I had lost my people.
> To Egyptian President Anwar el-Sadat, after the shah's overthrow, *Time* 10 Dec 79

4 My main mistake was to have made an ancient people advance by forced marches toward independence, health, culture, affluence, comfort.
> Recalled on his death 27 Jul 80

LESTER B PEARSON, Prime Minister of Canada

5 I accept now with equanimity the question so constantly addressed to me, "Are you an American?" and merely return the accurate answer, "Yes, I am a Canadian."
> 1941 statement recalled on his election as prime minister, news summaries 31 Dec 63

6 This is the flag of the future, but it does not dishonor the past.
> On his country's new Maple Leaf flag, to House of Commons 15 Dec 64

SHIMON PERES, Prime Minister of Israel

7 Nothing had excited me—the huge cars, the entourages, the bodyguards, the policeman jumping to attention, all meant nothing to me . . . till I came to the old man's office.
> On becoming prime minister two decades after his mentor David Ben Gurion, *People* 15 Oct 84

8 Why cross an ocean when you can cross a river? Why should we sail to Washington when we can meet right away 10 miles from here?
> On Middle East peace initiative by Jordan's King Hussein, *Time* 17 Jun 85

9 Leading the Jewish people is not easy—we are a divided, obstinate, highly individualistic people who have cultivated faith, sharp-wittedness and polemics to a very high level.
> "In Homage to Ben Gurion" NY *Times* 5 Oct 86

10 It is not only the psychology of the people that makes them so exacting—their geographical situation has been equally problematic.
> *ib*

11 He altered the image of the Jew from that of rabbi, merchant, wanderer, to that of scientist, farmer and soldier.
> On David Ben Gurion, *ib*

12 He restored the Bible to its people, he restored the people to the Bible.
> *ib*

JUAN D PERÓN, President of Argentina

13 It is not that we were so good, but those who followed us were so bad that they made us seem better than we were.
> 1972 interview in Spain, recalled on his return to power, NY *Times* 14 Jul 73

14 We are no longer interested in elections except as a means to reach our objectives.
> *ib*

SOUVANNA PHOUMA, Premier of Laos

15 I am a good friend to Communists abroad but I do not like them at home.
> On the art of remaining neutral, *Life* 3 Nov 61

GEORGES POMPIDOU, President of France

16 France is a widow.
> On death of Charles de Gaulle, *Newsweek* 23 Nov 70

17 The rest of the world cannot be expected to regulate its life by a clock which is always slow.
> On US dollar as a "basic monetary yardstick . . . that constantly loses value as a result of purely internal politics," Washington *Post* 26 May 71

MUAMMAR QADDAFI, Libyan head of state

18 If Abu Nidal is a terrorist, then so is George Washington.
> Reply to President Ronald Reagan in defense of Palestinian terrorist, *Newsweek* 20 Jan 86

19 I am sailing out along parallel 32.5 to stress that this is the Libyan border. This is the line of death where we shall stand and fight with our backs to the wall.
> On planning confrontation with US Sixth Fleet in Mediterranean, NY *Times* 26 Jan 86

20 American soldiers must be turned into lambs and eating them is tolerated.
> Address two months after US bombing raid on Tripoli, *ib* 15 Jun 86

21 We are capable of destroying America and breaking its nose.
> *ib*

22 The man who carried out the attack is still in power and still insane, so we shall expect another attack any minute.
> On President Ronald Reagan, quoted in *US News & World Report* 27 Oct 86

RONALD REAGAN, 40th US President

1 This administration is totally colorblind.
> On appropriating funds to investigate killing of black children in Atlanta, 13 Mar 81

2 We have the means to change the laws we find unjust or onerous. We cannot, as citizens, pick and choose the laws we will or will not obey.
> On dismissing 12,000 striking air traffic controllers, to United Brotherhood of Carpenters and Joiners, Chicago, 3 Sep 81

3 The Soviet Union would remain a one-party nation even if an opposition party were permitted—because everyone would join that party.
> To British Parliament 8 Jun 82

4 Democracy is not a fragile flower; still it needs cultivating.
> Introducing Project Democracy to foster democratic ideals in authoritarian regimes, *ib*

5 [We seek] a constitutional amendment to permit voluntary school prayer. God should never have been expelled from America's classrooms in the first place.
> State of the Union address 25 Jan 83

6 I call upon the scientific community in our country, those who gave us nuclear weapons, to turn their great talents now to the cause of mankind and world peace: to give us the means of rendering these nuclear weapons impotent and obsolete.
> Introducing the Strategic Defense Initiative, address to the nation 23 Mar 83

7 My belief has always been . . . that wherever in this land any individual's constitutional rights are being unjustly denied, it is the obligation of the federal government—at point of bayonet if necessary—to restore that individual's constitutional rights.
> Press conference 17 May 83

8 They don't worship at the altar of forced busing and mandatory quotas. They don't believe you can remedy past discrimination by mandating new discrimination.
> Defending his nominees for Civil Rights Commission, quoted by Jean Nathan Miller "Ronald Reagan and the Techniques of Discrimination" *Atlantic* Feb 84

9 If I thought there was some reason to be concerned about them, I wouldn't be sleeping in this house tonight.
> When asked about continued presence of Soviet nuclear submarines along US coastlines, press conference 22 May 84

10 Damn it, Pierre, what do you want me to do? We'll go sit with empty chairs to get those guys back to the table.
> To Pierre Trudeau, prime minister of Canada, who pressed for détente with the USSR when Soviet leadership changed, Washington *Post* 15 Jun 84

11 My fellow Americans: I'm pleased to tell you today that I've signed legislation that will outlaw Russia forever. We begin bombing in five minutes.
> Comment while testing a microphone before a broadcast 11 Aug 84

12 Anyone that's ever had their kitchen done over knows that it never gets done as soon as you wish it would.
> Attempting to explain delay in installing security devices in US embassy in Beirut after bombing that claimed many lives, NY *Times* 26 Sep 84

13 The war in Vietnam threatened to tear our society apart, and the political and philosophical disagreements that separated each side continue, to some extent. It's been said that these memorials reflect a hunger for healing.
> On privately financed Vietnam Veterans Memorial and statue in Washington DC, Veterans Day address 11 Nov 84

14 Some of your countrymen were unable to distinguish between their native dislike for war and the stainless patriotism of those who suffered its scars. But there has been a rethinking [and] now we can say to you, and say as a nation, thank you for your courage.
> *ib*

15 Some say it will bring war to the heavens, but its purpose is to deter war, in the heavens and on earth.
> On Strategic Defense Initiative, State of the Union address 6 Feb 85

16 The freedom fighters of Nicaragua . . . are the moral equal of our Founding Fathers and the brave men and women of the French Resistance.
> To National Conservative Political Action Conference 1 Mar 85

17 Someone must stand up to those who say, "Here's the key, there's the Treasury, just take as many of those hard-earned tax dollars as you want."
> On vetoing a bill that would have extended $2 billion in federal loan guarantees to farmers, *Time* 18 Mar 85

18 People don't start wars, governments do.
> On eve of Geneva arms negotiations meeting, *ib*

1 I have only one thing to say to the tax increasers. Go ahead—make my day.

> Picking up dialogue from Clint Eastwood's 1983 movie *Sudden Impact*, ib 25 Mar 85

2 Most [tax revisions] didn't improve the system, they made it more like Washington itself: complicated, unfair, cluttered with gobbledygook and loopholes designed for those with the power and influence to hire high-priced legal and tax advisers.

> Address to the nation 28 May 85

3 Even Albert Einstein reportedly needed help on his 1040 form.

> ib

4 The distance between the present system and our proposal is like comparing the distance between a Model T and the space shuttle. And I should know; I've seen both.

> ib

5 The little dictator who went to Moscow in his green fatigues to receive a bear hug did not forsake the doctrine of Lenin when he returned to the West and appeared in a two-piece suit.

> On Daniel Ortega Saavedra, president of Nicaragua, *Time* 17 Jun 85

6 The current tax code is a daily mugging.

> Labor Day address, Independence MO, 2 Sep 85

7 America's view of apartheid is simple and straightforward: We believe it is wrong. We condemn it. And we are united in hoping for the day when apartheid will be no more.

> On ordering sanctions against South Africa, announcement from the Oval Office 9 Sep 85

8 These young Americans sent a message to terrorists everywhere ... "You can run but you can't hide."

> On US pilots who captured four terrorists who had hijacked a ship in the Mediterranean, paraphrasing Joe Louis's 1946 comment, press conference 11 Oct 85

9 If we don't want to see the map of Central America covered in a sea of red, eventually lapping at our own borders, we must act now.

> Appeal to Congress for $100 million in aid for Nicaraguan rebels, White House statement 5 Mar 86

10 My fellow Americans, I must speak to you tonight about a mounting danger in Central America that threatens the security of the United States. This danger will not go away; it will grow worse, much worse, if we fail to take action now.

> On aid for Nicaraguan rebels, address to the nation 16 Mar 86

11 As long as there are guns, the individual that wants a gun for a crime is going to have one and going to get it. The only person who's going to be penalized and have difficulty is the law-abiding citizen, who then cannot have [it] if he wants protection—the protection of a weapon in his home, for home protection.

> On his support for removal of gun controls, White House interview 22 Mar 86

12 I've often wondered how some people in positions of this kind ... manage without having had any acting experience.

> Interview with Barbara Walters ABC TV 24 Mar 86

13 I have come to the conclusion that the 22nd Amendment [limiting the presidency to two terms] was a mistake. Shouldn't the people have the right to vote for someone as many times as they want to vote for him?

> ib

14 I think the presidency is an institution over which you have temporary custody.

> When asked what he would tell students about the presidency, interview with Hugh Sidey "In Search of History" *Time* 7 Apr 86

15 The White House is the leakiest place I've ever been in.

> On special measures to ensure secrecy of plans to bomb Libya, press conference 9 Apr 86

16 We know that this mad dog of the Middle East has a goal of a world revolution.

> On Muammar Qaddafi of Libya, *ib*

17 Today we have done what we had to do. If necessary, we shall do it again.

> Address to the nation an hour after US air attack on Muammar Qaddafi's Tripoli headquarters in reprisal for terrorist bombing of Berlin nightclub and other incidents in which American lives were lost, 14 Apr 86

18 [Qaddafi] counted on America to be passive. He counted wrong.

> ib

19 I don't have too much time for fiction.

> On memoirs of former budget director David A Stockman, NY *Times* 18 Apr 86

20 The nine most terrifying words in the English language are, "I'm from the government and I'm here to help."

> Opening Chicago press conference with acknowledgment of farmers' need for federal assistance, 12 Aug 86

21 There is bitter bile in my throat.

> Blaming a newspaper, "that rag in Beirut," for

leaking reports of US arms sales to Iran, *Time* 8 Dec 86

1 I've never seen the sharks circling like they now are with blood in the water.

Acknowledging criticism engendered by revelations that money from arms sales to Iran had gone to Contra forces in Nicaragua, *ib*

2 I do not feel betrayed. . . . He has a fine record. He is a national hero.

On Oliver L North's work on the National Security Council, *ib*

3 My only criticism is that I wasn't told everything.

ib

4 I just don't think it's good for us to be run out of town.

Refusing to cancel Secretary of State George P Shultz's visit to Moscow after discovery of bugs in new US embassy building, *ib* 20 Apr 87

ANWAR EL-SADAT, President of Egypt

5 Russians can give you arms but only the United States can give you a solution.

Newsweek 13 Jan 75

MARGARET THATCHER, Prime Minister of Great Britain

6 One hopes to achieve the zero option, but in the absence of that we must achieve balanced numbers.

On Soviet and Allied missiles in Europe, NY *Times* 20 Jan 83

7 I'm not a good butcher but I've had to learn to carve the joint. People expect a new look.

On changes in her cabinet after landslide victory, *ib* 11 Jun 83

8 I have a habit of comparing the phraseology of communiqués, one with another across the years, and noting a certain similarity of words, a certain similarity of optimism in the reports which followed the summit meetings and a certain similarity in the lack of practical results during the ensuing years.

London *Times* 1 Jun 84

9 Platitudes? Yes, there are platitudes. Platitudes are there because they are true.

ib

10 If you go into what I call a bubble boom, every bubble bursts.

On national economy, *ib*

11 I like Mr Gorbachev, we can do business together.

On meeting Mikhail S Gorbachev in London be-

fore he became Soviet premier, news summaries 17 Dec 84

12 We didn't have to do the minuets of diplomacy. We got down to business.

On Mikhail S Gorbachev, CBS TV 11 Mar 85

13 I have made it quite clear that a unified Ireland was one solution that is out. A second solution was a confederation of two states. That is out. A third solution was joint authority. That is out—that is a derogation of sovereignty.

After meeting with Irish Prime Minister Garret FitzGerald to discuss ways of ending conflict in Northern Ireland, NY *Times* 20 Nov 85

14 I always cheer up immensely if an attack is particularly wounding because I think, well, if they attack one personally, it means they have not a single political argument left.

On criticism, London *Daily Telegraph* 21 Mar 86

15 If you lead a country like Britain, a strong country, a country which has taken a lead in world affairs in good times and in bad, a country that is always reliable, then you have to have a touch of iron about you.

On references to her as the Iron Lady, *ib*

16 I do not know anyone who has got to the top without hard work. That is the recipe. It will not always get you to the top, but should get you pretty near.

ib

17 If you want to cut your own throat, don't come to me for a bandage.

To Robert Mugabe, prime minister of Zimbabwe, who called for sanctions against South Africa, quoted in *Time* 7 Jul 86

18 What is success? I think it is a mixture of having a flair for the thing that you are doing; knowing that it is not enough, that you have got to have hard work and a certain sense of purpose.

Parade 13 Jul 86

19 To wear your heart on your sleeve isn't a very good plan; you should wear it inside, where it functions best.

On governing, interview with Barbara Walters *20/20* ABC TV 18 Mar 87

20 A world without nuclear weapons would be less stable and more dangerous for all of us.

To Soviet Premier Mikhail S Gorbachev, *Time* 27 Apr 87

OMAR TORRIJOS HERRERA, President of Panama

1 I don't like Communism because it hands out wealth through rationing books.
NY *Times* 7 Sep 77

PIERRE ELLIOTT TRUDEAU, Prime Minister of Canada

2 Canada will be a strong country when Canadians of all provinces feel at home in all parts of the country, and when they feel that all Canada belongs to them.
To Liberal Convention, Ottawa, 5 Apr 68

3 The state has no business in the bedrooms of the nation.
Appeal for revised divorce laws, NY *Times* 16 Jun 68

4 Living next to you is in some ways like sleeping with an elephant. No matter how friendly and even-tempered is the beast, if I can call it that, one is affected by every twitch and grunt.
On relations with the US, *ib* 26 Mar 69

5 My life is one long curve, full of turning points.
New Yorker 5 Jul 69

HARRY S TRUMAN, 33rd US President

6 If I'd known how much packing I'd have to do, I'd have run again.
On leaving the White House, *Time* 26 Jan 53

7 Any man who has had the job I've had and didn't have a sense of humor wouldn't still be here.
News summaries 19 Apr 55

RICHARD VON WEIZSÄCKER, President of West Germany

8 There were many ways of not burdening one's conscience, of shunning responsibility, looking away, keeping mum. When the unspeakable truth of the Holocaust then became known at the end of the war, all too many of us claimed that they had not known anything about it or even suspected anything.
On 40th anniversary of end of World War II, quoted in NY *Times* 12 May 85

9 All of us, whether guilty or not, whether old or young, must accept the past. . . . It is not a case of coming to terms with the past. That is not possible. It cannot be subsequently modified or undone.
ib

10 Whoever refuses to remember the inhumanity is prone to new risks of infection.
ib

11 Seeking to forget makes exile all the longer; the secret of redemption lies in remembrance.
ib

HAROLD WILSON, Prime Minister of Great Britain

12 Given a fair wind, we will negotiate our way into the Common Market, head held high, not crawling in. Negotiations? Yes. Unconditional acceptance of whatever terms are offered us? No.
Address in Bristol 20 Mar 67

13 The main essentials of a successful prime minister [are] sleep and a sense of history.
The Governance of Britain Harper & Row 77

ZHOU ENLAI, Chinese Premier

14 All diplomacy is a continuation of war by other means.
Saturday Evening Post 27 Mar 54

15 China and North Vietnam are closely united to each other, like the lips and the teeth.
In Hanoi 5 Mar 71

16 For us, it is all right if the talks succeed, and it is all right if they fail.
On President Richard M Nixon's visit to China 5 Oct 71

17 China is an attractive piece of meat coveted by all . . . but very tough, and for years no one has been able to bite into it.
To Chinese Communist Party Congress, NY *Times* 1 Sep 73

Officials & Other Personages

ELLIOTT ABRAMS, US Assistant Secretary of State for Inter-American Affairs

18 There isn't any way for the people of Nicaragua to find out what's going on in Nicaragua.
Announcing US technical aid to Nicaraguan rebels for powerful new radio station to promote anti-Sandinista ideas, NY *Times* 9 Nov 86

19 I never said I had no idea about most of the things you said I said I had no idea about.
At Iran-Contra hearings 3 Jun 87

DEAN ACHESON, US Secretary of State

20 I will undoubtedly have to seek what is happily known as gainful employment, which I am glad to say does not describe holding public office.
On retiring to private life, *Time* 22 Dec 52

21 The greatest mistake I made was not to die in office.
After listening to funeral eulogies for his succes-

sor John Foster Dulles, news summaries 27 Mar 59

1 Great Britain has lost an empire and has not yet found a role.
Address at West Point 5 Dec 62

2 The most important aspect of the relationship between the president and the secretary of state is that they both understand who is president.
Quoted by Dean Rusk NBC TV 26 Mar 69

3 Washington is like a self-sealing tank on a military aircraft. When a bullet passes through, it closes up.
Quoted by Walter Isaacson and Evan Thomas *The Wise Men* Simon & Schuster 86

SPIRO T AGNEW, US Vice President

4 The lessons of the past are ignored and obliterated in a contemporary antagonism known as the generation gap.
Denouncing Moratorium Day protest against Vietnam War, NY *Times* 20 Oct 69

CHARLES E BOHLEN, US diplomat

5 A noncommunist premier with communist ministers would be like a woman trying to stay half pregnant.
On Winston Churchill's suggestion that the West share spheres of influence with Joseph Stalin in postwar government of the Balkans, quoted by Walter Isaacson and Evan Thomas *The Wise Men* Simon & Schuster 86

KINGMAN BREWSTER, US Ambassador to Great Britain

6 It is satisfying for the descendant of a dissident refugee from Elizabeth I to present his credentials to Elizabeth II.
London *Observer* 3 Jul 77

7 The function of a briefing paper is to prevent the ambassador from saying something dreadfully indiscreet. I sometimes think its true object is to prevent the ambassador from saying anything at all.
To English-Speaking Union, Edinburgh, 8 Sep 77

8 We all live in a televised goldfish bowl.
Lecture, St George's Chapel, Windsor, 5 May 78

9 I'm very curious to know what the hell they're saying on the phone, but I'd be more worried if they weren't talking.
On direct contact between heads of state, London *Observer* 10 Jun 79

MORTIMER CAPLIN, Commissioner, Internal Revenue Service

10 There is one difference between a tax collector and a taxidermist—the taxidermist leaves the hide.
Time 1 Feb 63

CLARK M CLIFFORD, US Secretary of Defense

11 I am not conscious of falling under any of those ornithological divisions.
When asked if he considered himself a hawk or a dove, NY *Times* 2 Jan 68

BARBER B CONABLE JR, US Congressman

12 Exhaustion and exasperation are frequently the handmaidens of legislative decision.
Time 22 Oct 84

13 [Congress is] functioning the way the Founding Fathers intended—not very well. They understood that if you move too quickly, our democracy will be less responsible to the majority.
ib

14 I don't think it's the function of Congress to function well. It should drag its heels on the way to decision.
ib

J EDWARD DAY, US Postmaster General

15 We cannot put the face of a person on a stamp unless said person is deceased. My suggestion, therefore, is that you drop dead.
Letter, never mailed, to a petitioner who wanted himself portrayed on a postage stamp, NY *Times* 7 Mar 62

JOHN DEAN, White House special counsel

16 I began by telling the president that there was a cancer growing on the presidency and that if the cancer was not removed . . . the president himself would be killed by it.
To Senate Watergate hearings 25 Jun 73

17 You really have to experience the feeling of being with the president in the Oval Office. . . . It's a disease I came to call Ovalitis.
After conviction for participation in Watergate cover-up, news summaries 1 Jan 75

BERNADETTE DEVLIN, Member of British Parliament

18 It wasn't long before people discovered the final horrors of letting an urchin into Parliament.
On being elected at age 21, *The Price of My Soul* Knopf 69

ROBERT J DOLE, US Senator

1 If you're hanging around with nothing to do
and the zoo is closed, come over to the Senate.
You'll get the same kind of feeling and you
won't have to pay.

Address on budget deficit to conference of NY
local officials, NY *Times* 9 May 85

2 As long as there are only 3 to 4 people on the
floor, the country is in good hands. It's only
when you have 50 to 60 in the Senate that you
want to be concerned.

ib

RAYMOND J DONOVAN, US Secretary of Labor

3 If you're in the contracting business in this
country, you're suspect. If you're in the contracting business in New Jersey, you're indict-
able. If you're in the contracting business in
New Jersey and are Italian, you're convicted.

In confirmation hearings before Senate Labor
Committee 27 Jan 81

4 Give me back my reputation!

As former secretary, on acquittal after nine-
month trial on charges of larceny and fraud, to
the prosecutor, *Time* 8 Jun 87

ALEC DOUGLAS-HOME, Foreign Secretary of Great Britain

5 Why employ intelligent and highly paid am-
bassadors and then go and do their work for
them? You don't buy a canary and sing
yourself.

NY *Times* 21 Apr 61

YURI V DUBININ

6 I only understand positive statements in English.

On becoming Soviet ambassador to the US,
quoted in NY *Times* 21 May 86

JOHN FOSTER DULLES, US Secretary of State

7 The ability to get to the verge without getting
into the war is the necessary art. . . . if you are
scared to go to the brink, you are lost.

Quoted by James Shepley "How Dulles Averted
War" *Life* 16 Jan 56

8 We walked to the brink and we looked it in the
face.

On US involvement in Korea, Indochina and
Formosa, *ib*

ABBA EBAN, Foreign Minister of Israel

9 Israel is not an aviary.

When asked if his country's policy was hawkish
or dovish, NY *Post* 8 Jul 67

10 I think that this is the first war in history that
on the morrow the victors sued for peace and
the vanquished called for unconditional surrender.

NY *Times* 9 Jul 67

11 Men and nations do behave wisely, once all
other alternatives have been exhausted.

Vogue 1 Aug 67

EDWARD, Duke of Windsor

12 It didn't work out.

On brief reign in 1936 as King Edward VIII,
quoted on *60 Minutes* CBS TV 8 Jun 80

ALLEN J ELLENDER, US Senator

13 First we just gave them these surpluses. Next
we agreed to pay freight on transportation to
ports. Then we agreed to mill the grain and
package it. The next thing [you know] we'll be
asked to cook it and serve it.

On complaints by charitable organizations about
food donated to them by the US, 1 Apr 56

GERALD R FORD, US Vice President

14 A coalition of groups . . . is waging a massive
propaganda campaign against the president of
the United States. . . . an all-out attack. Their
aim is total victory for themselves and total
defeat [for him].

On Watergate crisis, to Amer Farm Bureau Federation, Washington *Post* 17 Jan 74

15 It's the quality of the ordinary, the straight, the
square, that accounts for the great stability
and success of our nation. It's a quality to be
proud of. But it's a quality that many people
seem to have neglected.

Time 28 Jan 74

16 The political lesson of Watergate is this: Never
again must America allow an arrogant, elite
guard of political adolescents to by-pass the
regular party organization and dictate the
terms of a national election.

On the Committee for the Re-election of the
President, NY *Times* 31 Mar 74

17 I cannot imagine any other country in the
world where the opposition would seek, and
the chief executive would allow, the dissemi-
nation of his most private and personal conversations with his staff, which, to be honest,
do not exactly confer sainthood on anyone
concerned.

On taping of conversations in White House office of President Richard M Nixon, address at
University of Michigan, Ann Arbor, *ib* 4 May 74

BARNEY FRANK, US Congressman

1 This bill is the legislative equivalent of crack. It yields a short-term high but does long-term damage to the system and it's expensive to boot.

> On antidrug bill passed by House of Representatives, NY *Times* 12 Sep 86

J WILLIAM FULBRIGHT, US Senator

2 We have the power to do any damn fool thing we want to do, and we seem to do it about every 10 minutes.

> On Senate's right to change its mind, *Time* 4 Feb 52

EVAN G GALBRAITH, US Ambassador to France

3 There's something about the Foreign Service that takes the guts out of people.

> On resigning after four years as ambassador, NY *Times* 13 Feb 85

STEVEN GARFINKEL, Director, US Information Security Oversight Office

4 There are more secrets, but there is not more secrecy.

> On increase of espionage within government, NY *Times* 15 Apr 86

PETER C GOLDMARK JR, NY State Budget Director

5 Welfare is hated by those who administer it, mistrusted by those who pay for it and held in contempt by those who receive it.

> NY *Times* 24 May 77

ANDREI A GROMYKO, Soviet Foreign Minister

6 Every night, whisper "peace" in your husband's ear.

> To Nancy Reagan, at White House reception 28 Sep 84

7 My personality doesn't interest me.

> Refusing to answer personal questions, *Newsweek* 1 Oct 84

8 [The world may end up] under a Sword of Damocles . . . on a tightrope over the abyss.

> Criticizing US Strategic Defense Initiative, *Time* 11 Mar 85

9 Comrades, this man has a nice smile, but he's got iron teeth.

> On Mikhail S Gorbachev, quoted in NY *Times* 17 Jun 85

ALEXANDER M HAIG JR, US Secretary of State

10 As of now, I am in control here in the White House.

> After President Ronald Reagan was wounded in

an assassination attempt while Vice President George Bush was away from Washington DC, statement to the press 30 Mar 81

DORCAS HARDY, Director, Social Security System

11 The one with the primary responsibility to the individual's future is that individual.

> *Christian Science Monitor* 5 Mar 87

12 The business of government should be businesslike.

> *ib*

W AVERELL HARRIMAN, US diplomat

13 Conferences at the top level are always courteous. Name-calling is left to the foreign ministers.

> News summaries 1 Aug 55

14 [Americans wanted to] settle all our difficulties with Russia and then go to the movies and drink Coke.

> On wariness of sharing global responsibilities with the Soviets, quoted by Walter Isaacson and Evan Thomas *The Wise Men* Simon & Schuster 86

15 [He's] a margarine Communist.

> Prediction that Chairman Mao of China would break with Soviets, *ib*

16 I always read everything on the desks of people I went to see in Moscow, London, Paris . . . I found it quite useful.

> On his ability to read upside down, recalled on his death 26 Jul 86

PATRICIA ROBERTS HARRIS, US Secretary of Housing and Urban Development

17 Senator, I am one of them. You do not seem to understand who I am. I am a black woman, the daughter of a dining-car worker . . . If my life has any meaning at all, it is that those who start out as outcasts can wind up as being part of the system.

> Reply to Senator William Proxmire when asked if she would be able to defend the interests of the poor, *Newsweek* 24 Jan 77

ARTHUR A HARTMAN, US Ambassador to USSR

18 It is unacceptable to subject Americans in Moscow to any substance that is not present in the general environment.

> On "spy dust," powdery chemical used to track movements of US diplomats, NY *Times* 15 Feb 86

ORRIN G HATCH, US Senator

19 The marble columns will stand tall like silent

sentinels and the busts of the great Americans which line the upper wall will study our every move—sometimes approvingly, more often than not with raised eyebrows. As always.

> On waning days of 98th Congress, NY *Times* 17 Oct 84

DENIS HEALEY, Chancellor of the Exchequer

1 [It will] squeeze the rich until the pips squeak.

> On presenting budget to Parliament, *Illustrated London News* May 78

RICHARD M HELMS, Director, CIA

2 I have one president at a time. I only work for you.

> To President Richard M Nixon, who had promised not to use top-secret information to incriminate Helms, his predecessor or the CIA, quoted in *RN: Memoirs of Richard Nixon* Grosset & Dunlap 78

DONALD A HICKS, Research Director, US Defense Dept

3 Freedom works both ways. They're free to keep their mouths shut. . . . I'm also free not to give the money.

> Suggesting that federal research grants be denied scientists who oppose the Strategic Defense Initiative, Washington *Post* 13 May 86

JIM HIGHTOWER, Texas Agricultural Commissioner

4 The only difference between a pigeon and the American farmer today is that a pigeon can still make a deposit on a John Deere.

> On the financial crisis of the American farmer, to Chamber of Commerce, Dallas, NY *Times* 9 Mar 86

5 Do something. If it doesn't work, do something else. No idea is too crazy.

> Instructions to staff of activists dedicated to restoring farm profits, *ib*

LUTHER H HODGES, US Secretary of Commerce

6 If ignorance paid dividends, most Americans could make a fortune out of what they don't know about economics.

Wall Street Journal 14 Mar 62

ANNA ROSENBERG HOFFMAN, US Assistant Secretary of Defense

7 No form letters are sent out from this office. No husband was ever Section Three, Paragraph II-a, to his wife.

Newsweek 27 Feb 51

GEORGE M HUMPHREY, US Secretary of the Treasury

8 You can't set a hen in one morning and have chicken salad for lunch.

> On the impossibility of quick economic change, *Time* 26 Jan 53

9 It's a terribly hard job to spend a billion dollars and get your money's worth.

Look 23 Feb 54

WILLIAM G HYLAND, former national security adviser

10 Protectionism is the ally of isolationism, and isolationism is the Dracula of American foreign policy.

> Commencement address at Washington University, St Louis, NY *Times* 17 May 87

PETER JAY, former British Ambassador to US

11 He is just as entitled to be underwhelmed by the prospect of reigning over a fourth-class nation as the rest of us are by the prospect of living in it.

> On Charles, Prince of Wales, "Great is Little Britain" *London Illustrated News* Apr 86

CLAUDIA ("LADY BIRD") JOHNSON

12 The first lady is, and always has been, an unpaid public servant elected by one person, her husband.

> Quoted in *US News & World Report* 9 Mar 87

MAX M KAMPELMAN, chief US arms negotiator

13 We must be prepared to stay at the negotiating table one day longer than the Soviets.

Time 11 Mar 85

14 A dialogue is more than two monologues.

ib 6 May 85

PAUL KEATING, Federal Treasurer of Australia

15 I try to use the Australian idiom to its maximum advantage.

> On his use of colorful language in Parliament, *Wall Street Journal* 14 Nov 86

GEORGE F KENNAN, US diplomat

16 [One sometimes feels] a guest of one's time and not a member of its household.

> On view of himself as a pragmatist, quoted by Walter Isaacson and Evan Thomas *The Wise Men* Simon & Schuster 86

17 The best [an American] can look forward to is the lonely pleasure of one who stands at long

last on a chilly and inhospitable mountaintop where few have been before, where few can follow and where few will consent to believe he has been.

On trying to understand the Soviets, *ib*

1 [The accords were] fig leaves of democratic procedure to hide the nakedness of Stalinist dictatorship.

On postwar agreements to govern Eastern Europe, *ib*

ROBERT F KENNEDY, US Attorney General

2 I thought they'd get one of us, but Jack, after all he's been through, never worried about it . . . I thought it would be me.

On learning of his brother's assassination, quoted by Peter Collier and David Horowitz *The Kennedys* Summit 84

3 Did the CIA kill my brother?

To CIA Director John A McCone as speculation grew over US involvement in Bay of Pigs invasion, *ib*

HENRY A KISSINGER

4 No foreign policy—no matter how ingenious—has any chance of success if it is born in the minds of a few and carried in the hearts of none.

As national security adviser, to International Platform Assn 2 Aug 73

5 High office teaches decision making, not substance. [It] consumes intellectual capital; it does not create it. Most high officials leave office with the perceptions and insights with which they entered; they learn how to make decisions but not what decisions to make.

White House Years Little, Brown 79

6 The statesman's duty is to bridge the gap between his nation's experience and his vision.

Years of Upheaval Little, Brown 82

7 In crises the most daring course is often safest.

ib

8 [The] American temptation [is] to believe that foreign policy is a subdivision of psychiatry.

Commencement address at University of South Carolina, *Time* 17 Jun 85

9 If I should ever be captured, I want no negotiation—and if I should request a negotiation from captivity they should consider that a sign of duress.

Expressing strong opposition to bargaining with terrorists, *US News & World Report* 7 Oct 85

10 You can't make war in the Middle East without Egypt and you can't make peace without Syria.

Quoted by Ted Koppel *Nightline* ABC TV 21 May 86

11 Whatever must happen ultimately should happen immediately.

On handling of Iran-Contra scandal, *Time* 8 Dec 86

12 Any fact that needs to be disclosed should be put out now or as quickly as possible, because otherwise . . . the bleeding will not end.

ib

EDWARD KOCH, Mayor of NYC

13 In a neighborhood, as in life, a clean bandage is much, much better than a raw or festering wound.

On plan to improve the image of the Bronx by covering the windows of abandoned city-owned buildings with decals depicting pleasant interiors, NY *Times* 12 Nov 83

DELBERT L LATTA, US Congressman

14 I hold in my hand 1,379 pages of tax simplification.

On tax reform, quoted in *US News & World Report* 23 Dec 85

DREW LEWIS, presidential envoy

15 Saying sulfates do not cause acid rain is the same as saying that smoking does not cause lung cancer.

On meeting with New England governors to discuss industrial pollution, NY *Times* 14 Sep 85

HENRY CABOT LODGE JR

16 I guess it wouldn't discourage a real mob for very long, but it packs all the authority you can put in a desk drawer.

On keeping a small revolver in his desk while ambassador to South Vietnam, *Time* 15 May 64

NIALL MacDERMOT, Financial Secretary of British Treasury

17 "State intelligence," like "military intelligence" and "woman friend," is a contradiction in terms.

Quote 23 Jan 66

WILLIAM B MACOMBER, former US Ambassador to Jordan and Turkey

18 When it comes to an important portion of American ambassadorial appointments, we are still in the era of the Charge of the Light Brigade.

On campaign donations in exchange for ambassadorial appointments, NY *Times* 20 Nov 84

JEB STUART MAGRUDER, former Chairman, Committee to Re-elect the President

1 I know what I have done, and Your Honor knows what I have done. ... Somewhere between my ambition and my ideals, I lost my ethical compass.
> Confessing perjury in Watergate investigation, *Time* 3 Jun 74

GRAHAM A MARTIN, former US Ambassador to South Vietnam

2 In the end, we simply cut and ran. The American national will had collapsed.
> On 10th anniversary of fall of Saigon, NY *Times* 30 Apr 85

VINCENT MASSEY, Governor-General of Canada

3 What we do should have a Canadian character. Nobody looks his best in somebody else's clothes.
> Recalled on his death, *Time* 12 Jan 68

CHARLES McC MATHIAS JR, US Congressman

4 Most of us are honest all the time, and all of us are honest most of the time.
> On Congressional ethics, *Time* 31 Mar 67

JAMES A McCLURE, US Senator

5 In that hearing, we didn't hear anything.
> On why there were no leaks from a closed hearing, NY *Times* 24 Jan 87

ROBERT S McNAMARA, US Secretary of Defense

6 Neither conscience nor sanity itself suggests that the United States is, should or could be the global gendarme.
> To Amer Society of Newspaper Editors, NY *Times* 19 May 66

7 Coercion, after all, merely captures man. Freedom captivates him.
> *ib*

EDWIN MEESE 3RD, White House counsel

8 [An expert is] somebody who is more than 50 miles from home, has no responsibility for implementing the advice he gives, and shows slides.
> NY *Times* 24 Jan 84

9 Nicaragua is fast becoming a terrorist country club.
> On evidence that Nicaragua gave shelter to German, Italian, Irish, Spanish and Arab terrorists, news summaries 14 Sep 85

PAT NIXON

10 Being first lady is the hardest unpaid job in the world.
> Interview in Monrovia, Liberia, 15 Mar 72

OLIVER L NORTH, former staff member of National Security Council

11 I don't think there is another person in America that wants to tell this story as much as I do.
> Invoking Fifth Amendment right against self-incrimination in testimony to House committee investigating arms sales to Iran, NY *Times* 10 Dec 86

12 I came here to tell you the truth, the good, the bad and the ugly.
> Testifying at Iran-Contra hearings after being granted limited immunity, 7 Jul 87

13 I am here to accept responsibility for that which I did. I will not accept responsibility for that which I did not do.
> *ib*

14 I haven't, in the 23 years that I have been in the uniformed services of the United States of America ever violated an order—not one.
> *ib*

15 I thought using the Ayatollah's money to support the Nicaraguan resistance ... was a neat idea.
> On diversion of funds from arms sales to Iran 8 Jul 87

MILDRED PERLMAN, NY Civil Service Commission

16 You start by saying no to requests. Then if you have to go to yes, OK. But if you start with yes, you can't go to no.
> NY *Times* 1 Dec 75

PETER G PETERSON, former US Secretary of Commerce

17 The experience may have been costly, but it was also priceless.
> On his term in the Cabinet, *Quote* 18 Jan 73

PRINCE PHILIP, Duke of Edinburgh

18 If we are to recover prosperity we shall have to find ways of emancipating energy and enterprise from the frustrating control of timid ignoramuses.
> Quoted by Anthony Sampson *The Anatomy of Britain* Harper & Row 62

IGNACIO PICHARDO PAGAZA, Comptroller General of Mexico

19 The phenomenon of corruption is like the garbage. It has to be removed daily.
> NY *Times* 17 Apr 87

JOHN M POINDEXTER, former national security adviser

1 I made a very deliberate decision not to ask the president so that I could insulate him from the decision and provide some future deniability for the president if it ever leaked out.

> On diverting funds from arms sales, at Iran-Contra hearings 15 Jul 87

NANCY REAGAN

2 Today, there is a drug and alcohol abuse epidemic in this country. And no one is safe from it—not you, not me and certainly not our children, because this epidemic has their names written on it.

> Address to the nation with President Reagan 14 Sep 86

3 There is no moral middle ground. Indifference is not an option. . . . For the sake of our children, I implore each of you to be unyielding and inflexible in your opposition to drugs.

> ib

4 I don't think most people associate me with leeches or how to get them off. But I know how to get them off. I'm an expert at it.

> To Amer Camping Assn, Washington DC 2 Mar 87

DONALD T REGAN, White House chief of staff

5 I read all these stories that I don't know anything about politics. But I must know something. I've had some good victories in Congress, and I've survived this town for four years.

> NY Times 25 Jan 85

6 At dinner parties I sit below the salt now. There are a lot of interesting people there.

> Time 18 Mar 85

7 It's an ear job, not an eye job.

> ib

8 We do many things at the federal level that would be considered dishonest and illegal if done in the private sector.

> On efforts to alter federal budget, NY Times 25 Aug 86

9 Some of us are like a shovel brigade that follow a parade down Main Street cleaning up.

> On Iceland summit meeting between Ronald Reagan and Mikhail S Gorbachev, ib 16 Nov 86

10 By no means was it really teed up for him.

> On President Ronald Reagan's advance knowledge of arms sales to Iran, statement to Senate-appointed commission, quoted by William Safire "Teed Off over Teed Up" ib 19 Apr 87

11 I was trying to tell the commission that the issue had not been really defined well enough to be ready for the president.

> ib

12 When one goes through combat-patrol work, one quickly learns that the best target is the person who "stands on the skyline. . . ." Indians knew it, Indian scouts knew it, soldiers, sailors and all marines know it. . . . A chief of staff is supposed to know it, but sometimes there is no way a chief of staff can stay off the skyline.

> ib

ELLIOT L RICHARDSON

13 Conscience is the voice of values long and deeply infused into one's sinew and blood.

> On resigning as US attorney general rather than approve presidential firing of a Richardson appointee, Life Special Report 73

ELEANOR ROOSEVELT

14 Always be on time. Do as little talking as humanly possible. Remember to lean back in the parade car so everybody can see the president. Be sure not to get too fat, because you'll have to sit three in the back seat.

> On campaign behavior for first ladies, NY Times 11 Nov 62

DEAN RUSK, US Secretary of State

15 Let me say with a Georgia accent that we cannot solve this problem if it requires a diplomatic passport to claim the rights of an American citizen.

> On restaurants that admitted dark-skinned diplomats but not US blacks, Life 1 Jan 62

16 We were eyeball-to-eyeball and the other fellow just blinked.

> On the Cuban missile crisis, Saturday Evening Post 8 Dec 62

17 When you solve a problem, you ought to thank God and go on to the next one.

> On the Cuban missile crisis, Look 6 Sep 66

18 The United States is not just an old cow that gives more milk the more it's kicked in the flanks.

> Telling Senate Foreign Relations Committee that the US would not deliver a nuclear ultimatum to Vietnam, NY Times 5 May 67

19 The fidelity of the United States to security treaties is not just an empty matter. It is a pillar of peace in the world.

> On 10th anniversary of fall of Saigon, ib 30 Apr 85

1 Give a member of Congress a junket and a mimeograph machine and he thinks he is secretary of state.

> Quoted in *Time* 6 May 85

JEANNE SAUVÉ

2 I was asked to prepare a little program and I never stopped.

> On how she became first woman governor-general of Canada, London *Times* 29 Nov 85

GEORGE P SHULTZ, US Secretary of State

3 I learned in business that you had to be very careful when you told somebody that's working for you to do something, because the chances were very high he'd do it. In government, you don't have to worry about that.

> NY *Times* 14 Oct 84

4 Oh, you know. I am secretary of state. My trips aren't successful. I just talk to people.

> On global diplomacy, *ib* 17 May 85

5 [It was an attempt] to stick the Congress's finger in King Hussein's eye.

> On US Senate's nonbinding resolution to ban further arms sales to Jordan, press conference 4 Jun 85

6 Nothing ever gets settled in this town. . . . a seething debating society in which the debate never stops, in which people never give up, including me. And so that's the atmosphere in which you administer.

> On not being told about arms sales to Iran, to House investigating committee, NY *Times* 9 Dec 86

GERRY E STUDDS, US Congressman

7 It is the Edsel of the 1980s. It is overpriced, it has been oversold, it will not perform as advertised.

> On Strategic Defense Initiative, NY *Times* 21 Jun 85

GEORGE C WALLACE, Governor of Alabama

8 I draw the line in the dust and toss the gauntlet before the feet of tyranny, and I say segregation now, segregation tomorrow, segregation forever.

> 1963 inaugural address, quoted in *Life* 26 Dec 69

VERNON A WALTERS, US Ambassador to UN

9 The fact that I was a bachelor provided two opportunities or two handles that they might get on me, namely, girls or boys.

> On eluding traps for blackmail while a military attaché in France during the 1960s, *Silent Missions* Doubleday 78

10 Americans have always had an ambivalent attitude toward intelligence. When they feel threatened, they want a lot of it, and when they don't, they regard the whole thing as somewhat immoral.

> *ib*

EARL WARREN, Chief Justice, US Supreme Court

11 We may not know the whole story in our lifetime.

> On assassination of President John F Kennedy, quoted by Don Hewitt *Minute by Minute* Random House 85

JAMES G WATT, US Secretary of the Interior

12 I have a black, a woman, two Jews and a cripple. And we have talent.

> Comment on his staff that led to his resignation, to US Chamber of Commerce 21 Sep 83

JAIME WHEELOCK, Minister of Agriculture, Nicaragua

13 We prefer the loss of the coffee to the loss of the country.

> On diverting 20,000 student volunteers from harvest work to bolster defense against a possible US invasion, *Newsweek* 19 Nov 84

Politicians & Critics

HAROLD A ACKERMAN, Judge, US District Court, New Jersey

14 You reached for that honey pot and you got stung.

> On conviction of former Atlantic City Mayor Michael J Matthews for extortion, NY *Times* 1 Jan 85

15 You served the people shamefully. The people . . . thought they were electing a mayor.

> *ib*

KONRAD ADENAUER, Chancellor of West Germany

16 Kennedy cooked the soup that Johnson had to eat.

> On the Vietnam War, NY *Times* 24 Jan 73

SHANA ALEXANDER

17 What troubles me is not that movie stars run for office, but that they find it easy to get elected. It should be difficult. It should be difficult for millionaires, too.

> *Life* 8 Jul 66

AMERICAN BAR ASSOCIATION

1 The United States may become the first great power to falter because it lost its ability to collect taxes.
Quoted in *Wall Street Journal* 10 Apr 84

ANONYMOUS

2 The prime minister wishes to be obscene and not heard.
Opposition member's charge that Prime Minister Pierre Trudeau had mouthed an obscenity in Canadian House of Commons during debate on February 16, 1971, quoted in John Robert Colombo ed *Colombo's Canadian Quotations* Hurtig 74

3 She's a handbag economist who believes you pay as you go.
On Margaret Thatcher, quoted in *New Yorker* 10 Feb 86

HANNAH ARENDT

4 The most radical revolutionary will become a conservative the day after the revolution.
New Yorker 12 Sep 70

5 The trouble with lying and deceiving is that their efficiency depends entirely upon a clear notion of the truth that the liar and deceiver wishes to hide.
Crises of the Republic Harcourt Brace Jovanovich 72

RICHARD ARMEY, US Congressman

6 It's nothing but an eight-story microphone plugged into the Politburo.
On new US embassy building in Moscow found riddled with Soviet spying devices, *Time* 20 Apr 87

CLEMENT ATTLEE

7 The House of Lords is like a glass of champagne that has stood for five days.
Quoted by Leon A Harris *The Fine Art of Political Wit* Dutton 64

8 One layer was certainly 17th century. The 18th century in him is obvious. There was the 19th century, and a large slice, of course, of the 20th century; and another, curious layer which may possibly have been the 21st.
Comparing Winston Churchill to a cake, quoted by William Manchester *The Last Lion* Little, Brown 83

J EVANS ATTWELL

9 We are not going to have a racehorse pulling a milk wagon.
On appointing former Senate majority leader Howard H Baker Jr as head of the Washington office of his Texas law firm, NY *Times* 11 Dec 84

MARGARET ATWOOD

10 If the national mental illness of the United States is megalomania, that of Canada is paranoid schizophrenia.
The Journals of Susanna Moodie Oxford 70, quoted in John Robert Colombo ed *Colombo's Canadian Quotations* Hurtig 74

BEN BAGDIKIAN

11 He has been called "the Wizard of Ooze" and a man possessed of tonsils marinated in honey.
On Senator Everett M Dirksen, NY *Times* 14 Mar 65

HOWARD H BAKER JR, US Senator

12 The central question is simply put: What did the president know and when did he know it?
To John Dean, White House special counsel, at Watergate hearings 28 Jun 73

RUSSELL BAKER

13 A new star with a tremendous national appeal, the skill of a consummate showman.
On President John F Kennedy at his first televised press conference, NY *Times* 26 Jan 61

ALBEN W BARKLEY, former US Vice President

14 The best audience is intelligent, well-educated and a little drunk.
Recalled on his death 30 Apr 56

BERNARD BARUCH

15 Vote for the man who promises least; he'll be the least disappointing.
Quoted by Meyer Berger *Meyer Berger's New York* Random House 60

CAROL BELLAMY, President, NY City Council

16 I think he is an entertainer. I would prefer if he were a performer.
On Mayor Edward Koch, NY *Times* 31 Jan 85

GEORGES BIDAULT

17 I have plumbed the depth of human cowardice and I realized that there is only one way to be right, and that is to be in power.
Statement in 1962 shortly before he was exiled for attempting to overthrow Charles de Gaulle as president, recalled on Bidault's death 27 Jan 83

18 If we had not been dealing with the devil in person, we could have saved Algeria.
On de Gaulle, *ib*

1 Africa is destined to anarchy. It is turning into 36 Haitis, with 36 Duvaliers, full of Cadillacs, beggars and snarling dogs.
ib

JIMMY BRESLIN

2 The first funeral for Andrew Goodman was at night and it was a lot of work. To begin with they had to kill him.
On last rites for a 21-year-old civil-rights worker slain and secretly buried in Mississippi with two of his associates, NY *Herald Tribune* 10 Aug 64

3 Politics, where fat, bald, disagreeable men, unable to be candidates themselves, teach a president how to act on a public stage.
Table Money Ticknor & Fields 86

DAVID BRINKLEY

4 This is the first convention of the space age—where a candidate can promise the moon and mean it.
On 1960 Democratic National Convention, quoted in *Newsweek* 13 Mar 61

JOSEPH BRODSKY

5 No matter under what circumstances you leave it, home does not cease to be home. No matter how you lived there—well or poorly.
On leaving the USSR, NY *Times* 1 Oct 72

JAMES BROOKE

6 The blunt-spoken New Englander ran the White House as "the abominable 'no' man."
On President Dwight D Eisenhower's chief of staff Sherman Adams, recalled on Adams's death, NY *Times* 28 Oct 86

GEORGE BROWN, Foreign Secretary of Great Britain

7 I've got nothing against men wearing striped pants and black jackets if they want to, and they can wear Anthony Eden hats to their hearts' content. It's the wearing of striped pants in the soul that I object to, and having a Homburg hat where your heart ought to be.
Quoted in *Christian Science Monitor* 19 Aug 66

JOHN MASON BROWN

8 The more I observed Washington, the more I frequently I visited it, and the more people I interviewed there, the more I understood how prophetic L'Enfant was when he laid it out as a city that goes around in circles.
Through These Men Harper 56

ART BUCHWALD

9 Just when you think there's nothing to write about, Nixon says, "I am not a crook." Jimmy Carter says, "I have lusted after women in my heart." President Reagan says, "I have just taken a urinalysis test, and I am not on dope."
At Humor and the Presidency Symposium, Ford Museum, Grand Rapids MI, *Time* 29 Sep 86

GEORGE BURNS

10 Too bad that all the people who know how to run the country are busy driving taxicabs and cutting hair.
Life Dec 79

BARBARA BUSH

11 I can't say it, but it rhymes with *rich*.
On her husband's opponent, Democratic vice-presidential candidate Geraldine Ferraro; she later telephoned Ferraro to apologize for referring to her as a *witch*, NY *Times* 15 Oct 84

GEORGE BUSH, US Vice President

12 I haven't chosen her yet.
When asked what criteria he would use in selecting a 1988 vice-presidential candidate, to Republican meeting in NYC 27 Mar 87

CAPITOL STEPS, political satirists

13 Hark, when Gerald Ford was king,
We were bored with everything.
Unemployment 6 percent.
What a boring president.
Nothing major needed fixin'
So he pardoned Richard Nixon.
Lyrics for performance at Humor and the Presidency Symposium, Ford Museum, Grand Rapids MI, *Time* 22 Sep 86

JIMMY CARTER, 39th US President

14 I now understand more clearly than I ever had before why you won in November 1980 and I lost.
Thanking his successor Ronald Reagan for address during dedication of Carter Presidential Center in Atlanta, NY *Times* 2 Oct 86

HERVÉ DE CHARETTE, French cabinet minister

15 The French at heart are monarchists. They like to prostrate themselves in front of the monarch, whom they now call president, and every seven years or so they guillotine him.
NY *Times* 26 Nov 87

LAWTON CHILES, US Senator

1 We have entered the era of the "imperial" former presidency with lavish libraries, special staffs and benefits, around-the-clock Secret Service protection for life and other badges of privilege.
On his legislation to cut cost of presidential perquisites, *Wall Street Journal* 27 Jul 84

GEORGE J CHURCH

2 He is running not for election but for the history books.
On President Ronald Reagan halfway through his second term, *Time* 29 Sep 86

WINSTON CHURCHILL

3 In war, you can only be killed once, but in politics, many times.
Recalled on his death 24 Jan 65

4 Baldwin thought Europe was a bore, and Chamberlain thought it was only a greater Birmingham.
1953 comment quoted by Lord Moran *Churchill: Taken from the Diaries of Lord Moran* Houghton Mifflin 66

RAMSEY CLARK, former US Attorney General

5 If Rosa Parks had not refused to move to the back of the bus, you and I might never have heard of Dr Martin Luther King.
On effectiveness of individual protests, NY *Times* 14 Apr 87

CLARK M CLIFFORD

6 We're going through a kind of ancient, barbaric war dance now—it's almost an ultimate in absurdity.
On investigation of arms sales to Iran, *Christian Science Monitor* 9 Dec 86

FRANCIS X CLINES

7 If castaway cigar butts once were the floor symbol of the male-dominated convention, the equivalent symbol this year is a litter of women's pumps.
On Democratic National Convention in San Francisco, NY *Times* 18 Jul 84

RICHARD CORRIGAN

8 On Capitol Hill Congress runs by an internal clock: Legislative days are not counted the way calendar days are, and the seasons are marked not by the earth's orbit but by whether Congress is in session or out.
"Technology Focus" *National Journal* 25 Oct 86, quoted in NY *Times* 31 Oct 86

9 However time may be measured at the Naval Observatory, the clock seems to tick slowly here when Congress is out of town.
ib

MARIO CUOMO, Governor of NY

10 We must get the American public to look past the glitter, beyond the showmanship, to the reality, the hard substance of things. And we'll do it . . . not so much with speeches that will bring people to their feet as with speeches that bring people to their senses.
Keynote address to Democratic National Convention in San Francisco 16 Jul 84

11 I said I didn't want to run for president. I didn't ask you to believe me.
NY *Times* 12 Feb 85

12 You campaign in poetry. You govern in prose.
New Republic 8 Apr 85

13 I have no plans, and no plans to plan.
On presidential ambitions, NY *Times* 14 Sep 86

JOHN C DANFORTH, US Senator

14 I was to Japanese visitors to Washington what the Mona Lisa is to Americans visiting Paris.
On his criticism of trade deficit with Japan, NY *Times* 14 Sep 86

ROBERTSON DAVIES

15 The average politician goes through a sentence like a man exploring a disused mine shaft—blind, groping, timorous and in imminent danger of cracking his shins on a subordinate clause or a nasty bit of subjunctive.
The Papers of Samuel Marchbanks Viking 86, quoted in Boston *Globe* 5 Aug 86

BETTE DAVIS

16 I sent my flowers across the hall to Mrs Nixon but her husband remembered what a Democrat I am and sent them back.
On occupying one of the VIP suites at New York Hospital-Cornell Medical Center, Joan Rivers show 8 Apr 87

JOHN DAWKINS, Member of Australian Parliament

17 I heard his library burned down and that both books were destroyed—and one of them hadn't even been colored in yet.
On fellow member Wilson Tuckey, quoted in *Wall Street Journal* 14 Nov 86

CHARLES DE GAULLE, President of France

18 I have come to the conclusion that politics are

too serious a matter to be left to the politicians.

> Quoted by Clement Attlee *Twilight of Empire* Barnes 62

1 Roosevelt, a false witness; Truman, a merchant; Eisenhower, I am told that on the golf links he is better [with a putter] than he is with the long shots and that doesn't surprise me; Kennedy, the style of a hairdresser's assistant—he combed his way through problems; Johnson, a truck driver or a stevedore—or a legionnaire.

> *Time* 28 Feb 69

LEN DEIGHTON

2 In Mexico an air conditioner is called a politician because it makes a lot of noise but doesn't work very well.

> *Mexico Set* Knopf 85

DENG XIAOPING, Chinese Premier

3 The United States brags about its political system, but the president says one thing during the election, something else when he takes office, something else at midterm and something else when he leaves.

> Quoted by John F Burns "Deng Asserts Ties to West Are Vital to Fight Poverty" NY *Times* 2 Jan 85

GUSTAVO DÍAZ ORDOZ

4 I like to operate like a submarine on sonar. When I am picking up noise from both the left and right, I know my course is correct.

> While campaigning for presidency of Mexico, *US News & World Report* 13 Jul 64

JOHN G DIEFENBAKER, Prime Minister of Canada

5 The Liberals are the flying saucers of politics. No one can make head nor tail of them and they never are seen twice in the same place.

> Address at London, Ontario, 5 May 62

LLOYD DOGGETT

6 Sometimes when you get in a fight with a skunk, you can't tell who started it.

> On his opponent for a seat in the Texas legislature, *Time* 5 Nov 84

ROBERT J DOLE, US Senator

7 History buffs probably noted the reunion at a Washington party a few weeks ago of three ex-presidents: Carter, Ford and Nixon—See No Evil, Hear No Evil and Evil.

> To Washington Gridiron Club dinner 26 Mar 83

8 We'll all be riding that streetcar of desire.

> On 1988 Republican National Convention in New Orleans, NY *Times* 24 Jan 87

SEAN DONLON, Irish Ambassador to US

9 Democrats give away their old clothes; Republicans wear theirs. Republicans employ exterminators; Democrats step on the bugs. Democrats eat the fish they catch; Republicans stuff 'em and hang 'em on the wall.

> Quoted in Washington *Post* 23 Oct 81

T C DOUGLAS, leader of Canadian New Democratic Party

10 The Liberals talk about a stable government but we don't know how bad the stable is going to smell.

> News summaries 30 Oct 65

MAUREEN DOWD

11 His House colleagues still call him "Jackie One Note"—joking that if you ask him how to solve the problem of teenage pregnancy, he'll tell you to cut taxes.

> "Is Jack Kemp Mr Right?" NY *Times* 28 Jun 87

MARK DUFFY

12 In Louisiana we don't bet on football games ... We bet on whether a politician is going to be indicted or not.

> On winning wager that Governor Edwin W Edwards would be charged with racketeering and fraud, NY *Times* 3 Mar 85

JOHN P EAST, US Senator

13 The average American doesn't know the difference between a Contra and a caterpillar or between a Sandinista and a sardine.

> Opposing House-Senate conference agreement to continue ban on covert aid to Nicaraguan Contras, NY *Times* 12 Oct 84

EDWIN W EDWARDS, Governor of Louisiana

14 [He's] so slow that he takes an hour and a half to watch *60 Minutes*.

> On 1983 Republican opponent David C Treen, NY *Times* 22 Oct 83

15 People say I've had brushes with the law. That's not true. I've had brushes with overzealous prosecutors.

> On 12th grand jury probe in a decade, *ib* 24 Oct 83

16 [I could not lose unless I was] caught in bed with a dead girl or a live boy.

> On 1983 race against David C Treen, recalled on

his grand jury indictment for racketeering and fraud, *Time* 11 Mar 85

JOHN EHRLICHMAN, White House special assistant

1 I think we ought to let him hang there, let him twist slowly, slowly in the wind.
To presidential counsel John Dean on acting FBI Director L Patrick Gray, taped conversation 7 Mar 73

2 I was under the assumption that it would be conducted as a normal investigation, not as some kind of a second-story job.
On break-in of office of Daniel Ellsberg's psychiatrist after Ellsberg's leak of the Pentagon Papers, Washington *Post* 26 Jul 73

DWIGHT D EISENHOWER, 34th US President

3 Neither a wise man nor a brave man lies down on the tracks of history to wait for the train of the future to run over him.
Presidential campaign speech, quoted in *Time* 6 Oct 52

4 We are tired of aristocratic explanations in Harvard words.
1952 campaign remark that was recalled after more than a dozen Harvard men were named to high positions in the Eisenhower administration, *ib* 26 Jan 53

5 I thought it completely absurd to mention my name in the same breath as the presidency.
Recalling his initial reaction to suggestions that he run for office, *Mandate for Change* Doubleday 63

6 [I despise people who] go to the gutter on either the right or the left and hurl rocks at those in the center.
Time 25 Oct 63

7 I shall make that trip. I shall go to Korea.
1952 campaign promise that was credited with winning the election, quoted in *Life* 5 Jul 68

SAM ERVIN, US Senator

8 Divine right went out with the American Revolution and doesn't belong to the White House aides. What meat do they eat that makes them grow so great?
News conference during Watergate investigation, *Time* 16 Apr 73

9 I'm not going to let anybody come down at night like Nicodemus and whisper something in my ear that no one else can hear. That is not executive privilege; it is poppycock.
At Senate Watergate hearings, *US News & World Report* 28 May 73

10 If the many allegations made to this date are true, then the burglars who broke into the headquarters of the Democratic National Committee at the Watergate were, in effect, breaking into the home of every citizen.
ib

11 There is nothing in the Constitution that authorizes or makes it the official duty of a president to have anything to do with criminal activities.
At Senate Watergate hearings, Washington *Post* 12 Jul 73

12 I used to think that the Civil War was our country's greatest tragedy, but I do remember that there were some redeeming features in the Civil War in that there was some spirit of sacrifice and heroism displayed on both sides. I see no redeeming features in Watergate.
ib 24 Jul 73

LORD ESHER (Oliver S B Brett)

13 We are fortunate to have inherited an institution which we certainly should never have had the intelligence to create. We might have been landed with something like the American Senate.
On the House of Lords, *Wall Street Journal* 2 May 63

ROWLAND EVANS JR

14 The Kennedy organization doesn't run, it purrs.
On John F Kennedy's presidential campaign, quoted by Ralph G Martin *A Hero for Our Time* Macmillan 83

JAMES A FARLEY

15 A rigged convention is one with the other man's delegates in control. An open convention is when your delegates are in control.
Quoted in *Convention and Election Almanac* issued by NBC 64

JULES FEIFFER

16 I used to think I was poor. Then they told me I wasn't poor, I was needy. They told me it was self-defeating to think of myself as needy, I was deprived. Then they told me underprivileged was overused. I was disadvantaged. I still don't have a dime. But I have a great vocabulary.
1965 cartoon, quoted by William Safire *Safire's Political Dictionary* Random House 78

DIANNE FEINSTEIN, Mayor of San Francisco

1 Toughness doesn't have to come in a pinstripe suit.
> On women's role in government, *Time* 4 Jun 84

GERALDINE A FERRARO

2 Vice president—it has such a nice ring to it!
> Accepting Walter F Mondale's invitation to be his Democratic Party running mate, NY *Times* 13 Jul 84

3 I'd call it a new version of voodoo economics, but I'm afraid that would give witch doctors a bad name.
> On Republican Party platform, *ib* 25 Aug 84

TREVOR FISHLOCK

4 She ate a television journalist for breakfast and, feeling peckish, bit off some reporters' heads at a press conference.
> On Prime Minister Margaret Thatcher during a visit to Canada, London *Times* 28 Sep 83

DAVID FROST

5 Vote Labor and you build castles in the air. Vote Conservative and you can live in them.
> *That Was the Year That Was* BBC TV 31 Dec 62

CARLOS FUENTES

6 What the United States does best is to understand itself. What it does worst is understand others.
> *Time* 16 Jun 86

J WILLIAM FULBRIGHT, US Senator

7 The junior senator from Wisconsin, by his reckless charges, has so preyed upon the fears and hatreds and prejudices of the American people that he has started a prairie fire which neither he nor anyone else may be able to control.
> On Senator Joseph R McCarthy's charges of Communism in high places, news summaries 30 Nov 54

8 The biggest lesson I learned from Vietnam is not to trust [our own] government statements. I had no idea until then that you could not rely on [them].
> Recalling his years as chairman of US Senate Foreign Relations Committee during Vietnam War, NY *Times* 30 Apr 85

9 I'm sure that President Johnson would never have pursued the war in Vietnam if he'd ever had a Fulbright to Japan, or say Bangkok, or had any feeling for what these people are like

and why they acted the way they did. He was completely ignorant.
> *ib* 26 Jun 86

JOHN KENNETH GALBRAITH

10 Politics is not the art of the possible. It consists in choosing between the disastrous and the unpalatable.
> *Ambassador's Journal* Houghton Mifflin 69

11 Nothing is so admirable in politics as a short memory.
> Quoted in *A Guide to the 99th Congress* LTV Corp 85

GEORGE H GALLUP

12 Polling is merely an instrument for gauging public opinion. When a president or any other leader pays attention to poll results, he is, in effect, paying attention to the views of the people. Any other interpretation is nonsense.
> News summaries 1 Dec 79

JOHN NANCE GARNER, former US Vice President

13 You have to do a little bragging on yourself even to your relatives—man doesn't get anywhere without advertising.
> News summaries 15 Feb 54

BOB GELDOF

14 It's really very simple, Governor. When people are hungry they die. So spare me your politics and tell me what you need and how you're going to get it to these people.
> Discussing African famine relief with deputy governor of Eastern Region of the Sudan, NY *Times* 26 Jan 85

DAVID R GERGEN

15 When he hung up on Nancy Reagan, that's when he crossed his final threshold.
> On resignation of White House chief of staff Donald T Regan during Iran arms sales investigation, *Nightline* ABC TV 27 Feb 87

JACK GESCHEIDT

16 The *News* says, Khadafy
The *Times* says, Qaddafi
Time says, Gaddafi
Newsweek, Kaddafi;
MOO-a-mar
Mo-AH-mar;
LIB-ya
LIB-ee-a;
Let's blow the whole thing off.
> On variations in spelling of name of Libyan leader Muammar Qaddafi, NY *Times* 18 May 86

IAN GILMOUR, British Conservative Party leader

1 Politicians trim and tack in their quest for power, but they do so in order to get the wind of votes in their sails.
The Body Politic Hutchinson 69

BARRY M GOLDWATER, US Senator

2 Extremism in the defense of liberty is no vice. . . . Moderation in the pursuit of justice is no virtue.
Accepting Republican presidential nomination 16 Jul 64

3 To insist on strength . . . is not war-mongering. It is peace-mongering.
NY *Times* 11 Aug 64

4 It's political Daddyism and it's as old as demagogues and despotism.
On President Lyndon B Johnson's promise of federal aid without additional cost, *ib* 27 Nov 64

5 I wouldn't trust Nixon from here to that phone.
Newsweek 29 Sep 86

DORIS KEARNS GOODWIN

6 Once a president gets to the White House, the only audience that is left that really matters is history.
On presidential libraries, NY *Times* 13 Oct 85

7 They all start competing against Lincoln as the greatest president. And the [library] building becomes the symbol, the memorial to that dream.
ib

NADINE GORDIMER

8 Mumbling obeisance to abhorrence of apartheid [is] like those lapsed believers who cross themselves when entering a church.
On US policy of "constructive engagement" in South Africa, NY *Times* 8 Sep 85

HENRY GRAFF, Professor of History, Columbia University

9 He has a chance to make somebody move over on Mount Rushmore. He's working for his place on the coins and the postage stamps.
On President Ronald Reagan at start of his second term, *Newsweek* 28 Jan 85

ROGER L GREEN, Brooklyn Assemblyman and Chairman, Black and Puerto Rican Legislative Caucus

10 Everyone appears to be noticing only the statue's torch and not the manacles on her ankles.
On centennial of Statue of Liberty, NY *Times* 30 May 86

MEG GREENFIELD

11 In Washington it is an honor to be disgraced. . . . you have to have *been* somebody to fall.
Newsweek 2 Jun 86

ALEXANDER M HAIG JR

12 I probably carry more scar tissue on my derrière than any other candidate—that's political scar tissue.
On his qualifications for entering the 1988 presidential campaign, *MacNeil/Lehrer Newshour* 24 Mar 87

13 I'm the only American alive or dead who presided unhappily over the removal of a vice president and a president.
On his service at the White House during Richard M Nixon's presidency, *ib*

H R HALDEMAN, White House special assistant

14 Once the toothpaste is out of the tube, it's hard to get it back in.
On Watergate disclosures, news summaries 30 Aug 73

15 Every president needs an SOB—and I'm Nixon's.
ib

PETE HAMILL

16 Say what you will about him . . . Ed Koch is still the best show in town.
On NYC Mayor Edward Koch, "Act III" NY *Daily News* 1 Sep 85

17 He steps on stage and draws the sword of rhetoric, and when he is through, someone is lying wounded and thousands of others are either angry or consoled.
ib

GRACE HANSEN

18 I feel I'm as qualified for office as any of the other comedians who are running.
On her 1970 gubernatorial race against incumbent Tom McCall, recalled on her death, Eugene OR *Register-Guard* 14 Jan 85

19 For some time I've had my eye on Tom McCall's seat—which is a great deal more than he's had on it.
ib

GARY HART, US Senator

20 This is one Hart that you will not leave in San Francisco.
After his unsuccessful bid for the presidency at

the 1984 Democratic National Convention in San Francisco, London *Financial Times* 21 Jul 84

1 There is always some fig leaf being used.

On excuses for armed intervention abroad, *Time* 7 Apr 86

2 Follow me around. I don't care. . . . If anybody wants to put a tail on me, go ahead. They'd be very bored.

As presidential candidate, from interview that appeared the same day the Miami *Herald* reported that a woman had spent the night at his Washington town house, NY *Times* 3 May 87

3 I think there is one higher office than president and I would call that patriot.

On first television interview following his withdrawal from the presidential race, *Nightline* ABC TV 8 Sep 87

DENIS HEALEY, former Chancellor of the Exchequer

4 La Pasionaria of middle-class privilege.

On Prime Minister Margaret Thatcher, *New Yorker* 10 Feb 86

WILLIAM RANDOLPH HEARST

5 A politician will do anything to keep his job—even become a patriot.

Recalled on his death 14 Aug 51

LILLIAN HELLMAN

6 I cannot and will not cut my conscience to fit this year's fashions.

Letter to House Committee on Un-American Activities, *Nation* 31 May 52

7 Truth made you a traitor as it often does in a time of scoundrels.

On McCarthy era, *Scoundrel Time* Little, Brown 76

A P HERBERT, Member of British Parliament

8 I am sure that the party system is right and necessary. . . . there must be some scum.

Independent Member Doubleday 51

THEODORE M HESBURGH, President, Notre Dame

9 Voting is a civic sacrament.

Reader's Digest Oct 84

STEPHEN HESS

10 The presidency is a huge echo chamber magnifying every little thing he does.

On President Ronald Reagan, *Time* 6 Feb 84

GILBERT HIGHET

11 What is politics but persuading the public to vote for this and support that and endure these for the promise of those?

"The Art of Persuasion" *Vogue* Jan 51

GEORGE HILL

12 She is said to be inclined to cough noisily when he goes on too long at the rostrum; but this is a traditional prerogative of the political wife, and rather more necessary in this instance than in most.

On Glenys Kinnock, wife of Neil Kinnock, Labor Party candidate for prime minister, London *Times* 19 Feb 87

STANLEY HOFFMANN, Director, Harvard Center for European Studies

13 Arms control has to have a future, or none of us does. But it doesn't necessarily have to come in big packages of 600-page treaties.

Newsweek 1 Oct 84

SIMON HOGGART

14 The nanny seemed to be extinct until 1975, when, like the coelacanth, she suddenly and unexpectedly reappeared in the shape of Margaret Thatcher.

"At the Top: Margaret Thatcher" *Vanity Fair* Aug 83

15 She is the first head of government in history to give a whole country its second childhood.

ib

CHUCK HOLLANDER, National Student Assn

16 Hippiedom is more than a choice of lifestyle. It's an apolitical systemicide.

Time 7 Jul 67

HERBERT HOOVER, 31st US President

17 Honor is not the exclusive property of any political party.

Quoted in *Christian Science Monitor* 21 May 64

LUCY HOWARD

18 In the heat of a political lifetime, Ronald Reagan innocently squirrels away tidbits of misinformation and then, sometimes years later, casually drops them into his public discourse, like gum balls in a quiche.

Newsweek 11 Nov 85

JAMES C HUMES

19 Churchill wrote his own speeches. When a

leader does that, he becomes emotionally invested with his utterances. . . . If Churchill had had a speech writer in 1940, Britain would be speaking German today.
NY *Times* 15 Jun 86

HUBERT H HUMPHREY, US Senator

1 Underneath the beautiful exterior there was an element of ruthlessness and toughness that I had trouble either accepting or forgetting.
On presidential campaign of John F Kennedy, *The Education of a Public Man* Doubleday 76

HAROLD L ICKES

2 I am against government by crony.
On resigning in 1946 as secretary of the interior, recalled on his death 3 Feb 52

WALTER ISAACSON and EVAN THOMAS

3 Big, pink and lumbering, waving a trunklike arm, he indulged his love of phrase making with such clinkers as "our merific inheritances," "marcesant monarchyu," "nautical nimbus."
On Senator Arthur H Vandenberg as chairman of Foreign Relations Committee, *The Wise Men* Simon & Schuster 86

4 [John Foster Dulles] stirred whiskey with a thick forefinger, his socks drooped, his suits were green-hued, his ties were indifferent and his breath was chronically bad. Hunched forward as he talked, he droned on in a flat voice, pronouncing Anthony Eden "Ant-ny."
ib

HENRY M JACKSON, US Senator

5 The best politics is no politics.
On need for bipartisan approach to foreign affairs, to Amer Bar Assn, Chicago, 3 Feb 80

JESSE JACKSON

6 I cast my bread on the waters long ago. Now it's time for you to send it back to me—toasted and buttered on both sides.
Addressing black voters, *New York* 30 Jan 84

7 My constituency is the desperate, the damned, the disinherited, the disrespected and the despised.
Address to Democratic National Convention in San Francisco, 17 Jul 84

8 If there are occasions when my grape turned into a raisin and my joy bell lost its resonance, please forgive me. Charge it to my head and not to my heart.
ib

9 I am not a perfect servant. I am a public servant doing my best against the odds. As I develop and serve, be patient. God is not finished with me yet.
ib

10 Our flag is red, white and blue, but our nation is a rainbow—red, yellow, brown, black and white—and we're all precious in God's sight.
ib

11 America is not like a blanket—one piece of unbroken cloth, the same color, the same texture, the same size. America is more like a quilt—many patches, many pieces, many colors, many sizes, all woven and held together by a common thread.
ib

12 The white, the Hispanic, the black, the Arab, the Jew, the woman, the Native American, the small farmer, the businessperson, the environmentalist, the peace activist, the young, the old, the lesbian, the gay and the disabled make up the American quilt.
ib

13 We must not measure greatness from the mansion down, but from the manger up.
ib

14 From seeds of his body blossomed the flower that liberated a people and touched the soul of a nation.
Funeral oration for Martin Luther King Sr 15 Nov 84

JIANG QING, Gang of Four member

15 Man's contribution to human history is nothing more than a drop of sperm.
Newsweek 20 Feb 84

CLAUDIA ("LADY BIRD") JOHNSON

16 A politician ought to be born a foundling and remain a bachelor.
Time 1 Dec 75

LYNDON B JOHNSON, 36th US President

17 Every man has a right to a Saturday night bath.
London *Observer* 13 Mar 60

18 There are plenty of recommendations on how to get out of trouble cheaply and fast. Most of them come down to this: Deny your responsibility.
At Democratic fund-raising affair, news summaries 30 Sep 67

1 All that Hubert needs over there is a gal to answer the phone and a pencil with an eraser on it.
> On Vice President Hubert H Humphrey, recalled on Johnson's death 22 Jan 73

2 Jack was out kissing babies while I was out passing bills. Someone had to tend the store.
> On John F Kennedy's selection as Democratic presidential nominee, quoted by Ralph G Martin *A Hero for Our Time* Macmillan 83

3 I seldom think of politics more than 18 hours a day.
> Quoted in *A Guide to the 99th Congress* LTV Corp 85

4 A man can take a little bourbon without getting drunk, but if you hold his mouth open and pour in a quart, he's going to get sick on it.
> On political persuasion, "Love It or Loathe It, Here's the Wit and Wisdom of LBJ" *People* 2 Feb 87

5 The CIA is made up of boys whose families sent them to Princeton but wouldn't let them into the family brokerage business.
> *ib*

6 When things haven't gone well for you, call in a secretary or a staff man and chew him out. You will sleep better and they will appreciate the attention.
> *ib*

RYSZARD KAPUSCINSKI

7 Money changes all the iron rules into rubber bands.
> On fall of the shah of Iran, *Shah of Shahs* Harcourt Brace Jovanovich 85

GEORGE F KENNAN

8 The best thing we can do if we want the Russians to let us be Americans is to let the Russians be Russian.
> *US-Soviet Relations: The First 50 Years* WNET TV 17 Apr 84

EDWARD M KENNEDY, US Senator

9 Come out of the rose garden.
> Challenging President Jimmy Carter to a public debate, news summaries 10 Feb 80

10 Well, here I don't go again.
> On decision not to run in 1988 presidential campaign, press conference 20 Dec 85

11 Frankly, I don't mind not being president. I just mind that someone else is.
> To Washington Gridiron Club dinner 22 Mar 86

JOHN F KENNEDY, 35th US President

12 To exclude from positions of trust and command all those below the age of 44 would have kept Jefferson from writing the Declaration of Independence, Washington from commanding the Continental Army, Madison from fathering the Constitution, Hamilton from serving as secretary of the treasury, Clay from being elected speaker of the House and Christopher Columbus from discovering America.
> *NY Times* 5 Jul 60

13 We stand today on the edge of a new frontier—the frontier of the 1960s—a frontier of unknown opportunities and perils—a frontier of unfulfilled hopes and threats.
> Accepting the Democratic presidential nomination 15 Jul 60

14 The new frontier of which I speak is not a set of promises—it is a set of challenges. It sums up not what I intend to offer the American people, but what I intend to ask of them. It appeals to their pride, not their pocketbook—it holds out the promise of more sacrifice instead of more security.
> *ib*

15 I hope that no American ... will waste his franchise and throw away his vote by voting either for me or against me solely on account of my religious affiliation. It is not relevant.
> On being a Roman Catholic, *Time* 25 Jul 60

JOSEPH P KENNEDY

16 I have no political ambitions for myself or my children.
> Recalled on his death 18 Nov 69

JOSEPH P KENNEDY II, US Congressman

17 If you have 30 cousins, it's pretty easy.
> On fund-raising for his campaign, *Time* 8 Sep 86

18 I've had a tough time learning how to act like a congressman. Today I accidentally spent some of my own money.
> Quoted in *Newsweek* 9 Feb 87

ROBERT F KENNEDY

19 It will help erase the idea that politics is a second-rate profession and a dirty business.
> On John F Kennedy Library, *Newsweek* 9 Mar 64

20 Now I can go back to being ruthless again.
> On winning race for US Senate, *Esquire* Apr 65

Rose Kennedy

1 It's *our* money, and we're free to spend it any way we please.
> On her son John F Kennedy's presidential campaign, quoted by Ralph G Martin *A Hero for Our Time* Macmillan 83

Martin Luther King Jr

2 If you will protest courageously, and yet with dignity and Christian love, when the history books are written in future generations, the historians will have to pause and say, "There lived a great people—a black people—who injected new meaning and dignity into the veins of civilization."
> Address at Montgomery AL, news summaries 31 Dec 55

3 Discrimination is a hellhound that gnaws at Negroes in every waking moment of their lives to remind them that the lie of their inferiority is accepted as truth in the society dominating them.
> To Southern Christian Leadership Conference, Atlanta, 16 Aug 67

Jeane J Kirkpatrick, US Ambassador to UN

4 Look, I don't even agree with *myself* at times.
> On leaving Democratic Party to register as a Republican, NBC TV 3 Apr 85

5 [Democrats] can't get elected unless things get worse—and things won't get worse unless they get elected.
> *Time* 17 Jun 85

6 A government is not legitimate merely because it exists.
> On Sandinista government in Nicaragua, *ib*

Henry A Kissinger

7 Nixon had three goals: to win by the biggest electoral landslide in history; to be remembered as a peacemaker; and to be accepted by the "Establishment" as an equal. He achieved all these objectives at the end of 1972 and the beginning of 1973. And he lost them all two months later—partly because he turned a dream into an obsession.
> On president Richard M Nixon and the Watergate break-in, *Years of Upheaval* Little, Brown 82

8 It was a Greek tragedy. Nixon was fulfilling his own nature. Once it started it could not end otherwise.
> To James St Clair on August 8, 1974, after President Nixon's televised announcement of his resignation, *ib*

9 The Vietnam War required us to emphasize the national interest rather than abstract principles. . . . What President Nixon and I tried to do was unnatural. And that is why we didn't make it.
> On 10th anniversary of end of the Vietnam War, *Wall Street Journal* 11 Mar 85

10 When you meet the president, you ask yourself, "How did it ever occur to anybody that he should be governor much less president?"
> On President Ronald Reagan, *US* 2 Jun 86

Stanley Klein, FBI terrorism expert

11 Talk in a normal voice. Terrorists are suspicious of whispering.
> On how to behave if taken hostage, to conference of business travelers, NY *Times* 10 Oct 86

Edward Koch, Mayor of NYC

12 I'm not the type to get ulcers. I give them.
> NY *Times* 20 Jan 84

13 If you don't like the president, it costs you 90 bucks to fly to Washington to picket. If you don't like the governor, it costs you 60 bucks to fly to Albany to picket. If you don't like me, 90 cents.
> *ib* 28 Feb 85

14 We're in the hands of the state legislature and God, but at the moment, the state legislature has more to say than God.
> On requesting additional funds for NYC, *ib* 27 Jun 86

15 The knife of corruption endangered the life of New York City. The scalpel of the law is making us well again.
> On recent scandals, State of the City Address, *ib* 25 Jan 87

16 If you turn your back on these people, you yourself are an animal. You may be a well-dressed animal, but you are nevertheless an animal.
> Calling for civic compassion in AIDS epidemic, *ib* 16 Mar 87

Ted Koppel

17 Here is a guy who's had a stake driven through his heart. I mean, really nailed to the bottom of the coffin with a wooden stake, and a silver bullet through the forehead for good measure—and yet he keeps coming back.
> On former President Richard M Nixon, *New York* 13 Aug 84

WILLIAM KOVACH

1 We cannot encourage a process that has a political saliva test administered by candidates.
On allowing campaign managers to veto proposed panelists for presidential debates, *Time* 22 Oct 84

CHARLES KRAUTHAMMER

2 A three-year diet of rubber chicken and occasional crow.
On campaigning for the presidency, "The Appeal of Ordeal" *Time* 14 May 82

RICHARD LAMM, Governor of Colorado

3 Christmas is a time when kids tell Santa what they want and adults pay for it. Deficits are when adults tell the government what they want—and their kids pay for it.
To National League of Cities, Seattle, 10 Dec 85

4 Politics, like theater, is one of those things where you've got to be wise enough to know when to leave.
On stepping down after 12 years in office, *US News & World Report* 26 Jan 87

HAROLD D LASSWELL, Professor of Law and Political Science, Yale

5 Political science without biography is a form of taxidermy.
Quoted by Arnold A Rogow *James Forrestal* Macmillan 64

PAUL LAXALT, US Senator

6 A politician taking campaign money from gamblers in Nevada is like one taking campaign money from the auto people in Michigan. Gambling is our legal business.
On campaigning in Nevada, NY *Times* 21 Oct 84

IRVING LAYTON

7 In Pierre Elliott Trudeau, Canada has at last produced a political leader worthy of assassination.
The Whole Bloody Bird McClelland 69

MAX LERNER

8 The politics of surprise leads through the Gates of Astonishment into the Kingdom of Hope.
On announcement of presidential visit to China, quoted by Richard M Nixon *RN: Memoirs of Richard Nixon* Grosset & Dunlap 78

DON LESSEM

9 The former "first brat" [has] become a Yippie among yuppies.
On Amy Carter's radical activities, Boston *Globe* 28 Jun 87

DAVID LEVINE

10 [My philosophy] is that politicians should be jumped on as often as possible.
On his cartoons, *Time* 24 Sep 84

ANN F LEWIS, National Director, Americans for Democratic Action

11 Politicians have the same occupational hazard as generals—focusing on the last battle and overreacting to that.
NY *Times* 24 Sep 86

LIBYA RADIO

12 Oh, heroes of our Arab nation, let your missiles and suicide cells pursue American terrorist embassies and interests wherever they may be!
Exhorting Arab suicide squads to attack US targets in the Middle East, quoted in *Time* 7 Apr 86

G GORDON LIDDY, White House special assistant

13 Why is it there are so many more horses' asses than there are horses?
On Watergate hearings, news summaries 30 Aug 73

WALTER LIPPMANN

14 Successful . . . politicians are insecure and intimidated men. They advance politically only as they placate, appease, bribe, seduce, bamboozle or otherwise manage to manipulate the demanding and threatening elements in their constituencies.
The Public Philosophy Little, Brown 55

15 Brains, you know, are suspect in the Republican Party.
Recalled on his death 14 Dec 74

16 Once you touch the biographies of human beings, the notion that political beliefs are logically determined collapses like a pricked balloon.
From his 1913 book *A Preface to Morals*, quoted by Ronald Steel *Walter Lippmann and the American Century* Atlantic-Little, Brown 80

17 Certainly he is not of the generation that regards honesty as the best policy. However, he does regard it as a policy.
On President Richard M Nixon, quoted in *Newsweek* 12 May 80

LONDON DAILY TELEGRAPH

1 [She seems] a cross between Isadora Duncan and Lawrence of Arabia.
On Prime Minister Margaret Thatcher during NATO maneuvers, quoted in *Time* 29 Dec 86

EARL LONG, Governor of Louisiana

2 I consider myself 40 percent Catholic and 60 percent Baptist. ... but I'm in favor of *every* religion, with the possible exception of snake-chunking. Anybody that so presumes on how he stands with Providence that he will let a snake bite him, I say he deserves what he's got coming to him.
Quoted in *New Yorker* 4 Jun 60

3 The kind of thing I'm good at is knowing every politician in the state and remembering where he itches. And I know where to scratch him.
ib

RUSSELL B LONG, US Senator

4 Tax reform means "Don't tax you, don't tax me, tax that fellow behind the tree."
News summaries 31 Dec 76

5 I really think that it's better to retire, in Uncle Earl's terms, when you still have some snap left in your garters.
Referring to Earl Long, former governor of Louisiana, NY *Times* 18 Mar 85

6 [A tax loophole is] something that benefits the other guy. If it benefits you, it is tax reform.
Recalled on his retirement, *Time* 10 Nov 86

HAROLD MACMILLAN

7 He is forever poised between a cliché and an indiscretion.
On position of British foreign secretary, *Newsweek* 30 Apr 56

8 At home, you always have to be a politician; when you're abroad, you almost feel yourself a statesman.
Look 15 Apr 58

9 I have never found, in a long experience of politics, that criticism is ever inhibited by ignorance.
Wall Street Journal 13 Aug 63

10 You can hardly say boo to a goose in the House of Commons now without cries of "Ungentlemanly," "Not fair" and all the rest.
Quoted by Leon A Harris *The Fine Art of Political Wit* Dutton 64

11 If people want a sense of purpose they should get it from their archbishop. They should certainly not get it from their politicians.
Quoted by Henry Fairlie *The Life of Politics* Methuen 69

12 [She is] a brilliant tyrant surrounded by mediocrities.
On Prime Minister Margaret Thatcher, *Newsweek* 12 Jan 87

EDWARD MAHE

13 Senate races are about ideology. Governors are about jobs and contracts and schools and bridges and more contracts.
On study showing that a majority of voters care more about gubernatorial races than about Senate races, NY *Times* 12 Oct 86

ANDREW H MALCOLM

14 A Chicago alderman once confessed he needed physical exercise but didn't like jogging, because in that sport you couldn't hit anyone.
NY *Times* 5 May 85

WILLIAM MANCHESTER

15 It would be inaccurate to say that Churchill and I conversed. ... Like Gladstone speaking to Victoria, he addressed me as though I were a one-man House of Commons. It was superb.
On his initial meeting with Winston Churchill, recounted in *The Last Lion* Little, Brown 83

NELSON MANDELA

16 Only free men can negotiate; prisoners cannot enter into contracts. Your freedom and mine cannot be separated.
Refusing to bargain for freedom after 21 years in prison, *Time* 25 Feb 85

DONALD R MANES, former Queens Borough President

17 I apologize for what was said even though I didn't say it.
On report that he called NYC Mayor Edward Koch a crook, WQXR Radio 3 Feb 86

IMELDA MARCOS

18 I think that's a very kinky issue with the panties and bras. That's the thing that they will display: shoes, panties and bras.
On exhibition of thousands of pairs of shoes and other articles of clothing left behind when she and her husband fled the Philippines, NY *Times* 10 Apr 86

GROUCHO MARX

1 Politics is the art of looking for trouble, finding it everywhere, diagnosing it incorrectly and applying the wrong remedies.
　Recalled on his death 19 Aug 77

JANE MAYER

2 The campaign kickoff was so dismal that it needed a plastic surgeon instead of a press agent to put a face on it.
　On Mondale-Ferraro presidential campaign, *Wall Street Journal* 11 Sep 84

EUGENE J McCARTHY, US Senator

3 Have you ever tried to split sawdust?
　Reply to charge that he had divided the Democratic Party, NBC TV 23 Oct 69

JOSEPH R McCARTHY, US Senator

4 While I cannot take the time to name all of the men in the State Department who have been named as members of the Communist Party and members of a spy ring, I have here in my hand a list of 205 that were known to the secretary of state as being members of the Communist Party and who nevertheless are still working and shaping the policy of the State Department.
　February 9, 1950, address at Wheeling WV that began a period of unfounded accusations, quoted by Richard H Rovere *Senator Joe McCarthy* Harcourt, Brace 59

5 McCarthyism is Americanism with its sleeves rolled.
　Theme in successful campaign for re-election to US Senate in 1952, *ib*

MARY McCARTHY

6 Congress—these, for the most part, illiterate hacks whose fancy vests are spotted with gravy and whose speeches, hypocritical, unctuous and slovenly, are spotted also with the gravy of political patronage.
　On the Contrary Farrar, Straus & Cudahy 61

JOHN T McCUTCHEON

7 The political cartoon is a sort of pictorial breakfast food. It has the cardinal asset of making the beginning of the day sunnier.
　NY *Times* 3 Dec 75

JOE McGINNISS

8 We forgave, followed and accepted because we liked the way he looked. And he had a pretty wife. Camelot was fun, even for the peasants, as long as it was televised to their huts.
　On President John F Kennedy, *The Selling of the President 1968* Trident 69

GEORGE McGOVERN, US Senator

9 [I am] 1,000 percent for Tom Eagleton and I have no intention of dropping him from the ticket.
　On his 1972 presidential running mate Thomas F Eagleton after disclosure of Eagleton's health problems, statement issued less than a week before McGovern asked him to resign, quoted by Theodore H White *The Making of the President 1972* Atheneum 73

10 To those who charge that liberalism has been tried and found wanting, I answer that the failure is not in the idea, but in the course of recent history. The New Deal was ended by World War II. The New Frontier was closed by Berlin and Cuba almost before it was opened. And the Great Society lost its greatness in the jungles of Indochina.
　Lecture at Oxford University, NY *Times* 22 Jan 73

11 The whole campaign was a tragic case of mistaken identity.
　On his unsuccessful 1972 presidential campaign, *ib* 6 May 73

12 The trouble was, all people saw on television were a few of my outspoken supporters out front; and they came away thinking that was me.
　ib

13 When people ask if the United States can afford to place on trial the president, if the system can stand impeachment, my answer is, "Can we stand anything else?"
　Advocating impeachment of Richard M Nixon, San Francisco *Examiner* 29 Nov 73

SHEILA McKECHNIE, Director, Shelter National Campaign for the Homeless Ltd, London

14 People who are homeless are not social inadequates. They are people without homes.
　Christian Science Monitor 7 May 85

GEORGE MEANY

15 We heard from the abortionists and we heard from the people who looked like Jacks, acted like Jills and had the odors of Johns.
　On 1972 Democratic National Convention, quoted in *Wall Street Journal* 11 Jul 84

ROBERT G MENZIES, former Prime Minister of Australia

1 Never forget posterity when devising a policy. Never think of posterity when making a speech.

The Measure of the Years Cassell 70

2 The long-established and noble rule of Law, one of the greatest products of the character and tradition of British history, has suffered a deadly blow. Blackmail has become respectable.

On British government's cancellation of English tour by South African cricket players after public protests, recalled on his death 15 May 78

JEAN NATHAN MILLER

3 Through his mastery of storytelling techniques, he has managed to separate his character, in the public mind, from his actions as president. . . . He has, in short, mesmerized us with that steady gaze.

"Ronald Reagan and the Techniques of Deception" *Atlantic* Feb 84

4 The best advice one can offer to both press and public is the suggestion Ronald Reagan himself gave to students in Chicago . . . "Don't let me get away with it. Check me out. Don't be the sucker generation."

ib

WILLIAM ("FISHBAIT") MILLER, Congressional doorkeeper

5 Eighty percent were hypocrites, 80 percent liars, 80 percent serious sinners . . . except on Sundays. There is always boozing and floozying. . . . I don't have enough time to tell you everybody's name.

60 Minutes CBS TV 24 Apr 77

GEORGE J MITCHELL, US Senator

6 Although he's regularly asked to do so, God does not take sides in American politics.

At Iran-Contra hearings 13 Jul 87

JOHN N MITCHELL, Director, Committee for the Re-election of the President

7 In my mind, the re-election of Richard Nixon, compared with what was available on the other side, was so much more important that I put it in just that context.

On why he did not advise the president of the Watergate break-in, LA *Times* 11 Jul 73

HERBERT MITGANG

8 Johnson himself turned out to be so many different characters he could have populated all of *War and Peace* and still had a few people left over.

On President Lyndon B Johnson, in review of Merle Miller's *Lyndon: An Oral Biography* Putnam 80, NY *Times* 15 Aug 80

IRVIN MOLOTSKY

9 In a few days they are on the walls of the recipients, mementos of a once-in-a-lifetime visit to the president of the United States, pretty good cementers of future support.

On what White House photographer Michael Evans called "grip-and-grin" photographs of Ronald Reagan and visiting dignitaries, "Of Presidential Image and Presidential Focus" NY *Times* 15 Mar 85

WALTER F MONDALE

10 I don't want to spend the next two years in Holiday Inns.

Withdrawing from 1976 presidential campaign 21 Nov 74

11 I said I didn't want to spend most of my life in Holiday Inns, but I've checked and they've all been redecorated. They're marvelous places to stay and I've thought it over and that's where I'd like to be.

On accepting nomination as candidate for vice president, news summaries 16 Jul 76

12 In our system, at about 11:30 on election night, they just push you off the edge of the cliff—and that's it. You might scream on the way down, but you're going to hit the bottom, and you're not going to be in elective office.

On loss to Ronald Reagan in 1984 presidential election, NY *Times* 4 Mar 87

13 Do you want to tear your life apart and get rid of everything you've known as a lifestyle? Like seeing your family? Being with your friends? A fishing trip? A hunting trip? A night's sleep?

Comments to prospective presidential candidates, quoted in *Newsweek* 30 Mar 87

LANCE MORROW

14 The real 1960s began on the afternoon of November 22, 1963 . . . It came to seem that Kennedy's murder opened some malign trap door in American culture, and the wild bats flapped out.

Time 14 Nov 83

15 In the pageant of unity [at the Democratic National Convention], one speaker after another recited a Whitmanesque litany of races and

classes and minorities and interests and occupations—or unemployments. Some speakers, in fact, made the nation sound like an immense ingathering of victims—terrorized senior citizens, forsaken minorities, Dickensian children—warmed by the party's Frank Capra version of America: Say, it's a wonderful life!

"All Right, What Kind of People Are We?" *ib* 30 Jul 84

1 His campaign sounded a note of the bogusly grand. Hart is Kennedy typed on the eighth carbon.

After Gary Hart's withdrawal from the 1988 presidential campaign, *ib*, 18 May 87

ROBERT MOSES

2 If you elect a matinee idol mayor, you're going to have a musical comedy administration.

On John V Lindsay as mayor of NYC, NY *Times* 8 Jan 78

BILL MOYERS

3 Ideas are great arrows, but there has to be a bow. And politics is the bow of idealism.

Time 29 Oct 65

4 I work for him despite his faults and he lets me work for him despite my deficiencies.

As press secretary to President Lyndon B Johnson, NY *Times* 3 Apr 66

5 Hyperbole was to Lyndon Johnson what oxygen is to life.

ib 11 Sep 75

DANIEL P MOYNIHAN, US Senator

6 Citizen participation [is] a device whereby public officials induce nonpublic individuals to act in a way the officials desire.

The Public Interest Fall 69

7 Somehow liberals have been unable to acquire from life what conservatives seem to be endowed with at birth: namely, a healthy skepticism of the powers of government agencies to do good.

NY *Post* 14 May 69

8 The single most exciting thing you encounter in government is competence, because it's so rare.

NY *Times* 2 Mar 76

EDWARD R MURROW

9 No one can terrorize a whole nation, unless we are all his accomplices.

On Senator Joseph R McCarthy's accusations about Communists in government, *See It Now* CBS TV 7 Mar 54

10 If none of us ever read a book that was "dangerous," had a friend who was "different" or joined an organization that advocated "change," we would all be just the kind of people Joe McCarthy wants. Whose fault is that? Not really [McCarthy's]. He didn't create this situation of fear. He merely exploited it, and rather successfully.

ib

11 The politician in my country seeks votes, affection and respect, in that order. . . . With few notable exceptions, they are simply men who want to be loved.

October 19, 1959, address at London Guildhall, quoted by A M Sperber *Murrow* Freundlich 86

12 The politician is . . . trained in the art of inexactitude. His words tend to be blunt or rounded, because if they have a cutting edge they may later return to wound him.

ib

13 After last night's debate, the reputation of Messieurs Lincoln and Douglas is secure.

On September 26, 1960, televised debate between presidential candidates John F Kennedy and Richard M Nixon, *ib*

14 Difficulty is the excuse history never accepts.

On President John F Kennedy's inaugural address, *ib*

RALPH NADER

15 Our founders did not oust George III in order for us to crown Richard I.

On President Richard M Nixon during Watergate investigation, news summaries 23 Oct 73

16 President Reagan was elected on the promise of getting government off the backs of the people and now he demands that government wrap itself around the waists of the people.

On proposed legislation requiring air bags or automatic seat belts in all automobiles, NY *Times* 12 Jul 84

17 The networks are not some chicken-coop manufacturing lobby whose calls nobody returns.

On NBC President Robert C Wright's proposal that company employees support a political action committee, quoted by Edwin Diamond *New York* 19 Jan 87

V S NAIPAUL

18 Argentine political life is like the life of an ant

community or an African forest tribe: full of events, full of crisis and deaths, but life is always cyclical, and the year ends as it begins.
Quoted by Lydia Chavez NY *Times* 15 Dec 85

NEW YORK HERALD TRIBUNE

1 Truman lost his temper, MacArthur lost his job, Acheson lost his war, a million and a half people lost their lives and Stalin didn't even lose a night's sleep.
On Korean War and early 1950s, 6 Apr 64

REINHOLD NIEBUHR

2 The sad duty of politics is to establish justice in a sinful world.
Quoted by Jimmy Carter *Why Not the Best?* Broadman 75

RICHARD M NIXON, 37th US President

3 Any lady who is first lady likes being first lady. I don't care what they say, they like it.
Newsweek 22 Mar 71

4 My view is that one should not break up a winning combination.
On choice of Spiro T Agnew as vice-presidential running mate, CBS TV 2 Jan 72

5 If an individual wants to be a leader and isn't controversial, that means he never stood for anything.
Dallas *Times-Herald* 10 Dec 78

6 I wish I could give you a lot of advice, based on my experience of winning political debates. But I don't have that experience. My only experience is at losing them.
Letter to Robert Gray, Ronald Reagan's deputy campaign manager, quoted by Robert Sam Anson *Exile: The Unquiet Oblivion of Richard M Nixon* Simon & Schuster 84

JON NORDHEIMER

7 Louisiana has [no] monopoly on rogues, rapscallions, shakedowns and kickbacks. ... Nor is it the only place where a few officials have endeared themselves to the electorate by means of the utter disorder of their private lives.
NY *Times* 3 Mar 85

MICHAEL OAKESHOTT

8 In political activity ... men sail a boundless and bottomless sea; there is neither harbor for shelter nor floor for anchorage, neither starting point nor appointed destination.
"Rabble without a Cause" London *Times* 21 May 85

KIRK O'DONNELL

9 [Political theory] provides a common language with which people in this town communicate with each other.
On Washington DC, NY *Times* 18 Jan 83

10 Instant analysis is the occupational disease. ... There are no smokestacks, there's no black lung. Politics is the only industry.
ib

THOMAS P ("TIP") O'NEILL, Speaker of the House

11 Am I wrong in listening to women who live in Nicaragua and follow the Sermon on the Mount? Or am I supposed to just sit here and believe generals?
On crediting testimony of Maryknoll nuns against US aid to Nicaraguan Contras, quoted by Jimmy Breslin NY *Daily News* 29 Jun 86

ALAN PATON

12 I envision someday a great, peaceful South Africa in which the world will take pride, a nation in which each of many different groups will be making its own creative contribution.
Quoted in *New Yorker* 17 Dec 60

13 The Afrikaner has nowhere to go, and that's why he would rather destroy himself than capitulate.
On resistance to social change by descendants of the Dutch settlers in South Africa, *Christian Science Monitor* 17 Jan 78

LESTER B PEARSON, Prime Minister of Canada

14 We'll jump off that bridge when we come to it.
Quoted in John Robert Colombo ed *Colombo's Canadian Quotations* Hurtig 74

15 Politics is the skilled use of blunt objects.
From 1972 CBC TV presentation *The Tenth Decade*

CLAIBORNE PELL, US Senator

16 My opponent called me a cream puff. ... Well, I rushed out and got the baker's union to endorse me.
On his first political campaign, NY *Times* 3 Feb 87

17 The secret is to always let the other man have your way.
ib

CHARLES PETERS

18 Bureaucrats write memoranda both because they appear to be busy when they are writing

and because the memos, once written, immediately become proof that they were busy.

How Washington Really Works Addison-Wesley 80

1 The more bureaucrats do wrong to the public, the more favors congressmen can do for their constituents as they right the wrongs—or as they appear to try to right them.

ib

PRINCE PHILIP, Duke of Edinburgh

2 Most of the monarchies of Europe were really destroyed by their greatest and most ardent supporters. It was the most reactionary people who tried to hold onto something without letting it develop and change.

Quoted by John Pearson *The Selling of the Royal Family* Simon & Schuster 86

CABELL PHILLIPS

3 One gathers from talking with him, indeed, that he looks back upon the whole episode regretfully, as a virtuous husband might upon an extramarital fling with the office widow.

On Henry A Wallace's attitude toward his term as vice president, NY *Times* 6 Oct 63

WILLIAM PROXMIRE, US Senator

4 The biggest danger for a politician is to shake hands with a man who is physically stronger, has been drinking and is voting for the other guy.

NY *Herald Tribune* 16 Feb 64

5 He knows the tax code as thoroughly as the pope knows the Lord's Prayer.

On Senator Russell B Long, recalled on Long's retirement, *Time* 10 Nov 86

JEANETTE RANKIN, 1st US Congresswoman

6 We're half the people; we should be half the Congress.

Calling for more women in public office, *Newsweek* 14 Feb 66

SAM RAYBURN, Speaker of the House

7 They may be just as intelligent as you say. But I'd feel a helluva lot better if just one of them had ever run for sheriff.

To Vice President Lyndon B Johnson on associates of President John F Kennedy, quoted by Lance Morrow "After 20 Years, the Question: How Good a President?" *Time* 14 Nov 83

8 Wait a minute.

Advice recalled by Jack Valenti as "the three most important words in the English language," quoted by Peter W Kaplan "Are Movies a Fabulous Invalid, Too?" NY *Times* 5 May 85

RONALD REAGAN, 40th US President

9 The thought of being president frightens me. I do not think I want the job.

As governor of California, news summaries 31 Dec 73

10 To sit back hoping that someday, someway, someone will make things right is to go on feeding the crocodile, hoping he will eat you last—but eat you he will.

News summaries 7 Nov 74

11 Politics I supposed to be the second-oldest profession. I have come to realize that it bears a very close resemblance to the first.

LA *Herald-Examiner* 3 Mar 78

12 With our eyes fixed on the future, but recognizing the realities of today. ... we will achieve our destiny to be as a shining city on a hill for all mankind to see.

To Conservative Political Action Conference 17 Mar 78

13 I was alarmed at my doctor's report: He said I was sound as a dollar.

As Republican presidential nominee 17 Jul 80

14 I believe Moses was 80 when God first commissioned him for public service.

On running for president at age 73, address at Dixon IL 6 Feb 84

15 Thomas Jefferson once said, "We should never judge a president by his age, only by his works." And ever since he told me that I stopped worrying.

ib

16 There were so many candidates on the platform that there were not enough promises to go around.

On Democratic presidential primary debate in New Hampshire, *Newsweek* 6 Feb 84

17 Republicans believe every day is the Fourth of July, but Democrats believe every day is April 15.

NY *Times* 10 Oct 84

18 If I had as much make-up on as he did, I'd have looked younger, too.

On "age issue" during television debates with Walter F Mondale, *Wall Street Journal* 11 Oct 84

19 Shouldn't someone tag Mr Kennedy's bold new imaginative program with its proper age?

Under the tousled boyish haircut is still old Karl Marx—first launched a century ago. There is nothing new in the idea of a government being Big Brother.

1960 letter to Richard M Nixon disclosed in final weeks of 1984 presidential campaign, NY *Times* 27 Oct 84

1 I'll be like Scarlett O'Hara—I'll think about it tomorrow.

Refraining from endorsement of Vice President George Bush for 1988 Republican presidential nomination, *ib* 12 Feb 85

2 Die-hard conservatives thought that if I couldn't get everything I asked for, I should jump off the cliff with the flag flying—go down in flames. No, if I can get 70 or 80 percent of what it is I'm trying to get . . . I'll take that and then continue to try to get the rest in the future.

On criticism of early political compromises, *ib* 6 Oct 85

3 You know, it was only a generation ago that actors couldn't be buried in the churchyard.

Expressing belief that people underestimated him because of his acting background, *ib*

4 Recession is when your neighbor loses his job. Depression is when you lose yours. And recovery is when Jimmy Carter loses his.

1980 campaign remark recalled when Reagan participated in dedication of Carter Presidential Center in Atlanta, *ib* 2 Oct 86

JAMES RESTON

5 Half circus and half Supreme Court.

On national political conventions, NY *Times* 12 Jul 60

6 How Kennedy knew the precise drop in milk consumption in 1960, the percentage rise in textile imports from 1957 to 1960 and the number of speeches cleared by the Defense Department is not quite clear, but anyway, he did. He either overwhelmed you with decimal points or disarmed you with a smile and a wisecrack.

On President John F Kennedy's press conferences, quoted by Ralph G Martin *A Hero for Our Time* Macmillan 83

7 An election is a bet on the future, not a popularity test of the past.

NY *Times* 10 Oct 84

ELLIOT L RICHARDSON

8 Washington is . . . a city of cocker spaniels. It's a city of people who are more interested in being petted and admired, loved, than rendering the exercise of power.

NY *Times* 13 Jul 82

ALAN RICHMAN

9 She enjoys driving her restless mind in the express lane.

On Senator Paula Hawkins of Florida, *People* 20 Oct 86

HYMAN G RICKOVER

10 If you're going to sin, sin against God, not the bureaucracy. God will forgive you but the bureaucracy won't.

Quoted by William A Clinkscales Jr after Senate committee delayed confirming him as director of the Selective Service System, NY *Times* 3 Nov 86

PAT ROBERTSON

11 The first words I spoke as a baby were *Mommy*, *Daddy* and *constituency*.

On growing up in a prominent Virginia political family, NY *Times* 12 Feb 87

ANDY ROONEY

12 The only people who say worse things about politicians than reporters do are other politicians.

60 Minutes CBS TV 7 Oct 84

ETHEL AND JULIUS ROSENBERG

13 We are the first victims of American fascism.

Letter released by their attorney on the day they were electrocuted for espionage, news summaries 19 Jun 53

RICHARD H ROVERE

14 He stamped with his name a tendency, a whole cluster of tendencies in American life. The name survives. To many Americans, whatever is illiberal, anti-intellectual, repressive, reactionary, totalitarian or merely swinish will hereafter be *McCarthyism*. The word is imprecise, but it conveys a meaning and a powerful image.

On Senator Joseph R McCarthy, "The Frivolous Demagogue" *Esquire* Jun 58

15 He was a master of the scabrous and the scatological.

ib

16 McCarthy invented the Multiple Lie—the lie with so many tiny gears and fragile connecting rods that reason exhausted itself in the effort to combat it.

ib

MARK RUSSELL

1 He'll tell you he's a Texan
Though he's got those Eastern ways,
Eatin' lots of barbecue
With a sauce that's called béarnaise.

On George Bush's 1980 campaign, "Two-Gun Georgie Bush," set to tune of "Yellow Rose of Texas," quoted in NY *Times* 7 Oct 84

WILLIAM SAFIRE

2 I want my questions answered by an alert and experienced politician, prepared to be grilled and quoted—not my hand held by an old smoothie.

On artful dodging of difficult questions by President Ronald Reagan, NY *Times* 16 Aug 84

3 No one flower can ever symbolize this nation. America is a bouquet.

On Congressional designation of the rose as the official US flower, *ib* 25 Sep 86

4 One difference between French appeasement and American appeasement is that France pays ransom in cash and gets its hostages back while the United States pays ransom in arms and gets additional hostages taken.

ib 13 Nov 86

5 The first ladyship is the only federal office in which the holder can neither be fired nor impeached.

ib 2 Mar 87

6 Decide on some imperfect Somebody and you will win, because the truest truism in politics is: You can't beat Somebody with Nobody.

"The Perfect Candidate" *ib* 16 Apr 87

ANTHONY SAMPSON

7 The real rulers of England are not so much in the center of a solar system as in a cluster of interlocking circles, each one largely preoccupied with its own professionalism and expertise and touching others only at one edge. . . . They are not a single Establishment but a ring of Establishments, with slender connections.

The Anatomy of Britain Harper & Row 62

8 In the person of the prime minister several different strands come together. Dukes, Eton, Balliol, the Guards, clubs, the Church and Whitehall all jostle together behind that mustache.

On Harold Macmillan, *ib*

LORD SAMUEL (Edwin Herbert Samuel)

9 Where there are two PhDs in a developing country, one is head of state and the other is in exile.

NY *Times* 5 Jul 64

LORD SANDWICH (Alexander V E P Montague)

10 Lord Hailsham said the other day that the machinery of government was creaking. My Lords, it is not even moving sufficiently to emit a noise of any kind.

NY *Times* 21 Apr 63

ARTHUR SCARGILL, Marxist leader of British miners

11 [That] most dangerous duo, President Ray-Gun and the plutonium blonde, Margaret Thatcher.

Quoted in *Time* 3 Dec 84

JAMES R SCHLESINGER, former US Secretary of Defense

12 The notion of a defense that will protect American cities is one that will not be achieved, but it is that goal that supplies the political magic, as it were, in the president's vision.

To Senate Foreign Relations Committee, NY *Times* 7 Feb 87

13 Americans historically have embraced crusades—such as World War II—as well as glorious little wars. The difficulty is that the most likely conflicts of the future fall between crusades and such brief encounters as Grenada or Mayagüez.

ib

SERGE SCHMEMANN

14 In some circles Stalin has in fact been making a comeback. . . . His portrait hangs above the dashboard of trucks, a symbol of blue-collar nostalgia for a tough leader.

NY *Times* 31 Oct 86

DAVID SCHOENBRUN

15 There never was a France like the Madonna that Charles de Gaulle worships in the fresco of his imagination.

The Three Lives of Charles de Gaulle Atheneum 66

PATRICIA SCHROEDER, US Congresswoman

16 I have a brain and a uterus, and I use both.

On being an elected official and a mother, NY *Times* 6 May 77

17 I was cooking breakfast this morning for my

kids, and I thought, "He's just like a Teflon frying pan: Nothing sticks to him."

> August 1983 description of President Ronald Reagan, quoted by Michael Kenney Boston *Globe* 24 Oct 84

1 Spine transplants are what we really need to take Reagan on.

> On the military budget, NY *Times* 14 Jan 85

WALTER SHAPIRO

2 Geraldine Ferraro was undergoing one of the worst ordeals of a media age—trial by disclosure.

> On investigation of her family's finances, *Newsweek* 27 Aug 84

DAVID K SHIPLER

3 The Holocaust never quite leaves Israeli Jews alone. Arabs use it against them and they use it against Arabs. Jews use it against other Jews. Even the president of the United States, it seems, can use it against the prime minister of Israel.

> *Arab and Jew: Wounded Spirits in a Promised Land* Times Books 86

4 Watching foreign affairs is sometimes like watching a magician; the eye is drawn to the hand performing the dramatic flourishes, leaving the other hand—the one doing the important job—unnoticed.

> "For Israel and US, A Growing Military Partnership" NY *Times* 15 Mar 87

HUGH SIDEY

5 A White House dinner is the American family assembled, from labor leaders to billionaires, actors, architects, academicians and athletes.

> "Talking Peace and Pork Chops" *Time* 23 Jan 84

6 When people travel here from across the country, they shed jealousies and politics and prejudices. ... The mighty climb down. The humble are elevated.

> *ib*

7 [China's Premier] Zhao Ziyang, for all of his billion constituents, seemed in the evening's lovely flow like a favorite uncle, smiling a little too much, wanting to be a bit American, talking about peace and pork chops.

> *ib*

8 In this era of world leadership, the metal detector is the altar and the minicam may be god.

> "The New Style of Exposure" *ib* 18 Jun 84

9 In just 20 years terrorism, communications, the jet plane and the increase of wealth and knowledge have forced, to varying degrees, world leaders into a haunted and secret peerage whose links with the people they guide are meticulously cleansed and staged.

> *ib*

10 The problems seem so easy out there on the stump. Deficits shrink with a rhetorical flourish.

> On closing days of the 1984 presidential campaign, "Now Comes the Hard Part" *ib* 5 Nov 84

11 We love the blather and boast, the charge and countercharge of campaigning. Governing is a tougher deal.

> *ib*

12 The prime minister found something hopeful in the man's eyes and manner. The 30 or so people who run this world analyze one another that way and then make decisions of life and death for us. Scary, but true.

> On Margaret Thatcher's first meeting with Mikhail S Gorbachev, "Measure of the Man" *ib* 25 Mar 85

WILLIAM E SIMON, former US Secretary of the Treasury

13 Bad politicians are sent to Washington by good people who don't vote.

> Quoted in *A Guide to the 99th Congress* LTV Corp 85

ALAN K SIMPSON, US Senator

14 There is no "slippery slope" toward loss of liberties, only a long staircase where each step downward must first be tolerated by the American people and their leaders.

> NY *Times* 26 Sep 82

15 Welcome to the pit [and] the great hunters who have been out to tack the pelt of Bill Rehnquist on the wall of the den.

> To Supreme Court nominee Antonin Scalia on his appearance before the Senate Judiciary Committee after the committee's prolonged hearings to confirm William H Rehnquist as chief justice, *ib* 8 Aug 86

16 Here we can brag and bluster and blather and almost like a comic book character you could invent, Captain Bombast, pull the cape around the shoulders and shout the magic words, "Get him." And rise above it all in a blast of hot air.

> Characterizing his committee, *ib*

1 Stonewalling, wiretapping, cover-up, Lord's sake, if there isn't one of us here at this table that hasn't dabbled in that mystery.

ib

2 He has to do the heavy lifting and the windows and the wash, and also protect the president.

On role of Ronald Reagan's White House chief of staff Donald T Regan, *ib* 19 Feb 87

3 [You were doing a] sadistic little disservice to your country.

To reporters who shouted questions about the Iran arms deal to President Reagan as he boarded a helicopter, *Time* 30 Mar 87

4 You'd like to stick it in his gazoo.

ib

JOHN J SIRICA, Judge, US District Court, District of Columbia

5 An attempt is already underway to revise history—to leave the impression that the former president had nothing to do with Watergate. But there is no doubt about his obstruction of justice after the Watergate break-in.

NY *Times* 12 Aug 79

MICHAEL SMALL

6 To their credit, neither candidate said anything that would damage his campaign, and neither bit his opponent.

On mock debate between a German shepherd and a rottweiler, staged by Walter F Mondale's family the night before the actual debate in Louisville KY, *People* 5 Nov 84

MARGARET CHASE SMITH, US Senator

7 When people keep telling you that you can't do a thing, you kind of like to try it.

Announcing her presidential candidacy, *Time* 7 Feb 64

STEVEN SMITH

8 You've got to understand their reasoning. They think of this historian as one of their pocket-people, whom they feel they can count on.

On Kennedy family's approval of biographers, quoted by Peter Collier and David Horowitz *The Kennedys* Summit 84

ALEXANDER SOLZHENITSYN

9 I was in a state of witless shock, as though flames had suddenly enwrapped and paralyzed me so that for a moment I had no mind, no memory.

On arrest by Russian secret police, *The Oak and the Calf* Harper & Row 80

THEODORE C SORENSEN

10 The ambassador was never present, but his presence was never absent.

On Joseph P Kennedy's influence on his son John's presidential campaign, quoted by Ralph G Martin *A Hero for Our Time* Macmillan 83

11 Presidential candidates don't chew gum.

Aside to John F Kennedy overheard at a Nebraska airport, *ib*

12 I think he's informing himself, reaching out and getting ideas and information and advice. I haven't the slightest doubt that internally taking shape in that marvelous brain of his is a philosophy of foreign affairs. But it would be premature to say that one is fully formed.

On NY Governor Mario Cuomo, NY *Times* 1 May 86

ROGER STARR

13 Reality is the best possible cure for dreams.

On the near financial collapse of NYC in the mid 1970s, *The Rise and Fall of New York City* Basic Books 85

DAVID STEEL, leader of British Liberal Party

14 The cabinet has been shaken about a bit, but it's the same old jar of jellybeans.

On Prime Minister Margaret Thatcher's restructuring of her Conservative cabinet, *Newsweek* 16 Sep 85

15 [She has turned] the British bulldog into a Reagan poodle.

On Thatcher's decision to permit US bombers to take off from British bases for attack on Libya, *Time* 28 Apr 86

RONALD STEEL

16 Politics as battle has given way to politics as spectacle.

"The Vanishing Campaign Biography" NY *Times* 5 Aug 84

17 We are not a cynical people. The will to believe lingers on. We like to think that heroes can emerge from obscurity, as they sometimes do; that elections do matter, even though the process is at least part hokum; that through politics we can change our society and maybe even find a cause to believe in.

ib

18 He has not yet become an elder statesman, though his foreign policy credentials are considerable, but he is certainly our ancient mariner, forever tugging at our sleeve to let him tell his tale of what really happened.

On Richard M Nixon, *New York Review of Books* 30 May 85

1 He forever perplexes and annoys. Every time you think he is about to show the statesmanship for which his intelligence and experience have equipped him, he throws a spitball.
ib

GLORIA STEINEM

2 What has the women's movement learned from [Geraldine Ferraro's] candidacy for vice president? Never get married.
On personal and financial problems of Ferraro's family during 1984 presidential campaign, quoted in Boston *Globe* 14 May 87

ADLAI E STEVENSON

3 [They are] the dinosaur wing of the party.
On the Republican's extreme conservatives, address at Salt Lake City, news summaries 14 Oct 52

4 The general has dedicated himself so many times, he must feel like the cornerstone of a public building.
On his opponent Dwight D Eisenhower, *ib* 1 Nov 52

5 It is an ancient political vehicle, held together by soft soap and hunger and with front-seat drivers and back-seat drivers contradicting each other in a bedlam of voices, shouting "go right" and "go left" at the same time.
On the Republican Party, *ib* 15 Nov 52

6 I don't envy the driver and I don't think the American people will care to ride in his bus very far.
ib

7 To act coolly, intelligently and prudently in perilous circumstances is the test of a man—and also a nation.
Opposing US defense of islands off Chinese mainland, *ib* 11 Apr 55

8 Nixon is finding out there are no tails on an Eisenhower jacket.
On the 1960 presidential campaign, *ib* 30 Aug 60

9 The elephant has a thick skin, a head full of ivory, and as everyone who has seen a circus parade knows, proceeds best by grasping the tail of its predecessor.
ib

10 It will be helpful in our mutual objective to allow every man in America to look his neighbor in the face and see a man—not a color.
Foreword to booklet on interracial relations prepared by Anti-Defamation League of B'nai B'rith, quoted in NY *Times* 22 Jun 64

11 You know, you really can't beat a household commodity—the ketchup bottle on the kitchen table.
On running for president against Dwight D Eisenhower, recalled on Stevenson's death 14 Jul 65

12 He is the kind of politician who would cut down a redwood tree, then mount the stump and make a speech for conservation.
On Richard M Nixon, *ib*

DAVID A STOCKMAN

13 A veritable incubator of short cuts, schemes and devices to overcome the truth.
On his job as director of US Office of Management and Budget, *The Triumph of Politics* Harper & Row 86

14 He operated on the echo principle: He told the president what he wanted to hear.
On White House chief of staff Donald T Regan, *ib*

THEODORE STRAUSS

15 The vanquished themselves prove that history has not lied; like tourists in hell, they took snapshots.
On photographs of Nazi concentration camps, ABC TV 6 Mar 68

ROBERT A TAFT, US Senator

16 You really have to get to know Dewey to dislike him.
On Republican presidential candidate Thomas E Dewey, recalled on Taft's death 31 Jul 53

MARGARET THATCHER, Prime Minister of Great Britain

17 No woman in my time will be prime minister or chancellor or foreign secretary—not the top jobs. Anyway, I wouldn't want to be prime minister; you have to give yourself 100 percent.
On appointment as government spokesperson for education, London *Sunday Telegraph* 26 Oct 69

18 In politics if you want anything said, ask a man. If you want anything done, ask a woman.
People 15 Sep 75

19 What Britain needs is an iron lady.
Campaign slogan, quoted in *Newsweek* 14 May 79

20 Unless we change our ways and our direction, our greatness as a nation will soon be a footnote in the history books, a distant memory of

an offshore island, lost in the mists of time like Camelot, remembered kindly for its noble past.

>Campaign speech in Bolton, *ib*

1 Of course it's the same old story. Truth usually is the same old story.

>On her stand for sound money and competitive industry to cut inflation and unemployment, *Time* 16 Feb 81

2 We were told our campaign wasn't sufficiently slick. We regard that as a compliment.

>On winning an unprecedented third term as prime minister, NY *Times* 12 Jun 87

PAUL THEROUX

3 The Peace Corps is a sort of Howard Johnson's on the main drag into maturity.

>*Sunrise with Seamonsters* Houghton Mifflin 84

NORMAN THOMAS

4 [President John F] Kennedy said that if we had nuclear war we'd kill 300 million people in the first hour. [Secretary of Defense Robert S] McNamara, who is a good businessman and likes to save, says it would be only 200 million.

>Recalled on his death 19 Dec 68

5 The struggle against demagoguery scarcely fits the St George-against-the-dragon myth ... Our democratic St George goes out rather reluctantly with armor awry.

>Quoted on 30th anniversary of US Senate's censure of Joseph R McCarthy, NY *Times* 2 Dec 84

6 The struggle is confused; our knight wins by no clean thrust of lance or sword, but the dragon somehow poops out, and decent democracy is victor.

>*ib*

LORD THOMSON OF FLEET (Roy Herbert Thomson)

7 I've got money so I'm a Conservative.

>Recalled on his death 4 Aug 76

LORD THORNEYCROFT (Peter Thorneycroft), British Conservative Party leader

8 The choice in politics isn't usually between black and white. It's between two horrible shades of gray.

>London *Sunday Telegraph* 11 Feb 79

HARRY S TRUMAN, 33rd US President

9 In my opinion eight years as president is enough and sometimes too much for any man to serve in that capacity.

>Announcement that he would not seek election to a second full term, 29 Mar 52

10 You and I are stuck with the necessity of taking the worst of two evils or none at all. So— I'm taking the *immature* Democrat as the best of the two. Nixon is impossible.

>Letter to Dean Acheson on 1960 presidential campaign 26 Aug 60

11 I remember when I first came to Washington. For the first six months you wonder how the hell you ever got here. For the next six months you wonder how the hell the rest of them ever got here.

>Recalled on his death 26 Dec 72

12 He's one of the few in the history of this country to run for high office talking out of both sides of his mouth at the same time and lying out of both sides.

>On Richard M Nixon, quoted by Merle Miller *Plain Speaking: An Oral Biography of Harry S Truman* Berkley 74

13 He wasn't used to being criticized, and he never did get it through his head that's what politics is all *about*. He was used to getting his ass kissed.

>On President Dwight D Eisenhower, *ib*

14 Why, this fellow don't know any more about politics than a pig knows about Sunday.

>On 1952 presidential candidate Dwight D Eisenhower, quoted by Richard M Nixon *RN: Memoirs of Richard Nixon* Grosset & Dunlap 78

MARGARET TRUMAN

15 He took pride in belonging to the world's most exclusive club: the United States Senate.

>To joint session of Congress on centenary of the birth of her father President Harry S Truman 8 May 84

16 He was prouder still to be a member of that even more restricted group, Uncle Sam Rayburn's Board of Education—the Bourbon and Branch Water College of Congressional Knowledge.

>*ib*

17 He loved politicians—even Republicans.

>*ib*

T L TSIM

18 The destiny of Hong Kong is now the same as the destiny of China. There is no escaping.

>On 1984 agreement between Britain and China that life in the crown colony would continue virtually unchanged when it reverted to Chinese rule in 1997, NY *Times* 27 Sep 84

DESMOND TUTU, Bishop of Johannesburg

1 Be nice to whites, they need you to rediscover their humanity.
NY *Times* 19 Oct 84

2 I am a leader by default, only because nature does not allow a vacuum.
Christian Science Monitor 20 Dec 84

3 When a pile of cups is tottering on the edge of the table and you warn that they will crash to the ground, in South Africa you are blamed when that happens.
NY *Times* 3 Jan 85

4 For goodness sake, will they hear, will white people hear what we are trying to say? Please, all we are asking you to do is to recognize that we are humans, too.
ib

5 I am not interested in picking up crumbs of compassion thrown from the table of someone who considers himself my master. I want the full menu of rights.
Today NBC TV 9 Jan 85

6 Those who invest in South Africa should not think they are doing us a favor; they are here for what they get out of our cheap and abundant labor, and they should know that they are buttressing one of the most vicious systems.
Quoted by LA Mayor Tom Bradley in letter to the editor LA *Times* 13 May 85

JACK VALENTI, White House special assistant

7 I sleep each night a little better, a little more confidently, because Lyndon Johnson is my president.
In frontispiece to Jack Shepherd and Christopher S Wren comps *Quotations from Chairman LBJ* Simon & Schuster 68

GORE VIDAL

8 In writing and politicking, it's best not to think about it, just do it.
Quoted in *A Guide to the 99th Congress* LTV Corp 85

JOHN VINOCUR

9 On a strawberry sundae of a day, all daisies and June sun and pastoral posing by world leaders on the Lancaster House lawn.
On summit conference in London, NY *Times* 9 Jun 84

10 Like boilerplate, the final statements bear hundreds of hammer marks and rivets. And in their leaden way, they are perhaps as good a reflection of the mood that dominates the meetings at Lancaster House as the photogenic scenes behind the building this afternoon when President Reagan seemed to want to mow the old building's lawn.
ib

LOUDON WAINWRIGHT

11 Displaying a bland, even an eerie, disregard for what appeared to be the facts of the situation, he fell back on an old habit of looking ahead to the next defeat.
On perennial presidential candidate Harold E Stassen, *Life* 20 Mar 64

TERRY WAITE

12 Freeing hostages is like putting up a stage set, which you do with the captors, agreeing on each piece as you slowly put it together; then you leave an exit through which both the captor and the captive can walk with sincerity and dignity.
On trips to Middle East as emissary of the Archbishop of Canterbury to negotiate the release of hostages held by terrorists, ABC TV 3 Nov 86

GEORGE C WALLACE, Governor of Alabama

13 Being governor don't mean a thing anymore in this country. We're nothing. Just high-paid ornaments is all. I'm thinking of running for president myself.
Life 22 Jul 66

14 I'm the lamest lame duck there could be.
At farewell to political supporters after his retirement as governor, news summaries 22 Nov 86

HAROLD WASHINGTON, Mayor of Chicago

15 We have destroyed the dinosaur.
On defeating the Democratic machine in his 1983 election as mayor, quoted in *Time* 31 Mar 86

JOSEPH N WELCH

16 Until this moment, Senator, I think I had never gauged your cruelty or your recklessness.... Have you no sense of decency, sir, at long last? Have you left no sense of decency?
To Senator Joseph J McCarthy at the Army-McCarthy hearings after McCarthy had gratuitously smeared a young associate of Welch's, news summaries 9 Jun 54

THEODORE H WHITE

17 I happen to think that American politics is one of the noblest arts of mankind; and I cannot do anything else but write about it.
NY *Times* 22 Jun 65

1 The gusto of one, the indignation of the other; the challenge of the one party, the response of the other; the eloquence and the comedy, the passion and the issues were ours—no other country can provide them.

ib

2 He is like a good prewar house—solidly built. They don't build them that way anymore. He's also been repainted several times.

On Richard M Nixon's return to presidential politics, *Time* 16 Feb 68

3 His passion has aroused the best and the beast in man. And the beast waited for him in the kitchen.

On assassination of presidential candidate Robert F Kennedy in the kitchen of the Ambassador Hotel in Los Angeles, *The Making of the President 1968* Atheneum 69

4 The best time to listen to a politician is when he's on a stump on a street corner in the rain late at night when he's exhausted. Then he doesn't lie.

NY *Times* 5 Jan 69

5 The flood of money that gushes into politics today is a pollution of democracy.

Time 19 Nov 84

6 There is no excitement anywhere in the world, short of war, to match the excitement of an American presidential campaign.

On his role as "a storyteller of elections" in series of books on presidential campaigns, recalled on his death 15 May 86

7 A liberal is a person who believes that water can be made to run uphill. A conservative is someone who believes everybody should pay for his water. I'm somewhere in between: I believe water should be free, but that water flows downhill.

ib

8 With the end of the nominating process, American politics leaves logic behind.

Newsweek 26 May 86

9 Politics in America is the binding secular religion.

Time 29 Dec 86

RALPH WHITEHEAD JR

10 If Mike Dukakis were an automobile, he'd be a Honda Civic. Compact, efficient, reliable—short on style but long on utility.

On 1988 presidential candidate Michael S Dukakis, governor of Massachusetts, Boston *Globe* 17 Mar 87

TOM WICKER

11 [It is] a product of the media and by the media, if not just for the media.

On Senator Gary Hart's campaign for the 1984 Democratic presidential nomination, NY *Times* 13 Mar 84

AMY WILENTZ

12 The upcoming primaries will be a test of their old family football cheer: "Clap your hands! Stamp your feet! 'Cause Daddy's team can't be beat."

On concurrent Congressional campaigns of two of Robert F Kennedy's children, *Time* 8 Sep 86

GEORGE F WILL

13 They define themselves in terms of what they oppose.

On conservatives, *Newsweek* 30 Sep 74

14 Voters don't decide issues, they decide *who* will decide issues.

ib 8 Mar 76

15 The unpleasant sound Bush is emitting as he traipses from one conservative gathering to another is a thin, tinny "arf"—the sound of a lap dog.

On Vice President George Bush, Washington *Post* 30 Jan 86

16 All God's chillun got shoes or can get them in Mrs Marcos's closet, which is large enough to house Mr and Mrs Duvalier, itinerant nonlaborers.

On the 1986 flight into exile of Imelda Marcos of the Philippines, leaving behind a horde of shoes, and Haiti's ouster of President Jean Claude "Baby Doc" Duvalier, *Newsweek* 5 Jan 87

17 Stalin's henchman [V M] Molotov, 96, died old and in bed, a privilege he helped to deny to millions.

ib

HAROLD WILSON, Prime Minister of Great Britain

18 There is something utterly nauseating about a system of society which pays a harlot 25 times as much as it pays its prime minister, 250 times as much as it pays its members of Parliament and 500 times as much as it pays some of its ministers of religion.

To the House of Commons during Profumo Affair, news summaries 31 Mar 63

JAMES Q WILSON, Professor of Government, Harvard

19 There are no more liberals . . . They've all been mugged.

Time 21 Jan 85

Tom Wolfe

1 Radical chic invariably favors radicals who seem primitive, exotic and romantic, such as the grape workers who are not merely radical and "of the soil" but also Latin; the Panthers, with their leather pieces, Afros, shades and shoot-outs; and the Red Indians, who, of course, had always seemed primitive, exotic and romantic.

> On the fashionable rich who celebrated and supported radical views, *Radical Chic* Farrar, Straus & Giroux 70

2 At the outset, at least, all three groups had something else to recommend them, as well: They were headquartered 3,000 miles away from the East Side of Manhattan.

> *ib*

Stevie Wonder

3 [South Africa is] the land with tears in her eyes.

> At UN ceremony honoring his work against apartheid in South Africa, NY *Times* 14 May 85

Harriett Woods

4 The price of running for the Senate today is spending more time than you'd like to spend asking people for more money than they'd like to give.

> On campaigning for US Senate seat in Missouri, quoted by Steven V Roberts "Politicking Goes High-Tech" NY *Times* 2 Nov 86

James C Wright Jr, US Congressman

5 Here is an animal with a hide two feet thick, and no apparent interest in politics. What a waste.

> On the rhinoceros, NY *Times* 9 Dec 86

6 I have gone out already breaking the ice and floating ideas, saying the unsayable, and lightning has not struck me down.

> On becoming speaker of the House, quoted by Tom Wicker "The Wright Stuff" *ib* 11 Mar 87

Robert C Wright

7 Employees who earn their livings and support their families from the profits of our business must recognize the need to invest some portion of their earnings to ensure that the company is well represented in Washington.

> Memo to NBC employees on his desire for a company political action committee, quoted by Edwin Diamond *New York* 19 Jan 87

8 Employees who elect not to participate . . .
should question their own dedication to the company and their expectations.

> *ib*

Stefan Cardinal Wyszynski

9 You covered my windows with blotting paper so that people would not see the primate of Poland; but no one will be able to shield those windows from the world.

> *A Freedom Within: The Prison Notes of Cardinal Wyszynski* Hodder & Stoughton 85, quoted by Timothy Garton Ash London *Times* 17 Jan 85

David R Young, aide to US Secretary of State Henry A Kissinger

10 I'm a plumber. I fix leaks.

> On his assignment to prevent security leaks, quoted by Theodore H White *Breach of Faith: The Fall of Richard Nixon* Atheneum 75

Whitney Moore Young Jr

11 There is no such thing as a moderate in the civil-rights movement; everyone is a radical. The difference is whether or not one is all rhetoric or relevant.

> Recalled on his death 11 Mar 71

12 Personally, I am not nonviolent, but I'm not a fool either. I can count.

> *ib*

13 Should I . . . stand on 125th Street cussing out Whitey to show I am tough? Or should I go downtown and talk to an executive of General Motors about 2,000 jobs for unemployed Negroes?

> *ib*

UNITED NATIONS

Officials & Delegates

Afro-Asian Declaration on Colonialism

14 All peoples have the right of self-determination.

> NY *Times* 15 Dec 60

Nora Astorga, Nicaragua

15 We said nonsense but it was important nonsense.

> On conversing cordially with US Ambassador Vernon A Walters even though their countries were at odds, NY *Times* 28 Sep 86

Angie Brooks-Randolph, Liberia, President of General Assembly

16 The United Nations believes we cannot con-

tinue to ignore 800 million people. . . . to solve the problem we must have two Chinas.
LA *Herald-Examiner* 27 Feb 70

LORD CARADON (Hugh Mackintosh Foot), Great Britain

1 Now that he has changed the weather
Lion and lamb can vote together. God bless the Russian delegation,
I waive consecutive translation.
Poem read to Security Council in tribute to Soviet representative Vasily V Kuznetsov, NY *Times* 20 Jun 68

2 Better to make prime ministers out of prisoners than prisoners out of prime ministers.
Reply to criticism by Soviet representative, *International Herald Tribune* 5 Jun 79

3 I wanted to say in the Security Council, "There is no cause for alarm. The rumbling sound that you hear is the normal noise of the Soviet ambassador being lowered and locked into a fixed position." But I never got to say it, the time was never quite right.
Mimicking British pilots' explanation to passengers on lowering of landing gear, *ib*

HUMAYUN RASHEED CHOUDHURY, Bangladesh, President of General Assembly

4 If everyone did this, it would save us hundreds of thousands of dollars.
On Angolan Foreign Minister Afonso Van Dunem's decision to stop speaking 10 minutes into his 40-minute speech that was also available in print, NY *Times* 27 Sep 86

ANDREW COHEN, Great Britain

5 To campaign against colonialism is like barking up a tree that has already been cut down.
Quote 23 Feb 58

JOSÉ CORREA, Nicaragua

6 We do not believe in having happiness imposed upon us.
Reply to Soviet representative, NY *Times* 20 Jul 60

DECLARATION OF THE RIGHTS OF THE CHILD

7 Whereas mankind owes to the child the best it has to give . . .
Opening words of resolution approved by General Assembly's Social, Humanitarian and Cultural Committee, NY *Times* 20 Oct 59

8 The child shall be entitled from his birth to a name and a nationality.
ib

9 He shall be entitled to grow up and develop in health; to this end special care and protection shall be provided both to him and to his mother, including adequate prenatal and postnatal care.
ib

10 The child who is physically, mentally or socially handicapped shall be given the special treatment, education and care required by his particular condition.
ib

11 The child is entitled to receive education, which shall be free and compulsory at least in the elementary stages.
ib

12 The child shall in all circumstances be among the first to receive protection and relief.
ib

FRANÇOIS GIULIANI, spokesman for Secretary-General

13 Protocol is everything.
NY *Times* 24 Jul 83

ARTHUR J GOLDBERG, United States

14 Law not served by power is an illusion; but power not ruled by law is a menace which our nuclear age cannot afford.
Commencement address at Catholic University of America, *Time* 17 Jun 66

ANDREI A GROMYKO, USSR

15 Greece is a sort of American vassal; the Netherlands is the country of American bases that grow like tulip bulbs; Cuba is the main sugar plantation of the American monopolies; Turkey is prepared to kowtow before any United States proconsul and Canada is the boring second fiddle in the American symphony.
NY *Herald Tribune* 30 Jun 53

DAG HAMMARSKJÖLD, Sweden, Secretary-General

16 Everything will be all right—you know when? When people, just people, stop thinking of the United Nations as a weird Picasso abstraction and see it as a drawing they made themselves.
Time 27 Jun 55

17 "Freedom from fear" could be said to sum up the whole philosophy of human rights.
On 180th anniversary of Virginia Declaration of Human Rights, *Quote* 20 May 56

18 I never discuss discussions.
After talks with Soviet leaders, *Look* 19 Sep 56

1 The Assembly has witnessed over the last weeks how historical truth is established; once an allegation has been repeated a few times, it is no longer an allegation, it is an established fact, even if no evidence has been brought out in order to support it.

> Responding to Soviet Premier Nikita S Khrushchev's attack in General Assembly, NY *Times* 4 Oct 60

2 Those who invoke history will certainly be heard by history. And they will have to accept its verdict.

> *ib*

LOUIS LANCE JOSEPH, Australia

3 [It was] quite simply a massacre in the sky.

> On death of 269 persons aboard Korean airliner shot down when it entered Soviet airspace, to Security Council, NY *Times* 3 Sep 83

JEANE J KIRKPATRICK, United States

4 I was a woman in a man's world. I was a Democrat in a Republican administration. I was an intellectual in a world of bureaucrats. I talked differently. This may have made me a bit like an ink blot. People projected around me.

> On her resignation after four years as US ambassador, NY *Times* 1 Feb 85

5 When the Syrian ambassador acted up, what I really felt like saying to him was, "Go to your room!"

> Quoted in *US* 2 Jun 86

CHARLES M LICHENSTEIN, United States

6 If in the judicious determination of the members of the United Nations they feel they [are] not welcome and treated with the hostly consideration that is their due, the United States strongly encourages member states to seriously consider removing themselves and this organization from the soil of the United States.

> Responding to Soviet charges after the downing of a Korean passenger plane by Soviet jets prompted the US to deny Andrei Gromyko permission to land at Kennedy and Newark airports, NY *Times* 20 Sep 83

TRYGVE LIE, Norway, Secretary-General

7 I shall take all the troubles of the past, all the disappointments, all the headaches, and I shall pack them in a bag and throw them in the East River.

> On retiring as Secretary-General, news summaries 31 Dec 53

HENRY CABOT LODGE JR, United States

8 This organization is created to prevent you from going to hell. It isn't created to take you to heaven.

> On purpose of UN, news summaries 28 Jan 54

9 It has been well said that a hungry man is more interested in four sandwiches than four freedoms.

> Appealing to Senate Appropriations Committee for renewed support of UN technical assistance programs, news summaries 29 Mar 55

10 The primary, the fundamental, the essential purpose of the United Nations is to keep peace. Everything it does which helps prevent World War III is good. Everything which does not further that goal, either directly or indirectly, is at best superfluous.

> NY *Journal-American* 1 May 58

11 As you begin your tour of the United States, you may as well know that one American national trait which irritates many Americans and must be convenient for our critics is that we relentlessly advertise our imperfections.

> To Soviet Premier Nikita S Khrushchev, news summaries 18 Sep 59

12 May the United Nations ever be vigilant and potent to defeat the swallowing up of any nation, at any time, by any means—by armies with banners, by force or by fraud, by tricks or by midnight treachery.

> At dedication of plaque honoring 37,000 servicemen who died while fighting under UN's unified command in Korean War, NY *Times* 28 Jun 60

13 The fact that the talk may be boring or turgid or uninspiring should not cause us to forget the fact that it is preferable to war.

> On the UN, recalled on his death 27 Feb 85

14 Membership of the United Nations gives every member the right to make a fool of himself, and that is a right of which the Soviet Union in this case has taken full advantage.

> After Soviets denounced the US for aggressive actions, *ib*

PAUL J F LUSAKA, Zambia, President of General Assembly

15 There was no south, there was no north, no east and no west—just the 11 apostles.

> After conference with 10 former General Assembly presidents, NY *Times* 13 Jun 85

RODERIC M J LYNE, Great Britain

16 You can accidentally but deliberately bump

into someone at a party whose office you cannot enter.
> On diplomatic entertaining, NY *Times* 4 Oct 85

ANTONIO MONTEIRO, Portugal

1 It's group therapy for the world.
> On series of debates that mark the start of each General Assembly session, NY *Times* 27 Sep 86

CONOR CRUISE O'BRIEN, former UN representative to Katanga

2 The United Nations cannot do anything, and never could; it is not an animate entity or agent. It is a place, a stage, a forum and a shrine. . . . a place to which powerful people can repair when they are fearful about the course on which their own rhetoric seems to be propelling them.
> *New Republic* 4 Nov 85

3 The main thing that endears the United Nations to member governments, and so enables it to survive, is its proven capacity to fail, and to be seen to fail.
> *ib*

4 You can safely appeal to the United Nations in the comfortable certainty that it will let you down.
> *ib*

ANTHONY PARSONS, Great Britain

5 On the third Tuesday of every September, floodgates are opened in a tall building on the East River in New York and a Niagara of rhetoric gushes forth for three months.
> "Waffles But Still Worthwhile" London *Times* 6 Oct 79

6 Our view would be that the patient died yesterday at midday.
> On British-Argentine negotiations over the Falkland Islands after Secretary-General Javier Pérez de Cuéllar remarked, "The patient is in intensive care but still alive," news summaries 21 May 82

ABDUL RAHMAN PAZWAK, Afghanistan, President of General Assembly

7 Few, if any, calamities in our time have befallen the world without some advance notice . . . from this rostrum. Thus, if fools and folly rule the world, the end of man in our time may come as a rude shock, but it will no longer come as a complete surprise.
> On retiring 19 Sep 67

JAVIER PÉREZ DE CUÉLLAR, Peru, Secretary-General

8 The patient is in intensive care but still alive.
> Personifying the British-Argentine peace negotiations over the Falkland Islands, news summaries 21 May 82

ALEX QUAISON-SACKEY, Ghana, President of General Assembly

9 There is now a balance of terror.
> On worldwide representation of nations at the UN, *Quote* 27 Jun 65

IVOR RICHARD, Great Britain

10 The United Nations is messy because the world is messy.
> On retiring after five years as British ambassador, NY *Times* 18 May 79

11 The United Nations will not abolish sin, but it can make it more difficult for the sinners.
> *ib*

ELEANOR ROOSEVELT, United States

12 Without the United Nations our country would walk alone, ruled by fear instead of confidence and hope.
> Recalled on her death 7 Nov 62

ROSEMARY SPENCER, US Protocol Officer

13 Of course, everybody wants the permanent representative at their functions. You can only split the permanent representative 10 ways. Scheduling is a problem.
> NY *Times* 2 Oct 81

ADLAI E STEVENSON, United States

14 The first principle of a free society is an untrammeled flow of words in an open forum.
> NY *Times* 19 Jan 62

15 This is the first time I ever heard it said that the crime is not the burglary, but the discovery of the burglar.
> Comment to Soviet Ambassador Valerian A Zorin, who charged that the US threatened peace by exposing Soviet missile shipments to Cuba, 25 Oct 62

16 Do you, Ambassador Zorin, deny that the USSR has placed and is placing medium- and intermediate-range missiles and sites in Cuba? Yes or no? Don't wait for the translation. Yes or no?
> *ib*

17 You are in the courtroom of world opinion.

... You have denied they exist, and I want to know if I understood you correctly. ... I am prepared to wait for my answer until hell freezes over. And I am also prepared to present the evidence in this room!

ib

1 I believe in the forgiveness of sin and the redemption of ignorance.

Reply to a heckler who asked him to state his beliefs in a UN Day address at Dallas, *Time* 1 Nov 63

2 I don't want to send them to jail. I want to send them to school.

On pickets who attacked him in Dallas, *ib*

3 After four years at the United Nations I sometimes yearn for the peace and tranquillity of a political convention.

NY *Times* 14 Aug 64

U THANT, Burma, Secretary-General

4 The war we have to wage today has only one goal and that is to make the world safe for diversity.

On international tolerance, Dag Hammarskjöld Memorial Lecture, Columbia University, quoted in NY *Times* 8 Jan 64

5 I don't like to be disturbed at home; I tell the cable office not to call me before 6:30 AM, unless there's a war.

On beginning his ninth year as Secretary-General, *ib* 3 Nov 69

SEMYON K TSARAPKIN, USSR

6 I am not a gentleman. I am a representative of the Soviet Union here.

Answer to US Ambassador Henry Cabot Lodge Jr's inquiry on why "the gentleman" was asking for the floor; Lodge replied, "The two are not necessarily exclusive," news summaries 26 Jun 54

VERNON A WALTERS, United States

7 The United Nations has become a place where many countries seek to achieve a lynching of the United States by resolution.

On becoming US ambassador, NY *Times* 31 May 85

8 I'd describe myself as a pragmatist tinged with idealism.

ib

9 It is an endless procession of surprises. The expected rarely occurs and never in the expected manner.

On UN social circuit, *ib* 4 Oct 85

10 I'm a participant in the doctrine of constructive ambiguity.

On preference for keeping a low profile, *Christian Science Monitor* 18 Apr 86

11 I don't think we should tell them what we're going to do in advance. Let them think. Worry. Wonder. Uncertainty is the most chilling thing of all.

On how US should deal with terrorists and terrorism, *ib*

RUDIGER VON WECHMAR, West Germany, former President of General Assembly

12 Cut the fat, cut the fat.

Recommendation for UN, NY *Times* 13 Jun 85

RICHARD A WOOLCOTT, Australia

13 Apart from a good mind, the two most important assets for a United Nations diplomat are a good tailor and a strong liver.

NY *Times* 4 Oct 85

ANDREW YOUNG, United States

14 That was not a lie, it was just not the whole truth.

On disclosing an unauthorized meeting with the Palestine Liberation Organization that resulted in Young's resignation 14 Aug 79

VALERIAN A ZORIN, USSR

15 I am not in an American courtroom, sir, and therefore do not wish to answer a question that is put to me in the fashion in which a prosecutor puts questions. In due course, sir, you will have your reply.

Comments to US Ambassador Adlai E Stevenson when challenged to deny that the USSR had offensive missiles in Cuba, 25 Oct 62

Observers & Critics

CORAZON C AQUINO, President of the Philippines

16 As our country bled ... its leader's wife came to this podium piously to call for a new human order, this when thousands of Filipinos were political prisoners.

To General Assembly, speaking from the same lectern used a year earlier by Imelda Marcos, 22 Sep 86

17 One must be frank to be relevant.

Chiding UN for lack of support in opposing the Ferdinand Marcos regime, *ib*

ZULFIKAR ALI BHUTTO, Foreign Minister of Pakistan

1 Let's build a monument for the veto. Let's build a monument for impotence and incapacity.
> Denouncing Security Council after invasion of Pakistan by India, NY *Times* 16 Dec 71

JACQUES CHIRAC, Premier of France

2 Terrorism has become the systematic weapon of a war that knows no borders or seldom has a face.
> To General Assembly 24 Sep 86

NORMAN COUSINS

3 We will not have peace by afterthought.
> 1956 editorial on importance of preservation rather than breaches of world peace, recalled in summary of his comments, *Saturday Review* 15 Apr 80

4 If the United Nations is to survive, those who represent it must bolster it; those who advocate it must submit to it; and those who believe in it must fight for it.
> *ib*

JOHN FOSTER DULLES, US Secretary of State

5 The United Nations was not set up to be a reformatory. It was assumed that you would be good before you got in and not that being in would make you good.
> On UN Charter, news summaries 9 Jul 54

ABBA EBAN, Foreign Minister of Israel

6 When I was first here, we had the advantages of the underdog. Now we have the disadvantages of the overdog.
> On representing his country after its repulse of Egyptian invaders in the Six-Day War, *New Yorker* 1 Jul 67

7 Lest Arab governments be tempted out of sheer routine to rush into impulsive rejection, let me suggest that tragedy is not what men suffer but what they miss.
> Calling for peace in Middle East, to General Assembly, NY *Times* 9 Oct 68

8 Time and again these governments have rejected proposals today—and longed for them tomorrow.
> *ib*

DWIGHT D EISENHOWER, 34th US President

9 I feel impelled to speak today in a language that in a sense is new—one which I, who have spent so much of my life in the military profession, would have preferred never to use. That new language is the language of atomic warfare.
> Address to UN seeking establishment of international atomic energy agency, 8 Dec 53

10 The United States pledges ... its determination to help solve the fearful atomic dilemma—to devote its entire heart and mind to finding the way by which the miraculous inventiveness of man shall not be dedicated to his death but consecrated to his life.
> *ib*

11 If the United Nations once admits that international disputes can be settled by using force, then we will have destroyed the foundation of the organization and our best hope of establishing a world order.
> On Israel's invasion of Egypt, address to the nation 20 Feb 57

12 In most communities it is illegal to cry "fire" in a crowded assembly. Should it not be considered serious international misconduct to manufacture a general war scare in an effort to achieve local political aims?
> On Middle East crisis, address to General Assembly 13 Aug 58

WILLIAM FAULKNER

13 The last sound on the worthless earth will be two human beings trying to launch a homemade spaceship and already quarreling about where they are going next.
> To UNESCO Commission, NY *Times* 3 Oct 59

ESTHER B FEIN

14 If the United Nations is a country unto itself, then the commodity it exports most is words.
> NY *Times* 14 Oct 85

THOMAS M FRANCK, Director of Center for International Studies, NY University

15 We could probably win more often ... if we were willing to ... deploy seasoned personnel and equip them with sufficient carrots and sticks.
> *Nation against Nation: What Happened to the UN Dream and What the US Can Do about It* Oxford 85

HAILE SELASSIE, Emperor of Ethiopia

16 Today I stand before the world organization which has succeeded to the mantle discarded by its discredited predecessor.
> Opening a special session of the General Assem-

bly in Addis Ababa, thus becoming the first ruler to address both the League of Nations and the UN, 4 Oct 63

1 Throughout history it has been the inaction of those who could have acted, the indifference of those who should have known better, the silence of the voice of justice when it mattered most, that has made it possible for evil to triumph.
> *ib*

DAVID HARE

2 When they speak, dead frogs fall out of their mouths.
> On some UN representatives, *A Map of the World* Faber & Faber 83

LYNDON B JOHNSON, 36th US President

3 Peace is a journey of a thousand miles and it must be taken one step at a time.
> To General Assembly 17 Dec 63

JUAN CARLOS, King of Spain

4 Europe cannot confine itself to the cultivation of its own garden.
> To General Assembly 22 Sep 86

JOHN F KENNEDY, 35th US President

5 My God, in this job he's got the nerve of a burglar.
> On Ambassador Adlai E Stevenson, *Time* 24 Feb 61

6 We prefer world law in the age of self-determination to world war in the age of mass extermination.
> To General Assembly 25 Sep 61

7 We cannot expect that all nations will adopt like systems, for conformity is the jailer of freedom and the enemy of growth.
> *ib*

NIKITA S KHRUSHCHEV, Soviet Premier

8 All the sparrows on the rooftops are crying about the fact that the most imperialist nation that is supporting the colonial regime in the colonies is the United States of America.
> To General Assembly 1 Oct 60

9 What innocence, may I ask, is being played here when it is known that this virtuous damsel has already got a dozen illegitimate children?
> *ib*

HAROLD MACMILLAN, former Prime Minister of Britain

10 A colonial governor who ran out of countries.
> On Lord Caradon, British ambassador, *International Herald Tribune* 5 Jun 79

GOLDA MEIR, Foreign Minister of Israel

11 My delegation cannot refrain from speaking on this question—we who have such an intimate knowledge of boxcars and of deportations to unknown destinations that we cannot be silent.
> On Soviet actions in Hungary, to General Assembly, news summaries 21 Nov 56

ROBERT G MENZIES, Prime Minister of Australia

12 It is . . . a simple but sometimes forgotten truth that the greatest enemy to present joy and high hopes is the cultivation of retrospective bitterness.
> To General Assembly, NY *Times* 6 Oct 60

JAMES MORRIS

13 There it stands ablaze, like a slab of fire, with its parade of white flagstaffs gleaming in the street light, and the humped black limousines patient at the door.
> On the UN building, NY *Times* 2 Oct 60

14 When at last you . . . cross the road to the United Nations, it is like traversing some unmarked but crucial frontier.
> *ib*

DAVID ORMSBY-GORE, 5th Baron Harlech, Minister of State, Great Britain

15 It would indeed be the ultimate tragedy if the history of the human race proved to be nothing more noble than the story of an ape playing with a box of matches on a petrol dump.
> *Christian Science Monitor* 25 Oct 60

POPE PAUL VI

16 You have before you a humble man; your brother; and among you all, representatives of sovereign states, the least invested, if you wish to think of him thus, with a minuscule, as it were symbolic, temporal sovereignty, only as much as is necessary to be free to exercise his spiritual mission and to assure all those who deal with him that he is independent of every other sovereignty of this world.
> To General Assembly 4 Oct 65

17 You must strive to multiply bread so that it suffices for the tables of mankind, and not

rather favor an artificial control of birth, which would be irrational, in order to diminish the number of guests at the banquet of life.
ib

1 No more war! Never again war! . . . If you wish to be brothers, drop your weapons.
ib

SHIMON PERES, Prime Minister of Israel

2 The sons of Abraham have become quarrelsome, but remain family nonetheless.
Address to General Assembly in which he invited Jordan to peace talks, 21 Oct 85

ENOCH POWELL, Member of British Parliament

3 It is the very capital and new Jerusalem of humbug.
Listener 28 May 81

RONALD REAGAN, 40th US President

4 Maybe all those delegates should have six months . . . in Moscow and then six months in New York, and it would give them an opportunity to see two ways of life. . . . I think the gentleman [Charles Lichenstein] who spoke the other day had the hearty approval of most people in America in his suggestion that we weren't asking anyone to leave, but if they chose to leave, good-bye.
Press conference 21 Sep 83

5 The founders [of the United Nations] sought to replace a world at war with a world of civilized order. They hoped that a world of relentless conflict would give way to a new era, one where freedom from violence prevailed. . . . But the awful truth is that the use of violence for political gain has become more, not less, widespread in the last decade.
To General Assembly following Soviet downing of a Korean passenger plane, 26 Sep 83

6 What has happened to the dreams of the United Nations's founders? What has happened to the spirit which created the United Nations? The answer is clear: Governments got in the way of the dreams of the people.
ib

7 Dreams became issues of East versus West. Hopes became political rhetoric. Progress became a search for power and domination. Somewhere the truth was lost that people don't make war, governments do.
ib

8 The founders of the United Nations expected that member nations would behave and vote as individuals after they had weighed the merits of an issue—rather like a great, global town meeting. The emergence of blocks and the polarization of the United Nations undermine all that this organization initially valued.
ib

9 As caring, peaceful peoples, think what a powerful force for good we could be. Distinguished delegates, let us regain the dream the United Nations once dreamed.
ib

CARLOS P ROMULO, Ambassador to US and former representative from Philippines

10 I had hoped it would be the conscience of the world and it is.
On the UN, 16 years after he had addressed its founding session with the words, "Let us make this floor the last battlefield," *I Walked with Heroes* Holt, Rinehart & Winston 61

11 Can you imagine a policeman being required to secure the assent of parties to a street fight before breaking up the conflict?
On situation of the UN in 1984, recalled on his death 15 Dec 85

A M ROSENTHAL

12 Within a pitifully short time, the China that sat on the Council and was supposed to represent a billion people represented nothing but a steamy Pacific island.
Recalling effect of Chinese Revolution on Security Council representation, NY *Times* 25 Sep 85

13 There is a secret agreement between the United States and the Soviet Union . . . a simple but lucid treaty holding that when one side does something particularly fatheaded and self-destructive the other will respond by shooting itself in the foot within a period of from 17 to 30 days.
ib 14 Dec 86

HARRY S TRUMAN, 33rd US President

14 Our conference in 1945 did much more than draft an international agreement among 50 nations. [We] set down on paper the only principles which will enable civilized human life to continue to survive on this globe.
On UN's 10th anniversary, NY *Herald Tribune* 25 Jun 55

AFONSO VAN DUNEM, Foreign Minister of Angola

15 Mr President, I have decided not to speak the entire speech which I have.
To General Assembly when he was 10 minutes

into a 40-minute speech that was also available in print, NY *Times* 27 Sep 86

MOHAMMED YAZID, spokesman for Algerian rebels

1 Some of us throw bombs, I throw ideas. We have men to do the shooting but I do the shouting.
   NY *Times* 18 Mar 61

ARMED FORCES

Officers & Enlistees

GEN OMAR N BRADLEY, US Army

2 I am convinced that the best service a retired general can perform is to turn in his tongue along with his suit and to mothball his opinions.
   News summaries 17 May 59

MAJ JOSIAH BUNTING, US Army retired

3 Ennoblement is earned by merit in the American Army.
   The Lionheads Popular Library 72

4 These men are worthy heirs to the tradition of Washington and Lee and Marshall, men who know their business, and who because they hate war, have soldiered well.
   On soldiers in Vietnam, *ib*

ADM ARLEIGH BURKE, US Navy

5 The major deterrent [to war] is in a man's mind.
   US News & World Report 3 Oct 60

LT WILLIAM L CALLEY JR, US Army

6 That was the order of the day.
   On killing Vietnamese civilians at My Lai in 1968, news summaries 23 Feb 71

7 They were all enemy. They were all to be destroyed.
   ib

JIMMY CARTER, 39th US President

8 My decision to register women ... confirms what is already obvious throughout our society—that women are now providing all types of skills in every profession. The military should be no exception.
   Proposing that both men and women be required to register for conscription, 8 Feb 80

WINSTON CHURCHILL

9 If Hitler invaded hell I would make at least a favorable reference to the devil in the House of Commons.
   The Grand Alliance Houghton Mifflin 50

10 Before Alamein we never had a victory. After Alamein we never had a defeat.
   The Hinge of Fate Houghton Mifflin 50

11 There was unanimous, automatic, unquestioned agreement around our table.
   On decision at Potsdam Conference about US use of atom bomb on Japan, *Triumph and Tragedy* Houghton Mifflin 53

12 When the war of the giants is over the wars of the pygmies will begin.
   On the end of World War II, *ib*

13 Really I feel less keen about the Army every day. I think the Church would suit me better.
   Postscript on a letter home during early training at Sandhurst, quoted by William Manchester *The Last Lion* Little, Brown 83

14 War is a game that is played with a smile. If you can't smile, grin. If you can't grin, keep out of the way till you can.
   ib

MAX CLELAND, former head of US Veterans Administration

15 Within the soul of each Vietnam veteran there is probably something that says "Bad war, good soldier." [Only now are Americans beginning to] separate the war from the warrior.
   On dedication of Vietnam Veterans Memorial, Washington DC, *Time* 22 Nov 82

MOHAMMED DAOUD, Afghani rebel commander

16 History tells me that when the Russians come to a country they don't go back.
   Comments of 21-year-old leader of 50 men who had fought the Soviet-backed Afghan army since 1980, NY *Times* 28 Mar 85

GEN CHARLES DE GAULLE

17 And don't forget to get killed.
   To Romain Gary, permitting his return to combat in World War II, quoted by Romain Gary "To Mon Général" *Life* 9 May 69

18 You'll live. Only the best get killed.
   ib

DWIGHT D EISENHOWER, 34th US President

19 When you put on a uniform, there are certain inhibitions that you accept.
   As US Army general, on learning that President Harry S Truman had relieved Gen Douglas MacArthur of command, 11 Apr 51

1 The most terrible job in warfare is to be a second lieutenant leading a platoon when you are on the battlefield.
17 Mar 54

2 The purpose is clear. It is safety with solvency. The country is entitled to both.
Urging unification of ground, sea and air commands, 17 Apr 58

3 It is far more important to be able to hit the target than it is to haggle over who makes a weapon or who pulls a trigger.
ib

4 The sergeant *is* the Army.
NY *Times* 24 Dec 72

COL RALPH GAUER, US Army Intelligence

5 It's going to be a "come-as-you-are" war.
On future warfare, *Newsweek* 9 Jul 84

GEN JAMES M GAVIN, US Army

6 If you want a decision, go to the point of danger.
Quoted by Ralph G Martin *A Hero for Our Time* Macmillan 83

LT GEN ALFRED M GRAY, US Marine Corps

7 There's no such thing as a crowded battlefield. Battlefields are lonely places.
Address to officers, *Newsweek* 9 Jul 84

8 [I go] where the sound of thunder is.
On 34-year career that had given him more time in the field than most generals, including 2 years in Korea and 5 in Vietnam, *ib*

9 I don't run democracy. I train troops to defend democracy and I happen to be their surrogate father and mother as well as their commanding general.
To new officers, *ib*

10 All of you are assistant mothers and fathers. That is an awesome responsibility.
ib

LT GEN HUBERT R HARMON, Superintendent, Air Force Academy

11 The academy's long-range mission will be to train generals, not second lieutenants.
Newsweek 6 Jun 55

HO CHI MINH

12 You will kill 10 of our men, and we will kill 1 of yours, and in the end it will be you who tire of it.
Recalled on his death 3 Sep 69

BRIG GEN ELIZABETH P HOISINGTON, US Army

13 If I had learned to type, I never would have made brigadier general.
Comment of highest-ranking officer in Women's Army Corps, NY *Times* 20 Jun 70

REX HUNT, British Governor of Falkland Islands

14 I think it very uncivilized to invade British territory. You are here illegally.
To Argentine general, *Life* Jan 83

LYNDON B JOHNSON, 36th US President

15 We did not choose to be the guardians of the gate, but there is no one else.
On continued intervention in Vietnam, address to the nation 28 Jul 64

16 Curtis Le May wants to bomb Hanoi and Haiphong. You know how he likes to go around bombing.
To Walter Lippmann, quoted by Ronald Steel *Walter Lippmann and the American Century* Atlantic-Little, Brown 80

ADM C TURNER JOY, US Navy

17 The field of combat was a long, narrow, greenbaize covered table. The weapons were words.
On a year of truce talks in Korea, news summaries 31 Dec 52

JOHN F KENNEDY, 35th US President

18 There is always inequity in life. Some men are killed in war and some men are wounded, and some men are stationed in the Antarctic and some are stationed in San Francisco. It's very hard in military or personal life to assure complete equality. Life is unfair.
To reservists anxious to be released from active duty, 21 Mar 62

19 I look forward to ... a future in which our country will match its military strength with our moral restraint, its wealth with our wisdom, its power with our purpose.
Last major public address, at Amherst College 26 Oct 63

WILL KETTERSON, spokesman for US Air Force Academy

20 Quibbling is the creation of a false impression in the mind of the listener by cleverly wording what is said, omitting relevant facts or telling a partial truth when one does so with the intent to deceive or mislead.
On suspension of highest-ranking junior-class cadet for an offense considered to be the same as lying, NY *Times* 25 Sep 85

GEN BELA KIRALY, Commander, Hungarian National Guard

1 Even pirates, before they attack another ship, hoist a black flag.

> On Ambassador Yuri V Andropov's pretense of peace while Soviet forces were preparing to crush 1956 uprising in Hungary, recalled on Andropov's death 9 Feb 84

JOHN F LEHMAN JR, Secretary of the Navy

2 Contrary to the parlor-room Pershings around [Washington], we have a fully integrated multiservice unified command structure.

> NY Times 12 Oct 85

CAPT ROBERT LEWIS, US Army Air Corps

3 As the bomb fell over Hiroshima and exploded, we saw an entire city disappear. I wrote in my log the words: "My God, what have we done?"

> Comments of copilot of the Enola Gay, recalled on approach of 10th anniversary of bombing, NBC TV 19 May 55

GEN DOUGLAS MACARTHUR, US Army

4 The world has turned over many times since I took the oath on the plain at West Point, and the hopes and dreams have long since vanished; but I still remember the refrain of one of the most popular barracks ballads of that day which proclaimed most proudly that old soldiers never die; they just fade away.

> After being relieved of duties by President Harry S Truman, address to Congress 19 Apr 51

5 And like the old soldier in that ballad, I now close my military career and just fade away, an old soldier who tried to do his duty as God gave him the sight to see that duty.

> ib

6 I can recall no parallel in history where a great nation recently at war has so distinguished its former enemy commander.

> On receiving one of Japan's highest decorations, NY Times 22 Jun 60

7 Duty, honor, country: Those three hallowed words reverently dictate what you ought to be, what you can be, what you will be. They are your rallying point to build courage when courage seems to fail, to regain faith when there seems to be little cause for faith, to create hope when hope becomes forlorn.

> On receiving West Point's Sylvanus Thayer Award for service to the nation, 12 May 62

8 In my dreams I hear again the crash of guns, the rattle of musketry, the strange, mournful mutter of the battlefield. But in the evening of my memory always I come back to West Point. Always there echoes and re-echoes: duty, honor, country.

> ib

9 I've looked that old scoundrel death in the eye many times but this time I think he has me on the ropes.

> On entering Walter Reed Army Medical Center for surgery that ended in his death, ib

10 In war, you win or lose, live or die—and the difference is just an eyelash.

> In posthumous memoirs, "Reminiscences" ib 10 Jul 64

11 They died hard, those savage men—like wounded wolves at bay. They were filthy, and they were lousy, and they stunk. And I loved them.

> On troops who died in defense of Bataan and Corregidor in early days of World War II, ib

12 These proceedings are closed.

> Concluding Japan's surrender in Tokyo Bay on September 2, 1945, thereby ending World War II, quoted by Alistair Cooke America Knopf 73

13 My first recollection is that of a bugle call.

> Quoted by William Manchester American Caesar Little, Brown 78

MAO ZEDONG, Chinese premier

14 The enemy advances, we retreat.
The enemy camps, we harass.
The enemy tires, we attack.
The enemy retreats, we pursue.

> Slogan for his troops, recalled on his death 9 Sep 76

GEN GEORGE C MARSHALL, US Army

15 Morale is the state of mind. It is steadfastness and courage and hope. It is confidence and zeal and loyalty. It is élan, esprit de corps and determination.

> Recalled on his death 16 Oct 59

16 Don't fight the problem, decide it.

> Favorite advice, quoted by Walter Isaacson and Evan Thomas The Wise Men Simon & Schuster 86

ROBERT S MCNAMARA, Secretary of Defense

17 I don't object to its being called "McNamara's war." I think it is a very important war and I am pleased to be identified with it and do whatever I can to win it.

> On the Vietnam War, NY Times 25 Apr 64

1 One cannot fashion a credible deterrent out of an incredible action.

> On nuclear weapons, *The Essence of Security* Hodder & Stoughton 68

GOLDA MEIR, Prime Minister of Israel

2 We don't thrive on military acts. We do them because we have to, and thank God we are efficient.

> *Vogue* Jul 69

GEN JOHN H ("IRON MIKE") MICHAELIS, US Army

3 You're not here to die for your country. You're here to make those so-and-sos die for theirs.

> To troops fighting in Korea, recalled on his death, *Time* 11 Nov 85

FIELD MARSHAL BERNARD LAW MONTGOMERY, 1st Viscount Montgomery of Alamein, British Army

4 Decisions! And a general, a commander in chief who has not got the quality of decision, then he is no good.

> CBS TV 28 Apr 59

ADM THOMAS MOORER, US Navy retired

5 The Xerox machine is one of the biggest threats to national security ever devised.

> *Time* 17 Jun 85

MAJ MICHAEL DAVIS O'DONNELL, First Aviation Brigade, US Army

6 And in that time
When men decide and feel safe
To call the war insane,
Take one moment to embrace
Those gentle heroes
You left behind.

> From a 1970 poem written three months before his death in Vietnam, chosen for inscription across top of NY Vietnam War Memorial, *Newsweek* 20 May 85

ADM ARTHUR W RADFORD, US Navy, Chairman, Joint Chiefs of Staff

7 A decision is the action an executive must take when he has information so incomplete that the answer does not suggest itself.

> *Time* 25 Feb 57

RONALD REAGAN, 40th US President

8 We pray for the wisdom that this hero be America's last unknown.

> On the Unknown Soldier of the Vietnam War, 25 May 84

9 We're talking about a weapon that won't kill people. It'll kill weapons.

> On testing and development of Strategic Defense Initiative, *Newsweek* 30 Sep 85

ADM HYMAN G RICKOVER, US Navy

10 One of the most wonderful things that happened in our *Nautilus* program was that everybody knew it was going to fail—so they let us completely alone so we were able to do the job.

> On development of first nuclear submarine, *Reader's Digest* Jul 58

11 The more you sweat in peace, the less you bleed in war.

> 1983 retirement speech, recalled on his death 8 Jul 86

GEN MATTHEW B RIDGWAY, US Army

12 Sometimes, at night, it was almost as if I could hear the assurance that God the Father gave to another soldier, named Joshua: "I will not fail thee nor forsake thee."

> Recalling his World War II command of 82nd Airborne Division on D-day, *Time* 28 May 84

GEN BERNARD ROGERS, NATO Supreme Allied Commander Europe

13 The last thing we want to do is make Europe safe for a conventional war.

> Opposing removal of medium-range missiles because it could encourage nonnuclear conflict, *Time* 16 Mar 87

CAPT JOHN E SHEPHARD JR, Assistant Professor of Political Science, US Military Academy

14 The problem, evidently, was that God and President Truman did not see eye to eye.

> On President Truman's recall of Gen Douglas MacArthur from Korea and MacArthur's subsequent statement that he had "tried to do his duty as God gave him the sight to see that duty," *Wall Street Journal* 26 Mar 87

MAJ GEN C T SHORTIS, British Director of Infantry

15 The infantry doesn't change. We're the only arm [of the military] where the weapon is the man himself.

> NY *Times* 4 Feb 85

GEN DAVID M SHOUP, Commandant, US Marine Corps

16 Remember, God provides the best camouflage several hours out of every 24.

> On night fighting, NY *Herald Tribune* 5 Jan 61

MARGARET THATCHER, Prime Minister of Great Britain

1 It is only when you look now and see success that you say that it was good fortune. It was not. We lost 250 of our best young men. I felt every one.

On Falkland Islands War with Argentina, *New Yorker* 10 Feb 86

2 It was sheer professionalism and inspiration and the fact that you really cannot have people marching into other people's territory and staying there.

ib

HARRY S TRUMAN, 33rd US President

3 The Marine Corps is the Navy's police force and as long as I am president that is what it will remain. They have a propaganda machine that is almost equal to Stalin's.

Quoted in *Time* 18 Sep 56

GEN NATHAN F TWINING, Chief of Staff, US Air Force

4 If our air forces are never used, they have achieved their finest goal.

News summaries 31 Mar 56

LT GEN WALTER F ULMER, US Army

5 The essence of a general's job is to assist in developing a clear sense of purpose ... to keep the junk from getting in the way of important things.

Newsweek 9 Jul 84

LT RICHARD VAN DE GEER, US Air Force

6 I can envision a small cottage somewhere, with a lot of writing paper, and a dog, and a fireplace and maybe enough money to give myself some Irish coffee now and then and entertain my two friends.

Letter to a friend before he was killed on May 15, 1975, officially the last American to die in Vietnam War, *Time* 15 Apr 85

7 It isn't very easy for me to even tell myself what the motivation was to come here. I went into this searching for something. I have it now. If I could, I would probably go home. Adios, my friend.

Tape-recorded message to his closest friend, received the day of Van de Geer's death, *Newsweek* 20 May 85

GEN JOHN W VESSEY JR, US Army, Chairman, Joint Chiefs of Staff

8 [My job is] to give the president and secretary of defense military advice before they know they need it.

NY *Times* 15 Jul 84

9 "Resource-constrained environment" [are] fancy Pentagon words that mean there isn't enough money to go around.

ib

10 More has been screwed up on the battlefield and misunderstood in the Pentagon because of a lack of understanding of the English language than any other single factor.

ib

11 Our strategy is one of preventing war by making it self-evident to our enemies that they're going to get their clocks cleaned if they start one.

To soldiers at Schofield Barracks in Hawaii, *ib*

12 You have to set your "shove-it" tolerance someplace. But you also have to recognize that you, too, may be wrong, and that in two weeks' time you'll be "old what's-his-name" and won't be able to influence the situation at all.

On retiring after 46 years of service, *ib* 3 Sep 85

13 Don't get small units caught in between the forces of history.

Lesson learned from death of 237 US servicemen in terrorist bombing in Beirut, *ib*

ADM JAMES D WATKINS, former US Chief of Naval Operations

14 [This is] an era of violent peace.

Quoted by Richard Halloran "A Silent Battle Surfaces" NY *Times* 7 Dec 86

CASPAR W WEINBERGER, US Secretary of Defense

15 I think women are too valuable to be in combat.

To Defense Advisory Committee on Women in the Services, *US News & World Report* 19 May 86

GEN WILLIAM C WESTMORELAND, US Army

16 War is fear cloaked in courage.

McCall's Dec 66

17 Vietnam was the first war ever fought without any censorship. Without censorship, things can get terribly confused in the public mind.

Time 5 Apr 82

JOHN WHEELER, Chairman, Vietnam Veterans Memorial Committee

18 I had a picture of a seven-year-old throwing a Frisbee around on the grass ... but it's treated as a spiritual place.

On Vietnam Veterans Memorial, Washington DC, *Time* 15 Apr 85

ADM ELMO ZUMWALT JR, former US Chief of Naval Operations

1 I ordered the spraying of Agent Orange.

On defoliant he ordered used during Vietnam War, from *My Father, My Son,* with Lt Elmo Zumwalt 3rd, Macmillan 86, excerpted in NY *Times* 24 Aug 86

LT ELMO ZUMWALT 3RD

2 I am a lawyer and I don't think I could prove in court ... that Agent Orange is the cause of all the medical problems ... reported by Vietnam veterans, or of their children's serious birth defects. But I am convinced that it is.

On his cancer and his son's learning disability, from *My Father, My Son,* with Adm Elmo Zumwalt Jr, Macmillan 86, excerpted in NY *Times* 24 Aug 86

3 I realize that what I am saying may imply that my father is responsible for my illness and Russell's disability. ... I do not doubt for a minute that the saving of American lives was always his first priority. Certainly thousands, perhaps even myself, are alive today because of his decision to use Agent Orange.

ib

Observers & Critics

ANONYMOUS

4 This embattled shore, portal of freedom, is forever hallowed by the ideas, valor and sacrifice of our fellow countrymen.

Monument inscription on Normandy coast, quoted by John Vinocur "D-day Plus 40 Years" NY *Times* 13 May 84

LES ASPIN, US Congressman

5 Before we give you billions more, we want to know what you've done with the trillion you've got.

Letter to Secretary of Defense Caspar W Weinberger after Aspin became chairman of House of Representatives Armed Services Committee, NY *Times* 5 Feb 85

DANIEL BERRIGAN SJ

6 Don't just do something, stand there.

On importance of thought as well as action in 1960s war protests, recalled in Springfield MA *Valley Advocate* 17 Nov 86

WILLIAM BROYLES JR

7 "Why me?" That is the soldier's first question, asked each morning as the patrols go out and each evening as the night settles around the foxholes.

Memorial Day tribute, NY *Times* 26 May 86

ALISTAIR COOKE

8 These doomsday warriors look no more like soldiers than the soldiers of the Second World War looked like conquistadors. The more expert they become the more they look like lab assistants in small colleges.

On personnel of antiballistic missile complex, *America* Knopf 73

NELSON DEMILLE

9 It was no more than a black slash in the ground, a poignant contrast to the lofty white marble and limestone of this monumental city. It was cut into a gently rising slope of grass ... An al fresco mortuary.

On Vietnam Veterans Memorial, Washington DC, *Word of Honor* Warner 85

10 It's a gravestone.

ib

DAVID DIAZ

11 They say you can read faces. Well, if that is true, you can read the entire Vietnamese War in the crowds here.

On dedication of NY Vietnam War Memorial, NBC TV 5 May 85

BERNARD EDELMAN

12 They were called grunts, and many of them, however grudgingly, were proud of the name. They were the infantrymen, the foot soldiers of the war.

Dear America: Letters Home from Vietnam Norton 85

OWEN EDWARDS

13 A chest full of medals is nothing more than a résumé in 3-D and Technicolor.

On interviewing a US Marine general, NY *Times* 14 Jul 85

OTTO FRIEDRICH

14 The lessons that it teaches ... are fundamentally the lessons that all great battles teach ... That even the most carefully prepared plans often go wrong. That lucky breaks are very important.

On 40th anniversary of D-day Allied invasion of France, *Time* 28 May 84

15 [It teaches] that war is cruel and wasteful but

sometimes necessary. That a blundering victory is more to be valued than a heroic defeat. That might and right sometimes come to the same end. All these things happened on June 6, 1944.

ib

MICHAEL GLENDON JR

1 Hi, Daddy. I love you. This is Michael. I'm seven now.

Telephone conversation welcoming home Maj Michael Glendon, who had been shot down over North Vietnam in 1966, quoted by George Esper and the Associated Press *The Eyewitness History of the Vietnam War 1961-75* Ballantine 83

PETER GRIER

2 He smiles with the faraway, sea-remembering smile of all desk admirals.

On Adm James D Watkins, first nuclear submariner to become Chief of Naval Operations, *Christian Science Monitor* 4 Jun 86

3 It looks like a condominium with a cannon and tracks.

On introduction of US Army's 25-ton Bradley Fighting Vehicle, *ib* 19 Aug 86

THEODORE M HESBURGH, President, Notre Dame

4 It's like having a cobra in the nursery with your grandchildren. . . . You get rid of the cobra or you won't have any grandchildren.

On nuclear weapons, *60 Minutes* CBS TV 14 Mar 82

ERNEST F HOLLINGS, US Senator

5 If they've been put there to fight, there are far too few. If they've been put there to be killed, there are far too many.

On US Marines in Lebanon, *Time* 26 Dec 83

ALLAN KELLER

6 The only war is the war you fought in. Every veteran knows that.

NY *World-Telegram & Sun* 24 Aug 65

MRS MAHONEY

7 Dear Pete, Just a short note. Please don't do anything foolish. Seriously, Pete, please take care of yourself and don't be a hero. I don't need a Medal of Honor winner. I need a son. Love, Mom

Letter to her son Lt Peter P Mahoney, US Army, engraved on NY Vietnam War Memorial, *Newsweek* 20 May 85

WILLIAM MANCHESTER

8 He was a great thundering paradox of a man.

On Gen Douglas MacArthur, *American Caesar* Little, Brown 78

EDWARD MARSH

9 In war, resolution; in defeat, defiance; in victory, magnanimity; in peace, good will.

Epigram on World War I, used by Winston Churchill in his volumes on World War II, recalled on Marsh's death 13 Jan 53

10 In defeat, unbeatable; in victory, unbearable.

On Viscount Montgomery, *ib*

JOHN C METZLER, Superintendent, Arlington National Cemetery

11 I will tell each person what I have told others in the past—that exactly who the men on the hill are is not as important as the fact that they are there. Being there, they are not only representative of other men who died unknown, but of all men who have fought for America. For that reason, they belong to all of us.

Comment prior to burial of Unknown Soldiers of World War II and Korean War, *Cosmopolitan* May 58

LANCE MORROW

12 Like robots suffering an obscure sorrow, they carried the casket of the new Unknown Soldier, the one from Vietnam. [It] was a different kind of war for the United States [in] a shattering time, a bomb that originated a world away and went off in the middle of the American mind. [Now] the prevailing note was one of acceptance and reconciliation, as if in burying the Unknown Soldier, the nation were also interring another measure of its residual bitterness.

"War and Remembrance: A Bit of the Bitterness Is Buried Along with an Unknown Soldier" *Time* 11 Jun 84

13 As they marched, the crowds lining the route broke into applause, a sweet and deeply felt spontaneous pattering that was a sort of communal embrace. Welcome home.

ib

MALCOLM MUGGERIDGE

14 In Europe the ubiquitous GI, with his camera like a third eye, created wherever he went a little America, air-conditioned, steam-heated and neon-lighted. In American eyes he was a liberator and defender of freedom. In other

eyes he often seemed part of an American army of occupation. To all he symbolized Europe's enfeeblement and the shift of world power and wealth across the Atlantic.

The Titans: United States of America BBC TV 16 Jan 62

NEW YORK TIMES

1 Transfixed by the mysterious marble panels, glassy black windows reflecting the present and overlooking the past.

On visitors to Washington DC's Vietnam Veterans Memorial "The Black Gash of Shame" 14 Apr 85

2 A memorial at once national and personal. In each sharply etched name one reads the price paid by yet another family. In the sweeping pattern of names, chronological by day of death, 1959 to 1975, one reads the price paid by the nation.

ib

3 Ten years after the war, America may not yet comprehend the loss of those 58,000 lives; but it has at least found a noble way to remember them.

ib

GREG RUSHFORD, investigator for US House Select Committee on Intelligence

4 [They] acted like used-car salesmen rolling the mileage back.

On military personnel who calculated enemy strength in Vietnam, NY *Times* 1 Feb 85

WILLIAM SAFIRE

5 Modern war needs modern lingo.

Observing that "today's attackerese" refers to more than old terms such as *conduct a raid, mount an attack* or *deliver a blow,* NY *Times* 4 May 86

ALAN K SIMPSON, US Senator

6 He's a million rubber bands in his resilience.

Expressing respect for Secretary of Defense Caspar W Weinberger, whose budget was being reviewed, NY *Times* 3 Feb 85

FRANK SNEPP, former agent, CIA

7 Disinformation is most effective in a very narrow context.

Christian Science Monitor 26 Feb 85

8 You take a fraction of reality and expand on it. It's very seldom totally at odds with the facts. ... It's shaving a piece of reality off.

On disinformation, *ib*

BENJAMIN SPOCK

9 I'm not a pacifist. I was very much for the war against Hitler and I also supported the intervention in Korea, but in this war we went in there to steal Vietnam.

After indictment on charges of aiding and abetting resistance to Selective Service laws, news summaries 5 Jan 68

RICHARD STUBBING, US Office of Management and Budget

10 It's a middle-class welfare program for engineers.

On lack of competitive bidding that helps contractors keep large payrolls, NY *Times* 15 May 85

EVAN THOMAS

11 American boys should not be seen dying on the nightly news. Wars should be over in three days or less, or before Congress invokes the War Powers Resolution. Victory must be assured in advance. And the American public must be all for it from the outset.

On "unreal extremes" of modern warfare, "Week of the Big Stick" *Time* 7 Apr 86

TIME MAGAZINE

12 The rescuers had to rescue themselves.

On ill-fated attempt to free hostages in Iran, 5 May 80

PATRICIA L WALSH

13 We don't need to fabricate anything because the truth will make you weep.

On experiences as a civilian nurse in Vietnam, NY *Times* 12 Feb 85

JOHN WHEELER

14 It was the defining event ... and remains a thousand degrees hot.

On the Vietnam War, *Touched with Fire* Avon 85

JAMES WILDE

15 The stench of death massaged my skin; it took years to wash away.

On reporting the Vietnam War, *Time* 15 Apr 85

PETER WYDEN

16 Cataclysms from the Old Testament came to Truman's mind: "It may be the fire destruction prophesied in the Euphrates Valley era after Noah and his ark."

Day One: Before Hiroshima & After Simon & Schuster 84

1 Churchill also resorted to biblical terms. . . .
He brimmed over with exuberance: "What
was gunpowder? Trivial. What was electricity?
Meaningless. The atomic bomb is the Second
Coming in wrath."
ib

LAW
Attorneys & the Practice of Law

RENATA ADLER

2 In the strange heat all litigation brings to bear
on things, the very process of litigation fosters
the most profound misunderstandings in the
world.
Reckless Disregard Knopf 86

AMERICAN CIVIL LIBERTIES UNION

3 Liberty is always unfinished business.
Annual Report 55/56

HARRY S ASHMORE

4 We are going to have to decide what kind of
people we are—whether we obey the law only
when we approve of it or whether we obey it
no matter how distasteful we may find it.
On integration of Little Rock High School, Arkansas *Gazette* 4 Sep 57

ROBERT BADINTER, French Minister of Justice

5 One does not plead for a dead man, because
the lawyer of a dead man is nothing but a man
who remembers.
On capital punishment, London *Times* 19 Sep
81

F LEE BAILEY

6 Can any of you seriously say the Bill of Rights
could get through Congress today? It wouldn't
even get out of committee.
Newsweek 17 Apr 67

7 I use the rules to frustrate the law. But I didn't
set up the ground rules.
NY *Times* 20 Sep 70

HOWARD H BAKER JR, US Senator

8 You've got to guard against speaking more
clearly than you think.
Quoting his father's reaction to Baker's first
court appearance, Washington *Post* 24 Jun 73

ROGER N BALDWIN

9 [Our goal is] a society with a minimum of

compulsion, a maximum of individual freedom and of voluntary association and the abolition of exploitation and poverty.
Recalled on his death 26 Aug 81

RICHARD J BARTLETT, former Dean, Albany Law
School, Union University

10 Once someone uses the term "reasonable person," it's awfully hard to define it.
On defense of Bernhard H Goetz, accused of
shooting four youths he believed were attempting to rob him, NY *Times* 9 Jul 86

WILLIAM F BAXTER, Assistant US Attorney
General

11 I've never met a litigator who didn't think he
was winning—right up until the moment the
guillotine dropped.
News summaries 8 Jan 82

MELVIN BELLI

12 There is never a deed so foul that something
couldn't be said for the guy; that's why there
are lawyers.
LA *Times* 18 Dec 81

13 [A lawyer's] performance in the courtroom is
responsible for about 25 percent of the out-
come; the remaining 75 percent depends on
the facts.
US News & World Report 20 Sep 82

SIDNEY BERNARD

14 Jury duty [is] a bog of quicksand on the path
to justice.
"The Waiting Game" NY *Journal-American* 30
Dec 65

ALEXANDER M BICKEL, Professor of Legal History,
Yale

15 [The judiciary is] the least dangerous branch
of our government.
Quoted in *Christian Science Monitor* 11 Feb 86

ROSE ELIZABETH BIRD, Chief Justice, California
Supreme Court

16 You salivate on signal; they want a Pavlovian
justice.
On state law for periodic election and re-election
of judges, a statute that a year later resulted in
her removal from the bench, NY *Times* 22 Dec
85

HUGO L BLACK, Associate Justice, US Supreme
Court

17 The layman's constitutional view is that what

69

he likes is constitutional and that which he doesn't like is unconstitutional.

NY *Times* 26 Feb 71

HARRY A BLACKMUN, Associate Justice, US Supreme Court

1 Who is to say that 5 men 10 years ago were right whereas 5 men looking the other direction today are wrong.

On prior court decisions, especially 5-4 votes, LA *Herald-Examiner* 20 Apr 70

2 We're all eccentrics. We're nine prima donnas.

Time 6 Feb 84

DEREK BOK, President, Harvard

3 There is far too much law for those who can afford it and far too little for those who cannot.

Report to Board of Overseers 21 Apr 83

ib

WILLIAM J BRENNAN JR, Associate Justice, US Supreme Court

4 We current justices read the Constitution in the only way that we can: as 20th-century Americans.

Address at Georgetown University, NY *Times* 13 Oct 85

5 We look to the history of the time of framing and to the intervening history of interpretation. But the ultimate question must be, what do the words of the text mean in our time.

ib

CLAUS VON BÜLOW

6 This was a tragedy and it satisfied all of Aristotle's definitions of tragedy. Everyone is wounded, some fatally.

To Harvard Law School forum after his acquittal at trials for attempted murder of his wife, NY *Times* 16 Mar 86

WARREN E BURGER, Chief Justice, US Supreme Court

7 Concepts of justice must have hands and feet ... to carry out justice in every case in the shortest possible time and the lowest possible cost. This is the challenge to every lawyer and judge in America.

To Amer Bar Assn 1 Oct 72

8 We are more casual about qualifying the people we allow to act as advocates in the courtroom than we are about licensing electricians.

Address at Fordham University Law School, news summaries 28 Dec 73

9 The courtrooms of America all too often have Piper Cub advocates trying to handle the controls of Boeing 747 litigation.

ib

10 The trial of a case [is] a three-legged stool—a judge and two advocates.

To Amer Bar Assn 12 Feb 78

11 Doctors ... still retain a high degree of public confidence because they are perceived as healers. Should lawyers not be healers? Healers, not warriors? Healers, not procurers? Healers, not hired guns?

ib 12 Feb 84

12 It is not unprofessional to give free legal advice, but advertising that the first visit will be free is a bit like a fox telling chickens he will not bite them until they cross the threshold of the hen house.

ib 11 Aug 86

13 Judges ... rule on the basis of law, not public opinion, and they should be totally indifferent to pressures of the times.

Quoted by Charlotte Saikowski "The Power of Judicial Review" *Christian Science Monitor* 11 Feb 87

DAN M BURT

14 No individual should find the foot of a behemoth on his neck for no reason at all, without the ability to lift that foot off.

On Gen William C Westmoreland's libel suit against CBS TV, NY *Times* 31 May 84

RAMSEY CLARK, US Attorney General

15 A right is not what someone gives you; it's what no one can take from you.

NY *Times* 2 Oct 77

ROY M COHN

16 My scare value is high. My arena is controversy. My tough front is my biggest asset.

On his career as an attorney, recalled on his death 2 Aug 86

17 I don't write polite letters. I don't like to plea-bargain. I like to fight.

ib

18 I bring out the worst in my enemies and that's how I get them to defeat themselves.

Quoted by William Safire NY *Times* 4 Aug 86

ARCHIBALD COX, Professor of Law, Harvard

19 Through the centuries, men of law have been persistently concerned with the resolution of

disputes ... in ways that enable society to achieve its goals with a minimum of force and maximum of reason.
> News summaries 30 Dec 73

DONALD R CRESSEY, Professor of Criminology, University of California, Santa Barbara

1 Things in law tend to be black and white. But we all know that some people are a little bit guilty, while other people are guilty as hell.
> *Center Magazine* May/Jun 78

2 You cannot bring in a verdict that the defendant is a little bit guilty.
> *ib*

MARIO CUOMO, Governor of NY

3 If you can manipulate news, a judge can manipulate the law. A smart lawyer can keep a killer out of jail, a smart accountant can keep a thief from paying taxes, a smart reporter could ruin your reputation— unfairly.
> NBC TV 21 Aug 86

CHARLES CURTIS

4 Fraud is the homage that force pays to reason.
> *A Commonplace Book* Simon & Schuster 57

5 Bias and prejudice are attitudes to be kept in hand, not attitudes to be avoided.
> *ib*

ALAN M DERSHOWITZ, Professor of Law, Harvard

6 Judges are the weakest link in our system of justice, and they are also the most protected.
> *Newsweek* 20 Feb 78

7 All sides in a trial want to hide at least some of the truth.
> *US News & World Report* 9 Aug 82

8 The defendant wants to hide the truth because he's generally guilty. The defense attorney's job is to make sure the jury does not arrive at that truth.
> *ib*

9 The prosecution ... wants to make sure the process by which the evidence was obtained is not truthfully presented, because, as often as not, that process will raise questions.
> *ib*

10 The judge also has a truth he wants to hide: He often hasn't been completely candid in describing the facts or the law.
> *ib*

LORD PATRICK DEVLIN, Judge of the High Court

11 The judges of England have rarely been original thinkers or great jurists. Many have been craftsmen rather than creators.
> Quoted by Anthony Sampson *Anatomy of Britain Today* Harper & Row 65

12 The most important thing for a judge is—curiously enough—judgment.
> *ib*

WILLIAM O DOUGLAS, Associate Justice, US Supreme Court

13 The 5th Amendment is an old friend and a good friend. ... one of the great landmarks in men's struggle to be free of tyranny, to be decent and civilized.
> *An Almanac of Liberty* Doubleday 54

14 Common sense often makes good law.
> In court ruling 25 Mar 57

15 Since when have we Americans been expected to bow submissively to authority and speak with awe and reverence to those who represent us?
> Statement on unfair arrests for disorderly conduct, recalled on his retirement 12 Nov 75

16 We who have the final word can speak softly or angrily. We can seek to challenge and annoy, as we need not stay docile and quiet.
> *ib*

17 One who comes to the Court must come to adore, not to protest. That's the new gloss on the 1st Amendment.
> To Justice Potter Stewart on why Vietnam War veterans were arrested for peaceful protest on steps of the Supreme Court building, *The Court Years 1939-75* Random House 80

18 At the constitutional level where we work, 90 percent of any decision is emotional. The rational part of us supplies the reasons for supporting our predilections.
> *ib*

19 The Constitution is not neutral. It was designed to take the government off the backs of people.
> *ib*

20 It seemed to me that I had barely reached the Court when people were trying to get me off.
> On attempts to impeach him, *ib*

ADRIAN G DUPLANTIER, Louisiana State Senator

21 We are about to make motherhood a crime. No civilized government in the history of mankind has ever done this.
> Comment before legislators voted to make the

bearing of more than one illegitimate child a criminal act, NY *Herald Tribune* 15 Jun 60

RONALD D DWORKIN, Professor of Law, NY University

1 Moral principle is the foundation of law.
Law's Empire Belknap Press/Harvard 86, quoted in *Christian Science Monitor* 20 May 86

2 Integrity is the key to understanding legal practice. . . . Law's empire is defined by attitude, not territory or power or process.
ib

DWIGHT D EISENHOWER, 34th US President

3 The clearest way to show what the rule of law means to us in everyday life is to recall what has happened when there is no rule of law.
Address on first observance of Law Day 5 May 58

4 I deplore the need or the use of troops anywhere to get American citizens to obey the orders of constituted courts.
On Arkansas's defiance of Supreme Court school desegregation ruling, 14 May 58

5 There is no person in this room whose basic rights are not involved in any successful defiance to the carrying out of court orders.
ib

AUSTIN ELLIOT

6 Whoever said "Marriage is a 50-50 proposition" laid the foundation for more divorce fees than any other short sentence in our language.
"Some Observations on the Attorney-Secretary Function" *Law Office Economics and Management* Nov 64

MARTIN ERDMANN, NYC Legal Aid Society

7 Appellate Division judges [are] the whores who became madams.
Life 12 Mar 71

SAM ERVIN, US Senator

8 I'll have you understand I am running this court, and the law hasn't got a damn thing to do with it!
Recalling an old magistrate's words to a young attorney, quoted by Thad Stem Jr and Alan Butler comps *Senator Sam Ervin's Best Stories* Moore 73

9 The rain it raineth on the just
And also on the unjust fella;
But chiefly on the just, because
The unjust steals the just's umbrella.
ib

BENJAMIN F FAIRLESS, President, US Steel

10 What five members of the Supreme Court say the law is may be something vastly different from what Congress intended the law to be.
Address at Boston 18 May 50

11 If we persist in that kind of a system of law . . . virtually every business in America, big and small, is going to have to be run from Sing Sing, Leavenworth or Alcatraz.
ib

GEOFFREY FISHER, Archbishop of Canterbury

12 In a civilized society, all crimes are likely to be sins, but most sins are not and ought not to be treated as crimes. . . . Man's ultimate responsibility is to God alone.
Look 17 Mar 59

13 There is a sacred realm of privacy for every man and woman where he makes his choices and decisions—a realm of his own essential rights and liberties into which the law, generally speaking, must not intrude.
ib

MACKLIN FLEMING

14 Procrastination is a sin of lawyers, trial judges, reporters, appellate judges, in brief, everyone connected with the machinery of criminal law.
LA *Times* 24 Jul 74

ABE FORTAS, Associate Justice, US Supreme Court

15 For a justice of this ultimate tribunal, the opportunity for self-discovery and the occasion for self-revelation is usually great.
Quoted on his appointment to US Supreme Court, *Newsweek* 9 Aug 65

16 Judging is a lonely job in which a man is, as near as may be, an island entire.
ib

FELIX FRANKFURTER, Associate Justice, US Supreme Court

17 All our work, our whole life is a matter of semantics, because words are the tools with which we work, the material out of which laws are made, out of which the Constitution was written. Everything depends on our understanding of them.
Reply to counsel who said a challenge from the bench was "just a matter of semantics," *Reader's Digest* Jun 64

18 Litigation is the pursuit of practical ends, not a game of chess.
News summaries 9 Aug 64

1 As a member of this court I am not justified in writing my private notions of policy into the Constitution, no matter how deeply I may cherish them or how mischievous I may deem their disregard.

ib

2 Judicial judgment must take deep account ... of the day before yesterday in order that yesterday may not paralyze today.

Quoted in *National Observer* 1 Mar 65

DAVID FROST and ANTONY JAY

3 The whole paraphernalia of the criminal law and the criminal courts is based on the need of the upper class to keep the lower class in its place.

The English Avon 68

4 This is what has to be remembered about the law: Beneath that cold, harsh, impersonal exterior there beats a cold, harsh, impersonal heart.

ib

5 Nobody wants literate people to go to prison—they have a distressing way of revealing what it's actually like and destroying our illusions about training and rehabilitation with nasty stories about sadism and futility and buckets of stale urine.

ib

JACOB D FUCHSBERG, former President, Amer Trial Lawyers Assn

6 The average juror ... wraps himself in civic virtue. He's a judge now. He tries to act the part and do the right thing.

News summaries 6 Jun 69

JOHN W GARDNER

7 All laws are an attempt to domesticate the natural ferocity of the species.

San Francisco *Examiner & Chronicle* 3 Jul 74

LAWRENCE GIBBS, Commissioner, Internal Revenue Service

8 A taxpaying public that doesn't understand the law is a taxpaying public that can't comply with the law.

Wall Street Journal 3 Mar 87

ALBERT GORE JR, US Senator

9 When you have the facts on your side, argue the facts. When you have the law on your side, argue the law. When you have neither, holler.

Washington *Post* 23 Jul 82

WILLIAM T GOSSETT, President, Amer Bar Assn

10 The rule of law can be wiped out in one misguided, however well-intentioned, generation.

Address 11 Aug 69

MILTON S GOULD

11 When you soar like an eagle, you attract the hunters.

On his clients, corporate executives under government investigation, *Time* 8 Dec 67

LORD HAILSHAM OF MARYLEBON (Quintin Hogg)

12 A reasonable doubt is nothing more than a doubt for which reasons can be given. The fact that 1 or 2 men out of 12 differ from the others does not establish that their doubts are reasonable.

In support of changing jury vote necessary for conviction from unanimous to 10-2, *Time* 19 May 67

MARY HAMILTON

13 I will not answer until I am addressed correctly.

To an Alabama prosecutor who addressed her by her first name, an action that the US Supreme Court later ruled against as a familiarity contrary to the law barring segregation in courtrooms, *Newsweek* 13 Apr 64

LEARNED HAND

14 If we are to keep our democracy, there must be one commandment: Thou shalt not ration justice.

To NY Legal Aid Society 16 Feb 51

15 There is no surer way to misread any document than to read it literally.

Recalled on his death 18 Aug 61

16 Proceed. You have my biased attention.

To attorney who asked to review a motion already heard. *ib*

17 The spirit of liberty is the spirit which is not too sure that it is right.

ib

18 [The judge's authority] depends upon the assumption that he speaks with the mouth of others.

Quoted by William J Brennan Jr, Associate Justice, US Supreme Court, NY *Times* 6 Oct 63

GIDEON HAUSNER

19 No one can demand that you be neutral toward the crime of genocide. If ... there is a

judge in the whole world who can be neutral toward this crime, that judge is not fit to sit in judgment.

> Defending legality of trial of war criminal Adolf Eichmann, NY *Times* 27 Jun 61

MORTON J HORWITZ, Professor of Law, Harvard

1 [Law is] an odd profession that presents its greatest scholarship in student-run publications.

> On law-school reviews, *Newsweek* 15 Sep 75

PAUL E JOHNSON

2 A ruling like this will cause prejudice in people who have never been prejudiced before.

> On losing Supreme Court appeal against affirmative action employer who awarded a job to a woman with 4 years of experience and a test score of 73 as compared with his 13 years of experience and a score of 75, *Time* 6 Apr 87

NEAL JOHNSTON, Chief of Staff, NY City Council

3 The screening process through which law firms choose new partners is perhaps as well considered as anything this side of a papal election.

> NY *Times* 6 Mar 83

LUCILLE KALLEN

4 A lawyer's relationship to justice and wisdom . . . is on a par with a piano tuner's relationship to a concert. He neither composes the music, nor interprets it—he merely keeps the machinery running.

> *Introducing C B Greenfield* Crown 79

IRVING R KAUFMAN, Judge, US Court of Appeals, 2nd Circuit

5 To the extent that the judicial profession becomes the daily routine of deciding cases on the most secure precedents and the narrowest grounds available, the judicial mind atrophies and its perspective shrinks.

> To Institute of Judicial Administration 26 Aug 69

6 What most impresses us about great jurists is not their tenacious grasps of fine points, honed almost to invisibility; it is the moment when we are suddenly aware of the sweep and direction of the law, and its place in the lives of men.

> *ib*

7 No other profession is subject to the public contempt and derision that sometimes befalls

lawyers. . . . the bitter fruit of public incomprehension of the law itself and its dynamics.

> Quoted in San Francisco *Examiner & Chronicle* 17 Apr 77

8 The judge is forced for the most part to reach his audience through the medium of the press whose reporting of judicial decisions is all too often inaccurate and superficial.

> *ib*

9 Courtrooms contain every symbol of authority that a set designer could imagine. Everyone stands up when you come in. You wear a costume identifying you as, if not quite divine, someone special.

> *Time* 5 May 80

10 The judicial system is the most expensive machine ever invented for finding out what happened and what to do about it.

> *ib*

11 The ideal is to have the losing party feel that he is not the victim of the judge, but simply the object of a profession that is the same for all.

> *ib*

12 The [Supreme] Court's only armor is the cloak of public trust; its sole ammunition, the collective hopes of our society.

> "Keeping Politics out of the Court" NY *Times* 9 Dec 84

ROBERT F KENNEDY, US Attorney General

13 I'm tired of chasing people.

> On plans to pursue other interests after more than a decade as a criminal investigator, counsel and public official, NY *Times* 6 May 64

MARTIN LUTHER KING JR

14 It may be true that the law cannot make a man love me, but it can keep him from lynching me, and I think that's pretty important.

> *Wall Street Journal* 13 Nov 62

15 An individual who breaks a law that conscience tells him is unjust, and who willingly accepts the penalty of imprisonment in order to arouse the conscience of the community over its injustice, is in reality expressing the highest respect for the law.

> *Why We Can't Wait* Harper & Row 64

PAUL H KING, Judge, District Court, Dorchester MA

16 The police are not going to run this court. The defendants are not going to run this court. The defense attorneys are not going to run this

court. The district attorney is not going to run this court. I'm going to run this court.

> Reaction to 50 off-duty police officers who protested his bail procedures in 1980, Boston *Globe* 14 Nov 86

EDWARD KOCH, Mayor of NYC

1 If you seek violence, we will seek to put you in jail.

> To labor and management in hotel dispute, NY *Times* 2 Jun 85

STEVEN KUMBLE

2 The key thing that makes national law firms work is synergy; with the right combination, one and one can make three.

> NY *Times* 4 Oct 84

JEROME KURTZ, former Commissioner, Internal Revenue Service

3 If a person is an economic being and figures out the odds, then there is a very high incentive to cheat. That is, of course, putting aside honor, duty and patriotism.

> *Wall Street Journal* 10 Apr 84

RUSSELL R LEGGETT, Judge, Westchester County Court

4 You will be judges of the fact. You are the sole and exclusive judges of what the truth is. You will bring with you here your common sense.

> To prospective jurors in murder trial of Jean Harris for the death of Dr Herman Tarnower, quoted in her book *Stranger in Two Worlds* Macmillan 86

5 Your verdict will be "Guilty" or "Not Guilty." Your job is not to find innocence.

> *ib*

JONATHAN LUBELL

6 Given the state of libel law, whenever a public figure gets to face a jury, it is a victory.

> On representing Lt Col Anthony Herbert in unsuccessful libel suit against CBS TV, similar to action brought by Gen William C Westmoreland, *Time* 22 Oct 84

DAVID MARGOLICK

7 He takes hundreds of recent law graduates at their most vulnerable, dependent state and guides them, soothes them, suffers with them, flatters them, advises them, exhorts them, humors them and holds their hands over the last hurdle before they enter the practice of law.

> On eight-week course offered by John M Pieper to students preparing for NY State bar exams, NY *Times* 16 Jul 84

MICHELLE TRIOLA MARVIN

8 If a man wants to leave a toothbrush at my house, he can damn well marry me.

> On winning $104,000 California Superior Court case against common-law husband Lee Marvin, a decision regarded as a precedent for reciprocal property rights of unwed couples, NY *Times* 19 Apr 79

EDWIN MEESE 3RD, US Attorney General

9 [A Supreme Court] decision does not establish a "supreme law of the land" that is binding on all persons and parts of government, henceforth and forevermore.

> Address at Tulane University, quoted in NY *Times* 23 Oct 86

10 The implication that everyone would have to accept its judgments uncritically, that it was a decision from which there could be no appeal, was astonishing.

> On Supreme Court's assertion in 1958 that its earlier ruling requiring desegregation established "the supreme law of the land," *ib*

DAVID MELINKOFF, Professor of Law, UCLA

11 Lawyers as a group are no more dedicated to justice or public service than a private public utility is dedicated to giving light.

> San Francisco *Examiner & Chronicle* 22 Jun 73

MURRAY MEYERSON

12 Just think of the pleasure it would give a wealthy man to cut off his free-spending brother, then to explain it all in living color.

> On videotaped wills, *International Herald Tribune* 16 May 79

HENRY G MILLER, President, NY State Bar Assn

13 The legal system is often a mystery, and we, its priests, preside over rituals baffling to everyday citizens.

> "The Lawyer is Number 2, Not Number 1" NY *Times* 26 Jan 85

NEWTON MINOW

14 In Germany, under the law everything is prohibited except that which is permitted. In France, under the law everything is permitted except that which is prohibited. In the Soviet Union, everything is prohibited, including that which is permitted. And in Italy, under the law everything is permitted, especially that which is prohibited.

> On his comparative study of legal systems, *Time* 18 Mar 85

HOYT A MOORE

1 No one is under pressure. There wasn't a light on when I left at 2 o'clock this morning.
   Quoted by a partner in his Manhattan law firm, Cravath, Swaine & Moore, *Time* 24 Jun 64

ROBERT MORGENTHAU, District Attorney, NYC

2 I would rather have my fate in the hands of 23 representative citizens of the county than in the hands of a politically appointed judge.
   Defending secrecy of grand jury proceedings, *Time* 8 Apr 85

FRANCIS T MURPHY, President, Federation of NY State Judges

3 Society is pressed to its ancient defense against the violent criminal: the fear of swift and severe punishment. Either we take that road now, or we will live in the sickly twilight of a soulless people too weak to drive predators out of their own house.
   Calling on fellow judges to sentence anyone convicted of a serious crime, regardless of insufficient space in jails, NY *Times* 23 Apr 84

4 No more essential duty of government exists than the protection of the lives of its people. Fail in this, and we fail in everything.
   Harper's Jul 84

JON NEWMAN, Judge, US Court of Appeals, 2nd Circuit

5 [American liberty] is premised on the accountability of free men and women for what they have done, not for what they may do.
   On unconstitutionality of preventive detention, quoted in editorial "Fat Tony and the Bail Principle" NY *Times* 29 Nov 86

NEWSWEEK

6 Getting excused from jury duty without sufficient reason amounts to thumbing your nose at a distressed neighbor and at the most effective friend a free man ever had, the American courts.
   Public-service advertisement 24 Aug 64

7 It's called jury *duty*, not jury inconvenience. It is an obligation, not an interruption.
   ib

NEW YORK TIMES

8 They like to be seen wearing the robes of judicial restraint.
   Editorial on conservatism of Supreme Court Justices Warren E Burger, William H Rehnquist and Lewis F Powell Jr, "Good Old Federalism" 21 Feb 85

ROBERT N C NIX

9 Be prepared, be sharp, be careful, and use the King's English well. And you can forget all the [other rules] unless you remember one more: Get paid.
   Advice to young lawyers, recalled on inauguration of his son Robert N C Nix Jr as Chief Justice of Pennsylvania, NY *Times* 7 Jan 84

RICHARD M NIXON, 37th US President

10 Our chief justices have probably had more profound and lasting influence on their times and on the direction of the nation than most presidents.
   On appointment of Warren E Burger as Chief Justice of US Supreme Court, 21 May 69

LOUIS NIZER

11 When a man points a finger at someone else, he should remember that four of his fingers are pointing at himself.
   My Life in Court Doubleday 62

12 I know of no higher fortitude than stubborness in the face of overwhelming odds.
   ib

13 [Preparation] is the be-all of good trial work. Everything else—felicity of expression, improvisational brilliance—is a satellite around the sun. Thorough preparation is that sun.
   Newsweek 11 Dec 78

14 Yes, there's such a thing as luck in trial law but it only comes at 3 o'clock in the morning. . . . You'll still find me in the library looking for luck at 3 o'clock in the morning.
   Reader's Digest Oct 84

SANDRA DAY O'CONNOR, Associate Justice, US Supreme Court

15 My hope is that 10 years from now, after I've been across the street at work for a while, they'll all be glad they gave me that wonderful vote.
   On being confirmed unanimously by US Senate 21 Sep 81

STEWART ONEGLIA, US Department of Justice

16 [They are] social pariahs, irrationally ostracized by their communities because of medically baseless fears of contagion.
   On civil rights of AIDS patients, NY *Times* 26 Jun 86

PAUL O'NEIL

1 A criminal lawyer, like a trapeze performer, is seldom more than one slip from an awful fall.
On attorney Edward Bennett Williams, *Life* 22 Jun 59

2 No splints yet invented will heal a lawyer's broken reputation.
ib

JOSÉ ORTEGA Y GASSET

3 Law is born from despair of human nature.
Recalled on his death 18 Oct 55

MARGUERITE OSWALD

4 This young man—whether he's my son or a stranger—repeatedly declares, "I didn't do it, I didn't do it." And he's shot down. That's not the American way of life. A man is innocent until he's proved guilty.
On death of her son Lee Harvey Oswald less than 48 hours after the assassination of President John F Kennedy, NY *Post* 19 Feb 64

EDWARD PACKARD JR

5 Law students are trained in the case method, and to the lawyer everything in life looks like a case.
Columbia Forum Spring 67

6 The lawyer's first thought in the morning is how to handle the case of the ringing alarm clock.
ib

ROSA PARKS

7 All I was doing was trying to get home from work.
On her refusal to move to the back of a bus, an action leading to a boycott in Birmingham AL that sparked the civil-rights movement, recalled on 30th anniversary of her arrest, NBC TV 1 Dec 85

REGINALD WITHERS PAYNE, Judge of the High Court

8 The difficulty about a gentlemen's agreement is that it depends on the continued existence of the gentlemen.
NY *Times* 9 Feb 64

ROSCOE POUND, Dean Emeritus, Harvard Law School

9 Law is experience developed by reason and applied continually to further experience.
Christian Science Monitor 24 Apr 63

10 Law must be stable, and yet it cannot stand still.
Quoted by Kenneth R Redden and Enid L Veron *Modern Legal Glossary* Michie 80

LEWIS F POWELL JR, Associate Justice, US Supreme Court

11 I go onto the Court with deep personal misgivings whether I'll like it. In fact, I rather suppose I won't. . . . but it has a very special place in the life and attitude of any lawyer of my age, and for those of my generation it is a revered institution, the pinnacle of our profession.
Washington *Post* 24 Oct 71

12 For the most part . . . we function as nine small independent law firms.
NY *Times* 9 Dec 84

THOMAS REED POWELL

13 If you think that you can think about a thing, inextricably attached to something else, without thinking of the thing it is attached to, then you have a legal mind.
Recalled on his death 16 Aug 55

JANE BRYANT QUINN

14 Lawyers [are] operators of the toll bridge across which anyone in search of justice has to pass.
Newsweek 9 Oct 78

RONALD REAGAN, 40th US President

15 State problems should involve state solutions.
Restating a well-known viewpoint while at the same time supporting a federal law that would establish a national minimum age for drinking, address at Oradell NJ 20 Jun 84

WILLIAM H REHNQUIST, Associate Justice, US Supreme Court

16 The Supreme Court is an institution far more dominated by centrifugal forces, pushing toward individuality and independence, than it is by centripetal forces pulling for hierarchical ordering and institutional unity.
Address at University of Minnesota Law School, NY *Times* 20 Oct 84

17 Somewhere "out there," beyond the walls of the courthouse, run currents and tides of public opinion which lap at the courtroom door.
Address at Suffolk University Law School, Boston, *ib* 17 Apr 86

JOHN ROBERTSON, Professor of Law, University of Texas

1 Hiring a surrogate mother can be viewed as part of a constitutional right of married couples to reproduce.

NY *Times* 6 Oct 86

SOLLY ROBINS

2 We pioneered the field of catastrophe law.

On representing the government of India in negligence suit against Union Carbide Corp for industrial disaster at Bhopal, NY *Times* 12 Mar 85

FRED RODELL, Professor of Law, Yale

3 [The law is like the killy-loo bird, a creature that] insisted on flying backward because it didn't care where it was going but was mightily interested in where it had been.

NY *Times* 27 Jun 84

RICHARD ROME, Kansas magistrate

4 From her ancient profession she's been busted,
And to society's rules she must be adjusted,
If from all this a moral doth unfurl,
It's that pimps do not protect the working girl.

On prostitution conviction that drew disapproval from feminist groups, *National Observer* 4 Oct 75

BERTRAND RUSSELL

5 Obscenity is whatever happens to shock some elderly and ignorant magistrate.

Look 23 Feb 54

6 What is new in our time is the increased power of the authorities to enforce their prejudices.

Quoted on *Who Said That?* BBC TV 8 Aug 58

CARL SANDBURG

7 Why is there always a secret singing when a lawyer cashes in? Why does a hearse horse snicker hauling a lawyer away?

Quoted in NY *Times* 13 Jan 85

ANTONIN SCALIA, Associate Justice, US Supreme Court

8 [The Freedom of Information Act is] the Taj Mahal of the Doctrine of Unanticipated Consequences, the Sistine Chapel of Cost-Benefit Analysis Ignored.

Recalled on his appointment to Supreme Court, *Time* 30 Jun 86

LESLIE SCARMAN

9 Law reform is far too serious a matter to be left to the legal profession.

To NYC Bar Assn, *Record* Jan 55

ROBERT SCHMITT

10 The average lawyer is essentially a mechanic who works with a pen instead of a ball peen hammer.

Americans for Legal Reform Newsletter Spring 84

IRVING S SHAPIRO, Chairman, E I du Pont de Nemours

11 Litigation should be a last resort, not a knee-jerk reflex.

Christian Science Monitor 5 Dec 78

ARIEL SHARON, former Defense Minister of Israel

12 A lie . . . should be tried in a place where it will attract the attention of the world.

On bringing libel suit against *Time* magazine in NYC, NY *Times* 20 Nov 84

JOHN J SIRICA, Judge, US District Court, District of Columbia

13 In all candor, the Court fails to perceive any reason for suspending the power of courts to get evidence and rule on questions of privilege in criminal matters simply because it is the president of the United States who holds the evidence.

Statement on obtaining Watergate tapes from President Richard M Nixon, *Christian Science Monitor* 15 Sep 74

JAMES SISSERSON

14 [It's] like suing God in the Vatican.

On chances of a Florida court ruling against Walt Disney Productions, *Time* 11 May 85

ELIOT DUNLAP SMITH

15 The law is the only profession which records its mistakes carefully, exactly as they occurred, and yet does not identify them as mistakes.

Quoted by Louis Brown "Legal Autopsy" Amer Judicial Society *Journal* Nov 54

JOHN STERLING

16 [The] ideal client is the very wealthy man in very great trouble.

"Lawyers and the Laws of Economics" *ABA Journal* Apr 60

ADLAI E STEVENSON

17 I think that one of the most fundamental responsibilities . . . is to give testimony in a court of law, to give it honestly and willingly.

When asked why he had signed an affidavit supporting Alger Hiss after his conviction for perjury, recalled on Stevenson's death 14 Jul 65

1 Law is not a profession at all, but rather a business service station and repair shop.
The Papers of Adlai Stevenson Little, Brown 72

POTTER STEWART, Associate Justice, US Supreme Court

2 Swift justice demands more than just swiftness.
Time 20 Oct 58

3 Fairness is what justice really is.
ib

LLOYD PAUL STRYKER

4 A trial is still an ordeal by battle. For the broadsword there is the weight of evidence; for the battle-ax the force of logic; for the sharp spear, the blazing gleam of truth; for the rapier, the quick and flashing knife of wit.
Recalled on his death 21 Jun 55

5 Trying a case the second time is like eating yesterday morning's oatmeal.
ib

6 A tendency toward enthusiasm and a chivalrous instinct have more than once been weighed as evidence of a lack of judgment.
ib

BRENDAN J SULLIVAN JR

7 I'm not a potted plant. I'm here as the lawyer. That's my job.
On being told to allow his client Lt Col Oliver L North to object for himself if he wished to do so, at Iran-Contra hearings 9 Jul 87

GLEN TATHAM, Zimbabwe park warden

8 To kill a man for shooting an animal is a very delicate matter.
On executions of poachers of rare Zimbabwe valley rhinoceros, NY *Times* 6 May 86

TIME MAGAZINE

9 Late every night in Connecticut, lights go out in the cities and towns, and citizens by tens of thousands proceed zestfully to break the law.
On Connecticut law against contraceptives, 10 Mar 61

HARRY S TRUMAN, 33rd US President

10 Whenever you put a man on the Supreme Court he ceases to be your friend.
Recalled on his 75th birthday, NY *Times* 8 May 59

JOHN TURNER, Attorney General of Canada

11 Substantive and procedural law benefits and protects landlords over tenants, creditors over debtors, lenders over borrowers, and the poor are seldom among the favored parties.
To Canadian Bar Assn 7 Dec 69

MORRIS K UDALL, US Congressman

12 One puts on black robes to scare the hell out of white people, while the other puts on white robes to scare the hell out of blacks.
Contrasting US Supreme Court justices and Ku Klux Klan members, Washington Gridiron Club dinner 27 Mar 82

GORE VIDAL

13 Litigation takes the place of sex at middle age.
Quoted by Kenneth R Redden and Enid L Veron *Modern Legal Glossary* Michie 80

SOL WACHTLER, Judge, NY State Court of Appeals

14 You can, if you wish, think of it like the universe: Each case is a sun, and all the judges, lawyers and administrative personnel represent planets revolving around the case in fixed orbit, never getting closer.
NY *Times* 22 Apr 85

JOYCE WADLER

15 [He was] a lawyer who usually operated with the delicacy of a Lexington Avenue express train.
On Thomas Puccio, defense counsel in trial of Claus von Bülow, accused of attempting to murder his wife, *New York* 3 Jun 85

EARL WARREN, Chief Justice, US Supreme Court

16 In civilized life, law floats in a sea of ethics.
NY *Times* 12 Nov 62

17 The man of character, sensitive to the meaning of what he is doing, will know how to discover the ethical paths in the maze of possible behavior.
Quoted in editorial on moral codes, *Christian Science Monitor* 21 May 64

18 The police must obey the law while enforcing the law.
Condemning use of involuntary confessions, quoted in Milwaukee *Journal* 20 Sep 64

19 You sit up there, and you see the whole gamut of human nature. Even if the case being argued involves only a little fellow and $50, it involves justice. That's what is important.
Recalled on his death, *Time* 22 Jul 74

HERMAN WEINKRANTZ, Judge, NYC Criminal Court

1 This court will not deny the equal protection of the law to the unwashed, unshod, unkempt and uninhibited.

> Ruling that disapproval of hippies would not interfere with their civil rights, NY *Times* 1 Jul 68

BYRON R WHITE, Associate Justice, US Supreme Court

2 We're the only branch of government that explains itself in writing every time it makes a decision.

> *Time* 8 Oct 84

MARY BETH WHITEHEAD

3 [He considers me] just a uterus with legs.

> On NJ Superior Court Judge Harvey R Sorkow, who denied her the right to rear the child she had conceived as a surrogate mother, NY *Times* 8 Apr 87

HARRISON A WILLIAMS JR, former US Senator

4 A "dishonest crime" is when somebody else creates the situation for which you are convicted.

> On his prison sentence for accepting illegal funds, WNET TV 15 Jan 86

DOROTHY WRIGHT WILSON, Dean, University of Southern California Law Center

5 If criminals wanted to grind justice to a halt, they could do it by banding together and all pleading not guilty.

> On plea-bargaining and the criminal justice system, LA *Times* 11 Aug 74

JAMES Q WILSON, Professor of Government, Harvard

6 Arresting a single drunk or a single vagrant who has harmed no identifiable person seems unjust, and in a sense it is. But failing to do anything about a score of drunks or a hundred vagrants may destroy an entire community.

> *Thinking about Crime* Random House 77, quoted in *Time* 11 Mar 85

EVELLE J YOUNGER, Attorney General of California

7 An incompetent attorney can delay a trial for years or months. A competent attorney can delay one even longer.

> LA *Times* 3 Mar 71

FRANKLIN E ZIMRING, Professor of Law, University of Chicago

8 Because of plea-bargaining, I guess we can say,

"Gee, the trains run on time." But do we like where they are going?

> *Time* 28 Aug 78

Judicial Opinions

SIDNEY H ASCH, Judge, NY State Supreme Court, Appellate Division

9 Where sexual proclivity does not relate to job function, it seems clearly unconstitutional to penalize an individual in one of the most imperative of life's endeavors, the right to earn one's daily bread.

> Majority opinion in 3-1 ruling that upheld municipal authority to bar private agencies from discrimination on the basis of sexual orientation, 7 May 85
>
> *ib*

HUGO L BLACK, Associate Justice, US Supreme Court

10 Criticism of government finds sanctuary in several portions of the 1st Amendment. It is part of the right of free speech. It embraces freedom of the press.

> Dissenting opinion in 6-3 ruling that forbade a person summoned before a Congressional committee to refuse to answer the question, "Are you a member of the Communist Party?" 27 Feb 61

11 I was brought up to believe that Scotch whisky would need a tax preference to survive in competition with Kentucky bourbon.

> Dissenting opinion in 6-2 ruling that limited power of states to tax and restrict the liquor business, 1 Jun 64

12 Recalling that it is a Constitution intended to endure for ages to come, we also remember that the Founders wisely provided the means for that endurance: Changes in the Constitution, when thought necessary, are to be proposed by Congress or conventions and ratified by the states. The Founders gave no such amending power to this Court.

> Dissenting opinion in 6-3 ruling that prohibited racial discrimination in restaurants, 22 Jun 64

13 Our Constitution was not written in the sands to be washed away by each wave of new judges blown in by each successive political wind.

> Dissenting opinion in 6-2 ruling that upheld federal law making possession of heroin sufficient evidence of illegal importation of drugs, 20 Jan 70

14 The flagrant disregard in the courtroom of elementary standards of proper conduct should not and cannot be tolerated.

> Unanimous opinion that a disorderly defendant

may forfeit his constitutional right to be present in court, NY *Times* 1 Apr 70

1 We believe trial judges confronted with disruptive, contumacious, stubbornly defiant defendants must be given sufficient discretion to meet the circumstances in each case.
ib

2 It would degrade our country and our judicial system to permit our courts to be bullied, insulted and humiliated and the orderly progress thwarted and obstructed by defendants brought before them charged with crimes.
ib

3 Paramount among the responsibilities of a free press is the duty to prevent any part of the government from deceiving the people and sending them off to distant lands to die of foreign fevers and foreign shot and shell.
Concurring opinion in 6-3 ruling that upheld the press's right to publish the Pentagon Papers, 30 Jun 71

4 In my view, far from deserving condemnation for their courageous reporting, the New York *Times*, the Washington *Post* and other newspapers should be commended for serving the purpose that the Founding Fathers saw so clearly.
ib

5 In revealing the workings of government that led to the Vietnam War, the newspapers nobly did precisely that which the Founders hoped and trusted they would do.
ib

HARRY A BLACKMUN, Associate Justice, US Supreme Court

6 The states are not free, under the guise of protecting maternal health or potential life, to intimidate women into continuing pregnancies.
Majority opinion in 7-2 ruling that established the constitutional legality of abortion, 22 Jan 73

7 The mandated description of fetal characteristics at two-week intervals, no matter how objective, is plainly overinclusive. [It is] not medical information that is always relevant to the woman's decision, and it may serve to confuse and punish her and to heighten her anxiety.
ib

8 Controversy over the meaning of our nation's most majestic guarantees frequently has been turbulent. . . . Abortion raises moral and spiritual questions over which honorable persons

can disagree sincerely and profoundly. But those disagreements did not then and do not now relieve us of our duty to apply the Constitution faithfully.
ib

9 If there is any truth to the old proverb that "one who is his own lawyer has a fool for a client," the Court . . . now bestows a *constitutional* right on one to make a fool of himself.
Dissenting opinion in 6-3 ruling that allowed a defendant to refuse counsel, 30 Jun 75

10 The flaw in the statute [is] that in all its applications, it operates on a fundamentally mistaken premise that high solicitation costs are an accurate measure of fraud.
Majority opinion in 5-4 ruling that struck down a Maryland statute regulating how much charities may spend on fund raising, 26 Jun 84

11 By placing discretion in the hands of an official to grant or deny a license, such a statute creates a threat of censorship that by its very existence chills free speech.
ib

12 What the Court really has refused to recognize is the fundamental interest all individuals have in controlling the nature of their intimate associations.
Dissenting opinion in 5-4 ruling that upheld the right to prohibit deviant sexual behavior, 30 Jun 86

13 The right of an individual to conduct intimate relationships in the intimacy of his or her own home seems to me to be the heart of the Constitution's protection of privacy.
ib

WILLIAM J BRENNAN, Associate Justice, US Supreme Court

14 Sex and obscenity are not synonymous. Obscene material is material which deals with sex in a manner appealing to prurient interest.
Dissenting opinion in 5-4 ruling that established a new legal standard for obscenity, 24 Jun 57

15 Sex, a great and mysterious motive force in human life, has indisputably been a subject of absorbing interest to mankind through the ages.
ib

16 We hold that the Constitution does not forbid the states minor intrusions into an individual's body under stringently limited conditions.
Majority opinion in 5-4 ruling that blood tests of drunken drivers do not constitute self-incriminating evidence, 20 Jun 66

1 This Court inescapably has the duty, as the ultimate arbiter of the meaning of our Constitution, to say whether, when individuals condemned to death stand before our bar, "moral concepts" require us to hold that the law has progressed to the point where we should declare that the punishment of death, like punishments on the rack, the screw and the wheel, is no longer morally tolerable in our society.
> Dissenting opinion in 7-2 ruling that upheld the death penalty, 2 Jul 76

2 Death is not only an unusually severe punishment, unusual in its pain, in its finality and in its enormity, but it serves no penal purpose more effectively than a less severe punishment; therefore the principle inherent in the clause that prohibits pointless infliction of excessive punishment when less severe punishment can adequately achieve the same purposes invalidates the punishment.
> *ib*

3 Appellant constituted a legitimate class of one, and this provides a basis for Congress's decision to proceed with dispatch with respect to his materials.
> Majority opinion in 7-2 ruling that upheld Congressional seizure of Richard M Nixon's presidential papers, 28 Jun 77

4 We cannot . . . let colorblindness become myopia which masks the reality that many "created equal" have been treated within our lifetimes as inferior both by the law and by their fellow citizens.
> Dissenting opinion in 5-4 ruling in the Bakke case that prohibited racial quotas in university admissions policies, 28 Jun 78

5 No longer is the female destined solely for the home and the rearing of the family and only the male for the marketplace and the world of ideas.
> Majority opinion in 6-3 ruling that laws barring alimony for men are unconstitutional, 5 Mar 79

6 It would be ironic indeed if a law triggered by a nation's concern over centuries of racial injustice and intended to improve the lot of those who had "been excluded from the American dream for so long" constituted the first legislative prohibition of all voluntary, private, race-conscious efforts to abolish traditional patterns of racial segregation and hierarchy.
> Majority opinion in 5-2 ruling that a training program reserving places for blacks did not constitute illegal reverse discrimination, 27 Jun 79

7 It is difficult to understand precisely what the state hopes to achieve by promoting the creation and perpetuation of a subclass of illiterates within our boundaries, surely adding to the problems and costs of unemployment, welfare and crime. It is thus clear that whatever savings might be achieved by denying these children an education, they are wholly insubstantial in light of the costs involved to these children, the state and the nation.
> Majority opinion in 5-4 ruling that young illegal aliens have a constitutional right to public schooling, 15 Jun 82

8 Use of a mentally ill person's involuntary confession is antithetical to the notion of fundamental fairness embodied in the due process clause.
> Dissenting opinion in 7-2 ruling that confessions from the mentally ill may be used against them even if those confessions are not the product of free will, 10 Dec 86

9 Congress acknowledged that society's accumulated myths and fears about disability and disease are as handicapping as are the physical limitations that flow from actual impairment.
> Majority opinion in 7-2 ruling that people with contagious diseases are covered by law that prohibits discrimination against the handicapped in federally aided programs, 3 Mar 87

WARREN E BURGER, Chief Justice, US Supreme Court

10 It is indeed an odd business that it has taken this Court nearly two centuries to "discover" a constitutional mandate to have counsel at a preliminary hearing.
> Dissenting opinion in 6-2 ruling that declared right of the accused to court-appointed counsel at pretrial hearings, 22 Jun 70

11 For better or worse, editing is what editors are for; and editing is selection and choice of material. That editors—newspaper or broadcast—can and do abuse this power is beyond doubt, but that is no reason to deny the discretion Congress provided.
> Majority opinion in 7-2 ruling that allowed radio and television stations to refuse to sell time for political or controversial advertisements, 29 May 73

12 Calculated risks of abuse are taken in order to preserve higher values.
> *ib*

13 The president's need for complete candor and objectivity from advisers calls for great deference from the courts.
> Unanimous opinion on the Nixon tapes that

ruled the needs of the judicial process may outweigh presidential privilege, 24 Jul 74

1 Free speech carries with it some freedom to listen.

Majority opinion in 7-1 ruling that prohibited the closing of courtrooms to the press, 2 Jul 80

2 We reject the contention that in the remedial context the Congress must act in a wholly "colorblind" fashion. . . . It is fundamental that in no organ of government, state or federal, does there repose a more comprehensive remedial power than in the Congress, expressly charged by the Constitution with competence and authority to enforce equal protection guarantees.

Majority opinion in 6-3 ruling that upheld a federal law allotting 10 percent of public works contracts to minority businesses, *ib*

3 Respondent's expectation that his garden was protected from observation is unreasonable and is not an expectation that society is prepared to honor.

Majority opinion in 5-4 ruling that upheld aerial surveillance without a warrant of a fenced backyard where police suspected marijuana was being grown, 19 May 86

4 We may have lured judges into roaming at large in the constitutional field.

Dissenting opinion in 5-4 ruling that reaffirmed opinion establishing constitutional right to abortion, 11 Jun 86

5 To hold that the act of homosexual sodomy is somehow protected as a fundamental right would be to cast aside millennia of moral teaching.

Concurring opinion in 5-4 ruling that upheld the right to prohibit deviant sexual behavior, 30 Jun 86

CANADIAN SUPREME COURT

6 Kneeling to receive Communion is not a criminal offense.

Ruling against arrest of Roman Catholics in Nova Scotia for "disturbing the solemnity of a church service" by refusing to follow new directive to stand while receiving the Eucharist, news summaries 30 Sep 85

TOM C CLARK, Associate Justice, US Supreme Court

7 In the relationship between man and religion, the state is firmly committed to a position of neutrality.

Majority opinion in 8-1 ruling that religious exercises in public schools are unconstitutional, 17 Jun 63

8 To so interpret the language of the act is to extract more sunbeams from cucumbers than did Gulliver's mad scientist.

Dissenting opinion in 7-2 ruling that upheld the constitutionality of loyalty oaths, 1 Jun 64

9 To conjure up such ridiculous questions, the answers to which we all know or should know are in the negative, is to build up a whimsical and farcical straw man which is not only grim but Grimm.

ib

10 A defendant on trial for a specific crime is entitled to his day in court, not in a stadium or a city or nationwide arena.

Majority opinion in 5-4 ruling that the principles of a fair trial are violated when telecasting is allowed, 7 Jun 65

11 The heightened public clamor resulting from radio and television coverage will inevitably result in prejudice. Trial by television is, therefore, foreign to our system.

ib

LYNN COMPTON, Judge, California Court of Appeals, 2nd District

12 Whatever choice Elizabeth Bouvia may ultimately make, I can only hope that her courage, persistence and example will cause our society to deal realistically with the plight of those unfortunate individuals to whom death beckons as a welcome respite from suffering.

Unanimous opinion that the right to refuse medical treatment is basic and fundamental in the case of a quadriplegic cerebral palsy victim who requested she not be force-fed, 16 Apr 86

LAWRENCE H COOKE, Judge, NY State Court of Appeals

13 Ordinarily, death will be determined according to the traditional criteria of irreversible cardiorespiratory repose. When, however, the respiratory and circulatory functions are maintained by mechanical means, their significance, as signs of life, is at best ambiguous.

Unanimous opinion that a person may be deemed legally dead when the brain has ceased to function, even if heartbeat and breathing are being maintained artificially, 30 Oct 84

RICHARD L CURRY, Judge, Cook County Circuit Court, Chicago

14 The scheme which has major-league baseball trashing a residential community and tinkering with the quality-of-life aspirations of countless households so that television royal-

ties might more easily flow into the coffers of 25 distant sports moguls not consonant with present-day concepts of right and justice.

Supporting citizens' protest against night baseball at Chicago's Wrigley Field, 25 Mar 85

WILLIAM O DOUGLAS, Associate Justice, US Supreme Court

1 We do not sit as a superlegislature to weigh the wisdom of legislation.

Majority opinion in 8-1 ruling that upheld right of states to legislate internal affairs, 3 Mar 52

2 We are a religious people whose institutions presuppose a Supreme Being.

Majority opinion in 6-3 ruling that allowed release of public school students for religious instruction, 28 Apr 52

3 The right to be let alone is indeed the beginning of all freedoms.

Dissenting opinion in 7-1 ruling that allowed radios to be played on streetcars, 26 May 52

4 The critical point is that the Constitution places the right of silence beyond the reach of government.

Dissenting opinion in 7-2 ruling that upheld Immunity Act of 1954, 26 Mar 56

5 Free speech is not to be regulated like diseased cattle and impure butter. The audience ... that hissed yesterday may applaud today, even for the same performance.

Dissenting opinion in 5-4 ruling that banned sale of obscene books, 24 Jun 57

6 We deal with a right of privacy older than the Bill of Rights—older than our political parties, older than our school system.

Majority opinion in 6-2 ruling that overturned state birth control laws, 7 Jun 65

7 Marriage is a coming together for better or for worse, hopefully enduring, and intimate to the degree of being sacred.

ib

8 The association promotes a way of life, not causes; a harmony in living, not political faiths; a bilateral loyalty, not commercial or social projects. Yet it is an association for as noble a purpose as any involved in any prior decisions.

ib

9 If discrimination based on race is constitutionally permissible when those who hold the reins can come up with "compelling" reasons to justify it, then constitutional guarantees acquire an accordionlike quality.

Dissenting opinion in 7-2 ruling that upheld dis-

criminatory university admissions policies, 23 Apr 74

FELIX FRANKFURTER, Associate Justice, US Supreme Court

10 Lincoln's appeal to "the better angels of our nature" failed to avert a fratricidal war. But the compassionate wisdom of Lincoln's first and second inaugurals bequeathed to the Union, cemented with blood, a moral heritage which, when drawn upon in times of stress and strife, is sure to find specific ways and means to surmount difficulties that may appear to be insurmountable.

Concurring opinion in unanimous ruling that ordered racial desegregation of schools in Little Rock AR, 29 Sep 58

11 Time and experience have forcefully taught that the power to inspect dwelling places, either as a matter of systematic area-by-area search or, as here, to treat a specific problem, is of indispensable importance in the maintenance of community health; a power that would be greatly hobbled by the blanket requirement of the safeguards necessary for a search of evidence of criminal acts.

Majority opinion in 5-4 ruling that allowed health inspectors to enter a private home without a search warrant, 4 May 59

ARTHUR J GOLDBERG, Associate Justice, US Supreme Court

12 The basic guarantees of our Constitution are warrants for the here and now, and unless there is an overwhelmingly compelling reason, they are to be promptly fulfilled.

Unanimous opinion that ordered Memphis TN to desegregate immediately its recreational facilities, NY *Times* 27 May 63

13 The concept of neutrality can lead to ... a brooding and pervasive devotion to the secular and a passive, or even active, hostility to the religious. Such results are not only not compelled by the Constitution, but, it seems to me, are prohibited by it.

Concurring but mitigating opinion in 8-1 ruling that declared religious exercises in public schools unconstitutional, 17 Jun 63

JOHN MARSHALL HARLAN, Associate Justice, US Supreme Court

14 The Constitution is not a panacea for every blot upon the public welfare. Nor should this Court, ordained as a judicial body, be thought of as a general haven for reform movements.

Dissenting opinion in 6-3 ruling that required

both houses of state legislatures to be apportioned on a population basis, 15 Jun 64

ROBERT H JACKSON, Associate Justice, US Supreme Court

1 The petitioner's problem is to avoid Scylla without being drawn into Charybdis.

Majority opinion in 5-4 ruling that prohibited federal jurisdiction over utility rates, 7 May 51

2 Men are more often bribed by their loyalties and ambitions than by money.

Dissenting opinion in 6-3 ruling that upheld authority of department heads in awarding government contracts, 26 Nov 51

3 We can afford no liberties with liberty itself.

Dissenting opinion in 5-3 ruling that upheld the constitutionality of forced deportation, 7 Apr 52

4 The day that this country ceases to be free for irreligion, it will cease to be free for religion.

Dissenting opinion in 6-3 ruling that allowed release of public school children for religious instruction, 28 Apr 52

5 We are not unaware that we are not final because we are infallible; we know that we are infallible only because we are final.

Concurring opinion in 6-3 ruling that upheld Supreme Court as the court of last appeal, 9 Feb 53

6 In this court the parties changed positions as nimbly as if dancing a quadrille.

Majority opinion in 6-3 ruling that armed forces personnel have no constitutional right to a particular assignment based on education or preparation, 9 Mar 53

7 The validity of a doctrine does not depend on whose ox it gores.

Dissenting opinion in 5-3 ruling that upheld state laws setting statute of limitations on cases of wrongful death, 18 May 53

THURGOOD MARSHALL, Associate Justice, US Supreme Court

8 If the 1st Amendment means anything, it means that a state has no business telling a man, sitting alone in his own house, what books he may read or what films he may watch.

Unanimous opinion that the 1st Amendment guarantees the right to possess in one's home material that might be regarded as obscene in public, 7 Apr 69

9 Our whole constitutional heritage rebels at the thought of giving government the power to control men's minds.

ib

10 Surely the fact that a uniformed police officer is wearing his hair below his collar will make him no less identifiable as a policeman.

Dissenting opinion in 7-2 ruling that upheld the

right of police departments to order officers to have short haircuts and no beards, NY Times 6 Apr 76

11 Mere access to the courthouse doors does not by itself assure a proper functioning of the adversary process.

Majority opinion in 8-1 ruling that allowed defendants who plead not guilty by reason of insanity to seek a psychiatrist's help in preparing and presenting their cases, 26 Feb 85

12 [It is] a historic step toward eliminating the shameful practice of racial discrimination in the selection of juries.

Majority opinion in 7-2 ruling that made it more difficult for blacks to be excluded from juries trying black defendants, 30 Apr 86

13 [Ending racial discrimination in jury selection] can be accomplished only by eliminating peremptory challenges entirely.

ib

14 [Jurors who are opposed to capital punishment are] more likely to believe that a defendant's failure to testify is indicative of his guilt, more hostile to the insanity defense, more mistrustful of defense attorneys and less concerned about the danger of erroneous convictions.

Dissenting opinion in 6-3 ruling that opponents of the death penalty may be barred from juries in capital cases, 5 May 86

MASSACHUSETTS SUPREME JUDICIAL COURT

15 [It is time to end] antediluvian assumptions concerning the role and status of women in marriage.

Ruling that wives have a right to sue their husbands, 30 Jul 80

JAMES B M McNALLY, Judge, NY State Supreme Court, Appellate Division

16 Slovenliness is no part of my religion, nor is it conducive to rest. Scripture commands cleanliness.

Unanimous opinion declaring it legal to use a coin-operated laundry on Sunday, NY Times 19 Jun 59

SANDRA DAY O'CONNOR, Associate Justice, US Supreme Court

17 A moment of silence is not inherently religious.

Concurring opinion in 6-3 ruling that an Alabama law authorizing voluntary prayer or meditation in public schools violated the 1st Amendment by encouraging religious practice, 4 Jun 85

1 Statutes authorizing unreasonable searches were the core concern of the framers of the 4th Amendment.

> Minority opinion in 5-4 ruling that broadened an exception to the 4th Amendment rule barring use of unconstitutionally seized evidence in criminal trials, 9 Mar 87

2 We hold that the reckless disregard for human life implicit in knowingly engaging in criminal activity known to carry a grave risk of death represents a highly culpable mental state ... that may be taken into account in making a capital sentencing judgment when that conduct causes its natural, though also not inevitable, lethal result.

> Majority opinion in 5-4 ruling that some accomplices in crimes leading to death may be executed even if they did not personally kill or intend to kill, 21 Apr 87

LAWRENCE PIERCE, Judge, US Court of Appeals, 2nd Circuit

3 Although the employer may perhaps lawfully destroy its own reputation, its employees should be and are barred from destroying their employer's reputation by misappropriating their employer's informational property.

> Majority opinion in 2-1 ruling that upheld conviction of former *Wall Street Journal* reporter for insider trading, 27 May 86

LEWIS F POWELL JR, Associate Justice, US Supreme Court

4 The guarantee of equal protection cannot mean one thing when applied to one individual and something else when applied to a person of another color. If both are not accorded the same protection, then it is not equal.

> Majority opinion in 5-4 ruling that affirmed the constitutionality of college admission programs favoring minorities, 28 Jun 78

5 The states' role in our system of government is a matter of constitutional law, not of legislative grace.

> Dissenting opinion in 5-4 ruling that upheld imposition of federal standards for mass transit workers, 19 Feb 85

WILLIAM H REHNQUIST, Associate Justice, US Supreme Court

6 A father's interest in having a child—perhaps his only child—may be unmatched by any other interest in his life. It is truly surprising that the state must assign a greater value to a mother's decision to cut off a potential human life by abortion than to a father's decision to let it mature into a live child.

> Minority opinion in 6-3 ruling that prohibited states from requiring women to obtain their husbands' consent for abortions, 1 Jul 76

7 Pregnancy is of course confined to women, but it is in other ways significantly different from the typical covered disease or disability.

> Majority opinion in 6-3 ruling that allowed private employers to refuse to compensate women for absences due to pregnancy, 7 Dec 76

8 This result ... will daily stand as a veritable sword of Damocles over every succeeding president and his advisers.

> Dissenting opinion in 7-2 ruling that upheld Congressional seizure of Richard M Nixon's presidential papers, 28 Jun 77

9 [The majority has created] a scenario in which the government appears as the Big Bad Wolf and Pacifica as Little Red Riding Hood. A more appropriate analogy [would be] Faust and Mephistopheles.

> Dissenting opinion in 5-4 ruling that lifted ban on editorializing by public broadcasting's Pacifica Foundation, 3 Jul 84

10 [Jury selection] is best based upon seat-of-the-pants instincts, which are undoubtedly crudely stereotypical and may in many cases be hopelessly mistaken.

> Dissenting opinion in 7-2 ruling that made it more difficult for blacks to be excluded from juries trying black defendants, 30 Apr 86

CHARLES RICHEY, Judge, US District Court, District of Columbia

11 The court must admit that it is not comfortable with racially based distinctions. [But] no decision of [the Supreme] Court has ever adopted the proposition that the Constitution must be colorblind.

> Rejecting Justice Department's argument that a 1984 Supreme Court decision "precludes the use of any race-conscious affirmative action plan," 1 Apr 85

H LEE SAROKIN, Judge, US District Court, New Jersey

12 Why should a claim for a damaged leg survive one's death where a claim for a damaged name does not? After death, the leg cannot be healed, but the reputation can. To say that a man's defamed reputation dies with him is to ignore the realities of life and the bleak legacy he leaves behind.

> Ruling that the family of a deceased man may sue for libel to clear his name, 13 Jan 83

13 The invidious effects of such mass, roundup urinalysis is that it casually sweeps up the innocent with the guilty.

> Ruling that mandatory testing of government

employees to determine presence of illegal drugs is unconstitutional, 18 Sep 86

ANTONIN SCALIA, Associate Justice, US Supreme Court

1 There is nothing new in the realization that the Constitution sometimes insulates the criminality of a few in order to protect the privacy of us all.

Majority opinion in 6-3 ruling that refused to expand police powers to search or seize evidence that they suspect may be stolen, 3 Mar 87

2 A search is a search, even if it happens to disclose nothing but the bottom of a turntable.

ib

3 We are unwilling to send police and judges into a new thicket of 4th Amendment law, to seek a creature of uncertain description that is neither a plain-view inspection nor yet a "fullblown search."

ib

4 The Court today completes the process of converting [Title VII of the Civil Rights Act of 1964] from a guarantee that race or sex will not be the basis for employment determinations, to a guarantee that it often will.

Dissenting opinion in 6-3 ruling that employers may sometimes favor women and members of minorities over better-qualified men and whites in hiring and promoting in order to achieve better balance in their work forces, 25 Mar 87

5 Ever so subtly, without even alluding to the last obstacles preserved by earlier opinions that we now push out of our path, we effectively replace the goal of a discrimination-free society with the quite incompatible goal of proportionate representation by race and by sex in the workplace.

ib

6 A law can be both economic folly and constitutional.

Concurring opinion in 6-3 ruling that upheld state law restricting hostile takeover offers for companies incorporated within that state, 21 Apr 87

HARVEY R SORKOW, Judge, New Jersey Superior Court

7 To make a new concept fit into an old statute makes tortured law with tortured results.

Ruling in the Baby M case that a surrogacy agreement was a valid contract and did not violate prior laws governing adoption, custody and the cessation of parental rights, 31 Mar 87

JOHN PAUL STEVENS, Associate Justice, US Supreme Court

8 When the commission finds that a pig has entered the parlor, the exercise of its regulatory power does not depend on proof that the pig is obscene.

Majority opinion in 5-4 ruling that allowed the Federal Communications Commission to prohibit the broadcasting of words that are offensive but fall short of the Court's definition of obscenity, 3 Jul 78

9 The 4th Amendment protects the individual's privacy in a variety of settings. In none is the zone of privacy more clearly defined than when bounded by the unambiguous physical dimensions of an individual's home—a zone that finds its roots in clear and specific constitutional terms: "the right of the people to be secure in their . . . houses . . . shall not be violated."

Majority opinion in 6-3 ruling that required police to have a warrant before entering a suspect's home to make an arrest, 15 Apr 80

10 It is not our job to apply laws that have not yet been written.

Majority opinion in 5-4 ruling that allowed consumers to use videotape recorders to tape television programs for their own use, 17 Jan 84

11 They may not be conscripted against their will as the foot soldiers in a federal crusade.

Majority opinion in 5-3 ruling that struck down Reagan administration regulations requiring life-prolonging medical treatment for infants with severe handicaps, 9 Jun 86

12 To show a "well-founded fear of persecution," an alien need not prove that it is more likely than not that he or she will be persecuted in his or her home country.

Majority opinion in 6-3 ruling that the government must ease its rule for deciding whether aliens are eligible for political asylum, 9 Mar 87

POTTER STEWART, Associate Justice, US Supreme Court

13 It must always be remembered that what the Constitution forbids is not all searches and seizures, but unreasonable searches and seizures.

Majority opinion in 5-4 ruling that prohibited the federal government from using evidence improperly seized by state officials, 27 Jun 60

14 The 4th Amendment and the personal rights it secures have a long history. At the very core stands the right of a man to retreat into his own home and there be free from unreasonable governmental intrusion.

Unanimous opinion that Constitution bars police from electronic eavesdropping, 5 Mar 61

1 For me this is not something that can be swept under the rug and forgotten in the interest of forced Sunday togetherness.

> Dissenting opinion in 6-3 ruling that upheld blue laws, 29 May 61

2 I shall not today attempt further to define the kinds of material . . . but I know it when I see it.

> Concurring opinion in 6-3 ruling that overturned ban on pornographic films, 22 Jun 64

3 At the very least, the freedom that Congress is empowered to secure . . . includes the freedom to buy whatever a white man can buy, the right to live wherever a white man can live. If Congress cannot say that being a freeman means at least this much, then the 13th Amendment made a promise it cannot keep.

> Majority opinion in 7-2 ruling that upheld a 102-year-old law prohibiting racial discrimination in the sale and rental of real estate, 17 Jun 68

4 The dichotomy between personal liberties and property rights is a false one. Property does not have rights. People have rights.

> Majority opinion in 4-3 ruling that upheld a district court's refusal to hear a case involving property rights, 23 Mar 72

5 In fact, a fundamental interdependence exists between the personal right to liberty and the personal right in property.

> *ib*

6 These death sentences are cruel and unusual in the same way that being struck by lightning is cruel and unusual.

> Concurring opinion in 5-4 ruling that struck down state death penalty laws, 29 Jun 72

7 The Court today holds the Congress may say that some of the poor are too poor even to go bankrupt. I cannot agree.

> Dissenting opinion in 5-4 ruling that a person must pay a $50 legal fee when filing for bankruptcy, 10 Jan 73

8 To force a lawyer on a defendant can only lead him to believe that the law contrives against him.

> Majority opinion in 6-3 ruling that a defendant may not be forced to accept state-appointed counsel, 30 Jun 75

9 It may be assumed that parents have a 1st Amendment right to send their children to educational institutions that promote the belief that racial segregation is desirable, and that the children have an equal right to attend such institutions. But it does not follow that the practice of excluding racial minorities from such institutions is also protected by the same principle.

> Majority opinion in 7-2 ruling that prohibited private schools from excluding children because of their race, 25 Jun 76

10 We are concerned here only with the imposition of capital punishment for the crime of murder, and when a life has been taken deliberately by the offender, we cannot say that the punishment is invariably disproportionate to the crime. It is an extreme sanction suitable to the most extreme of crimes.

> Majority opinion in 7-2 ruling that the death penalty is a constitutionally acceptable form of punishment for premeditated murder, 2 Jul 76

11 Regardless of whether the freedom of a woman to choose to terminate her pregnancy for health reasons lies at the core or the periphery of the due process [of] liberty . . . it simply does not follow that a woman's freedom of choice carries with it a constitutional entitlement to the financial resources to avail herself of the full range of protected choices.

> Majority opinion in 5-4 ruling that upheld the Congressional ban on federal payments for abortion, 30 Jun 80

12 Abortion is inherently different from other medical procedures because no other procedure involves the purposeful termination of a potential life.

> *ib*

13 [It took many decades after adoption of the 14th Amendment] before the states and the federal government were finally directed to eliminate detrimental classifications based on race. Today, the Court derails this achievement and places its imprimatur on the creation once again by government of privileges based on birth.

> Dissenting opinion in 6-3 ruling that upheld a federal law setting aside 10 percent of public works contracts for minority businesses, 2 Jul 80

MATTHEW TOBRINER, Judge, California Supreme Court

14 Man's drive for self-expression, which over the centuries has built his monuments, does not stay within set bounds; the creations which yesterday were the detested and the obscene become the classics of today.

> Ruling that Henry Miller's *Tropic of Cancer* was not pornographic, *Wall Street Journal* 3 Feb 64

15 The quicksilver of creativity will not be solidi-

fied by legal pronouncement; it will necessarily flow into new and sometimes frightening fields.

ib

UNITED STATES COURT OF APPEALS, District of Columbia Circuit

1 Man has discovered no technique for long preserving free government except that the executive be under the law.

5-2 ruling that President Richard M Nixon must turn over to investigators the tape recordings he was withholding, NY *Times* 14 Oct 73

2 Sovereignty remains at all times with the people and they do not forfeit through elections the rights to have the law construed against and applied to every citizen.

ib

FREDERICK M VINSON, Chief Justice, US Supreme Court

3 There is a vast difference—a constitutional difference—between restrictions imposed by the state which prohibit the intellectual commingling of students, and the refusal of individuals to commingle where the state presents no such bar.

Unanimous opinion that black students admitted to state universities may not be restricted in their access to university facilities and functions, 5 Jun 50

SOL WACHTLER, Judge, NY State Court of Appeals

4 A marriage license should not be viewed as a license for a husband to forcibly rape his wife with impunity.

Unanimous opinion that a man may be prosecuted for raping his wife, 20 Dec 84

5 A married woman has the same right to control her own body as does an unmarried woman.

ib

6 In the past, those who had ideas they wished to communicate to the public had the unquestioned right to disseminate those ideas in an open marketplace. Now that the marketplace has a roof over it and is called a mall, we should not abridge that right.

Dissenting opinion in 5-2 ruling that permitted owners of shopping malls to restrict the distribution of leaflets, 19 Dec 85

7 We cannot lightly . . . allow the perpetrator of a serious crime to go free simply because that person believed his actions were reasonable

and necessary to prevent some perceived harm.

Ruling that Bernhard H Goetz should be prosecuted for shooting four youths whom he feared were about to rob him, 8 Jul 86

EARL WARREN, Chief Justice, US Supreme Court

8 In these days, it is doubtful that any child may reasonably be expected to succeed in life if he is denied the opportunity of an education.

Unanimous opinion in Brown *v* Board of Education of Topeka that declared segregated schools unconstitutional, 17 May 54

9 Such an opportunity, where the state has undertaken to provide it, is a right which must be made available to all on equal terms.

ib

10 Separate educational facilities are inherently unequal.

ib

11 We come then to the question presented: Does segregation of children in public schools solely on the basis of race, even though the physical facilities and other "tangible" factors may be equal, deprive the children of the minority group of equal education opportunities? We believe that it does.

ib

12 To separate [children] from others of similar age and qualifications solely because of their race generates a feeling of inferiority as to their status in the community that may affect their hearts and minds in a way unlikely ever to be undone.

ib

13 We conclude that in the field of public education the doctrine of "separate but equal" has no place.

ib

14 All provisions of federal, state or local law requiring or permitting discrimination in public education must yield.

Unanimous opinion that ordered the desegregation of public schools, 31 May 55

15 The police must obey the law while enforcing the law.

Unanimous opinion that confessions obtained under duress must be excluded from criminal proceedings, 22 Jun 59

16 Life and liberty can be as much endangered from illegal methods used to convict those thought to be criminals as from the actual criminals themselves.

ib

1 The censor's sword pierces deeply into the heart of free expression.

> Dissenting opinion in 5-4 ruling that allowed municipalities to ban the showing of motion pictures that do not meet certain moral standards, 23 Jan 61

2 Legislatures represent people, not acres or trees.

> Majority opinion in 6-3 ruling that required both houses of state legislatures to be apportioned on a population basis, 15 Jun 64

3 Prior to any questioning, the person must be warned that he has a right to remain silent, that any statement he does make may be used as evidence against him and that he has a right to the presence of an attorney, either retained or appointed.

> Majority opinion in 6-3 ruling in the Miranda case that prohibited prosecution from using information obtained in violation of a suspect's 5th Amendment rights, 13 Jun 66

CLINTON R WEIDNER, Judge, Court of Common Pleas, Cumberland County PA

4 By analogy, Miss Frick might as well try to enjoin publication and distribution of the Holy Bible because, being a descendant of Eve, she does not believe that Eve gave Adam the forbidden fruit in the Garden of Eden and . . . her senses are offended by such a statement about an ancestor of hers.

> Dismissing Helen Frick's lawsuit charging that her father Henry Clay Frick had been libeled by a historian's biography, NY *Times* 26 May 67

BYRON R WHITE, Associate Justice, US Supreme Court

5 [Rape] is highly reprehensible, both in a moral sense and in its almost total contempt for the personal integrity and autonomy of the female victim and for the latter's privilege of choosing those with whom intimate relations are to be established.

> Majority opinion in 6-2 ruling that forbade death penalty for rape, 29 Jun 77

6 To exclude all jurors who would be in the slightest way affected by the prospect of the death penalty would be to deprive the defendant of the impartial jury to which he or she is entitled under the law.

> Majority opinion in 8-1 ruling that overturned a Texas law barring opponents of the death penalty from jury duty in capital cases, 25 Jun 80

7 The Court, casually, but candidly, abandons the functional approach to immunity that has run through all of our decisions. Indeed, the majority turns this rule on its head by declaring that because the functions of the president's office are so varied and diverse and some of them so profoundly important, the office is unique and must be clothed with office-wide, absolute immunity. This is a policy, not law, and in my view, very poor policy.

> Dissenting opinion in 5-4 ruling that granted former President Richard M Nixon immunity from civil suits concerning damages he might have caused while in office, 24 Jun 82

8 Maintaining order in the classrooms has never been easy [and] it is evident that the school setting requires some easing of the restrictions to which searches by public authorities are ordinarily subject.

> Majority opinion in 6-3 ruling that allowed the search of students for drugs or weapons, 15 Jan 85

9 The 1st Amendment protects the right to speak, not the right to spend.

> Dissenting opinion in 7-2 ruling that struck down $1,000 legal limit on spending by political action committees on behalf of presidential candidates, 18 Mar 85

10 Where the suspect poses no immediate threat to the officer and no threat to others, the harm resulting from the failing to apprehend him does not justify the use of deadly force to do so.

> Majority opinion in 6-3 ruling that forbade police to shoot to kill fleeing suspects who are not armed, 27 Mar 85

11 The risk of racial prejudice infecting a capital sentencing proceeding is especially serious in light of the complete finality of the death sentence.

> Majority opinion in 7-2 ruling that allowed a defendant facing capital punishment to have prospective jurors questioned on prejudice, 30 Apr 86

12 However one answers the metaphysical or theological question whether the fetus is a "human being" or the legal question whether it is a "person" as that term is used in the Constitution, one must at least recognize, first, that the fetus is an entity that bears in its cells all the genetic information that characterizes a member of the species *Homo sapiens* and distinguishes an individual member of that species from all others and, second, that there is no nonarbitrary line separating a fetus from a child or, indeed, an adult human being.

> Dissenting opinion in 5-4 ruling that reaffirmed the constitutional right to abortion, 11 Jun 86

1 Respondent would have us announce ... a fundamental right to engage in homosexual sodomy. This we are quite unwilling to do.

> Majority opinion in 5-4 ruling that upheld the right to prohibit deviant sexual behavior, 30 Jun 86

2 The Court is most vulnerable and comes nearest to illegitimacy when it deals with judge-made constitutional law having little or no cognizable roots in the language or design of the Constitution.

> *ib*

3 The law ... is constantly based on notions of morality, and if all laws representing essentially moral choices are to be invalidated under the due process clause, the courts will be very busy indeed.

> *ib*

ROBERT N WILENTZ, Chief Justice, New Jersey Supreme Court

4 It is the upheaval of prior norms by a society that has finally recognized that it must change its habits and do whatever is required, whether it means a small change or a significant one, in order to stop the senseless loss inflicted by drunken drivers.

> Majority opinion in 6-1 ruling that a host may be held liable for serving alcohol to persons later involved in drunk-driving incidents, 27 Jun 84

5 The common characteristics of a battered wife [include] her inability to leave despite such constant beatings; her "learned helplessness"; her lack of anywhere to go; her feeling that if she tried to leave, she would be subjected to even more merciless treatment; her belief in the omnipotence of her battering husband; and sometimes her hope that her husband will change his ways.

> Majority opinion in 6-1 ruling that called for a new trial for a woman convicted of killing her abusive husband, 24 Jul 84

Criminology

GAIL ABARBANELA, Rape Treatment Center, Santa Monica

6 If a girl says no and the boy perceives it as yes, he acts on his belief and you have trouble.

> On date rape, news summaries 25 May 85

DAVID ABRAHANSEN, psychoanalyst

7 The American dream is, in part, responsible for a great deal of crime and violence because people feel that the country owes them not only a living but a good living.

> Quoted in San Francisco *Examiner & Chronicle* 18 Nov 75

8 Frustration is the wet nurse of violence.

> *ib*

PETER ACKROYD

9 Murderers will try to recall the sequence of events, they will remember exactly what they did just before and just after.... But they can never remember the actual moment of killing. ... This is why [they] will always leave a clue.

> *Hawksmoor* Harper & Row 86

FREDA ADLER

10 [Rape] is the only crime in which the victim becomes the accused.

> *Sisters in Crime* McGraw-Hill 75

11 Woman throughout the ages has been mistress to the law, as man has been its master.

> *ib*

POLLY ADLER

12 What it comes down to is this: The grocer, the butcher, the baker, the merchant, the landlord, the druggist, the liquor dealer, the policeman, the doctor, the city father and the politician— these are the people who make money out of prostitution, these are the real reapers of the wages of sin.

> *A House Is Not a Home* Rinehart 53

ELI ADORNO

13 Do you think someone who is about to rape you is going to stop and think about a condom?

> On uselessness of issuing condoms to fellow prisoners in Riker's Island penitentiary, quoted in NY *Times* 5 Mar 87

MEHMET ALI AGCA

14 To me [the pope] was the incarnation of all that is capitalism.

> On attempted assassination of Pope John Paul II, *Time* 18 Feb 85

15 Bulgaria is guilty.

> On plot to kill the pope, news summaries 7 Jun 85

GENNARO ANGUILO, Boston organized crime boss

16 When a guy knocks ya down, never get up unless he's gonna kill ya.

> From compilation of FBI tapes in "Anguilo's Republic" *New England Monthly* Jul 86, quoted in *Harper's* Oct 86

17 When a man assumes leadership, he forfeits the right to mercy.

> *ib*

1 I wouldn't be in a legitimate business for all the ... money in the world.
ib

ANONYMOUS

2 There was a blue wall of silence.
On lack of official response to reports of police brutality, NY *Daily News* 6 May 85

3 Crack down on crack.
Police motto for campaign against potent new drug, NY *Times* 21 May 86

4 Even the bugs have bugs.
On police and organized crime spying, *NBC Evening News* NBC TV 8 Sep 86

BILL ARMONTROUT, Warden, Missouri State Penitentiary

5 I look at the criminal justice system as a sewer pipe and I'm just at the end of it. The police did their job, the courts did their job, now I have to do my job.
On his role as executioner, *Wall Street Journal* 6 Nov 84

WILLIAM ATTWOOD

6 *Payola* is the year's new word. It doesn't sound as ugly as *bribe*, but it means the same thing.
Look 29 Mar 60

BRUCE BABBITT, former Governor of Arizona

7 [It] is like living in a wilderness of mirrors. No fact goes unchallenged.
On 10-year controversy surrounding murder of investigative reporter Don Bolles, *Wall Street Journal* 23 Feb 87

BRUCE A BAIRD, AARON R MARCU and FRANK H SHERMAN, US Prosecuting Attorneys, NYC

8 Carmine Persico was born in August 1933 and killed his first human being in 1951, before his 18th birthday.
Sentencing memorandum on organized crime boss Carmine Persico, quoted in NY *Times* 18 Nov 86

JOSEPH BALL, President, Amer College of Trial Lawyers

9 Most of the clients that I represent in a criminal case I detest.
LA *Herald-Examiner* 23 Aug 70

10 The more I become involved emotionally in my client's cause, the less I am able to do for him.
ib

J HOPPS BARKER, Florida State Probation and Parole Commission

11 When you punish someone, you pay for it later. There was a time when pickpockets were publicly hanged, but other pickpockets took advantage of the large crowds attracted to the executions to ply their trade.
McCall's May 65

PEGGY BARLOW

12 Television nearly always showed the bandits in masks and using violence, but I wanted to go about it in a kind and gentle way.
Comment of 70-year-old widow who tried to rob London's National Westminster Bank, London *Times* 6 Oct 84

13 Agatha Christie would have been in her element with the plot.
ib

SYDNEY BIDDLE BARROWS

14 Never say anything on the phone that you wouldn't want your mother to hear at your trial.
Advice to women she employed in escort service, *Mayflower Madam*, with William Novak, Arbor House 86

15 I was naughty. I wasn't bad. Bad is hurting people, doing evil. Naughty is not hurting anyone. Naughty is being amusing.
Quoted by Marian Christy "'Mayflower Madam' Tells All" Boston *Globe* 10 Sep 86

16 I ran the wrong kind of business, but I did it with integrity.
ib

ED BATES, Sheriff, Madera County CA

17 I long for the days of good honest crooks.
On the kidnapping of 26 children and their bus driver, news summaries 19 Jul 76

REX BEABER, clinical psychologist, UCLA

18 The little child in each of us would kill any person who infringed our slightest right.
Time 8 Apr 85

DAVID BERKOWITZ, known as "Son of Sam"

19 It was a command. I had a sign and I followed it. Sam told me what to do and I did it.
Confession to police of killing six persons and wounding seven others on orders from his dog Sam, *Time* 22 Aug 77

20 And huge drops of lead

Poured down upon her head
Until she was dead.
Yet the cats still come out at night to mate;
And the sparrows still sing in the morning.
> Poem found in suspect's car, *ib*

1 I am a spirit roaming the night. Thirsty, hungry, seldom stopping to rest, anxious to please Sam. I love my work.
> Letter to Jimmy Breslin, quoted in *ib*

WALTER AUGUSTUS BOWE, gang member

2 We could knock the head and the arms off that damned old bitch.
> On plot to destroy the Statue of Liberty, NY *Times* 17 Feb 65

JIMMY BRESLIN

3 The number 1 rule of thieves is that nothing is too small to steal.
> NBC TV 15 May 74

SUSAN BROWNMILLER

4 We are unalterably opposed to the presentation of the female body being stripped, bound, raped, tortured, mutilated and murdered in the name of commercial entertainment and free speech.
> On pornography, *Against Our Will: Men, Women and Rape* Simon & Schuster 75

WARREN E BURGER, Chief Justice, US Supreme Court

5 Guilt or innocence becomes irrelevant in the criminal trials as we flounder in a morass of artificial rules poorly conceived and often impossible [to apply].
> As judge, US Court of Appeals, District of Columbia Circuit, news summaries 26 May 69

6 Crime and the fear of crime have permeated the fabric of American life.
> To Amer Bar Assn, Houston, 8 Feb 81

7 A far greater factor [than abolishing poverty] is the deterrent effect of swift and certain consequences: swift arrest, prompt trial, certain penalty and—at some point—finality of judgment.
> On lowering the crime rate, *ib*

8 There may be some incorrigible human beings who cannot be changed except by God's own mercy to that one person.
> *ib*

JOHN CASEY, NYC police officer

9 It's 90 percent boredom and 10 percent sheer terror.
> On Emergency Service Unit, quoted in NY *Times* 11 Feb 85

MARK DAVID CHAPMAN

10 I've pent up all my aggression, kept swallowing it and swallowing it.
> Statement to his attorney in first week after fatally shooting John Lennon, *People* 23 Feb 87

11 I found out Lennon was more accessible.
> On choosing to shoot Lennon instead of other public figures, *ib*

12 I remember thinking, "The bullets are working" ... I think I felt a little regret that they were working.
> *ib* 2 Mar 87

CARYL CHESSMAN, convicted murderer

13 The California executioner keeps banker's hours. He never kills before 10 o'clock in the morning, never after 4 in the afternoon.
> Letter written in San Quentin Prison on eve of his execution, quoted in NY *Post* 3 May 60

JAMES CHILES

14 The rise of computer crime and armed robbery has not eliminated the lure of caged cash.
> "Age-Old Battle to Keep Safes Safe from Creepers, Soup Men and Yeggs" *Smithsonian* Jul 84

15 Safe-breaking and vault-breaking are at least as old as the pyramids and burial chambers of Egypt. ... Poking holes in vaults and safes for profit appears to be as durable as greed.
> *ib*

16 Burglars know there's more than one way to skin a vault.
> *ib*

17 Organized crime is the dirty side of the sharp dollar.
> *ib*

AGATHA CHRISTIE

18 Oh dear, I never realized what a terrible lot of explaining one has to do in a murder!
> From her 1956 play *Spider's Web*, recalled on her death 12 Jan 76

BILL CLARK, Brooklyn detective

19 You want to make a guy comfortable enough to confess to murder.
> *New York* 24 Dec 84

RAMSEY CLARK, US Attorney General

20 A humane and generous concern for every individual, his health and his fulfillment, will do more to soothe the savage heart than the fear of state-inflicted death, which chiefly serves to remind us how close we remain to the jungle.
> Urging abolishment of the death penalty for fed-

eral crimes, to Senate Judiciary Committee, *NY Times* 3 Jul 68

1 Our history shows that the death penalty has been unjustly imposed, innocents have been killed by the state, effective rehabilitation has been impaired, judicial administration has suffered. It is the poor, the weak, the ignorant, the hated who are executed [and] racial discrimination occurs in the administration of capital punishment.
> *ib*

ARMAND COURVILLE

2 If the Mafia exists in Montreal, it's probably like the Knights of Columbus.
> Testifying at Quebec Police Commission inquiry on organized crime, Toronto *Globe & Mail* 27 May 75

MARIO CUOMO, Governor of NY

3 The mugger who is arrested is back on the street before the police officer, but the person mugged may not be back on the street for a long time, if ever.
> Calling for hiring of more police, *New Republic* 8 Apr 85

4 I'd say, "That's it, Charlie, you're going to be by yourself for a hundred years."
> Favoring life sentences without parole instead of capital punishment, *Time* 2 Jun 86

GERALD CVETKO, police officer

5 We don't have professional burglars here. We have opportunists.
> On burglary in South Plainfield NJ, *NY Times* 15 Mar 79

6 Burglars, judging by our statistics, define opportunity as an unoccupied, unlocked house stocked with portable television sets.
> *ib*

RICHARD J DALEY, Mayor of Chicago

7 The policeman isn't there to create disorder; the policeman is there to preserve disorder.
> Quoted by Laurence J Peter *Why Things Go Wrong: The Peter Principle Revisited* Morrow 84

EDMUND DAVIES

8 Let us clear any romantic notion of daredevil-try from our minds. It is nothing less than a sordid crime of violence inspired by vast greed.
> On sentencing 12 men convicted in Britain's Great Train Robbery, the theft of more than £20 million from the Royal Mail, *Time* 24 Apr 64

WILLIAM J DEAN

9 In New York City we need police officers to protect even the dead.
> On desecration of graves in Potter's Field, *Time* 29 Aug 83

WILFRED DENNO, Warden, Sing Sing Prison, NY

10 It may sound incredible, but they seemed more interested in the ball game.
> On reaction of death row inmates to abolishment of capital punishment in the state, *NY Times* 2 Jun 65

PETE ("THE GREEK") DIOPOULIS

11 A good hit man has no conscience at all.
> *60 Minutes* CBS TV 25 Apr 76

F W DUPREE

12 From Jesse James to Loeb and Leopold, from the perpetrators of the St Valentine's Day's massacre to the Lindbergh kidnapper and beyond, our celebrated delinquents have become a part of the national heritage.
> *New York Review of Books* 3 Feb 66

13 They figure in a sort of *musée imaginaire*, half Madame Tussaud's, half Smithsonian, of American crime.
> *ib*

ADOLF EICHMANN

14 To sum it all up, I must say that I regret nothing.
> While awaiting trial in Israel for death of 6 million Jews during World War II, *Life* 5 Dec 60

DORIS ANN FOSTER, convicted murderer

15 Death row is a state of mind.
> London *Times* 31 Aug 84

JAMES ALAN FOX, Professor of Criminal Justice, Northeastern University

16 The typical mass murderer is extraordinarily ordinary.
> Quoted in *NY Times* 27 Aug 84

ALADENA T ("JIMMY THE WEASEL") FRATIANNO, convicted murderer

17 Some people are a little better [at it] than others.
> When asked if he was a good killer, *60 Minutes* CBS TV 6 Jan 80

LYNETTE ("SQUEAKY") FROMME

18 Anybody can kill anybody.
> On her attempted assassination of President Gerald R Ford, news summaries 30 Sep 75

JOHN WAYNE GACY, convicted serial killer

1 [All the police] are going to get me for is running a funeral parlor without a license.
Quoted by James Alan Fox and Jack Levin *Mass Murder* Plenum 85

THOMAS E GADDIS

2 Alcatraz, the federal prison with a name like the blare of a trombone, [is] a black molar in the jawbone of the nation's prison system.
Birdman of Alcatraz Random House 55

DAVID GATES

3 The pseudonymous perpetrator of America's only unsolved airline hijacking [is] a folk hero as shadowy as Deep Throat and as morally troublesome as Jesse James.
On celebration of D B Cooper Day in Ariel WA, *Newsweek* 26 Dec 83

WILLARD GAYLIN, psychiatrist

4 A street thug and a paid killer are professionals—beasts of prey, if you will, who have dissociated themselves from the rest of humanity and can now see human beings in the same way that trout fishermen see trout.
The Killing of Bonnie Garland Simon & Schuster 82

JEAN GENET

5 I give the name *violence* to a boldness lying idle and enamored of danger.
The Thief's Journal Grove 64

6 Violence is a calm that disturbs you.
ib

RUDOLPH W GIULIANI, US Attorney, Southern District, NY

7 It's about time law enforcement got as organized as organized crime.
Quoted by Peter Stoler "The Sicilian Connection" *Time* 15 Oct 84

8 If we take back the labor unions, the legitimate businesses, eventually they become just another street gang. Spiritually, psychologically, they've always been just a street gang.
Quoted by Robert D McFadden "The Mafia of the 1980s: Divided and Under Siege" NY *Times* 11 Mar 87

MILLS E GODWIN, Governor of Virginia

9 Men of faith know that throughout history the crimes committed in liberty's name have been exceeded only by those committed in God's name.
On burning of crosses by Ku Klux Klan members, *Quote* 1 Jan 67

BERNARD H GOETZ

10 When you are surrounded by four people, one of them smiling, taunting, demanding, terrorizing, you don't have a complete grasp or perfect vision.
On shooting four youths who allegedly accosted him on a NYC subway, *Newsweek* 11 Mar 85

RONALD GOLDSTOCK, Director, NY State Organized Crime Task Force

11 The people who join the mob now are second- and third-generation and don't have the values their predecessors had.
NY *Times* 21 Mar 87

12 They prey on their own with extortion and protection rackets, in a culture where people don't go to the police and where most police don't speak the language.
On Chinese organized crime members, *ib*

JOHN GOTTI, organized crime leader

13 Don't carry a gun. It's nice to have them close by, but don't carry them. You might get arrested.
Quoted in NY *Times* 3 Dec 86

CHESTER GOULD

14 I decided that if the police couldn't catch the gangsters, I'd create a fellow who could.
On his comic strip *Dick Tracy*, recalled on his death 11 May 85

WILLIAM R GREER

15 Officers from the 44th Precinct in the High Bridge section of the Bronx arrested two men in a blue van who were trying to make off with the corner of 161st Street and Jerome Avenue.
On growing theft of paving stones, NY *Times* 12 Jan 85

PETE HAMILL

16 There is a growing feeling that perhaps Texas *is* really another country, a place where the skies, the disasters, the diamonds, the politicians, the women, the fortunes, the football players and the murders are all bigger than anywhere else.
After sniper at University of Texas killed 14 people and injured 30, Boston *Globe* 2 Aug 66

JEAN HARRIS, convicted murderer

17 [We were] two persons who never argued over anything except the use of a subjunctive.
Testimony in trial for her fatal shooting of Dr Herman Tarnower, NY *Times* 30 Jan 81

1 I had led a private life and wanted to die a private death.

> On intention to kill herself after a final visit to Dr Tarnower, *ib* 31 Jan 81

2 Overnight I became a cottage industry.

> On intense journalistic interest in her arrest and trial, *Stranger in Two Worlds* Macmillan 86

3 It would be ugly to watch people poking sticks at a caged rat. It is uglier still to watch rats poking sticks at a caged person.

> On life in prison, *ib*

4 What do you do in hell? Every day within this grim, ridiculous cinder block pile I play Horatio at small bridges, having easily convinced myself that what stands at risk on the other side is Human Decency, always in capital letters, or even that ephemeral little Tinker Bell called justice.

> *ib*

LAWRENCE S HARRIS, North Carolina State Medical Examiner

5 Are we taking the drunken drivers off the road only to turn them into drunken pedestrians?

> On traffic deaths of persons whose driver's licenses had been revoked for drunk driving, NY *Times* 30 Jun 86

G H HATHERILL, Commander, Scotland Yard

6 There are only about 20 murders a year in London and not all are serious—some are just husbands killing their wives.

> News summaries 1 Jul 54

GIDEON HAUSNER

7 He is responsible because of the conspiracy and the plots for all that happened to the Jewish people—from the shores of the Arctic Ocean to the Aegean Sea, from the Pyrenees to the Urals.

> Summation in trial of war criminal Adolf Eichmann, NY *Times* 27 Jun 61

WALTER HEADLEY, Chief of Police, Miami

8 I'm so used to pressure I'm afraid if it stopped I'd get the bends.

> NY *Times* 17 Nov 68

HENRY HILL, accused mob member

9 I'm an average nobody. I get to live the rest of my life like a schnook.

> After providing information on other mobsters in exchange for a new identity, quoted by Nicholas Pileggi *Wiseguy* Simon & Schuster 86

MORTON A HILL SJ, member of President's Commission on Pornography

10 It is a Magna Carta for pornography.

> 1970 comment about Attorney General's Report on Pornography that concluded pornography is harmless and should be legalized, recalled after 1986 report declared that pornography could lead to violence, NY *Times* 23 Oct 86

JOHN W HINCKLEY JR

11 Guns are neat little things, aren't they? They can kill extraordinary people with very little effort.

> Statement introduced by Hinckley's attorney in insanity defense for March 30, 1981, attempted assassination of President Ronald Reagan, quoted in *Time* 17 May 82

12 Your prodigal son has left again to exorcise some demons.

> Farewell note to parents in February 1981, *ib*

13 Jodie Foster may continue to outwardly ignore me for the rest of my life, but I have . . . made her one of the most famous actresses in the world.

> On actress who rebuffed his calls and letters, quoted in NY *Times* 9 Jul 82

ALGER HISS

14 In the future the way that Whittaker Chambers was able to carry out forgery by typewriter will be disclosed.

> On how stolen documents were allegedly forged, news summaries 25 Jan 50

XAVIERA HOLLANDER

15 If my business could be made legal. . . . I and women like me could make a big contribution to what Mayor Lindsay calls "Fun City," and the city and state could derive the money in taxes and licensing fees that I pay off to crooked cops and political figures.

> *The Happy Hooker* Dell 72

MARK HOLTHAUS, social worker

16 Guys die down here on a regular basis—that's the reality. They die here for a nickel. They are killed for a piece of change or because somebody looks at somebody wrong.

> On frequent murders of homeless people on Los Angeles's Skid Row, NY *Times* 3 Nov 86

J EDGAR HOOVER, Director, FBI

17 Banks are an almost irresistible attraction for that element of our society which seeks unearned money.

> News summaries 7 Apr 55

1 We are a fact-gathering organization only. We don't clear anybody. We don't condemn anybody.
Look 14 Jun 56

2 Just the minute the FBI begins making recommendations on what should be done with its information, it becomes a Gestapo.
ib

ROBERT HUGHES

3 [The prisons are] the monuments of Australia—the Paestums [of] an extraordinary time—an effort to exile en masse a whole class.
On 18th-century British practice of transporting criminals to Australia, quoted in NY *Times* 25 Jan 87

4 Transportation made sublimation literal. It conveyed evil to another world.
The Fatal Shore Knopf 86, quoted in *Time* 2 Feb 87

DEREK HUMPHRY, Director, Hemlock Society

5 Ninety-nine percent of requested deaths go unrecorded. It's a secret crime.
On mercy killings, *Newsweek* 9 Sep 85

BRUCE JACKSON, Professor of Law and Jurisprudence, State University of NY, Buffalo

6 America has the longest prison sentences in the West, yet the only condition long sentences demonstrably cure is heterosexuality.
NY *Times* 12 Sep 68

RICHARD LEOFRIC JACKSON, President, Interpol

7 I am devoted to detective novels. They make such a nice change from my work.
Saturday Evening Post 28 Oct 61

ROGER A JASKE, convicted murderer

8 Mercenary looking for male Caucasian partner 18-25. Willing to accept the risk. Must have guts, be able to travel and start work immediately. No special skills required. High pay guaranteed. Ask for Sundance.
Ad placed to arrange his rescue from a courtroom; he was foiled by undercover police who answered the ad, NY *Times* 10 Mar 86

ANN JONES

9 Unlike men, who are apt to stab a total stranger in a drunken brawl or run amuck with a high-powered rifle, we women usually kill our intimates: We kill our children, our husbands, our lovers.
Women Who Kill Holt, Rinehart & Winston 80

JOSEPH KALLINGER, convicted murderer

10 Picking our first victim seemed as right as going to church on Sunday.
On acting with his son in the murder of his older son and another boy, quoted by Flora Rheta Schreiber *The Shoemaker* Simon & Schuster 83

KITTY KELLEY

11 [He] ordered killings as easily as he ordered linguine.
On Chicago organized crime boss Sam Giancana, *His Way* Bantam 86

RICHARD KELLY, US Congressman

12 Does it show?
On stuffing his pockets with $25,000 in cash, to FBI agents posing as Arab businessmen during Abscam probe, videotape recording 8 Jan 80

STEPHEN P KENNEDY, Police Commissioner, NYC

13 A policeman's gun is his cross and he carries it always.
Saturday Evening Post 8 Sep 56

14 In the dark all men were the same color. In the dark our fellow man was seen more clearly than in the normal light of a New York night.
On "zero" crime rate during a blackout in Manhattan, *Time* 31 Aug 59

JAMES C KIMBROUGH, Judge, Superior Court, Lake County IN

15 We would not want our children to be beaten with extension cords, but we would not expect them to go out and kill little old ladies because of it.
On abused girl who fatally stabbed an aged woman, NY *Times* 2 Nov 86

MARTIN LUTHER KING JR

16 It is incontestable and deplorable that Negroes have committed crimes; but they are derivative crimes. They are born of the greater crimes of the white society.
To Southern Christian Leadership Conference 16 Aug 67

PAUL H KING, Judge, District Court, Dorchester MA

17 When they drag me down the aisle the final time I'll be singing "I Did It My Way."
On being barred from the bench for allegedly flouting the Massachusetts domestic abuse law, Boston *Globe* 14 Nov 86

PETER KIRK, Professor of Criminalistics, University of California

1 I hate this "crime doesn't pay" stuff. Crime in the United States is perhaps one of the biggest businesses in the world today.
Wall Street Journal 16 Feb 60

EDWARD KOCH, Mayor of NYC

2 The person who is bent on killing you will follow you wherever you are.
On murder of John Lennon, quoted in NY *Times* 10 Dec 80

ANNA M KROSS, Corrections Commissioner, NYC

3 Let time serve you, don't serve time!
Address at Riker's Island penitentiary, NY *Herald Tribune* 29 Dec 65

J WALLACE LAPRADE, FBI agent

4 We will not close that case until we know that he is not findable or found. And not findable means we find his bones.
On search for man accused of murdering his own wife, mother and three children in Westfield NJ, NY *Times* 2 Jun 74

JONATHAN LARSEN

5 His achievements read like the graffiti on the walls of a hangman's changing room.
On Rudolph W Giuliani, US attorney for Southern District, NY, "The Avenger" *Manhattan Inc* Feb 85

6 The criminal justice system [is] accurately symbolized by a large sculpture that sits at the foot of the United States attorney's building: four metal circles that interlock. The wheels of justice, as it were, frozen in legal and social gridlock.
ib

JOHN LE CARRÉ

7 You should have died when I killed you.
Lines for a bureaucrat speaking to a reassigned agent. *A Perfect Spy* Knopf 86

NATHAN LEOPOLD, convicted murderer

8 What a rotten writer of detective stories life is!
Life Plus 99 Years Doubleday 58

LAWRENCE LIEF, industrial security analyst

9 Those you trust the most can steal the most.
Quoted by David Pauly "Stealing from the Boss" *Newsweek* 26 Dec 83

DAVID LIVINGSTONE

10 It's been busier than ever . . . I guess they were having a going-out-of-business sale.
On increase in drug traffic from neighborhood home following court order to evict dealers, NY *Times* 11 Dec 86

LONDON POLICE

11 We have reason to believe you have committed an offense.
Printed form for overtime parking, quoted by John Crosby NY *Herald Tribune* 4 Nov 63

HENRY LEE LUCAS, convicted serial murderer

12 Once I've done a crime, I just forget it. I go from crime to crime.
On belief that he may have committed as many as 360 murders, 142 of which had been verified, *Life* Aug 84

CHARLES MANSON, convicted murderer

13 From the world of darkness I did loose demons and devils in the power of scorpions to torment.
From his unsuccessful plea for parole from life sentence for ritualistic murders, NY *Times* 9 Feb 86

14 I'd probably try to stop the rain forests from being cut down. I'd probably join the revolution down south somewhere and try to save my life on the planet Earth. I might go to Libya. I might go see the Ayatollah. I might go to France, catch somebody in France I'm upset with.
What he would do if paroled, *ib*

ROBERT MARK, Commissioner, London Metropolitan Police

15 The criminal trial today is . . . a kind of show-jumping contest in which the rider for the prosecution must clear every obstacle to succeed.
Washington *Post* 23 Nov 71

ED McBAIN

16 A detective sees death in all the various forms at least five times a week.
Ten Plus One Simon & Schuster 63

OWEN J McCLAIN, Yonkers NY police officer

17 We don't believe the nation is smothered with tainted Tylenol.
On death of a young woman from cyanide-laced over-the-counter medication, NY *Times* 12 Feb 86

ROBERT D McFADDEN

1 The old images seem like a caricature now: the shadowy world of secret rituals, the aging dons behind high-walled estates, the passion for vengeance and power over other men. For years, the Mafia was the stuff of novels and movies and whispers on Mulberry Street.

"The Mafia of the 1980s: Divided and Under Siege" NY *Times* 11 Mar 87

2 Behind the façades of respectability, family life and surprisingly modest homes [are] fathers who hate drugs but sell tons of heroin, gambling czars who lose heavily on the horses, murderers who take offense at off-color language around women and Runyonesque characters with funny nicknames who beat people to death with hammers.

On evidence presented in trials of organized crime figures, *ib*

3 The myths die hard, especially within the Mafia.

ib

JOHN McGEORGE, Australian psychiatrist

4 A woman has a much better chance than a man of acquittal on a murder charge. . . . If she happens to be a blonde her chances rise about 45 percent.

Quote 12 Mar 60

5 With attractive women . . . juries sometimes have to be restrained from handing them a medal for their crimes.

ib

ANN McMILLAN, psychologist

6 Sometimes it's not going to matter who raises them. If the parents were Mary and Joseph, it would still turn out the same.

On background of serial killers, quoted in *Newsweek* 26 Nov 84

EDWIN MEESE 3RD, US Attorney General

7 The idea that the police cannot ask questions of the person that knows most about the crime is an infamous decision.

On Supreme Court's 1966 Miranda decision requiring police to advise criminal suspects of their right to remain silent, NY *Times* 1 Sep 85

J REID MELOY, forensic psychologist

8 Once they start to murder, the act becomes habitual. As it becomes habitual, it becomes easier.

On serial killers, *Time* 9 Sep 85

KARL A MENNINGER

9 Is it hard for the reader to believe that suicides are sometimes committed to forestall the committing of murder? There is no doubt of it. Nor is there any doubt that murder is sometimes committed to avert suicide.

The Crime of Punishment Viking 68

10 We need criminals to identify ourselves with, to secretly envy and to stoutly punish. They do for us the forbidden, illegal things we wish to do.

ib

11 Police are not all bad guys. Nobody is all bad guys.

ib

W WALTER MENNINGER

12 [Members of the commission] simply state that smoking marijuana in the privacy of your home should be perfectly legal—as long as no one gave it to you [or] sold it to you and you didn't grow it yourself.

On report by President's Commission on Marijuana and Drug Abuse, San Francisco *Examiner & Chronicle* 23 Apr 72

MARIO MEROLA, District Attorney, Bronx NY

13 These guys commit their crimes with a pencil instead of a gun.

On corporate crime, NY *Times* 9 Jun 85

14 Pretty soon, there will not be any debate in this city about overcrowded prisons. AIDS will take care of that.

On reluctance to prosecute AIDS victims, *ib* 5 Mar 87

GEORGE METESKY

15 One thing I can't understand is why the newspapers labeled me the Mad Bomber. That was unkind.

On his arrest for placing 20 bombs in public places over a 17-year period, NY *Journal-American* 22 Jan 57

GREGORY MILLER, Assistant US Attorney

16 When artwork is involved, it's almost assumed that it's going to travel. It's too hot to stay here.

On calling in FBI after the theft of a painting from Philadelphia Museum of Art, NY *Times* 1 Jan 85

ELISEO MORENO, convicted murderer

17 I'm here because I'm guilty. . . . I'm willing to

pay according to the laws of Texas because I know I'm guilty.

> On scheduled execution for killing 6 people during 50-hour rampage, NY *Times* 5 Mar 87

JAMES D C MURRAY, defense attorney

1 Juvenile delinquency starts in the highchair and ends in the death chair.

> NY *World-Telegram & Sun* 8 Sep 56

BESS MYERSON

2 The accomplice to the crime of corruption is frequently our own indifference.

> Quoted by Claire Safran "Impeachment?" *Redbook* Apr 74

VLADIMIR NABOKOV

3 You can always count on a murderer for a fancy prose style.

> *Lolita* Putnam 58

NEVADA DEPARTMENT OF PRISONS

4 After each execution, sinks, plugs, pot and entire inside of cabinet should be washed down with warm water and a detergent; add two ounces of aqua ammonia to each gallon of water.

> On cleaning of gas chamber after an execution, quoted by John Gregory Dunne *Esquire* Oct 86

NEW YORK TIMES

5 The eternal man in the street says the street's no place for anyone anymore.

> Editorial on series of unprovoked assaults, 29 Dec 80

EUGENE H NICKERSON, Judge, US District Court, Eastern NY

6 She can refresh his recollection with a piece of green cheese, if that will help.

> Permitting prosecutor's use of another person's testimony to refresh a witness's memory, NY *Times* 4 Dec 86

JOHN NORTON, Public Safety Commissioner, Pittsburgh

7 There is absolutely no doubt in my mind that rap music spurs violence.

> *Time* 1 Sep 86

JOAN O'SULLIVAN

8 Today, the Harvard-educated proprietor of a boutique brothel on the East Side would be photographed attending first nights and would discuss her next book on television chat shows

with respectful psychoanalysts who would treat her, not without justification, as a professional colleague.

> Possible result of the legalization of prostitution, London *Times* 11 Feb 85

9 [The madam] would contribute her favorite recipes to *Cosmopolitan* magazine. And she would eventually achieve complete respectability by either posing for a *Playboy* centerfold or being elected to Congress.

> *ib*

MARINA OSWALD

10 Sometimes in the dark of night I begin to think. And I wonder if Lee started all this violence.

> On 10th anniversary of the death of her husband Lee Harvey Oswald, alleged assassin of President John F Kennedy, *People* 4 Mar 74

11 The memory is like a cat scratching my heart.

> *ib*

ROBERT PERRY, prosecuting attorney

12 For a plot hatched in hell, don't expect angels for witnesses.

> In summation to jury at conspiracy trial of John De Lorean, 6 Aug 84

NICHOLAS PILEGGI

13 Ever since Damon Runyon wrote the first preppy handbook for the city's Guys and Dolls, back in the 1930s, New York's tough-talking, double-breasted, blue-serge hoods have been the prototype for gangsters all over the world.

> "The Boss of Bosses" *New York* 24 Dec 84

14 He had never lit a fire that wasn't a felony.

> On a smalltime hoodlum, *Wiseguy* Simon & Schuster 86

RICHARD RAMÍREZ, confessed murderer

15 I killed about 20 people. I was a super criminal. No one could catch me. [Then] they caught me.

> Confession to a Los Angeles jail guard, NY *Times* 9 May 86

16 I love to kill people.

> *ib*

RONALD REAGAN, 40th US President

17 The criminal element now calculates that crime really does pay.

> To crime victims invited to the White House 18 Apr 84

ROBERT RICE

1 Crime is a logical extension of the sort of behavior that is often considered perfectly respectable in legitimate business.
    The Business of Crime Farrar, Straus & Cudahy 56

ANGELO RIZZO

2 He's just a kid, and he's dying fast. . . . trapped inside a cell sick as a dog and made to lay in his own filth. All he did was drugs. Mass killers get treated better.
    On fellow inmate in AIDS cell block at Riker's Island penitentiary, NY *Times* 5 Mar 87

BENJAMIN RUGGIERO

3 Keep a neat appearance at all times . . . a wise guy doesn't have a bushy mustache and long hair.
    Advice to man about to be initiated into an organized crime family, NY *Times* 11 Mar 87

BERTRAND RUSSELL

4 Americans need rest, but do not know it. I believe this to be a large part of the explanation of the crime wave in the United States.
    Quoted by Alan Wood *Bertrand Russell* Simon & Schuster 58

DIANA E RUSSELL

5 A large percentage of the male population has a propensity to rape.
    The Politics of Rape Stein & Day 84

WILLIAM SAFIRE

6 One out of 10 guests turns out to be a lexiklept.
    On people who steal dictionaries from hotels, NY *Times* 12 Apr 87

7 Departing guests leave The Word and grab the words.
    On preference for dictionaries over Bibles, *ib*

ANTHONY SALERNO

8 If it wasn't for me, there wouldn't be no mob left. I made all the guys. And everybody's a good guy. This guy don't realize that.
    Wiretapped conversation about a disrespectful young mobster, NY *Times* 11 Mar 87

JACK SCAFF

9 The idea is to make the woman so repulsive that the attacker runs away. It sounds funny until you smell it.
    On perfume for protection against assaults, *Wall Street Journal* 11 Sep 85

MARC SCHREUDER

10 My mother asked me to.
    Testimony on motive for murder of his grandfather, quoted by Shana Alexander *Nutcracker* Doubleday 85

SCOTLAND YARD

11 This appeal is urgently directed to all those women whose means of livelihood places them in danger.
    Warning possible future victims of a prostitute murderer, NY *Times* 28 Apr 64

ALFRED SETT, LA County Sheriff's Dept

12 Los Angeles is the serial mass murder capital of the world.
    After a killer had shot to death 10 Skid Row people in 2 months, NY *Times* 3 Nov 86

GAIL SHEEHY

13 It is a silly question to ask a prostitute why she does it. . . . These are the highest-paid "professional" women in America.
    Hustling Delacourt 73

THOMAS L SHEER, FBI bureau chief, NYC

14 They move into a legitimate business and they take it over and compete with other businesses, but if they feel they are losing out, they will revert to breaking legs. True American corporate competition does not include breaking legs.
    On organized crime members, NY *Times* 11 Mar 87

SIRHAN SIRHAN

15 They can gas me, but I am famous. I have achieved in one day what it took Robert Kennedy all his life to do.
    On fatal shooting of Senator Robert F Kennedy, *Time* 13 Apr 81

BARRY SLOTNICK

16 If the district attorney wanted, a grand jury would indict a ham sandwich.
    Quoted by Sydney Biddle Barrows *Mayflower Madam*, with William Novak, Arbor House 86

JOHN JUSTIN SMITH

17 Nathan Leopold walked out of Stateville Prison Thursday into the wonderful world of free men. He promptly got sick.
    On release of a convicted murderer after 33 years in prison, Chicago *Daily News* 13 Mar 58

PERRY SMITH, convicted murderer

1 I thought he was a very nice gentleman. .... I thought so right up to the moment I cut his throat.

> Quoted by Truman Capote *In Cold Blood* Random House 66

ALEXANDER SOLZHENITSYN

2 I can say without affectation that I belong to the Russian convict world no less . . . than I do to Russian literature. I got my education there, and it will last forever.

> *The Oak and the Calf* Harper & Row 80

CLYDE STOW, forensic pathologist

3 Having a policeman dig up a skeleton is like having a chimpanzee do a heart transplant.

> On careful exhumation of skeleton believed to be that of Nazi "angel of death" Joseph Mengele, ABC TV 7 Jun 85

WILLIE SUTTON

4 There was the South Ozone National Bank looking as though it had been waiting for me.

> Quoted by Quentin Reynolds *I, Willie Sutton: The Personal Story of the Most Daring Bank Robber and Jail Breaker of Our Time* Farrar, Straus 53

EMMANUEL TENEY, Professor of Psychiatry, Wayne State University, Detroit

5 Murder is not the crime of criminals, but that of law-abiding citizens.

> *Time* 12 Aug 66

STUDS TERKEL

6 Chicago is not the most corrupt American city, it's the most theatrically corrupt.

> Dick Cavett show PBS TV 9 Jun 78

OTTIS ELWOOD TOOLE

7 I killed people I didn't think was worth living anyhow.

> On his confessed series of 50 murders that began when he was age 14, *Life* Aug 84

JOE VALACHI, convicted racketeer

8 In the circle in which I travel, a dumb man is more dangerous than a hundred rats.

> Expressing confidence in his ability to testify to US Senate subcommittee, NY *Herald Tribune* 27 Sep 63

9 You live by the gun and knife, and die by the gun and knife.

> Secret code of crime syndicate, NY *Times* 21 Oct 63

10 You can imagine my embarrassment when I killed the wrong guy.

> Quoted in Robert Singer comp *The Bad Guys' Quote Book* Avon 84

DUDLEY VARNEY, LA homicide detective

11 There could be a guy signing his name on the ass of some dead body back on the East Coast, and we wouldn't know about it.

> On lack of time to read nationwide teletype messages, *Newsweek* 26 Nov 84

ANTHONY VIDLER, architect

12 Any precinct captain in New York could have told the grandmother that latches of that nature could not guard against the wolf.

> On design of lock on Little Red Riding Hood's grandmother's cottage, NY *Times* 5 Mar 84

JOHN P VUKASIN JR, Judge, US District Court, Northern California

13 [He was] not a Soviet apologist. [He] did not believe in anything at all. He is the type of modern man whose highest expression lies in his amorality.

> Prior to sentencing former US Navy officer Jerry A Whitworth for espionage, NY *Times* 29 Aug 86

JOSEPH WAMBAUGH

14 Perhaps it had nothing to do with sin and everything to do with sociopathy, that most incurable of human disorders because all so afflicted consider themselves *blessed* rather than cursed.

> On partnership of Main Line murderers, *Echoes in the Darkness* Morrow 87, quoted in *Time* 23 Feb 87

BENJAMIN WARD, NYC Police Commissioner

15 If you come to New York to buy crack, bring carfare and be prepared to take the bus back.

> On stopping 43 motorists and impounding 30 automobiles cruising in areas where drugs were sold, NY *Times* 5 Aug 86

HERBERT WARD, Episcopal priest

16 Child abuse casts a shadow the length of a lifetime.

> Annual report, St Jude's Ranch, Boulder City NV, 85

EDWIN WARNER

17 People have always accused kids of getting away with murder. Now that is all too literally true.

> "The Youth Crime Plague" *Time* 11 Jul 77

KEITH WHEELER

1 They are pure, unduplicatable Chicago. ... they help explain why—in Chicago—it is unwise to take your eyes off any asset smaller than a locomotive.

> On the Panczko brothers, arrested 214 times in 25 years, *Life* 6 Aug 65

HERBERT EMERSON WILSON

2 The safe that night looked like a soft one [and] the explosion made no more noise than a pig's grunt.

> On his first break-in of a Detroit department store, quoted by James Chiles "Age-Old Battle to Keep Safes Safe from Creepers, Soup Men and Yeggs" *Smithsonian* Jul 84

3 In all my years on the prowl, I never got over the thrill of hearing the first boom and seeing what it did to a massive block of steel.

> *ib*

BUSINESS

Executives

AGHA HASAN ABEDI, President, Bank of Credit and Commerce International, Luxembourg

4 The conventional definition of management is getting work done through people, but real management is developing people through work.

> *Leaders* Jul 84

TADASHI ADACHI, President, Chamber of Commerce of Japan

5 If the lion and dragon fight, they will both die.

> On the belief that the shame of failure is exceeded only by the shame of causing someone else's failure, *Newsweek* 17 May 65

DONALD G ADAMS, Vice President, Addressograph-Multigraph Corp

6 Copying has become a national disease.

> On the heavy use of photocopying machines, *Newsweek* 7 Sep 64

ANONYMOUS

7 The most important marketer in our company is the man or woman on the loading dock who decides not to drop the damned box into the back of the truck.

> Executive of a high-tech company, quoted by Thomas J Peters and Nancy K Austin *A Passion for Excellence* Random House 85, excerpted in *Fortune* 13 May 85

8 If my boss calls, be sure to get his name.

> Comment of ABC executive, quoted by William S Rukeyser in report on the swift shifts of personnel in television management, *Fortune* 14 Apr 86

ELIZABETH ARDEN, cosmetics executive

9 Dear, never forget one little point. It's my business. You just work here.

> To her husband, quoted by Alfred Lewis and Constance Woodworth *Miss Elizabeth Arden* Coward, McCann & Geoghegan 72

MARY KAY ASH, Chairman, Mary Kay Cosmetics Inc

10 If you think you can, you can. And if you think you can't, you're right.

> NY *Times* 20 Oct 85

MORTON BAHR, President, Communications Workers of America

11 We are beginning to recognize that it is more important to organize the unorganized than to argue about who will get the workers when they are organized.

> On cooperation in labor negotiations, NY *Times* 4 May 86

SYDNEY BIDDLE BARROWS

12 The more you act like a lady, the more he'll act like a gentleman.

> Instructions to employees of her escort service, *Mayflower Madam*, with William Novak, Arbor House 86

BRUCE BARTON, Chairman, Batten, Barton, Durstine & Osborn

13 In good times, people want to advertise; in bad times, they have to.

> *Town & Country* Feb 55

BERNARD BARUCH

14 Always do one thing less than you think you can do.

> On maintaining good health, *Newsweek* 28 May 56

WILLIAM BERNBACH, advertising executive

15 An idea can turn to dust or magic, depending on the talent that rubs against it.

> NY *Times* 6 Oct 82

BARRY BINGHAM JR

16 There were board meetings when my wife was doing needlepoint, one sister was addressing

Christmas cards and another didn't bother to attend.

> On breakdown of the family media business, *Fortune* 17 Feb 86

ROGER BLOUGH, President, US Steel Corp

1 Steel prices cause inflation like wet sidewalks cause rain.

> *Forbes* 1 Aug 67

FRANK BORMAN, Chief Executive Officer, Eastern Airlines

2 Capitalism without bankruptcy is like Christianity without hell.

> Quoted in *US* 21 Apr 86

WILLIAM BOURKE, Executive Vice President, Ford Motor Co

3 Other people set off firecrackers. We drop atomic bombs.

> On forced resignation of company president Lee Iacocca, NY *Times* 18 Jul 78

RICHARD BRANSON, Chairman, Virgin Atlantic Airlines

4 Like getting into a bleeding competition with a blood bank.

> On competing with British Airways, London *Times* 20 Sep 84

EDGAR BRONFMAN, Chairman, Seagram Co

5 To turn $100 into $110 is work. To turn $100 million into $110 million is inevitable.

> *Newsweek* 2 Dec 85

L E J BROUWER, Senior Managing Director, Royal Dutch/Shell Oil Co

6 Oil is seldom found where it is most needed, and seldom most needed where it is found.

> *Time* 4 May 70

CHARLES BROWER, President, Batten, Barton, Durstine & Osborn

7 There is no such thing as "soft sell" and "hard sell." There is only "smart sell" and "stupid sell."

> Comments to national convention of sales executives, news summaries 20 May 58

ARTHUR BRYAN, Chairman, Josiah Wedgwood & Sons Ltd

8 Hiccups in the international business scene are not new to us. Wedgwood china has survived upheavals before—the Napoleonic Wars, the Franco-Prussian War, the world wars. We do have a sense of continuity.

> Quoted in NY *Times* 30 Mar 80

LEO BURNETT, Chairman, Leo Burnett Co Inc

9 When you reach for the stars, you may not quite get one, but you won't come up with a handful of mud either.

> *Reader's Digest* Jan 85

H S M BURNS, President, Shell Oil Co

10 A good manager is a man who isn't worried about his own career but rather the careers of those who work for him.

> Quoted by Osborn Elliott *Men at the Top* Harper 59

11 Take care of those who work for you and you'll float to greatness on their achievements.

> *ib*

DONALD C BURR, Chairman, People Express Airlines Inc

12 Coffee stains on the flip-down trays mean [to the passengers] that we do our engine maintenance wrong.

> Quoted by Thomas J Peters and Nancy K Austin *A Passion for Excellence* Random House 85, excerpted in *Fortune* 13 May 85

CLIVE CHAJET, President, Lippincott & Margulies

13 There is an idea, broadly held on Wall Street, that names with X's are more memorable and tend to capture the attention of analysts. It is not held by us.

> On advising clients about corporate name changes, quoted by Lisa Belkin "How American Can Became Primerica" NY *Times* 8 Mar 87

LORD CHANDOS (Oliver Lyttelton), international banking and metals executive

14 In business a reputation for keeping absolutely to the letter and spirit of an agreement, even when it is unfavorable, is the most precious of assets, although it is not entered in the balance sheet.

> *Memoirs of Lord Chandos: An Unexpected View From the Summit* New American Library 63

15 Power in a corporation becomes residual and dwells in the background. It is the ability to exercise nice matters of judgment.

> *ib*

ALVIN CHERESKIN, President, AC & R advertising agency

16 Sex! What is that but *life*, after all? We're all of us selling sex, because we're all selling life.

> Quoted by Kennedy Fraser "As Gorgeous As It Gets" *New Yorker* 15 Sep 86

JOHN CHERRY, Florida undertaker

1 Celestis is a postcremation service.... We further reduce and encapsulate them, identify each by name, Social Security number and a religious symbol and place them into the payloader.

> Comments of one of a group of morticians arranging to send human ashes into a permanent orbit 1,900 miles above the earth, NY *Times* 25 Jan 85

L L COLBERT, President, Chrysler Corp

2 When I've had a rough day, before I go to sleep I ask myself if there's anything more I can do right now. If there isn't, I sleep sound.

> *Newsweek* 22 Aug 55

BARBER B CONABLE JR, President, World Bank

3 Women do two thirds of the world's work.... Yet they earn only one tenth of the world's income and own less than one percent of the world's property. They are among the poorest of the world's poor.

> To annual meeting of World Bank and International Monetary Fund, NY *Times* 1 Oct 86

FAIRFAX CONE, advertising executive

4 Advertising is what you do when you can't go see somebody. That's all it is.

> *Christian Science Monitor* 20 Mar 63

E GERALD CORRIGAN

5 I am very careful about bringing people into my confidence. I want to see the color of their eyes.

> On becoming president of Federal Reserve Bank in Minneapolis, NY *Times* 30 Dec 84

HARLOW H CURTICE, President, General Motors Corp

6 General Motors has no bad years, only good years and better years.

> Quoted by Alfred P Sloan Jr *My Years with General Motors* Doubleday 64

KITTY D'ALESSIO, President, Chanel Inc

7 As times change, you want to really revere your heredity, but you don't want to be a shrine. ... to light candles and kneel.

> On conflict between tradition and modernity after she succeeded company founder Coco Chanel, NY *Times* 28 Jul 85

8 Open the windows, let in the year we're living in.

> *ib*

LEON A DANCO, President, Center for Family Business

9 They look upon retirement as something between euthanasia and castration.

> On company founders who view "giving up" as tantamount to planning their own funerals, NY *Times* 11 Jun 86

JERRY DELLA FEMINA, advertising executive

10 Thank you for making me *nouveau riche*.

> Engraving on silver box presented to attorney Mort Janklow after successful sale of Della Femina's advertising agency, *New York* 2 Feb 87

11 It goes back to all of us wanting to be in Hollywood. We're all dying to win an Oscar.

> On plethora of awards in advertising industry, *Wall Street Journal* 26 Mar 87

RICHARD DONAT, store manager, Marshall Field & Co, Chicago

12 Another day, another million dollars.

> On the Christmas shopping season, *Wall Street Journal* 29 Nov 84

FREDERICK HUDSON ECKER, Chairman, Metropolitan Life

13 I don't think anybody yet has invented a pastime that's as much fun, or keeps you as young, as a good job.

> Recalled on his death at age 96, 20 Mar 64

BILL EVANS, President, Clio Awards

14 We use the people who are in the bullpen producing.

> On importance of having young judges in advertising competition, *Wall Street Journal* 26 Mar 87

15 It's like having a designer dress compared with one from Woolworth's. Which one is more impressive when you go to the debutante ball?

> On the Clio's prestige as one of the oldest and best-known advertising awards, *ib*

JONI EVANS, President, Trade Division, Simon & Schuster

16 People assume you slept your way to the top. Frankly, I couldn't sleep my way to the middle.

> Comments to conference of women executives on her beginnings as a reader of manuscripts, NY *Times* 22 Jul 86

HAL FAIR, National Product Coordinator, Brother International Corp

17 Don't expect the typewriter to ever completely disappear.

> On the widespread use of word processors, NY *Times* 23 Nov 84

JIM FISHEL, direct-mail specialist

1 She doesn't want to touch it. She doesn't want to smell it. She doesn't want to hear it. Lord love her. She's a Mail Order Freak.
> Advertisement for direct marketing, quoted by Philip H Dougherty "Advertising: The Fishels of Fairfax at Compton" NY *Times* 30 Dec 80

BERNICE FITZ-GIBBON, Director of Advertising, Macy's

2 Teenagers travel in droves, packs, swarms. . . . To the librarian, they're a gaggle of geese. To the cook, they're a scourge of locusts. To department stores they're a big beautiful exaltation of larks. . . . all lovely and loose and jingly.
> NY *Times* 6 Jun 60

B C FORBES

3 If you don't drive your business, you will be driven out of business.
> *Forbes* 1 Apr 74

MALCOLM S FORBES

4 Executives who get there and stay suggest solutions when they present the problems.
> *Forbes* 12 May 80

GEORGE KEITH FUNSTON, President, New York Stock Exchange

5 Automation does not make optimism obsolete.
> Address at George Peabody College for Teachers, Vanderbilt University, Nashville TN, 11 Mar 64

CORNELIUS GALLAGHER, Realtor

6 After all, the three major sources of apartments are death, divorce and transfer.
> On reading obituaries for leads in the tight Manhattan housing market, NY *Times* 2 May 85

HAROLD S GENEEN, former Chairman, International Telephone and Telegraph

7 In the business world, everyone is paid in two coins: cash and experience. Take the experience first; the cash will come later.
> *Managing*, with Alvin Moscow, Doubleday 84

8 Every company has two organizational structures: The formal one is written on the charts; the other is the everyday relationship of the men and women in the organization.
> *ib*

9 Management must manage!
> *ib*

10 Managers in all too many American companies do not achieve the desired results because nobody makes them do it.
> *ib*

11 It is much more difficult to measure nonperformance than performance.
> On why management sometimes accepts underachievement, *ib*

12 Performance stands out like a ton of diamonds. Nonperformance can always be explained away.
> *ib*

13 You can know a person by the kind of desk he keeps. . . . If the president of a company has a clean desk . . . then it must be the executive vice president who is doing all the work.
> *ib*

14 The worst disease which can afflict business executives in their work is not, as popularly supposed, alcoholism; it's egotism.
> *ib*

15 It is an immutable law in business that words are words, explanations are explanations, promises are promises—but only performance is reality.
> *ib*

16 If you keep working you'll last longer and I just want to keep vertical. . . . I'd hate to spend the rest of my life trying to outwit an 18-inch fish.
> On establishing a new business after retiring from ITT, NY *Times* 18 Nov 84

J PAUL GETTY

17 No one can possibly achieve any real and lasting success or "get rich" in business by being a conformist.
> *International Herald Tribune* 10 Jan 61

18 Oil is like a wild animal. Whoever captures it has it.
> Quoted by Robert Lenzner *The Great Getty* Crown 85

19 There are one hundred men seeking security to one able man who is willing to risk his fortune.
> *ib*

20 I buy when other people are selling.
> *ib*

21 The meek shall inherit the earth, but not the mineral rights.
> *ib*

22 If you can count your money, you don't have a billion dollars.
> *ib*

STEVEN GILLIATT, Director of Design, Lippincott & Margulies

1 A one-syllable word sounds better with Inc. A longer word has better rhythm with Corporation.

> On making corporate name changes, quoted by Lisa Belkin "How American Can Became Primerica" NY *Times* 8 Mar 87

2 [A logo] should look just as good in 15-foot letters on top of company headquarters as it does one sixteenth of an inch tall on company stationery.

> *ib*

ROBERT GREENLEAF, Director of Management Research, AT&T

3 Many attempts to communicate are nullified by saying too much.

> *Servant Leadership: A Journey into the Nature of Legitimate Power and Greatness* Paulist Press 77

4 Even the frankest and bravest of subordinates do not talk with their boss the same way they talk with colleagues.

> *ib*

DEIL O GUSTAFSON, real estate executive

5 Inequality of knowledge is the key to a sale.

> *Newsweek* 20 May 74

ROBERT W HAACK, President, New York Stock Exchange

6 The public may be willing to forgive us for mistakes in judgment but it will not forgive us for mistakes in motive.

> *Wall Street Journal* 17 Oct 67

MARION HARPER JR, President, McCann-Erickson

7 I have been captured by what I chased.

> On marketing organization that grew out of his advertising agency, *Newsweek* 30 Mar 64

JOHN B HARTNETT, Chairman, Xerox Corp

8 A word beginning with X ... the more we thought about it, the more we were ready to try it. And we got it into the dictionary.

> On the trademark *Xerox*, recalled on his death 3 Jun 82

KEN HAYASHIBARA, Japanese manufacturer

9 If the person is over 40 years old, I tell him he should do something because it is first good for Japan, good for the company, good for his family and finally good for him. If the person is under 40, I tell him he should do it because first it is good for him, good for his family, good for the company and finally good for Japan.

> On social changes introduced during US military occupation of Japan, NY *Times* 9 May 84

H L HUNT, Texas oil billionaire

10 I didn't go to high school, and I didn't go to grade school either. Education, I think, is for refinement and is probably a liability.

> *60 Minutes* CBS TV 1 Apr 69

NELSON BUNKER HUNT, Texas billionaire

11 People who know how much they're worth aren't usually worth that much.

> Testimony to Congressional subcommittee, *Time* 12 May 80

ROBERT HUNTER, Director, National Insurance Consumer Organization

12 At the top of the cycle you write [policies for] everybody, no matter how bad, and at the bottom you cancel everybody, no matter how good. It's a manic-depressive cycle.

> On the insurance business, quoted by George J Church "Sorry, Your Policy Is Cancelled" *Time* 24 Mar 86

LEE IACOCCA

13 One of the things the government can't do is run anything. The only things our government runs are the post office and the railroads, and both of them are bankrupt.

> As president of Ford Motor Co, *Quote* 17 Jun 73

14 People want economy and they will pay any price to get it.

> NY *Times* 13 Oct 74

15 When future historians look back on our way of curing inflation ... they'll probably compare it to bloodletting in the Middle Ages.

> *Fortune* 27 Jun 83

16 We at Chrysler borrow money the old-fashioned way. We pay it back.

> As chairman of Chrysler Corp, which borrowed $1.2 billion under US Loan Guarantee Act of 1979 and repaid the loan seven years before it was due, news summaries 13 Jul 83

17 I gotta tell ya, with our $2.4 billion in profits last year, they gave me a great big bonus. Really, it's almost obscene.

> Addressing market analysts in Detroit, quoted in *Time* 1 Apr 85

18 If a guy is over 25 percent jerk, he's in trouble. And Henry was 95 percent.

> On Henry Ford II, *ib*

1 Are we going to be a services power? The double-cheeseburger-hold-the-mayo kings of the whole world?

> To Japan Society of NY, *Fortune* 7 Jul 86

ERIC JOHNSTON, President, US Chamber of Commerce

2 The dinosaur's eloquent lesson is that if some bigness is good, an overabundance of bigness is not necessarily better.

> Warning businesses against excessive growth, *Quote* 23 Feb 58

J BRUCE JOHNSTON, Executive Vice President, US Steel Corp

3 There are not enough seats in the steel lifeboat for everybody.

> From a letter warning striking employees that the company was facing "an economic showdown with nonunion competitors, bankrupt competitors and foreign competitors," NY *Times* 10 Aug 86

ERNEST A JONES, advertising executive

4 Only for the phony is commercialism—the bending of creativity to common utility—a naughty word. To the truly creative, it is a bridge to the great audience, a means of sharing rather than debasing.

> Address at Cranbrook Academy of Art, NY *Herald Tribune* 2 Jun 64

5 Creativity not committed to public purpose is merely therapy or ego satisfaction.

> *ib*

HENRY J KAISER, industrialist

6 Problems are only opportunities in work clothes.

> Recalled on his death 24 Aug 67

FREDERICK R KAPPEL, Chairman, AT&T

7 The Bell System is like a damn big dragon. You kick it in the tail, and two years later it feels it in its head.

> Quoted by J Robert Moskin "The Surprising Story of Ma Bell" *Look* 28 Aug 62

JOSEPH P KENNEDY, former US Ambassador to Britain

8 Whenever you're sitting across from some important person, always picture him sitting there in a suit of long red underwear. That's the way I always operated in business.

> Quoted by Lawrence O'Brien *No Final Victories* Doubleday 74

MARILYN MOATS KENNEDY, Managing Partner, Career Strategies, Chicago

9 Politics is the process of getting along with the querulous, the garrulous and the congenitally unlovable.

> Quoted in "Playing Office Politics" *Newsweek* 16 Sep 85

LANE KIRKLAND, President, AFL-CIO

10 To hear the Japanese plead for free trade is like hearing the word *love* on the lips of a harlot.

> NY *Times* 28 Jul 85

11 We must be part of the general staff at the inception, rather than the ambulance drivers at the bitter end.

> On bargaining disputes that impede contract negotiations, *ib* 4 May 86

CARL A KROCH, Chairman, Kroch's & Brentano's Inc, Chicago

12 The independent bookstore—you know we're almost dinosaurs.

> On turning over the 80-year-old family firm to its employees, NY *Times* 22 Jun 86

EDWIN HERBERT LAND, founder, Polaroid Corp

13 The bottom line is in heaven!

> When asked what a new product called Polavision might contribute to "the bottom line," *Boston Business* Fall 86

ESTÉE LAUDER, cosmetics executive

14 When you stop talking, you've lost your customer. When you turn your back, you've lost her.

> To conference of sales personnel, quoted by Kennedy Fraser "As Gorgeous As It Gets" *New Yorker* 15 Sep 86

15 Touch a face. Touch a hand. Say, "This is for you, this is what I want *you* to wear."

> *ib*

16 If you don't sell, it's not the product that's wrong, it's *you*.

> *ib*

MARY WELLS LAWRENCE, advertising executive

17 In this business, you can never wash the dinner dishes and say they are done. You have to keep doing them constantly.

> On need for fresh approaches, *Time* 3 Oct 66

JOHN L LEWIS, President, United Mine Workers

18 I don't think the federation has a head; its neck has just grown up and haired over.

> On World Federation of Trade Unions, recalled in news summaries 11 Jan 80

RAYMOND LOEWY

1 Good design keeps the user happy, the manufacturer in the black and the aesthete unoffended.

> Comment of "the father of streamlining," recalled on his death 14 Jul 86

BERNARD LOOMIS, toy manufacturing executive

2 The trouble with research is that it tells you what people were thinking about yesterday, not tomorrow. It's like driving a car using a rearview mirror.

> *International Herald Tribune* 9 Oct 85

FRANK P LOUCHHEIM, Chairman, Right Associates, management placement firm

3 "You're fired!" No other words can so easily and succinctly reduce a confident, self-assured executive to an insecure, groveling shred of his former self.

> "The Art of Getting Fired" *Wall Street Journal* 16 Jul 84

4 Handled creatively, getting fired allows an executive . . . to actually experience a sense of relief that he never wanted the job he has lost.

> *ib*

F R MANN, retired Chairman, National Container Corp

5 There's a little bit of the dictator in all of us. Fortunately, I was blessed with a disproportionately generous share.

> NY *Times* 16 Jun 76

HERBERT MARCUS, cofounder, Neiman-Marcus

6 There is never a good *sale* for Neiman-Marcus unless it's a good *buy* for the customer.

> 1926 comment to his son, quoted by Stanley Marcus *Minding the Store* Little, Brown 74

TOM McELLIGOTT, advertising executive

7 You're never too bad to win.

> On plethora of awards in advertising industry, *Wall Street Journal* 26 Mar 87

ROBERT MILLER, Chairman, Chrysler Financial Corp

8 Are these guys really Robin Hood and his Merry Men as they claim, or Genghis Khan and the Mongol hordes?

> On corporate raiders, address at Harvard Business School, *US News & World Report* 26 Jan 87

ROGER MILLER, Codirector, Mergers and Acquisitions, Salomon Brothers Inc

9 Junk bonds are the Holy Grail for hostile takeovers.

> NY *Times* 14 Apr 85

GEORGE MORROW, President, Morrow Inc

10 Being in the microcomputer business is like going 55 miles an hour 3 feet from a cliff.

> On his company's bankruptcy, *Fortune* 14 Apr 86

CHARLES G MORTIMER, President, General Foods Corp

11 Today convenience is the success factor of just about every type of product and service that is showing steady growth.

> To Amer Marketing Assn, quoted by NY *Herald Tribune* 14 May 59

12 The creeping notion that additives are baddatives.

> Calling for campaign against the ban on food coloring, *Wall Steet Journal* 29 Dec 60

CLINT W MURCHISON, Texas financier

13 Money is like manure. If you spread it around, it does a lot of good, but if you pile it up in one place, it stinks like hell.

> Quoted by his son Clint Murchison Jr, *Time* 16 Jun 61

PAUL NEILD, Managing Director, Phillips & Drew, London

14 The aristocracy is in decline in the City, and the cloth-cap professionals are in the ascent. And we will take over.

> On aggressive new breed in London's financial district, NY *Times* 25 Sep 86

DONALD NEUENSCHWANDER, Chairman, Medical Center Bank, Houston

15 You can't be all things to all people. But I can be all things to the people I select.

> Commenting on his bank, whose clients are physicians and wealthy customers, *Time* 3 Dec 84

ALBERT NEWGARDEN, Arthur Young & Co

16 Accountants are perpetually fighting their shiny pants, green eyeshades, number-cruncher image.

> *Wall Street Journal* 26 Apr 84

DAVID OGILVY, advertising executive

17 The most important word in the vocabulary of

advertising is TEST. If you pretest your product with consumers, and pretest your advertising, you will do well in the marketplace.

Confessions of an Advertising Man Atheneum 63

1 Never stop testing, and your advertising will never stop improving.

ib

2 Leaders . . . grasp nettles.

To Amer Marketing Assn 10 May 72

WILLIAM S PALEY, founder, CBS

3 There's a certain amount of disorder that has to be reorganized.

On return as CBS chairman after his retirement, Boston *Globe* 16 Sep 86

COLA PARKER, President, National Assn of Manufacturers

4 We have gone completely overboard on security. Everything has to be secured, jobs, wages, hours— although the ultimate in security is jail, the slave labor camp and the salt mine.

News summaries 9 Dec 55

PAUL J PAULSON, President, Doyle Dane Bernbach

5 You can learn a lot from the client. . . . Some 70 percent doesn't matter, but that 30 percent will kill you.

NY *Times* 4 May 79

JAMES CASH PENNEY, founder, JC Penney Corp

6 I wouldn't be human if I didn't feel pride and something that transcends pride—humility.

At dedication of his company's Manhattan headquarters, NY *Herald Tribune* 30 May 65

TOMMY PERSE, co-owner, Maxfield boutique, Los Angeles

7 The store forces people to cleanse their mind and allows them to do the major damage to their credit cards that we appreciate so much.

On effect of minimalist décor, *Newsweek* 10 Nov 86

T BOONE PICKENS, Chairman, Mesa Petroleum Co

8 Chief executives, who themselves own few shares of their companies, have no more feeling for the average stockholder than they do for baboons in Africa.

Harvard Business Review May/Jun 86

GIFFORD PINCHOT III, management consultant

9 Corporate risk takers are very much like entre-preneurs. They take personal risks to make new ideas happen.

Intrapreneuring Harper & Row 85

ROBERT PLISKIN, Vice President, Benton & Bowles

10 Market research can establish beyond the shadow of a doubt that the egg is a sad and sorry product and that it obviously will not continue to sell. Because after all, eggs won't stand up by themselves, they roll too easily, are too easily broken, require special packaging, look alike, are difficult to open, won't stack on the shelf.

To National Packaging Forum 16 Oct 63

B EARL PUCKETT, President, Allied Stores Corp

11 It is our job to make women unhappy with what they have.

Recalled on his death, *Newsweek* 23 Feb 76

CLARENCE B RANDALL

12 The leader must know, must know that he knows and must be able to make it abundantly clear to those about him that he knows.

Making Good in Management McGraw-Hill 64

ROSSER REEVES, Chairman, Ted Bates & Co Inc

13 If he isn't a salesman, he can't write selling copy. If he isn't a writer, he can't be a salesman in print.

On the making of a copywriter, *Advertising Age* 19 Apr 65

14 Some of the people that float around in this business and are allegedly great copywriters at great salaries, we wouldn't pay $50 a week to at this agency. I think a great many copywriters in this business earn their living because they haven't been caught.

ib

CHARLES REVSON, founder of Revlon Inc

15 I don't meet competition. I crush it.

Time 16 Jun 58

AL RIES, Chairman, Trout & Ries Advertising Inc

16 Today, communication itself is the problem. We have become the world's first overcommunicated society. Each year we send more and receive less.

Positioning: The Battle for Your Mind, with Jack Trout, McGraw-Hill 80

17 Changing the direction of a large company is like trying to turn an aircraft carrier. It takes a mile before anything happens. And if it was a

wrong turn, getting back on course takes even longer.
ib

1 Don't overlook the importance of worldwide thinking. A company that keeps its eye on Tom, Dick and Harry is going to miss Pierre, Hans and Yoshio.
ib

ROBERTO RISSO

2 If I can get every rich girl with a rose garden to use guano, that's it.
On his attempt to market $80,000 worth of Peruvian bat dung as the "Rolls Royce of fertilizers," *Wall Street Journal* 24 Jul 84

FELIX G ROHATYN, Chairman, Municipal Assistance Corp, NYC

3 Two-tier tender offers, Pac-Man and poison-pill defenses, crown-jewel options, greenmail, golden parachutes, self-tenders—all have become part of our everyday business.
Quoted by William Safire NY *Times* 27 Jan 85

4 [Bankruptcy would be] like stepping into a tepid bath and slashing your wrists: You might not feel yourself dying, but that's what would happen.
ib 2 Jul 85

WILLIAM ROOTES, industrialist

5 No other manmade device since the shields and lances of the knights quite fulfills a man's ego like an automobile.
Quoted on *Who Said That?* BBC TV 14 Jan 58

RAYMOND RUBICAM, cofounder, Young & Rubicam Inc

6 The best identification of a great advertisement is that its public is not only strongly sold by it, but that both the public and the advertising world remember it for a long time as an admirable piece of work.
Quoted by David Ogilvy *Confessions of an Advertising Man* Atheneum 63

DAVID SARNOFF, Chairman, RCA

7 I hitched my wagon to an electron rather than the proverbial star.
NY *Times* 4 Apr 58

JIM SCHWARTZ, stockholder in Manhattan's East Side Sauna

8 From a business point of view, we make as much money from one person having sex with one person as one person having sex with 40.
On remaining open for business despite the AIDS epidemic, NY *Times* 14 Oct 85

ROBERT F SIX, President, Continental Airlines

9 "My door is always open—bring me your problems." This is guaranteed to turn on every whiner, lackey and neurotic on the property.
Quoted in Robert W Kent ed *Money Talks* Pocket Books 86

RANDY SMITH, marketing official, People Express Airlines Inc

10 We built the Model T; it was black and a lot of people bought it. But we found out not everybody wanted it.
On no-frills flying, NY *Times* 25 Jun 86

ROGER B SMITH, Chairman, General Motors Corp

11 We hope this car will be less labor intensive, less material intensive, less everything intensive than anything we have done before.
On the Saturn model, *Time* 21 Jan 85

BENJAMIN SONNENBERG, public relations pioneer

12 I supply the Listerine to the commercial dandruff on the shoulders of corporations.
Time 12 Feb 79

A ALFRED TAUBMAN, owner of 650 A&W Root Beer Stands and Chairman, Sotheby Galleries

13 There is more similarity in a precious painting by Degas and a frosted mug of root beer than you ever thought possible.
NY *Times* 3 Feb 85

14 God help us if we ever take the theater out of the auction business or anything else. It would be an awfully boring world.
Wall Street Journal 18 Sep 85

BERNARD TRESNOWSKI, Director, Blue Cross and Blue Shield Assn

15 In the past, employers were like an absentee host who paid the bill but never showed up at the table. Now they are intimately involved in planning the menu.
On new role of employers in determining health care, *Newsweek* 2 Jul 84

DONALD J TRUMP, real estate developer

16 When I build something for somebody, I always add $50 million or $60 million onto the price. My guys come in, they say it's going to cost $75 million. I say it's going to cost $125 million, and I build it for $100 million. Basically, I did a lousy job. But they think I did a great job.
To 1984 meeting of US Football League owners, NY *Times* 1 Jul 86

TED TURNER

1 If I only had a little humility, I'd be perfect.
Quoted in news summaries 8 Jun 80

JAMES R UFFELMAN, President, Technimetrics Inc

2 The work is often deadly and boring, but it requires a keen intelligence, and the only way I can compete with large corporations is to treat my employees better, move them up faster, give them more money and put mirrors in the bathrooms.
Wall Street Journal 21 Aug 84

3 If you can make an employee happy by spending $800 on a comfortable office chair, what's $800?
ib

KAREN VALENSTEIN, Vice President, E F Hutton Group Inc

4 I never go out of my way to screw someone, but I'm always looking over my shoulder.
Quoted by Jane Gross "Against the Odds" NY *Times* 6 Jan 85

5 There's a place for corporate wives, but there's no place for corporate husbands.
ib

KENNETH J VAUGHAN, former Director, Winnebago Industries Inc

6 John K probably won't stop working for Winnebago until six weeks after he dies.
On the company's founder John K Hanson, NY *Times* 18 May 86

AN WANG

7 Success is more a function of consistent common sense than it is of genius.
Boston Magazine Dec 86

8 I founded Wang Laboratories . . . to show that Chinese could excel at things other than running laundries and restaurants.
ib

GORDON WEBBER, Vice President, Benton & Bowles

9 To dare every day to be irreverent and bold. To dare to preserve the randomness of mind which in children produces strange and wonderful new thoughts and forms. To continually scramble the familiar and bring the old into new juxtaposition.
Advertising Age 31 Oct 60

WILLIAM K WHITEFORD, Chairman, Gulf Corp

10 Smell that! That's gasoline you smell in there. You can't buy any perfume in the world that smells as sweet.
Forbes 1 May 64

KING WHITNEY JR, President, Personnel Laboratory Inc

11 Change has considerable psychological impact on the human mind. To the fearful it is threatening because it means that things may get worse. To the hopeful it is encouraging because things may get better. To the confident it is inspiring because the challenge exists to make things better. Obviously, then, one's character and frame of mind determine how readily he brings about change and how he reacts to change that is imposed on him.
To a sales meeting, quoted by *Wall Street Journal* 7 Jun 67

WALTER B WRISTON

12 When you retire . . . you go from who's who to who's that, [like] stepping off the pier [or] achieving statutory senility.
On retiring as chairman of Citibank Corp, NY *Times* 21 Apr 85

PETE ZAMARELLO, real estate developer

13 I'd rather be a pimp with a purple hat . . . than be associated with banks.
In bankruptcy court in Anchorage, *Wall Street Journal* 24 Feb 87

14 I will not build nothing in Alaska, even my tomb.
ib

Observers & Critics

DEAN ACHESON

15 Time spent in the advertising business seems to create a permanent deformity like the Chinese habit of foot-binding.
Quoted in David S McLellan and David C Acheson eds *Among Friends* Dodd, Mead 80

WOODY ALLEN

16 Eighty percent of success is showing up.
Quoted by Thomas J Peters & Robert H Waterman *In Search of Excellence* Harper & Row 82

ANONYMOUS

17 He carves you up but leaves the skin around the body.
Comments of a Ford Motor Co executive on

Philip Caldwell, president of international operations, quoted in NY *Times* 13 Mar 77

1 The problem when solved will be simple.
Sign on the wall of General Motors research laboratory, Dayton, quoted by Al Ries and Jack Trout *Positioning: The Battle for Your Mind* McGraw-Hill 81

2 You know what the difference is between a dead skunk and a dead banker on the road? There's skid marks by the skunk.
Quoted by Andrew H Malcolm *Final Harvest: An American Tragedy* Times Books 86

3 Oilfield prayer: Lord, let there be one more Boom. And don't let us screw it up.
Sign in Texas diner, quoted in "A Dream Dies in Texas" *People* 10 Nov 86

4 Either lead, follow or get out of the way.
Sign on desk of broadcasting executive Ted Turner, pictured in *Fortune* 5 Jan 87

PETER BAIDA

5 I have received memos so swollen with managerial babble that they struck me as the literary equivalent of assault with a deadly weapon.
"Management Babble" *American Heritage* Apr 85

LISA BELKIN

6 Dozens of meetings, hundreds of man-hours, millions of dollars and months of angst . . . went into the name change. . . . the most sweeping of changes brought about by the most persnickity attention to detail.
"How American Can Became Primerica" NY *Times* 8 Mar 87

7 Corporate identity specialists . . . spend their time rechristening other companies, [conducting] a legal search [and] a linguistic search to insure that the name is not an insult in another language.
ib

PAULA BERNSTEIN

8 Today's corporate family is headed by a "father" who finds the child he never had, the child he always wanted, at the office and guides him (sometimes her) up the ladder.
Employing metaphors of family life to explain office scenarios, *Family Ties, Corporate Bonds* Doubleday 85

DEREK BOK, President, Harvard

9 The oldest of the arts and the youngest of the professions.
Conferring the degree Master of Business Administration, quoted by Kingman Brewster, US Ambassador, in address to British Institute of Management 13 Dec 77

FRANCIS J BRACELAND, Chief Psychiatrist, Institute for Living, Hartford CT

10 Whereas the well-functioning executive encourages the best in brains and skills, the one who is paranoid or even less morbidly insecure must have inadequates about him, men who will take punishment.
"Living with Executive Tensions" *National Observer* 28 Dec 64

JIMMY BRESLIN

11 Men in the uniform of Wall Street retirement: black Chesterfield coat, rimless glasses and the *Times* folded to the obituary page.
The Gang Who Couldn't Shoot Straight Viking 69

12 People born in Queens, raised to say that each morning they get on the subway and "go to the city," have a resentment of Manhattan, of the swiftness of its life and success of the people who live there.
Table Money Ticknor & Fields 86

13 Those of Manhattan are the brokers on Wall Street and they talk of people who went to the same colleges; those from Queens are margin clerks in the back offices and they speak of friends who live in the same neighborhood.
ib

KINGMAN BREWSTER, US Ambassador to Britain

14 Incomprehensible jargon is the hallmark of a profession.
To British Institute of Management 13 Dec 77

D W BROGAN

15 Man does not live by bread alone, even presliced bread.
On decline of US baking industry, quoted in *Forbes* 1 Mar 64

HELEN GURLEY BROWN

16 No office anywhere on earth is so puritanical, impeccable, elegant, sterile or incorruptible as not to contain the yeast for at least one affair, probably more. You can say it couldn't happen *here*, but just let a yeast raiser into the place and first thing you know—bread!
Sex and the Office Geis 64

ROBERT FARRAR CAPON

17 The shock of unemployment becomes a pathology in its own right.
"Being Let Go" NY *Times* 5 Aug 84

DALE CARNEGIE

1 The ideas I stand for are not mine. I borrowed them from Socrates. I swiped them from Chesterfield. I stole them from Jesus. And I put them in a book. If you don't like their rules, whose would you use?
   On his 1936 book *How to Win Friends and Influence People, Newsweek* 8 Aug 55

DICK CAVETT

2 Show people tend to treat their finances like their dentistry. They assume the man handling it knows what he is doing.
   On investigation of his investment broker, *Time* 6 May 85

CENTURY CLUB OF NEW YORK

3 If this were the best of all possible worlds and the spirit of the Century were perfectly honored here, no business would ever be discussed in the clubhouse. In any case, business papers should never be displayed in the common rooms of the first, second and third floors.
   Announcement from the House Committee, *Century Customs: The Spirit and The Letter* 85

JOHN CLEESE

4 I find it rather easy to portray a businessman. Being bland, rather cruel and incompetent comes naturally to me.
   On appearing in industrial-training films, quoted in *Newsweek* 15 Jun 87

WILLIAM G CONNOLLY

5 The mortgage market changes virtually from day to day, so you can wait a few weeks and, if you haven't committed suicide in the meantime, try again, even with the same lenders.
   The New York Times Guide to Buying or Building a Home Quadrangle 79

JOHN C DANFORTH, Chairman, US Senate Subcommittee on Trade

6 Japan is a great nation. It should begin to act like one.
   Address in Tokyo 13 Jan 86

RICHARD G DARMAN, US Deputy Secretary of the Treasury

7 "Corpocracy" [is] large-scale corporate America's tendency to be like the government bureaucracy.
   NY *Times* 9 Nov 86

GIANNI DE MICHELIS, Minister of Labor, Italy

8 Culture is Italy's oil, and it must be exploited.
   Quoted by Roberto Suro "Saving the Treasures of Italy" NY *Times* 21 Dec 86

ALMA DENNY

9 The feminist surge will crest when a lady named Arabella, flounces and ruffles and all, can rise to the top of a Fortune 500 corporation.
   NY *Times* 30 Aug 85

NED DEWEY, Harvard Business School, Class of '49

10 These kids are smart. But I'd as soon take a python to bed as hire one.
   On recent graduates, *Business Week* 24 Mar 86

11 He'd suck my brains, memorize my Rolodex and use my telephone to find some other guy who'd pay him twice the money.
   ib

PHILIP H DOUGHERTY

12 It is embellished with a print of Cabbage Patch Kids in muted hues of pink, blue and green, done not quite in Empire style and without either a court train or redingote, but flared about the bottom in an alençon lace effect [and] sprinkled throughout with tiny pink dots not unlike stephanotis adorning the Plaza Hotel's Grand Ballroom.
   On introduction of world's first designer diaper with the claim that "babies go gaga over it," NY *Times* 1 Oct 84

PETER F DRUCKER

13 Innovation is the specific instrument of entrepreneurship. . . . the act that endows resources with a new capacity to create wealth.
   Innovation and Entrepreneurship Harper & Row 85, quoted in *Harvard Business Review* May/Jun 86

PETER EVANS

14 He needed to make deals. . . . a deal meant an opponent, an opponent meant confrontation and confrontation was the source of his strength.
   On Aristotle Onassis, *Ari* Summit 86

15 He could not live without adversaries, no more than a tree can live without soil; like mangrove trees, which make their own soil, he could create enemies from within himself.
   ib

D W EWING

1 A zealous sense of mission is only possible where there is opposition to it.
   "Tension Can Be an Asset" *Harvard Business Review* Sep/Oct 64

CLIFTON FADIMAN

2 He has made a profession out of a business and an art out of a profession.
   On Alfred A Knopf, recalled on Knopf's death 11 Aug 84

ED FINKELSTEIN

3 A consultant is someone who takes your watch away to tell you what time it is.
   NY *Times* 29 Apr 79

CHARLES FOUNTAIN

4 In the acquire-or-be-acquired corporate mayhem of the 1980s, the mantle of management has passed to investment bankers and number-crunchers whose vision extends no further than the next quarterly earnings statement.
   Christian Science Monitor 10 Dec 86

5 Were David Sarnoff alive today, there would almost surely be no place for him in the company [RCA] he had shepherded to greatness.
   ib

KENNEDY FRASER

6 For the camera and for posterity, Stanley Marcus and Estée Lauder greeted each other with an embrace ... a pair of elderly merchant monarchs who had tested each other's titanic shrewdness for decades formally exchanging a kiss of peace.
   On launching a new perfume at Neiman-Marcus in Dallas, "As Gorgeous As It Gets" *New Yorker* 15 Sep 86

ROBERT FROST

7 Take care to sell your horse before he dies. The art of life is passing losses on.
   From "The Ingenuities of Debt" in *The Poetry of Robert Frost* Holt, Rinehart & Winston 79

MERYL GARDNER, Assistant Professor of Marketing, NY University

8 Just as there is a trend toward high tech today, there is another trend toward high touch—homemade and wholesome.
   On Ben & Jerry's Homemade Inc, a Vermont ice-cream company, NY *Times* 29 Mar 85

ERIC GELMAN

9 Sharks have been swimming the oceans unchallenged for thousands of years; chances are, the species that roams corporate waters will prove just as hardy.
   "Macho Men of Capitalism" *Newsweek* 1 Oct 84

JOHN GIBBONS, Chairman, Congressional Office of Technology Assessment

10 They recruit their managers from the factory floor; we get ours out of law schools.
   On Japanese success in world trade, NY *Times* 28 Jul 85

LOUIS J GLICKMAN, real estate owner

11 The best investment on earth is earth.
   NY *Post* 3 Sep 57

JACK GOULD

12 One does not allow the plumbers to decide the temperature, depth and timing of a bath.
   Declaring that "old line carriers" such as AT&T should not be allowed to dominate national communications, NY *Times* 7 Aug 66

PAUL GRAY

13 Paperbacks blink in and out of print like fireflies. They also, as older collectors have ruefully discovered, fade and fall apart even more rapidly than their owners.
   Time 3 May 82

EDGAR A GUEST

14 I take the family shopping round
   The markets of the world.
   Poem on cover of 1934 Fall/Winter Sears, Roebuck Catalogue, quoted in profile of Sears Chairman Edward Riggs Telling, *Time* 20 Aug 84

ANDREW HACKER, Professor of Political Science, Queens College

15 Advertising has always been the Peck's Bad Boy of American business ... urging us to buy things we probably don't need and often can't afford.
   NY *Times* 24 Jun 84

16 Every time a message seems to grab us, and we think, "I just might try it," we are at the nexus of choice and persuasion that is advertising.
   ib

ALAN HARRINGTON

17 A corporation prefers to offer a job to a man who already has one ... To obtain entry into

paradise, in terms of employment, you should be in a full state of grace.
Life In the Crystal Palace Knopf 59

JOSEPH HELLER

1 I think in every country that there is at least one executive who is scared of going crazy.
Something Happened Knopf 74

MICHAEL deCOURCY HINDS

2 Single-family homes in New York generally come in two price ranges: expensive and unbelievably expensive.
"Living with Tenants: An Owner's Guide" NY *Times* 5 May 85

JEAN HOLLANDS, psychotherapist

3 The person who says "I'm not political" is in great danger. . . . Only the fittest will survive, and the fittest will be the ones who understand their office's politics.
Quoted in "Playing Office Politics" *Newsweek* 16 Sep 85

ROBERT HUGHES

4 It was the basilica of gossip, the Vatican of inside dope.
On Gramercy Park residence of NY public relations pioneer Benjamin Sonnenberg, *Time* 12 Feb 79

IOWA CITY PRESS-CITIZEN

5 If there's one thing that is clear from Monday's tragic series of murder and suicide, it is that the farm crisis is not numbers and deficits and bushels of corn. It is people and pride and tears and blood.
On financially troubled farmer who killed a bank president and two others before taking his own life, quoted in NY *Times* 12 Dec 85

HAYES B JACOBS

6 Contentment, in Telephone Ad-land, is a conversation, and happiness is a warm receiver.
On AT&T advertisements, NY *Times* 1 Mar 64

JOSEPH D JAMAIL JR

7 There are more pompous, arrogant, self-centered mediocre . . . people running corporate America . . . Their judgments and misjudgments have made me rich.
On $10.5-billion settlement he won for Pennzoil Co against Texaco Inc, NY *Times* 21 Nov 85

GEORGE KATONA, Director, University of Michigan Business Survey Research Bureau

8 Business is like sex. When it's good, it's very, very good; when it's not so good, it's still good.
Wall Street Journal 9 Apr 69

MERVYN A KING, professor, London School of Economics

9 When I was a graduate student at Harvard, I learned about showers and central heating. Ten years later, I learned about breakfast meetings. These are America's three great contributions to civilization.
On value of "power breakfasts," quoted in NY *Times* 4 Mar 87

ROBERT KRULWICH

10 As soon as the boss decides he wants his workers to do something, he has two problems: making them do it and monitoring what they do.
"Motivating the Help" NY *Times* 4 Jul 82

H LANCE LESSMAN, arbitrage assistant to Ivan Boesky

11 If you perceive the pregnancy early, then you don't get beat up too badly if you're wrong, and you make a fortune if you're right.
Quoted by Connie Bruck in profile of Boesky, "My Master Is My Purse" *Atlantic* Dec 84

PETER H LEWIS

12 The new version has page previewing known as WYSIWYG (pronounced wizzy-wig, for What You See Is What You Get).
On new program from Microsoft, "A Way With Words" NY *Times* 4 Nov 86

SINCLAIR LEWIS

13 Damn the great executives, the men of measured merriment, damn the men with careful smiles . . . oh, damn their measured merriment.
From his 1925 novel *Arrowsmith*, recalled on his death 10 Jan 51

ASSAR LINDBECK, Nobel Prize Committee for economics

14 The true test of a brilliant theory [is] what first is thought to be wrong is later shown to be obvious.
On Franco Modigliani's award-winning theory of corporate finance, NY *Times* 16 Oct 85

JOANNE LIPMAN

1 Hollywood has its Oscars. Television has its Emmys. Broadway has its Tonys. And advertising has its Clios. And its Andys, Addys, Effies and Obies. And 117 other assorted awards. And those are just the big ones.

"Ad Creators Collect Prizes Ad Nauseam, Almost Ad Infinitum" *Wall Street Journal* 26 Mar 87

STEVE LOHR

2 A new breed of broker making $300,000 a year in London . . . hot traders [who] are likely to be thirtyish, a bit cheeky and more interested in piling up commissions than meeting club cronies for a late afternoon brandy at Boodle's or White's.

On changing financial community in Great Britain, "London's Brokers Start Taking Off the Gloves" NY *Times* 25 Sep 86

JAY W LORSCH, professor, Harvard Business School

3 I think a lot more decisions are made on serendipity than people think. Things come across their radar screens and they jump at them.

Quoted in "For a Company Chief, When There's a Whim There's Often a Way" *Wall Street Journal* 1 Oct 84

RUSSELL LYNES

4 Cynicism is the intellectual cripple's substitute for intelligence. It is the dishonest businessman's substitute for concience. It is the communicators substitute, whether he is advertising man or editor or writer, for self-respect.

To Amer Assn of Advertising Agencies 25 Apr 63

ANDREW H MALCOLM

5 Farmers now are members of a capital-intensive industry that values good bookwork more than backwork. So several times a year almost every farmer must seek operating credit from the college fellow in the white shirt and tie—in effect, asking financial permission to work hard on his own land.

"Murder on the Family Farm" NY *Times* 23 Mar 86

LEON MANDEL, Editor, *Autoweek*

6 Lights shine more brightly at Ford, but they go out overnight.

On short careers of Ford Motor Co executives, NY *Times* 3 Oct 84

DEXTER MASTERS

7 In the jungle of the marketplace, the intelligent buyer must be alert to every commercial sound, to every snapping of a selling twig, to every rustle that may signal the uprising arm holding the knife pointed toward the jugular vein.

The Intelligent Buyer and the Telltale Seller Knopf 66

MARTIN MAYER

8 Except for the con men borrowing money they shouldn't get and the widows who have to visit with the handsome young men in the trust department, no sane person ever enjoyed visiting a bank.

The Money Bazaars Dutton 84

9 This is the twilight of the banks. It would be a more cheerful spectacle if we could envision the dawn of the institutions that will replace them.

ib

MARSHALL MCLUHAN

10 Advertising is the greatest art form of the 20th century.

Advertising Age 3 Sep 76

EDWARD SHEPHERD MEAD

11 Not even computers will replace committees, because committees buy computers.

Wall Street Journal 18 Jun 64

JESSE MEYERS, Publisher, *Beverage Digest*

12 [The battle is for the] shelf space in our stomachs.

On competition between soft-drink bottlers, *Fortune* 7 Jan 85

MORTON MINTZ

13 The human being who would not harm you on an individual, face-to-face basis, who is charitable, civic-minded, loving and devout, will wound or kill you from behind the corporate veil.

On the marketing of a damaging birth-control device, *At Any Cost: Corporate Greed, Women and the Dalkon Shield* Pantheon 85

JESSICA MITFORD

14 Gracious dying is a huge, macabre and expensive joke on the American public.

On funeral directors, *The American Way of Death* Simon & Schuster 63

WALTER F MONDALE

15 What do we want our kids to do? Sweep up around Japanese computers?

To electrical workers union, Washington *Post* 7 Oct 82

117

TED MORGAN

1 In America, the land of the permanent revolution, ulcers and cancer often become, for the men at the top, the contemporary equivalent of the guillotine.
> On Robert Lacey's *Ford: The Men and the Machine* Little, Brown 86, NY *Times* 13 Jul 86

2 [It is a story] to satisfy the expectations of the average man, who wants awful things to happen to overprominent people.
> *ib*

JAN MORRIS

3 The language of economics is seldom limpid, but in H Street they usually manage to remove from it the very last flickering colophon of charm.
> On the World Bank in Washington DC, *The Road to Huddersfield* Pantheon 63

FRANK MUMNY

4 To write a book is a task needing only pen, ink and paper; to print a book is rather more difficult, because genius often expresses itself illegibly; to read a book is more difficult still, for one has to struggle with sleep; but to sell a book is the most difficult task of all.
> "The Romance of Bookselling" *The Reader's Adviser* Bowker 60

RALPH NADER

5 For almost 70 years the life insurance industry has been a smug sacred cow feeding the public a steady line of sacred bull.
> Testimony to US Senate subcommittee, NY *Times* 19 May 74

6 I don't think meals have any business being deductible. I'm for separation of calories and corporations.
> *Wall Street Journal* 15 Jul 85

BRUCE NUSSBAUM

7 The organization man is dead. He thrived when smokestack America thrived. When airlines, banks and telephones were highly regulated. When Japan built shoddy cars. When computers were huge and an apple was something you ate.
> "The New Corporate Elite" *Business Week* 21 Jan 85

JACK O'LEARY

8 Simon and Schuster runs a sales contest every year. The winners get to keep their jobs.
> On high turnover of salespeople, *Newsweek* 2 Jul 84

C NORTHCOTE PARKINSON

9 Work expands to fill the time available for its completion.
> *Economist* 19 Nov 55

KEN PATTON, NYC Economic Development Administrator

10 We have yet to find a significant case where the company did not move in the direction of the chief executive's home.
> On corporate relocations, NY *Times* 5 Feb 71

LAURENCE J PETER

11 In a hierarchy, every employee tends to rise to his level of incompetence; the cream rises until it sours.
> *The Peter Principle* Morrow 69

12 Work is accomplished by those employees who have not yet reached their level of incompetence.
> *ib*

13 Competence, like truth, beauty and contact lenses, is in the eye of the beholder.
> *ib*

14 Incompetence knows no barriers of time or place.
> *Why Things Go Wrong: The Peter Principle Revisited* Morrow 84

15 Equal opportunity means everyone will have a fair chance at becoming incompetent.
> *ib*

THOMAS J PETERS and NANCY K AUSTIN

16 The brand of leadership we propose has a simple base of MBWA (Managing By Wandering Around). To "wander," with customers and vendors and our own people, is to be in touch with the first vibrations of the new.
> *A Passion for Excellence* Random House 85, excerpted in *Fortune* 13 May 85

DIANE RAVITCH, professor, Columbia University Teachers College

17 The person who knows "how" will always have a job. The person who knows "why" will always be his boss.
> Commencement address at Reed College, Portland OR, *Time* 17 Jun 85

RONALD REAGAN, 40th US President

18 Inflation is as violent as a mugger, as frightening as an armed robber and as deadly as a hit man.
> At Republican Party fund-raising dinner, LA *Times* 20 Oct 78

ROBERT REINHOLD

1 As welcome as a rattlesnake at a square dance.
> On Thomas R Procopio, FDIC "liquidator-in-charge" during Texas bank failure, "US Helps Texans Survive Death of Bank" NY *Times* 14 Oct 84

RANDALL ROBINSON, TransAfrica lobby

2 They are supplying the legs on which this monster walks.
> On US firms doing business with South Africa, *Time* 25 Nov 85

WILLIAM SAFIRE

3 The CEO era gave rise to the CFO (not certified flying object, as you might imagine, but chief financial officer) and, most recently, the CIO, chief investment officer, a nice boost for the bookkeeper you can't afford to give a raise, unless he is a member of the Congress of Industrial Organizations, in which case you can stick your title in your ear.
> "Hail to the CEO" NY *Times* 28 Sep 86

ANTHONY SAMPSON

4 The great body of managers ... spend their whole careers climbing up inside one great Leviathan, with little contact with anyone outside.
> *The Anatomy of Britain* Harper & Row 62

PAUL SAMUELSON

5 Profits are the lifeblood of the economic system, the magic elixir upon which progress and all good things depend ultimately. But one man's lifeblood is another man's cancer.
> To Forum of European and Amer Economists, Harvard, *Time* 16 Aug 76

ARTHUR M SCHLESINGER JR

6 Anti-intellectualism has long been the anti-Semitism of the businessman.
> *Partisan Review* 4 Mar 53

E R SHIPP

7 The rest is hamburger history.
> On the aftermath of Ray Kroc's 1961 buy-out of the original McDonald's holdings, NY *Times* 27 Feb 85

GERALD M SLATON, personnel consultant

8 There are the daddies, who want to be in charge, the mommies, who do the nurturing, and the various children vying for their attention.
> Quoted in "Playing Office Politics" *Newsweek* 16 Sep 85

JOSEPH SMITH, consumer research specialist

9 The laundry has its hands on *my* dirty shirts, sheets, towels and tablecloths, and who knows what tales they tell.
> On business relationships with people in service industries, quoted by Margot Slade "Butchers, Bakers and Intimacy" NY *Times* 11 Aug 86

LEE SMITH

10 The subordinate is likely to feel that the examiner has taken a sample of his bone marrow.
> On the reason Keizo Saji, chairman of Suntory Ltd, asks "Why?" five times in rapid succession during meetings, *Fortune* 7 Jan 84

GERRY SPENCE, trial lawyer

11 What the insurance companies have done is to reverse the business so that the public at large insures the insurance companies.
> *Time* 24 Mar 86

GEORGE STEINER, Professor of Comparative Literature, University of Geneva

12 More and more lower-middle-income families either live their lives in debt or leave the city altogether. The boom is strictly at the penthouse level.
> To Royal Society of Arts, London, NY *Times* 26 May 85

TIME MAGAZINE

13 The world's biggest company is a bundle of paradoxes wrapped in a string of superlatives. It makes a product that cannot be bought and lives on a commodity that cannot be seen.
> On AT&T, 29 May 64

14 Kodak is one of a growing number of recession-plagued companies that are trying to make their payrolls lean without being mean.
> On early-retirement policies, 21 Feb 83

ANDREW TOBIAS

15 In a world where the time it takes to travel (supersonic) or to bake a potato (microwave) or to process a million calculations (microchip) shrinks inexorably, only three things have remained constant and unrushed: the nine months it takes to have a baby, the nine months it takes to untangle a credit card dispute and the nine months it takes to publish a hardcover book.
> "Hot Leads and Lead Time" *Savvy* May 80

ROBERT TOWNSEND

16 If you don't do it excellently, don't do it at all.

Because if it's not excellent, it won't be profitable or fun, and if you're not in business for fun or profit, what the hell are you doing there?
Further Up the Organization Knopf 84

1 One of the most important tasks of a manager is to eliminate his people's excuses for failure.
ib

2 Most people in big companies are administered, not led. They are treated as personnel, not people.
ib

3 "Top" management is supposed to be a tree full of owls—hooting when management heads into the wrong part of the forest. I'm still unpersuaded they even know where the forest is.
ib

4 If you have to have a policy manual, publish the Ten Commandments.
ib

JAY L TUROFF, Chairman, NYC Taxi and Limousine Commission

5 When a man owns the tin, he has a vested interest in it.
On independent taxi drivers who purchase the required tin medallions from the city for as much as $100,000, NY *Times* 16 Dec 85

GORE VIDAL

6 Until the rise of American advertising, it never occurred to anyone anywhere in the world that the teenager was a captive in a hostile world of adults.
Rocking the Boat Little, Brown 62

PAUL A VOLCKER, Chairman, Federal Reserve System

7 What's the subject of life—to get rich? All of those fellows out there getting rich could be dancing around the real subject of life.
Newsweek 24 Feb 86

JOAN WALKER

8 It took at least 200 people, in 5 states, 4 months to turn out a Ford Thunderbird commercial that lasted 90 seconds.
NY *Herald Tribune* 5 Jul 64

MIKE WALLACE

9 There are more queens crowned in one night in Dallas than in 400 years in Westminster Abbey.
On sales incentive awards from Mary Kay Cosmetics, *60 Minutes* CBS TV 25 Jul 82

THOMAS L WHISLER, Professor of Business, University of Chicago

10 Men are going to have to learn to be managers in a world where the organization will come close to consisting of all chiefs and one Indian. The Indian, of course, is the computer.
Christian Science Monitor 21 Apr 64

WILLIAM H WHYTE JR

11 The onlooker had better wipe the sympathy off his face. What he has seen is a revolution, not the home of little cogs and drones. What he has seen is the dormitory of the next managerial class.
On Levittown, Long Island, and similar suburbs, *Fortune* May 53

LEON WIESELTIER

12 Her book about the money in sex gives you the feeling of the sex in money.
On Sydney Biddle Barrows's *Mayflower Madam*, with Michael Novak, Arbor House 86, *Vanity Fair* Dec 86

13 The effort was to summon to the bosoms of her personnel the sort of man that Barrows likes to call "nice." Nice meant rich.
ib

DAVID WILD

14 Greenmail is, quite logically, blackmail of a different color.
On how takeover buyers increase stock prices for resale to management, "The Tax Adviser" *Esquire* Apr 85

MICHAEL WINERIP

15 If Jack Kerouac had set out to find a real bookstore in the suburbs, he would still be on the road, Phileas Fogg would still be in the air, the Ancient Mariner wouldn't have had time to tell anyone his story.
On bookstore chains, NY *Times* 28 Oct 86

WALTER WRISTON

16 Our banking system grew by accident; and whenever something happens by accident, it becomes a religion.
Business Week 20 Jan 75

BERNARD WYSOCKI

17 Confusing for AT&T shareholders, frustrating for many AT&T customers, a mixed blessing for AT&T competitors and a boon, if sometimes a boondoggle, for a small army of lawyers, consultants and stockbrokers.
On breakup of AT&T, in review of W Brooke

Tunstall's *Disconnecting Parties* McGraw-Hill 85, *Wall Street Journal* 8 Apr 85

PHILIP YOUNG, economist, Pace University, NYC

1 For Hispanics, the store is the end, the goal. For Koreans, it's entry level.

On motivation of ethnic merchants, NY *Times* 19 Mar 85

EDUCATION
Educators & Participants

ANONYMOUS

2 If you promise not to believe everything your child says happens at this school, I'll promise not to believe everything he says happens at home.

Note to students' parents from an English schoolmaster, quoted in *Wall Street Journal* 4 Jan 85

SYLVIA ASHTON-WARNER

3 The truth is that I am enslaved. . . . in one vast love affair with 70 children.

On life of a teacher, *Spinster* Simon & Schuster 59

4 I see the mind of the 5-year-old as a volcano with two vents: destructiveness and creativeness.

Teacher Simon & Schuster 63

THOMAS BAILEY, Florida State Superintendent of Schools

5 There must be such a thing as a child with average ability, but you can't find a parent who will admit that it is his child.

Wall Street Journal 17 Dec 61

6 Start a program for gifted children, and every parent demands that his child be enrolled.

ib

EDWARD C BANFIELD, Professor of Government, Harvard

7 A good professor is a bastard perverse enough to think what *he* thinks is important, not what government thinks is important.

Life 9 Jun 67

JACQUES BARZUN, Dean of Graduate School, Columbia University

8 Teaching is not a lost art, but the regard for it is a lost tradition.

Newsweek 5 Dec 55

9 The test and the use of man's education is that he finds pleasure in the exercise of his mind.

"Science vs the Humanities" *Saturday Evening Post* 3 May 58

WILLIAM J BENNETT, US Secretary of Education

10 [The shortage of student loans] may require . . . divestiture of certain sorts—stereo divestiture, automobile divestiture, three-weeks-at-the-beach divestiture.

NY *Times* 12 Feb 85

11 The secretary of education does not work for the education establishment. The secretary works for the American people.

Christian Science Monitor 12 Mar 85

12 Our common language is . . . English. And our common task is to ensure that our non-English-speaking children learn this common language.

NY *Times* 26 Sep 85

13 The elementary school must assume as its sublime and most solemn responsibility the task of teaching every child in it to read. Any school that does not accomplish this has failed.

Report on condition of elementary schools, quoted in *ib* 3 Sep 86

BARBARA ARONSTEIN BLACK, Dean, Columbia Law School

14 Where I am today has *everything* to do with the years I spent hanging on to a career by my fingernails.

On appointment as dean after raising a family and then returning to studies, NY *Times* 2 Jan 86

DEREK BOK, President, Harvard

15 I won't say there aren't any Harvard graduates who have never asserted a superior attitude. But they have done so to our great embarrassment and in no way represent the Harvard I know.

M Jun 84

LEON BOTSTEIN, President, Bard College

16 At best, most college presidents are running something that is somewhere between a faltering corporation and a hotel.

Center Mar 77

FRANK L BOYDEN, Headmaster, Deerfield Academy, MA

1 Work 'em hard, play 'em hard, feed 'em up to the nines and send 'em to bed so tired that they are asleep before their heads are on the pillow.
News summaries 2 Jan 54

2 I never reprimand a boy in the evening—darkness and a troubled mind are a poor combination.
Life 30 Nov 62

ERNEST BOYER, President, Carnegie Foundation for Advancement of Teaching

3 A poor surgeon hurts 1 person at a time. A poor teacher hurts 130.
People 17 Mar 86

KINGMAN BREWSTER, President, Yale

4 If I take refuge in ambiguity, I assure you that it's quite conscious.
On appointment as president, quoted in NY *Herald Tribune* 14 Oct 63

5 Universities should be safe havens where ruthless examination of realities will not be distorted by the aim to please or inhibited by the risk of displeasure.
Inaugural address 11 Apr 64

6 Maybe you are the "cool" generation ... If coolness means a capacity to stay calm and use your head in the service of ends passionately believed in, then it has my admiration.
Baccalaureate address 12 Jun 66

PETER BRODIE, classics teacher, Foxcroft School, Middleburg VA

7 What is important—what lasts—in another language is not what is said but what is written. For the essence of an age, we look to its poetry and its prose, not its talk shows.
NY *Times* 18 Jul 84

8 One attraction of Latin is that you can immerse yourself in the poems of Horace and Catullus without fretting over how to say, "Have a nice day."
ib

9 There is a negative proof of the value of Latin: No one seems to boast of not knowing it.
ib

MARY INGRAHAM BUNTING, President, Radcliffe College

10 When her last child is off to school, we don't want the talented woman wasting her time in work far below her capacity. We want her to come out running.
On establishing institute for women's independent study, *Life* 13 Jan 61

HERBERT BUTTERFIELD, Vice Chancellor, Cambridge

11 The academic mind can eat away the very basis of its own assurance ... produce contortions when it tries to bend over backward ... allow itself to be dismayed by the picture it has created of relentless historical process.
Address on his retirement 2 Oct 61

12 The very fact of its finding itself in agreement with other minds perturbs it, so that it hunts for points of divergence, feeling the urgent need to make it clear that at least it reached the same conclusions by a different route.
ib

GUIDO CALABRESI, Dean, Yale Law School

13 You never replace a great scholar who retires. If you try to do that, you end up with burnt-out volcanoes.
On A Bartlett Giamatti's retirement as president of Yale, NY *Times* 12 Dec 85

BRAD CARTER, Chairman, Religious Studies Department, Southern Methodist University

14 They wanted a great university without building a great university. They knew a lot about football, but not a lot about academia.
On National Collegiate Athletic Assn's suspension of SMU's football program for recruiting violations, NY *Times* 5 Mar 87

DORA CHAPLIN, Professor of Christian Education, General Theological Seminary, NYC

15 Everyone knows a good deal about one child—himself.
The Privilege of Teaching Morehouse-Barlow 62

SIDNEY M B COULLING, Professor of English, Washington and Lee University

16 Of all the threats to Phi Beta Kappa ... probably none is more pervasive than that of the so-called counterculture, with its elevation of instinct over intellect, mysticism over reason, consciousness over scholarship, sensitivity over discipline.
Wall Street Journal 7 Mar 71

ARCHIBALD COX, Professor of Law, Harvard

17 A great many college graduates come here

thinking of lawyers as social engineers arguing the great Constitutional issues.
> San Francisco *Examiner & Chronicle* 6 Jun 82

JOHN SLOAN DICKEY, President, Dartmouth

1 The American male at the peak of his physical powers and appetites, driving 160 big white horses across the scenes of an increasingly open society, with weekend money in his pocket and with little prior exposure to trouble and tragedy, personifies "an accident going to happen."
> "Conscience and the Undergraduate" *Atlantic* Apr 55

2 There is no more vulnerable human combination than an undergraduate.
> *ib*

OTIS C EDWARDS, Episcopal priest

3 To be loose with grammar is to be loose with the worst woman in the world.
> Lecture at Nashotah House Episcopal Seminary, Nashotah WI, 10 Jan 66

ELLIOT EISNER, professor, Stanford School of Education

4 We have inadvertently designed a system in which being good at what you do as a teacher is not formally rewarded, while being poor at what you do is seldom corrected nor penalized.
> NY *Times* 3 Sep 85

SISTER EVANGELIST RSM

5 I have one rule—attention. They give me theirs and I give them mine.
> On teaching high-school students, Billings MT *Gazette* 4 May 80

JOHN FISCHER, Dean, Teachers College, Columbia University

6 The essence of our effort to see that every child has a chance must be to assure each an equal opportunity, not to become equal, but to become different—to realize whatever unique potential of body, mind and spirit he or she possesses.
> San Francisco *Examiner* 19 Mar 73

CLAUDE M FUESS

7 I was still learning when I taught my last class.
> After 40 years at Phillips Academy, Andover MA, *Independent Schoolmaster* Atlantic Monthly Press 52

JOHN KENNETH GALBRAITH

8 The commencement speech is not, I think, a wholly satisfactory manifestation of our culture.
> Commencement address at American University, Washington DC, *Time* 18 Jun 84

9 Commencement oratory . . . must eschew anything that smacks of partisan politics, political preference, sex, religion or unduly firm opinion. Nonetheless, there must be a speech: Speeches in our culture are the vacuum that fills a vacuum.
> *ib*

DAVID P GARDNER, President, University of Utah, Salt Lake City

10 Much that passes for education . . . is not education at all but ritual. The fact is that we are being educated when we know it least.
> *Vital Speeches* 15 Apr 75

11 We learn simply by the exposure of living, and what we learn most natively is the tradition in which we live.
> *ib*

A BARTLETT GIAMATTI, President, Yale

12 A liberal education is at the heart of a civil society, and at the heart of a liberal education is the act of teaching.
> "The American Teacher" *Harper's* Jul 80

13 Teaching is an instinctual art, mindful of potential, craving of realizations, a pausing, seamless process.
> *ib*

14 Teachers believe they have a gift for giving; it drives them with the same irrepressible drive that drives others to create a work of art or a market or a building.
> *ib*

15 On a good day, I view the job [of president] as directing an orchestra. On the dark days, it is more like that of a clutch—engaging the engine to effect forward motion, while taking greater friction.
> NY *Times* 6 Mar 83

16 There are many who lust for the simple answers of doctrine or decree. They are on the left and right. They are not confined to a single part of the society. They are terrorists of the mind.
> Final baccalaureate address, *ib* 26 May 86

Virginia Gildersleeve, Dean Emeritus, Barnard College

1 I was resolved to sustain and preserve in my college the bite of the mind, the chance to stand face to face with truth, the good life lived in a small, various, highly articulate and democratic society.
Many a Good Crusade Macmillan 54

2 The ability to think straight, some knowledge of the past, some vision of the future, some skill to do useful service, some urge to fit that service into the well-being of the community—these are the most vital things education must try to produce.
ib

Robert F Goheen, President, Princeton

3 If you feel that you have both feet planted on level ground, then the university has failed you.
Baccalaureate address, *Time* 23 Jun 61

4 In the realm of ideas it is better to let the mind sally forth, even if some precious preconceptions suffer a mauling.
Commencement address, NY *Times* 19 Jun 66

Samuel Gould, Chancellor, University of California, Santa Barbara

5 If the state of oratory that inundates our educational institutions during the month of June could be transformed into rain for southern California, we should all be happily awash or waterlogged.
Time 27 Jun 60

Hanna Holborn Gray, President, University of Chicago

6 There was a perception that life here was—I won't say gray, that's hard for me—but beige.
On a guidebook's observation that "studying is the U of C student's favorite pastime," *Time* 28 May 84

7 The university's characteristic state may be summarized by the words of the lady who said, "I have enough money to last me the rest of my life, unless I buy something."
Christian Science Monitor 25 Nov 86

A Whitney Griswold, President, Yale

8 A Socrates in every classroom.
On his ambitious standard for faculty, *Time* 11 Jun 51

9 Could *Hamlet* have been written by a committee, or the *Mona Lisa* painted by a club? Could the New Testament have been composed as a conference report? Creative ideas do not spring from groups. They spring from individuals. The divine spark leaps from the finger of God to the finger of Adam.
Baccalaureate address 8 Jun 57

S I Hayakawa, President, San Francisco State College

10 How anybody dresses is indicative of his self-concept. If students are dirty and ragged, it indicates they are not interested in tidying up their intellects either.
LA *Herald-Examiner* 8 Apr 73

Theodore M Hesburgh, President, Notre Dame

11 Anyone who refuses to speak out off campus does not deserve to be listened to on campus.
Quoted by Clark Kerr NY *Times* 18 Sep 84

Richard Hofstadter, Professor of American History, Columbia University

12 The delicate thing about the university is that it has a mixed character, that it is suspended between its position in the eternal world, with all its corruption and evils and cruelties, and the splendid world of our imagination.
1968 commencement address, quoted in "Parting Shots: A Century of Commencement Speeches" *Saturday Review* 12 May 79

13 A university's essential character is that of being a center of free inquiry and criticism—a thing not to be sacrificed for anything else.
ib

14 A university is not a service station. Neither is it a political society, nor a meeting place for political societies. With all its limitations and failures, and they are invariably many, it is the best and most benign side of our society insofar as that society aims to cherish the human mind.
ib

Michael K Hooker, Chancellor, University of Maryland

15 What I'm concerned about is the people who *don't* dwell on the meaninglessness of their lives, or the meaningfulness of it—who just pursue mindless entertainment.
Quoted by Rushworth M Kidder *Christian Science Monitor* 1 Oct 86

SHIRLEY M HUFSTEDLER, US Secretary of Education

1 I'm bilingual. I speak English and I speak educationese.
   Newsweek 12 May 80

ROBERT M HUTCHINS, Chancellor, University of Chicago

2 Education is a kind of continuing dialogue, and a dialogue assumes ... different points of view.
   On academic freedom, *Time* 8 Dec 52

3 It is not so important to be serious as it is to be serious about the important things. The monkey wears an expression of seriousness which would do credit to any college student, but the monkey is serious because he itches.
   Quote 3 Aug 58

4 It has been said that we have not had the three R's in America, we had the six R's: remedial readin', remedial 'ritin' and remedial 'rithmetic.
   NY *Herald Tribune* 22 Apr 63

LOUIS JOHANNOT, Headmaster, Institut Le Rosey, Switzerland

5 The only reason I always try to meet and know the parents better is because it helps me to forgive their children.
   Life 7 May 65

BARNABY C KEENEY, President, Brown University

6 The scramble to get into college is going to be so terrible in the next few years that students are going to put up with almost anything, even an education.
   Time 29 Aug 55

7 At college age, you can tell who is best at taking tests and going to school, but you can't tell who the best people are. That worries the hell out of me.
   Recalled on his death 18 Jun 80

GEORGE F KENNAN, Professor Emeritus, Institute for Advanced Study, Princeton NJ

8 The very concept of history implies the scholar and the reader. Without a generation of civilized people to study history, to preserve its records, to absorb its lessons and relate them to its own problems, history, too, would lose its meaning.
   On receiving Gold Medal for History from the Amer Academy and Institute of Arts and Letters, NY *Times* 27 May 84

9 Not only the studying and writing of history but also the honoring of it both represent affirmations of a certain defiant faith—a desperate, unreasoning faith, if you will—but faith nevertheless in the endurance of this threatened world—faith in the total essentiality of historical continuity.
   ib

CLARK KERR, President, University of California, Berkeley

10 A university anywhere can aim no higher than to be as British as possible for the sake of the undergraduates, as German as possible for the sake of the public at large—and as confused as possible for the preservation of the whole uneasy balance.
   Lecture at Harvard, "The Uses of the University," quoted in NY *Times* 26 Apr 63

ROBERT J KIBBEE, Chancellor, City University of NY

11 The quality of a university is measured more by the kind of student it turns out than the kind it takes in.
   NY *Times* 27 Jul 71

12 Over the years, we have come to identify quality in a college not by whom it serves but by how many students it excludes. Let us not be a sacred priesthood protecting the temple, but rather the fulfillers of dreams.
   In defense of open admissions, recalled on his death 16 Jun 82

GRAYSON KIRK, President, Columbia University

13 The most important function of education at any level is to develop the personality of the individual and the significance of his life to himself and to others. This is the basic architecture of a life; the rest is ornamentation and decoration of the structure.
   Quote 27 Jan 63

SUSANNA KLEIN, senior, Wellesley College

14 I have lived in three dormitories over four years and I have never seen a naked man, other than in the privacy of my own room.
   Defending classmates against charges of "sexual immorality" brought by a student's father, NY *Times* 1 May 76

JONATHAN KOZOL

15 Pick battles big enough to matter, small enough to win.
   On Being a Teacher Continuum 81

LEON LESSINGER, Dean, College of Education, USC

1 Human beings are full of emotion, and the teacher who knows how to use it will have dedicated learners. It means sending dominant signals instead of submissive ones with your eyes, body and voice.
  Newsweek 8 Mar 76

WILMARTH S LEWIS, Selections Committee, Yale

2 The Yale president must be a Yale man. Not too far to the right, too far to the left or a middle-of-the-roader. Ready to give the ultimate word on every subject under the sun from how to handle the Russians to why undergraduates riot in the spring. Profound with a wit that bubbles up and brims over in a cascade of brilliance. You may have guessed who the leading candidate is, but there is a question about him: Is God a Yale man?
  1950 statement recalled in 1970s when Yale considered a woman president, NY *Times* 24 Apr 77

FRANK J MACCHIAROLA, Schools Chancellor, NYC

3 If Chrysler had an assembly line in which the same number of cars got through as kids do in our school system, people would be scandalized.
  NY *Times* 9 Jan 83

CHARLES C MARSHALL III, former member, Students for a Democratic Society

4 I think a lot of it was puberty.
  On student rioting of 1960s, *Time* 14 Apr 80

SYBIL MARSHALL

5 I had learned to respect the intelligence, integrity, creativity and capacity for deep thought and hard work latent somewhere in every child; they had learned that I differed from them only in years and experience, and that as I, an ordinary human being, loved and respected them, I expected payment in kind.
  On 18 years as teacher in a one-room school in rural England, *An Experiment in Education* Cambridge 63

BENJAMIN E MAYS, former President, Morehouse College, Atlanta GA

6 The tragedy of life doesn't lie in not reaching your goal. The tragedy lies in having no goal to reach.
  Quoted by Marian Wright Edelman in commencement address at Barnard College, NY *Times* 16 May 85

CHRISTA MCAULIFFE, teacher, Concord NH

7 I cannot join the space program and restart my life as an astronaut, but this opportunity to connect my abilities as an educator with my interests in history and space is a unique opportunity to fulfill my early fantasies.
  From her winning essay in NASA's nationwide search for the first teacher to travel in space, released after her death with six others aboard the space shuttle Challenger 28 Jan 86

R M MCCALLUM, Master, Pembroke College, Oxford

8 Fulbright is responsible for the greatest movement of scholars across the face of the earth since the fall of Constantinople in 1453.
  On US Senator J William Fulbright's sponsorship of Fulbright scholarships, *Saturday Evening Post* 23 Mar 63

WILLIAM H MCNEILL, Professor of History, University of Chicago

9 My job is to bore you and let the hardness of your seat and the warmth of your robe prepare you for what is to come.
  Commencement address at Bard College 26 May 84

JOHN MERRIMAN, Professor of History and Master, Branford College, Yale

10 Yale is more than going to classes. Yale is staggering on in the best fashion possible.
  On 10-week strike of workers, NY *Times* 1 Dec 84

V S NAIPAUL

11 Ignorant people in preppy clothes are more dangerous to America than oil embargoes.
  After a year of teaching at Wesleyan University, *Time* 21 May 79

MAURICE NATANSON, Professor of Philosophy, Yale

12 What a teacher doesn't say . . . is a telling part of what a student hears.
  NY *Times* 6 Jan 85

NEW YORK CITY BOARD OF EDUCATION

13 It's like being grounded for 18 years.
  Poster warning against teen pregnancy, pictured in NY *Times* 12 Oct 86

14 Don't make a baby if you can't be a father.
  ib

EWALD B NYQUIST, NY State Education Commissioner

1 Equality is not when a female Einstein gets promoted to assistant professor: Equality is when a female schlemiel moves ahead as fast as a male schlemiel.
   NY *Times* 9 Oct 75

JACK W PELTASON, President, Amer Council on Education

2 The Greeks had their laurel wreaths. The English have their honors list. The French are always wearing ribbons in their lapels. In this country honorary degrees from universities serve that function.
   NY *Times* 27 May 84

JAMES A PERKINS, President, Cornell

3 The acquisition of knowledge is the mission of research, the transmission of knowledge is the mission of teaching and the application of knowledge is the mission of public service.
   From Stafford Little Lectures at Princeton, quoted in NY *Times* 3 Nov 66

JOHN PHILLIPS, President, National Assn of Independent Colleges and Universities

4 The real test is whether we are going to have an efficient, program-oriented department or just another federal bureaucracy run by a group of people with their feet caught in their underwear.
   On new US Department of Education, *Newsweek* 12 May 80

NATHAN M PUSEY, President, Harvard

5 The teacher's task is not to implant facts but to place the subject to be learned in front of the learner and, through sympathy, emotion, imagination and patience, to awaken in the learner the restless drive for answers and insights which enlarge the personal life and give it meaning.
   NY *Times* 22 Mar 59

6 We live in a time of such rapid change and growth of knowledge that only he who is in a fundamental sense a scholar—that is, a person who continues to learn and inquire—can hope to keep pace, let alone play the role of guide.
   The Age of the Scholar Belknap Press/Harvard 63

JOHN A RASSIAS, Professor of Romance Languages, Dartmouth

7 Language study is a route to maturity. Indeed, in language study as in life, if a person is the same today as he was yesterday, it would be an act of mercy to pronounce him dead and to place him in a coffin, rather than in a classroom.
   Quote 26 May 74

8 Language is a living, kicking, growing, flitting, evolving reality, and the teacher should spontaneously reflect its vibrant and protean qualities.
   ib

PHILIP RIEFF, Professor of Sociology, University of Pennsylvania

9 Scholarship is polite argument.
   NY *Herald Tribune* 1 Jan 61

MANLEY E ROGERS, Director of Admissions, West Point

10 Robert E Lee didn't make it the first time and Jefferson Davis took the vacancy. Pershing didn't make it for two years, MacArthur couldn't get in the first year and Eisenhower took an extra year of high school to get in. [Patton] took three years to get in and five to get out.
   On prominent alumni who were not initially accepted by West Point, NY *Times* 7 May 85

11 Harvard doesn't consider anyone a loss until he dies without a diploma, because they say he can always come back and finish.
   On West Point's 33 percent attrition rate compared with that of private institutions, *ib*

RUTHERFORD D ROGERS, librarian, Yale

12 We're drowning in information and starving for knowledge.
   On the enormous number of books, periodicals and other documents published each year, quoted in NY *Times* 25 Feb 85

HENRY ROSOVSKY, former Dean, Faculty of Arts and Sciences, Harvard

13 Harvard admissions is an exercise in social engineering.
   Quoted by Colin Campbell "The Harvard Factor" NY *Times* 20 Jul 86

GEORGE C ST JOHN, Headmaster, Choate School, Wallingford CT

14 We save a boy's soul at the same time we are saving his algebra.
   Recalled on his death 21 Jan 66

Benno C Schmidt Jr, President, Yale

1 Yale is a crucible in American life for the accommodation of intellectual achievement, of wisdom, of refinement, with the democratic ideals of openness, of social justice and of equal opportunity.

> On election as president, quoted in NY *Times* 11 Dec 85

2 Yale's greatness carries an urgent need to guard against the fall of excellence into exclusivity, of refinement into preciousness, of elegance into class and convention.
> *ib*

3 To take the measure of oneself by reference to one's colleagues leads to envy or complacency rather than constructive self-examination.

> On competition in academia, *Christian Science Monitor* 12 Dec 85

Charles Seymour, President, Yale

4 We seek the truth and will endure the consequences.

> Recalled on his death 11 Aug 63

George N Shuster, President Emeritus, Hunter College

5 You ought not to educate a woman as if she were a man, or to educate her as if she were not.

> *The Ground I Walked On* Farrar, Straus 61

Alan Simpson, President, Vassar College

6 An educated man . . . is thoroughly inoculated against humbug, thinks for himself and tries to give his thoughts, in speech or on paper, some style.

> On becoming president, *Newsweek* 1 Jul 63

Harold Taylor, President, Sarah Lawrence College

7 A student is not a professional athlete. . . . He is not a little politician or junior senator looking for angles . . . an amateur promoter, a gladhander, embryo Rotarian, café-society leader, quiz kid or man about town. A student is a person who is learning to fulfill his powers and to find ways of using them in the service of mankind.

> News summaries 3 Sep 56

8 Most of the most important experiences that truly educate cannot be arranged ahead of time with any precision.

> "The Private World of the Man with a Book" *Saturday Review* 7 Jan 61

John Thorn, Headmaster, Winchester College

9 Whatever else I do before finally I go to my grave, I hope it will not be looking after young people.

> Quoted by Martin O'Brien "Inside Britain's Brainiest School" *M* Feb 85

Hugh Trevor-Roper, Professor of Modern History, Oxford

10 The function of a genius is not to give new answers, but to pose new questions which time and mediocrity can resolve.

> *Man and Events* Harper 57

Barbara M White, President, Mills College

11 The basic purpose of a liberal arts education is to liberate the human being to exercise his or her potential to the fullest.

> *Christian Science Monitor* 8 Sep 76

Eugene S Wilson, Dean of Admissions, Amherst

12 Only the curious will learn and only the resolute overcome the obstacles to learning. The quest quotient has always excited me more than the intelligence quotient.

> *Reader's Digest* Apr 68

Mary J Wilson, elementary school teacher

13 I'm never going to be a movie star. But then, in all probability, Liz Taylor is never going to teach first and second grade.

> *Newsweek* 4 Jul 76

Nancy Zerby

14 The girls aren't going to know what they're doing because they're freshmen, and the school's not going to know what it's doing because we're girls.

> On being among the first women admitted to Yale, NY *Times* 30 Apr 69

Observers & Critics

J Donald Adams

15 There are times when I think that the ideal library is composed solely of reference books. They are like understanding friends—always ready to meet your mood, always ready to change the subject when you have had enough of this or that.

> NY *Times* 1 Apr 56

Edward Albee

16 American critics are like American universi-

ties. They both have dull and half-dead faculties.

> To NY Cultural League, news summaries 6 May 69

CHRISTOPHER ANDREAE

1 Ignorance is a *right*! Education is eroding one of the few democratic freedoms remaining to us.

> *Christian Science Monitor* 21 Feb 80

ANONYMOUS

2 A major cause of deterioration in the use of the English language is very simply the enormous increase in the number of people who are using it.

> Quoted by Robert McCrum, William Cran and Robert MacNeil *The Story of English* Viking 86

BERNARD BARUCH

3 I am quite sure that in the hereafter she will take me by the hand and lead me to my proper seat.

> On one of his early teachers, news summaries 29 Aug 55

SIMONE DE BEAUVOIR

4 These worthy schoolteachers were not over-burdened with diplomas, but as far as devotion and morality were concerned, they were second to none; they wore plum-colored silk blouses that caressed my cheeks when they pressed me to their bosoms.

> On her early teachers, *When Things of the Spirit Come First* Pantheon 82

JIM BENCIVENGA

5 The single-room worlds remain strong icons at the heart of our national memory, permanent as any church spire piercing the New England sky.

> On country schools, *Christian Science Monitor* 13 Feb 85

6 From facing down rattlesnakes in broom closets with the spring thaw to fending off ranch-hand bullies (or lovelorn cowboys), teachers had to be wise in the ways of the world.

> *ib*

BERNARD BERENSON

7 German is of stone, limestone, pudding stone, marble, granite even, and so to a considerable degree is English, whereas French is bronze and gives out a metallic resonance with tones that neither German nor English tolerate.

> Quoted by Meryle Secrest *Being Bernard Berenson* Holt, Rinehart & Winston 79

LEONARD BERNSTEIN

8 [It was] an initiation into the love of learning, of learning how to learn, that was revealed to me by my BLS masters as a matter of interdisciplinary cognition—that is, learning to know something by its relation to something else.

> On Boston Latin School, NY *Times* 22 Nov 84

LISA BIRNBACH

9 The University of Miami is not a campus with visible school spirit, just visible tan lines.

> *Lisa Birnbach's College Book* Ballentine 84

DANIEL J BOORSTIN, Librarian of Congress

10 Knowledge is not simply another commodity. On the contrary. Knowledge is never used up. It increases by diffusion and grows by dispersion.

> To House Appropriations Subcommittee, quoted in NY *Times* 23 Feb 86

WILLIAM E BROCK, US Secretary of Labor

11 It's an insane tragedy that 700,000 people get a diploma each year and can't read the damned diploma.

> To Senate Committee on Labor and Human Resources, NY *Times* 14 Jan 87

JOHN MASON BROWN

12 She knows what is the best purpose of education: not to be frightened by the best but to treat it as part of daily life.

> Tribute to classical scholar Edith Hamilton, *Publishers Weekly* 17 Mar 58

JEROME BRUNER

13 The shrewd guess, the fertile hypothesis, the courageous leap to a tentative conclusion—these are the most valuable coins of the thinker at work. But in most schools guessing is heavily penalized and is associated somehow with laziness.

> *The Process of Education* Harvard 60

WILLIAM F BUCKLEY JR

14 The majority of the senior class of Vassar does not desire my company and I must confess, having read specimens of their thought and sentiments, that I do not desire the company of the majority of the senior class of Vassar.

> Withdrawing as commencement speaker after students protested his conservative record, NY *Times* 20 May 80

ROBERT W BURCHFIELD

1 American English is the greatest influence of English everywhere.

On completing lexicographical work on *A Supplement to the Oxford English Dictionary*, quoted in *Newsweek* 2 Jun 86

WARREN E BURGER, Chief Justice, US Supreme Court

2 [We must have] a program to "learn the way out of prison."

Calling for programs that teach convicts to read and write, to Amer Bar Assn, Houston, 8 Feb 81

CARNEGIE CORPORATION OF NEW YORK

3 Teachers will not come to the school knowing all they have to know, but knowing how to figure out what they need to know, where to get it and how to help others make meaning out of it.

On establishment of a committee to set teaching standards, *A Nation Prepared*, report quoted in NY *Times* 16 May 86

4 Teachers must think for themselves if they are to help others think for themselves.
ib

WINSTON CHURCHILL

5 Study history, study history. In history lies all the secrets of statecraft.

Quoted by James Humes *Churchill* Stein & Day 80

6 I got into my bones the essential structure of the ordinary British sentence—which is a noble thing.

On studying remedial English for three terms, quoted by William Manchester *The Last Lion* Little, Brown 83

CYRIL CONNOLLY

7 [The headmistress] was an able instructress in French and history and we learned with her as fast as fear could teach us.

From his essay "Such, Such Were the Joys," quoted in *Newsweek* 19 Mar 84

NORMAN COUSINS

8 A library, to modify the famous metaphor of Socrates, should be the delivery room for the birth of ideas—a place where history comes to life.

Amer Library Assn *Bulletin* Oct 54

JEAN SPARKS DUCEY, librarian

9 People ought to listen more slowly!

On confused requests such as "Do you have the wrath of grapes?" and "I want a book about the Abdominal Snowman," *Christian Science Monitor* 9 Dec 86

JOHN FOSTER DULLES, US Secretary of State

10 I wouldn't attach too much importance to these student riots. I remember when I was a student at the Sorbonne in Paris, I used to go out and riot occasionally.

On Indonesian demonstrations, news summaries 15 Apr 58

RUDOLF FLESCH

11 Johnny couldn't read . . . for the simple reason that nobody ever showed him how.
Why Johnny Can't Read Harper 55

E M FORSTER

12 They go forth with well-developed bodies, fairly developed minds and undeveloped hearts. An undeveloped heart—not a cold one. The difference is important.

On British public school students, *Life* 2 Apr 51

ROBERT FROST

13 Education is the ability to listen to almost anything without losing your temper or your self-confidence.
Reader's Digest Apr 60

14 Education doesn't change life much. It just lifts trouble to a higher plane of regard.
Quote 9 July 61

15 College is a refuge from hasty judgment.
ib

J WILLIAM FULBRIGHT, US Senator

16 The exchange program is the thing that reconciles me to all the difficulties of political life.

On Fulbright scholarships established after World War II, *New Yorker* 10 May 58

17 To avoid a nuclear war. . . . you may think that's pretentious but that's its main purpose.

On rationale for establishing Fulbright scholarships, NY *Times* 26 Jun 86

VARTAN GREGORIAN, President, NY Public Library

18 It meant that New York philanthropists, New York society, would now rediscover the library. . . . that learning, books, education have glamour, that self-improvement has glamour, that hope has glamour.

On Brooke Astor's decision to devote herself to raising money for the library, NY *Times* 20 May 84

1 The book is here to stay. What we're doing is symbolic of the peaceful coexistence of the book and the computer.

On computerization of card catalog, *Time* 25 Feb 85

2 Libraries keep the records on behalf of all humanity. . . . the unique and the absurd, the wise and [the] fragments of stupidity.

New Yorker 14 Apr 86

HENRY ANATOLE GRUNWALD

3 Everything can be learned, including, to a very large extent, to be what you are not. You can learn to be pretty if you are plain, charming if you are dull, thin if you are fat, youthful if you are aging, how to write though you are inarticulate, how to make money though you are not good with figures.

Time 5 Jul 76

4 Nagging questions remain: Where is the line between making the most of one's potential and reaching for the unattainable? Where is the line between education as a tool and education as a kind of magic? The line is blurred and that is why when education fails, disillusionment is so bitter.

ib

EDITH HAMILTON

5 To be able to be caught up into the world of thought—that is educated.

Saturday Evening Post 27 Sep 58

SYDNEY J HARRIS

6 Nothing is as easy to make as a promise this winter to do something next summer; this is how commencement speakers are caught.

Chicago *Daily News* 20 Feb 58

GENE R HAWES

7 Intellect won, though not easily or decisively. Gradually, painfully, the upper-class colleges severed as amicably as possible their links with the least-qualified members of the prominent families.

Analysis of Social Register and Ivy League college enrollments, NY *Times* 14 Mar 64

LARRY HAWKINS, founder, Institute for Athletics and Education

8 We need programs that will teach athletes how to *spell* "jump shot" rather than how to shoot it.

Quoted by Preston Greene "A Mind *Is* a Terrible Thing to Waste" *Christian Science Monitor* 13 Aug 86

GILBERT HIGHET

9 A teacher must believe in the value and interest of his subject as a doctor believes in health.

The Art of Teaching Knopf 50

E D HIRSCH JR

10 We have ignored cultural literacy in thinking about education . . . We ignore the air we breathe until it is thin or foul. Cultural literacy is the oxygen of social intercourse.

Cultural Literacy: What Every American Needs to Know Houghton Mifflin 87

ERIC HOFFER

11 The education explosion is producing a vast number of people who want to live significant, important lives but lack the ability to satisfy this craving for importance by individual achievement. The country is being swamped with nobodies who want to be somebodies.

Wall Street Journal 23 Mar 78

HERBERT HOOVER, 31st US President

12 No greater nor more affectionate honor can be conferred on an American than to have a public school named after him.

At dedication of Herbert Hoover Junior High School, San Francisco, 5 Jun 56

JESSE JACKSON

13 [Today's students] can put dope in their veins or hope in their brains. . . . If they can conceive it and believe it, they can achieve it. They must know it is not their aptitude but their attitude that will determine their altitude.

Washington *Post* 21 May 78

LYNDON B JOHNSON, 36th US President

14 We have entered an age in which education is not just a luxury permitting some men an advantage over others. It has become a necessity without which a person is defenseless in this complex, industrialized society. . . . We have truly entered the century of the educated man.

As vice president, commencement address at Tufts University, 9 Jun 63

15 Poverty must not be a bar to learning and learning must offer an escape from poverty.

Calling for an educational system that "grows in excellence as it grows in size," commencement address at University of Michigan 22 May 64

1 I believe the destiny of your generation—and your nation—is a rendezvous with excellence.
> Commencement address at College of the Holy Cross, Worcester MA, 10 Jun 64

2 I greet you as the shapers of American society.
> To National Educational Assn 3 Jul 65

ALFRED KAZIN

3 If we practiced medicine like we practice education, we'd look for the liver on the right side and left side in alternate years.
> Quoted by US Secretary of Education William J Bennett in address to National Press Club 27 Mar 85

HELEN KELLER

4 A child . . . must feel the flush of victory and the heart-sinking of disappointment before he takes with a will to the tasks distasteful to him and resolves to dance his way through a dull routine of textbooks.
> NY Times 12 Sep 65

JOHN F KENNEDY, 35th US President

5 The human mind is our fundamental resource.
> Message to Congress on state of education 20 Feb 61

6 A child miseducated is a child lost.
> State of the Union address 11 Jan 62

7 It might be said now that I have the best of both worlds. A Harvard education and a Yale degree.
> On receiving honorary degree from Yale, NY Times 12 Jun 62

8 Modern cynics and skeptics . . . see no harm in paying those to whom they entrust the minds of their children a smaller wage than is paid to those to whom they entrust the care of their plumbing.
> Address on 90th anniversary of Vanderbilt University 19 May 63

CHARLES F KETTERING

9 My definition of an educated man is the fellow who knows the right thing to do at the time it has to be done. . . . You can be sincere and still be stupid.
> Quoted by T A Boyd Professional Amateur Dutton 57

EDWARD KOCH, Mayor of NYC

10 The fireworks begin today. Each diploma is a lighted match. Each one of you is a fuse.
> Commencement address to graduates of Poly-

technic Institute of NY, during which fire broke out briefly, NY Times 10 Jun 83

C S LEWIS

11 The real Oxford is a close corporation of jolly, untidy, lazy, good-for-nothing humorous old men, who have been electing their own successors ever since the world began and who intend to go on with it. They'll squeeze under the Revolution or leap over it when the time comes, don't you worry.
> Quoted in Jan Morris ed The Oxford Book of Oxford Oxford 78

ARTHUR LUBOW

12 Behind closed doors each winter the college admissions committee riffles through the folders of concerto-writing East Coast preppies, football stars from the Corn Belt and ghetto valedictorians.
> On Harvard's selection of students, Newsweek 10 Jul 78

13 Diversity wasn't always cultivated along the banks of the Charles.
> On effort since the 1950s to make Harvard a less homogeneous institution, ib

ARCHIBALD MACLEISH

14 Once you permit those who are convinced of their own superior rightness to censor and silence and suppress those who hold contrary opinions, just at that moment the citadel has been surrendered. For the American citadel is a man. Not man in general. Not man in the abstract. Not the majority of men. But man. That man. His worth. His uniqueness.
> 1951 commencement address at Wellesley College, quoted in "Parting Shots: A Century of Commencement Speeches" Saturday Review 12 May 79

JOHN MASEFIELD

15 There are few earthly things more beautiful than a university . . . a place where those who hate ignorance may strive to know, where those who perceive truth may strive to make others see.
> News summaries 10 Jun 63

CHARLES McC MATHIAS JR, US Senator

16 I cannot help but wonder whether, by continuing and expanding the school lunch program, we aren't witnessing, if not encouraging, the slow demise of yet another American tradition: the brown bag. . . . Perhaps we are be-

holding yet another break in the chain that links child to home.
> *Time* 16 Aug 76

H L Mencken

1 A professor must have a theory as a dog must have fleas.
> Quoted by Geoffrey H Hartman *Easy Pieces* Columbia University 85

William Menninger

2 It is just as important, perhaps more important, for the teacher to have the benefit of personal counseling when he needs it as it is for the student.
> To National Assn of Secondary School Principals, news summaries 24 Feb 54

Thomas Merton

3 October is a fine and dangerous season in America. ... a wonderful time to begin anything at all. You go to college, and every course in the catalogue looks wonderful.
> Recalled on his death 10 Dec 68

Sue Mittenthal

4 As the youngsters grow attached to their teachers and classmates ... they can finally say good-bye to their mothers without re-enacting the death scene from *Camille*.
> NY *Times* 6 Sep 84

Bernard Law Montgomery, 1st Viscount Montgomery of Alamein

5 I was well beaten myself, and I am better for it.
> On corporal punishment in schools, news summaries 8 Nov 55

Ted Morgan

6 The elective system ... offered a bewildering freedom of choice, leaving some graduates with the impression that they had nibbled at dozens of canapés of knowledge and never had their fill.
> On Harvard's experimentation with elective courses, *FDR* Simon & Schuster 85

Daniel P Moynihan, US Senator

7 The United States in the 1980s may be the first society in history in which children are distinctly worse off than adults.
> On problems in US education system, NY *Times* 6 May 86

Stephen Neill

8 The bad teacher imposes his ideas and his methods on his pupils, and such originality as they may have is lost in the second-rate art of imitation.
> *A Genuinely Human Existence* Doubleday 59

9 The good teacher ... discovers the natural gifts of his pupils and liberates them by the stimulating influence of the inspiration that he can impart. The true leader makes his followers twice the men they were before.
> *ib*

Richard M Nixon, 37th US President

10 It is not too strong a statement to declare that this is the way civilizations begin to die ... None of us has the right to suppose it cannot happen here.
> On tumult on college campuses, address 22 Mar 69

11 Violence or the threat of violence [must] never be permitted to influence the actions or judgments of the university community. Once it does, the community, almost by definition, ceases to be a university. It is for this reason that from time immemorial expulsion has been the primary instrument of university discipline.
> *ib*

Seán O'Faoláin

12 It is really the undergraduate who makes a university, gives it its lasting character, smell, feel, quality, tradition ... whose presence creates it and whose memories preserve it.
> *Harvard Alumni Bulletin* 24 Oct 64

Vance Packard

13 You can't tell a millionaire's son from a billionaire's.
> On democracy at prep schools, *The Status Seekers* McKay 59

Georges Pompidou, President of France

14 The most dangerous thing about student riots is that adults take them seriously.
> *Life* 20 Feb 70

Nelson A Rockefeller, Governor of NY

15 There are many other possibilities more enlightening than the struggle to become the local doctor's most affluent ulcer case.
> Urging Syracuse University graduates to enter public service, *Quote* 3 Jul 66

ROCKEFELLER BROTHERS FUND

1 A degree is not an education, and the confusion on this point is perhaps the gravest weakness in American thinking about education.
Prospect for America Doubleday 61

STEVEN RUNCIMAN

2 Faced by the mountainous heap of the minutiae of knowledge and awed by the watchful severity of his colleagues, the modern historian too often takes refuge in learned articles or narrowly specialized dissertations, small fortresses that are easy to defend from attack.
London *Times* 7 Jul 83

MICHAEL SADLER

3 Education is the established church of the United States. It is one of the religions that Americans believe in. It has its own orthodoxy, its pontiffs and its noble buildings.
Quoted in NY *Times* 1 Sep 56

WILLIAM SAFIRE

4 I think we have a need to know what we do not need to know.
"Class Cleavage" NY *Times* 1 Jun 86

NORMAN ST JOHN-STEVAS, Member of British Parliament

5 How amazing that the language of a few thousand savages living on a fog-encrusted island in the North Sea should become the language of the world.
Quoted by Jack Valenti NY *Times* 10 Jul 84

ELOISE SALHOLZ

6 Living up to basic ethical standards in the classroom—discipline, tolerance, honesty—is one of the most important ways children learn how to function in society at large.
"Morals Mine Field" *Newsweek* 13 Oct 86

ANTHONY SAMPSON

7 In Britain, the segregated world of public schools crops up in all kinds of institutions: A boy can pass from Eton to the Guards to the Middle Temple to Parliament and still retain the same male world of leather armchairs, teak tables and nicknames. They need never deal closely with other kinds of people, and some never do.
The Anatomy of Britain Harper & Row 62

CHARLES SCRIBNER JR

8 Language is the soul of intellect, and reading is the essential process by which that intellect is cultivated beyond the commonplace experiences of everyday life.
Publishers Weekly 30 Mar 84

9 Beyond the formative effects of reading on the individuals composing society, the fact that they have read the same books gives them experiences and ideas in common. These constitute a kind of shorthand of ideas which helps make communication quicker and more efficient. That is what we mean when we say figuratively of another person, "We speak the same language."
ib

C A SIMPSON, Dean, Christ Church College, Oxford

10 It is a rare thing for a student to be taught by only one tutor. If he should by rare chance have been indoctrinated by Mr A, he will certainly be liberated by Mr B.
Answering charge that US students at Oxford might acquire a preference for the British system, *Saturday Evening Post* 23 Mar 63

B F SKINNER

11 Education is what survives when what has been learned has been forgotten.
"Education in 1984" *New Scientist* 21 May 64

MURIEL SPARK

12 All my pupils are the crème de la crème. Give me a girl of an impressionable age, and she is mine for life.
The Prime of Miss Jean Brodie Dell 64

JOSEPH STALIN

13 Education is a weapon whose effects depend on who holds it in his hands and at whom it is aimed.
Recalled on his death 5 Mar 53

ADLAI E STEVENSON

14 We must recover the element of quality in our traditional pursuit of equality. We must not, in opening our schools to everyone, confuse the idea that all should have equal chance with the notion that all have equal endowments.
To United Parents Assn, NY *Times* 6 Apr 58

15 Respect for intellectual excellence, the restoration of vigor and discipline to our ideas of study, curricula which aim at strengthening in-

tellectual fiber and stretching the power of young minds, personal commitment and responsibility—these are the preconditions of educational recovery in America today; and, I believe, they have always been the preconditions of happiness and sanity for the human race.

ib

TIME MAGAZINE

1 Balliol College is a Victorian Gothic pile of no great distinction. . . . Yet it sits at the head of Oxford's intellectual table—a proud hatchery of prime ministers, archbishops, cardinals and viceroys.

On the college's 700th anniversary, 12 Jul 63

2 Whether or not Balliol really was 700—an agreed age more than a historic fact—they cheerily drank the ancient toast, *Floreat domus de Balliol*, meaning roughly, boola, boola Balliol.

ib

3 Shocked to the tips of its sweat socks.

Recalling Dartmouth's switch to coeducation in 1972, 12 Mar 79

GARDNER TUCKER

4 A towered city, set within a wood,
Far from the world, upon a mountain crest,
There storms of life burst not, nor cares intrude,
There Learning dwells, and Peace is Wisdom's guest.

Quoted in William Strode and William Butt eds *Sewanee: The University of the South* Harmony House 84

JOHN UPDIKE

5 Four years was enough of Harvard. I still had a lot to learn, but had been given the liberating notion that now I could teach myself.

Quoted in *Life* Sep 86

EVELYN WAUGH

6 The truth is that Oxford is simply a very beautiful city in which it is convenient to segregate a certain number of the young of the nation while they are growing up.

Quoted in Donat Gallagher ed *A Little Order: Selections from His Journalism* Little, Brown 81

ORSON WELLES

7 He is as unaffected as Albert Einstein.

On Joel Kufferman at age 6, recalled in reunion of child prodigies who appeared on the radio show *The Quiz Kids,* CBS TV 16 Nov 86

MARK WHITE, Governor of Texas

8 The rest of the world is sweeping past us. The oil and gas of the Texas future is the well-educated mind. But we are still worried about whether Midland can beat Odessa at football.

Supporting law that bans failing students from participating in extracurricular activities, NY *Times* 25 Nov 85

THEODORE H WHITE

9 Generally students are the best vehicles for passing on ideas, for their thoughts are plastic and can be molded and they can adjust the ideas of old men to the shape of reality as they find it in villages and hills of China or in ghettos and suburbs of America.

In Search of History: A Personal Adventure Harper & Row 78

GEORGE F WILL

10 A society that thinks the choice between ways of living is just a choice between equally eligible "lifestyles" turns universities into academic cafeterias offering junk food for the mind.

Newsweek 29 May 78

11 In the 1940s a survey listed the top seven discipline problems in public schools: talking, chewing gum, making noise, running in the halls, getting out of turn in line, wearing improper clothes, not putting paper in wastebaskets. A 1980s survey lists these top seven: drug abuse, alcohol abuse, pregnancy, suicide, rape, robbery, assault. (Arson, gang warfare and venereal disease are also-rans.)

ib 5 Jan 87

W WILLARD WIRTZ, US Secretary of Labor

12 Commencement speakers have a good deal in common with grandfather clocks: Standing usually some six feet tall, typically ponderous in construction, more traditional than functional, their distinction is largely their noisy communication of essentially commonplace information.

Commencement address at University of Iowa, *Time* 19 Jun 65

JOHN WOLFENDEN

13 Schoolmasters and parents exist to be grown out of.

London *Sunday Times* 13 Jun 58

JOHN A WOLTER, Director, Geography and Map Division, Library of Congress

1 Remember civics? It wasn't this bouillabaisse they call social studies today.
Time 16 Sep 85

LOUIS BOOKER WRIGHT, Director, Folger Shakespearean Library, Washington DC

2 We're trying to show that we're not a little bit of England in America, but a place for Americans to gain a better perspective on their own history.
News summaries 9 May 55

3 All the fundamental concepts which make up the kind of people we are today had their modern conception in the Tudor and Stuart periods. For us, that's the milk in the coconut.
ib

MEDICINE

Physicians & the Medical World

DR DAVID ALLMAN, President, Amer Medical Assn

4 The dedicated physician is constantly striving for a balance between personal, human values, scientific realities and the inevitabilities of God's will.
"The Brotherhood of Healing," address to National Conference of Christians and Jews 12 Feb 58

5 Life is precious to the old person. He is not interested merely in thoughts of yesterday's good life and tomorrow's path to the grave. He does not want his later years to be a sentence of solitary confinement in society. Nor does he want them to be a death watch.
ib

AMERICAN DENTAL ASSOCIATION

6 Brush them and floss them and take them to the dentist, and they will stay with you. Ignore them, and they'll go away.
Advertisement in *Time* 11 Feb 85

DR GEORGE J ANNAS, Professor of Health Law, Boston University School of Medicine

7 The more things doctors are able to do, the more likely that at least a few doctors won't do them. And the result will be more people suing for negligence.
Wall Street Journal 7 Jun 85

ANONYMOUS

8 Drill, fill and bill.
Standard of old-fashioned dentistry, quoted in *Newsweek* 5 May 86

9 Please come to my being alive party.
Patient's invitation to physician after treatment for drug addiction, quoted in advertisement for St Vincent's Hospital and Medical Center, NY *Times* 7 May 86

DR VINCENT ASKEY, President, Amer Medical Assn

10 When it comes to your health, I recommend frequent doses of that rare commodity among Americans—common sense.
Address at Bakersfield CA 20 Oct 60

DR MICHAEL M BADEN, Chief Medical Examiner, NYC

11 A cancer is not only a physical disease, it is a state of mind.
NY *Times* 17 Jun 79

DR TAZEWELL BANKS, Director of Heart Program, DC General Hospital

12 It would be better if they told their children, "Go out and play in traffic."
On parents who allow their children to eat foods rich in unsaturated fats at fast-food restaurants, NY *Times* 15 Nov 85

DR ALVAN BARACH, developer of the first practical oxygen tent

13 Remember to cure the patient as well as the disease.
Recalled on his death 15 Dec 77

DR CHRISTIAAN N BARNARD, South African surgeon

14 It is infinitely better to transplant a heart than to bury it to be devoured by worms.
Time 31 Oct 69

BERNARD BARUCH

15 I am interested in physical medicine because my father was. I am interested in medical research because I believe in it. I am interested in arthritis because I have it.
NY *Post* 1 May 59

DR THOMAS J BASSLER, pathologist

16 Two out of every three deaths are premature; they are related to loafer's heart, smoker's lung and drinker's liver.
Quoted by James Fixx *The Complete Book of Running* Random House 77

DR ANNE C BAYLEY

17 It was like coming home from work and find-

ing that your spaniel had turned into a wolf . . . so against one's expectations.

> On Kaposi's sarcoma as it changed to an AIDS-related virus in Zambia, NY *Times* 9 Dec 85

CAL BEACOCK

1 A bunch of germs were whooping it up
In the Bronchial Saloon.
The bacillus handling the larynx
Was jazzing a gag-time tune,
While back of the tongue in a solo game
Sat Dangerous Ah Kerchoo.
And watching his luck was his light of love
The malady known as Flu.

> From *The Pundit*, published by International Save the Pun Foundation, quoted in *Reader's Digest* Jan 86

DR ARTHUR BENJAMIN

2 We all basically go back to being a child when we're in a dentist's chair.
Newsweek 5 May 86

DR HARRY BENJAMIN

3 I ask myself, in mercy, or in common sense, if we cannot alter the conviction to fit the body, should we not, in certain circumstances, alter the body to fit the conviction?

> To Jan Morris, who as a man approached Dr Benjamin for sex-change surgery, quoted in NY *Times* 27 Aug 86

DR NORMAN BETHUNE

4 How beautiful the body is . . . How terrible when torn. The little flame of life sinks lower and lower and, with a flicker, goes out. It goes out like a candle goes out. Quietly and gently. It makes its protest at extinction, then submits. It has its say, then is silent.

> From 1940 article on his experiences in China, quoted in *New Frontiers* Fall 52

JEFF BLECKNER

5 It attacks the most precious thing we have as human beings, our mental faculties.

> On Alzheimer's disease, quoted by Stephen Farber NY *Times* 11 Mar 85

SHANNON BOFF

6 I think I'm going into retirement. Any more babies coming from me are going to be keepers.

> Comments of a 23-year-old woman who had twice been a surrogate mother, quoted in *Time* 28 Apr 86

DR JOSEPH F BOYLE, President-elect, Amer Medical Assn

7 We believe that doctors have the same concerns as their patients and will share in all the sacrifices that are necessary to keep the economy strong.

> Appeal to physicians to help the economy by voluntarily freezing their fees for a year, NY *Times* 24 Feb 84

DR SANDY BURSTEIN

8 What is most interesting in family practice is not what the problem is but what motivates people to seek help for it. Something in the family, a hidden factor, will make the mundane interesting.
New Yorker 23 Jul 84

DR JOHN BUTTON JR

9 We sit at breakfast, we sit on the train on the way to work, we sit at work, we sit at lunch, we sit all afternoon . . . a hodgepodge of sagging livers, sinking gallbladders, drooping stomachs, compressed intestines and squashed pelvic organs.

> To Amer Osteopathic Assn, quoted in *Newsweek* 6 Aug 56

DR ARTHUR CAPLAN, Associate Director, Hastings Center, Hastings-on-Hudson, NY

10 Bodies aren't the same as Coca-Cola cans.

> Quoted by Lindsey Gruson "Signs of Traffic in Cadavers Seen, Raising Ethical Issues" NY *Times* 25 Sep 86

11 The use of fetuses as organ and tissue donors is a ticking time bomb of bioethics.

> On fetal-cell surgery, quoted by Joe Levine "Help from the Unborn" *Time* 12 Jan 87

DR DONALD J CIAGLIA, Assistant Professor of Community Medicine, University of Rochester, NY

12 They learn that once they enter the court, they are in someone else's operating room.

> On teaching legal procedures to medical students, NY *Times* 5 Mar 86

DR JAMES CIMINO, Medical Director, Calvary Hospital, NY Institute for the Terminally Ill

13 You die as you've lived. If you were paranoid in life, you'll probably be paranoid when you're dying.
NY *Times* 6 Mar 79

MATT CLARK

14 In Alzheimer's [disease] the mind dies first:

Names, dates, places—the interior scrapbook of an entire life—fade into mists of nonrecognition.

"A Slow Death of the Mind" *Newsweek* 3 Dec 84

Dr Stanley N Cohen, geneticist, Stanford

1 Nature [is] that lovely lady to whom we owe polio, leprosy, smallpox, syphilis, tuberculosis, cancer.

Quoted by David N Leff in letter to the editor NY *Times* 15 Mar 87

Dr John P Conomy, Chairman of Neurology, Cleveland Clinic Foundation

2 It's very hard to live a productive life when a piece of your brain is missing. And that's what stroke is, a hole in the brain.

Wall Street Journal 16 Jul 84

Norman Cousins

3 The more serious the illness, the more important it is for you to fight back, mobilizing all your resources—spiritual, emotional, intellectual, physical.

Anatomy of an Illness Norton 79

4 Your heaviest artillery will be your will to live. Keep that big gun going.

ib

5 Laughter is a form of internal jogging. It moves your internal organs around. It enhances respiration. It is an igniter of great expectations.

ib

Dr Theresa Crenshaw, President, Amer Assn of Sex Educators, Counselors and Therapists

6 You're not just sleeping with one person, you're sleeping with everyone *they* ever slept with.

Interviewed on *Men, Women, Sex and AIDS* NBC TV 13 Jan 87

Dr Bruce B Dan

7 Sedentary people have shriveled hearts and most of us who do not exercise have an atrophied body.

On evidence that even moderate exercise helps prolong life, quoted in NY *Times* 27 Jul 84

8 We can now prove that large numbers of Americans are dying from sitting on their behinds.

ib

Dr Michael E De Bakey

9 If you can think of how much love there would be in hundreds of hearts, then that is how much love there is in a plastic heart and when you grow up you will understand how very much love that is.

In reply to a child who asked, "Does a plastic heart have love in it?" *Newsweek* 6 Jun 66

Dr William C DeVries

10 I would have picked up the artificial heart and thrown it on the floor and walked out and said he's dead if the press had not been there.

On his frustration in implanting the first artificial heart, NY *Times* 12 Apr 83

Dr Seymour Diamond

11 Patients with migraines know precisely when and how often and how long their headaches strike. They often come in with long lists. When you have a patient with lists, you have a patient with migraine.

Quoted in Washington *Post* 28 Dec 79

Dr Francis Dudley-Hart

12 Some consulting rooms are full of complainers . . . professionals for whom pain is a career.

To British Medical Assn, quoted in London *Daily Telegraph* 17 Jul 74

David W Dunlap

13 The subject no longer has to be mentioned by name. Someone is sick. Someone else is feeling better now. A friend has just gone back into the hospital. Another has died. The unspoken name, of course, is AIDS.

NY *Times* 23 Apr 85

Dr Robert S Eliot, Professor of Cardiology, University of Nebraska

14 Rule Number 1 is, don't sweat the small stuff. Rule Number 2 is, it's all small stuff. And if you can't fight and you can't flee, flow.

On coping with stress, *Time* 6 Jun 83

Theodor Geisel ("Dr Seuss")

15 When at last we are sure
You've been properly pilled,
Then a few paper forms
Must be properly filled
So that you and your heirs
May be properly billed.

You're Only Old Once! Random House 86

PETER GOLDMAN and LUCILLE BEACHY

1 He is one in a sad new specialty in our medicine, a thin white line of plague doctors doing battle with the most fearsome epidemic of our time.

> On physicians who treat patients with AIDS, "One Against the Plague" *Newsweek* 21 Jul 86

DR BURTON GREBIN, Executive Director, St Mary's Hospital for Children, Bayside, Queens

2 The death of a child is the single most traumatic event in medicine. To lose a child is to lose a piece of yourself.

> On opening of NYC's first facility for terminally ill children, NY *Times* 30 Oct 84

JANE GROSS

3 Rarely does anyone speak of fear for his own life, as if an unspoken etiquette prevails.

> On regular meetings of persons who have lost their lovers to AIDS, "AIDS: The Next Phase" NY *Times* 16 Mar 87

4 Over and over, these men cry out against the weight of so many losses—not just a lover dead, but friends and friends of friends, dozens of them, until it seems that AIDS is all there is and all there ever will be.

> *ib*

DR GUNNAR GUNDERSEN, former President, Amer Medical Assn

5 When I began practice . . . I was relatively safe in assuming [that abdominal pain] was appendicitis or green apples. Today it is also highly probable that the patient is suffering from the fact that his wife of 40 years wants to leave him for the Peace Corps or Richard Burton.

> Commencement address at Strich School of Medicine, Loyola University, Chicago, 7 Jun 62

6 While the patient wants the best and most modern treatment available, he is also badly in need of the old-fashioned friend that a doctor has always personified and which you must continue to be.

> *ib*

DR MICHAEL J HALBERSTAM

7 [The joy of medicine is] the challenge of making a solid diagnosis, the delight in besting (if only momentarily) an intern or resident, the satisfaction (if rare) of actually helping someone, the sheer cantankerousness of being able to tell the bureaucracy to "stuff it."

> Recalled on his death 5 Dec 80

DR ROBERT P HEANEY, endocrinologist, Creighton University, Omaha NE

8 It's just like remodeling an office. The body tears out partitions, puts up dry walls and paints.

> On how the body takes calcium from its bones when there is a shortage of calcium in the blood stream, *Newsweek* 27 Jan 86

DR HERMAN HELLERSTEIN, School of Medicine, Case Western Reserve University, Cleveland OH

9 Coronary heart disease is a silent disease and the first manifestation frequently is sudden death.

> *Newsweek* 6 Aug 84

DR ELMER HESS, President, Amer Medical Assn

10 If a man is good in his heart, then he is an ethical member of any group in society. If he is bad in his heart, he is an unethical member. To me, the ethics of medical practice is as simple as that.

> *American Weekly* 24 Apr 55

11 There is no greater reward in our profession than the knowledge that God has entrusted us with the physical care of his people.

> *ib*

DR ARTHUR HOLLEB, Vice President for Medical Affairs, Amer Cancer Society

12 We do not know what we mean by cure because there is a great difference between cure and long-term survival.

> On the society's slogan "We want to cure cancer in your lifetime," NY *Times* 17 Apr 79

DR CHARLES BRENTON HUGGINS, Professor of Surgery, University of Chicago

13 One pits his wits against apparently inscrutable nature, wooing her with ardor [but] nature is blind justice who cannot recognize personal identity.

> On scientific research, *National Observer* 21 Nov 66

14 [Nature] can refuse to speak but she cannot give a wrong answer.

> *ib*

15 We wanted to see if hormone therapy would do for elderly gentlemen what it would do for their best friends, elderly male dogs.

> On cancer research, Chicago *Sun Times* 27 Nov 66

Dr Ernest Johnson, Ohio State University

1 Back fusions are like killing a fly on the windowpane with a sledgehammer. The fly is dead, but you've also broken the glass.

> Quoted in "That Aching Back" *Time* 14 Jul 80

Dr David Jones

2 Doctors coin money when they do procedures [but] family medicine doesn't have any procedures.

> *New Yorker* 23 Jul 84

Dr Sara Murray Jordan, gastroenterologist

3 Every businessman over 50 should have a daily nap and nip—a short nap after lunch and a relaxing highball before dinner.

> *Reader's Digest* Oct 58

4 Nobody should smoke cigarettes—and smoking with an ulcer is like pouring gasoline on a burning house.

> *ib*

5 A much more effective and lasting method of facelifting than surgical technique is happy thinking, new interests and outdoor exercise.

> *ib*

6 In medicine, as in statecraft and propaganda, words are sometimes the most powerful drugs we can use.

> NY *Times* 23 Nov 59

Dr Hugo A Keim, orthopedist

7 If you believe in evolution . . . you can trace all of our lower back problems to the time when the first hominid stood erect.

> Quoted in "That Aching Back" *Time* 14 Jul 80

Geraldine Kidston, mother of a drug victim

8 I guess he got into what we now call designer drugs.

> Testimony to Senate committee on the need for protection against unregulated drugs, NY *Times* 19 Jul 85

Dr John Kirklin, heart surgeon, Mayo Clinic, Rochester MN

9 Surgery is always second best. If you can do something else, it's better.

> *Time* 3 May 63

10 Surgery is limited. It is operating on someone who has no place to go.

> *ib*

Dr C Everett Koop, US Surgeon General

11 You can't talk of the dangers of snake poisoning and not mention snakes.

> On need to discuss sexual conduct as part of AIDS education in schools, quoted by John Leo "Sex and Schools" *Time* 24 Nov 86

Martha Weinman Lear

12 No other surgery affects people in quite this way. For it is unthinkable, finally, that one's heart should be cut open. It is the one unthinkable cut.

> On her husband's double by-pass coronary operation, *Heartsounds* Simon & Schuster 80

13 Women agonize . . . over cancer; we take as a personal threat the lump in every friend's breast.

> *ib*

Dr Frederick Leboyer, French obstetrician

14 Yes, hell exists. It is not a fairy tale. One indeed burns there. This hell is not at the end of life. It is here. At the beginning. Hell is what the infant must experience before he gets to us.

> Comments from proponent of "birth without violence," NY *Times* 8 Dec 74

15 This tragic brow, these closed eyes, eyebrows raised and knotted.

> *ib*

16 This howling mouth, this head which rolls back and tries to escape.

> *ib*

17 These hands which stretch out, implore, beg, then rise to the head in a gesture of calamity.

> *ib*

18 These feet which kick furiously, legs which bend in to protect a tender stomach. This flesh which is but a mass of spasms, starts and shakes.

> *ib*

19 He doesn't speak, the newborn? Why his entire being shouts out, "Don't touch me! Don't touch me!" And yet at the same time, imploringly, begging, "Don't leave me! Don't leave me!" . . . This is birth. This is the torture, the Calvary.

> *ib*

Dr Thomas C Lee, Professor of Surgery, Georgetown University Medical School

20 Eagles: When they walk, they stumble. They are not what one would call graceful. They were not designed to walk. They fly. And when

they fly, oh, how they fly, so free, so graceful. They see from the sky what we never see. Steve, you are an eagle.

> Inscription given with painting of an eagle to a paraplegic medical student, quoted in Washington *Post* 29 May 80

DAVID N LEFF, Editor in Chief, *Biotechnology Newswatch*

1 The gene-spliced product is safer by far than the natural one.

> On superiority of genetically engineered hormones to those taken from cadavers, letter to the editor NY *Times* 15 Mar 87

2 This genie can't be pushed back into the bottle.

> On impossibility of halting genetic research, *ib*

DR IAN LUSTBADER

3 When you get that close to the abyss, you can always jump tomorrow.

> On critically ill patients who may decide whether or not artificial means will be used to prolong their lives, NY *Times* 16 Jan 85

DR WALTER MARTIN, President, Amer Medical Assn

4 The very success of medicine in a material way may now threaten the soul of medicine.

> "Medicine and the Public Welfare," inaugural address 23 Jun 54

WILLIAM F MAY, Professor of Medical Ethics, Southern Methodist University

5 You convert the whole medical system into a giant jaws and the individual's only possible response is a yelp of protest.

> On acquisition of bodily parts for transplants and research, quoted by Lindsey Gruson "Signs of Traffic in Cadavers Seen, Raising Ethical Issues" NY *Times* 25 Sep 86

JOHN McPHEE

6 If the social status of a urologist, a nephrologist, a gastroenterologist, can send a wistful moment through the thoughts of a family practitioner, that is nothing compared with this hovering ghost, this image afloat above the family practitioner's head: Superdoc, the Great American GP, *omniscie ubiquitous*.

> "A Reporter at Large: Heirs of General Practice" *New Yorker* 23 Jul 84

DR WILLIAM MONTAGNA, dermatological researcher, Brown University

7 Interest in hair today has grown to the propor-

tions of a fetish. Think of the many loving ways in which advertisements refer to scalp hair—satiny, glowing, shimmering, breathing, living. Living indeed! It is as dead as rope.

> NY *Herald Tribune* 11 Apr 63

ASHLEY MONTAGU

8 One goes through school, college, medical school and one's internship learning little or nothing about goodness but a good deal about success.

> *Northwestern University Alumni News* Summer 75

9 There have been some medical schools ... in which somewhere along the assembly line, a faculty member has informed the students, not so much by what he said but by what he did, that there is an intimate relation between curing and caring.

> *ib*

10 Human beings are the only creatures who are able to behave irrationally in the name of reason.

> NY *Times* 30 Sep 75

11 The [doctor] has been taught to be interested not in health but in disease. What the public is taught is that health is the cure for disease.

> *ib*

JAN MORRIS (James Morris)

12 I told him everything and it was from him that I learned what my future would be.

> On consultation with Dr Harry Benjamin, who coined the term *transsexualism* and performed Morris's sex-change operation, recalled on Benjamin's death, NY *Times* 27 Aug 86

DR BERNARD NATHANSON

13 We can see the child moving rather serenely in the uterus. ... The child senses aggression in its sanctuary. ... We see the child's mouth wide open in a silent scream.

> From narration of *The Silent Scream*, 1984 film on the abortion of a 12-week-old fetus, quoted in NY *Times* 11 Mar 85

EDWARD R NIDA, US Food and Drug Administration

14 How you lose or keep your hair depends on how wisely you choose your parents.

> On barring sale of nonprescription cures for baldness, NY *Times* 15 Jan 85

MEDICINE

DR JOEL J NOBEL, cofounder, Emergency Care Research Institute

1 The purpose of medicine is to prevent significant disease, to decrease pain and to postpone death when it is meaningful to do so. Technology has to support these goals—if not, it may even be counterproductive.

On the development and maintenance of high-technology medical systems, NY *Times* 1 Jan 85

DR WILLIS POTTS, heart surgeon

2 The heart is a tough organ: a marvelous mechanism that, mostly without repairs, will give valiant service up to a hundred years.

The Surgeon and the Child Saunders 59

DR JOSEPH PURSCH, Medical Director, Comprehensive Care Corp

3 Coroners (they always have the final word) know why cocaine's nickname is *killer*.

"Cocaine in the Board Room" *Leaders* Jul 84

4 Cocaine is quickly supplanting alcohol as the most dangerous occupational hazard in executive suites.

ib

5 The irony is that as the user gets sicker, he is less able to see it. The magic of the powder is that every noseful tells you that you don't really have a problem.

ib

RONALD REAGAN, 40th US President

6 I've noticed that everybody that is for abortion has already been born.

As presidential candidate, quoted in NY *Times* 22 Sep 80

7 Surgeons now speak of "the patient" in the womb [and] for the first time . . . we're able to see with our own eyes, on film, the abortion of a 12-week-old unborn child. [It] provides chilling documentation of the horror of abortion.

On 1984 film *The Silent Scream*, to antiabortion demonstrators, Washington DC, 22 Jan 85

DONNA REGAN, surrogate mother

8 They're borrowing one tiny little egg and some space.

On surrogate motherhood, *Newsweek* 4 Nov 85

DR ARNOLD RELMAN, Editor, New England Journal of Medicine

9 Health care is being converted from a social service to an economic commodity, sold in the marketplace and distributed on the basis of who can afford to pay for it.

Criticizing the takeover of public hospitals by commercial businesses, NY *Times* 25 Jan 85

PATRICK REYNOLDS, grandson of tobacco manufacturer R J Reynolds

10 Am I biting the hand that feeds me? If the hand that once fed me is the tobacco industry, then that hand has killed 10 million people and may kill millions more.

On the eve of testifying before Congressional hearing on the banning of cigarette advertising, NY *Times* 17 Jul 86

MARION ROACH

11 She was losing her mind in handfuls.

On her mother, a victim of Alzheimer's disease, *Another Name for Madness* Houghton Mifflin 85

DR OLIVER SACKS, British neurologist

12 There is only one cardinal rule: One must always *listen* to the patient.

Quoted by Walter Clemons "Listening to the Lost" *Newsweek* 20 Aug 84

DR JONAS SALK

13 It is courage based on confidence, not daring, and it is confidence based on experience.

On administering the experimental vaccine for polio to himself and his wife and three sons, news summaries 9 May 55

14 I feel that the greatest reward for doing is the opportunity to do more.

On receiving Congressional Medal for Distinguished Civilian Achievement 23 Apr 58

DR CECILY SAUNDERS

15 I think very soon the right to die will become the duty to die.

On euthanasia, *60 Minutes* CBS TV 24 Jul 83

MARGARET SCHROEDER

16 I wish Bill had written down on the consent form at what point he would want to say, "Stop this, I've had enough."

On her husband William Schroeder, artificial-heart recipient, after he suffered a series of strokes, *People* 16 Dec 85

DR ALBERT SCHWEITZER

17 I wanted to be a doctor that I might be able to work without having to talk because for years I had been giving myself out in words.

Recalled on his death 4 Sep 65

1 This new form of activity [medicine] I could not represent to myself as talking about the religion of love, but only as an actual putting it into practice.
ib

2 Whosoever is spared personal pain must feel himself called to help in diminishing the pain of others.
ib

3 Serious illness doesn't bother me for long because I am too inhospitable a host.
Quoted by Norman Cousins *Anatomy of an Illness* Norton 79

NORBERT SEGARD

4 I am not going to fight against death but for life.
On suffering from cancer, London *Times* 2 Feb 81

DR HANS SELYE, Director, Institute of Experimental Medicine and Surgery, University of Montreal

5 Man should not try to avoid stress any more than he would shun food, love or exercise.
The Stress of Life McGraw-Hill 56, quoted in *Newsweek* 31 Mar 58

6 Every stress leaves an indelible scar, and the organism pays for its survival after a stressful situation by becoming a little older.
Emphasis, paper from Smith, Kline & French, Winter 69

DR RICHARD SELZER

7 I contemplate the body, dead and diseased as well as alive and healthy.
Mortal Lessons Simon & Schuster 77

8 Surgery is the red flower that blooms among the leaves and thorns that are the rest of medicine.
Letters to a Young Doctor Simon & Schuster 82, quoted in NY *Times* 29 Aug 82

DR MARK SIEGLER, Director, Center for Clinical Medical Ethics, University of Chicago

9 The coming together of two laudable movements—death with dignity and cost containment—concerns me. You start with those in a permanent vegetative state. Then you move to the mentally retarded, the permanently senile, seriously ill defective newborns and the physically handicapped. Patients have a right to die. But do they have a duty to die?
Quoted in NY *Times* 18 Aug 86

DR GEORGE D SNELL

10 I was on a hunt for 30 years. I wore a laboratory gown, not a Maine guide's red wool jacket.
On winning the 1980 Nobel Prize for his explanation of how cell structure relates to organ transplants, *Life* Feb 81

DR BENJAMIN SPOCK

11 You know more than you think you do.
First sentence of *Baby and Child Care*, quoted in *Ladies' Home Journal* Mar 60

12 In automobile terms, the child supplies the power but the parents have to do the steering.
ib

13 I really learned it all from mothers.
On the 40th-anniversary edition of his book that had already sold more than 28 million copies, *Time* 8 Apr 85

DR MARTIN R STEINBERG, Director, Mt Sinai Hospital, NYC

14 The most important thing we have learned about the aged is the necessity to give them the shortest possible period "down," the longest period "up." When a patient is "up," he is a citizen, an individual. When he is "down," he and his doctor are in trouble. .... "Down" is bad, "up" is life.
Saturday Evening Post 20 May 67

PINCHAS STOLPER, Executive Vice President, Union of Orthodox Jewish Congregations of America

15 A person is entitled to be buried whole.
On acquisition of bodily parts for transplants and research, quoted by Lindsey Gruson "Signs of Traffic in Cadavers Seen, Raising Ethical Issues" NY *Times* 25 Sep 86

JEROME H STONE, President, National Alzheimer's Disease and Related Disorders Assn

16 It is the disease that robs the mind of the victim and breaks the hearts of the family.
NY *Times* 23 Nov 83

DR LEWIS THOMAS, President, Memorial Sloan-Kettering Institute for Cancer Research

17 The great secret of doctors, known only to their wives, but still hidden from the public, is that most things get better by themselves; most things, in fact, are better in the morning.
NY *Times* 4 Jul 76

CALVIN TRILLIN

18 Keeping off a large weight loss is a phenome-

non about as common in American medicine as an impoverished dermatologist.
Alice, Let's Eat Random House 78

UNITED STATES SURGEON GENERAL

1 Warning: Quitting smoking now greatly reduces serious risk to your health.
One of four warnings printed on cigarette packages, quoted by NY *Times* 12 Feb 86

DR CECIL VAUGHN, St Luke's Hospital, Phoenix

2 There's a greater law than the FDA, and that is an obligation of a doctor to try to do anything he can to save a life when he thinks that there's a chance.
Defending a decision to implant an experimental mechanical heart without the approval of the US Food and Drug Administration, NY *Times* 8 Mar 85

CLAUDIA WALLIS

3 Tooth decay was a perennial national problem that meant a mouthful of silver for patients, and for dentists a pocketful of gold.
On decreasing occurrence of tooth decay, "Today's Dentistry: A New Drill" *Time* 9 Sep 85

ELIZABETH WHELAN, Amer Council on Science and Health

4 We recommend that no one eat more than two tons of turkey—that's what it would take to poison someone.
On toxins and carcinogens in holiday meals, *US News & World Report* 8 Dec 86

DR PAUL DUDLEY WHITE

5 The country will be very pleased—the country is so bowel-minded anyway . . . and it is important.
Reporting President Dwight D Eisenhower's condition following a heart attack, news summaries 10 Oct 55

FRED WITCH, District Staff Officer, St John's Ambulance Brigade

6 This is the moment when we get the most casualties. The adrenaline runs quick when the queen enters.
On Buckingham Palace garden parties, NY *Times* 15 Jul 83

DR ERNST WUNDER, President, Amer Health Foundation

7 Clearly, if disease is manmade, it can also be man-prevented. It should be the function of medicine to help people die young as late in life as possible.
NY *Times* 30 Sep 75

BARBARA YUNCKER

8 In the medical sense now, birth is not the beginning but just a developmental transition.
"The Riddle of Birth" NY *Post* 23 May 69

Psychiatry & Psychology

RICHARD ABELL

9 Anxiety is the space between the "now" and the "then."
Own Your Own Life McKay 76

DR VICTOR ALTZHUL, Professor of Psychiatry, Yale

10 The practicing psychotherapist is perhaps better qualified than other serious human beings to discuss boredom.
New York 7 Apr 80

DR RUTH TIFFANY BARNHOUSE

11 Maturity is coming to terms with that other part of yourself.
News summaries 1 Mar 82

DR FRANK BARRON, Professor of Psychology, University of California, Santa Cruz

12 The creative person is both more primitive and more cultivated, more destructive and more constructive, a lot madder and a lot saner, than the average person.
Think Nov 62

DR JOHN V BASMAJIAN, McMaster University, Hamilton, Ontario

13 Back pain is just a tension headache that has slipped down the back.
On psychological aspects of backaches, *Time* 14 Jul 80

DR REX JULIAN BEABER, clinical psychologist, UCLA

14 A reservoir of rage exists in each person, waiting to burst out. We fantasize about killing or humiliating our boss or the guy who took our parking space. It is only by growing up in a civilized society of law that we learn the idea of proportionate response.
Quoted by Ed Magnuson "Up in Arms over Crime" *Time* 8 Apr 85

NEIL G BENNETT, Associate Professor of Sociology, Yale

1 It appears . . . that much of this marriage deferral is translating into marriage forgone.
> On current marriage patterns, NY *Times* 22 Feb 86

DR RUTH BERKELEY

2 Heterosexuality is an attribute of the mature personality.
> *NY State Journal of Medicine* 15 Nov 51

3 I see adult sexuality more as an expression of an emotional attitude than as a function of anatomy.
> *ib*

DR ERIC BERNE

4 Losers spend time explaining why they lost. Losers spend their lives thinking about what they're going to do. They rarely enjoy doing what they're doing.
> *Games People Play* Random House 64

5 Games are a compromise between intimacy and keeping intimacy away.
> *ib*

DR LUDWIG BINSWANGER, Swiss psychiatrist

6 Loneliness is an unhappy compound of having lost one's point of reference, of suffering the fate of individual and collective discontinuity and of living through or dying from a crisis of identity to the point of alienation of one's self.
> On his "naked horror" theory of loneliness, *National Observer* 12 Aug 72

DR PHILIP BONNET, psychiatrist, Princeton Brain Biological Center

7 The patient is always the ultimate source of knowledge.
> *W* 27 Aug 76

DR FRANCIS J BRACELAND, Chief Psychiatrist, Institute for Living, Hartford CT

8 The sorrow which has no vent in tears may make other organs weep.
> On psychosomatic disorders, "Living With Executive Tensions" *National Observer* 28 Dec 64

9 We can be sure that the greatest hope for maintaining equilibrium in the face of any situation rests within ourselves. Persons who are secure with a transcendental system of values and a deep sense of moral duties are possessors of values which no man and no catastrophe can take from them.
> *ib*

DR NORMAN M BRADBURN, psychologist, University of Chicago

10 It is the lack of joy in Mudville, rather than the presence of sorrow that makes the difference.
> *In Pursuit of Happiness: A Pilot Study of Behavior Related to Mental Health* National Opinion Research Center 63

JIMMY BRESLIN

11 When you stop drinking, you have to deal with this marvelous personality that started you drinking in the first place.
> *Table Money* Ticknor & Fields 86

STEPHEN BROOK

12 Unpinned even by rudimentary notions of time and space, dreams float or flash by, leaving in their wake trails of unease, hopes, fears and anxieties.
> *The Oxford Book of Dreams* Oxford 84

DR JOYCE BROTHERS

13 I don't give advice. I can't tell anybody what to do. Instead I say this is what we know about this problem at this time. And here are the consequences of these actions.
> *American Way* 79

DR DONALD BROWN, Director, Morrisania Neighborhood Family Care Center, NYC

14 It's getting hard to find a pure schizophrenic anymore.
> On the difficulty of differentiating between drug abuse and mental illness in the inner city, NY *Times* 17 Mar 86

DR MARY S CALDERONE

15 Before the child ever gets to school it will have received crucial, almost irrevocable sex education and this will have been taught by the parents, who are not aware of what they are doing.
> *People* 21 Jan 80

VIOLET DE LAZLO

16 The edifice of C G Jung's work is reminiscent of a cathedral . . . With its altar, its cross and its rose window, this edifice has been erected *ad majorem Dei gloriam*, as is true of all valid creative efforts, often those which appear to be agnostically motivated.
> Comment in her edition of Carl Jung *Psyche and Symbol* Doubleday 58

DR WILLIAM C DEMENT

17 Dreaming permits each and every one of us to

be quietly and safely insane every night of our lives.
Newsweek 30 Nov 59

BELLA DEPAULO, psychologist, University of Virginia

1 People tell about two lies a day, or at least that is how many they will admit to.
On a study in which participants kept a daily diary of lies, NY *Times* 12 Feb 85

PHIL DONAHUE

2 Suicide is a permanent solution to a temporary problem.
NBC TV 23 May 84

DR ROBERT L DUPONT, Director, Center of Behavioral Medicine, Washington DC

3 The malignant disease of the "what-ifs."
On phobias, quoted by Jerry Adler "The Fight to Conquer Fear" *Newsweek* 23 Apr 84

PAUL EKMAN, psychologist, University of California, San Francisco

4 Most liars can fool most people most of the time.
On research showing people to be surprisingly inept at detecting lies, NY *Times* 12 Feb 85

DR ERIK ERIKSON

5 Children love and want to be loved and they very much prefer the joy of accomplishment to the triumph of hateful failure. Do not mistake a child for his symptom.
Childhood and Society Norton 50

6 Doubt is the brother of shame.
ib

DR JACK R EWALT

7 The result was like preparing a plan to build a new airplane and ending up [with only] a wing and a tail.
On US policy that released many mentally ill people from institutional care, quoted in NY *Times* 30 Oct 84

DR VIKTOR E FRANKL, Professor of Neurology and Psychiatry, University of Vienna

8 Ultimately, man should not ask what the meaning of his life is, but rather he must recognize that it [is] he who is asked.
Man's Search for Meaning Beacon 59

9 Each man is questioned by life; and he can only answer to life by answering for his own

life; to life he can only respond by being responsible.
ib

DR ERICH FROMM

10 In the 19th century inhumanity meant cruelty; in the 20th century it means schizoid self-alienation.
The Sane Society Holt, Rinehart & Winston 55

11 One cannot be deeply responsive to the world without being saddened very often.
ABC TV 25 May 58

12 Both dreams and myths are important communications from ourselves to ourselves. If we do not understand the language in which they are written, we miss a great deal of what we know and tell ourselves in those hours when we are not busy manipulating the outside world.
NY *Times* 5 Jan 64

DR RALPH GERARD, neurophysiologist

13 Activity of the nervous system improves the capacity for activity, just as exercising a muscle makes it stronger.
Time 29 Nov 63

DR HAIM GINOTT

14 Each of us carries within himself a collection of instant insults.
Between Parent and Teenager Macmillan 69

DR ERNEST HARTMANN, Professor of Psychiatry, School of Medicine, Tufts University

15 One important aspect of what makes a person an artist is having a psychological make-up of thin boundaries, which includes the ability to experience and take in a great deal from inside and outside, to experience one's own inner life in a very direct fashion and (sometimes an unwanted ability) to experience the world more directly, more painfully than others.
The Nightmare Basic Books 85, previewed in NY *Times* 23 Oct 84

ERNEST HAVEMANN

16 All of us, even the myriads among us who have emotional problems ranging from the light to the serious, have far more hope for the future.
On the outlook of modern psychiatry, *Life* 4 Feb 57

LESLEY HAZELTON

17 When depression is stigmatized as illness and

weakness, a double bind is created: If we admit to depression, we will be stigmatized by others; if we feel it but do not admit it, we stigmatize ourselves, internalizing the social judgment. ... The only remaining choice may be truly sick behavior: to experience no emotion at all.

The Right to Feel Bad Dial 84

1 Suffering, once accepted, loses its edge, for the terror of it lessens, and what remains is generally far more manageable than we had imagined.

ib

2 There is no perfect solution to depression, nor should there be. And odd as this may sound ... we should be glad of that. It keeps us human.

ib

Dr Stanley A Herring

3 We don't consider a patient cured when his sprain has healed or he's been restored to a minimal level of functioning. The patient is cured when he can again do the things he loves to do.

On a survey showing that several hundred orthopedists and neurosurgeons had never referred a patient to a psychiatrist for postoperative rehabilitation, NY *Times* 16 Apr 85

Dr Karen Horney

4 Life itself still remains a very effective therapist.

Recalled on her death 4 Dec 52

Howard Hughes

5 Wash four distinct and separate times, using lots of lather each time from individual bars of soap.

Instructions from his procedure manual for staff who handled anything that he was to touch, quoted by Michael Drosnin *Citizen Hughes* Holt, Rinehart & Winston 85

6 The door to the cabinet is to be opened using a minimum of 15 Kleenexes.

ib

Kathryn Hulme

7 The dark-veiled silhouette ... that solitary form patrolling without visible strain or vainglory a demented dreamland of fearful potential.

On a nun working in a psychiatric ward, *The Nun's Story* Little, Brown 56

Morton Hunt

8 Being a good psychoanalyst, in short, has the same disadvantage as being a good parent: The children desert one as they grow up.

"How the Analyst Stands the Pace" NY *Times* 24 Nov 57

Jill Johnston

9 The inmates are ghosts whose dreams have been murdered.

On Bellevue Hospital's psychiatric wards, *Paper Daughter* Knopf 85, quoted in NY *Times* 28 Jul 85

Carl Jung

10 The brain is viewed as an appendage of the genital glands.

On Freudian theory of sexuality, *Time* 14 Feb 55

11 Understanding does not cure evil, but it is a definite help, inasmuch as one can cope with a comprehensible darkness.

Psyche and Symbol, edited by Violet de Lazlo, Doubleday 58

12 How indeed? He copes, like everybody else, as well as he can, that's all. And it's usually deplorably enough.

On how a psychiatrist deals with his personal problems, quoted by Yousuf Karsh *Portraits of Greatness* Nelson 60

13 Shrinking away from death is something unhealthy and abnormal which robs the second half of life of its purpose.

Recalled on his death 6 Jun 61

14 The greatest and most important problems of life are all fundamentally insoluble. They can never be solved but only outgrown.

ib

15 Neurosis is always a substitute for legitimate suffering.

ib

16 Man's task is to become conscious of the contents that press upward from the unconscious.

Memories, Dreams, Reflections Atlantic Monthly Press 62

17 As far as we can discern, the sole purpose of human existence is to kindle a light in the darkness of mere being.

ib

18 Everything that irritates us about others can lead us to an understanding of ourselves.

ib

19 Your vision will become clear only when you

can look into your own heart. .... Who looks outside, dreams; who looks inside, awakes.

> To patient in Cambridge MA, quoted in Gerhard Adler ed *Letters Vol I* Princeton 73

1 Nobody, as long as he moves about among the chaotic currents of life, is without trouble.

> To patient whose only son had drowned at age 21 while sailing off the coast of Maine, *ib*

DR RALPH KAUFMAN, Director of Psychiatry, Mt Sinai Hospital, NYC

2 Anybody who is 25 or 30 years old has physical scars from all sorts of things, from tuberculosis to polio. It's the same with the mind.

> *Newsweek* 29 May 61

EUGENE KENNEDY, Professor of Psychology, Loyola University, Chicago

3 The future is religion and commerce, aphrodisiac and Benzedrine, a mother of mysterious comfort and a mistress of familiar ravishments ever on the verge of embracing or destroying us.

> *NY Times* 2 Dec 79

4 We not only romanticize the future; we have also made it into a growth industry, a parlor game and a disaster movie all at the same time.

> *ib*

DR NATHAN S KLINE

5 There is nothing more productive of problems than a really good solution.

> On tranquilizers and related drugs, *Time* 24 Apr 64

DR ELISABETH KÜBLER-ROSS

6 Those who have the strength and the love to sit with a dying patient in *the silence that goes beyond words* will know that this moment is neither frightening nor painful, but a peaceful cessation of the functioning of the body.

> *On Death and Dying* Macmillan 69

7 Watching a peaceful death of a human being reminds us of a falling star; one of a million lights in a vast sky that flares up for a brief moment only to disappear into the endless night forever.

> *ib*

WESTON LA BARRE

8 [We] feed upon each other's mouths and minds like ants with social stomachs.

> *The Human Animal* University of Chicago 64

JOHN LE CARRÉ

9 The monsters of our childhood do not fade away, neither are they ever wholly monstrous. But neither, in my experience, do we ever reach a plane of detachment regarding our parents, however wise and old we may become. To pretend otherwise is to cheat.

> *Book-of-the-Month Club News* May 86

DR ROBERT LINDNER

10 *You must adjust.* .... This is the legend imprinted in every schoolbook, the invisible message on every blackboard.

> *Must You Conform?* Holt, Rinehart & Winston 56

JANET MALCOLM

11 Analysts keep having to pick away at the scab that the patient tries to form between himself and the analyst to cover over his wounds. [The analyst] keeps the surface raw, so that the wound will heal properly.

> *Psychoanalysis: The Impossible Profession* Knopf 81, quoted in *Time* 28 Sep 81

DR ARNOLD J MANDELL, Professor of Psychology, University of California, San Diego

12 We will learn to think of ourselves, our personalities, as an orchestra of chemical voices in our heads.

> *Time* 2 Apr 79

MICHAEL R MANTELL, San Diego police psychologist

13 You know what happens to scar tissue. It's the strongest part of your skin.

> On psychological recovery of disaster victims, NY *Daily News* 14 Dec 86

DR VERNON H MARK, Chief of Neurosurgery, Harvard Medical School

14 The proclivity for extraordinary violence is not just an ailment of the mind, as psychologists like to think. Nor is it only a malaise of the society, as sociologists believe. It is both of these things, but it is also a sickness of the body as distinct and definite as cancer or leprosy.

> *Life* Aug 84

DR WILLIAM H MASTERS, codirector, Masters & Johnson Institute

15 The best sex education for kids is when Daddy pats Mommy on the fanny when he comes home from work.

> NBC TV 16 Aug 71

1 Sex is a natural function. You can't make it happen, but you can teach people to let it happen.

NY *Times* 29 Oct 84

2 When things don't work well in the bedroom, they don't work well in the living room either.

NBC TV 23 Jun 86

Dr Rollo May

3 If we admit our depression openly and freely, those around us get from it an experience of freedom rather than the depression itself.

Paulus Harper & Row 73

Dr Joost Meerloo

4 It's among the intelligentsia ... that we often find the glib compulsion to explain everything and to understand nothing.

The Rape of the Mind World 56

Dr Karl A Menninger

5 The voice of the intelligence ... is drowned out by the roar of fear. It is ignored by the voice of desire. It is contradicted by the voice of shame. It is biased by hate and extinguished by anger. Most of all it is silenced by ignorance.

The Progressive Oct 55

6 Psychoanalysis has changed American psychiatry from a diagnostic to a therapeutic science, not because so many patients are cured by the psychoanalytic technique, but because of the new understanding of psychiatric patients it has given us and the new and different concepts of illness and health.

News summaries 29 Apr 56

7 It was his optimism that Freud bequeathed to America and it was the optimism of our youthfulness, our freedom from the sterner, sadder tradition of Europe which enabled us to seize his gift.

ib

8 Unrest of spirit is a mark of life.

This Week 16 Oct 58

9 Hope is a necessity for normal life and the major weapon against the suicide impulse.

Newsweek 2 Nov 59

10 To "know thyself" must mean to know the malignancy of one's own instincts and to know, as well, one's power to deflect it.

Vogue Jun 61

Dr William Menninger

11 Mental health problems do not affect three or four out of every five persons but one out of one.

NY *Times* 22 Nov 57

Arthur Miller

12 What is the most innocent place in any country? Is it not the insane asylum? These people drift through life truly innocent, unable to see into themselves at all.

On his 1964 play *After the Fall*, quoted in *Life* 7 Feb 64

Dr John W Money, Professor of Medical Psychology, Johns Hopkins Medical School

13 It puts an eggbeater in people's brains.

On the "liberating" aspects of pornographic films, NY *Times* 21 Jan 73

Dr Willibald Nagler, Psychiatrist in Chief, NY Hospital-Cornell Medical Center

14 A psychiatrist has to be a person who commits himself to making a person better. Nothing should be too menial for a psychiatrist to do.

NY *Times* 16 Apr 85

Ulric Neisser, cognitive psychologist, Emory University, Atlanta

15 Most of our oldest memories are the product of repeated rehearsal and reconstruction.

Quoted by Sharon Begley "Memory" *Newsweek* 29 Sep 86

Dr Barry M Panter, Associate Professor of Psychiatry, UCLA, and director of annual conference on creativity and madness

16 The material artists use for their art comes from the primitive levels of their inner lives—aggression, sexual fantasy, polymorphous sexuality. ... As we mature and are "civilized," we suppress [these drives]. But the artist stays in touch with and struggles to understand them. And to remain so in touch with that primitive self is to be on the fine line between sanity and madness.

NY *Times* 17 Nov 85

Dr M Scott Peck

17 It is only because of problems that we grow mentally and spiritually.

The Road Less Traveled Touchstone 80

DR WILDER G PENFIELD, Montreal Neurological Institute

1 Among the millions of nerve cells that clothe parts of the brain there runs a thread. It is the thread of time, the thread that has run through each succeeding wakeful hour of the individual's past life.
Reader's Digest Jul 58

V S PRITCHETT

2 The whole influence of psychology has turned our interest to . . . the failures of the will, the fulfillment of the heart, the vacillations of the sensibility, the perception of self-interest.
The Living Novel and Later Associations Random House 64

HARRY REASONER

3 We're all controlled neurotics.
TV Guide 20 Mar 71

THEODOR REIK

4 The repressed memory is like a noisy intruder being thrown out of the concert hall. You can throw him out, but he will bang on the door and continue to disturb the concert. The analyst opens the door and says, "If you promise to behave yourself, you can come back in."
Saturday Review 11 Jan 58

5 In our civilization, men are afraid that they will not be men enough and women are afraid that they might be considered only women.
Quoted by Arthur M Schlesinger Jr "The Crisis of American Masculinity" *Esquire* Nov 58

6 Work and love—these are the basics. Without them there is neurosis.
Of Love and Lust Grove 59

ANN ROIPHE

7 In the office there was an old, soft and worn blue velvet couch, above which a hundred thousand dissected dreams floated in the peaceful, still air.
Recalling an interview with psychoanalyst Helene Deutsch, NY *Times* 13 Feb 71

DR MILTON ROKEACH

8 To say that a particular psychiatric condition is incurable or irreversible is to say more about the state of our ignorance than about the state of the patient.
The Three Christs of Ypsilanti Knopf 64

DR THEODORE I RUBIN

9 I must learn to love the fool in me—the one who feels too much, talks too much, takes too many chances, wins sometimes and loses often, lacks self-control, loves and hates, hurts and gets hurt, promises and breaks promises, laughs and cries. It alone protects me against that utterly self-controlled, masterful tyrant whom I also harbor and who would rob me of human aliveness, humility and dignity but for my fool.
Love Me, Love My Fool McKay 76

DR JOSEPH SANDLER

10 Blushing fulfills a most important function in propagation of the human species and is all the more interesting because it is involuntary and shows a readiness to be courted.
News summaries 9 Sep 55

JOHN SANFORD, priest-therapist

11 We can never cure a neurosis; the neurosis cures us and is resolved as the need for it no longer exists.
Your Church Jan 80

DR IRWIN SARASON, psychologist, University of Washington

12 Good friends are good for your health.
NY *Times* 27 Aug 85

DR STANLEY J SARNOFF, physiologist, National Institute of Health

13 The process of living is the process of reacting to stress.
Time 29 Nov 63

DR R W SHEPHERD

14 You handle depression in much the same way you handle a tiger.
Vogue Jul 78

15 If depression is creeping up and must be faced, learn something about the nature of the beast: You may escape without a mauling.
ib

DR JUNE SINGER

16 Is it sufficient that you have learned to drive the car, or shall we look and see what is under the hood? Most people go through life without ever knowing.
Boundaries of the Soul Doubleday 72

17 The first half of life is spent mainly in finding

out who we are through seeing ourselves in our interaction with others.

ib

PATRICIA MEYER SPACKS

1 Gossip, even when it avoids the sexual, bears around it a faint flavor of the erotic.

Gossip Knopf 85, quoted in NY *Times* 1 Sep 85

2 Poring over fragments of other people's lives, peering into their bedrooms when they don't know we're there, we thrill to the glamour and the power of secret knowledge, partly detoxified but also heightened by being shared.

ib

KARL STERN

3 Psychoanalysis . . . shows the human infant as the passive recipient of love, unable to bear hostility. Development is the learning to love actively and to bear rejection.

The Pillar of Fire Harcourt, Brace & World 51

ANTHONY STORR

4 With the exception of certain rodents, no other vertebrate [except *Homo sapiens*] habitually destroys members of his own species.

Human Destructiveness Morrow 75

CAROL TAVRIS

5 The second sweetest set of three words in English is "I don't know," and it is to R D Laing's credit that he uses it often.

On R D Laing's *Wisdom, Madness and Folly* McGraw-Hill 85, NY *Times* 8 Sep 85

DR PAUL TOURNIER

6 Recounting of a life story, a mind thinking aloud . . . leads one inevitably to the consideration of problems which are no longer psychological but spiritual.

The Meaning of Persons Harper 57

DR DAVID VISCOTT

7 This is really America in therapy, people trying to get themselves together and be whole.

On popularity of "nonoccasion" greeting cards, *Time* 12 May 86

DR CARL WHITAKER

8 The problem is that you have a disease, but the disease is abnormal integrity, loyalty to a view of the world that the schizophrenic is willing to stake his life on.

On schizophrenia, *Time* 23 Dec 85

TENNESSEE WILLIAMS

9 If I am no longer disturbed myself, I will deal less with disturbed people, but I don't regret having concerned myself with them because I think most of us are disturbed.

On psychological condition of his characters, NY *Herald Tribune* 5 Jan 58

DR STANLEY F YOLLES, Director, National Institute of Mental Health

10 It is rebellion without a cause, rejection without a program and a refusal of what is, without a vision of what should be.

On alienation as a major cause of drug abuse, NY *Times* 10 Mar 68

DR NORMAN ZINBERG, Professor of Psychiatry, Harvard

11 Nobody in the United States is more than one handshake away from virtually any drug they want to get.

NY *Times* 21 Mar 83

SCIENCE

WILTON ROBERT ABBOTT, aerospace engineer

12 To understand the place of humans in the universe is to solve a complex problem. Therefore I find it impossible to believe that an understanding based entirely on science or one based entirely on religion can be correct.

Quoted in *Who's Who in America, 43rd Edition 1984-85* Marquis 84

EDWIN E ("BUZZ") ALDRIN JR, US astronaut

13 Beautiful! Beautiful! Magnificent desolation.

On joining Neil A Armstrong in first walk on the moon 20 Jul 69

AMERICAN LIBRARY ASSOCIATION

14 The computer is only a fast idiot, it has no imagination; it cannot originate action. It is, and will remain, only a tool to man.

On Univac computer exhibited at the 1964 NY World's Fair

AMERICAN MUSEUM OF NATURAL HISTORY, NYC

15 A zebra is a light-colored animal with dark stripes; not a dark one with light stripes.

After discovery in South Africa that dark parts of zebras fade while light parts remain unchanged, *Newsweek* 16 Dec 57

GEORGE ARCHIBALD, Director, International Crane Foundation

1 [They] thought the whole thing was a riot. I thought it was a miracle.

> On the artificial insemination of a crane with sperm flown in from Maryland's Patuxent Wildlife Research Center and carried in a picnic cooler by stewardesses, *Life* Jul 86

NEIL A ARMSTRONG, US astronaut

2 Houston, Tranquillity Base here. The Eagle has landed.

> First message to the earth from the Apollo 11 lunar module Eagle after landing on the moon 20 Jul 69

3 That's one small step for man, one giant leap for mankind.

> Message to the earth from the first man to walk on the moon 20 Jul 69; also reported as "That's one small step for *a* man"

SHARON BEGLEY

4 The mind can store an estimated 100 trillion bits of information—compared with which a computer's mere billions are virtually amnesiac.

> "Memory: Science Achieves Important New Insights into the Mother of the Muses" *Newsweek* 29 Sep 86

KURT BENIRSCHKE

5 Extinct is forever.

> On work with endangered species at San Diego Zoo, *Christian Science Monitor* 29 May 80

LUCIEN M BIBERMAN, Associate Director, University of Chicago Military Research Laboratory

6 I think the school's involvement in the development of atomic energy and the bomb left a deep scar on the moral fiber of this place.

> *NY Times* 7 Jun 63

JIM BISHOP

7 Archaeology . . . is the peeping Tom of the sciences. It is the sandbox of men who care not where they are going; they merely want to know where everyone else has been.

> "Sifting the Sea for Time's Treasures" NY *Journal-American* 14 Mar 61

FRANK BORMAN, US astronaut

8 We have company tonight.

> Message from Gemini 7 on sighting Gemini 6 before they became the first two craft to rendezvous in space, NY *Times* 16 Dec 65

9 Exploration is really the essence of the human spirit.

> Address to joint session of Congress, NY *Times* 10 Jan 69

RAY BRADBURY

10 Touch a scientist and you touch a child.

> LA *Times* 9 Aug 76

LEWIS M BRANSCOMB, Director, National Bureau of Standards

11 Science is some kind of cosmic apple juice from the Garden of Eden. Those who drink of it are doomed to carry the burden of original sin.

> News summaries 9 Apr 71

WERNHER VON BRAUN

12 It will free man from the remaining chains, the chains of gravity which still tie him to this planet.

> On the meaning of space travel, *Time* 10 Feb 58

JACOB BRONOWSKI

13 You will die but the carbon will not; its career does not end with you. . . . it will return to the soil, and there a plant may take it up again in time, sending it once more on a cycle of plant and animal life.

> "Biography of an Atom—And the Universe" NY *Times* 13 Oct 68

14 The most wonderful discovery made by scientists is science itself.

> *A Sense of the Future* New American Library 77

MICHAEL CAREY

15 The thing about farming is it's so easy, half of it is learning to kill.

> On plowing under overabundant corn and soybean crops on his Iowa farm, quoted by Hugh Sidey "Bitter Harvest" *Time* 8 Sep 86

RACHEL CARSON

16 Over increasingly large areas of the United States, spring now comes unheralded by the return of the birds, and the early mornings are strangely silent where once they were filled with the beauty of bird song.

> On the effect of chemical insecticides and fertilizers, *Silent Spring* Houghton Mifflin 62

17 As crude a weapon as a cave man's club, the chemical barrage has been hurled against the fabric of life.

> *ib*

ROGER B CHAFFEE, US astronaut

1 Problems ... look mighty small from 150 miles up.

In his last public interview before he died with astronauts Virgil I Grissom and Edward H White II in a fire aboard Apollo 1 during a simulated launch, *This Week* 23 Apr 67

ERWIN CHARGAFF, Professor of Biological Chemistry, Columbia University

2 Science is wonderfully equipped to answer the question "How?" but it gets terribly confused when you ask the question "Why?"

Columbia Forum Summer 69

STEVEN CHU, Director, Quantum Electronics Research, Bell Laboratories

3 The atoms become like a moth, seeking out the region of higher laser intensity.

On isolating atoms with a laser for close study, NY *Times* 13 Jul 86

RUSSELL L CIOCHON

4 [It] is not a monkey, not an ape and not a human, but it's a common ancestor of them all.

On the discovery in Burma of a jawbone of the earliest known higher primate, NY *Times* 16 Aug 85

MICHAEL COLLINS, US astronaut

5 I think a future flight should include a poet, a priest and a philosopher ... we might get a much better idea of what we saw.

News summaries 9 Nov 69

6 I knew I was alone in a way that no earthling has ever been before.

On his solo flight in the Apollo 11 command module while astronauts Neil A Armstrong and Edwin E Aldrin Jr explored the lunar surface, *Time* 11 Dec 72

JACQUES COUSTEAU

7 The sea is the universal sewer.

On the sea as a place "where all kinds of pollution wind up," to House Committee on Science and Astronautics 28 Jan 71

8 We must plant the sea and herd its animals ... using the sea as farmers instead of hunters. That is what civilization is all about—farming replacing hunting.

Interview 17 Jul 71

9 Farming as we do it is hunting, and in the sea we act like barbarians.

ib

10 If we go on the way we have, the fault is our greed [and] if we are not willing [to change], we will disappear from the face of the globe, to be replaced by the insect.

ib

11 What is a scientist after all? It is a curious man looking through a keyhole, the keyhole of nature, trying to know what's going on.

Christian Science Monitor 21 Jul 71

12 I am not a scientist. I am, rather, an impresario of scientists.

Describing his role as an explorer and filmmaker associated with scientists in underwater exploration, *ib* 24 Jul 86

LEILA M COYNE, researcher, San Jose State University

13 The more science learns what life is, the more reluctant scientists are to define it.

On study of clay as an energy storehouse and transfer agent, *Christian Science Monitor* 4 Apr 85

LORRAINE LEE CUDMORE

14 We are a sad lot, the cell biologists. Like the furtive collectors of stolen art, we are forced to be lonely admirers of spectacular architecture, exquisite symmetry, dramas of violence and death, mobility, self-sacrifice and, yes, rococo sex.

The Center of Life Quadrangle 77

ROBERT GORHAM DAVIS

15 In Genesis, seeing the world filled with violence, God decided to drown all mankind except Noah's family. But because that family carried the same genes as those who had drowned, violence continued unabated.

Letter to the editor NY *Times* 15 Mar 87

JEANNETTE DESOR, research scientist, General Foods

16 Humans can learn to like anything, that's why we are such a successful species.

Smithsonian May 86

17 You can drop humans anywhere and they'll thrive—only the rat does as well.

ib

PAUL EHRLICH, Professor of Biological Sciences, Stanford

18 [The National Academy of Sciences] would be unable to give a unanimous decision if asked whether the sun would rise tomorrow.

Look 1 Apr 70

ALBERT EINSTEIN

1 The grand aim of all science is to cover the greatest number of empirical facts by logical deduction from the smallest number of hypotheses or axioms.
Life 9 Jan 50

2 I assert that the cosmic religious experience is the strongest and the noblest driving force behind scientific research.
Recalled on his death 18 Apr 55

3 I think and think for months and years. Ninety-nine times, the conclusion is false. The hundredth time I am right.
ib

4 The most beautiful experience we can have is the mysterious. . . . the fundamental emotion which stands at the cradle of true art and true science.
From his 1931 book *Living Philosophies, ib*

5 When I examine myself and my methods of thought, I come close to the conclusion that the gift of fantasy has meant more to me than my talent for absorbing positive knowledge.
Recalled on 100th anniversary of his birth, 18 Feb 79

6 I made one great mistake in my life—when I signed the letter to President Roosevelt recommending that atom bombs be made . . . but there was some justification—the danger that the Germans would make them.
Quoted by Ted Morgan *FDR* Simon & Schuster 85

7 Concern for man and his fate must always form the chief interest of all technical endeavors . . . Never forget this in the midst of your diagrams and equations.
Quoted in "Science and Values" London *Times* 1 Jul 85

LOREN EISELEY

8 One could not pluck a flower without troubling a star.
The Immense Journey Random House 57

RICHARD P FEYNMAN, 1965 Nobel laureate in physics

9 If I could explain it to the average person, I wouldn't have been worth the Nobel Prize.
People 22 Jul 85

10 Reality must take precedence over public relations, for nature cannot be fooled.
On pinpointing reason for explosion of the space shuttle Challenger by showing that O-rings grow brittle when immersed in water, *Life* Jan 87

YURI A GAGARIN, Soviet cosmonaut

11 I could have gone on flying through space forever.
On the first manned space flight, NY *Times* 14 Apr 61

ROBERT PETER GALE, bone-marrow specialist

12 There is a silent enemy lurking there.
On dangerous radiation levels in western Russia, after his visit to treat victims of Chernobyl nuclear accident, *Time* 23 Jun 86

PAUL H GEBHARD, Director, Kinsey Institute for Sex Research, Indiana University

13 A crossing of a Rubicon in life history.
On one's initial experience of sexual intercourse, to Amer Assn for the Advancement of Science, NY *Times* 30 Dec 67

RICCARDO GIACCONI, Director, Space Telescope Science Institute, Johns Hopkins University

14 The universe is popping all over the place.
NY *Times* 8 May 84

HAROLD M GIBSON, Chief Meteorologist, NYC Weather Bureau

15 The best weather instrument yet devised is a pair of human eyes.
NY *Times* 30 Mar 84

JOHN GLENN, former astronaut

16 This is a day we have managed to avoid for a quarter of a century.
On loss of seven lives in the explosion of the space shuttle Challenger, news summaries 28 Jan 86

ALBERT GORE JR, US Senator

17 To use a Southern euphemism, our space program has been snake-bit.
On unsuccessful launch of an unmanned rocket shortly after the explosion of the space shuttle Challenger, *Nightline* ABC TV 5 May 86

ROBERT GROVE JR, satellite engineer

18 It's like a big parking lot up there. There are lots of empty places, and you can park in one as long as it doesn't belong to someone else.
On monitoring and transmitting satellite communications, *Newsweek* 29 Sep 86

EDMUND HILLARY

19 I am hell-bent for the South Pole—God willing and crevasses permitting.
Comment eight days before he reached the South

Pole via an overland route, news summaries 5 Jan 58

1 We knocked the bastard off.
On his successful ascent of Mt Everest, London *Sunday Times* 21 Jul 74

2 Better if he had said something natural like, "Jesus, here we are."
Commenting on Neil A Armstrong's 1969 message from the moon, "That's one small step for man, one giant leap for mankind," *ib*

JOHN F KENNEDY, 35th US President

3 Let both sides seek to invoke the wonders of science instead of its terrors.
On US and Soviet joint scientific ventures, inaugural address 21 Jan 61

4 In a very real sense, it will not be one man going to the moon . . . it will be an entire nation. For all of us must work to put him there.
State of the Union address 30 Jan 61

5 America has tossed its cap over the wall of space.
Quoted by William Safire NY *Times* 19 Aug 84

CHARLES F KETTERING, Vice President and Manager of Research, General Motors

6 People think of the inventor as a screwball, but no one ever asks the inventor what he thinks of other people.
Recalled on his death 25 Nov 58

7 The Wright brothers flew right through the smoke screen of impossibility.
ib

NIKITA S KHRUSHCHEV

8 He was . . . a crystal of morality among our scientists.
On Andrei D Sakharov's concern for dangerous potential of experimental nuclear explosions, recalled at end of Sakharov's detention in Gorky, NY *Times* 20 Dec 86

ALFRED C KINSEY, founder, Institute for Sex Research, Indiana University

9 There are some who have questioned the applicability of scientific methods to an investigation of human sexual behavior. . . . as though the dietitian and biochemist were denied the right to analyze foods and the process of nutrition, because the cooking and proper serving of food may be rated a fine art, and because the eating of certain foods has been considered a matter for religious regulation.
On critics of his pioneering investigations into human sexual behavior, *The Right to Investigate* Saunders 53

10 We are recorders and reporters of the facts—not judges of the behavior we describe.
Recalled on his death 25 Aug 56

DANIEL KLEPPNER, Professor of Physics, MIT

11 Big machines are the awe-inspiring cathedrals of the 20th century.
On large-scale equipment for physics experiments, NY *Times* 11 Jun 85

BRUCE KNAPP, physicist, Nevis Laboratory, Columbia University

12 It means you can try to answer questions you thought the universe was going to have to do without.
On supercomputers, NY *Times* 3 Jul 84

ARTHUR KOESTLER

13 [They are] peeping Toms at the keyhole of eternity.
Description of scientists, *The Roots of Coincidence* Hutchinson 72

VLADIMIR M KOMAROV, Soviet cosmonaut

14 In orbit now we have a small but harmonious collection of Soviet people.
Message from the first spaceship to carry three people, NY *Times* 13 Oct 64

ARTHUR KORNBERG, biochemist, Stanford, and 1959 Nobel laureate

15 A scientist . . . shouldn't be asked to judge the economic and moral value of his work. All we should ask the scientist to do is find the truth—and then not keep it from anyone.
San Francisco *Examiner & Chronicle* 19 Dec 71

STEPHEN LABERGE, research associate, Stanford

16 Not all lucid dreams are useful but they all have a sense of wonder about them. If you must sleep through a third of your life, why should you sleep through your dreams, too?
Quoted by Anne Fadiman "The Doctor of Dreams" *Life* Nov 86

17 Dream research is a wonderful field. All you do is sleep for a living.
ib

MARY LEAKEY, paleontologist

18 I've found him—found our man!
On 1959 discovery in Tanzania of a 1.8-million-year-old hominid skull, one of the earliest traces of human origin, quoted in NY *Times* 30 Oct 84

WILLIAM N LIPSCOMB JR, 1976 Nobel laureate in chemistry

1 For me, the creative process, first of all, requires a good nine hours of sleep a night. Second, it must not be pushed by the need to produce practical applications.
> NY *Times* 7 Dec 77

THOMAS E LOVEJOY, Executive Vice President, World Wildlife Fund

2 Natural species are the library from which genetic engineers can work.
> *Time* 13 Oct 86

3 Genetic engineers don't make new genes, they rearrange existing ones.
> *ib*

JAMES A LOVELL, US astronaut

4 The moon is essentially gray, no color. It looks like plaster of Paris, like dirty beach sand with lots of footprints in it.
> Washington *Post* 25 Dec 68

SPYRIDON MARINATOS, Professor of Archaeology, University of Athens

5 To excavate is to open a book written in the language that the centuries have spoken into the earth.
> NY *Times* 11 Jan 72

WILLIAM H MASTERS

6 Science by itself has no moral dimension. But it does seek to establish truth. And upon this truth morality can be built.
> *Life* 24 Jun 66

BARBARA MCCLINTOCK, 1983 Nobel laureate

7 It might seem unfair to reward a person for having so much pleasure over the years, asking the maize plant to solve specific problems and then watching its responses.
> On her lifelong research into the genetic characteristics of Indian corn plants, *Newsweek* 24 Oct 83

JAMES S MCDONNELL, builder of Mercury and Gemini space capsules

8 America is now a space-faring nation. . . . a frontier good for millions of years. The only time remotely comparable was when Columbus discovered a whole new world.
> *Time* 31 Mar 67

9 The creative conquest of space will serve as a wonderful substitute for war.
> *ib*

MARGARET MEAD

10 [Anthropology demands] the open-mindedness with which one must look and listen, record in astonishment and wonder that which one would not have been able to guess.
> *Sex and Temperament in Three Primitive Societies* Morrow 63

11 The way to do fieldwork is never to come up for air until it is all over.
> Letter from New Guinea, quoted by Jane Howard *Margaret Mead* Simon & Schuster 84

MIKE MELVILLE

12 I've got tooth marks on my heart.
> Comment after *Voyager* pilot Richard G Rutan's plane dropped 3,000 feet during the last leg of the first nonstop flight around the world on one load of fuel, NY *Times* 24 Dec 86

13 What you want to do, and what you can do, is limited only by what you can dream.
> Quoted by Charles Kuralt *Sunday Morning* CBS TV 28 Dec 86

DESMOND MORRIS

14 There are 193 species of monkeys and apes, 192 of them are covered with hair. The exception is a naked ape self-named *Homo sapiens*.
> *The Naked Ape* McGraw-Hill 68

15 This unusual and highly successful species spends a great deal of time examining his higher motives and an equal amount of time ignoring his fundamental ones.
> *ib*

NATIONAL GEOGRAPHIC SOCIETY

16 Comets are the nearest thing to nothing that anything can be and still be something.
> Announcing discovery of a comet visible only by telescope, 31 Mar 55

DAVID R NELSON, Professor of Physics, Harvard

17 The main satisfaction we're getting . . . is the intellectual excitement. For me, that's plenty. Isn't that really the driving force of science?
> On crystal research, NY *Times* 30 Jul 85

STEPHEN A NESBITT, NASA Public Affairs Officer

18 Obviously a major malfunction.
> Announcement moments after the space shuttle Challenger exploded, quoted in NY *Times* 29 Jan 86

19 The vehicle has exploded.
> *ib*

J ROBERT OPPENHEIMER

1 The open society, the unrestricted access to knowledge, the unplanned and uninhibited association of men for its furtherance—these are what may make a vast, complex, ever growing, ever changing, ever more specialized and expert technological world, nevertheless a world of human community.
  Science and the Common Understanding Simon & Schuster 53

2 Both the man of science and the man of action live always at the edge of mystery, surrounded by it.
  Address at Columbia University 26 Dec 54

3 The atomic bomb . . . made the prospect of future war unendurable. It has led us up those last few steps to the mountain pass; and beyond there is a different country.
  Quoted by Richard Rhodes *The Making of the Atomic Bomb* Simon & Schuster 87

DR LOUIS ORR, President, Amer Medical Assn

4 Science will never be able to reduce the value of a sunset to arithmetic. Nor can it reduce friendship or statesmanship to a formula.
  Commencement address at Emory University, Atlanta, 6 Jun 60

HEINZ R PAGELS, Executive Director, NY Academy of Sciences

5 The world changed from having the determinism of a clock to having the contingency of a pinball machine.
  On quantum theory's break with classical Newtonian physics, *The Cosmic Code* Simon & Schuster 82

6 Stars are like animals in the wild. We may see the young but never the actual birth, which is a veiled and secret event.
  Perfect Symmetry Simon & Schuster 85

7 There was emptiness more profound than the void between the stars, for which there was no here and there and before and after, and yet out of that void the entire plenum of existence sprang forth.
  Reflecting on origin of the universe, *Vogue* Jan 86

LINUS C PAULING, 1954 and 1962 Nobel laureate

8 I like people. I like animals, too—whales and quail, dinosaurs and dodos. But I like human beings especially, and I am unhappy that the pool of human germ plasm, which determines the nature of the human race, is deteriorating.
  From 1959 paper on the effect of radioactive fall-out on heredity, recalled on winning 1962 Nobel Peace Prize, NY *Times* 13 Oct 62

JOHN PIKE, Federation of Amer Scientists

9 Some agencies have a public affairs office. NASA is a public affairs office that has an agency.
  Criticism of statements made by image-conscious NASA officials after explosion of the space shuttle Challenger, NY *Times* 25 Apr 86

MICHAEL POTTS, spokesman, Beech Aircraft

10 The Wright brothers' design . . . allowed them to survive long enough to learn how to fly.
  On the wing formation used in the first successful powered flight, NY *Times* 17 Apr 84

T R REID

11 It was a seminal event of postwar science, one of those rare demonstrations that changes everything.
  On the development of the microchip, *The Chip* Simon & Schuster 85, quoted in NY *Times* 11 Feb 85

BERTRAND RUSSELL

12 Science is what you know, philosophy is what you don't know.
  Quoted by Alan Wood *Bertrand Russell* Simon & Schuster 58

CARL SAGAN, astronomer, Cornell University

13 To make an apple pie from scratch, you must first invent the universe.
  Cosmos PBS TV 23 Nov 80

ROALD Z SAGDEYEV, Soviet astrophysicist

14 I was looking at them as extraterrestrials.
  Recalling his first meeting with US scientists, NY *Times* 10 Mar 86

DAVID SARNOFF, Chairman, RCA

15 Freedom is the oxygen without which science cannot breathe.
  "Electronics—Today and Tomorrow," in Emily Davie ed *Profile of America* Crowell 54

16 Atoms for peace. Man is still the greatest miracle and the greatest problem on this earth.
  First message sent with atomic-powered electricity 27 Jan 54

17 I have learned to have more faith in the scientist than he does in himself.
  Recalled on his death, *Newsweek* 27 Dec 71

R TUCKER SCULLY, Director, US State Department Office of Oceans and Polar Affairs

1 You don't have three guys holed up there all winter with an American flag for nothing.
> In support of ad hoc exploratory missions rather than the establishment of a permanent Arctic research station, *Smithsonian* Nov 84

STUART LUMAN SEATON

2 The presence of humans, in a system containing high-speed electronic computers and high-speed, accurate communications, is quite inhibiting.
> To Amer Institute of Engineering, *Time* 17 Feb 58

FREDERICK SEITZ, President, Rockefeller University

3 A good scientist is a person in whom the childhood quality of perennial curiosity lingers on. Once he gets an answer, he has other questions.
> *Fortune* Apr 76

HUGH SIDEY

4 The Corn Belt is like John Bunyan's idyllic Beulah—or a dark Gehenna.
> "Bitter Harvest" *Time* 8 Sep 86

LORD SKELMERSDALE (Roger Bootle-Wilbraham), British Undersecretary of the Environment

5 This is the first time I've actually held a toad. And my sympathy goes very much to the toad.
> On opening of tunnel under highway to protect migrating toads during mating season, NY *Times* 14 Mar 87

C P SNOW

6 Technology . . . is a queer thing. It brings you great gifts with one hand, and it stabs you in the back with the other.
> NY *Times* 15 Mar 71

JOHN SPENCER, Professor of Science and Mathematics, Highlands University, Las Vegas NM

7 [The research rat of the future] allows experimentation without manipulation of the real world. This is the cutting edge of modeling technology.
> On computer program that simulates a human body's reaction to surgery, NY *Times* 12 Nov 85

ELVIN STACKMAN, President, Amer Assn for the Advancement of Science

8 Science cannot stop while ethics catches up . . . and nobody should expect scientists to do all the thinking for the country.
> *Life* 9 Jan 50

THOMAS P STAFFORD, US astronaut

9 Houston, this is Apollo 10. You can tell the world we have arrived.
> On reaching a lunar orbit that brought the spacecraft within nine miles of the moon's surface, NY *Times* 22 May 69

ALBERT SZENT-GYÖRGYI, 1937 Nobel laureate

10 Research is four things: brains with which to think, eyes with which to see, machines with which to measure and, fourth, money.
> Recalled on his death 22 Oct 86

LEWIS THOMAS

11 The uniformity of earth's life, more astonishing than its diversity, is accountable by the high probability that we derived, originally, from some single cell, fertilized in a bolt of lightning as the earth cooled.
> *The Lives of a Cell* Viking 74

12 It is from the progeny of this parent cell that we all take our looks; we still share genes around, and the resemblance of the enzymes of grasses to those of whales is in fact a family resemblance.
> *ib*

STEWART L UDALL, US Secretary of the Interior

13 Mining is like a search-and-destroy mission.
> *1976—Agenda for Tomorrow* Harcourt, Brace & World 68

14 Over the long haul of life on this planet, it is the ecologists, and not the bookkeepers of business, who are the ultimate accountants.
> To Congress of Optimum Population and Environment 9 Jun 70

HAROLD C UREY, 1934 Nobel laureate

15 I thought it might have a practical use in something like neon signs.
> On developing heavy water, vital to the atomic bomb, *Quote* 4 Apr 65

LARRY VAN GOETHEM

16 They travel with a constant companion, autumn.
> "Southward Stream of Birds of Prey" NY *Times* 14 Oct 84

LANCE A WALLACE, environmental scientist

1 We're all living in a chemical soup.
   Newsweek 7 Jan 85

CLAUDIA WALLIS

2 They are babies in waiting, life on ice.
   On sperm cells frozen for preservation, "Quickening Debate over Life on Ice" *Time* 2 Jul 84

JAMES D WATSON, 1962 Nobel laureate and Director of Research, Cold Spring Harbor Laboratory, NY

3 Biology has at least 50 more interesting years.
   News summaries 31 Dec 84

4 Take young researchers, put them together in virtual seclusion, give them an unprecedented degree of freedom and turn up the pressure by fostering competitiveness.
   On his formula for breakthroughs in research, *ib*

HARVEY WHEELER

5 The same system that produced a bewildering succession of new-model, style-obsolescent autos and refrigerators can also produce an endless outpouring of new-model, style-obsolescent science.
   NY *Times* 11 Aug 75

EDWARD H WHITE II, US astronaut

6 I felt red, white and blue all over.
   On his walk in space, *Life* 25 Jan 65

JOHN NOBLE WILFORD

7 Alone among all creatures, the species that styles itself wise, *Homo sapiens*, has an abiding interest in its distant origins, knows that its allotted time is short, worries about the future and wonders about the past.
   On paleontology, NY *Times* 30 Oct 84

EDWARD O WILSON, Professor of Science, Harvard

8 It's like having astronomy without knowing where the stars are.
   On disappearance of plants and animals more quickly than scientists can find and describe them, *Time* 13 Oct 86

9 When you have seen one ant, one bird, one tree, you have not seen them all.
   ib

TOM WOLFE

10 What is it that makes a man willing to sit up on top of an enormous Roman candle, such as a Redstone, Atlas, Titan or Saturn rocket, and wait for someone to light the fuse?
   The Right Stuff Farrar, Straus & Giroux 79

TRAVEL
Travelers on Traveling

AMERICAN EXPRESS

11 When your business trip is running late, your room will be waiting up for you.
   Guaranteeing the holding of advance reservations, advertisement in *New York* 16 Sep 85

ANONYMOUS

12 Is forbidden to steal towels, please. If you are not person to do such is please not to read notice.
   Sign in Tokyo hotel, quoted in *Holiday* 5 May 69

RUSSELL BAKER

13 When it comes to cars, only two varieties of people are possible—cowards and fools.
   On use of seat belts, "The Belted Coward" NY *Times* 2 Feb 85

14 A railroad station? That was sort of a primitive airport, only you didn't have to take a cab 20 miles out of town to reach it.
   ib 5 Nov 86

ELEANOR R BELMONT

15 A private railroad car is not an acquired taste. One takes to it immediately.
   The Fabric of Memory Farrar, Straus 57

HARVEY BERGENHOLTZ, NYC taxi driver

16 Our back seats are like psychiatrists' couches.
   NY *Times* 18 Jul 84

SHELLEY BERMAN

17 The sooner you are there, the sooner you will find out how long you will be delayed.
   On "getting to the airport in plenty of time," CNN TV 12 Dec 86

JAMES BRADY

18 One very clear impression I had of all the Beautiful People was their prudence. It may be that they paid for their own airline tickets, but they paid for little else.
   Superchic Little, Brown 74

FRANK BRAYNARD

19 We are all sailors on the spaceship Earth.
   On his idea for Operation Sail, which brought

225 vessels from throughout the world to NY Harbor for US Bicentennial, *Newsweek* 4 Jul 76

PAT BUCKLEY

1 I've never made the trip to or from Connecticut without its resembling the worst excesses of the French Revolution.
Quoted in NY *Times* 20 Nov 84

CHARLES, Prince of Wales

2 I'd rather go by bus.
When asked at age six if he was excited about sailing to Tobruk on the royal yacht, news summaries 21 May 54

ELLEN CHURCH

3 We could never get our coffee hot when flying out of Cheyenne because of the altitude—and we were too dumb to know why.
Recollection of being among the first airline hostesses in 1930, NY *Times* 15 May 60

CHARLOTTE CURTIS

4 His venture sounds like a banana peel awaiting its victim.
On plans of Nigel Nicolson to tour half the US while his son toured the other half for a book entitled *Two Roads to Dodge City*, NY *Times* 12 Nov 85

ELIZABETH DAVID

5 Provence is a country to which I am always returning, next week, next year, any day now, as soon as I can get on a train.
W 12 Sep 80

RAYMOND DAVIDSON

6 I'm fed up with it. I'm sick and tired of the delays, tired of the waiting. I'm hanging it up. You can have it. This flight will be my last flight.
Announcement of Eastern Airlines pilot who taxied back to the terminal and walked off his plane in protest against delays at Atlanta's Hartsfield Airport, NY *Times* 25 Jul 86

LUIGI DONZELLI, restaurant manager, Claridge's Hotel, London

7 Kings are no trouble. It's the queens.
Newsweek 5 Jun 78

LAWRENCE DURRELL

8 Journeys, like artists, are born and not made. A thousand differing circumstances contribute to them, few of them willed or determined by the will—whatever we may think.
Bitter Lemons Dutton 57, quoted in Washington *Post* 29 May 86

9 Travel can be one of the most rewarding forms of introspection.
ib

TEMPLE FIELDING

10 As a member of an escorted tour, you don't even have to know the Matterhorn isn't a tuba.
Fielding's Guide to Europe Sloane 63

BETTY FORD

11 Have a nice trip, Dick.
Bidding farewell to resigning President Richard M Nixon, quoted in *RN: Memoirs of Richard Nixon* Grosset & Dunlap 78

OTTO FRIEDRICH

12 Americans have always been eager for travel, that being how they got to the New World in the first place.
Time 22 Apr 85

PAUL GOLDBERGER

13 Riding on the IRT is usually a matter of serving time in one of the city's most squalid environments—noisy, smelly, crowded and overrun with a ceaseless supply of graffiti.
On NYC subways, NY *Times* 27 Jul 85

DAN GREENBERG

14 Storing your car in New York is safer than entering it in a demolition derby. But not much.
On parking garages, *New York* 25 Jan 71

ROBERT HUGHES

15 [It] was a secular cathedral, dedicated to the rites of travel.
On the Gare d'Orsay in Paris, *Time* 8 Dec 86

ADA LOUISE HUXTABLE

16 Nothing was more up-to-date when it was built, or is more obsolete today, than the railroad station.
On railroad terminals in the air age, NY *Times* 19 Nov 72

JEROME A JACKSON

17 There is no way to avoid the birds in the air, but the pilots can avoid being where the birds are.
On studying migration patterns to avoid aviation accidents, NY *Times* 7 May 85

FRANCES G KNIGHT, Director, Passport Division, US State Department

18 I was well acquainted with the gag that if you

looked like your passport picture, you needed a trip. I was unprepared for the proponderance of thuglike pictures which I found in the course of processing passports.

Ruling that it is all right to smile in passport photographs, NY *Herald Tribune* 21 Feb 57

HANS KONING

1 The *Queen Elizabeth II* provides vast amounts of entertainment for an age that has forgotten how to amuse itself unaided.

International Herald Tribune 15 Nov 85

CHARLES KURALT

2 Thanks to the interstate highway system, it is now possible to travel across the country from coast to coast without seeing anything.

On the Road Putnam 85

PHILIP LARKIN

3 I wouldn't mind seeing China if I could come back the same day.

NY *Times* 3 Dec 85

BOB LAVNER, spokesman for Automobile Club of NY

4 If a man needs his appendix taken out, his gall-bladder treated and some brain surgery as well, I don't think too many doctors would do the jobs simultaneously.

On concurrent road repairs clogging traffic, NY *Times* 29 Jun 84

BEA LILLIE

5 When does this place get to England?

Aboard the *Queen Mary,* quoted in NY *Times* 3 Sep 67

LONDON TIMES

6 There are good dukes and bad dukes and they cannot all be worthy of the ultimate in airport lounges.

On British Airport Authority's list of 42 official positions that rate use of VIP facilities, "Heathrow's Many Mansions" 15 Aug 78

ANITA LOOS

7 On a plane . . . you can pick up more and better people than on any other public conveyance since the stagecoach.

NY *Times* 26 Apr 73

HAROLD MACMILLAN

8 But, my dear boy, it always has been.

On being told that Cliveden, the Astor estate, had been turned into a hotel, NY *Times* 4 May 86

ANDREW H MALCOLM

9 Calling [O'Hare] an airport is like calling the *Queen Elizabeth II* a boat.

On intersection near O'Hare Airport, NY *Times* 5 May 85

RAZA MANJI

10 You don't watch for potholes around here, you watch for a little roadway between them.

Quoted by William E Geist "The Pothole: A Source of Perverse Civic Pride" NY *Times* 14 Jul 84

PAMELA MARSH

11 Enough scraps and rocks and countries are conveniently distributed across the face of the earth so that the sun still always shines on something British.

In review of Simon Winchester's *The Sun Never Sets* Prentice-Hall 86, *Christian Science Monitor* 3 Jul 86

GROUCHO MARX

12 I'm leaving because the weather is too good. I hate London when it's not raining.

News summaries 28 Jun 54

NEIL H McELROY, US Secretary of Defense

13 In the space age, man will be able to go around the world in two hours—one for flying and the other to get to the airport.

Look 18 Feb 58

JAMES A MICHENER

14 If you reject the food, ignore the customs, fear the religion and avoid the people, you might better stay home.

Quoted by William Safire and Leonard Safir *Good Advice* Times Books 82

JAN MYRDAL

15 There is a third dimension to traveling, the longing for what is beyond.

The Silk Road Random House 80, previewed in NY *Times* 25 Aug 79

16 Traveling is not just seeing the new; it is also leaving behind. Not just opening doors; also closing them behind you, never to return. But the place you have left forever is always there for you to see whenever you shut your eyes. And the cities you see most clearly at night are

the cities you have left and will never see again.
ib

ENID NEMY

1 My husband was getting his sea legs—rereading Joseph Conrad with a side order of C S Forester.
"In Search of Glamour on the Sea" *International Herald Tribune* 15 Feb 85

SYLVAINE ROUY NEVES

2 Dress impressively like the French, speak with authority like the Germans, have blond hair like the Scandinavians and speak of no American presidents except Lincoln, Roosevelt and Kennedy.
On how to gain respect while traveling in Europe, NY *Times* 30 Sep 84

NEW YORK STATE DRIVERS ASSOCIATION

3 When in doubt, don't start out.
Warning motorists not to drink and drive, NBC TV 3 May 85

PATRICK B OLIPHANT

4 Correct me if I'm wrong—the gizmo is connected to the flingflang connected to the watzis, watzis connected to the doo-dad connected to the ding dong.
Cartoon caption on questionable airline maintenance, *Time* 7 Jul 80

CYNTHIA OZICK

5 Traveling is *seeing*; it is the implicit that we travel by.
"Enchanters at First Encounter" NY *Times* 17 Mar 85

6 Travelers are fantasists, conjurers, seers—and what they finally discover is that every round object everywhere is a crystal ball: stone, teapot, the marvelous globe of the human eye.
ib

GLADYS PARRISH

7 The hotel was a forcing house for situations ... every shade of behavior in public had significance, so that the choice of a seat could constitute a victory or a reverse, and a few words aside change the complexion of half the day.
Madame Solario Penguin 84

DAVID PAULY

8 If airport traffic continues to snarl, the only

sure way to get there on Tuesday will be to leave on Monday.
"Airport '84: Stalled Out" *Newsweek* 30 Jul 84

NANCY POND-SMITH, flight attendant

9 They are the passengers of the future, and we want them to have a good experience the first time they fly.
On increasing number of children who are traveling alone between homes of divorced parents, NY *Times* 21 Jun 86

WILLIAM PROXMIRE, US Senator

10 The limousine is the ultimate ego trip, the supreme sign of success. It shouts: "Hey, this guy is really and truly Mr Big."
Testimony to House Committee on Government Operations, NY *Times* 20 Sep 85

ANTHONY RAMIREZ

11 Flying first class is déclassé.
"The Decline of First Class" *Fortune* 26 May 86

ROBERT REINHOLD

12 The main ... divorce routes are along the heavily traveled corridor between Boston and Washington in the Northeast and between nearby cities, such as Houston and Dallas in Texas and San Francisco and Los Angeles in California.
On increasing number of children who are traveling alone between homes of divorced parents, "Have Toys, Will Travel" NY *Times* 21 Jun 86

CHARLES RITZ

13 The Ritz is not ritzy.
Denying ostentatious luxury in his family's Parisian hotel, recalled on his death, NY *Times* 14 Jul 76

14 The guest is always right—even if we have to throw him out.
ib

WILLIAM ROBBINS

15 It provides an excuse for morning tardiness and an alibi for late returns. It provides grist for party talk and harrowing tales of accidents narrowly missed, potholes hit, tires blown and hubcaps lost.
On Philadelphia's Schuylkill Expressway, sometimes called "Surekill Stressway," NY *Times* 13 Jul 84

ANDY ROONEY

16 Crossing the street in New York keeps old people young—if they make it.
60 Minutes CBS TV 6 Jan 85

VICTOR ROSS, spokesman for NY Bureau of Traffic Operations

1 This was not a day of *Titanic* proportions. Maybe just *Lusitania*.
> On road congestion after Labor Day, NY *Times* 5 Sep 84

2 My expressway runneth over.
> After tractor trailer filled with wine casks split open on the Brooklyn-Queens Expressway, *ib* 7 May 85

RUMANIAN NATIONAL AIRLINES

3 Exit according to rule, first leg and then head. Remove high heels and synthetic stockings before evacuation: Open the door, take out the recovery line and throw it away.
> Emergency instructions quoted in letter to London *Times* 27 Sep 84

ROBERT RUNCIE, Archbishop of Canterbury

4 I sometimes think that Thomas Cook should be numbered among the secular saints. He took travel from the privileged and gave it to the people.
> *Canadian Churchman* Mar 80

MARY LEE SETTLE

5 She dreamed, lulled by the train, of getting off at heaven or New York City, whichever she got to first.
> *The Scapegoat* Random House 80

GEORGE BERNARD SHAW

6 The great advantage of a hotel is that it is a refuge from home life.
> Quoted in NY *Times* 10 Jul 83

MARGARET MARY SHEERIN

7 I read it all beforehand—"How to ditch without a hitch."
> On preparing for a European flight that took her out of her Georgetown Visitation Convent for the first time in nearly 40 years, Washington *Post* 7 Jun 64

IGOR SIKORSKY

8 The helicopter . . . approaches closer than any other [vehicle] to fulfillment of mankind's ancient dreams of the flying horse and the magic carpet.
> On the 20th anniversary of the initial flight of his invention, NY *Times* 13 Sep 59

RONALD STEEL

9 Discount air fares, a car in every parking space and the interstate highway system have made every place accessible—and every place alike.
> "Life in the Last 50 Years" *Esquire* Jun 83

JOHN STEINBECK

10 Four hoarse blasts of a ship's whistle still raise the hair on my neck and set my feet to tapping.
> *Travels with Charley* Viking 62

11 The sound of a jet, an engine warming up, even the clopping of shod hooves on pavement brings on the ancient shudder, the dry mouth and vacant eye, the hot palms and the churn of stomach high up under the rib cage.
> *ib*

ESTHER TALLAMY

12 I'm as self-contained as a turtle. When I put my key in the ignition, I have my home right behind me.
> On convenience of motor homes for long-distance travel, NY *Times* 26 Jun 86

HENRIETTA, LADY TAVISTOCK

13 Traveling with a tiara is such a performance. Your hair has to be woven into [it], and I wouldn't think you would be able to find a hairdresser here who knows how.
> Comment when a case of her tiaras was included in "The Treasure Houses of Britain" exhibit at Washington DC's National Gallery of Art, NY *Times* 31 Oct 85

PAUL THEROUX

14 You define a good flight by negatives: you didn't get hijacked, you didn't crash, you didn't throw up, you weren't late, you weren't nauseated by the food. So you are grateful.
> *The Old Patagonian Express* Houghton Mifflin 79

PAUL TOURNIER

15 The real meaning of travel, like that of a conversation by the fireside, is the discovery of oneself through contact with other people, and its condition is self-commitment in the dialogue.
> *The Meaning of Persons* Harper 57

ANNE TYLER

16 While armchair travelers dream of going places, traveling armchairs dream of staying put.
> *The Accidental Tourist* Knopf 85, quoted in *Christian Science Monitor* 4 Oct 85

DONALD WEEKS

1 The crossroads of yesterday and tomorrow, Gatwick Airport.

In biography of Frederick William Rolfe, *Corvo, "Saint or Madman?"* McGraw-Hill 71

EUDORA WELTY

2 Writers and travelers are mesmerized alike by knowing of their destinations.

One Writer's Beginnings Harvard 84

ROBIN WILLIAMS

3 The only people flying to Europe will be terrorists, so it will be, "Will you be sitting in armed or unarmed?"

Quoted in *US* 3 Nov 86

DARYL WYCKOFF

4 The airlines were always ending up like my beagle, 15 blocks from home and panting.

On bankruptcy of airlines that expanded routes too quickly after deregulation in 1978, *Time* 8 Oct 84

MELISSA ZEGANS

5 You have to run ahead of people sometimes and try to kill them.

On catching cabs in Manhattan, NY *Times* 18 Dec 86

The Eye of the Traveler

ANSEL ADAMS

6 Yosemite Valley, to me, is always a sunrise, a glitter of green and golden wonder in a vast edifice of stone and space.

The Portfolios of Ansel Adams NY Graphic Society/Little, Brown 81

JAMES AGEE

7 This continent, an open palm spread frank before the sky.

"The Great American Roadside" *Fortune* Sep 54

SHANA ALEXANDER

8 The graceful Georgian streets and squares, a series of steel engravings under a wet sky.

"Dublin Is My Sure Thing" *Life* 2 Sep 66

NELSON ALGREN

9 Chicago is an October sort of city even in spring.

Quoted by George F Will *Newsweek* 13 Aug 84

ANONYMOUS

10 London is a bad habit one hates to lose.

Quoted by William Sansom *Blue Skies, Brown Studies* Hogarth 61

11 If the United States is a melting pot, then New York makes it bubble.

Sign in Times Square, quoted in *US News & World Report* 14 Apr 86

R W APPLE JR

12 Aspects of life here—civility, courtesy, coziness—have always bound Britons to their country ... They are part of the British myth, along with lovely countryside, dogs and horses, rose gardens, the Armada, the Battle of Britain.

NY *Times* 9 Oct 85

ANTHONY AUSTIN

13 The city charms you out of any mood of protest or anger or hopelessness. It is a city of sky and water, of stone lions and sphinxes gazing out over the Neva River, of delicate iron grillwork hanging over the canals, of sunsets that paint the riverfront houses with tender violet and pink.

On Leningrad, NY *Times* 2 Jun 80

14 It is a city of fantasy, as Dostoyevsky called it, and sometimes, adrift amid so much beauty, one almost shares the expectation he described: that any moment one can imagine the city rising and floating away, leaving nothing but the swamp on which it was built.

ib

ANTHONY BAILEY

15 As one comes down the Henry Hudson Parkway along the river in the dusk, New York is never real; it is always fabulous.

New Yorker 29 Jul 67

MONICA BALDWIN

16 The Sussex lanes were very lovely in the autumn. ... spendthrift gold and glory of the year-end ... earth scents and the sky winds and all the magic of the countryside which is ordained for the healing of the soul.

On the English countryside, *I Leap over the Wall* Rinehart 50

DJUNA BARNES

17 What is a ruin but time easing itself of endurance?

Selected Works of Djuna Barnes Farrar, Straus & Giroux 62

CHARLES EDWIN WOODROW BEAN

1 Australia is a big blank map, and the whole people is constantly sitting over it like a committee, trying to work out the best way to fill it in.

> Quoted in Stephen Murray-Smith ed *The Dictionary of Australian Quotations* Heinemann 84

ARBIT BLATAS

2 In the winter, Venice is like an abandoned theater. The play is finished, but the echoes remain.

> Quoted by Erica Jong "A City of Love and Death: Venice" NY *Times* 23 Mar 86

MARY BLUME

3 The Englishman's telephone box is his castle. Like the London taxi, it can be entered by a gentleman in a top hat. It protects the user's privacy, keeps him warm and is large enough for a small cocktail party.

> Protesting replacement of Britain's bright-red phone booths, *International Herald Tribune* 30 Aug 85

ALAN BRIEN

4 The blue-rinse warbler and her horn-rimmed mate are rare and overdue this year.

> On annual migration of Americans to Great Britain, London *Sunday Times* 21 Jul 74

ANATOLE BROYARD

5 Rome was a poem pressed into service as a city.

> NY *Times* 25 Mar 74

HOLLY BRUBACH

6 Nothing makes you feel that you've overstayed your welcome like a flower arrangement that has withered and died.

> In survey of London hotels, *Harper's* 8 Sep 84

7 Claridge's [is] elegant but determinedly unglamorous. . . . The only fantasy it has to offer is the illusion that the world is in good working order.

> *ib*

8 It's the punctilious attention to detail, in a time when nobody even bothers to get the spelling of your name right.

> *ib*

LENNY BRUCE

9 Miami Beach is where neon goes to die.

> Quoted by Barbara Gordon *Saturday Review* 20 May 72

TOM BUCKLEY

10 The voluptuous curve of the riverbank at 79th Street . . . escapes from the city's rigid grid of streets and avenues like a fat woman slipping out of a corset.

> On New York City, NY *Times* 13 Apr 75

TRUMAN CAPOTE

11 Venice is like eating an entire box of chocolate liqueurs in one go.

> News summaries 26 Nov 61

CHARLES, Prince of Wales

12 I sometimes wonder if two thirds of the globe is covered in red carpet.

> After Australian and US tour, quoted in *US* 16 Dec 85

AGATHA CHRISTIE

13 It is ridiculous to set a detective story in New York City. New York City is itself a detective story.

> *Life* 14 May 56

WINSTON CHURCHILL

14 I shall always be glad to have seen it—for the same reason Papa gave for being glad to have seen Lisbon—namely, "that it will be unnecessary ever to see it again."

> On Calcutta, in 1896 letter to his mother, quoted by John Colville *The Fringes of Power* Norton 85

RICHARD COBB

15 France is getting younger. I am not.

> *London Illustrated News* Mar 86

ROBERT TRISTRAM COFFIN

16 Vermont's a place where barns come painted
Red as a strong man's heart,
Where stout carts and stout boys in freckles
Are highest forms of art.

> "Vermont Looks Like a Man," last poem contributed to NY *Herald Tribune* editorial page before his death 20 Jan 55

PAT COLANDER

17 Chicago is a city of contradictions, of private visions haphazardly overlaid and linked together.

> "A Metropolis of No Little Plans" NY *Times* 5 May 85

CHARLOTTE CURTIS

18 The new, young, chic and acquisitive rich, the

restless young Europeans and the beautiful people ... still flit from Palm Beach's polo fields to Newport's yachts with refueling stops at Gucci, Yves Saint Laurent and Tiffany.

NY *Times* 7 Aug 84

BOB DODSON

1 The Mississippi meanders down the spine of America.

CBS TV 26 Aug 84

ROBIN DOUGLAS-HOME

2 Scotland, thank God, is not for everyone.

"Scotland: The Dour and the Beautiful" *Vogue* 15 Apr 64

MARGARET DRABBLE

3 The yearning of the provincial for the capital is a quite exceptional passion. It sets in early, and until it is satisfied it does not let go. It draws its subjects into a strange world where trains and hotels take on an exceptional significance. Many suffering from it become travelers, but perhaps they are aware that travel is simply an extension of that first uprooting, a desire to repeat that first incomparable shock.

Arnold Bennett Knopf 74

JOHN FLEISCHMAN

4 Living as you do in New York, the navel of the universe, it is easy to confuse the Midwest and the South.

Letter to the editor NY *Times* 7 Jun 85

5 North Carolina is the place you fly over on the way to Florida. Ohio is the flat place between Hoboken and Malibu.

ib

WILLIAM E GEIST

6 New York is a city of conversations overheard, of people at the next restaurant table (micrometers away) checking your watch, of people reading the stories in your newspaper on the subway train.

"A Quiet Sendoff at the Barbershop" NY *Times* 25 Oct 86

PENELOPE GILLIATT

7 Prague is like a vertical Venice ... steps everywhere.

Vanity Fair Jan 85

WILLIAM GOLDING

8 He who rides the sea of the Nile must have sails woven of patience.

An Egyptian Journal Faber & Faber 85

NIGEL GOSLIN

9 New York is a granite beehive, where people jostle and whir like molecules in an overheated jar. . . . Houston is six suburbs in search of a center.

Saturday Review 7 Oct 67

ROBERT GRAVES

10 I was last in Rome in ad 540 when it was full of Goths and their heavy horses. It has changed a great deal since then.

NY *Times* 6 Jan 58

CEDRIC HARDWICKE

11 England is my wife, America my mistress. It is very good sometimes to get away from one's wife.

NY *Herald Tribune* 7 Aug 64

ERNEST HEMINGWAY

12 If you are lucky enough to have lived in Paris as a young man, then wherever you go for the rest of your life it stays with you, for Paris is a moveable feast.

A Moveable Feast Scribner's 64

JOHN HILLABY

13 Few things are more pleasant than a village graced with a good church, a good priest and a good pub.

On cross-country walking in England, *Journey Home* Holt, Rinehart & Winston 84

PAUL HOGARTH and STEPHEN SPENDER

14 Chicago is at the base of that congress of lakes—Superior, Huron and Michigan—which, on the map, makes it look like the sensitive area of some vital organ—lungs or heart or liver drawing in and giving out blood—a meeting of waterways, airways and railways—the pulse of the continent.

America Observed Potter 79, quoted in NY *Times* 1 Jul 79

ELSPETH HUXLEY

15 [Africa] is a cruel country; it takes your heart and grinds it into powdered stone—and no one minds.

The Flame Trees of Thika Morrow 59

ISRAELI TOURIST BUREAU

16 If you liked the book, you'll love the country.

Urging tourists to visit Israel after reading the Old Testament, quoted by Episcopal Diocese of Chicago *Advance* Jul 79

BRIAN JACKMAN

1 Everything in Africa bites, but the safari bug is worst of all.

"Close Encounters of the Rare and Violent Kind" London *Times* 15 Oct 83

ERICA JONG

2 It is the city of mirrors, the city of mirages, at once solid and liquid, at once air and stone.

"A City of Love and Death: Venice" NY *Times* 23 Mar 86

3 The stones themselves are thick with history, and those cats that dash through the alleyways must surely be the ghosts of the famous dead in feline disguise.

ib

GEORGE F KENNAN

4 Russia, Russia—unwashed, backward, appealing Russia, so ashamed of your own backwardness, so orientally determined to conceal it from us by clever deceit.

Quoted by Walter Isaacson and Evan Thomas *The Wise Men* Simon & Schuster 86

5 I shall always remember you—slyly, touchingly, but with great shouting and confusion—pumping hot water into our sleeping car in the frosty darkness of a December morning in order that we might not know, in order that we might never realize, to how primitive a land we had come.

ib

GEORGE KIMBLE

6 The darkest thing about Africa has always been our ignorance of it.

"Africa Today: The Lifting Darkness" *Reporter* 15 May 51

JOHN LE CARRÉ

7 Berlin. What a garrison of spies! ... what a cabinet full of useless, liquid secrets, what a playground for every alchemist, miracle worker and rat piper that ever took up the cloak.

A Perfect Spy Knopf 86

ANNE MORROW LINDBERGH

8 I have been overcome by the beauty and richness of our life together, those early mornings setting out, those evenings gleaming with rivers and lakes below us, still holding the last light.

War Within and Without Harcourt Brace Jovanovich 80

9 Those fields of daisies we landed on, and dusty fields and desert stretches. Memories of many skies and earths beneath us—many days, many nights of stars.

ib

CHARLES A LINDBERGH

10 I owned the world that hour as I rode over it. ... free of the earth, free of the mountains, free of the clouds, but how inseparably I was bound to them.

On flying above the Rocky Mountains, quoted by Leonard Mosley *Lindbergh* Doubleday 78

RICHARD E LINGENFELTER

11 The valley we call Death, isn't really that different from much of the rest of the desert West. It's just a little deeper, a little hotter and a little drier. What sets it apart more than anything else is the mind's eye.

Death Valley and the Amargosa University of California 86, quoted in NY *Times* 6 Jun 86

WALTER LIPPMANN

12 There is nothing so good for the human soul as the discovery that there are ancient and flourishing civilized societies which have somehow managed to exist for many centuries and are still in being though they have had no help from the traveler in solving their problems.

Quoted by Ronald Steel *Walter Lippmann and the American Century* Atlantic-Little, Brown 80

LONDON TIMES

13 After the annual festival, Edinburgh reverts to its staid character, a stern old lady counting the cash from her annual fling.

17 Aug 81

BERYL MARKHAM

14 I have a trunk containing continents.

Quoted on *World without Walls: Beryl Markham's African Memoir* WNET TV 8 Oct 86

FELIX MARTI-IBÁÑEZ

15 In Amsterdam the water is the mistress and the land the vassal. ... throughout the city there are as many canals and drawbridges as bracelets on a Gypsy's bronzed arms.

MD Mar 80

MILTON MAYER

16 The American goes to Paris, always has, and comes back and tells his neighbor, always

does, how exorbitant and inhospitable it is, how rapacious and selfish and unaccommodating and unresponsive it is, how dirty and noisy it is—and the next summer his neighbor goes to Paris.

"Paris as a State of Mind" NY *Times* 9 Jun 85

DAVE MAZUR, Canisius College freshman

1 Beaches, beer and bikinis . . . sand, surf and sex.

On Ft Lauderdale FL during spring break, *Time* 7 Apr 86

PHYLLIS MCGINLEY

2 The East is a montage. . . . It is old and it is young, very green in summer, very white in winter, gregarious, withdrawn and at once both sophisticated and provincial.

"The East Is Home" *Woman's Home Companion* Jul 56

JOHN MCKAY, Lord Provost of Edinburgh

3 We are Boston, Glasgow is Cleveland.

Wall Street Journal 25 Oct 85

TED MILLS and STEVEN WHITE

4 In every building of Paris there is a concierge, to serve as a human watchdog. Whoever you are, she knows about you.

Maurice Chevalier's Paris NBC TV 6 Mar 57

NICHOLAS MONSARRAT

5 The marvelous maturity of London! I would rather be dead in this town than preening my feathers in heaven.

Breaking In, Breaking Out Morrow 66

JAN MORRIS (James Morris)

6 There it stands, with a toss of curls and a flounce of skirts, a Carmen among the cities. . . . the last of the Middle Eastern fleshpots. . . . a junction of intrigue and speculation.

On Beirut, *Among the Cities* Oxford 85

7 Its origins are ancient but it burgeons with brash modernity, and it lounges upon its delectable shore, halfway between the Israelis and the Syrians, in a posture that no such city, at such a latitude, in such a moment of history, has any reasonable excuse for assuming.

ib

8 To the stern student of affairs, Beirut is a phenomenon, beguiling perhaps, but quite, quite impossible.

ib

9 Brooded over by mist more often than swirled about by cloud, drizzled rather than storm-swept, on the western perimeter of Europe lies the damp, demanding and obsessively interesting country called by its own people Cymru . . . and known to the rest of the world, if it is known at all, as Wales.

The Matter of Wales Oxford 85

10 Its smallness is not petty; on the contrary, it is profound.

ib

V S NAIPAUL

11 I came to London. It had become the center of my world and I had worked hard to come to it. And I was lost.

An Area of Darkness André Deutsch 64

V S PRITCHETT

12 The very name London has tonnage in it.

London Perceived Harcourt, Brace & World 62

STEPHEN J PYNE

13 In Antarctica . . . foreground and background were difficult to establish . . . On shelf and plateau the vision was of an immutable nothingness.

The Ice: A Journey to Antarctica University of Iowa 86, quoted in NY *Times* 25 Jan 87

DAVID QUAMMEN

14 Stonehenge nowadays is a zoo animal, an imposing but humbled beast, captive behind a wire fence and a turnstile, embarrassed by the near presence of a visitors' car park.

Christian Science Monitor 12 May 80

JONATHAN RABAN

15 They'll like you because you're a foreigner. They love foreigners; it's just strangers they hate.

Citing a subtle distinction given him on a Mississippi River cruise, *Old Glory: An American Voyage* Simon & Schuster 81

16 In this part of the country taxidermy seemed as much a part of everyday culture as psychoanalysis in Manhattan.

Visiting hunters and fishermen in the upper Midwest, *ib*

JOHN RUSSELL

17 The bedrooms are just large enough for a well-behaved dwarf and a greyhound on a diet.

On modern European hotels, NY *Times* 4 Aug 77

ERNESTO SÁBATO

1 The first time I passed through the country I had the impression it was swept down with a broom from one end to the other every morning by housewives who dumped all the dirt on Italy.

On Switzerland, *On Heroes and Tombs* Godine 81

MORLEY SAFER

2 Arrogance and snobbism live in adjoining rooms and use a common currency.

On the Ritz Hotel in Paris, *60 Minutes* CBS TV 27 Jul 80

HARRISON E SALISBURY

3 Here when I walk the hutungs of a summer's evening as the moon rises over the city I can hear a lover's flute sending a tender message beyond the courtyard walls or the mournful monotony of a three-stringed lute.

"Capturing Old Echoes in the New Peking" NY *Times* 10 Feb 85

DOROTHY L SAYERS

4 There ... within a stone's throw, stood the twin towers of All Souls, fantastic, unreal as a house of cards, clear-cut in the sunshine, the drenched oval in the quad beneath brilliant as an emerald in the bezel of a ring.

On Oxford University, from her 1935 book *Gaudy Night*, recalled on her death 17 Dec 57

SERGE SCHMEMANN

5 [Leningrad] sits astride the Neva, frozen in time, a haunting mélange of pale hues, glorious façades and teeming ghosts.

"Majesty Fading from Russia's Window on the West" NY *Times* 7 Apr 84

ROBERT B SEMPLE JR

6 In Britain it will connect you to all sorts of people you had no intention of speaking to in the first place.

On London's telephone system, NY *Times* 6 Aug 76

LUCKY SEVERSON

7 Nome is as far west as west goes before it becomes east.

On Nome AK, *1986* NBC TV 30 Dec 86

8 If you don't believe hell freezes over, you haven't been to Nome.

ib

PETER SHAFFER

9 If London is a watercolor, New York is an oil painting.

NY *Times* 13 Apr 75

R Z SHEPPARD

10 The San Francisco Bay Area [is] the playpen of countercultures.

Time 8 Sep 86

DAVID K SHIPLER

11 Jerusalem is a festival and a lamentation. Its song is a sigh across the ages, a delicate, robust, mournful psalm at the great junction of spiritual cultures.

Arab and Jew: Wounded Spirits in a Promised Land Times Books 86

TERENCE SMITH

12 The whole peninsula ... remains what it has always been: one of the last great wildernesses of the world, a place of stunning beauty and harsh reality where history, religion and modern politics come together as nowhere else.

"The Harsh Splendor of the Sinai" NY *Times* 18 Nov 84

PETER STOREY

13 Once a place becomes special, it's no longer special.

On transformation of Cannes from fishing village to stylish resort, quoted by C David Heymann *Poor Little Rich Girl* Lyle Stuart 84

HORACE SUTTON

14 Ireland's ruins are historic emotions surrendered to time.

Saturday Review 25 Jun 66

TIME MAGAZINE

15 Spain is a land of mystery where the dust of isolation has often settled on men's work and obscured their lives.

6 Jul 53

ARNOLD TOYNBEE

16 The immense cities lie basking on the beaches of the continent like whales that have taken to the land.

On Australia, *East to West* Oxford 58

17 Angkor is not orchestral; it is monumental. It is an epic poem which makes its effect, like the *Odyssey* and like *Paradise Lost,* by the grandeur of its structure as well as by the beauty of

the details. .... an epic in rectangular forms imposed upon the Cambodian jungle.

ib

JOHN UPDIKE

1 The city overwhelmed our expectations. The Kiplingesque grandeur of Waterloo Station, the Eliotic despondency of the brick row in Chelsea ... the Dickensian nightmare of fog and sweating pavement and besmirched cornices.

On London, in "A Madman" *New Yorker* 22 Dec 62

CRAIG R WHITNEY

2 A city of private lives, led in quiet resignation.

On Dresden, East Germany, NY *Times* 6 Nov 76

Humankind

FAMILY LIFE

Family Members

CAROL BURNETT

1 [This is to explain] just how your mom turned out to be the kind of hairpin she is.
> Note to her daughters in *One More Time* Random House 86, quoted in NY *Times* 19 Oct 86

LILLIAN CARTER

2 Sometimes when I look at all my children, I say to myself, "Lillian, you should have stayed a virgin."
> Comment to 1980 Democratic Convention that nominated her son for a second term as president, quoted in *Newsweek* 29 Dec 80

JOHN CHEEVER

3 When I remember my family, I always remember their backs. They were always indignantly leaving places.
> Quoted by Susan Cheever *Home before Dark* Houghton Mifflin 84

MAY ROPER COKER

4 I never thought that you should be rewarded for the greatest privilege of life.
> On being chosen Mother of the Year, NY *Daily News* 7 May 58

CLAUDETTE COLBERT

5 Why do grandparents and grandchildren get along so well? They have the same enemy—the mother.
> *Time* 14 Sep 81

PAT CONROY

6 The children of warriors in our country learn the grace and caution that come from a permanent sense of estrangement.
> *Book-of-the-Month Club News* Dec 86

MARIO CUOMO, Governor of NY

7 I talk and talk and talk, and I haven't taught people in 50 years what my father taught by example in one week.
> *Time* 2 Jun 86

8 I am a trial lawyer. ... Matilda says that at dinner on a good day I sound like an affidavit.
> NY *Times* 10 Nov 86

LOUISE SEVIER GIDDINGS CURREY

9 Spoil your husband, but don't spoil your children—that's my philosophy.
> On being chosen Mother of the Year, NY *Post* 14 May 61

BETTE DAVIS

10 If you've never been hated by your child, you've never been a parent.
> On publication of her daughter B D Hyman's book, CBS TV 5 May 85

DOROTHY DeBOLT

11 Of course I don't always enjoy being a mother. At those times my husband and I hole up somewhere in the wine country, eat, drink, make mad love and pretend we were born sterile and raise poodles.
> On receiving 1980 National Mother's Day Committee Award as the natural mother of 6 and adoptive mother of 14, San Francisco *Chronicle* 22 Apr 80

YVONNE DE GAULLE

12 The presidency is temporary—but the family is permanent.
> On her priorities as wife of French President Charles de Gaulle, quoted by Richard M Nixon *RN: Memoirs of Richard Nixon* Grosset & Dunlap 78

FRANCO DILIGENTI

13 A man who has raised quintuplets has had enough of babies.
> *Saturday Evening Post* 25 Jan 64

OLIVA DIONNE

14 I ought to be shot.
> On becoming father of quintuplets in 1934, recalled on his death 15 Nov 79

DWIGHT D EISENHOWER, 34th US President

15 There's no tragedy in life like the death of a

child. Things never get back to the way they were.

On the death of his first son, recalled on *Ike* PBS TV 15 Oct 86

GERALD R FORD, 38th US President

1 All my children have spoken for themselves since they first learned to speak, and not always with my advance approval, and I expect that to continue in the future.

NY *Post* 13 Aug 74

HENRY FORD II

2 My grandfather killed my father in my mind. I know he died of cancer—but it was because of what my grandfather did to him.

On Henry and Edsel Ford, quoted by Robert Lacey *Ford: The Men and the Machine* Little, Brown 86

KATHARINE HOUGHTON HEPBURN

3 If you want to sacrifice the admiration of many men for the criticism of one, go ahead, get married.

Advice to her daughter Katharine before the actress's 1928 marriage to Ludlow Ogden Smith, quoted by Anne Edwards *A Remarkable Woman* Morrow 85

MARY JARRELL

4 Jarrell was not so much a father . . . as an affectionate encyclopedia.

On her husband, *Randall Jarrell's Letters* Houghton Mifflin 85

NATASHA JOSEFOWITZ

5 My father died
many years ago,
and yet when something special
happens to me,
I talk to him secretly
not really knowing
whether he hears,
but it makes me feel better
to half believe it.

Is This Where I Was Going? Warner 83

JULIANA, Queen of the Netherlands

6 Our child will not be raised in tissue paper! We don't even want her to hear the word *princess*.

On hiring a nurse for her first child, *Ladies' Home Journal* Mar 55

EDWARD M KENNEDY, US Senator

7 Dad, I'm in some trouble. There's been an ac-

cident and you're going to hear all sorts of things about me from now on. Terrible things.

Informing his father of Chappaquiddick incident in which Mary Jo Kopechne was drowned, quoted by Peter Collier and David Horowitz *The Kennedys* Summit 84

JACQUELINE KENNEDY

8 Dear God, please take care of your servant John Fitzgerald Kennedy.

Inscription for mass cards at her husband's funeral 25 Nov 63

JOHN F KENNEDY JR

9 The three of us have been alone for such a long time. We welcome a fourth person.

Toast to Edwin Schlossberg at rehearsal dinner for his wedding to Caroline Kennedy, quoted in *People* 4 Aug 86

JOSEPH P KENNEDY

10 Jack doesn't belong anymore to just a family. He belongs to the country.

Comment a few weeks before his son's inauguration, quoted by Hugh Sidey *John F Kennedy, President* Atheneum 63

11 If there's anything I'd hate as a son-in-law, it's an actor; and if there's anything I think I'd hate worse than an actor as a son-in-law, it's an English actor.

Tongue-in-cheek comment on Patricia Kennedy's marriage to English actor Peter Lawford, *ib*

12 He may be president, but he still comes home and swipes my socks.

On his son John, *ib*

13 He's a great kid. He hates the same way I do.

On his son Bobby, quoted by Richard J Whalen *The Founding Father* New American Library 64

ROSE KENNEDY

14 I looked on child rearing not only as a work of love and duty but as a profession that was fully as interesting and challenging as any honorable profession in the world and one that demanded the best that I could bring to it.

Times to Remember Doubleday 74

15 Make sure you never, never argue at night. You just lose a good night's sleep, and you can't settle anything until morning anyway.

Advice to her first married granddaughter, *People* 6 Jun 83

LOUISE HEATH LEBER

16 There's always room for improvement, you know—it's the biggest room in the house.

On being chosen Mother of the Year, NY *Post* 14 May 61

MADELEINE L'ENGLE

1 I love my mother, not as a prisoner of atherosclerosis, but as a person; and I must love her enough to accept her as she is, now, for as long as this dwindling may take.

The Summer of the Great-Grandmother Farrar, Straus & Giroux 74

2 She seems to have had the ability to stand firmly on the rock of her past while living completely and unregretfully in the present.

ib

CHARLES A LINDBERGH

3 He makes fuzz come out of my bald patch!

On his son's driving ability, quoted by Leonard Mosley *Lindbergh* Doubleday 76

ALISON LURIE

4 There is a peculiar burning odor in the room, like explosives. . . . the kitchen fills with smoke and the hot, sweet, ashy smell of scorched cookies. The war has begun.

On a wife's discovery of her husband's infidelity, *The War between the Tates* Warner 74

DOUGLAS MACARTHUR

5 Build me a son, O Lord, who will be strong enough to know when he is weak, and brave enough to face himself when he is afraid, one who will be proud and unbending in honest defeat, and humble and gentle in victory.

"A Father's Prayer," quoted by Courtney Whitney *MacArthur* Knopf 55

PETER MALKIN

6 Even a secret agent can't lie to a Jewish mother.

On his mother's suspicion that he was going on an important mission, NY *Times* 28 Apr 86

PHYLLIS MCGINLEY

7 To be a housewife is . . . a difficult, a wrenching, sometimes an ungrateful job if it is looked on only as a job. Regarded as a profession, it is the noblest as it is the most ancient of the catalogue. Let none persuade us differently or the world is lost indeed.

Sixpence in Her Shoe Macmillan 64

MARGARET MEAD

8 The pains of childbirth were altogether different from the enveloping effects of other kinds of pain. These were pains one could follow with one's mind.

Quoted by Nancy Caldwell Sorel *Ever Since Eve: Personal Reflections on Childbirth* Oxford 84

LIZA MINNELLI

9 Whenever we were on a plane, we had a family.

On life with her mother Judy Garland and father Vincente Minnelli, NBC TV 15 Jan 74

CHARLOTTE MONTGOMERY

10 One of my children wrote in a third-grade piece on how her mother spent her time. . . . "one-half time on home, one-half time on outside things, one-half time writing."

Good Housekeeping May 59

RICHARD M NIXON, 37th US President

11 President Johnson and I have a lot in common. We were both born in small towns . . . and we're both fortunate in the fact that we think we married above ourselves.

5 Sep 69

NOOR, Queen of Jordan

12 Our planning may leave something to be desired, but our designs, thank God, have been flawless.

On birth of fourth child in six years, *Time* 10 Mar 86

RICHARD OLTON

13 When I held you in my arms at your baptism, I wanted it to be a fresh start, for you to be more complete than we had ever been ourselves, but I wonder if we expected too much.

Eulogy for 18-year-old nephew who committed suicide, quoted by James S Newton "Three Suicide Victims Buried in Jersey" NY *Times* 15 Mar 87

ALEXANDER ONASSIS

14 My father loves names and Jackie loves money.

On marriage of his father Aristotle Onassis to Jacqueline Kennedy, quoted by Peter Evans *Ari* Summit 86

KATHERINE D ORTEGA, Treasurer of the US

15 In the next year or so, my signature will appear on $60 billion of United States currency. More important to me, however, is the signature that appears on my life—the strong, proud, assertive handwriting of a loving father and mother.

Quoted by William Safire NY *Times* 19 Aug 84

MARGUERITE OSWALD

16 Lee was such a fine, high-class boy. . . . If my

son killed the president he would have said so. That's the way he was brought up.

On Lee Harvey Oswald, alleged assassin of President John F Kennedy, *Time* 13 Dec 63

RAINIER, Prince of Monaco

1 I can be a good father but I'm a terrible mother.

After his daughter Stephanie went swimming fully clad alongside models wearing swimwear she had designed, *Life* Oct 85

RONALD REAGAN, 40th US President

2 You get a little stir crazy during the week.

On living in the White House, NY *Times* 27 Sep 83

ARTUR RUBINSTEIN

3 It took great courage to ask a beautiful young woman to marry me. Believe me, it is easier to play the whole of Petrushka on the piano.

Quoted by Samuel Chotzinoff *A Little Nightmusic* Harper & Row 64

ANTONIN SCALIA

4 [In a big family] the first child is kind of like the first pancake. If it's not perfect, that's okay, there are a lot more coming along.

Recalled on his appointment to US Supreme Court, *Newsweek* 30 Jun 86

WALTER M SCHIRRA SR

5 You don't raise heroes, you raise sons. And if you treat them like sons, they'll turn out to be heroes, even if it's just in your own eyes.

This Week 3 Feb 63

MAUDE SHAW

6 Your daddy's upstairs. You can call him "Mr President" now.

To Caroline Kennedy on morning after 1960 presidential election, quoted by Ralph G Martin *A Hero for Our Time* Macmillan 83

EARL SIMPSON

7 They say the best product off a farm is the children.

After losing 90 percent of corn crop to drought, quoted by Hugh Sidey "Bitter Harvest" *Time* 8 Sep 86

MARGARET THATCHER, Prime Minister of Great Britain

8 I just owe almost everything to my father [and] it's passionately interesting for me that the things that I learned in a small town, in a very modest home, are just the things that I believe have won the election.

Quoted in *New Yorker* 10 Feb 86

HARRY S TRUMAN, 33rd US President

9 It is terrible—and I mean terrible—nuisance to be kin to the president of the United States.

Letter to his mother and sister two weeks after assuming the presidency in 1945, *Year of Decision* Doubleday 55

10 I have found the best way to give advice to your children is to find out what they want and then advise them to do it.

CBS TV 27 May 55

11 My father was not a failure. After all, he was the father of a president of the United States.

Mr Citizen Geis 60

12 It seems like there was always somebody for supper.

On life in the White House, quoted by Merriman Smith *The Good New Days* Bobbs-Merrill 62

13 I was the only calm one in the house. You see I've been shot at by experts.

Recalling service in World War I after assassination attempt on November 1, 1950, quoted by Margaret Truman *Bess W Truman* Macmillan 86

14 We're going to be buried out here. I like the idea because I may just want to get up some day and stroll into my office. And I can hear you saying, "Harry—you oughtn't!"

To his wife, on plans to be buried together at Truman Library, Independence MO, *ib*

MARGARET TRUMAN

15 It's only when you grow up, and step back from him, or leave him for your own career and your own home—it's only then that you can measure his greatness and fully appreciate it. Pride reinforces love.

Address to joint session of Congress on centennial of birth of her father President Harry S Truman, 8 May 84

EVELYN WAUGH

16 Of children as of procreation—the pleasure momentary, the posture ridiculous, the expense damnable.

May 5, 1954, letter to Nancy Mitford, news summaries 31 Dec 54

MARY BETH WHITEHEAD

17 I gave her life, I can take life away.

On her role as surrogate mother to Baby M, quoted in Washington *Post* 14 Oct 86

MARY GILLIGAN WONG

1 My husband would be Catholic and, I hoped, Irish, and if he happened to have played for Notre Dame, so much the better.

    Nun Harcourt Brace Jovanovich 83

2 We would have a picture of the Sacred Heart in the living room and holy-water fonts by each doorway, we would say the family rosary together every night and every Thursday night we would watch Bishop Fulton J Sheen on television.

    ib

JAMES C WRIGHT JR, Speaker of the House

3 That was the year when our family ate the piano.

    On his childhood during the Great Depression, NY *Times* 10 Dec 86

Observers & Critics

AHARON APPELFELD

4 People who lose their parents when young are permanently in love with them.

    To the Land of the Cattails Weidenfeld & Nicolson 86, quoted by Herbert Mitgang "Writing Holocaust Memories" NY *Times* 15 Nov 86

JOSEPH BARTH

5 Marriage is our last, best chance to grow up.

    Ladies' Home Journal Apr 61

ALAN BECK

6 Boys are found everywhere—on top of, underneath, inside of, climbing on, swinging from, running around or jumping to. Mothers love them, little girls hate them, older sisters and brothers tolerate them, adults ignore them and Heaven protects them. A boy is Truth with dirt on its face, Beauty with a cut on its finger, Wisdom with bubble gum in its hair and the Hope of the future with a frog in its pocket.

    "What Is a Boy?" pamphlet distributed by New England Life Insurance Co Boston 56

7 A boy is a magical creature—you can lock him out of your workshop, but you can't lock him out of your heart. You can get him out of your study, but you can't get him out of your mind. Might as well give up—he is your captor, your jailer, your boss and your master—a freckled-faced, pint-sized, cat-chasing bundle of noise. But when you come home at night with only the shattered pieces of your hopes and dreams, he can mend them like new with two magic words—"Hi, Dad!"

    ib

8 Little girls are the nicest things that happen to people. They are born with a little bit of angel-shine about them, and though it wears thin sometimes there is always enough left to lasso your heart—even when they are sitting in the mud, or crying temperamental tears, or parading up the street in mother's best clothes.

    "What Is a Girl?" *ib*

9 A little girl can be sweeter (and badder) oftener than anyone else in the world. She can jitter around, and stomp, and make funny noises that frazzle your nerves, yet just when you open your mouth she stands there demure with that special look in her eyes. A girl is Innocence playing in the mud, Beauty standing on its head, and Motherhood dragging a doll by the foot.

    ib

10 What is a husband? He is the one who, with a touch, can bring back the starlight and glow of years long ago. At least he hopes he can—don't disappoint him.

    "What Is a Husband?" *Good Housekeeping* Jul 57

11 A girl becomes a wife with her eyes wide open. She knows that those sweetest words, "I take thee to be my wedded husband," really mean, "I promise thee to cook three meals a day for 60 years; thee will I clean up after; thee will I talk to even when thou art not listening; thee will I worry about, cry over and take all manner of hurts from."

    "What Is a Wife?" *ib*

MARY KAY BLAKELY

12 Divorce is the psychological equivalent of a triple coronary by-pass. After such a monumental assault on the heart, it takes years to amend all the habits and attitudes that led up to it.

    Quoted in *Parade* 12 Jul 87

NADIA BOULANGER

13 Loving a child doesn't mean giving in to all his whims; to love him is to bring out the best in him, to teach him to love what is difficult.

    Quoted by Bruno Monsaingeon *Mademoiselle* Carcanet 85

ANTHONY BRANDT

14 Other things may change us, but we start and end with the family.

    "Bloodlines" *Esquire* Sep 84

BARNETT BRICKNER

1 Success in marriage does not come merely through finding the right mate, but through being the right mate.

> Quoted in Samuel Silver comp *The Quoteable American Rabbis* Droke House 67

BRITISH FAMILY PLANNING ASSOCIATION

2 Would you be more careful if it was you that got pregnant?

> Urging birth control by men, advertisement quoted in *Time* 28 Apr 86

ANATOLE BROYARD

3 The first divorce in the world may have been a tragedy, but the hundred-millionth is not necessarily one.

> On overemphasis on divorce in contemporary fiction, NY *Times* 25 Jun 80

GAIL LUMET BUCKLEY

4 Family faces are magic mirrors. Looking at people who belong to us, we see the past, present and future.

> *The Hornes: An American Family* Knopf 86

ROBERT C BYRD, US Senator

5 One's family is the most important thing in life. I look at it this way: One of these days I'll be over in a hospital somewhere with four walls around me. And the only people who'll be with me will be my family.

> NY *Times* 27 Mar 77

MARY S CALDERONE

6 Our children are not going to be just "our children"—they are going to be other people's husbands and wives and the parents of our grandchildren.

> NBC TV 18 Jan 74

RACHEL CARSON

7 If a child is to keep alive his inborn sense of wonder, he needs the companionship of at least one adult who can share it, rediscovering with him the joy, excitement and mystery of the world we live in.

> *The Sense of Wonder* Harper & Row 65

STANLEY H CATH

8 Middle age is Janus-faced. As we look back on our accomplishments and our failures to achieve the things we wanted, we look ahead to the time we have left to us. . . . Our children are gaining life, and our parents are losing it.

> NY *Times* 18 Apr 83

CHILDREN'S DEFENSE FUND

9 Will your child learn to multiply before she learns to subtract?

> Poster on teen pregnancies, quoted in *Christian Science Monitor* 13 Mar 86

JEROME CHODOROV and JOSEPH FIELDS

10 I'll tell you the real secret of how to stay married. Keep the cave clean. They want the cave clean and spotless. Air-conditioned, if possible. Sharpen his spear, and stick it in his hand when he goes out in the morning to spear that bear; and when the bear chases him, console him when he comes home at night, and tell him what a big man he is, and then hide the spear so he doesn't fall over it and stab himself.

> *Anniversary Waltz* Random House 54

FRANCIS X CLINES

11 He sits at the kitchen table, which is the only authentic way to touch down at home in Queens.

> On a man's return home from prolonged hospitalization, NY *Times* 16 Jun 79

COLETTE

12 The faults of husbands are often caused by the excess virtues of their wives.

> Recalled on her death 3 Aug 54

LAURIE COLWIN

13 That family glaze of common references, jokes, events, calamities—that sense of a family being like a kitchen midden: layer upon layer of the things daily life is made of. The edifice that lovers build is by comparison delicate and one-dimensional.

> *The Lone Pilgrim* Knopf 81

HENRY STEELE COMMAGER

14 It's awfully hard to be the son of a great man and also of a half-crazy woman.

> On Robert Todd Lincoln, NY *Times* 12 Feb 85

JOHN CORRY

15 Loneliness seems to have become the great American disease.

> On NBC TV documentary *Second Thoughts on Being Single*, NY *Times* 25 Apr 84

JO COUDERT

16 The divorced person is like a man with a black patch over one eye: He looks rather dashing

but the fact is that he has been through a maiming experience.

Advice from a Failure Stein & Day 65

QUENTIN CREWE

1 The children despise their parents until the age of 40, when they suddenly become just like them—thus preserving the system.

On British upper class, *Saturday Evening Post* 1 Dec 62

PATRICK DENNIS

2 The Upsons lived the way every family in America wants to live—not rich, but well-to-do. They had two of everything: two addresses, the flat on Park and a house in Connecticut; two cars, a Buick sedan and a Ford station wagon; two children, a boy and a girl; two servants, man and maid; two clubs, town and country; and two interests, money and position.

Auntie Mame Vanguard 55

3 Mrs Upson had two fur coats and two chins. Mr Upson had two chins, two passions—gold and business—and two aversions, Roosevelt and Jews.

ib

ANN DIEHL

4 I think we're seeing in working mothers a change from "Thank God it's Friday" to "Thank God it's Monday." If any working mother has not experienced that feeling, her children are not adolescent.

Vogue Jan 85

MARLENE DIETRICH

5 A king, realizing his incompetence, can either delegate or abdicate his duties. A father can do neither. If only sons could see the paradox, they would understand the dilemma.

NY *Journal-American* 21 Jun 64

MARGARET DRABBLE

6 Family life itself, that safest, most traditional, most approved of female choices, is not a sanctuary: It is, perpetually, a dangerous place.

Christian Science Monitor 10 Apr 85

DAVID ELKIND, Professor of Child Study, Tufts University

7 We see these adolescents mourning for a lost childhood.

On children "pushed into sports or music or academics," quoted in NY *Times* 24 Sep 84

RALPH ELLISON

8 Some people are your relatives but others are your ancestors, and you choose the ones you want to have as ancestors. You create yourself out of those values.

Time 27 Mar 64

DELIA EPHRON

9 As complicated as joint custody is, it allows the delicious contradiction of having children and maintaining the intimacy of life-before-kids.

Funny Sauce Viking 86, quoted in NY *Times* 14 Sep 86

10 Your basic extended family today includes your ex-husband or -wife, your ex's new mate, your new mate, possibly your new mate's ex and any new mate that your new mate's ex has acquired.

ib 12 Oct 86

11 [It] consists entirely of people who are not related by blood, many of whom can't stand each other.

ib

NORA EPHRON

12 Summer bachelors, like summer breezes, are never as cool as they pretend to be.

"The Truth about Summer Bachelors" NY *Post* 22 Aug 65

13 There are plenty of men who philander during the summer, to be sure, but they are usually the same lot who philander during the winter—albeit with less convenience.

ib

TONI FALBO, Associate Professor, University of Texas

14 The only child is a world issue now.

On importance of population control, NY *Times* 13 Aug 84

ELIZABETH FISHEL

15 A sister is both your mirror—and your opposite.

People 2 Jun 80

16 Comparison is a death knell to sibling harmony.

ib

TREVOR FISHLOCK

17 Babies here seem to be almost as rare as panda cubs.

On New York City, London *Times* 9 May 85

F Scott Fitzgerald

1 Family quarrels are bitter things. They don't go according to any rules. They're not like aches or wounds, they're more like splits in the skin that won't heal because there's not enough material.
   Quoted by Nancy Milford *Zelda* Harper & Row 70

Betty Friedan

2 Each suburban wife struggled with it alone. As she made the beds, shopped for groceries, matched slipcover material, ate peanut butter sandwiches with her children, chauffered Cub Scouts and Brownies, lay beside her husband at night—she was afraid to ask even of herself the silent question—"Is this all?"
   The Feminine Mystique Norton 63

3 American housewives have not had their brains shot away, nor are they schizophrenic in the clinical sense. But if . . . the fundamental human drive is not the urge for pleasure or the satisfaction of biological needs, but the need to grow and to realize one's full potential, their comfortable, empty, purposeless days are indeed cause for a nameless terror.
   ib

Robert Frost

4 You don't have to deserve your mother's love. You have to deserve your father's.
   Quoted in George Plimpton ed *Writers at Work* Viking 63

5 The father is always a Republican toward his son, and his mother's always a Democrat.
   ib

6 Home is the place where, when you have to go there,
   They have to take you in.
   From 1914 poem "Death of the Hired Man," recalled on his death 29 Jan 63

7 The greatest thing in family life is to take a hint when a hint is intended—and not to take a hint when a hint isn't intended.
   Quoted in *Vogue* 15 Mar 63

Lavina Christensen Fugal

8 Love your children with all your hearts, love them enough to discipline them before it is too late. . . . Praise them for important things, even if you have to stretch them a bit. Praise them a lot. They live on it like bread and butter and they need it more than bread and butter.
   On being chosen Mother of the Year, news summaries 3 May 55

Gallup Poll

9 Only one woman in ten recognizes her husband as the same man he was before she married him. Nine out of ten say he's changed. One in three says he's changed for the worse.
   "The Woman's Mind" *Ladies' Home Journal* Feb 62

Vartan Gregorian

10 Dignity is not negotiable. Dignity is the honor of the family.
   New Yorker 14 Apr 86

Henry Anatole Grunwald

11 Home is the wallpaper above the bed, the family dinner table, the church bells in the morning, the bruised shins of the playground, the small fears that come with dusk, the streets and squares and monuments and shops that constitute one's first universe.
   "Home Is Where You Are Happy" *Time* 8 Jul 85

12 Home is one's birthplace, ratified by memory.
   ib

Richard C Halverson, Chaplain, US Senate

13 I like to remind them to be spouses and parents when they go home.
   Wall Street Journal 31 Jan 85

Elizabeth Hardwick

14 I am alone here in New York, no longer a we.
   On being divorced, *Sleepless Nights* Random House 79

Brooks Hays

15 Back of every achievement is a proud wife and a surprised mother-in-law.
   NY *Herald Tribune* 2 Dec 61

Suzanne Heller

16 Misery is when you make your bed and then your mother tells you it's the day she's changing the sheets.
   Misery Eriksson 64

17 Misery is when grown-ups don't realize how miserable kids can feel.
   ib

Heloise (Heloise Cruse)

18 I think housework is the reason most women go to the office.
   Editor & Publisher 27 Apr 63

LEWIS B HERSHEY

1 A boy becomes an adult three years before his parents think he does, and about two years after he thinks he does.
> News summaries 31 Dec 51

THEODORE M HESBURGH

2 The most important thing a father can do for his children is to love their mother.
> *Reader's Digest* Jan 63

MARJORIE HOLMES

3 What feeling is so nice as a child's hand in yours? So small, so soft and warm, like a kitten huddling in the shelter of your clasp.
> *Calendar of Love and Inspiration* Doubleday 81

4 A child's hand in yours—what tenderness it arouses, what power it conjures. You are instantly the very touchstone of wisdom and strength.
> *ib*

THOMAS HOLMES

5 A person often catches a cold when a mother-in-law comes to visit. Patients mentioned mothers-in-law so often that we came to consider them a common cause of disease in the United States.
> *Time* 6 Jun 83

J EDGAR HOOVER

6 Above all, I would teach him to tell the truth . . . Truth-telling, I have found, is the key to responsible citizenship. The thousands of criminals I have seen in 40 years of law enforcement have had one thing in common: Every single one was a liar.
> "What I Would Tell a Son" *Family Weekly* 14 Jul 63

MCCREADY HUSTON

7 She invoked the understood silence of the long married.
> *The Platinum Yoke* Lippincott 63

KENNETH HUTCHIN

8 The wife who always insists on the last word often has it.
> On keeping husbands alive, NY *Times* 26 Feb 60

POPE JOHN XXIII

9 The family [is] the first essential cell of human society.
> *Pacem in Terris* 10 Apr 63

POPE JOHN PAUL II

10 The great danger for family life, in the midst of any society whose idols are pleasure, comfort and independence, lies in the fact that people close their hearts and become selfish.
> Sermon, Washington DC, 7 Oct 79

11 To maintain a joyful family requires much from both the parents and the children. Each member of the family has to become, in a special way, the servant of the others.
> *ib*

NORA JOHNSON

12 I doubt if there is one married person on earth who can be objective about divorce. It is always a threat, admittedly or not, and such a dire threat that it is almost a dirty word.
> "A Marriage on the Rocks" *Atlantic* Jul 62

THOMAS H KEAN, Governor of New Jersey

13 The most painful death in all the world is the death of a child. When a child dies, when one child dies—not the 11 per 1,000 we talk about statistically, but the one that a mother held briefly in her arms—he leaves an empty place in a parent's heart that will never heal.
> NY *Times* 20 Mar 85

ANN KENT

14 Grief and greed are as inextricably entwined as love and marriage should be.
> "The Bitter Inheritance of Bereavement" London *Times* 12 Aug 85

LAWRENCE KUBIE

15 Today's family is built like a pyramid; with all the intrafamilial rivalries, tensions, jealousies, angers, hatreds, loves and needs focused on the untrained, vulnerable, insecure, young, inexperienced and incompetent parental apex . . . about whose incompetence our vaunted educational system does nothing.
> *Newsweek* 7 Mar 60

NORMAN LEAR

16 Edith, stifle yourself!
> Line for Archie Bunker to his wife, *All in the Family* ABC TV series 73

DAVID LEAVITT

17 Childhood smells of perfume and brownies.
> On a son embracing his mother, *Family Dancing* Knopf 84, quoted in NY *Times* 30 Oct 84

George Levinger

1 What counts in making a happy marriage is not so much how compatible you are, but how you deal with incompatibility.

> Quoted by Daniel Goleman "Marriage: Research Reveals Ingredients of Happiness" NY *Times* 16 Apr 85

Guy Lombardo

2 Many a man wishes he were strong enough to tear a telephone book in half—especially if he has a teenage daughter.

> News summaries 19 Apr 54

Norman Mailer

3 There are four stages in a marriage. First there's the affair, then the marriage, then children and finally the fourth stage, without which you cannot know a woman, the divorce.

> News summaries 31 Dec 69

Andrew H Malcolm

4 The car trip can draw the family together, as it was in the days before television when parents and children actually talked to each other.

> "The Annual Automobile Migration" NY *Times* 21 Apr 85

François Mauriac

5 Where does discipline end? Where does cruelty begin? Somewhere between these, thousands of children inhabit a voiceless hell.

> *Second Thoughts* World 61

André Maurois

6 A successful marriage is an edifice that must be rebuilt every day.

> Quoted by Jacob Brande comp *Speaker's Encyclopedia* Prentice-Hall 55

7 Without a family, man, alone in the world, trembles with the cold.

> Quoted by John D MacDonald *The Lonely Silver Rain* Knopf 85

Millicent Carey McIntosh

8 The most important phase of living with a person [is] respect for that person as an individual.

> "The Art of Living with Your Children" *Vogue* 1 Feb 53

Margaret Mead

9 Of all the peoples whom I have studied, from city dwellers to cliff dwellers, I always find that at least 50 percent would prefer to have at least one jungle between themselves and their mothers-in-law.

> Recalled on her death 15 Nov 78

Maurice Merleau-Ponty

10 Divorces as well as marriages can fail.

> *Signs* Northwestern University 64

Lance Morrow

11 He vanished to the public in order to materialize for his family.

> On Senator Paul Tsongas, who was diagnosed with cancer, *Time* 13 May 85

David Nasaw

12 The street bred a gritty self-reliance in its children. It was their frontier.

> *Children of the City* Anchor 85, quoted in *People* 20 May 85

Ogden Nash

13 An occasional lucky guess as to what makes a wife tick is the best a man can hope for,
Even then, no sooner has he learned how to cope with the tick than she tocks.

> *Marriage Lines* Little, Brown 64

14 To keep your marriage brimming,
With love in the loving cup,
Whenever you're wrong, admit it;
Whenever you're right, shut up.

> *ib*

15 Parents were invented to make children happy by giving them something to ignore.

> Recalled on his death 19 May 71

New York Times

16 To be an American is to aspire to a room of one's own.

> "Dream House" 19 Apr 87

Pope Paul VI

17 Every mother is like Moses. She does not enter the promised land. She prepares a world she will not see.

> Quoted by Jean Guitton *Conversations with Pope Paul* Meredith Press 67

Ivy Baker Priest, Treasurer of the US

18 Any woman who has a career and a family automatically develops something in the way of two personalities, like two sides of a dollar bill, each different in design. . . . Her problem is to keep one from draining the life from the other.

> *Green Grows Ivy* McGraw-Hill 58

RANDOLPH RAY

1 Kindness is the life's blood, the elixir of marriage. Kindness makes the difference between passion and caring. Kindness is tenderness. Kindness is love, but perhaps greater than love ... Kindness is good will. Kindness says, "I want you to be happy." Kindness comes very close to the benevolence of God.
My Little Church around the Corner Simon & Schuster 57

PHILIP ROTH

2 A Jewish man with parents alive is a 15-year-old boy.
Portnoy's Complaint Random House 69

BERTRAND RUSSELL

3 The fundamental defect of fathers is that they want their children to be a credit to them.
NY *Times* 9 Jun 63

ELOISE SALHOLZ

4 To Tennessee Williams, children were "no-neck monsters," while William Wordsworth apotheosized the newborn infant as a "Mighty Prophet! Seer Blest!" Most adults know the truth is somewhere in between.
"Morals Minefield" *Newsweek* 13 Oct 86

CARL SANDBURG

5 A baby is God's opinion that the world should go on.
Remembrance Rock Harcourt, Brace 48, recalled on his death 22 Jul 67

GEORGE BERNARD SHAW

6 Never fret for an only son, the idea of failure will never occur to him.
Quoted by Alistair Cooke *America* Knopf 73

DAVID SHIRE

7 You can sort of be married, you can sort of be divorced, you can sort of be living together, but you can't sort of have a baby.
Quoted in *Time* 2 Jan 84

C W SMITH

8 Divorced fathers are forced to recognize that there's no substitute for being there; or rather, there are only substitutes for it.
"Uncle Dad" *Esquire* Mar 84

ELINOR GOULDING SMITH

9 It sometimes happens, even in the best of families, that a baby is born. This is not necessarily cause for alarm. The important thing is to keep your wits about you and borrow some money.
The Complete Book of Absolutely Perfect Baby and Child Care Harcourt, Brace 57

MARGARET SMITH

10 The best contraceptive is the word *no*—repeated frequently.
To Women's Liberation Federation, Blackpool, England, *Quote* 27 Jun 71

BENJAMIN SPOCK

11 What good mothers and fathers instinctively feel like doing for their babies is usually best after all.
Quoted in *Life* 26 Jun 50

12 All the time a person is a child he is both a child and learning to be a parent. After he becomes a parent he becomes predominantly a parent reliving childhood.
Quote 29 Aug 65

SPORTS ILLUSTRATED

13 Any parent who has ever found a rusted toy automobile buried in the grass or a bent sand bucket on the beach knows that objects like these can be among the powerful things in the world. They can summon up in an instant, in colors stronger than life, the whole of childhood at its happiest—the disproportionate affection lavished on some strange possession, the concentrated self-forgetfulness of play, the elusive expressions of surprise or elation that pass so transparently over youthful features.
"The Timeless House of Children's Games" 26 Dec 60

RONALD STEEL

14 Children, for whom suburban life was supposed to make wholesome little Johns and Wendys, became the acid-dropping, classroom-burning hippies of the 1960s.
"Life in the Last 50 Years" *Esquire* Jun 83

JOHN STEINBECK

15 The impulse of the American woman to geld her husband and castrate her sons is very strong.
Quoted in Elaine Steinbeck and Robert Wallsten comps *Steinbeck: A Life in Letters* Penguin 76

PRESTON STURGES

16 Daughters are a mess no matter how you look

at 'em, a headache till they get married—if they get married—and, after that, they get worse. ... Either they leave their husbands and come back with four children and move into your guest room or their husband loses his job and the whole *caboodle* comes back. Or else they're so homely you can't get rid of them at all and they hang around the house like Spanish moss.

> From screenplay for his 1944 film *The Miracle of Morgan's Creek*, recalled on his death 6 Aug 59

Patricia Sullivan

1 We had our own baby boom.

> On sailing to America on the *Queen Mary* during World War II, NY *Times* 15 Apr 85

St Clair Adams Sullivan

2 Our children are here to stay, but our babies and toddlers and preschoolers are gone as fast as they can grow up—and we have only a short moment with each. When you see a grandfather take a baby in his arms, you see that the moment hasn't always been long enough.

> *The Father's Almanac* Doubleday 80

John Tarkov

3 This Melting Pot of ours absorbs the second generation over a flame so high that the first is left encrusted on the rim.

> "Fitting In" NY *Times* 7 Jul 85

Alvin Toffler

4 Parenthood remains the greatest single preserve of the amateur.

> *Future Shock* Random House 70

Desmond Tutu

5 You don't choose your family. They are God's gift to you, as you are to them.

> Address at enthronement as Anglican archbishop of Cape Town 7 Sep 86

Alan Valentine

6 For thousands of years, father and son have stretched wistful hands across the canyon of time, each eager to help the other to his side, but neither quite able to desert the loyalties of his contemporaries. The relationship is always changing and hence always fragile; nothing endures except the sense of difference.

> *Fathers to Sons: Advice without Consent* University of Oklahoma 63

Abigail Van Buren

7 First, there is the rocket-boosted mother-in-law.... queen of the melodrama when her acts of self-sacrifice and martyrdom go unnoticed and unrewarded. Her banner is the tear-stained hanky. She is as phony as a colic cure, transparent as a soap bubble. And as harmless as a barracuda. But she is really more wretched than wicked and needs more help than she can give.

> "After the Honeymoon" *McCall's* Sep 62

8 Then, there's the modern mother-in-law. In her mid 40s, she is the compact car of her breed: efficient, trim, attractive and in harmony with her times. ... She's pretty stiff competition for the plain young matron who's overweight and underfinanced. If there is going to be friction in this relationship, it could start from envy and resentment in the younger woman. But Father Time is on her side, even if Mother Nature played her a dirty trick.

> *ib*

John Van de Kamp

9 If we can ... get them to understand that saying "no" to drugs is rebelling against their parents and the generations of the past, we'd make it an enormous success.

> On campaigning against drugs in rock videos, LA *Times* 16 Jul 86

Amy Vanderbilt

10 [Parents] must get across the idea that "I love you always, but sometimes I do not love your behavior."

> On raising teenagers, *New Complete Book of Etiquette* Doubleday 63

Gore Vidal

11 All children alarm their parents, if only because you are forever expecting to encounter yourself.

> From his 1968 play *Weekend*

Evelyn Waugh

12 Perhaps host and guest is really the happiest relation for father and son.

> "Father and Son" *Atlantic* Mar 63

Rebecca West

13 She was like the embodiment of all women who have felt an astonished protest because their children have died before them.

> On Queen Mary at funeral of her son King George VI, *Life* 25 Feb 52

GEORGE F WILL

1 Some parents ... say it is toy guns that make boys warlike. ... But give a boy a rubber duck and he will seize its neck like the butt of a pistol and shout "Bang!"
Newsweek 11 Dec 78

2 Childhood is frequently a solemn business for those inside it.
ib

EARL WILSON

3 For the parents of a Little Leaguer, a baseball game is simply a nervous breakdown into innings.
News summaries 31 Dec 79

CHARLES EDDIE WISEMAN

4 We're going to raise a lost generation of children unless they are properly disciplined and properly spanked.
On why members of the Northeast Kingdom Community Church, Island Pond VT, physically punish their children, NY *Times* 11 Jul 84

WORLD BANK

5 Parents may feel the need to have many babies to be sure that a few survive.
On high infant mortality rate in developing countries, *World Development Report*, quoted in NY *Times* 11 Jul 84

GEOFFREY WRANGHAM

6 Distrust all mothers-in-law. They are completely unscrupulous in what they say in court.
Boston *Herald* 10 Oct 60

7 The wife's mother is always more prejudiced against the husband than even the most ill-treated wife. If I had my way, I am afraid I would abolish mothers-in-law entirely.
ib

JONATHAN YARDLEY

8 An entire generation grew up unacquainted with the thwack of paddle against bottom.
On parental permissiveness promoted by Benjamin Spock's books, *American Heritage* Apr 85

LOVE

MORTIMER ADLER

9 There is only one situation I can think of in which men and women make an effort to read better than they usually do. [It is] when they are in love and reading a love letter.
Quote 26 Dec 61

ANTONY, Russian Orthodox Archbishop of England

10 So often when we say "I love you" we say it with a huge "I" and a small "you."
Beginning to Pray Paulist Press 70

W H AUDEN

11 Among those whom I like, I can find no common denominator, but among those whom I love, I can; all of them make me laugh.
The Dyer's Hand Random House 62

PHYLLIS BATTELLE

12 If you haven't had at least a slight poetic crack in the heart, you have been cheated by nature.
NY *Journal-American* 1 Jun 62

13 A broken heart is what makes life so wonderful five years later, when you see the guy in an elevator and he is fat and smoking a cigar and saying long-time-no-see.
ib

ELIZABETH BLACK

14 He spoke of love and the Supreme Court.
On marriage proposal from Hugo L Black, quoted in *Christian Science Monitor* 27 Feb 86

ERMA BOMBECK

15 For years [my wedding ring] has done its job. It has led me not into temptation. It has reminded my husband numerous times at parties that it's time to go home. It has been a source of relief to a dinner companion. It has been a status symbol in the maternity ward.
Moneysworth Mar 80

CHARLES BOYER

16 A Frenchwoman, when double-crossed, will kill her rival; the Italian woman would rather kill her deceitful lover; the Englishwoman simply breaks off relations—but they all will console themselves with another man.
News summaries 20 Jul 54

ROBERT FARRAR CAPON

17 I talk marriage; they talk weddings!
On counseling engaged couples, *Bed and Board: Plain Talk about Marriage* Simon & Schuster 65

GABRIELLE ("COCO") CHANEL

18 I never wanted to weigh more heavily on a man than a bird.
On why she never married her lovers, NY *Herald Tribune* 18 Oct 64

ILKA CHASE

1 On the whole, I haven't found men unduly loath to say, "I love you." The real trick is to get them to say, "Will you marry me?"
This Week 5 Feb 56

NIKOLAI CHEPIK

2 Believing that a girl will wait is just like jumping with a parachute packed by someone else.
From diary of Soviet farm boy who died in action in Afghanistan, quoted by Seth Mydans NY *Times* 16 Jan 85

MAURICE CHEVALIER

3 Many a man has fallen in love with a girl in a light so dim he would not have chosen a suit by it.
News summaries 17 Jul 55

4 The crime of loving is forgetting.
Look 28 May 68

AGATHA CHRISTIE

5 An archaeologist is the best husband any woman can have: The older she gets, the more interested he is in her.
News summaries 9 Mar 54

NOEL COWARD

6 I've sometimes thought of marrying—and then I've thought again.
Theatre Arts Nov 56

E E CUMMINGS

7 Be of love (a little) more careful than of anything.
Line adapted for serigraph by artist Corita Kent, quoted in *Newsweek* 17 Dec 84

MARLENE DIETRICH

8 How do you know love is gone? If you said that you would be there at seven and you get there by nine, and he or she has not called the police—it's gone.
ABC Doubleday 62

9 Grumbling is the death of love.
ib

ISAK DINESEN

10 Man reaches the highest point of lovableness at 12 to 17—to get it back, in a second flowering, at the age of 70 to 90.
Shadows on the Grass Random House 60

DAVID HERBERT DONALD

11 Their correspondence was something like a duet between a tuba and a piccolo.
On love letters of Thomas Wolfe and Aline Bernstein, *Look Homeward* Little, Brown 87

MARTHA DUFFY

12 A fastidious person in the throes of love is a rich source of mirth.
In review of A N Wilson's *Wise Virgin* Viking 83, *Time* 5 Dec 83

WILL DURANT

13 The love we have in our youth is superficial compared to the love that an old man has for his old wife.
On his 90th birthday, NY *Times* 6 Nov 75

EDWARD, Duke of Windsor

14 I have found it impossible to carry the heavy burden of responsibility and to discharge my duties as king as I would wish to do without the help and support of the woman I love.
December 11, 1936, abdication broadcast, recalled on his death 28 May 72

HARRY EMERSON FOSDICK

15 Bitterness imprisons life; love releases it. Bitterness paralyzes life; love empowers it. Bitterness sours life; love sweetens it. Bitterness sickens life; love heals it. Bitterness blinds life; love anoints its eyes.
Riverside Sermons Harper 58

ERICH FROMM

16 Love is the only sane and satisfactory answer to the problem of human existence.
The Art of Loving Harper 56, recalled on his death 18 Mar 80

17 If a person loves only one other person and is indifferent to all others, his love is not love but a symbiotic attachment, or an enlarged egotism.
ib

ROBERT FROST

18 Two such as you with such a master speed
Cannot be parted nor be swept away
From one another once you are agreed
That life is only life forevermore
Together wing to wing and oar to oar.
From "The Master Speed," inscribed on gravestone of Frost and his wife Elinor, *National Observer* 6 Jul 64

GEORGE GILDER

1 This is what sexual liberation chiefly accomplishes—it liberates young women to pursue married men.
Quoted in *Newsweek* 8 Dec 86

HELEN HAYES

2 The truth [is] that there is only one terminal dignity—love. And the story of a love is not important—what is important is that one is capable of love. It is perhaps the only glimpse we are permitted of eternity.
Guideposts Jan 60

SHIRLEY HAZZARD

3 The tragedy is not that love doesn't last. The tragedy is the love that lasts.
The Transit of Venus Viking 80

BEN HECHT

4 Love is a hole in the heart.
From his 1958 play *Winkelberg*

KATHARINE HEPBURN

5 Marriage [is] a series of desperate arguments people feel passionately about.
Quoted by Charles Higham *Kate* Norton 75

ALDOUS HUXLEY

6 No man ever dared to manifest his boredom so insolently as does a Siamese tomcat when he yawns in the face of his amorously importunate wife.
NY *Times* 2 Nov 63

CARL JUNG

7 Where love rules, there is no will to power; and where power predominates, there love is lacking. The one is the shadow of the other.
Recalled on his death 6 Jun 61

ESTÉE LAUDER

8 Look for a sweet person. Forget rich.
Advice on choosing a spouse, *New Yorker* 15 Sep 86

JOHN LE CARRÉ

9 Love is whatever you can still betray ... Betrayal can only happen if you love.
A Perfect Spy Knopf 86

ISABEL G MACCAFFREY

10 Love is the source of language, and also its destroyer.
In Frank Doggett and Robert Buttel eds *Wallace Stevens: A Celebration* Princeton 80

SOMERSET MAUGHAM

11 The love that lasts longest is the love that is never returned.
Recalled on his death 16 Dec 65

MIGNON MCLAUGHLIN

12 A successful marriage requires falling in love many times, always with the same person.
Atlantic Jul 65

H L MENCKEN

13 No normal man ever fell in love after 30 when the kidneys begin to disintegrate.
Recalled on his death 29 Jan 56

14 Love is the delusion that one woman differs from another.
ib

KARL A MENNINGER

15 Love cures people, the ones who receive love and the ones who give it, too.
Sparks Crowell 73

ANDRÉ DE MISSAN

16 You study one another for 3 weeks, you love each other 3 months, you fight for 3 years, you tolerate the situation for 30.
Pink and Black privately published 53

MISTINGUETT

17 A kiss can be a comma, a question mark or an exclamation point. That's basic spelling that every woman ought to know.
Theatre Arts Dec 55

W STANLEY MOONEYHAM

18 Love talked about can be easily turned aside, but love demonstrated is irresistible.
Come Walk the World Word Books 78, quoted in *Reader's Digest* Oct 84

CHARLES MORGAN

19 There is no surprise more magical than the surprise of being loved: It is God's finger on man's shoulder.
Recalled on his death 6 Feb 58

RICHARD J NEEDHAM

20 Every woman needs one man in her life who is strong and responsible. Given this security, she can proceed to do what she really wants to do—fall in love with men who are weak and irresponsible.
The Garden of Needham Macmillan 68

JOYCE CAROL OATES

1 Love commingled with hate is more powerful than love. Or hate.

On Boxing Doubleday 87, quoted in NY *Times* 15 Mar 87

SEÁN O'FAOLÁIN

2 Love lives in sealed bottles of regret.

"The Jungle of Love" *Saturday Evening Post* 13 Aug 66

JOSÉ ORTEGA Y GASSET

3 Love is that splendid triggering of human vitality . . . the supreme activity which nature affords anyone for going out of himself toward someone else.

McCall's Feb 82

M SCOTT PECK

4 Falling in love is not an extension of one's limits or boundaries; it is a partial and temporary collapse of them.

The Road Less Traveled Simon & Schuster 78

5 Real love is a permanently self-enlarging experience. Falling in love is not.

ib

RANDOLPH RAY

6 I would like to have engraved inside every wedding band *Be kind to one another*. This is the Golden Rule of marriage and the secret of making love last through the years.

My Little Church around the Corner Simon & Schuster 57

THEODOR REIK

7 Love is an attempt to change a piece of a dream world into reality.

Recalled on his death 31 Dec 69

GINGER ROGERS

8 When two people love each other, they don't look at each other, they look in the same direction.

Quoted by Dotson Rader "'I Don't Want to Live without Love'" *Parade* 8 Mar 87

NED ROREM

9 Quarrels in France strengthen a love affair, in America they end it.

The Paris Diary of Ned Rorem Braziller 66

HOWARD SACKLER

10 Affairs, like revolutions, should only have beginnings.

From his 1980 play *Good-bye Fidel*

RICHARD SCHICKEL

11 That common cold of the male psyche, fear of commitment.

Time 28 Nov 83

LIZ SMITH

12 The marriage didn't work out but the separation is great.

On a Hollywood relationship, NBC TV 13 Nov 85

13 All weddings, except those with shotguns in evidence, are wonderful.

NY *Daily News* 13 Apr 86

MURIEL SPARK

14 It is impossible to repent of love. The sin of love does not exist.

New Yorker 10 Jul 65

WALLACE STEGNER

15 It is something—it can be everything—to have found a fellow bird with whom you can sit among the rafters while the drinking and boasting and reciting and fighting go on below.

On finding a loved one, *The Spectator Bird* Doubleday 76

JESSICA TANDY

16 When he's late for dinner, I know he's either having an affair or is lying dead in the street. I always hope it's the street.

On her husband Hume Cronyn, *Kennedy Center Honors* CBS TV 26 Dec 86

JAMES THURBER

17 A lady of 47 who has been married 27 years and has 6 children knows what love really is and once described it for me like this: "Love is what you've been through with somebody."

Life 14 Mar 60

PAUL TILLICH

18 The first duty of love is to listen.

Recalled on his death 22 Oct 65

HARRY S TRUMAN, 33rd US President

19 In my Sunday School class there was a beautiful little girl with golden curls. I was smitten at once and still am.

On his wife Bess, news summaries 31 Dec 52

JUDITH VIORST

20 One advantage of marriage, it seems to me, is

that when you fall out of love with him, or he falls out of love with you, it keeps you together until you maybe fall in again.
"What *Is* This Thing Called Love?" *Redbook* Feb 75

DAVID VISCOTT

1 To love and be loved is to feel the sun from both sides.
How to Live with Another Person Arbor House 74

GLENWAY WESCOTT

2 It is not love, but lack of love, which is blind.
NY *Herald Tribune* 19 Dec 65

MATTIE WHITE

3 I never married. Nobody ever asked me.
On her 100th birthday, *Newsweek* 4 Jul 76

EMLYN WILLIAMS

4 Cupid's dart had hit both targets and set the Nile on fire. And the Tiber. Even the Thames sizzled a bit.
On 1963 romance of Richard Burton and Elizabeth Taylor while filming *Cleopatra* in Egypt, recalled on Burton's death, *People* 17 Sep 84

WOODROW WYATT

5 A man falls in love through his eyes, a woman through her ears.
"To the Point" London *Sunday Times* 22 Mar 81

RELIGION

Spirituality

THOMAS J ALTIZER, Associate Professor of Religion, Emory University, Atlanta

6 We must recognize that the death of God is a historical event: God has died in our time, in our history, in our existence.
Time 22 Oct 65

ANONYMOUS

7 God was more exciting then than he is now.
Child's comment on the Old Testament, quoted by Gerald Kennedy *The Seven Worlds of the Minister* Harper & Row 68

8 I sought my soul but my soul I could not see. I sought my God but my God eluded me. I sought my brother—and I found all three.
Quoted by London Church News Service May 86

W H AUDEN

9 Health is the state about which medicine has nothing to say: Sanctity is the state about which theology has nothing to say.
Atlantic May 70

KARL BARTH

10 Conscience is the perfect interpreter of life.
The Word of God and the Word of Man Harper 57

HILAIRE BELLOC

11 The grace of God is courtesy.
Quoted by Monica Baldwin *I Leap over the Wall* Rinehart 50

ROBERT McAFEE BROWN

12 Prayer for many is like a foreign land. When we go there, we go as tourists. Like most tourists, we feel uncomfortable and out of place. Like most tourists, we therefore move on before too long and go somewhere else.
Introduction to John B Coburn *Prayer and Personal Religion* Westminster 67

MARTIN BUBER

13 God is the *mysterium tremendum* that appears and overthrows, but he is also the mystery of the self-evident, nearer to me than my I.
Recalled on his death 13 Jun 65

FREDERICK BUECHNER

14 It is as impossible for man to demonstrate the existence of God as it would be for even Sherlock Holmes to demonstrate the existence of Arthur Conan Doyle.
Wishful Thinking: A Theological ABC Harper & Row 73

15 In his holy flirtation with the world, God occasionally drops a handkerchief. These handkerchiefs are called saints.
On the Eucharist, *ib*

WILLIAM SLOANE COFFIN JR, Senior Minister, Riverside Church, NYC

16 Hope arouses, as nothing else can arouse, a passion for the possible.
Once to Every Man Atheneum 77, quoted in *Christian Science Monitor* 5 Jan 78

HARVEY COX, Professor of Divinity, Harvard

17 There has never been a better raconteur than Jesus of Nazareth.
The Seduction of the Spirit Simon & Schuster 73

RICHARD CARDINAL CUSHING, Archbishop of Boston

1 Mindful of the fact you live in an agricultural country, I presume you know what an ass is. We read in the New Testament that our blessed Lord rode on an ass in triumph into the city of Jerusalem. Today the Lord rides on another ass: I myself.
> Preaching in the slums of Lima, Peru, *Time* 21 Aug 64

DALAI LAMA

2 Sleep is the best meditation.
> *People* 10 Sep 79

ANTHONY DALLA VILLA, Roman Catholic priest

3 What you are is God's gift to you; what you make of it is your gift to God.
> Eulogy at memorial Mass for Andy Warhol at NYC's St Patrick's Cathedral 1 Apr 87

4 Death gives life its fullest reality.
> *ib*

LAKDASA J DE MEL, Anglican Metropolitan of India

5 Faith must not be slow to reason, nor reason to adore.
> Sermon closing 10th Lambeth Conference, St Paul's Cathedral, London, 25 Aug 68

JEREMIAH A DENTON JR

6 A man does a lot of praying in an enemy prison. Prayer, even more than sheer thought, is the firmest anchor.
> Quoted by George Esper and the Associated Press *The Eyewitness History of the Vietnam War 1961-75* Ballantine 83

ANGUS DUN, former Episcopal Bishop of Washington DC

7 I have learned that human existence is essentially tragic. It is only the love of God, disclosed and enacted in Christ, that redeems the human tragedy and makes it tolerable. No, more than tolerable. Wonderful.
> Recalled on his death 12 Aug 71

WILL AND ARIEL DURANT

8 The soul of a civilization is its religion, and it dies with its faith.
> *The Age of Reason Begins* Simon & Schuster 61

ALBERT EINSTEIN

9 God does not play dice [with the universe].
> Quoted by Banesh Hoffman *Albert Einstein* New American Library 73

AUSTIN FARRER, Warden, Keble College, Oxford

10 One of the silliest of all discussions is the question whether God is personal—it would be more useful to inquire whether ice is frozen.
> *Saving Belief* Hodder & Stoughton 64

11 Religion is more like response to a friend than it is like obedience to an expert.
> *ib*

RABBI LOUIS FINKELSTEIN

12 [A rabbi] should not despair if people do not do as much as they should. Every parent has that with children. God is merciful.
> NY *Times* 1 Sep 85

MARIE DE FLORIS OSB

13 Hunting God is a great adventure.
> To novices making their vows, quoted by Peter Beach and William Dunphy *Benedictine and Moor* Holt, Rinehart & Winston 60

HARRY EMERSON FOSDICK

14 I would rather live in a world where my life is surrounded by mystery than live in a world so small that my mind could comprehend it.
> "The Mystery of Life" in *Riverside Sermons* Harper 58

R BUCKMINSTER FULLER

15 God, to me, it seems, is a verb not a noun, proper or improper.
> *No More Secondhand God* Southern Illinois University 63

ERIC GILL

16 Without philosophy man cannot know what he makes; without religion he cannot know why.
> Quoted in *Christian Science Monitor* 14 Aug 80

RUMER GODDEN

17 The motto was "Pax," but the word was set in a circle of thorns.
> On a Benedictine motto, *In This House of Brede* Viking 69

LEON GOOD

18 Let us maintain our ability to wince as a people of faith.
> On his Mennonite beliefs, NY *Times* 29 Nov 84

GRAHAM GREENE

19 You think it more difficult to turn air into wine than to turn wine into blood?
> On a priest who pantomimes Mass, *Monsignor Quixote* PBS TV 13 Feb 87

DAG HAMMARSKJÖLD

1 I am the vessel. The draft is God's. And God is the thirsty one.
> *Markings* Knopf 64

HENRY HANCOCK, Dean, St Mark's Cathedral, Minneapolis MN

2 Out of our beliefs are born deeds; out of our deeds we form habits; out of our habits grows our character; and on our character we build our destiny.
> *Alpha Xi Delta Magazine* 57

ABRAHAM JOSHUA HESCHEL, Jewish Theological Seminary of America, NYC

3 A religious man is a person who holds God and man in one thought at one time, at all times, who suffers harm done to others, whose greatest passion is compassion, whose greatest strength is love and defiance of despair.
> NY *Journal-American* 5 Apr 63

REUEL HOWE, Director, Institute of Advanced Pastoral Studies, Bloomfield Hills MI

4 I want them "dunked"—plunged deeply into life, brought up gasping and dripping, and returned to us humble and ready to learn.
> On candidates for the priesthood, *Anglican World* Epiphany/Lent 64

KATHRYN HULME

5 Never forget that [God] tests his real friends more severely than the lukewarm ones.
> *The Nun's Story* Little, Brown 56

JEWISH THEOLOGICAL SEMINARY OF AMERICA, NYC

6 A human life is like a single letter in the alphabet. It can be meaningless. Or it can be part of a great meaning.
> From advertisement on Rosh Hashanah, "Who Takes Delight in Life" NY *Herald Tribune* 5 Sep 56

POPE JOHN XXIII

7 I am made to tremble and I fear!
> On learning of his election to succeed Pius XII, 29 Oct 58

POPE JOHN PAUL I

8 You know that I try to maintain a continuous conversation with you. I take comfort in the thought that the important thing is not for one person to write to Christ but for many people to love and emulate [you]. Fortunately, despite everything, this still occurs today.
> Letter to Jesus Christ, in volume of letters to historical figures published when he was patriarch of Venice, recalled on his death 28 Sep 78

POPE JOHN PAUL II

9 This people draws its origin from Abraham, our father in faith . . . The very people that received from God the commandment "Thou shalt not kill" itself experienced in a special measure what is meant by killing. It is not permissible for anyone to pass by this inscription with indifference.
> On visiting Auschwitz concentration camp that he called "the Golgotha of the modern world," *ib*

10 Do not abandon yourselves to despair. . . . We are the Easter people and hallelujah is our song.
> Address in Harlem 2 Oct 79

11 Social justice cannot be attained by violence. Violence kills what it intends to create.
> To workers in São Paulo, Brazil, news summaries 4 Jul 80

12 [I kiss the soil] as if I placed a kiss on the hands of a mother, for the homeland is our earthly mother. I consider it my duty to be with my compatriots in this sublime and difficult moment.
> On arriving in Poland during period of martial law, *Time* 27 Jun 83

CARL JUNG

13 I have treated many hundreds of patients. . . . Among [those] in the second half of life—that is to say, over 35—there has not been one whose problem in the last resort was not that of finding a religious outlook on life.
> *Time* 14 Feb 55

14 Knowing your own darkness is the best method for dealing with the darknesses of other people.
> Letter to a former student on reassessing religious values outlined to Sigmund Freud a half century earlier, quoted in Gerhard Adler ed *Letters, Vol 1* Princeton 73

YASUNARI KAWABATA

15 Because you cannot see him, God is everywhere.
> Quoted by Susan Cheever *Home before Dark* Houghton Mifflin 84

HELEN KELLER

16 I can see, and that is why I can be happy, in what you call the dark, but which to me is golden. I can see a God-made world, not a man-made world.
> Reply to question,"Can you see a world?" in 1955 documentary *The Unconquered*

JOHN F KENNEDY, 35th US President

1 I know there is a God—I see the storm coming and I see his hand in it—if he has a place then I am ready—we see the hand.

> Paraphrasing Abraham Lincoln in notes on program for prayer breakfast, NY *Times* 15 May 64

C S LEWIS

2 I believe in Christianity as I believe that the sun has risen, not only because I see it but because I see everything in it.

> Recalled on his death 22 Nov 63

3 Aim at heaven and you will get earth thrown in. Aim at earth and you get neither.

> *ib*

4 The safest road to hell is the gradual one—the gentle slope, soft underfoot, without sudden turnings, without milestones, without signposts.

> *ib*

5 I gave in, and admitted that God was God.

> On relinquishing atheism at age 31 in 1929, quoted by William Griffin *Clive Staples Lewis* Harper & Row 86

MOTHER MARY MADELEVA CSC

6 I like to go to Marshall Field's in Chicago just to see how many things there are in the world that I do not want.

> *My First Seventy Years* Macmillan 59

ERIC MASCALL, Lecturer in Philosophy of Religion, Christ Church, Oxford

7 A very large amount of human suffering and frustration is caused by the fact that many men and women are not content to be the sort of beings that God has made them, but try to persuade themselves that they are really beings of some different kind.

> *The Importance of Being Human* Columbia University 58

WILLIAM McGILL, Episcopal priest

8 The value of persistent prayer is not that he will hear us ... but that we will finally hear him.

> "Prayer Unceasing" *Living Church* 28 Sep 86

MARGARET MEAD

9 Prayer does not use up artificial energy, doesn't burn up any fossil fuel, doesn't pollute.

> Quoted by Jane Howard *Margaret Mead* Simon & Schuster 84

THOMAS MERTON OCSO

10 The very contradictions in my life are in some ways signs of God's mercy to me.

> Preface to *Thomas Merton Reader* Harcourt, Brace & World 62

11 So Brother Matthew locked the gate behind me, and I was enclosed in the four walls of my new freedom.

> On entering the Trappist Monastery of Our Lady of Gethsemani, *The Seven Storey Mountain* Harcourt, Brace 48, recalled on his death 10 Dec 68

DEWI MORGAN, Rector, St Bride's, Fleet Street, London

12 Christianity is different from all other religions. They are the story of man's search for God. The Gospel is the story of God's search for man.

> *St Mary's Messenger* Sep/Oct 66

ROBERT R MOTON, President, Tuskegee Institute

13 When you eat fish, you don't eat the bones. You eat the flesh. Take the Bible like that.

> NY *Post* 17 May 64

MALCOLM MUGGERIDGE

14 Every happening, great and small, is a parable whereby God speaks to us, and the art of life is to get the message.

> News summaries 31 Dec 78

JACK ("MURPH THE SURF") MURPHY

15 God had a sense of humor, a style of his own.

> On his parole 10 Nov 86

JOHN COURTNEY MURRAY SJ

16 Today's barbarian may wear a Brooks Brothers suit and carry a ball-point pen. In fact, even beneath the academic gown there may lurk a child of the wilderness, untutored in the high tradition of civility, who goes busily and happily about his work, a domesticated and law-abiding man, engaged in the concoction of a philosophy to put an end to all philosophy.

> Recalled on his death 16 Aug 67

MOHAMMED NAGUIB

17 Religion is a candle inside a multicolored lantern. Everyone looks through a particular color, but the candle is always there.

> News summaries 31 Dec 53

REINHOLD NIEBUHR

18 Nothing that is worth doing can be achieved in

a lifetime; therefore we must be saved by hope.

The Irony of American History Scribner's 52

1 Nothing which is true or beautiful or good makes complete sense in any immediate context of history; therefore we must be saved by faith.

ib

2 Nothing we do, however virtuous, can be accomplished alone; therefore we are saved by love.

ib

3 The final test of religious faith ... is whether it will enable men to endure insecurity without complacency or despair, whether it can so interpret the ancient verities that they will not become mere escape hatches from responsibilities but instruments of insights into what civilization means.

Saturday Evening Post 23 Jul 60

4 God, give us grace to accept with serenity the things that cannot be changed, courage to change the things which should be changed and the wisdom to distinguish the one from the other.

Originally part of a sermon in 1943 and later used by Alcoholics Anonymous, quoted by June Bingham *Courage to Change* Scribner's 61

D T NILES

5 Christianity is one beggar telling another beggar where he found bread.

NY *Times* 11 May 86

WILLIAM BARR OGLESBY JR, Professor of Pastoral Counseling, Union Theological Seminary, Richmond VA

6 The presence of faith is no guarantee of deliverance from times of distress and vicissitude but there can be a certainty that nothing will be encountered that is overwhelming.

Virginia Seminary Journal May 83

C NORTHCOTE PARKINSON

7 Where life is colorful and varied, religion can be austere or unimportant. Where life is appallingly monotonous, religion must be emotional, dramatic and intense. Without the curry, boiled rice can be very dull.

East and West Houghton Mifflin 63

POPE PAUL VI

8 Of all human activities, man's listening to God is the supreme act of his reasoning and will.

Quoted by Curtis Pepper *The Pope's Backyard* Farrar, Straus & Giroux 66

PIO DA PIETREICINA, Capuchin monk

9 The wretchedness of men equals the mercy of God.

Time 24 Apr 64

POPE PIUS XII

10 I shall be able to rest one minute after I die.

To physicians who asked him to curtail his work, *Look* 22 Aug 55

MICHAEL RAMSEY, Archbishop of Canterbury

11 The supreme question is not what we make of the Eucharist but what the Eucharist is making of us.

To men about to be ordained, quoted by James B Simpson *The Hundredth Archbishop of Canterbury* Harper & Row 62

12 Reason is an action of the mind; knowledge is a possession of the mind; but faith is an attitude of the person. It means you are prepared to stake yourself on something being so.

ib

13 To be with God wondering, that is adoration. To be with God gratefully, that is thanksgiving. To be with God ashamed, that is contrition. To be with God with people and things we care about in our hearts, that is intercession. But the center of it in desire and in design will be the being with God.

"The Heart of Prayer" *Christian World* 7 Dec 78

RONALD REAGAN, 40th US President

14 I miss going to church, but I think the Lord understands.

Explaining that security precautions prevented him from joining in public worship, reply in debate with Democratic candidate Walter F Mondale, Louisville KY, 7 Oct 84

BETTY ROBBINS

15 I sing what is in my heart. My only thought now is to sing as I have never sung before.

On being first woman cantor in Jewish history, news summaries 15 Aug 55

ROBERT RUNCIE, Archbishop of Canterbury

16 The New Testament never simply says "remember Jesus Christ." That is a half-finished sentence. It says "remember Jesus Christ is risen from the dead."

1980 Easter sermon, recalled in *Seasons of the Spirit* Eerdmans 83

1 The priest is concerned with other people for the sake of God and with God for the sake of other people.

> Ordination sermon, "The Character of a Priest," *ib*

2 If our faith delivers us from worry, then worry is an insult flung in the face of God.

> Address during April 1982 tour of Nigeria, *ib*

FRANCIS B SAYRE, Dean, National Cathedral, Washington DC

3 Religion isn't yours firsthand until you doubt it right down to the ground.

> *Life* 2 Apr 65

4 I don't think man comes to faith firsthand except through despair or to knowledge of God except through doubt. It has to be a kind of watershed experience.

> *ib*

ALBERT SCHWEITZER

5 Do not let Sunday be taken from you ... If your soul has no Sunday, it becomes an orphan.

> Quoted by Erica Anderson *The Schweitzer Album* Harper & Row 65

6 Example is not the main thing in influencing others. It is the only thing.

> Recalled on his death 4 Sep 65

FULTON J SHEEN, retired Roman Catholic Bishop of Rochester NY

7 The only way to win audiences is to tell people about the life and death of Christ. Every other approach is a waste.

> To National Conference of Catholic Bishops, Chicago, NY *Times* 4 May 78

8 Show me your hands. Do they have scars from giving? Show me your feet. Are they wounded in service? Show me your heart. Have you left a place for divine love?

> Good Friday sermon, quoted in *ib* 14 Apr 79

CARROLL SIMCOX, Editor, *Living Church*

9 When you want it, it's a handout; when I want it, it's seed money. When you're that way, you're naive; when I'm that way, I'm open. When you have it, it's a hang-up; when I have it, it's a priority. When you're that way, you're uptight; when I'm that way, I'm liberated. When you're that way, you're not hearing me; when I'm that way, I'm telling it like it is. When you're that way, you're being irrelevant; when I'm that way, I'm being prophetic.

> On "semantic distinctions," at Episcopal convention 28 Sep 69

ISAAC BASHEVIS SINGER

10 Life is God's novel. Let him write it.

> Quoted in Dom Moraes ed *Voices for Life* Praeger 75

11 Doubt is part of all religion. All the religious thinkers were doubters.

> NY *Times* 3 Dec 78

SOONG MEI-LING

12 No one who has had a unique experience with prayer has a right to withhold it from others.

> "The Power of Prayer" *Reader's Digest* Aug 55

RABBI PINCHAS STOLPER, Executive Vice President, Union of Orthodox Jewish Congregations

13 [The yarmulke] is an indication that one recognizes that there is something above you. It says, "Above my intellect is a sign of godliness."

> On Supreme Court ruling that allowed the military to prohibit an Orthodox Jewish officer from wearing a yarmulke indoors while in uniform, NY *Times* 26 Mar 86

MOTHER TERESA MC

14 I do not pray for success, I ask for faithfulness.

> When asked if she was ever discouraged, NY *Times* 18 Jun 80

15 I am a little pencil in the hand of a writing God who is sending a love letter to the world.

> News summaries 1 Sep 82

MOTHER CATHERINE THOMAS

16 A Carmelite nun should be, by the very nature of her vocation, a specialist in prayer. Or, to give it a more modern twist, she is a career woman in the field of prayer and contemplation.

> *My Beloved: The Story of a Carmelite Nun* McGraw-Hill 55

PAUL TILLICH

17 Being religious means asking passionately the question of the meaning of our existence and being willing to receive answers, even if the answers hurt.

> *Saturday Evening Post* 14 Jun 58

RABBI MATTHEW TROPP

18 We're looking into a mirror of godliness.

> On studying the Talmud, NY *Times* 7 Apr 86

ANN BELFORD ULANOV, Professor of Psychiatry and Mental Health, Union Theological Seminary, NYC

1 To be religious is to have a life that flows with the presence of the extraordinary.
Vogue Dec 85

ARTHUR VOGEL, Professor of Apologetics and Dogmatic Theology, Nashotah House Episcopal Seminary, Nashotah WI

2 There can be no true response without responsibility; there can be no responsibility without response.
The Christian Person Seabury 63

KURT VONNEGUT JR

3 It is a very mixed blessing to be brought back from the dead.
Palm Sunday sermon at St Clement's Episcopal Church, NYC, quoted by John Leonard NY *Times* 30 Apr 80

4 People don't come to church for preachments, of course, but to daydream about God.
ib

SIMONE WEIL

5 The danger is not lest the soul should doubt whether there is any bread, but lest, by a lie, it should persuade itself that it is not hungry.
Waiting for God Putnam 51

EDWARD N WEST, former Subdean, Cathedral Church of St John the Divine, NYC

6 There is nothing in the world more dreary than a prayer that attempts to inform God of anything at all.
To NY School of Theology 2 Oct 83

MORRIS WEST

7 Once you accept the existence of God—however you define him, however you explain your relationship to him—then you are caught forever with his presence in the center of all things.
The Clowns of God Morrow 81

THORNTON WILDER

8 Hope, like faith, is nothing if it is not courageous; it is nothing if it is not ridiculous.
The Eighth Day Harper & Row 67

9 Man is not an end but a beginning. We are at the beginning of the second week. We are children of the eighth day.
ib

P J WINGATE

10 "Give us this day our daily bread" is probably the most perfectly constructed and useful sentence ever set down in the English language.
Wall Street Journal 8 Aug 77

STEFAN CARDINAL WYSZYNSKI, Primate of Poland

11 I tell you, you will serve only your God, because man is too noble to serve anyone but God.
Sermon against Communist adversaries, NY *Times* 20 Mar 61

HUMOR & WIT

JONATHAN ADASHEK, age 12

12 To the best of my knowledge there has been no child in space. I would like to learn about being weightless, and I'd like to get away from my mother's cooking.
Letter to President Ronald Reagan, *Life* Oct 84

FRED ALLEN

13 I have just returned from Boston. It is the only thing to do if you find yourself up there.
Letter to Groucho Marx 12 Jun 53

14 A vice president in an advertising agency is a "molehill man" [who] has until 5 PM to make [a] molehill into a mountain. An accomplished molehill man will often have his mountain finished even before lunch.
Treadmill to Oblivion Little, Brown 54

15 A celebrity is a person who works hard all his life to become well known, then wears dark glasses to avoid being recognized.
ib

16 Batten, Barton, Durstine & Osborne—sounds like a trunk falling down a flight of stairs.
On NYC advertising agency, recalled on his death 17 Mar 56

STEVE ALLEN

17 The hair is real—it's the head that's a fake.
When asked if he wore a toupee, NBC TV 15 Dec 57

KINGSLEY AMIS

18 He resolved, having done it once, never to move his eyeballs again.
On recovering from a hangover, *Lucky Jim* Jonathan Clowes 58

CLEVELAND AMORY

19 The New England conscience . . . does not stop

you from doing what you shouldn't—it just stops you from enjoying it.
> *New York* 5 May 80

RICHARD ARMOUR

1 I've suffered from all of the hang-ups known, And none is as bad as the telephone.
> *Wall Street Journal* 11 Jul 85

ANONYMOUS

2 If you drink, don't dial.
> Reply to caller who dialed his social security number instead of the number he wished to reach, quoted in NY *Herald Tribune* 30 Apr 58

3 To hell with you. Offensive letter follows.
> Irate citizen's telegram, quoted by Alec Douglas-Home, British foreign secretary, *Wall Street Journal* 11 Jul 62

4 Wanted: Playpen, cot and highchair. Also two single beds.
> Advertisement in *Evening Standard*, quoted by David Frost and Antony Jay *The English* Stein & Day 68

5 To our wives and sweethearts ... and may they never meet.
> Favorite toast of the Royal Navy, quoted by Hugo Vickers *Cecil Beaton* Little, Brown 85

6 Don't cross this field unless you can do it in 9.9 seconds. The bull can do it in 10.
> Sign on bison range above underground quarters of Fermi National Accelerator Laboratory, Batavia IL, pictured in *People* 18 Nov 85

7 Mr Holmes thanks you for your letter. At the moment he is in retirement in Sussex, keeping bees.
> Reply of a bank at 221B Baker Street, London, to 40 or so letters addressed daily to fictional sleuth Sherlock Holmes, quoted in *US News & World Report* 19 Jan 87

NANCY, LADY ASTOR

8 My vigor, vitality and cheek repel me. I am the kind of woman I would run from.
> To Washington reporters, news summaries 29 Mar 55

BERNARD BARUCH

9 To me, old age is always 15 years older than I am.
> On his 85th birthday, news summaries 20 Aug 55

PHYLLIS BATTELLE

10 For her fifth wedding, the bride wore black and carried a scotch and soda.
> On Barbara Hutton's marriage to Porfirio Rubirosa, quoted by Cleveland Amory and Earl Blackwell eds *Celebrity Register* Harper & Row 63

STEPHEN BAYNE

11 I am rather like a mosquito in a nudist camp; I know what I ought to do, but I don't know where to begin.
> On becoming first executive officer of the Anglican Communion, *Time* 25 Jan 60

LORD BEAVERBROOK (William Maxwell Aitken)

12 Buy old masters. They fetch a better price than old mistresses.
> Recalled on his death 9 Jun 64

MAX BEERBOHM

13 Most women are not so young as they are painted.
> "A Defense of Cosmetics," recalled on his death 20 May 56

BRENDAN BEHAN

14 New York is my Lourdes, where I go for spiritual refreshment. . . . a place where you're least likely to be bitten by a wild goat.
> Recalled on his death, NY *Post* 22 Mar 64

GUY BELLAMY

15 Life is a sexually transmitted disease.
> *The Sinner's Congregation* Secker & Warburg 84

SAUL BELLOW

16 I've never turned over a fig leaf yet that didn't have a price tag on the other side.
> PBS TV 27 Jan 82

JACK BENNY

17 Age is strictly a case of mind over matter. If you don't mind, it doesn't matter.
> NY *Times* 15 Feb 74

MILTON BERLE

18 A committee is a group that keeps minutes and loses hours.
> News summaries 1 Jul 54

ERMA BOMBECK

19 Guilt: the gift that keeps on giving.
> Quoted by John Skow *Time* 2 Jul 84

BOY GEORGE

20 I can do anything. In *GQ*, I appeared as a man.
> Quoted in *US* 21 Apr 86

WERNHER VON BRAUN

1 We can lick gravity, but sometimes the paperwork is overwhelming.

   On bureaucracy, Chicago *Sun Times* 10 Jul 58

HANK BRENNAN

2 His baroque is worse than his bite.

   On Cecil Beaton, quoted by Hugo Vickers *Cecil Beaton* Little, Brown 85

MARIO BUATTA

3 Dust is a protective coating for fine furniture.

   Quoted by John Taylor "Fringe Lunatic" *Manhattan Inc* Jul 86

ART BUCHWALD

4 A bad liver is to a Frenchman what a nervous breakdown is to an American. Everyone has had one and everyone wants to talk about it.

   NY *Herald Tribune* 16 Jan 58

5 People are broad-minded. They'll accept the fact that a person can be an alcoholic, a dope fiend, a wife beater and even a newspaperman, but if a man doesn't drive, there's something wrong with him.

   Have I Ever Lied to You? Putnam 68

LUIS BUÑUEL

6 Thank God, I am still an atheist.

   Time 29 Nov 69

CAROL BURNETT

7 Adolescence is just one big walking pimple.

   Phil Donahue show NBC TV 16 Oct 86

GEORGE BURNS

8 Happiness? A good cigar, a good meal, a good cigar and a good woman—or a bad woman; it depends on how much happiness you can handle.

   NBC TV 16 Oct 84

9 I don't believe in dying. It's been done. I'm working on a new exit. Besides, I can't die now—I'm booked.

   News summaries 20 Jan 87

AL CAPP

10 The public is like a piano. You just have to know what keys to poke.

   News summaries 1 Mar 54

JEROME CAVANAGH, former Mayor of Detroit

11 He played football too long without a helmet.

   On Congressman Gerald R Ford, quoted by Lyndon B Johnson and recalled when Richard M Nixon chose Ford as his vice president, *Newsweek* 22 Oct 73

HARRY CHAPMAN

12 Having served on various committees, I have drawn up a list of rules: Never arrive on time; this stamps you as a beginner. Don't say anything until the meeting is half over; this stamps you as being wise. Be as vague as possible; this avoids irritating the others. When in doubt, suggest that a subcommittee be appointed. Be the first to move for adjournment; this will make you popular; it's what everyone is waiting for.

   Greater Kansas City Medical Bulletin 63

ZEV CHAVETS

13 In Tel Aviv the weekends last 48 hours. In Jerusalem they last 6 months.

   On moving from Jerusalem to Tel Aviv, Boston *Globe* 10 Apr 87

LYDIA CHAVEZ

14 An Argentine is an Italian who speaks Spanish and thinks he is British.

   NY *Times* 9 Feb 86

WINSTON CHURCHILL

15 A fanatic is one who can't change his mind and won't change the subject.

   News summaries 5 Jul 54

16 An appeaser is one who feeds a crocodile—hoping it will eat him last.

   Reader's Digest Dec 54

17 When you took your seat I felt as if a woman had come into my bathroom and I had only the sponge to defend myself.

   To Nancy Astor, first women to sit in British Parliament, recalled on her death 2 May 64

18 Although present on the occasion, I have no clear recollection of the events leading up to it.

   On his birth, recalled on his death 24 Jan 65

19 We have always found the Irish a bit odd. They refuse to be English.

   ib

20 The monarchy is so extraordinarily *useful*. When Britain wins a battle she shouts, "God save the Queen"; when she loses, she votes down the prime minister.

   Quoted by Anne Edwards *Matriarch* Morrow 84

JEAN COCTEAU

21 The trouble about the Académie is that by the

195

time they get around to electing us to a seat, we really need a bed.

On election to Académie Française, recalled on his death 11 Oct 63

BOB CONSIDINE

1 I believe in opening mail once a month, whether it needs it or not.

NY *Journal-American* 21 Jan 60

HENRY S F COOPER

2 A man who thinks too much about his ancestors is like a potato—the best part of him is underground.

Recalled on his death 10 Sep 84

BILL COSBY

3 When you become senile, you won't know it.

On growing older, quoted in NY *Times* 17 Mar 87

NOEL COWARD

4 Success took me to her bosom like a maternal boa constrictor.

On having three hit plays running simultaneously in London, recalled on his death 26 Mar 73

5 It was not Café Society, it was Nescafé Society.

On entertaining at Desert Inn, Las Vegas, *ib*

6 I like long walks, especially when they are taken by people who annoy me.

ib

RODNEY DANGERFIELD

7 I'm at the age where food has taken the place of sex in my life. In fact, I've just had a mirror put over my kitchen table.

New York 5 May 80

BETTE DAVIS

8 She is the original good time that was had by all.

On another actress, *Parade* 15 Feb 81

CHARLES DE GAULLE, President of France

9 I always thought I was Jeanne d'Arc and Bonaparte. How little one knows oneself.

Reply to someone who compared him to Robespierre, *Time* 16 Jun 58

10 How can you be expected to govern a country that has 246 kinds of cheese?

Newsweek 1 Oct 62

ANNA DE NOAILLES

11 If God exists, I'd be the first to be told.

To Jean Cocteau, *Vogue* May 84

NORMAN DOUGLAS

12 Never take a solemn oath. People think you mean it.

Recalled on his death 9 Feb 52

JAMES DUFFECY

13 A dead atheist is someone who's all dressed up with no place to go.

NY *Times* 21 Aug 64

RONALD DUNCAN

14 E M Forster was like a tea cozy, but I quite liked him. I was at a wedding party with him once, sitting opposite Queen Mary. I asked if he would like to be presented. "Good Lord," he said. "I thought it was the wedding cake."

London *Sunday Times* 14 Sep 80

EDWARD, Duke of Windsor

15 The thing that impresses me most about America is the way parents obey their children.

Look 5 Mar 57

ALBERT EINSTEIN

16 When a man sits with a pretty girl for an hour, it seems like a minute. But let him sit on a hot stove for a minute—and it's longer than any hour. That's relativity.

Recalled on his death 18 Apr 55

DWIGHT D EISENHOWER, 34th US President

17 Oh yes, I studied dramatics under him for 12 years.

When asked if he knew Douglas MacArthur, quoted in *By Quentin Reynolds* McGraw-Hill 63

WILLIAM FAULKNER

18 This is a free country. Folks have a right to send me letters, and I have a right not to read them.

On discarding unopened mail, recalled on his death 6 Jul 62

HARVEY FIERSTEIN

19 The great thing about suicide is that it's not one of those things you have to do now or you lose your chance. I mean, you can always do it *later*.

New York 22 Aug 83

GEOFFREY FISHER, Archbishop of Canterbury

20 The long and distressing controversy over capital punishment is very unfair to anyone meditating murder.

London *Sunday Times* 24 Feb 57

ERROL FLYNN

1 My problem lies in reconciling my gross habits with my net income.
> Recalled on his death 14 Oct 59

MARTIN FREUD

2 I didn't know the full facts of life until I was 17. My father never talked about his work.
> On being the son of Sigmund Freud, news summaries 15 Nov 57

ROBERT FROST

3 I'm not confused. I'm just well mixed.
> *Wall Street Journal* 5 Aug 69

ZSA ZSA GABOR

4 A man in love is incomplete until he has married. Then he's finished.
> *Newsweek* 28 Mar 60

5 We were both in love with him. ... I fell out of love with him, but he didn't.
> On ex-husband George Sanders, Chicago *American* 4 Sep 66

ERLE STANLEY GARDNER

6 It's a damn good story. If you have any comments, write them on the back of a check.
> Note on manuscript submitted to hard-to-please editors, quoted by Dorothy B Hughes *Erle Stanley Gardner* Morrow 78

ANDRÉ GIDE

7 It is unthinkable for a Frenchman to arrive at middle age without having syphilis and the Cross of the Legion of Honor.
> Recalled on his death 19 Feb 51

FRANK L GILL, State Senator, Colorado

8 Last week we passed a birth-control bill. Now we are trying to pass a law to put the people to bed an hour earlier.
> On daylight-saving time legislation, *Quote* 18 Apr 65

SAMUEL GOLDWYN

9 Any man who goes to a psychiatrist ought to have his head examined.
> One of many Goldwynisms attributed to him, recalled on his death 31 Jan 74

BARRY GRAY

10 I get my exercise running to the funerals of my friends who exercise.
> *New York* 19 May 80

VARTAN GREGORIAN, President, NY Public Library

11 Everybody is somebody, so you don't have to introduce anybody.
> At dinner honoring authors, NY *Times* 13 Nov 84

GRACE HANSEN

12 A wedding is just like a funeral except that you get to smell your own flowers.
> Recalled on her death, Eugene OR *Register-Guard* 14 Jan 85

BOB HOPE

13 When she started to play, Steinway came down personally and rubbed his name off the piano.
> On comedian Phyllis Diller, WNEW TV 7 May 85

ROBERT HUGHES

14 One gets tired of the role critics are supposed to have in this culture: It's like being the piano player in a whorehouse; you don't have any control over the action going on upstairs.
> *Publishers Weekly* 12 Dec 86

POPE JOHN XXIII

15 Here I am at the end of the road and at the top of the heap.
> On succeeding Pius XII, *Time* 24 Nov 58

LYNDON B JOHNSON, 36th US President

16 When the burdens of the presidency seem unusually heavy, I always remind myself it could be worse. I could be a mayor.
> To US Mayors' Convention, *Newsweek* 3 Oct 66

17 It's probably better to have him inside the tent pissing out, than outside the tent pissing in.
> On FBI director J Edgar Hoover, quoted in NY *Times* 31 Oct 71

ERICA JONG

18 Jealousy is all the fun you think they had.
> *Fear of Flying* Holt, Rinehart & Winston 73

YOUSUF KARSH

19 The trouble with photographing beautiful women is that you never get into the dark room until after they've gone.
> NY *Mirror* 2 May 63

GARRISON KEILLOR

20 It was luxuries like air conditioning that

brought down the Roman Empire. With air conditioning their windows were shut, they couldn't hear the barbarians coming.
Lake Wobegon Days Viking 85

WALT KELLY

1 We have met the enemy and he is us.
From his comic strip *Pogo*, recalled on his death 18 Oct 73

JOHN F KENNEDY, 35th US President

2 I am the man who accompanied Jacqueline Kennedy to Paris, and I have enjoyed it.
Press conference 3 Jun 61

3 I think this is the most extraordinary collection of talent, of human knowledge, that has ever been gathered at the White House—with the possible exception of when Thomas Jefferson dined alone.
At dinner for 49 Nobel laureates 29 Apr 62

4 It was absolutely involuntary. They sank my boat.
On how he became a war hero, quoted in Bill Adler ed *The Kennedy Wit* Citadel 64

5 Let's not talk so much about vice. I'm against vice in all forms.
Rejecting efforts to make him 1960 Democratic candidate for vice president, quoted by Ralph G Martin *A Hero for Our Time* Macmillan 83

6 The pay is good and I can walk to work.
On becoming president, *ib*

CLARK KERR, President, University of California

7 I find that the three major administrative problems on a campus are sex for the students, athletics for the alumni and parking for the faculty.
Time 17 Nov 58

JEAN KERR

8 I'm tired of all this nonsense about beauty being only skin-deep. . . . What do you want—an adorable pancreas?
The Snake Has All the Lines Doubleday 60

9 A lawyer is never entirely comfortable with a friendly divorce, anymore than a good mortician wants to finish his job and then have the patient sit up on the table.
Time 14 Apr 61

10 Life with Mary was like being in a telephone booth with an open umbrella—no matter which way you turned, you got it in the eye.
Mary, Mary Doubleday 63

11 Being divorced is like being hit by a Mack truck—if you survive you start looking very carefully to the right and left.
ib

LISA KIRK

12 A gossip is one who talks to you about others; a bore is one who talks to you about himself; and a brilliant conversationalist is one who talks to you about yourself.
NY *Journal-American* 9 Mar 54

HENRY A KISSINGER

13 Next week there can't be any crisis. My schedule is already full.
NY *Times* 28 Oct 73

14 The illegal we do immediately. The unconstitutional takes a little longer.
On Watergate, *ib*

15 People are generally amazed that I would take an interest in any form that would require me to stop talking for three hours.
On his fondness for opera, *Time* 15 Sep 80

16 Even a paranoid has some real enemies.
Newsweek 13 Jun 83

17 The nice thing about being a celebrity is that when you bore people, they think it's their fault.
Reader's Digest Apr 85

ANN LANDERS

18 You need that guy like a giraffe needs strep throat.
Red Bank NJ *Register* 12 Oct 73

GYPSY ROSE LEE

19 I have everything now I had 20 years ago—except now it's all lower.
Newsweek 16 Sep 68

SAM LEVENSON

20 Insanity is hereditary—you get it from your children.
Diner's Club Magazine Nov 63

C S LEWIS

21 There are two kinds of people: those who say to God, "Thy will be done," and those to whom God says, "All right, then, have it your way."
From his 1943 book *The Screwtape Letters*, recalled on his death 22 Nov 63

LIBERACE

1 I cried all the way to the bank.
> On criticism of his flamboyant appearance and style as an entertainer, news summaries 30 Jun 54

2 You know that bank I used to cry all the way to? I bought it.
> Recalled on his death, *Newsweek* 16 Feb 87

ALICE ROOSEVELT LONGWORTH

3 My father always wanted to be the corpse at every funeral, the bride at every wedding and the baby at every christening.
> On President Theodore Roosevelt, quoted in Cleveland Amory and Earl Blackwell eds *Celebrity Register* Harper & Row 63

4 If you can't say something good about someone, sit right here by me.
> Motto embroidered on sofa pillow, quoted in *Time* 9 Dec 66

CLARE BOOTHE LUCE

5 I'm in my anecdotage.
> At age 77, *Town & Country* Jan 81

RUSSELL LYNES

6 The true snob never rests; there is always a higher goal to attain, and there are, by the same token, always more and more people to look down upon.
> *Snobs* Harper 50

HAROLD MACMILLAN, former Prime Minister of Great Britain

7 No man should ever lose sleep over *public* affairs.
> Interview with Dick Cavett ABC TV 16 Aug 82

MARCEL MARCEAU

8 Never get a mime talking. He won't stop.
> *US News & World Report* 23 Feb 87

FREDRIC MARCH

9 He has a terrific way with women. I don't think he has missed more than half a dozen.
> On Richard Burton, recalled on Burton's death, NY *Times* 6 Aug 84

GROUCHO MARX

10 A hospital bed is a parked taxi with the meter running.
> *Reader's Digest* Mar 73

11 I never forget a face, but in your case I'll make an exception.
> Quoted in news summaries 29 Jul 81

GALE W McGEE, US Senator

12 I'm going to introduce a resolution to have the postmaster general stop reading dirty books and deliver the mail.
> On efficiency over censorship, *Quote* 13 Sep 59

MIGNON McLAUGHLIN

13 A woman telling her true age is like a buyer confiding his final price to an Armenian rug dealer.
> Chicago *Tribune* 13 Sep 64

GEORGE MEANY, President, AFL

14 Anybody who has any doubt about the ingenuity or the resourcefulness of a plumber never got a bill from one.
> CBS TV 8 Jan 54

BETTE MIDLER

15 When it's three o'clock in New York, it's still 1938 in London.
> London *Times* 21 Sep 78

EDNA ST VINCENT MILLAY

16 Please give me some good advice in your next letter. I promise not to follow it.
> As an undergraduate at Vassar, quoted in Allen Ross Macdougall ed *Letters of Edna St Vincent Millay* Harper 52

MARILYN MONROE

17 I've been on a calendar, but never on time.
> *Look* 5 Mar 57

18 It's not true that I had nothing on. I had the radio on.
> On posing nude for a calendar, news summaries 31 Dec 57

PETER MULLEN, Anglican priest

19 Even the end of the world is described as if it were only an exceptionally hot afternoon.
> Criticizing the *New English Bible* translation, *Fair of Speech* Oxford 85, quoted in NY *Times* 22 Sep 85

GEORGE JEAN NATHAN

20 I drink to make other people interesting.
> Recalled on his death 8 Apr 58

NEW YORK TIMES

21 A New Yorker is a person with an almost inordinate interest in mental health, which is only natural considering how much of that it takes to live here.
> "New Yorkers, By the Book" 4 Oct 86

ERIC NICOL

1 Was Lenin pro-Communist?

> *Russia, Anyone? A Completely Uncalled-for History of the USSR* Harper & Row 63

CRAIG NOVA

2 She's got what I call bobsled looks: going downhill fast.

> From his novel *Incandescence* Harper & Row 79

CAROL AND NEIL OFFEN

3 Kenya—along with Hollywood Boulevard—boasts one of the main animal crossings in the world.

> *Esquire* Apr 86

ARISTOTLE ONASSIS

4 [Find a priest] who understands English and doesn't look like Rasputin.

> To a business associate on planning Greek Orthodox marriage ceremony with Jacqueline Kennedy, quoted by Peter Evans *Ari* Summit 86

5 She's got to learn to reconcile herself to being Mrs Aristotle Onassis because the only place she'll find sympathy from now on is in the dictionary between shit and syphilis.

> *ib*

ROBERT ORBEN

6 Life was a lot simpler when what we honored was father and mother rather than all major credit cards.

> *Wall Street Journal* 17 Mar 80

DOROTHY PARKER

7 He and I had an office so tiny that an inch smaller and it would have been adultery.

> On sharing space with Robert Benchley while working on *Vanity Fair* magazine, quoted in Malcolm Cowley ed *Writers at Work* Viking 58

PRINCE PHILIP, Duke of Edinburgh

8 Dontopedology is the science of opening your mouth and putting your foot in it. I've been practicing it for years.

> To Britain's General Dental Council, *Time* 21 Nov 60

IVY BAKER PRIEST, Treasurer of the US

9 We women don't care too much about getting our pictures on money as long as we can get our hands on it.

> *Look* 10 Aug 54

V S PRITCHETT

10 I shall never be as old as I was between 20 and 30.

> NY *Times* 16 Dec 85

RONALD REAGAN, 40th US President

11 Middle age is when you're faced with two temptations and you choose the one that will get you home by 9 o'clock.

> On his 66th birthday, quoted in Washington *Post* 7 Feb 77

12 A hippie is someone who looks like Tarzan, walks like Jane and smells like Cheetah.

> Quoted by Nat Shapiro ed *Whatever It Is, I'm Against It* Simon & Schuster 84

13 I was recovering from young Mr Hinckley's unwelcome attentions.

> To Al Smith Memorial Dinner, recalling Terence Cardinal Cooke's visit to the White House after assassination attempt by John W Hinckley Jr, news summaries 18 Oct 84

14 My doctors told me this morning my blood pressure is down so low that I can start reading the newspapers.

> On recovering from prostate surgery, quoted in *US News & World Report* 23 Feb 87

15 Do you remember when I said bombing would begin in five minutes? Remember when I fell asleep during my audience with the pope? . . . Those were the good old days.

> Washington Gridiron Club dinner 28 Mar 87

NAN ROBERTSON

16 Ever since Eve gave Adam the apple, there has been a misunderstanding between the sexes about gifts.

> On Christmas shopping, NY *Times* 28 Nov 57

BILLY ROSE

17 Never invest your money in anything that eats or needs repainting.

> NY *Post* 26 Oct 57

STANLEY RUDIN

18 Frustrate a Frenchman, he will drink himself to death; an Irishman, he will die of angry hypertension; a Dane, he will shoot himself; an American, he will get drunk, shoot you, then establish a million-dollar aid program for your relatives. Then he will die of an ulcer.

> To International Congress of Psychology, NY *Times* 22 Aug 63

RITA RUDNER

1 If you never want to see a man again, say, "I love you, I want to marry you, I want to have children"—they leave skid marks.
NY *Times* 2 Aug 85

ROBERT O RUPP

2 We stopped counting his mistresses and started counting his accomplishments.
On commemorating Marion OH's best-known citizen, President Warren G Harding, NY *Times* 3 Nov 86

J D SALINGER

3 He probably passed on . . . of an overdose of garlic, the way all New York barbers eventually go.
Seymour: An Introduction Little, Brown 63

ANTHONY SAMPSON

4 London clubs remain insistent on keeping people out, long after they have stopped wanting to come in.
On royal decorations ranging from Commander, Knight Commander and Grand Commander to the Order of St Michael and St George, *The Anatomy of Britain* Harper & Row 62

CHARLES M SCHULZ

5 You're a good man, Charlie Brown.
From *Peanuts* comic strip 75

6 No problem is too big to run away from.
Quoted by Al Ries and Jack Trout *Positioning: The Battle for Your Mind* McGraw-Hill 81

FRED ("THE FURRIER") SCHWARTZ

7 You have to remember. In the beginning we were *all* furriers.
Quoted in *Newsweek* 29 Dec 86

F R SCOTT

8 I am dying by honorary degrees.
On his many academic honors, news summaries 31 Dec 65

ARTIE SHAW

9 You have no idea of the people I *didn't* marry.
On his many marriages, NBC TV 8 Apr 85

FULTON J SHEEN, Auxiliary Bishop of NYC

10 Baloney is the unvarnished lie laid on so thick you hate it. Blarney is flattery laid on so thin you love it.
News summaries 22 Mar 54

11 I feel it is time that I also pay tribute to my four writers, Matthew, Mark, Luke and John.
On receiving award for television appearances, NY *World-Telegram & Sun* 24 Dec 54

12 An atheist is a man who has no invisible means of support.
Look 14 Dec 55

NEIL SIMON

13 People with honorary awards are looked upon with disfavor. Would you let an honorary mechanic fix your brand-new Mercedes?
On receiving honorary degree from Williams College, NY *Times* 4 Jun 84

EDITH SITWELL

14 The aim of flattery is to soothe and encourage us by assuring us of the truth of an opinion we have already formed about ourselves.
Quoted by Elizabeth Salter *The Last Years of a Rebel* Houghton Mifflin 76

JOHN SKOW

15 Housework, if it is done right, can kill you.
"Erma in Bomburbia" *Time* 2 Jul 84

GERALD B H SOLOMON, US Congressman

16 [My dog] can bark like a congressman, fetch like an aide, beg like a press secretary and play dead like a receptionist when the phone rings.
Entry in contest to identify Capitol Hill's Great American Dog, NY *Times* 9 Aug 86

SALLY STANFORD, madam and former Mayor of Sausalito CA

17 Madaming is the sort of thing that happens to you—like getting a battlefield commission or becoming the dean of women at Stanford University.
The Lady of the House Putnam 66

WILL STANTON

18 Republicans sleep in twin beds—some even in separate rooms. That is why there are more Democrats.
"How to Tell a Democrat from a Republican" *Ladies' Home Journal* Nov 62

JOHN STEINBECK

19 One man was so mad at me that he ended his letter: "Beware. You will never get out of this world alive."
"The Mail I've Seen" *Saturday Review* 3 Aug 56

GLORIA STEINEM

1 She has become the Julia Child of sex.
    On "Dr Ruth" Westheimer, *Today* NBC TV 12
    Feb 87

ADLAI E STEVENSON

2 Man does not live by words alone, despite the
    fact that sometimes he has to eat them.
    Recalled on his death 14 Jul 65

3 The relationship of the toastmaster to speaker
    should be the same as that of the fan to the fan
    dancer. It should call attention to the subject
    without making any particular effort to cover
    it.
    ib

4 Flattery is all right—if you don't inhale.
    ib

5 Do you know the difference between a beauti-
    ful woman and a charming one? A beauty is a
    woman you notice, a charmer is one who no-
    tices you.
    ib

CASKIE STINNETT

6 Working for a federal agency was like trying to
    dislodge a prune skin from the roof of the
    mouth. More enterprise went into the job than
    could be justified by the results.
    Out of the Red Random House 60

7 A diplomat is a person who can tell you to go
    to hell in such a way that you actually look for-
    ward to the trip.
    ib

LEWIS THOMAS

8 Ants are so much like human beings as to be
    an embarrassment. They farm fungi, raise
    aphids as livestock, launch armies into war,
    use chemical sprays to alarm and confuse ene-
    mies, capture slaves, engage in child labor, ex-
    change information ceaselessly. They do
    everything but watch television.
    The Lives of a Cell Viking 74

GORE VIDAL

9 A narcissist is someone better looking than
    you are.
    NY *Times* 12 Mar 81

ANDY WARHOL

10 It would be very glamorous to be reincarnated
    as a great big ring on Liz Taylor's finger.
    Quoted in eulogy at memorial mass, St Patrick's
    Cathedral, NY *Times* 2 Apr 87

ROBERT PENN WARREN

11 Storytelling and copulation are the two chief
    forms of amusement in the South. They're in-
    expensive and easy to procure.
    Newsweek 25 Aug 80

CHAIM WEIZMANN, President of Israel

12 Einstein explained his theory to me every day,
    and on my arrival I was fully convinced that
    he understood it.
    On transatlantic crossing with Albert Einstein,
    quoted by Nigel Calder *Einstein's Universe* Vi-
    king 79

ORSON WELLES

13 When you are down and out something always
    turns up—and it is usually the noses of your
    friends.
    NY *Times* 1 Apr 62

RUTH WESTON

14 A fox is a wolf who sends flowers.
    NY *Post* 8 Nov 55

E B WHITE

15 I arise in the morning torn between a desire to
    improve (or save) the world and a desire to en-
    joy (or savor) the world. This makes it hard to
    plan the day.
    Recalled on his death, *Newsweek* 14 Oct 85

16 I can only assume that your editorial writer . . .
    tripped over the First Amendment and
    thought it was the office cat.
    Letter to NY *Herald Tribune* on its post-World
    War II insistence that its employees should
    "state their beliefs," *ib*

THYRA SAMTER WINSLOW

17 Platonic love is love from the neck up.
    News summaries 10 Aug 52

P G WODEHOUSE

18 There is only one cure for gray hair. It was in-
    vented by a Frenchman. It is called the guil-
    lotine.
    The Old Reliable Doubleday 51

HENNY YOUNGMAN

19 I once wanted to become an atheist, but I gave
    up—they have no holidays.
    Quoted in Irving Wallace et al *Book of Lists #2*
    Morrow 80

20 When God sneezed, I didn't know what to say.
    NBC TV 28 Aug 86

WISDOM, PHILOSOPHY & OTHER MUSINGS

LIONEL ABEL

1 I have noted that persons with bad judgment are most insistent that we do what they think best.

Important Nonsense Prometheus 86, quoted in NY *Times* 6 Feb 87

DEAN ACHESON

2 The manner in which one endures what must be endured is more important than the thing that must be endured.

Quoted by Merle Miller *Plain Speaking: An Oral Biography of Harry S Truman* Putnam 73

MORTIMER ADLER

3 Not to engage in the pursuit of ideas is to live like ants instead of like men.

Saturday Review 22 Nov 58

RENATA ADLER

4 Bored people, unless they sleep a lot, are cruel.

Speedboat Random House 76

BRIAN ALDISS

5 When childhood dies, its corpses are called adults.

Manchester *Guardian* 31 Dec 77

SHANA ALEXANDER

6 Letters are expectation packaged in an envelope.

"The Surprises of the Mail" *Life* 30 Jun 67

MUHAMMAD ALI

7 The man who views the world at 50 the same as he did at 20 has wasted 30 years of his life.

Playboy Nov 75

MAYA ANGELOU

8 Self-pity in its early stages is as snug as a feather mattress. Only when it hardens does it become uncomfortable.

Gather Together in My Name Random House 74

ANONYMOUS

9 Man himself is a visitor who does not remain.

From proposed legislation to designate up to 10 million acres of government-owned land as wilderness preserves, quoted in NY *Times* 15 Jul 84

10 After ecstasy, the laundry.

Zen statement, quoted in *Newsweek* 17 Dec 84

11 A person's right to smoke ends where the next person's nose begins.

Public service announcement WNET TV 23 May 86

12 A neat house has an uninteresting person in it.

Inscription on china plate, quoted by Enid Nemy NY *Times* 2 Nov 86

ROBERT ANTHONY

13 We neither get better or worse as we get older, but more like ourselves.

Think Again Berkley 86

14 If you are not learning, no one will ever let you down.

ib

15 If you let other people do it *for* you, they will do it *to* you.

ib

ELIZABETH ARDEN

16 Treat a horse like a woman and a woman like a horse. And they'll both win for you.

Quoted by Alfred Allen Lewis *Miss Elizabeth Arden* Coward-McCann 72

NANCY, LADY ASTOR

17 The penalty of success is to be bored by people who used to snub you.

Recalled on her death 2 May 64

MARGARET ATWOOD

18 A divorce is like an amputation; you survive, but there's less of you.

Time 19 Mar 73

DOROTHY AUCHTERLONIE (Dorothy Green)

19 Evil is the stone on which the good sharpens itself.

St Mark's Review Jun 76

W H AUDEN

20 Death is the sound of distant thunder at a picnic.

The Dyer's Hand Random House 68

HAROLD AZINE

21 Happiness in the older years of life, like happiness in every year of life, is a matter of choice—*your* choice for yourself.

The House in Webster Groves NBC TV 16 Feb 58

RICHARD BACH

22 The more I want to get something done, the less I call it work.

Illusions Delacorte 77

FAITH BALDWIN

1 Time is a dressmaker specializing in alterations.
Face toward the Spring Rinehart 56

JAMES BALDWIN

2 I imagine one of the reasons people cling to their hates so stubbornly is because they sense, once hate is gone, they will be forced to deal with pain.
Notes of a Native Son Beacon 55

MONICA BALDWIN

3 I have always felt that the moment when first you wake up in the morning is the most wonderful of the 24 hours. No matter how weary or dreary you may feel, you possess the certainty that ... absolutely anything may happen. And the fact that it practically always *doesn't*, matters not one jot. The possibility is always there.
I Leap over the Wall Holt, Rinehart & Winston 50

GEORGE BALL

4 Nostalgia is a seductive liar.
Newsweek 22 Mar 71

MARGARET CULKIN BANNING

5 Regrets are as personal as fingerprints.
"Living With Regrets" *Reader's Digest* Oct 58

CHRISTIAAN N BARNARD

6 Suffering isn't ennobling, recovery is.
Quoted in NY *Times* 28 Apr 85

BRUCE BARTON

7 Conceit is God's gift to little men.
Coronet Sep 58

CECIL BEATON

8 Perhaps the world's second-worst crime is boredom; the first is being a bore.
Recalled on his death 18 Jan 80

SIMONE DE BEAUVOIR

9 One is not born, but rather becomes, a woman.
The Second Sex Knopf 53

LUCIUS BEEBE

10 All I want is the best of everything and there's very little of that left.
Quoted by Richard Kluger *The Paper: The Life*

and Death of the New York Herald Tribune
Knopf 86

GUY BELLAMY

11 Hindsight is an exact science.
The Sinner's Congregation Secker & Warburg 84

ELEANOR ROBSON BELMONT

12 I was trained by my husband. He said, "If you want a thing done—go. If not—send." I belong to that group of people who move the piano themselves.
NY *Times* 18 Dec 60

BERNARD BERENSON

13 A complete life may be one ending in so full an identification with the nonself that there is no self left to die.
Recalled on his death, *Time* 19 Oct 59

14 Life has taught me that it is not for our faults that we are disliked and even hated but for our qualities.
The Passionate Sightseer Abrams 60

15 Boast is always a cry of despair except in the young, when it is a cry of hope.
Quoted by Umberto Morra *Conversations with Berenson* Houghton Mifflin 65

16 I would willingly stand at street corners, hat in hand, begging passers-by to drop their unused minutes into it.
Quoted on *A Renaissance Life* PBS TV 12 Apr 71

JOHN BERRY

17 The bird of paradise alights only upon the hand that does not grasp.
Flight of White Crows Macmillan 61

STEPHEN BIRMINGHAM

18 What is known as success assumes nearly as many aliases as there are those who seek it.
"Young Men of Manhattan" *Holiday* Mar 61

JIM BISHOP

19 It is difficult to live in the present, ridiculous to live in the future and impossible to live in the past. Nothing is as far away as one minute ago.
NY *Journal-American* 7 May 61

20 Death is as casual—and often as unexpected—as birth. It is as difficult to define grief as joy. Each is finite. Each will fade.
Red Bank NJ *Register* 13 Aug 73

LAWRENCE BIXBY

1 Each handicap is like a hurdle in a steeple-chase, and when you ride up to it, if you throw your heart over, the horse will go along, too.
"Comeback from a Brain Operation" *Harper's* Nov 52

HARRY BLACKSTONE JR

2 Nothing I do can't be done by a 10-year-old . . . with 15 years of practice.
On being a magician, *Newsweek* 16 Oct 78

RONALD BLYTHE

3 He longed to be lost but he couldn't bear not to be found.
On T E Lawrence, *The Age of Illusion* Houghton Mifflin 64

4 The ordinariness of living to be old is too novel a thing to appreciate.
The View in Winter Harcourt Brace Jovanovich 79

GEOFFREY BOCCA

5 Wit is a treacherous dart. It is perhaps the only weapon with which it is possible to stab oneself in one's own back.
The Woman Who Would Be Queen: A Biography of the Duchess of Windsor Rinehart 54

HUMPHREY BOGART

6 The whole world is about three drinks behind.
Recalled on his death 14 Jan 57

SISSELA BOK

7 Liars share with those they deceive the desire not to be deceived.
Lying Random House 78

EDWARD BOND

8 The English sent all their bores abroad, and acquired the Empire as a punishment.
Narrow Road to the Deep North Hill & Wang 68

DANIEL J BOORSTIN, Librarian of Congress

9 Technology is so much fun but we can drown in our technology. The fog of information can drive out knowledge.
On computerization of libraries, NY *Times* 8 Jul 83

10 The greatest obstacle to discovery is not ignorance—it is the illusion of knowledge.
Washington *Post* 29 Jan 84

VICTOR BORGE

11 Humor [is] something that thrives between man's aspirations and his limitations. There is more logic in humor than in anything else. Because, you see, humor is truth.
London *Times* 3 Jan 84

ELIZABETH BOWEN

12 Fate is not an eagle, it creeps like a rat.
Recalled on her death 22 Feb 73

13 There is no end to the violations committed by children on children, quietly talking alone.
The House in Paris Avon 79

KINGMAN BREWSTER

14 There is no greater challenge than to have someone relying upon you; no greater satisfaction than to vindicate his expectation.
Baccalaureate address as president of Yale 12 Jun 66

15 Judgment is more than skill. It sets forth on intellectual seas beyond the shores of hard indisputable factual information.
Address at University of Exeter as US ambassador to Great Britain 26 Oct 78

JOSEPH BRODSKY

16 Life—the way it really is—is a battle not between Bad and Good but between Bad and Worse.
NY *Times* 1 Oct 72

VAN WYCK BROOKS

17 Nothing is so soothing to our self-esteem as to find our bad traits in our forebears. It seems to absolve us.
From a Writer's Notebook Dutton 58

JOHN MASON BROWN

18 A good conversationalist is not one who remembers what was said, but says what someone wants to remember.
Esquire Apr 60

ROSELLEN BROWN

19 When it comes time to do your own life, you either perpetuate your childhood or you stand on it and finally kick it out from under.
Civil Wars Knopf 84

ANATOLE BROYARD

20 When friends stop being frank and useful to each other, the whole world loses some of its radiance.
NY *Times* 1 Sep 85

MARTIN BUBER

1 An animal's eyes have the power to speak a great language.
I and Thou Scribner's 70

GERALD BURRILL, retired Episcopal Bishop of Chicago

2 The difference between a rut and a grave is the depth.
Advance Jul 79

RICHARD E BYRD

3 A static hero is a public liability. Progress grows out of motion.
Recalled on his death 11 Mar 57

JAMES BRANCH CABELL

4 The optimist proclaims that we live in the best of all possible worlds, the pessimist fears this is true.
Quoted on *Who Said That?* BBC TV 19 Sep 58

ALBERT CAMUS

5 There is no fate that cannot be surmounted by scorn.
The Myth of Sisyphus Knopf 55

6 Don't wait for the last judgment—it takes place every day.
The Fall Knopf 57

7 There is but one truly serious philosophical problem and that is suicide.
Recalled on his death 4 Jan 60

8 An intellectual is someone whose mind watches itself.
ib

TRUMAN CAPOTE

9 Failure is the condiment that gives success its flavor.
The Dogs Bark Random House 73

BENNETT CERF

10 For me, a hearty "belly laugh" is one of the beautiful sounds in the world.
Foreword to *An Encyclopedia of Modern American Humor* Doubleday 54

JOHN CHANCELLOR

11 The avenues in my neighborhood are Pride, Covetousness and Lust; the cross streets are Anger, Gluttony, Envy and Sloth. I live over on Sloth, and the style on our street is to avoid the other thoroughfares.
New York 24 Dec 84

LORD CHANDOS (Oliver Lyttelton)

12 Flattery is the infantry of negotiation.
Memoirs New American Library 63

GABRIELLE ("COCO") CHANEL

13 Nature gives you the face you have at 20; it is up to you to merit the face you have at 50.
Ladies' Home Journal Sep 56

14 How many cares one loses when one decides not to be something, but to be someone.
This Week 20 Aug 61

15 Those who create are rare; those who cannot are numerous. Therefore, the latter are stronger.
ib

16 Some people think luxury is the opposite of poverty. It is not. It is the opposite of vulgarity.
Recalled on her death 10 Jan 71

SUSAN CHEEVER

17 Death is terrifying because it is so ordinary. It happens all the time.
On her father's last illness, *Home before Dark* Houghton Mifflin 84

MAURICE CHEVALIER

18 Old age isn't so bad when you consider the alternative.
At age 72, NY *Times* 9 Oct 60

SUSAN CHITTY

19 Never answer a question, other than an offer of marriage, by saying Yes or No.
The Intelligent Woman's Guide to Good Taste MacGibbon & Kee 58

WINSTON CHURCHILL

20 If you have an important point to make, don't try to be subtle or clever. Use a pile driver. Hit the point once. Then come back and hit it again. Then hit it a third time—a tremendous whack.
On public speaking, quoted by Edward, Duke of Windsor, *A King's Story* Putnam 51

21 Working hours are never long enough. Each day is a holiday, and ordinary holidays . . . are grudged as enforced interruptions in an absorbing vocation.
On work and pleasure, quoted by John Mason Brown "The Art of Keeping the Mind Refueled" *Vogue* 1 May 53

1 I am bored with it all.
   Last words, recalled on his death 24 Jan 65

JOHN CIARDI

2 Nothing . . . goes further toward a man's liberation than the act of surviving his need for
character.
   Saturday Review 4 Aug 62

3 Intelligence recognizes what has happened.
Genius recognizes what will happen.
   Quote 30 Oct 66

4 The day will happen whether or not you get
up.
   Reader's Digest May 83

EMILE M CIORAN

5 No one recovers from the disease of being
born, a deadly wound if there ever was one.
   The Fall into Time Quadrangle 70

JAY COCKS

6 Yearning is not only a good way to go crazy
but also a pretty good place to hide out from
hard truth.
   Time 15 Oct 84

JEAN COCTEAU

7 You've never seen death? Look in the mirror
every day and you will see it like bees working
in a glass hive.
   Quoted by Ned Rorem, Dick Cavett show PBS
   TV 6 Oct 81

8 I have lost my seven best friends, which is to
say God has had mercy on me seven times
without realizing it. He lent a friendship, took
it from me, sent me another.
   Vogue May 84

WILLIAM SLOAN COFFIN

9 The world is too dangerous for anything but
truth and too small for anything but love.
   Address at Trinity Institute, San Francisco, 7
   Feb 81

10 The woman most in need of liberation is the
woman in every man and the man in every
woman.
   ib

LESLEY CONGER

11 Every act of dishonesty has at least two victims: the one we think of as the victim, and the
perpetrator as well. Each little dishonesty . . .
makes another little rotten spot somewhere in
the perpetrator's psyche.
   Adventures of an Ordinary Mind Norton 63

CYRIL CONNOLLY

12 Our memories are card indexes—consulted,
and then put back in disorder, by authorities
whom we do not control.
   The Unquiet Grave Harper & Row 72

JULIO CORTÁZAR

13 After the age of 50 we begin to die little by little in the deaths of others.
   A Certain Lucas Knopf 84

NORMAN COUSINS

14 Life is an adventure in forgiveness.
   Saturday Review 15 Apr 78

15 History is a vast early warning system.
   ib

16 Wisdom consists of the anticipation of consequences.
   ib

17 If something comes to life in others because of
you, then you have made an approach to immortality.
   Anatomy of an Illness Norton 79

18 What was most significant about the lunar
voyage was not that men set foot on the moon
but that they set eye on the earth.
   Reader's Digest Sep 80

19 Optimism doesn't wait on facts. It deals with
prospects. Pessimism is a waste of time.
   Human Options Norton 81

20 Cynicism is intellectual treason.
   ib

NOEL COWARD

21 I'll go through life either first class or third, but
never in second.
   NY *Post* 28 Mar 73

DONALD CREIGHTON

22 History is the record of an encounter between
character and circumstances.
   Toward the Discovery of Canada Macmillan 72

ROBERTSON DAVIES

23 Fanaticism is . . . overcompensation for
doubt.
   The Manticore Viking 72

CHARLES DE GAULLE

24 Old age is a shipwreck.
   Quoted by Orson Welles NBC TV 14 Oct 85

MORARJI R DESAI, Prime Minister of India

1 Self-help must precede help from others. Even for making certain of help from heaven, one has to help oneself.

At conference of nonallied nations, NY *Times* 8 Apr 77

JOAN DIDION

2 To cure jealousy is to see it for what it is, a dissatisfaction with self, an impossible claim that one should be at once Rose Bowl princess, medieval scholar, Saint Joan, Milly Theale, Temple Drake, Eleanor of Aquitaine, one's sister and a stranger in a pink hat seen once and admired on the corner of 55th and Madison—as well as oneself, mysteriously improved.

"Jealousy: Is It a Curable Illness?" *Vogue* Jun 61

NIELS DIFFRIENT

3 Today the ringing of the telephone takes precedence over everything. It reaches a point of terrorism, particularly at dinnertime.

NY *Times* 16 Oct 86

ISAK DINESEN

4 God made the world round so we would never be able to see too far down the road.

Recalled on her death 7 Sep 62

MACNEILE DIXON

5 Ideas, like individuals, live and die. They flourish, according to their nature, in one soil or climate and droop in another. They are the vegetation of the mental world.

Quoted by Norman Cousins *Human Options* Norton 81

ANGELO DONGHIA

6 Assumption is the mother of screw-up.

NY *Times* 20 Jan 83

JOHN DOS PASSOS

7 People don't choose their careers; they are engulfed by them.

NY *Times* 25 Oct 59

JOHN FOSTER DULLES

8 A man's accomplishments in life are the cumulative effect of his attention to detail.

Quoted by Leonard Mosley *Dulles* Dial 78

WILL DURANT

9 To speak ill of others is a dishonest way of praising ourselves. . . . Nothing is often a good thing to say, and always a clever thing to say.

NY *World-Telegram & Sun* 6 Jun 58

10 In my youth I stressed freedom, and in my old age I stress order. I have made the great discovery that liberty is a product of order.

Time 13 Aug 65

11 When people ask me to compare the 20th century to older civilizations, I always say the same thing: "The situation is normal."

On winning Pulitzer Prize with his wife Ariel, NY *Times* 7 May 68

12 The ego is willing but the machine cannot go on. It's the last thing a man will admit, that his mind ages.

At age 90, NY *Times* 6 Nov 75

13 The trouble with most people is that they think with their hopes or fears or wishes rather than with their minds.

Recalled on his death 7 Nov 81

UMBERTO ECO

14 The real hero is always a hero by mistake; he dreams of being an honest coward like everybody else.

Travels in Hyper Reality Harcourt Brace Jovanovich 86

ALBERT EINSTEIN

15 If A equals success, then the formula is A equals X plus Y plus Z. X is work. Y is play. Z is keep your mouth shut.

Recalled on his death 18 Apr 55

16 Anger dwells only in the bosom of fools.

ib

17 The tragedy of life is what dies inside a man while he lives.

ib

DWIGHT D EISENHOWER, 34th US President

18 Speeches are for the younger men who are going places. And I'm not going anyplace except six feet under the floor of that little chapel adjoining the museum and library at Abilene.

On eve of his 75th birthday, NY *Times* 11 Oct 65

ALEXANDER ELIOT

19 Life is a fatal adventure. It can only have one end. So why not make it as far-ranging and free as possible?

NY *Post* 28 Nov 62

WILLIAM EMERSON

20 Beware of the man who will not engage in idle conversation; he is planning to steal your walking stick or water your stock.

Newsweek 29 Oct 73

PAUL ENGLE

1 Wisdom is knowing when you can't be wise.
Poems in Praise Random House 59

CLIFTON FADIMAN

2 A sense of humor ... is the ability to understand a joke—and that the joke is oneself.
Santa Barbara *Center Magazine* Jul/Aug 77

WILLIAM FAULKNER

3 A gentleman can live through anything.
The Reivers Random House 62

4 I love Virginians because Virginians are all snobs and I like snobs. A snob has to spend so much time being a snob that he has little time left to meddle with you.
Recalled on his death, Memphis *Commercial Appeal* 7 Jul 62

HERMAN FEIFEL

5 It is a myth to think death is just for the old. Death is there from the very beginning.
NY *Times* 21 Jul 74

CHARLES W FERGUSON

6 The essence of tragedy is to know the end.
Naked to Mine Enemies: The Life of Cardinal Wolsey Little, Brown 58

GEOFFREY FISHER, Archbishop of Canterbury

7 Who knows whether in retirement I shall be tempted to the last infirmity of mundane minds, which is to write a book.
On retiring, *Time* 12 May 61

HARRY EMERSON FOSDICK

8 He who cannot rest, cannot work; he who cannot let go, cannot hold on; he who cannot find footing, cannot go forward.
"Finding Unfailing Resources" in *Riverside Sermons* Harper 58

GENE FOWLER

9 Men are not against you; they are merely for themselves.
Skyline Viking 61

10 Love and memory last and will so endure till the game is called because of darkness.
ib

JOHN FOWLES

11 Duty largely consists of pretending that the trivial is critical.
The Magus Little, Brown 66

ERICH FROMM

12 The danger of the past was that men became slaves. The danger of the future is that men may become robots.
The Sane Society Holt, Rinehart & Winston 55

ROBERT FROST

13 You have freedom when you're easy in your harness.
News summaries 10 May 54

14 A civilized society is one which tolerates eccentricity to the point of doubtful sanity.
Quoted in *New Republic* 25 Oct 58

15 Forgive, O Lord, my little jokes on thee and I'll forgive thy great big one on me.
From *In the Clearing* Holt, Rinehart & Winston 62

16 Thinking isn't agreeing or disagreeing. That's voting.
Quoted in George Plimpton ed *Writers at Work* Viking 63

R BUCKMINSTER FULLER

17 Everyone is born a genius, but the process of living de-geniuses them.
Address at Ripon College, Ripon WI, NY *Post* 20 May 68

WILLIAM GADDIS

18 Stupidity's the deliberate cultivation of ignorance.
Carpenter's Gothic Viking 85, quoted in *Newsweek* 15 Jul 85

JOHN W GARDNER, President, Carnegie Foundation

19 The society which scorns excellence in plumbing because plumbing is a humble activity, and tolerates shoddiness in philosophy because philosophy is an exalted activity, will have neither good plumbing nor good philosophy. Neither its pipes nor its theories will hold water.
Saturday Evening Post 1 Dec 62

20 Self-pity is easily the most destructive of the nonpharmaceutical narcotics; it is addictive, gives momentary pleasure and separates the victim from reality.
The Recovery of Confidence Norton 70

ANDRÉ GIDE

21 Sin is whatever obscures the soul.
Recalled on his death 19 Feb 51

1 The most decisive actions of life . . . are most often unconsidered actions.
   ib

2 Believe those who are seeking the truth; doubt those who find it.
   ib

BERNARD GIMBEL

3 Two things are bad for the heart—running uphill and running down people.
   Reader's Digest Apr 67

GOOD LIFE ALMANAC

4 No man is the whole of himself. His friends are the rest of him.
   Solway Community Press 76

5 When in charge, ponder. When in trouble, delegate. When in doubt, mumble.
   ib

RUTH GORDON

6 Courage is very important. Like a muscle, it is strengthened by use.
   L'Officiel Summer 80

SUZANNE GORDON

7 To be alone is to be different, to be different is to be alone.
   Lonely in America Simon & Schuster 76

WILLIAM GORDON, Episcopal Bishop of Alaska

8 I believe that all of us have the capacity for one adventure inside us, but great adventure is facing responsibility day after day.
   Time 19 Nov 65

BILLY GRAHAM

9 Courage is contagious. When a brave man takes a stand, the spines of others are often stiffened.
   "A Time for Moral Courage" *Reader's Digest* Jul 64

MARTHA GRAHAM

10 You are unique, and if that is not fulfilled, then something has been lost.
   Newsweek 7 Apr 58

CARY GRANT

11 My formula for living is quite simple. I get up in the morning and I go to bed at night. In between, I occupy myself as best I can.
   News summaries 28 Oct 79

ROBERT GRUDIN

12 Happiness may well consist primarily of an attitude toward time.
   Time and the Art of Living Harper & Row 82

ALBERT GUERARD

13 Chivalry is the most delicate form of contempt.
   Bottle in the Sea Harvard 54

DAG HAMMARSKJÖLD

14 Friendship needs no words—it is a loneliness relieved of the anguish of loneliness.
   Markings Knopf 64

15 I believe that we should die with decency so that at least decency will survive.
   ib

16 Do not seek death. Death will find you. But seek the road which makes death a fulfillment.
   ib

OSCAR HAMMERSTEIN II

17 What is a sophisticate? He is a man who thinks he can swim better than he can and sometimes he drowns.
   NY *Mirror* 15 Apr 60

KNUT HAMSUN

18 In old age . . . we are like a batch of letters that someone has sent. We are no longer in the past, we have arrived.
   The Wanderer Farrar, Straus & Giroux 75

GRACE HANSEN

19 Don't be afraid your life will end; be afraid that it will never begin.
   Recalled on her death, Eugene OR *Register-Guard* 14 Jan 85

HAN SUYIN

20 I really can't hate more than 5 or 10 years. Wouldn't it be terrible to be always burdened with those primary emotions you had at one time?
   NY *Times* 25 Jan 85

SYDNEY J HARRIS

21 An idealist believes the short run doesn't count. A cynic believes the long run doesn't matter. A realist believes that what is done or left undone in the short run determines the long run.
   Reader's Digest May 79

BARBARA GRIZZUTI HARRISON

1 Beware of people carrying ideas. Beware of ideas carrying people.
> *Foreign Bodies* Doubleday 84, quoted in *ib* 6 Jun 84

JOSEPH HELLER

2 When I grow up I want to be a little boy.
> *Something Happened* Knopf 74

LILLIAN HELLMAN

3 People change and forget to tell each other.
> *Toys in the Attic* Random House 60

ERNEST HEMINGWAY

4 All things truly wicked start from innocence.
> Quoted by R Z Sheppard in review of Hemingway's posthumously published *The Garden of Eden* Scribner's 86, *Time* 26 May 86

ABRAHAM J HESCHEL

5 Self-respect is the fruit of discipline; the sense of dignity grows with the ability to say no to oneself.
> Quoted in Ruth M Goodhill ed *The Wisdom of Heschel* Farrar, Straus & Giroux 75

GEORGE HIGGINS, Minister, Congregational Church, Briarcliff NY

6 Egotism: The art of seeing in yourself what others cannot see.
> Quoted in *Suburban People News* 2 Mar 86

ERIC HOFFER

7 Craving, not having, is the mother of a reckless giving of oneself.
> *The True Believer* Harper 51

MARJORIE HOLMES

8 The man who treasures his friends is usually solid gold himself.
> *Love and Laughter* Doubleday 67

IRVING HOWE

9 The knowledge that makes us cherish innocence makes innocence unattainable.
> Quoted by Louis Mumford *The City in History* Harcourt, Brace & World 61

ALDOUS HUXLEY

10 Most ignorance is vincible ignorance. We don't know because we don't want to know.
> Recalled on his death 22 Nov 63

POPE JOHN XXIII

11 Every man has the right to life, to bodily integrity.
> *Pacem in Terris* 10 Apr 63

CARL JUNG

12 The greatest and most important problems of life are all fundamentally insoluble. They can never be solved but only outgrown.
> Recalled on his death 6 Jun 61

CONSTANTINE KARAMANLIS, Prime Minister of Greece

13 You do what you have to do in life, when you form a philosophy that you can't talk yourself out of.
> News summaries 14 Nov 56

14 People who decide they came to earth to work, who make work their personal philosophy, are kept very busy.
> *ib*

YOUSUF KARSH

15 If there is a single quality that is shared by all great men, it is vanity.
> *Cosmopolitan* Dec 55

NIKOS KAZANTZAKIS

16 Beauty . . . is merciless. You do not look at it, it looks at you and does not forgive.
> *Report to Greco* Simon & Schuster 65

HELEN KELLER

17 Death . . . is no more than passing from one room into another. But there's a difference for me, you know. Because in that other room I shall be able to see.
> To a five-year-old, recalled on her death 1 Jun 68

JOHN F KENNEDY, 35th US President

18 The courage of life is often a less dramatic spectacle than the courage of a final moment; but it is no less than a magnificent mixture of triumph and tragedy.
> As senator, *Profiles In Courage* Harper & Row 55

19 A man does what he must—in spite of personal consequences, in spite of obstacles and dangers and pressures—and that is the basis of all human morality.
> *ib*

20 The credit belongs to the man who is actually in the arena, whose face is marred by dust and sweat and blood, who knows the great enthusi-

asms, the great devotions, and spends himself in a worthy cause; who at best, if he wins, knows the thrills of high achievement, and, if he fails, at least fails daring greatly, so that his place shall never be with those cold and timid souls who know neither victory nor defeat.

> 1961 comment quoted by William Manchester in frontispiece for *The Last Lion* Little, Brown 83

1 If I had to live my life over again, I would have a different father, a different wife and a different religion.

> To John Sharon, former aide to Adlai Stevenson, quoted by Ralph G Martin *A Hero for Our Time* Macmillan 83

CORITA KENT

2 Love the moment and the energy of that moment will spread beyond all boundaries.

> *Moments of 1984* Beacon 84

3 Damn everything but the circus.

> Quotation used on serigraph, *Newsweek* 17 Dec 84

4 Life is a succession of moments,
To live each one is to succeed.

> *ib*

CHARLES F KETTERING

5 I object to people running down the future. I am going to live all the rest of my life there.

> Quoted by T A Boyd *Professional Amateur* Dutton 57

6 Thinking is one thing no one has ever been able to tax.

> Recalled on his death 25 Nov 58

NIKITA S KHRUSHCHEV, Soviet Premier

7 If you cannot catch a bird of paradise, better take a wet hen.

> Quoted in *Time* 6 Jan 58

MARTIN LUTHER KING JR

8 I want to be the white man's brother, not his brother-in-law.

> NY *Journal-American* 10 Sep 62

9 A nation or civilization that continues to produce soft-minded men purchases its own spiritual death on the installment plan.

> *Strength to Love* Walker 63

10 We are not makers of history. We are made by history.

> *ib*

11 Shallow understanding from people of good will is more frustrating than absolute misunderstanding from people of ill will.

> Letter from a Birmingham jail 16 Jan 63

12 I have a dream that one day on the red hills of Georgia, the sons of former slaves and the sons of former slave owners will be able to sit together at the table of brotherhood.

> Address at Lincoln Memorial during March on Washington 28 Aug 63

13 I have a dream that my four little children will one day live in a nation where they will not be judged by the color of their skin, but by the content of their character.

> *ib*

14 I have a dream that one day every valley shall be exalted, every hill and mountain shall be made low, the rough places will be made straight and the glory of the Lord shall be revealed and all flesh shall see it together.

> *ib*

15 From the prodigious hilltops of New Hampshire, let freedom ring. From the mighty mountains of New York, let freedom ring. From the heightening Alleghenies of Pennsylvania, let freedom ring. But not only that: Let freedom ring from every hill and molehill of Mississippi.

> *ib*

16 When this happens, when we let it ring, we will speed the day when all of God's children, black men and white men, Jews and Gentiles, Protestants and Catholics, will be able to join hands and sing in the words of the old Negro spiritual: "Free at last, free at last, thank God Almighty, we're free at last."

> *ib*

17 A riot is the language of the unheard.

> On blacks in America, address at Birmingham AL, news summaries 31 Dec 63

18 Nonviolence is a powerful and just weapon. . . . which cuts without wounding and ennobles the man who wields it. It is a sword that heals.

> *Why We Can't Wait* Harper & Row 64

19 I just want to do God's will. And he's allowed me to go to the mountain. And I've looked over, and I've seen the promised land! I may not get there with you, but I want you to know tonight that we as a people will get to the promised land.

> Address in Memphis the night before his assassination, 3 Apr 68

1 So I'm happy tonight. I'm not worried about anything. I'm not fearing any man. Mine eyes have seen the glory of the coming of the Lord!
ib

LOUIS KRONENBERGER

2 The trouble with our age is all signposts and no destination.
Look 17 May 54

3 Highly educated bores are by far the worst; they know so much, in such fiendish detail, to be boring about.
Forbes 1 May 64

WAUHILLAU LA HAY

4 Find a nice man, marry him, have babies and shut up.
Advice to career women, *Advertising Age* 26 Oct 59

STANISLAW LEM

5 To torture a man you have to know his pleasures.
Holiday Sep 63

6 Cannibals prefer those who have no spines.
ib

7 Do not trust people. They *are* capable of greatness.
ib

MADELEINE L'ENGLE

8 The great thing about getting older is that you don't lose all the other ages you've been.
Quoted in NY *Times* 25 Apr 85

OSCAR LEVANT

9 Happiness isn't something you experience; it's something you remember.
Recalled on his death, *Time* 28 Aug 72

C S LEWIS

10 Courage is not simply one of the virtues, but the form of every virtue at the testing point.
Recalled on his death 22 Nov 63

11 An explanation of cause is not a justification by reason.
ib

12 The long, dull, monotonous years of middle-aged prosperity or middle-aged adversity are excellent campaigning weather for the devil.
ib

13 The future is something which everyone reaches at the rate of 60 minutes an hour, whatever he does, whoever he be.
ib

14 It's so much easier to pray for a bore than to go and see one.
Letters to Malcolm Harcourt, Brace & World 64

ANNE MORROW LINDBERGH

15 The punctuation of anniversaries is terrible, like the closing of doors, one after another between you and what you want to hold on to.
Diary entry on the first anniversary of her son's kidnapping and death, *Locked Rooms and Open Doors* Harcourt Brace Jovanovich 74

WALTER LIPPMANN

16 Industry is a better horse to ride than genius.
Quoted in Cleveland Amory and Earl Blackwell eds *Celebrity Register* Harper & Row 63

17 Men who are orthodox when they are young are in danger of being middle-aged all their lives.
ib

CLARE BOOTHE LUCE

18 Courage is the ladder on which all the other virtues mount.
Reader's Digest May 79

RUSSELL LYNES

19 The only gracious way to accept an insult is to ignore it; if you can't ignore it, top it; if you can't top it, laugh at it; if you can't laugh at it, it's probably deserved.
Reader's Digest Dec 61

JOHN D MACDONALD

20 Friendships, like marriages, are dependent on avoiding the unforgivable.
The Last One Left Doubleday 67

ROBERT D MACDONALD

21 One German makes a philosopher, two a public meeting, three a war.
From his play *Summit Conference*, quoted in *International Herald Tribune* 13 May 82

ARCHIBALD MACLEISH

22 The dissenter is every human being at those moments of his life when he resigns momentarily from the herd and thinks for himself.
"In Praise of Dissent" NY *Times* 16 Dec 56

HAROLD MACMILLAN

1 Tradition does not mean that the living are dead, it means that the dead are living.
Manchester *Guardian* 18 Dec 58

2 A man who trusts nobody is apt to be the kind of man nobody trusts.
NY *Herald Tribune* 17 Dec 63

3 When the curtain falls, the best thing an actor can do is to go away.
On withdrawing from Parliament in 1964, recalled on his death, *Time* 12 Jan 87

BERNARD MALAMUD

4 Life is a tragedy full of joy.
NY *Times* 29 Jan 79

5 If you ever forget you're a Jew, a Gentile will remind you.
Quoted by Joseph Heller *Good as Gold* Pocket Books 80

MARYA MANNES

6 For every five well-adjusted and smoothly functioning Americans, there are two who never had the chance to discover themselves. It may well be because they have never been alone with themselves.
"To Save the Life of 'I'" *Vogue* 1 Oct 64

PRINCESS MARGRETHE OF DENMARK

7 I have always had a dread of becoming a passenger in life.
On necessity of independent achievement, *Life* 12 Jan 68

FÉLIX MARTÍ-IBÁÑEZ

8 Even as a coin attains its full value when it is spent, so life attains its supreme value when one knows how to forfeit it with grace when the time comes.
"A Doctor Looks at Death" *MD* Sep 63

ANDRÉ MAUROIS

9 We owe to the Middle Ages the two worst inventions of humanity—romantic love and gunpowder.
Quoted on *Who Said That?* BBC TV 21 Jan 58

10 Growing old is no more than a bad habit which a busy man has no time to form.
Quoted by Milton Barron *The Aging American* Crowell 61

ELSA MAXWELL

11 Under pressure, people admit to murder, setting fire to the village church or robbing a bank, but never to being bores.
How to Do It Little, Brown 57

12 I make enemies deliberately. They are the sauce piquante to my dish of life.
NY *Journal-American* 2 Nov 63

DAVID C McCULLOUGH

13 A nation that forgets its past can function no better than an individual with amnesia.
LA *Times* 23 Apr 78

14 History is a guide to navigation in perilous times. History is who we are and why we are the way we are.
Address at Wesleyan University 3 Jun 84

PHYLLIS McGINLEY

15 Gossip isn't scandal and it's not merely malicious. It's chatter about the human race by lovers of the same.
"A New Year and No Resolutions" *Woman's Home Companion* Jan 57

MIGNON McLAUGHLIN

16 What you have become is the price you paid to get what you used to want.
The Neurotic's Notebook Bobbs-Merrill 63

17 For the happiest life, days should be rigorously planned, nights left open to chance.
Atlantic Jul 65

MARSHALL McLUHAN

18 The new electronic independence re-creates the world in the image of a global village.
The Gutenberg Galaxy: The Making of Typographical Man University of Toronto 62

19 Publication is a self-invasion of privacy.
Counterblast Harcourt, Brace & World 69

20 The winner is one who knows when to drop out in order to get in touch.
Quoted by Peter Newman "The Table Talk of Marshall McLuhan" *Maclean's* Jun 71

FRANK MEDLICOTT

21 Some people mistake weakness for tact. If they are silent when they ought to speak and so feign an agreement they do not feel, they call it being tactful. Cowardice would be a much better name.
Reader's Digest Jul 58

ELISSA MELAMED

22 Men look *at* themselves in mirrors. Women look *for* themselves.
Mirror, Mirror: The Terror of Not Being Young Linden Press 83

GIAN CARLO MENOTTI

1 A man only becomes wise when he begins to calculate the approximate depth of his ignorance.
NY *Times* 14 Apr 74

THOMAS MERTON

2 A daydream is an evasion.
Conjectures of a Guilty Bystander Doubleday 66

3 The biggest human temptation is . . . to settle for too little.
Forbes 4 Aug 80

JAMES A MICHENER

4 Character consists of what you do on the third and fourth tries.
Chesapeake Random House 78

ARTHUR MILLER

5 Where choice begins, Paradise ends, innocence ends, for what is Paradise but the absence of any need to choose this action?
Foreword to 1964 play *After the Fall*, quoted in *Saturday Evening Post* 1 Feb 64

6 You specialize in something until one day you find it is specializing in you.
From his 1967 play *The Price*

LLEWELLYN MILLER

7 It's a sad truth that everyone is a bore to someone.
The Encyclopedia of Etiquette Crown 68

PHILLIP MOFFITT

8 A house is a home when it shelters the body and comforts the soul.
"Everyman's Xanadu" *ib* Apr 86

ASHLEY MONTAGU

9 Human beings are the only creatures who are able to behave irrationally in the name of reason.
NY *Times* 30 Sep 75

MICHAEL MOONEY

10 When a civilization takes up the study of itself, it is always high noon.
"The Ministry of Culture" *Harper's* Aug 80

BRIAN MOORE

11 If misery loves company, then triumph demands an audience.
An Answer from Limbo Atlantic-Little, Brown 62

MARIANNE MOORE

12 The passion for setting people right is in itself an afflictive disease.
Recalled on her death 5 Feb 72

LORD MORAN (Charles McMoran Wilson)

13 Courage is a moral quality; it is not a chance gift of nature like an aptitude for games. It is a cold choice between two alternatives, the fixed resolve not to quit; an act of renunciation which must be made not once but many times by the power of the will.
The Anatomy of Courage Houghton Mifflin 67

ALBERTO MORAVIA

14 In life there are no problems, that is, objective and external choices; there is only the life which we do not resolve as a problem but which we live as an experience, whatever the final result may be.
The Time of Desecration Farrar, Straus & Giroux 80

NEIL MORGAN

15 California is where you can't run any farther without getting wet.
"California: The Nation within a Nation" *Saturday Review* 23 Sep 67

CHRISTOPHER MORLEY

16 There is only one success—to be able to spend your life in your own way.
Recalled on his death 28 Mar 57

17 There are three ingredients in the good life: learning, earning and yearning.
ib

18 When you sell a man a book you don't sell him just 12 ounces of paper and ink and glue—you sell him a whole new life.
From his 1955 book *Parnassus on Wheels, ib*

MALCOLM MUGGERIDGE

19 Bad humor is an evasion of reality; good humor is an acceptance of it.
BBC Publications 68

LEWIS MUMFORD

20 I would die happy if I knew that on my tombstone could be written these words, "This man was an absolute fool. None of the disastrous things that he reluctantly predicted ever came to pass!"
To National Book Awards Committee, *My Works and Days* Harcourt Brace Jovanovich 79

EDWARD R MURROW

1 People say conversation is a lost art; how often I have wished it were.

Quoted by George F Will *The Pursuit of Virtue and Other Tory Notions* Simon & Schuster 82

MIKE NICHOLS

2 Being with an insanely jealous person is like being in the room with a dead mammoth.
NY *Times* 27 May 84

MARTIN NIEMÖLLER

3 First they came for the Jews. I was silent. I was not a Jew. Then they came for the Communists. I was silent. I was not a Communist. Then they came for the trade unionists. I was silent. I was not a trade unionist. Then they came for me. There was no one left to speak for me.

On resistance to Nazis, recalled on his death 6 Mar 84

RICHARD M NIXON, 37th US President

4 A man is not finished when he is defeated. He is finished when he quits.
Dallas *Times-Herald* 10 Dec 78

LAURENCE OLIVIER

5 I take a simple view of living. It is keep your eyes open and get on with it.
LA *Times* 26 Feb 78

WILLIAM O'ROURKE

6 Regret is an odd emotion because it comes only upon reflection. Regret lacks immediacy, and so its power seldom influences events when it could do some good.
Idle Hands Delacorte 81

JOSÉ ORTEGA Y GASSET

7 I am I plus my circumstances.
Time 31 Oct 55

BOB PACKWOOD, US Senator

8 Judgment comes from experience and great judgment comes from bad experience.
NY *Times* 30 May 86

MARCEL PAGNOL

9 The most difficult secret for a man to keep is his own opinion of himself.
News summaries 15 Mar 54

DOROTHY PARKER

10 As only New Yorkers know, if you can get through the twilight, you'll live through the night.
Esquire Nov 64

KENNETH PATCHEN

11 Now is then's only tomorrow.
Hallelujah Anyway New Directions 66

ALAN PATON

12 There is only one way in which one can endure man's inhumanity to man and that is to try, in one's own life, to exemplify man's humanity to man.
"The Challenge of Fear" *Saturday Review* 9 Sep 67

NORMAN VINCENT PEALE

13 Getting people to like you is merely the other side of liking them.
The Power of Positive Thinking Prentice-Hall 52

WALTER PERSEGATI

14 Is life worth living? It is, so you take the risk of getting up in the morning and going through the day's work.
NY *Times* 9 Jul 84

WILLIAM PHILLIPS

15 Boredom, after all, is a form of criticism.
A Sense of the Present Chilmark 67

BELVA PLAIN

16 All [life] is pattern . . . but we can't always see the pattern when we're part of it.
Crescent City Delacorte 84

KATHERINE ANNE PORTER

17 I'm not afraid of life and I'm not afraid of death: Dying's the bore.
At age 80, NY *Times* 3 Apr 70

18 You learn something the day you die. You learn how to die.
Recalled on her death 18 Sep 80

PETER S PRESCOTT

19 Sociologists [are] academic accountants who think that truth can be shaken from an abacus.
Newsweek 14 Apr 72

J B PRIESTLEY

20 One of the delights known to age, and beyond the grasp of youth, is that of Not Going.
Delight Heinemann 66

V S Pritchett

1 The mark of genius is an incessant activity of mind. Genius is a spiritual greed.
The Tale Bearers Random House 80

2 The secret of happiness is to find a congenial monotony.
Collected Stories Random House 82, quoted in NY *Times* 24 Apr 82

Roger Allan Raby

3 A bad attitude is the worst thing that can happen to a group of people. It's infectious.
Wall Street Journal 12 Apr 84

Ayn Rand

4 Ever since Kant divorced reason from reality, his intellectual descendants have been diligently widening the breach.
"The Cashing-In: The Student Rebellion" in *The New Left* New American Library 71

Ronald Reagan, 40th US President

5 Heroes may not be braver than anyone else. They're just braver five minutes longer.
Awarding Young American Medal for Bravery 22 Dec 82

Nelson A Rockefeller

6 There are three periods in life: youth, middle age and "how well you look."
NY *Times* 16 Dec 76

Leonard Rubinstein

7 Curiosity is a willing, a proud, an eager confession of ignorance.
"Writing: A Habit of Mind" *Reader's Digest* Oct 84

Bertrand Russell

8 Work is of two kinds: first, altering the position of matter at or near the earth's surface relatively to other such matters; second, telling other people to do so.
Recalled on his death 2 Feb 70

9 Boredom is a vital problem for the moralist, since at least half the sins of mankind are caused by the fear of it.
Life 13 Feb 70

William Safire

10 When duty calls, that is when character counts.
On the abdication of King Edward VIII, "'Lov'd I Not Honor More'" NY *Times* 23 May 86

George Santayana

11 Friendship is almost always the union of a part of one mind with a part of another: People are friends in spots.
Recalled on his death 26 Sep 52

12 There are books in which the footnotes or comments scrawled by some reader's hand in the margin are more interesting than the text. The world is one of these books.
ib

William Saroyan

13 The greatest happiness you can have is knowing that you do not necessarily require happiness.
News summaries 16 Dec 57

14 Good people are good because they've come to wisdom through failure. We get very little wisdom from success, you know.
NY *Journal-American* 23 Aug 61

15 Everybody has got to die, but I always believed an exception would be made in my case. Now what?
May 13, 1981, phone call to Associated Press reporter, quoted by Samuel G Freedman "Saroyan and His Plays Are Recalled at Tribute" NY *Times* 31 Oct 83

Jean Paul Sartre

16 Hell is other people.
From his 1947 play *No Exit*, recalled on his death 15 Apr 80

Thomas Savage

17 Cosmic upheaval is not so moving as a little child pondering the death of a sparrow in the corner of a barn.
Her Side of It Little, Brown 81

Richard Schickel

18 The law of unintended consequences pushes us ceaselessly through the years, permitting no pause for perspective.
Time 28 Nov 83

Jonathan Schwartz

19 Most of us are only tuned in to distant stations where all kinds of things are happening to other people. We listen through the static to their heartbreaks as if we were in some well-protected receiving chamber.
Distant Stations Doubleday 79

ALBERT SCHWEITZER

1 An optimist is a person who sees a green light everywhere, while the pessimist sees only the red stoplight. . . . The truly wise person is colorblind.

    News summaries 14 Jan 55

2 Reverence for life is the highest court of appeal.

    Recalled on his death 4 Sep 65

3 The tragedy of life is what dies inside a man while he lives.

    ib

RICHARD SENNETT

4 Authority . . . is itself inherently an act of imagination.

    Authority Random House 80, quoted in *Newsweek* 5 May 80

ERIC SEVAREID

5 The chief cause of problems is solutions.

    Reader's Digest Mar 74

GEORGE BERNARD SHAW

6 A perpetual holiday is a good working definition of hell.

    Quoted by Charles Krauthammer "Holiday: Living on a Return Ticket" *Time* 27 Aug 84

FULTON J SHEEN, former Bishop of Rochester NY

7 Jealousy is the tribute mediocrity pays to genius.

    Quoted by Daniel P Noonan *The Passion of Fulton Sheen* Dodd, Mead 72

ALISTAIR SIM

8 It was revealed to me many years ago with conclusive certainty that I was a fool and that I had always been a fool. Since then I have been as happy as any man has a right to be.

    Time 30 Aug 76

GEORGES SIMENON

9 I adore life but I don't fear death. I just prefer to die as late as possible.

    International Herald Tribune 26 Nov 81

ISAAC BASHEVIS SINGER

10 The analysis of character is the highest human entertainment.

    NY *Times* 26 Nov 78

11 When you betray somebody else, you also betray yourself.

    ib

12 Our knowledge is a little island in a great ocean of nonknowledge.

    ib 3 Dec 78

EDITH SITWELL

13 The aim of flattery is to soothe and encourage us by assuring us of the truth of an opinion we have already formed about ourselves.

    Quoted by Elizabeth Salter *The Last Years of a Rebel* Houghton Mifflin 67

B F SKINNER

14 I did not direct my life. I didn't design it. I never made decisions. Things always came up and made them for me. That's what life is.

    Particulars of My Life Knopf 76

C R SMITH

15 A problem is something you have hopes of changing. Anything else is a fact of life.

    Publishers Weekly 8 Sep 69

SUSAN SONTAG

16 He who despises himself esteems himself as a self-despiser.

    Death Kit Farrar, Straus & Giroux 67

MURIEL SPARK

17 It is impossible to persuade a man who does not disagree, but smiles.

    The Prime of Miss Jean Brodie Lippincott 62

FRANCIS CARDINAL SPELLMAN

18 When you do say Yes, say it quickly. But always take a half hour to say No, so you can understand the other fellow's side.

    Advice to Terence Cooke, recalled on Cooke's death 6 Oct 83

DANIELLE STEEL

19 If you see the magic in a fairy tale, you can face the future.

    Family Album Delacorte 85, quoted in *Christian Science Monitor* 21 Mar 85

WALLACE STEGNER

20 Most things break, including hearts. The lessons of life amount not to wisdom, but to scar tissue and callus.

    The Spectator Bird Doubleday 76

HARRY STEIN

21 Envy is as persistent as memory, as intractable as a head cold.

    "Thy Neighbor's Life" *Esquire* Jul 80

JOHN STEINBECK

1 It is a common experience that a problem difficult at night is resolved in the morning after the committee of sleep has worked on it.
Recalled on his death 20 Dec 68

WALLACE STEVENS

2 The most beautiful thing in the world is, of course, the world itself.
Quoted in Frank Doggett and Robert Buttel eds *Wallace Stevens* Princeton 80

ADLAI E STEVENSON

3 You will find that the truth is often unpopular and the contest between agreeable fancy and disagreeable fact is unequal. For, in the vernacular, we Americans are suckers for good news.
Commencement address at Michigan State, NY *Times* 9 Jun 58

4 Freedom is not an ideal, it is not even a protection, if it means nothing more than the freedom to stagnate.
Putting First Things First Random House 60

5 We have confused the free with the free and easy.
ib

HENRY L STIMSON

6 The only way to make a man trustworthy is to trust him.
Recalled on his death 20 Oct 50

TOM STOPPARD

7 Life is a gamble, at terrible odds—if it was a bet you wouldn't take it.
Rosencrantz and Guildenstern Are Dead Grove 67

8 Age is a very high price to pay for maturity.
ib

9 The bad end unhappily, the good unluckily. That is what tragedy means.
ib

THOMAS SZASZ

10 People often say that this or that person has not yet found himself. But the self is not something that one finds. It is something that one creates.
The Second Sin Doubleday 73

BARRY TARGAN

11 Adventure is hardship aesthetically considered.
Kingdoms State University of New York 81

EDWARD TELLER

12 Life improves slowly and goes wrong fast, and only catastrophe is clearly visible.
The Pursuit of Simplicity Pepperdine University 80

MARGARET THATCHER

13 Why do you climb philosophical hills? Because they are worth climbing . . . There are no hills to go down unless you start from the top.
Recalling childhood maxims, *New Yorker* 10 Feb 86

DYLAN THOMAS

14 Do not go gentle into that good night.
Title and first line of 1952 poem

RODERICK THORP

15 We have to learn to be our own best friends because we fall too easily into the trap of being our worst enemies.
Rainbow Drive Summit 86, quoted in NY *Times* 4 Nov 86

JAMES THURBER

16 Last night I dreamed of a small consolation enjoyed only by the blind: Nobody knows the trouble I've *not* seen!
On his failing eyesight, *Newsweek* 16 Jun 58

17 Humor is emotional chaos remembered in tranquillity.
NY *Post* 29 Feb 60

PAUL TILLICH

18 Decision is a risk rooted in the courage of being free.
Systematic Theology Vol I University of Chicago 51

19 Astonishment is the root of philosophy.
Life 5 Nov 65

MIKE TODD

20 I've never been poor, only broke. Being poor is a frame of mind. Being broke is only a temporary situation.
Newsweek 31 Mar 58

ALVIN TOFFLER

21 Future shock [is] the shattering stress and disorientation that we induce in individuals by subjecting them to too much change in too short a time.
Future Shock Random House 70

J R R Tolkien

1 All that is gold does not glitter; not all those that wander are lost.
The Fellowship of the Ring Houghton Mifflin 54

Paul Tournier

2 Acceptance of one's life has nothing to do with resignation; it does not mean running away from the struggle. On the contrary, it means accepting it as it comes, with all the handicaps of heredity, of suffering, of psychological complexes and injustices.
The Meaning of Persons Harper 57

Arnold Toynbee

3 Civilization is a movement and not a condition, a voyage and not a harbor.
Reader's Digest Oct 58

4 I do not believe that civilizations have to die because civilization is not an organism. It is a product of wills.
Recalled on his death, *Time* 3 Nov 75

5 History is a vision of God's creation on the move.
ib

Claire Trevor

6 What a holler would ensue if people had to pay the minister as much to marry them as they have to pay a lawyer to get them a divorce.
NY *Journal-American* 12 Oct 60

Desmond Tutu

7 A person is a person because he recognizes others as persons.
Address at enthronement as Anglican archbishop of Cape Town 7 Sep 86

John Updike

8 A healthy male adult bore consumes each year one and a half times his own weight in other people's patience.
Assorted Prose Knopf 65

Gore Vidal

9 Every time a friend succeeds, I die a little.
Quoted in Nat Shapiro ed *Whatever It Is, I'm Against It* Simon & Schuster 84

Andy Warhol

10 In the future everyone will be famous for 15 minutes.
Prediction in the 1960s, quoted in Washington *Post* 15 Nov 79

11 I'm bored with that line. I never use it anymore. My new line is "In 15 minutes everybody will be famous."
ib

12 I never think that people die. They just go to department stores.
Manchester *Guardian* 3 Aug 86

13 I always wished I had died, and I still wish that, because I could have gotten the whole thing over with.
On being gravely wounded in 1968, recalled on his death, *Newsweek* 9 Mar 87

14 The most exciting thing is not doing it. If you fall in love with someone and never do it, it's much more exciting.
ib

Alan Watts

15 Trying to define yourself is like trying to bite your own teeth.
Life 21 Apr 61

Evelyn Waugh

16 Punctuality is the virtue of the bored.
Quoted in Michael Davie ed *The Diaries of Evelyn Waugh* Little, Brown 76

17 We cherish our friends not for their ability to amuse us, but for ours to amuse them.
Forbes 12 May 80

18 What is youth except a man or woman before it is ready or fit to be seen?
Quoted in Donat Gallagher ed *A Little Order: A Selection from His Journalism* Little, Brown 81

Lee Weiner

19 We are all refugees of a future that never happened.
On failure to achieve goals of the 1960s, *People* 12 Sep 77

Rebecca West

20 If the whole human race lay in one grave, the epitaph on its headstone might well be: "It seemed a good idea at the time."
NY *Times* 2 Oct 77

John Hall Wheelock

21 It's almost two societies, the living and the dead, and you live with them both.
To National Institute of Arts and Letters, NY *Times* 9 Apr 76

ELIE WIESEL

1 Not to transmit an experience is to betray it.
Christian Science Monitor 18 Sep 79

2 I do not recall a Jewish home without a book on the table.
"Echoes of Yesterday" in advertisement marking centennial of Yeshiva University, *ib* 28 Sep 86

3 In Jewish history there are no coincidences.
Quoted by Joseph Berger "Witness to Evil" *ib* 15 Oct 86

4 I decided to devote my life to telling the story because I felt that having survived I owe something to the dead. . . . and anyone who does not remember betrays them again.
On writing about the Holocaust, *ib*

5 Indifference, to me, is the epitome of evil.
US News & World Report 27 Oct 86

6 The opposite of love is not hate, it's indifference. The opposite of art is not ugliness, it's indifference. The opposite of faith is not heresy, it's indifference. And the opposite of life is not death, it's indifference.
ib

7 Because of indifference, one dies before one actually dies.
ib

8 No one is as capable of gratitude as one who has emerged from the kingdom of night.
Accepting Nobel Peace Prize 10 Dec 86

9 Because I remember, I despair. Because I remember, I have the duty to reject despair.
Nobel lecture, Oslo, 11 Dec 86

10 Mankind must remember that peace is not God's gift to his creatures; peace is our gift to each other.
ib

GEORGE F WILL

11 There may be more poetry than justice in poetic justice.
The Pursuit of Virtue and Other Tory Notions Simon & Schuster 82

TENNESSEE WILLIAMS

12 Time rushes toward us with its hospital tray of infinitely varied narcotics, even while it is preparing us for its inevitably fatal operation.
The Rose Tattoo New Directions 51

13 All cruel people describe themselves as paragons of frankness.
The Milk Train Doesn't Stop Here Anymore New Directions 64

TOM WOLFE

14 The idea was to prove at every foot of the way up . . . that you were one of the elected and anointed ones who had *the right stuff* and could move higher and higher and even— ultimately, God willing, one day—that you might be able to join that special few at the very top, that elite who had the capacity to bring tears to men's eyes, the very Brotherhood of the Right Stuff itself.
The Right Stuff Farrar, Straus & Giroux 79

LOUIS B WRIGHT

15 More common sense can be induced by observation of the diversity of human beings in a small town than can be learned in academia.
Barefoot in Arcadia University of South Carolina 74

MAX WYLIE

16 Heartbreak is gratuitous wreckage. It is futility.
Response to murder of his daughter, *Ladies' Home Journal* Mar 64

Communications & the Arts

ARCHITECTURE

Architects on Architecture

EMILIO AMBASZ

1 The large executive chair elevates the sitter.
. . . and it is covered with the skin of some animal, preferably your predecessor.
  Smithsonian Apr 86

GAE AULENTI

2 Light *is* impressionism.
  On positioning galleries for impressionist and postimpressionist paintings at the top of her design for Paris's Musée d'Orsay, *Time* 8 Dec 86

LUIS BARRAGÁN

3 Any work of architecture that does not express serenity is a mistake.
  Time 12 May 80

4 Art is made by the alone for the alone.
  ib

R BUCKMINSTER FULLER

5 My ideas have undergone a process of emergence by emergency. When they are needed badly enough, they are accepted.
  On geodesic domes, *Time* 10 Jun 64

6 I just invent, then wait until man comes around to needing what I've invented.
  ib

7 I look for what needs to be done. . . . After all, that's how the universe designs itself.
  Christian Science Monitor 3 Nov 64

8 Tension is the great integrity.
  On his belief that "tensegrity" gives coherence to the structure of the universe, *ib*

9 When I am working on a problem, I never think about beauty . . . but when I have finished, if the solution is not beautiful, I know it is wrong.
  Reply to student at MIT about aesthetics in engineering and architecture, quoted by Clifton Fadiman comp *The Little, Brown Book of Anecdotes* Little, Brown 85

WALTER GROPIUS

10 Architecture begins where engineering ends.
  To Harvard Department of Architecture, quoted in Paul Heyer ed *Architects on Architecture* Walker 78

HUGH NEWELL JACOBSEN

11 When you look at a city, it's like reading the hopes, aspirations and pride of everyone who built it.
  NY *Times* 31 May 84

12 It is our art that has an opportunity to leave a footprint in the sand. They don't wrap fish in our work.
  ib

PHILIP JOHNSON

13 The best thing to do with water is to use a lot of it.
  On designing fountains, *New Yorker* 9 Jul 66

14 All architecture is shelter, all great architecture is the design of space that contains, cuddles, exalts, or stimulates the persons in that space.
  1975 address at Columbia University, quoted in *Philip Johnson: Writings* Oxford 79

15 I'm about four skyscrapers behind.
  On excusing himself from a dinner party, *Wall Street Journal* 20 Jun 84

LOUIS KAHN

16 A great building . . . must begin with the unmeasurable, must go through measurable means when it is being designed and in the end must be unmeasurable.
  On architecture for academia, *Fortune* May 63

17 Consider . . . the momentous event in architecture when the wall parted and the column became.
  Quoted by John Lobell *Between Silence and Light* Shambhala 79

LE CORBUSIER

18 I prefer drawing to talking. Drawing is faster, and leaves less room for lies.
  Time 5 May 61

1 A hundred times have I thought New York is a catastrophe and 50 times: It is a beautiful catastrophe.
NY *Herald Tribune* 6 Aug 61

2 Space and light and order. Those are the things that men need just as much as they need bread or a place to sleep.
On need for spaciously separated skyscrapers, recalled on his death 27 Aug 65

3 Architecture is the learned game, correct and magnificent, of forms assembled in the light.
ib

Ludwig Mies van der Rohe

4 A chair is a very difficult object. A skyscraper is almost easier. That is why Chippendale is famous.
Time 18 Feb 57

5 Less is more.
On restraint in design, NY *Herald Tribune* 28 Jun 59

6 Architecture starts when you carefully put two bricks together. There it begins.
ib

7 Architecture is the will of an epoch translated into space.
ib

Miyoko Ohno

8 Balance is beautiful.
On designing bridges, *Christian Science Monitor* 22 May 86

John Portman

9 Thank God this isn't a play. Critics can kill a play. But not a hotel.
On opening of Manhattan's Marriott Marquis Hotel, NY *Times* 12 Oct 85

10 It's like saying trousers with two legs is a design cliché.
On criticism of his use of cavernous atriums, *ib*

Eero Saarinen

11 To me, the drawn language is a very revealing language; one can see in a few lines whether a man is really an architect.
NY *Times* 5 Jun 77

Eliel Saarinen

12 Always design a thing by considering it in its next larger context—a chair in a room, a room in a house, a house in an environment, an environment in a city plan.
Quoted by his son Eero, *Time* 2 Jun 77

Robert A M Stern

13 The dialogue between client and architect is about as intimate as any conversation you can have, because when you're talking about building a house, you're talking about dreams.
NY *Times* 13 Jan 85

14 Our greatest responsibility is not to be pencils of the past.
ib

Robert Venturi

15 Less is a bore.
1969 reaction to Mies van der Rohe's statement "Less is more," recalled on 100th anniversary of Mies's birth, *Time* 3 Mar 86

Harold E Wagoner

16 The great thing about being an architect is you can walk into your dreams.
Quoted by Episcopal priest Edward Chinn in tribute to Wagoner's restoration of All Saints' Church in Philadelphia, *Episcopalian* Oct 86

Frank Lloyd Wright

17 I doubt if there is anything in the world uglier than a Midwestern city.
Address at Evanston IL, news summaries 8 Aug 54

18 Clear out 800,000 people and preserve it as a museum piece.
On Boston, NY *Times* 27 Nov 55

19 New York: Prison towers and modern posters for soap and whiskey. Pittsburgh: Abandon it.
ib

20 If you're going to have centralization, why not have it!
Announcing plans for 510-story Chicago office building, news summaries 10 Sep 56

21 Early in life I had to choose between honest arrogance and hypocritical humility. I chose honest arrogance and have seen no occasion to change.
Recalled on his death 8 Apr 59

22 Architecture is life, or at least it is life itself taking form and therefore it is the truest record of life as it was lived in the world yesterday, as it is lived today or ever will be lived.
An Organic Architecture MIT 70

Observers & Critics

Russell Baker

23 The lobbies of the new hotels and the Pan

American Building exhale a chill as from the unopened Pharaonic tombs. . . . And in their marble labyrinths there is an evil presence that hates warmth and sunlight.

NY *Times* 19 May 64

ALAN BIRD, English master builder

1 Most buildings now are glorified wallpaper.

Comparing modern structures with his stonework for the Cathedral Church of St John the Divine, NY *Times* 19 Mar 86

PETER BLAKE

2 This book is not written in anger. It is written in fury.

On his study of deteriorating towns and landscapes, *God's Own Junkyard* Holt, Rinehart & Winston 63

3 There isn't much wrong with most of those summerhouses that a really good hurricane wouldn't cure [and] when it comes it may do for the Hamptons what Mrs O'Leary's cow did for Chicago.

"Summerhouses: Eyefuls and Eyesores" *New York* 24 Aug 70

DANIEL J BOORSTIN, Librarian of Congress

4 When they built this building they were afraid to say that beauty is truth for fear that it wouldn't be by the time it was completed.

On the library's 1980 Madison Building with its glass walls and unornamented linear spaces, NY *Times* 8 Jul 83

DAVID BRINKLEY

5 The House Office Building is costing more than the combined cost of the Great Pyramids at Giza, the Colossus of Rhodes and the Hanging Gardens of Babylon. Three of the Seven Wonders of the World combined cost less money than an office building for 200 congressmen.

NY *Herald Tribune* 16 Apr 64

BRITISH TRAVEL ASSOCIATION

6 A cathedral transcends the noblest single work of art. It is a pinnacle of faith and act of centuries. It is an offering of human hands as close to Abraham as it is to Bach.

Advertisement in *New Yorker* 17 Jan 59

JOHN CANADAY

7 The Solomon R Guggenheim Museum . . . is a war between architecture and painting in which both come out badly maimed.

On Manhattan museum designed by Frank Lloyd Wright, NY *Times* 21 Oct 59

CHARLES, Prince of Wales

8 [It's] a kind of vast municipal fire station . . . a monstrous carbuncle on the face of a much-loved friend.

On Peter Ahrends's design for an office building housing additional space for the National Gallery, address at 150th anniversary celebration of the Royal Institute of British Architects, NY *Times* 12 Oct 84

WINSTON CHURCHILL

9 We shape our buildings; thereafter they shape us.

Time 12 Sep 60

CONGRESSIONAL MANAGEMENT FOUNDATION

10 Face it: Here you've got American government at its visual best: the marble, the columns, the rotundas, the sweeping staircases. You've got goals, you've got commitments, you've got aspirations and inspirations. . . . But have you got a place to sit?

Report on overcrowding of legislative offices, quoted in NY *Times* 12 Nov 84

ROBERT DiLEONARDO

11 My job is to create an environment that relaxes morality.

On Atlantic City casinos, *Wall Street Journal* 10 Jan 83

DAVID W DUNLAP

12 An unusually tranquil skyscraping vantage—a kind of front porch 850 feet in the air.

On closing of a midtown Manhattan observation deck to make room for the new entrance to a high-rise restaurant and nightclub, "A Quiet Place at RCA's Summit Drifts onto the Pages of the Past" NY *Times* 18 Jun 86

RICHARD T FELLER, Clerk of the Works and Chairman of the Building Committee, National Cathedral, Washington DC

13 The Gothic style historically, more perhaps than any other, released architecture from its earthbound confines.

An Act of Optimism, 1980 cathedral booklet

EDWARD FINLASON, British Army

14 Even the Germans did not succeed in doing the damage you propose to do.

Protest against Mies van der Rohe's high-rise building in Mansion House Square, London *Times* 10 Jun 85

HENRY GELDZAHLER, Commissioner, NYC Department of Cultural Affairs

1 It is the theater God would have built if he had the money.
> On preservation of Radio City Music Hall, NY *Times* 2 Apr 78

WILLIAM HAMILTON

2 Concrete is, essentially, the color of bad weather.
> *Gourmet* Dec 86

C DAVID HEYMANN

3 [It was] the last word in mortuary chintz.
> On dime-store magnate F W Woolworth's mausoleum, *Poor Little Rich Girl* Lyle Stuart 84

ROBERT HUGHES

4 Nothing they design ever gets in the way of a work of art.
> On Kevin Roche, John Dinkeloo & Associates' design for new wing at the Metropolitan Museum of Art, *ib* 2 Feb 87

ADA LOUISE HUXTABLE

5 The New York Hilton is laid out with a competence that would make a computer blush.
> NY *Times* 30 Jun 63

6 Superfluous curtains that needlessly cover glass would give Salome a lifetime supply of veils.
> *ib*

7 The building is a national tragedy ... a cross between a concrete candy box and a marble sarcophagus in which the art of architecture lies buried.
> On John F Kennedy Center for the Performing Arts in Washington DC, *ib* 6 Sep 71

JOHN F KENNEDY, 35th US President

8 I know that the White House was designed by [James] Hoban, a noted Irish-American architect, and I have no doubt that he believed by incorporating several features of the Dublin style he would make it more homelike for any president of Irish descent. It was a long wait, but I appreciate his efforts.
> Addressing the Irish Parliament in Dublin, assembled in a Georgian mansion that was the seat of Kennedy's maternal ancestors, NY *Times* 28 Jun 63

9 I look forward to an America which will not be afraid of grace and beauty, which will protect the beauty of our natural environment, which will preserve the great old American houses and squares and parks of our national past and which will build handsome and balanced cities for our future.
> Last major public address, at Amherst College 26 Oct 63

NEIL KINNOCK, Labor Party leader

10 The Parthenon without the marbles is like a smile with a tooth missing.
> Promising return of the Elgin marbles to Greece, London *Times* 5 Jan 84

RUSSELL LYNES

11 The bungalow had more to do with how Americans live today than any other building that has gone remotely by the name of architecture in our history.
> *The Domesticated Americans* Harper & Row 63

JOHN MAZZOLA, President, Lincoln Center, NYC

12 We patch and patch and patch and patch, but we work on the assumption that you can only keep a place beautiful by maintaining the hell out of it.
> On $6-million renovation during the center's 20th year, NY *Times* 11 Sep 81

DAVID McCORD

13 The high-ceilinged rooms, the little balconies, alcoves, nooks and angles all suggest sanctuary, escape, creature comfort. The reader, the scholar, the browser, the borrower is king.
> On the Boston Athenaeum, *Time* 15 Nov 82

BRYAN MILLER

14 The Polo Lounge is like a fine old mink coat: opulent, dignified and warm.
> On the Westbury Hotel's bar, NY *Times* 9 Nov 84

MALCOLM MILLER

15 This building is like a book. Its architecture is the binding, its text is in the glass and sculpture.
> *Chartres Cathedral* Pitkin 80

FREDERIC MORTON

16 A grand old odalisque should never deign to turn housewife.
> On trend to turn Manhattan's older hotels into cooperative apartment houses, *Holiday* Nov 64

ROBERT MOSES, NYC Parks Commissioner

17 Frank Lloyd Wright's inverted oatmeal dish

and silo with their awkward cantilevering, their jaundiced skin and the ingenious spiral ramp leading down past the abstractions which mirror the tortured maladjustments of our time.

> On the Guggenheim Museum, NY *Times* 21 May 59

1 [It is] the most hideous waterfront structure ever inflicted on a city by a combination of architectural conceit and official bad taste. . . . the Cathedral of Asphalt.

> On arch-shaped municipal asphalt plant, recalled 40 years later when the structure had become a registered landmark and centerpiece for Manhattan's largest playing field, *ib* 24 Oct 84

Lewis Mumford

2 New York is the perfect model of a city, not the model of a perfect city.

> *My Work and Days* Harcourt, Brace Jovanovich 79

3 Forget the damned motor car and build the cities for lovers and friends.

> *ib*

Enid Nemy

4 Windows . . . are as essential to office prestige as Christmas is to retailing.

> NY *Times* 13 Aug 80

5 Even at the United Nations, where legend has it that the building was designed so that there could be no corner offices, the expanse of glass in individual offices is said to be a dead giveaway as to rank. Five windows are excellent, one window not so great.

> *ib*

New York Times

6 Any city gets what it admires, will pay for and, ultimately, deserves.

> On demolition of Pennsylvania Station, 30 Oct 63

7 We want and deserve tin-can architecture in a tin-horn culture. And we will probably be judged not by the monuments we build but by those we have destroyed.

> *ib*

Richard Oulahan

8 The building has all the requisites of a great aunt. She is neither very pretty nor elegant, but she has enduring qualities of character.

> On Old Executive Office Building in Washington DC, *Smithsonian* Mar 86

Paige Rense, Editor, *Architectural Digest*

9 Everyone has, I think, in some quiet corner of his mind, an ideal home waiting to become a reality.

> Foreword to *Designers' Own Homes* Knapp 84

John Richardson

10 While American interiors are often designed to provide an idealized picture of their owner's circumstances, English interiors tend to tell the truth about the people who live in them.

> Quoted in NY *Times* 29 Jul 84

Andy Rooney

11 An arch is two curves trying to fall.

> *An Essay on Bridges* CBS TV 15 Feb 65

12 Man has made a sewer of the river—and spanned it with a poem.

> On completion of world's longest suspension span, the Verrazano-Narrows Bridge linking Brooklyn and Staten Island, *Time* 11 Jul 69

A L Rowse, Emeritus Fellow, All Souls College, Oxford

13 It is the quintessence of England: gray, white and silvery stone, rose-red and rust-colored brick, embowered in greenery, ancient lawns running down to the water, and in spring starred with a million daffodils.

> "Cambridge through Oxford Eyes" NY *Times* 17 Mar 85

John Russell

14 Houses are like theater. . . . What is played out in them may be comedy or tragedy, historical drama or farce; but no matter what is on the program for the day, every house has its exits and its entrances, its upstage and its downstage, its good seats and its bad seats and, all too often, its prompter's box in full use.

> "Design Notebook" NY *Times* 5 Jul 79

Carl Sandburg

15 We live in the time of the colossal upright oblong.

> To Chicago Dynamic Committee, *Life* 4 Nov 57

San Diego Tribune

16 A Gothic cathedral is a hymn to God.

> On National Cathedral, Washington DC, 5 Jul 86

ALBERT SCARDINO

1 Not since the Battle of Britain has control over air space generated so much conflict.
On air rights for Manhattan skyscrapers, NY *Times* 21 Feb 86

ROGER SCRUTON

2 Architecture, like dress, is an exercise in good manners, and good manners involve the habit of skillful insincerity—the habit of saying "good morning" to those whose mornings you would rather blight, and of passing the butter to those you would rather starve.
London *Times* 14 Aug 84

RALPH STEPHENSON, counterman at Savarin Restaurant

3 The city's got the right name—New York. Nothing ever gets old around here.
On demolition of Pennsylvania Station, NY *Times* 29 Oct 63

HARRY S TRUMAN, 33rd US President

4 I don't want it torn down. I think it's the greatest monstrosity in America.
1958 statement on the Old Executive Office Building, 19th-century structure adjoining the White House, quoted by Carleton Knight III "Dusting off History" *Christian Science Monitor* 1 Aug 86

DAVID UTZ

5 There were no floors, no walls, no ceilings, no windows and the plumbing was nonexistent. Of course, I fell in love.
On renovating a loft apartment, NY *Times* 8 Jul 82

JOHN VINOCUR

6 No one has the right to change Paris, the protesters say, and argue that the city is the patrimony of all mankind.
On protests against building a glass pyramid in the courtyard of the Louvre, NY *Times* 18 Mar 85

ART

Painters & Sculptors

LEONARD BASKIN

7 Pop art is the inedible raised to the unspeakable.
Publishers Weekly 5 Apr 65

GEORGES BRAQUE

8 Painting is a nail to which I fasten my ideas.
Recalled on his death 31 Aug 63

ALEXANDER CALDER

9 I paint with shapes.
On suspended sculptures that move with air—"mobiles," as Marcel Duchamp called them in 1932, *Saturday Evening Post* 27 Feb 65

MARC CHAGALL

10 I work in whatever medium likes me at the moment.
Recalled on his death 28 Mar 85

11 Great art picks up where nature ends.
Time 30 Dec 85

WINSTON CHURCHILL

12 The first quality that is needed is audacity.
Painting as a Pleasure Whittesay House 50

13 My hand seemed arrested by a silent veto.
On trying to paint a pale-blue sky, quoted by William Manchester *The Last Lion* Little, Brown 83

JEAN COCTEAU

14 An artist cannot speak about his art any more than a plant can discuss horticulture.
Newsweek 16 May 55

SALVADOR DALI

15 Drawing is the honesty of the art. There is no possibility of cheating. It is either good or bad.
People 27 Sep 76

16 Each morning when I awake, I experience again a supreme pleasure—that of being Salvador Dali.
NY *Times* 1 Jan 80

17 Let my enemies devour each other.
Replying at age 80 to reports that his assistants did much of his painting, *ib* 19 Mar 85

18 Painting is an infinitely minute part of my personality.
ib

STUART DAVIS

19 The value of impermanence is to call attention to the permanent.
Recalled on his death 24 Jun 64

LUIS FRANGELLA

20 When something needs to be painted it lets me know.
Esquire Apr 86

CHESTER GOULD

1 I usually start with a repulsive character and go on from there.

> On his *Dick Tracy* cartoons, NY *Daily News* 18 Dec 55

MORRIS GRAVES

2 I paint to rest from the phenomena of the external world—to pronounce and to make notations of its essences with which to verify the inner eye.

> On his unconventional paintings of conventional subjects, *Christian Science Monitor* 19 Feb 64

EDWARD HOPPER

3 What I wanted to do was to paint sunlight on the side of a house.

> Recalled on his death to mean "I want to paint the human soul," *Newsweek* 29 May 67

J STEWARD JOHNSON JR

4 The common strain in my work is that in each case I celebrate a moment when the individual responded to his or her own humanity.

> On his sculptures, "Capturing Moments" *Leaders* Oct 84

ROCKWELL KENT

5 If to the viewer's eyes, *my* world appears less beautiful than his, I'm to be pitied and the viewer praised.

> Recalled on his death 13 Mar 71

DONG KINGMAN

6 Most artists are surrealists. . . . always dreaming something and then they paint it.

> Quoted in Mary Ann Guitar ed *Twenty-two Famous Painters and Illustrators Tell How They Work* McKay 64

7 Three men riding on a bicycle which has only one wheel, I guess that's surrealist.

> *ib*

ALEXANDER LIBERMAN

8 All art is solitary and the studio is a torture area.

> NY *Times* 13 May 79

ROY LICHTENSTEIN

9 I don't have big anxieties. I wish I did. I'd be much more interesting.

> Quoted by Deborah Solomon "The Art behind the Dots" NY *Times* 8 Mar 87

10 I like to pretend that my art has nothing to do with me.

> *ib*

MAYA LIN

11 It terrified me to have an idea that was solely mine to be no longer a part of my mind, but totally public.

> On her design for Vietnam Veterans Memorial in Washington DC, *National Geographic* May 85

JACQUES LIPCHITZ

12 Copy nature and you infringe on the work of our Lord. Interpret nature and you are an artist.

> NY *Times* 28 Apr 64

13 Imagination is a very precise thing, you know—it is not fantasy; the man who invented the wheel while he was observing another man walking—that is imagination!

> Chicago *Tribune* 4 Jun 67

14 Cubism is like standing at a certain point on a mountain and looking around. If you go higher, things will look different; if you go lower, again they will look different. It is a point of view.

> *ib*

15 All my life as an artist I have asked myself: What pushes me continually to make sculpture? I have found the answer..... art is an action against death. It is a denial of death.

> *ib*

HENRI MATISSE

16 A picture must possess a real power to generate light [and] for a long time now I've been conscious of expressing myself through light or rather *in* light.

> Quoted by Pierre Schneider *Matisse* Rizzoli 84

17 Impressionism is the newspaper of the soul.

> *ib*

18 Drawing is like making an expressive gesture with the advantage of permanence.

> Quoted by Theodore F Wolff in review of "The Drawings of Henri Matisse" exhibit at Manhattan's Museum of Modern Art, *Christian Science Monitor* 25 Mar 85

19 I have been no more than a medium, as it were.

> Quoted in *Smithsonian* Nov 86

JOAN MIRÓ

20 My way is to seize an image that moment it

has formed in my mind, to trap it as a bird and to pin it at once to canvas. Afterward I start to tame it, to master it. I bring it under control and I develop it.

London *Observer* 10 Jun 79

HENRY MOORE

1 It is a mistake for a sculptor or a painter to speak or write very often about his job. It releases tension needed for his work.

Henry Moore on Sculpture Viking 67

2 A sculptor is a person who is interested in the shape of things, a poet in words, a musician by sounds.

ib

3 A sculptor is a person obsessed with the form and shape of things, and it's not just the shape of one thing, but the shape of anything and everything: the growth in a flower; the hard, tense strength, although delicate form of a bone; the strong, solid fleshiness of a beech tree trunk.

ib

ROBERT MOTHERWELL

4 Most painting in the European tradition was painting the mask. Modern art rejected all that. Our subject matter was the person behind the mask.

On relationship between torment and creativity, NY *Times* 17 Nov 85

GEORGIA O'KEEFFE

5 [Sun-bleached bones] were most wonderful against the blue—that blue that will always be there as it is now after all man's destruction is finished.

On desert skies of New Mexico, *Newsweek* 17 Mar 86

PABLO PICASSO

6 When one starts from a portrait and seeks by successive eliminations to find pure form . . . one inevitably ends up with an egg.

Look 6 Jun 56

7 If only we could pull out our brain and use only our eyes.

On painting objectively, *Saturday Review* 1 Sep 56

8 Ah, good taste! What a dreadful thing! Taste is the enemy of creativeness.

Quote 24 Mar 57

9 Art is a lie that makes us realize the truth.

ib 21 Sep 58

10 The people no longer seek consolation in art. But the refined people, the rich, the idlers seek the new, the extraordinary, the extravagant, the scandalous.

Parade 3 Jan 65

11 There are painters who transform the sun into a yellow spot, but there are others who, thanks to their art and intelligence, transform a yellow spot into the sun.

Quote 21 Mar 65

12 Those trying to explain pictures are as a rule completely mistaken.

Quoted in Dore Ashton ed *Picasso on Art* Viking 72

13 Every child is an artist. The problem is how to remain an artist once he grows up.

Recalled on his death 8 Apr 73

14 For a long time I limited myself to one color— as a form of discipline.

On his blue and rose periods, *ib*

15 For those who know how to read, I have painted my autobiography.

ib

16 [He] must have an angel in his head.

On Marc Chagall, recalled on Chagall's 97th birthday, NY *Times* 12 Jul 84

17 Everything I need to know about Africa is in these objects.

On symbolism of primitive sculpture, quoted in *Time* 15 Oct 84

JACKSON POLLOCK

18 Abstract painting is abstract. It confronts you.

Quoted by Francis V O'Connor *Jackson Pollock* Museum of Modern Art 67

FAIRFIELD PORTER

19 To ask the meaning of art is like asking the meaning of life: Experience comes before a measurement against a value system.

Quoted by Kay Larson *New York* 18 Jun 84

NORMAN ROCKWELL

20 I unconsciously decided that, even if it wasn't an ideal world, it should be and so painted only the ideal aspects of it—pictures in which there are no drunken slatterns or self-centered mothers . . . only foxy grandpas who played baseball with the kids and boys who fished from logs and got up circuses in the backyard.

Washington *Post* 27 May 72

21 I cannot convince myself that a painting is

good unless it is popular. If the public dislikes one of my *Post* covers, I can't help disliking it myself.
> Quoted by Arthur C Danto "Freckles for the Ages" NY *Times* 28 Sep 86

SAUL STEINBERG

1 I am among the few who continue to draw after childhood is ended, continuing and perfecting childhood drawing—without the traditional interruption of academic training.
Christian Science Monitor 25 Nov 85

MACEDONLO DE LA TORRE

2 You cannot hear the waterfall if you stand next to it. I paint my jungles in the desert.
NY *Times* 3 Feb 60

3 The imagination must not be given too much material. It must be denied food so that it can work for itself.
ib

MARTINE VERMEULEN

4 Clay. It's rain, dead leaves, dust, all my dead ancestors. Stones that have been ground into sand. Mud. The whole cycle of life and death.
On her pottery, NY *Times* 3 Dec 75

ANDY WARHOL

5 If you want to know all about Andy Warhol, just look at the surface of my paintings and films and me, and there I am. There's nothing behind it.
Recalled on his death, *Newsweek* 9 Mar 87

JON WITCOMB

6 Portraits are supposed to "look within," but in my opinion very few people have an interior significantly different from the outside portrait.
> Quoted in Mary Ann Guitar ed *Twenty-two Famous Painters and Illustrators Tell How They Work* McKay 64

GRANT WOOD

7 All the really good ideas I ever had came to me while I was milking a cow.
News summaries 1 Mar 54

ANDREW WYETH

8 I prefer winter and fall, when you feel the bone structure in the landscape—the loneliness of it—the dead feeling of winter. Something waits beneath it—the whole story doesn't show.
> Quoted by Richard Meryman *The Art of Andrew Wyeth* NY Graphic Society 73

9 I'm like a prostitute. . . . never off duty.
Time 18 Aug 86

10 I don't really have studios. I wander around—around people's attics, out in fields, in cellars, anyplace I find that invites me.
ib

11 I dream a lot. I do more painting when I'm not painting. It's in the subconscious.
ib

JAMIE WYETH

12 Had I been born in New York, I'd probably be painting taxis . . . but because I live on this farm, I paint objects and landscapes I know and love.
> Interviewed in his studio at Chadds Ford PA, *M* Aug 84

DEAN YOUNG

13 I don't deal in controversy. I deal in fun. It's separate from reality.
> On continuing the comic strip *Blondie* begun by his father Chic Young, *Newsweek* 1 Oct 84

Photographers

ANSEL ADAMS

14 The negative is comparable to the composer's score and the print to its performance. Each performance differs in subtle ways.
> *The Portfolios of Ansel Adams* NY Graphic Society/Little, Brown 81

15 There is nothing worse than a brilliant image of a fuzzy concept.
Recalled on his death 22 Apr 84

16 Not everybody trusts paintings but people believe photographs.
ib

RICHARD AVEDON

17 It's in trying to direct the traffic between Artiface [*sic*] and Candor, without being run over, that I'm confronted with the questions about photography that matter most to me.
On maintaining authenticity, NY *Times* 27 Dec 85

DAVID BAILEY

18 When I die I want to go to *Vogue*.
International Herald Tribune 15 Nov 85

CECIL BEATON

19 Mrs Woolf's complaint should be addressed to her creator, who made her, rather than me.
Answering Virginia Woolf's protest about his

drawing of her, quoted by Hugo Vickers *Cecil Beaton* Little, Brown 85

MARGARET BOURKE-WHITE

1 The beauty of the past belongs to the past.
On modern photojournalism, quoted by Mary Warner Marien *Christian Science Monitor* 5 Dec 86

ALFRED EISENSTAEDT

2 I don't like to work with assistants. I'm already one too many; the camera alone would be enough.
On his 50-year career as a *Life* magazine photographer, *New York* 15 Sep 86

PHILIPPE HALSMAN

3 Of the thousands of people, celebrated and unknown, who have sat before my camera, I am often asked who was the most difficult subject, or the easiest, or which picture is my favorite. This last question is like asking a mother which child she likes the most.
Recalled on his death 25 Jun 79

YOUSUF KARSH

4 Character, like a photograph, develops in darkness.
Parade 3 Dec 78

NORMAN PARKINSON

5 A photographer without a magazine behind him is like a farmer without fields.
New Yorker 10 Dec 84

6 The camera can be the most deadly weapon since the assassin's bullet. Or it can be the lotion of the heart.
ib

EDWARD STEICHEN

7 Photography is a major force in explaining man to man.
Time 7 Apr 61

8 When that shutter clicks, anything else that can be done afterward is not worth consideration.
Recalled on his death 25 Mar 73

Collectors & Curators

FRANÇOISE CACHIN, Director, Musée d'Orsay, Paris

9 Certainly we have bad paintings. We have only the "greatest" bad paintings.
Time 8 Dec 86

GISBERTO MARTELLI, Superintendent of Monuments, Milan

10 Imagine 500 friars eating 500 plates of steaming minestrone every night—that's pollution.
On the restoration of *The Last Supper,* Leonardo da Vinci's 1498 refectory fresco, NY *Times* 20 Aug 80

WALTER PERSEGATI, Secretary-Treasurer, Vatican Museum

11 You can't lock up art in a vault and keep it frozen for posterity. Then the artist is betrayed, history is betrayed.
NY *Times* 9 Jul 84

GAILLARD F RAVENEL, National Gallery of Art, Washington DC

12 You begin with a group of objects and then you build a room like a glove to hold them.
On the gallery's exhibit "The Treasure Houses of Britain," NY *Times* 10 Sep 85

ELIZABETH SHAW, Public Relations Director, Museum of Modern Art

13 Dead artists always bring out an older, richer crowd.
On a fauvism exhibition that drew 2,000 people, NY *Times* 26 Mar 76

BARON HANS HEINRICH THYSSEN-BORNEMISZA

14 I chase works of art the way others chase *les jolies maîtresses.*
M Jul 85

PETER C WILSON, Chairman, Sotheby's

15 Works of art are all that survive of incredibly gifted people.
London Illustrated News Dec 78

Observers & Critics

BERNARD BERENSON

16 I am only a picture-taster, the way others are wine-or tea-tasters.
Sunset and Twilight Harcourt, Brace & World 63

JONATHAN BROWN, Professor of Fine Arts, NY University

17 Whenever the occasion arose, he rose to the occasion.
On Diego de Velázquez, quoted by Susan Heller Anderson NY *Times* 10 Aug 86

WINSTON CHURCHILL

18 Without tradition, art is a flock of sheep with-

out a shepherd. Without innovation, it is a corpse.

To Royal Academy of Arts, *Time* 11 May 53

RICHARD CORLISS

1 Every artist undresses his subject, whether human or still life. It is his business to find essences in surfaces, and what more attractive and challenging surface than the skin around a soul?

On Andrew Wyeth's studies of Helga Testorf, *Time* 18 Aug 86

ARTHUR C DANTO, Johnsonian Professor of Philosophy, Columbia University

2 The Rockwell [magazine] cover was more a part of the American reality than a record of it.

In review of Laurie Norton Moffat's *Norman Rockwell: A Definitive Catalogue* Norman Rockwell Museum/University Press of New England 86, NY *Times* 28 Sep 86

3 His was a landscape of amiable codgers, nurturing moms, adorable dogs, callow soldiers with hearts of gold—grown-up Boy Scouts all.
ib

4 It really is impossible not to like him. His success was his failure.
ib

PETER DE VRIES

5 Murals in restaurants are on a par with the food in museums.
Madder Music Little, Brown 77

ALEXANDER ELIOT

6 So-called art restoration is at least as tricky as brain surgery. Most pictures expire under scalpel and sponge.
NY *Times* 20 Dec 86

HANS MAGNUS ENZENSBERGER

7 Culture is a little like dropping an Alka-Seltzer into a glass—you don't see it, but somehow it does something.

Quoted by painter Hans Haacke NY *Times* 25 Jan 87

EMILY GENAUER

8 Since nudes in all countries and centuries possess standard equipment, it's difficult to say precisely why the pictures at the Brooklyn Museum right now are so thoroughly American.

Reviewing a historical survey of the nude in American painting, NY *Herald Tribune* 10 Oct 61

BIL GILBERT

9 Audubon biographers and scholars [have noted], by various euphemisms, that all great men have their flaws, and their man's principal flaw was that he, well, he lied a lot.

On John James Audubon, *Sports Illustrated* 23 Dec 85

GRACE GLUECK

10 The studio, a room to which the artist consigns himself for life, is naturally important, not only as workplace, but as a source of inspiration. And it usually manages, one way or another, to turn up in his product.
NY *Times* 29 Jun 84

ALDOUS HUXLEY

11 A competent portraitist knows how to imply the profile in the full face.

Quoted in John Gassner and Sidney Thomas eds *The Nature of Art* Crown 64

ALEXANDRA JOHNSON

12 [It] is that rare impressionist painting where people don't judge the light, but rather are judged by it.

On *Terrace at Sainte-Adresse* by Claude Monet, *Christian Science Monitor* 1 Oct 80

CARL JUNG

13 A "scream" is always just that—a noise and not music.

On Pablo Picasso, *Letters Vol 1* Princeton 73

JESSE KORNBLUTH

14 Although one of his long-standing fantasies was to open a house of prostitution, the fantasy role he chose for himself was that of cashier.

On Andy Warhol, *New York* 9 Mar 87

RICHARD LACAYO

15 A museum show is the acid test for photojournalism.

On retrospective of Carl Mydans's work, *Time* 19 Aug 85

MADELEINE L'ENGLE

16 Artistic temperament . . . sometimes seems a battleground, a dark angel of destruction and a bright angel of creativity wrestling.

A Severed Wasp Farrar, Straus & Giroux 82

17 When the bright angel dominates, out comes a great work of art, a Michelangelo *David* or a Beethoven symphony.
ib

MICHAEL LESY

1 Photographers represented occasions once. You dressed for them as you might for church, they cost money, they recorded important moments.
Wisconsin Death Trip Pantheon 73

RUSSELL LYNES

2 The Art Snob will stand back from a picture at some distance, his head cocked slightly to one side. .... After a long period of gazing (during which he may occasionally squint his eyes), he will approach to within a few inches of the picture and examine the brushwork; he will then return to his former distant position, give the picture another glance and walk away.
Snobs Harper 50

3 The Art Snob can be recognized in the home by the quick look he gives the pictures on your walls, quick but penetrating, as though he were undressing them. This is followed either by complete and pained silence or a comment such as "That's really a very pleasant little water color you have there."
ib

ANDRÉ MALRAUX, French Minister of Culture

4 Some pictures are in the gallery because they belong to humanity and others because they belong to the United States.
On visiting the National Gallery of Art, Washington DC, NY *Herald Tribune* 12 May 62

5 There has been talk of the risks this painting took by leaving the Louvre. ... But the risks taken by the boys who landed one day in Normandy—to say nothing of those who had preceded them 25 years before—were much more certain.
At dinner honoring the exhibition of the *Mona Lisa* at the National Gallery, *ib* 8 Jan 63

6 An art book is a museum without walls.
Quoted by Jonathan Cott *Conversations with Glenn Gould* Little, Brown 84

NIGEL McGILCHRIST

7 It has always been difficult to get very close to the spirit of the Sistine Chapel; now that it is cleaned, it is like trying to get close to a trumpet.
London *Times* 14 Apr 86

MARSHALL McLUHAN

8 I think of art, at its most significant, as a DEW line, a Distant Early Warning system that can always be relied on to tell the old culture what is beginning to happen to it.
Understanding Media McGraw-Hill 64

GEORGE MENDOZA

9 You never saw any husband writing an alimony check in Norman Rockwell's America.
Quoted in NY *Times* 20 Aug 85

BRIAN O'DOHERTY

10 He searched disorder for its unifying principle.
On Stuart Davis, abstractionist whose work prefigured pop art, NY *Times* 26 Jun 64

RONALD REAGAN, 40th US President

11 In an atmosphere of liberty, artists and patrons are free to think the unthinkable and create the audacious; they are free to make both horrendous mistakes and glorious celebrations.
To recipients of the National Medal of Arts, *Newsweek* 13 May 85

12 Where there's liberty, art succeeds.
ib

PAUL RICHARD

13 A mood of gloom or longing that people mistake for profundity.
On Andrew Wyeth's paintings, *Newsweek* 18 Aug 86

FRIDA KAHLO RIVERA

14 I cannot speak of Diego as my husband because that term, when applied to him, is an absurdity. He never has been, nor will he ever be, anybody's husband.
Acknowledging that art overruled everything in her husband's life, quoted by William Weber Johnson "The Tumultuous Life and Times of the Painter Diego Rivera" *Smithsonian* Feb 86

15 His capacity for work breaks clocks and calendars.
ib

JOHN RUSSELL

16 What makes people the world over stand in line for Van Gogh is not that they will see beautiful pictures [but] that in an indefinable way they will come away feeling better human beings. And that is exactly what Van Gogh hoped for.
NY *Times* 19 Oct 84

GEORGE SANTAYANA

1 Art is delayed echo.
   Quoted in John Gassner and Sidney Thomas eds
   The Nature of Art Crown 64

2 Nothing is so poor and melancholy as an art that is interested in itself and not in its subject.
   ib

JEAN PAUL SARTRE

3 What I see is teeming cohesion, contained dispersal. . . . For him, to sculpt is to take the fat off space.
   On Alberto Giacometti's work, *Situations* Braziller 65

SUSAN SONTAG

4 Life is not significant details, illuminated by a flash, fixed forever. Photographs are.
   On Photography Farrar, Straus & Giroux 77

MARK STEVENS

5 Shouldn't a great museum foster serious seeing before all else?
   On poor presentation of a Van Gogh exhibit at the Metropolitan Museum of Art, *Newsweek* 15 Oct 84

6 One of the best things about paintings is their silence—which prompts reflection and random reverie.
   Decrying guided tours by headphone, *ib*

GENE THORNTON

7 Magazine photography is the mural painting of modern times.
   NY *Times* 15 Jul 79

TIME MAGAZINE

8 The doodle is the brooding of the hand.
   16 Oct 78

LUCIE UTRILLO

9 I picked him up in a gutter, and saved him for France.
   On her husband Maurice, recalled on his death 5 Nov 55

LILA ACHESON WALLACE

10 A painting is like a man. If you can live without it, then there isn't much point in having it.
   Recalled on her death 8 May 84

FASHION
Designers

MANOLO BLAHNIK

11 About half my designs are controlled fantasy, 15 percent are total madness and the rest are bread-and-butter designs.
   W 25 Aug 86

BILL BLASS

12 When in doubt wear red.
   News summaries 31 Dec 82

MARIO BUATTA, interior designer

13 I like all the chairs to talk to one another and to the sofas and not those parlor-car arrangements that create two Siberias.
   New York 28 Jan 85

PIERRE CARDIN

14 The jean! The jean is the destructor! It is a dictator! It is destroying creativity. The jean must be stopped!
   People 28 Jun 76

GABRIELLE ("COCO") CHANEL

15 I love luxury. And luxury lies not in richness and ornateness but in the absence of vulgarity. Vulgarity is the ugliest word in our language. I stay in the game to fight it.
   Life 19 Aug 57

16 Luxury must be comfortable, otherwise it is not luxury.
   NY *Times* 23 Aug 64

17 Fashion is made to become unfashionable.
   ib

18 Look for the woman in the dress. If there is no woman, there is no dress.
   ib

19 It is the unseen, unforgettable, ultimate accessory of fashion. . . . that heralds your arrival and prolongs your departure.
   On perfume, NY *Herald Tribune* 18 Oct 64

20 Elegance is not the prerogative of those who have just escaped from adolescence, but of those who have already taken possession of their future.
   McCall's Nov 65

ANGELA CUMMINGS, jewelry designer

21 I think of Bergdorf's as being something like pastel sapphires.
   On a fashionable clothing store, NY *Times* 20 Aug 84

LILLY DACHÉ

1 Glamour is what makes a man ask for your telephone number. But it also is what makes a woman ask for the name of your dressmaker.
News summaries 3 Dec 54

NIELS DIFFRIENT, industrial designer

2 The less there is of a phone, the more I like it.
At a Manhattan Phone City display, NY *Times* 16 Oct 86

3 It looks like a galosh with electronics in it.
On a rubber Italian telephone, *ib*

CHRISTIAN DIOR

4 My dream is to save them from nature.
On his desire to make all women look beautiful, *Collier's* 10 Jun 55

ANNE FOGARTY

5 If you adore her, you must adorn her. There lies the secret of a happy marriage.
Wife Dressing Messner 59

FREDDIE FOX, milliner to Queen Elizabeth II

6 She is not a fashion plate, she is a monarch; you can't have both.
Replying to criticism of the queen's "awful hats," London *Times* 6 Oct 84

RUDI GERNREICH

7 It was just a whimsical idea that escalated when so many crazy ladies took it up.
On his design for a topless bathing suit, Chicago *American* 26 Nov 66

HUBERT DE GIVENCHY

8 I absolutely believe my talent is God-given. I ask God for a lot, but I also thank him. I'm a very demanding believer.
W 12 Oct 79

9 Hair style is the final tip-off whether or not a woman really knows herself.
Vogue Jul 85

HALSTON

10 You are only as good as the people you dress.
Quoted by Lisa Belkin "The Prisoner of Seventh Avenue" NY *Times* 15 Mar 87

NORMAN HARTNELL

11 I despise simplicity. It is the negation of all that is beautiful.
London *Times* 30 Apr 85

EDITH HEAD, eight-time Oscar winner for costume design

12 A designer is only as good as the star who wears her clothes.
Saturday Evening Post 30 Nov 63

CALVIN KLEIN

13 I think there's something incredibly sexy about a woman wearing her boyfriend's T-shirt and underwear.
People 24 Dec 84

EILEEN ("BUTCH") KRUTCHIK

14 I don't do glitz, I do reverse chic.
On customized invitations and announcements, NY *Times* 21 Dec 85

RALPH LAUREN

15 I don't design clothes, I design dreams.
NY *Times* 19 Apr 86

MAINBOCHER

16 To be well turned out, a woman should turn her thoughts in.
Vogue 1 Apr 64

17 I have never known a really chic woman whose appearance was not, in large part, an outward reflection of her inner self.
ib

WILLIAM PAHLMANN, interior designer

18 Ambiance is an unstudied grace . . . the grace of human dignity.
Insider's Newsletter 18 Jan 65

MRS HENRY PARISH ("Sister" Parish)

19 All decorating is about memories.
Architectural Digest May 81

20 I *am* taste.
W 14 Jun 85

MARY QUANT

21 Legs stay throughout a woman's life.
On ageless appeal of miniskirts, quoted by Marylin Bender *The Beautiful People* Coward-McCann 67

NETTIE ROSENSTEIN

22 It's what you leave off a dress that makes it smart.
Recalled on her death 13 Mar 80

YVES SAINT LAURENT

23 I wish I had invented blue jeans. They have ex-

pression, modesty, sex appeal, simplicity—all I hope for in my clothes.
New York 28 Nov 83

1 Dressing is a way of life.
ib

2 Isn't elegance forgetting what one is wearing?
ib

VIDAL SASSOON

3 We have come a long way from the youths who wore so much long hair it became a uniform—its own form of uniformity.
Quote 13 Apr 75

VALENTINA

4 Mink is for football games ... Please. Out in the fresh air, sit in it, eat hot dogs in it, anything. But not evening, not elegance, I beg of you.
Ladies' Home Journal Mar 58

Manufacturers & Merchandisers

BROOKS BROTHERS

5 The well-dressed man still doffs his hat.
On hats as "the classic finishing touch ... a confident statement of your personal good taste," advertisement in NY *Times* 16 Sep 85

FLORENCE EISEMAN, manufacturer of children's clothing

6 Please do not have a fit in the fitting room. Your fashion life begins there.
Advertisement in *New Yorker* 19 Mar 66

MAX FACTOR, cosmetics executive

7 A woman who doesn't wear lipstick feels undressed in public. Unless she works on a farm.
Time 16 Jun 58

IRWIN GROSSMAN, Vice President, Groshire-Austin Leeds

8 If we knew how to get the label on the outside, we'd all be in clover.
On men's suits, *Time* 28 Feb 64

JACK LIPMAN, Drizzle Inc

9 The trench coat is the only thing that has kept its head above water.
Wall Street Journal 11 Oct 84

ARTHUR ORTENBERG

10 Men's wear is an eight-lane highway with nobody on it.
On opportunities in the manufacturing of men's fashions, NY *Times* 4 May 86

HELENA RUBINSTEIN, cosmetics executive

11 All the American women had purple noses and gray lips and their faces were chalk white from terrible powder. I recognized that the United States could be my life's work.
Recalling her arrival in America on a cold day in 1914, *Time* 9 Apr 65

12 Some women won't buy anything unless they can pay a lot.
ib

Observers & Critics

NORA ASTORGA, UN delegate, Nicaragua

13 You can't expect me to wear blue jeans to the Security Council.
Defending her clothing expenditures, NY *Times* 28 Sep 86

LETITIA BALDRIGE

14 She changed the White House from a plastic to a crystal bowl.
On Jacqueline Kennedy, quoted by Ralph G Martin *A Hero for Our Time* Macmillan 83

DAVE BARRY

15 [There is] a breed of fashion models ... who weigh no more than an abridged dictionary.
NY *News* 9 Nov 86

16 The leading cause of death among fashion models is falling through street grates.
ib

ANNE BAXTER

17 My grandfather Frank Lloyd Wright wore a red sash on his wedding night. *That* is glamour!
Time 5 May 52

CECIL BEATON

18 What is elegance? Soap and water!
NY *Times* 30 Jan 59

19 Never in the history of fashion has so little material been raised so high to reveal so much that needs to be covered so badly.
On miniskirts, news summaries 17 Jan 69

STELLA BLUM, Costume Institute, Metropolitan Museum of Art

20 Fashion is a social agreement.... the result of a consensus of a large group of people.
Recalled on her death 31 Jul 85

21 After World War II society had to settle back

for a moment before it picked up the 20th century.

On Christian Dior's 1947 "New Look," characterized by full skirts and corseted waistlines suggestive of Victorian styles, *ib*

DAVIS BUSHNELL

1 They are certainly fit to be tied.

On designer shoelaces, *People* 10 May 82

TRUMAN CAPOTE

2 She is pure *Alice in Wonderland,* and her appearance and demeanor are a nicely judged mix of the Red Queen and a flamingo.

On Diana Vreeland, quoted by Colin McDowell *Country Life* 15 May 86

PATRICK DENNIS

3 Chinchilla is said to be more chic than mink, though personally it reminds me of unborn burlap.

Life 7 Dec 62

STEPHEN DRUCKER

4 The Lawson chair is the little black dress of the upholsterer: comfortable and safe.

"A Revival of the Shapely Drawing-room Chair" NY *Times* 10 Jan 85

GEORGIA DULLEA

5 The Prince of Chintz . . . wears well and resists stains.

On interior designer Mario Buatta, NY *Times* 24 Jan 86

JOHN FAIRCHILD, Publisher, *Women's Wear Daily*

6 "Style" is an expression of individualism mixed with charisma. Fashion is something that comes after style.

Quoted in Dallas *Times Herald* 15 Jul 75

GEORGE V HIGGINS

7 She had rouged her cheeks to a color otherwise seen only on specially ordered Pontiac Firebirds, and in her ears she wore two feathered appliances resembling surfcasting jigs especially appetizing to striped bass.

On Diana Vreeland, *Wall Street Journal* 9 Jul 84

8 Rental formal wear of the sky-blue, brocade and shiny varieties [is] favored by upwardly mobile young gangsters drafted as groomsmen for weddings.

ib 5 Feb 85

CHAUNCEY HOWE

9 Eclectic means you can put anything together as long as it's expensive.

On decorators' show houses, NBC TV 6 May 85

JACQUELINE KENNEDY

10 A newspaper reported I spend $30,000 a year buying Paris clothes and that women hate me for it. I couldn't spend that much unless I wore sable underwear.

Replying to charges that she was too chic to become First Lady, NY *Times* 15 Sep 60

11 It looks like it's been furnished by discount stores.

Contemplating her move to the White House, quoted by Ralph G Martin *A Hero for Our Time* Macmillan 83

RENÉ KONIG

12 Fashion is as profound and critical a part of the social life of man as sex, and is made up of the same ambivalent mixture of irresistible urges and inevitable taboos.

The Restless Image: A Sociology of Fashion Allen & Unwin 73

DORIS LILLY

13 Men who wear turtlenecks look like turtles.

NY *Post* 18 Dec 67

JOHN V LINDSAY, Mayor of NYC

14 The miniskirt enables young ladies to run faster, and because of it, they may have to.

NY *Times* 8 Jun 67

LIN YUTANG

15 All women's dresses are merely variations on the eternal struggle between the admitted desire to dress and the unadmitted desire to undress.

This Week 17 Feb 67

ANITA LOOS

16 I've had my best times when trailing a Mainbocher evening gown across a sawdust floor. I've always loved high style in low company.

NY *Times* 28 Mar 61

SOPHIA LOREN

17 A woman's dress should be like a barbed-wire fence: serving its purpose without obstructing the view.

Quoted on *Good Morning, America* ABC TV 10 Aug 79

MICHEIL MACDONALD, Scottish Tartans Museum, Comrie, Scotland

1 I called it the McVomit.

On a computer-designed tartan for the state of Ohio, combining red for its steel and automotive industries, green and gold for its agriculture, blue for its lakes and white for its winter snows, London *Times* 21 Dec 84

LOUIS MOUNTBATTEN, 1st Earl Mountbatten of Burma

2 If you've got it, wear it.

Advice to Prince Charles on use of royal insignia and other medals, quoted by Stephen Barry *Royal Secrets* Villard 85

CARL M MUELLER, President of the Board of River House, exclusive NYC co-op

3 She is better known for her jeans than for her genes.

On rejecting applications made by Gloria Vanderbilt, *People* 9 Jun 80

NEW YORK JOURNAL-AMERICAN

4 They held on tight going around the curves.

On gowns worn by actress Elizabeth Taylor, 22 Jun 64

NAVEEN PATNAIK

5 That left shoulder really has an aura of its own; it holds everything together.

On wearing a sari, quoted by Marina Warner "Woven Winds" *Connoisseur* Apr 86

JOHN RUSSELL

6 It is possible in England to dress up by dressing down, but it's a good idea to be a duke before you try it.

NY *Times* 9 Mar 86

CAROLINE SEEBOHM

7 World War I, that tiresome European engagement that threatened to close down French couture.

The Man Who Was Vogue Viking 82

GEORGE BERNARD SHAW

8 A fashion is nothing but an induced epidemic.

Recalled on his death 2 Nov 50

EUGENIA SHEPPARD

9 To call a fashion wearable is the kiss of death. No new fashion worth its salt is ever wearable.

NY *Herald Tribune* 13 Jan 60

UPTON SINCLAIR

10 I just put on what the lady says. I've been married three times, so I've had lots of supervision.

Interviewed at age 85, NY *Times* 7 Sep 62

EDITH SITWELL

11 The trouble with most Englishwomen is that they *will* dress as if they had been a mouse in a previous incarnation . . . they do not want to attract attention.

Recalled on her death 9 Dec 64

12 Why not be oneself? That is the whole secret of a successful appearance. If one is a greyhound, why try to look like a Pekingese?

ib

SUZANNE SLESIN

13 Chintz, it could rightly be said, is the basic black dress of the English-style interior.

"Floral Attributes" NY *Times* 14 Apr 85

CARMEL SNOW

14 Elegance is good taste *plus* a dash of daring.

The World of Carmel Snow McGraw-Hill 62

STEPHEN J SOLARZ, US Congressman

15 Compared to Imelda [Marcos], Marie Antoinette was a bag lady.

On viewing the elaborate wardrobe left behind by the wife of the overthrown Philippines president, NY *Times* 9 Mar 86

SUSAN SONTAG

16 "Camp" is a vision of the world in terms of style—but a particular style. It is the love of the exaggerated.

Against Interpretation and Other Essays Farrar, Straus & Giroux 66

TIME MAGAZINE

17 The first thing the first couple did after committing the first sin was to get dressed. Thus Adam and Eve started the world of fashion, and styles have been changing ever since.

"Gilding the Lily" 8 Nov 63

18 Pierre Cardin is a designer whose name can be worn, walked on, slept in, set upon, munched on, drunk, flown, pedaled or driven.

Quoted in introducing Cardin on *Good Morning America* ABC TV 22 Oct 86

DIANA VREELAND

19 The only real elegance is in the mind; if you've got that, the rest really comes from it.

Newsweek 10 Dec 62

1 What do I think about the way most people dress? Most people are not something one thinks about.
ib 2 Jan 78

2 [Blue jeans are] the most beautiful things since the gondola.
NY *Times* 14 Sep 80

3 Elegance is innate. It has nothing to do with being well dressed. Elegance is refusal.
ib

4 The two greatest mannequins of the century were Gertrude Stein and Edith Sitwell—unquestionably. You just couldn't take a bad picture of those two old girls.
Newsweek 22 Sep 80

5 I always wear my sweater back-to-front; it is so much more flattering.
Country Life 15 May 86

6 In a Balenciaga you were the only woman in the room—no other woman *existed*.
ib

7 No one cuts backs like he did. No one knows what a back *is* anymore.
On Cristóbal Balenciaga, *ib*

WALL STREET JOURNAL

8 If anything is worse than your own tuxedo that doesn't fit, it's a borrowed one that doesn't fit.
1 Dec 58

FILMS
Actors & Actresses

FRED ALLEN

9 You can take all the sincerity in Hollywood, place it in the navel of a fruit fly and still have room enough for three caraway seeds and a producer's heart.
Quoted by John Robert Colombo *Popcorn in Paradise* Holt, Rinehart & Winston 80

LAUREN BACALL

10 How many women do we know who were continually kissed by Clark Gable, William Powell, Cary Grant, Spencer Tracy and Fredric March? Only one: Myrna Loy.
Hosting Carnegie Hall tribute to Myrna Loy, NY *Times* 16 Jan 85

TALLULAH BANKHEAD

11 They made me sound as if I'd been castrated.
On early talking pictures, *People* 9 Feb 87

THEDA BARA

12 The reason good women like me and flock to my pictures is that there is a little bit of vampire instinct in every woman.
On her roles as the Vamp, recalled on her death 7 Apr 55

BRIGITTE BARDOT

13 I have been very happy, very rich, very beautiful, much adulated, very famous and very unhappy.
Interviewed on her 50th birthday, London *Times* 28 Sep 84

ETHEL BARRYMORE

14 Fundamentally I feel that there is as much difference between the stage and the films as between a piano and a violin. Normally you can't become a virtuoso in both.
NY *Post* 7 Jun 56

WARREN BEATTY

15 When you mutilate movies for mass media, you tamper with the hearts and minds of America.
On refusal to grant television rights for his movies because of cuts made for commercials, NY *Times* 21 Apr 85

INGRID BERGMAN

16 Hitch is a gentleman farmer who raises goose flesh.
On Alfred Hitchcock, recalled on his death 29 Apr 80

HUMPHREY BOGART

17 I came out here with one suit and everybody said I looked like a bum. Twenty years later Marlon Brando came out with only a sweatshirt and the town drooled over him. That shows how much Hollywood has progressed.
Recalled on his death 14 Jan 57

18 They'll nail anyone who ever scratched his ass during the National Anthem.
On House Un-American Activities Committee, *ib*

MARLON BRANDO

19 An actor's a guy who, if you ain't talking about him, ain't listening.
British *Vogue* Aug 74

LOUISE BROOKS

20 Every actor has a natural animosity toward ev-

ery other actor, present or absent, living or dead.
Lulu in Hollywood Knopf 82

GEORGE BURNS

1 The most important thing in acting is honesty. If you can fake that, you've got it made.
News summaries 31 Dec 84

RICHARD BURTON

2 You may be as vicious about me as you please. You will only do me justice.
On being interviewed for cover story, *Time* 26 Apr 63

3 Well, I don't want to kill myself.
When asked why he refused to see his performance in *Cleopatra*, quoted in NY *Times* 6 Aug 84

4 If you're going to make rubbish, be the best rubbish in it.
On his films, quoted in *Newsweek* 20 Aug 84

MICHAEL CAINE

5 The best research [for playing a drunk] is being a British actor for 20 years.
Quoted in *US* 2 Jun 86

CHARLIE CHAPLIN

6 All my pictures are built around the idea of getting in trouble and so giving me the chance to be desperately serious in my attempt to appear as a normal little gentleman.
Quoted by David Robinson *Chaplin* McGraw-Hill 85

JOAN CRAWFORD

7 I think that the most important thing a woman can have—next to talent, of course—is her hairdresser.
Quoted by Helen Lawrenson "Star Gazing" *Esquire* Apr 57

BETTE DAVIS

8 Evil people ... you never forget them. And that's the aim of any actress—never to be forgotten.
Quoted in NY State Theater program Jun 66

9 The best time I ever had with Joan Crawford was when I pushed her down the stairs in *Whatever Happened to Baby Jane?*
Quoted by John Robert Colombo *Popcorn in Paradise* Holt, Rinehart & Winston 80

10 You know what I'm going to have on my gravestone? "She did it the hard way."
CBS TV 5 May 85

11 I am just too much.
When asked by Barbara Walters to describe herself in five words, ABC TV 30 Mar 87

AVA GARDNER

12 After my screen test, the director clapped his hands gleefully and yelled: "She can't talk! She can't act! She's sensational!"
On "crashing" Hollywood, news summaries 11 Dec 54

13 What's the point? My face, shall we say, looks lived in.
On not lying about her upcoming 65th birthday, *People* 10 Jun 85

JUDY GARLAND

14 I've never looked through a keyhole without finding someone was looking back.
On her lack of privacy, NBC TV 16 Mar 67

VITTORIO GASSMAN

15 A totally healthy actor is a paradox.
Quoted in *Wall Street Journal* 2 Oct 84

LILLIAN GISH

16 Young man, if God had wanted you to see me that way, he would have put your eyes in your bellybutton.
On a low camera angle, quoted by Richard Thomas on Amer Film Institute's *Salute to Lillian Gish* CBS TV 17 Apr 84

WHOOPI GOLDBERG

17 I told her I would play a Venetian blind, dirt on the floor, anything.
Letter to Alice Walker, author of *The Color Purple,* in which Goldberg eventually played a leading role, *Today* NBC TV 13 Jan 86

18 An actress can only play a woman. I'm an actor, I can play anything.
ib

RUTH GORDON

19 If I don't make it today, I'll come in tomorrow.
From her 1976 autobiography *My Side,* recalled on her death 28 Aug 85

CARY GRANT

20 I pretended to be somebody I wanted to be until finally I became that person. Or he became me.
On shaping his personality early in his career, *Parade* 22 Sep 85

CEDRIC HARDWICKE

1 I believe that God felt sorry for actors so he created Hollywood to give them a place in the sun and a swimming pool. The price they had to pay was to surrender their talent.

> *A Victorian in Orbit*, with James Brough, Doubleday 61

KATHARINE HEPBURN

2 It's a rather rude gesture, but at least it's clear what you mean.

> On spitting in the eye of director Joseph L Mankiewicz, quoted by Anne Edwards *A Remarkable Woman* Morrow 85

ELSA LANCHESTER

3 She looked as if butter wouldn't melt in her mouth—or anywhere else.

> On Maureen O'Hara, news summaries 30 Jan 50

ROBERT MITCHUM

4 Every two or three years I knock off for a while. That way I'm constantly the new girl in the whorehouse.

> On maintaining his success in Hollywood, London *Observer* 18 Aug 68

MARILYN MONROE

5 The body is meant to be seen, not all covered up.

> Handwritten response to query about posing nude, which sold for $2,600 at auction in Boston, quoted in *International Herald Tribune* 5 Oct 84

6 Say good-bye to Pat, say good-bye to Jack and say good-bye to yourself, because you're a nice guy.

> Last words in 1962 to actor Peter Lawford, his wife Patricia and Patricia's brother President John F Kennedy, disclosed in the official report of Monroe's suicide released on September 23, 1985, quoted in *US News & World Report* 7 Oct 85

PAUL NEWMAN

7 I picture my epitaph: "Here lies Paul Newman, who died a failure because his eyes turned brown."

> Quoted by Maureen Dowd "Testing Himself" NY *Times* 28 Sep 86

RONALD REAGAN

8 Someplace along the line the audience discovered you. In my case it was playing the Gipper.

> On his role as Notre Dame football hero George Gipp in the 1940 film *Knute Rockne—All American, ib*

9 No one goes Hollywood—they were that way before they came here. Hollywood just exposed it.

> *People* 9 Feb 87

ROBERT REDFORD

10 I would go into life for a year. Go on the bum, so to speak.

> Advising Dartmouth film students to skip graduate school, Boston *Globe* 8 Feb 87

BURT REYNOLDS

11 You can only hold your stomach in for so many years.

> On retiring briefly from films, *Time* 9 Jan 78

MICKEY ROONEY

12 I was a 14-year-old boy for 30 years.

> On his film roles, quoted in NY *Journal-American* 15 Apr 58

13 It's confusing. I've had so many wives and so many children I don't know which house to go to first on Christmas.

> On his frequent marriages, quoted in NY *Post* 13 Nov 60

GEORGE SANDERS

14 I am leaving because I am bored.

> Suicide note 25 Apr 72

ELIZABETH TAYLOR

15 I have a woman's body and a child's emotions.

> On her short-lived marriage at age 19 to Nicky Hilton, *Time* 4 Jan 51

16 Success is a great deodorant. It takes away all your past smells.

> ABC TV 6 Apr 77

17 The Frank Sinatra of Shakespeare.

> On Richard Burton, NY *Times* 6 Aug 84

SHIRLEY TEMPLE

18 When I was 14, I was the oldest I ever was. . . . I've been getting younger ever since.

> *Parade* 7 Dec 86

SPENCER TRACY

19 Know your lines and don't bump into the furniture.

> Favorite advice to young actors, recalled on his death 10 Jun 67

20 Not much meat on her, but what's there is cherce.

> Description of Katharine Hepburn, quoted by *People* 17 Mar 86

ORSON WELLES

1 The word *genius* was whispered into my ear, the first thing I ever heard, while I was still mewling in my crib. So it never occurred to me that I wasn't until middle age.
> Talking to biographer Barbara Leaming, quoted in *Wall Street Journal* 20 Sep 85

OSKAR WERNER

2 I'm married to the theater but my mistress is the films.
> *Vogue* 1 Sep 65

SHELLEY WINTERS

3 He had a quality of sexual lightning.
> On Montgomery Clift, NBC TV 19 Jun 80

Writers, Producers & Directors

MICHELANGELO ANTONIONI

4 Hollywood is like being nowhere and talking to nobody about nothing.
> London *Sunday Times* 20 Jun 71

INGMAR BERGMAN

5 I write scripts to serve as skeletons awaiting the flesh and sinew of images.
> NY *Times* 22 Jan 78

RITA MAE BROWN

6 You sell a screenplay like you sell a car. If someone drives it off a cliff, that's it.
> *Newsweek* 19 Aug 85

LEON CLORE

7 If Americans didn't speak English, we'd have no problem.
> On marketing British films in the US, NY *Times* 13 Jul 80

JEAN COCTEAU

8 A film is a petrified fountain of thought.
> Quoted in *Esquire* Feb 61

CECIL B DE MILLE

9 Creation is a drug I can't do without.
> NY *Times* 12 Aug 56

BARRY DILLER, Chairman, 20th Century-Fox

10 This is a world in which reasons are made up because reality is too painful.
> On the film industry, *Time* 3 Feb 86

WALT DISNEY

11 There's nothing funnier than the human animal.
> On changing from films with animals to films with people, news summaries 5 Dec 54

FEDERICO FELLINI

12 Even if I set out to make a film about a fillet of sole, it would be about me.
> On autobiographical nature of his films, *Atlantic* Dec 65

13 All art is autobiographical; the pearl is the oyster's autobiography.
> *ib*

14 Cinema is an old whore, like circus and variety, who knows how to give many kinds of pleasure. Besides, you can't teach old fleas new dogs.
> *ib*

SAMUEL GOLDWYN

15 A wide screen just makes a bad film twice as bad.
> *Quote* 9 Sep 56

16 The reason so many people turned up at his funeral is that they wanted to make sure he was dead.
> On producer Louis B Mayer, recalled on Goldwyn's death 31 Jan 74

17 Where they got lesbians, we'll use Albanians.
> When an associate questioned the taste of filming Radclyffe Hall's 1928 book *The Well of Loneliness, ib*

18 Too caustic? To hell with the costs, we'll make the picture anyway.
> *ib*

BEN HECHT

19 The honors Hollywood has for the writer are as dubious as tissue-paper cuff links.
> *Charlie* Harper 57

20 People's sex habits are as well known in Hollywood as their political opinions, and much less criticized.
> NY *Mirror* 24 Apr 59

ALFRED HITCHCOCK

21 I am a typed director. If I made *Cinderella*, the audience would immediately be looking for a body in the coach.
> *Newsweek* 11 Jun 56

22 Give them pleasure—the same pleasure they have when they wake up from a nightmare.
> On audiences, Asbury Park NJ *Press* 13 Aug 74

JOHN HUSTON

1 The directing of a picture involves coming out of your individual loneliness and taking a controlling part in putting together a small world. A picture is made. You put a frame around it and move on. And one day you die. That is all there is to it.
NY *Journal-American* 31 Mar 60

HERMAN J MANKIEWICZ

2 There, but for the grace of God, goes God.
On Orson Welles, NY *Times* 11 Oct 85

JOSEPH L MANKIEWICZ

3 I've been in on the beginning, the rise, peak, collapse and end of the talking picture.
Washington *Post* 1 Jun 86

VINCENTE MINNELLI

4 I work to please myself. I'm still not sure if movies are an art form. And if they're not, then let them inscribe on my tombstone what they could about any craftsman who loves his job: "Here lies Vincente Minnelli. He died of hard work."
Recalled on his death 25 Jul 86

DOROTHY PARKER

5 Hollywood money isn't money. It's congealed snow.
On writing film scripts, *Paris Review* Summer 56

SAM PECKINPAH

6 I'm a student of violence because I'm a student of the human heart.
Defending the violence in his films, *Newsweek* 7 Jan 85

S J PERELMAN

7 A dreary industrial town controlled by hoodlums of enormous wealth, the ethical sense of a pack of jackals and taste so degraded that it befouled everything it touched.
On Hollywood, *Paris Review* Spring 64

8 There were times, when I drove along the Sunset Strip and looked at those buildings or when I watched the fashionable film colony arriving at some première . . . that I fully expected God in his wrath to obliterate the whole shebang.
ib

ROMAN POLANSKI

9 It's easy to direct while acting—there's one less person to argue with.
NY *Times* 22 Feb 76

STEVEN SPIELBERG

10 I dream for a living.
Time 15 Jul 85

FRANÇOIS TRUFFAUT

11 An actor is never so great as when he reminds you of an animal—falling like a cat, lying like a dog, moving like a fox.
New Yorker 20 Feb 60

JACK VALENTI, President, Motion Picture Association of America

12 I don't know any other business that tells you not to go in and buy their product.
On the rating of films, NY *Times* 5 May 85

JACK WARNER

13 I have a theory of relatives, too. Don't hire 'em.
During a 1930s studio visit by Albert Einstein, quoted by Stephen Farber and Marc Green *Hollywood Dynasties* Delilah Books 84

BILLY WILDER

14 Hollywood didn't kill Marilyn Monroe, it's the Marilyn Monroes who are killing Hollywood.
Quoted in Nat Shapiro ed *Whatever It Is, I'm Against It* Simon & Schuster 84

FRANCO ZEFFIRELLI

15 I am a sultan in a harem of three women: Opera, Theater and Film!
Zeffirelli: An Autobiography Weidenfeld & Nicolson 86

Observers & Critics

CECELIA AGER

16 Miss Hepburn's voice was lilting along as before: She is oblivious of her impact. Or inured to it. Or stuck with it.
On Katharine Hepburn, NY *Times* 18 Jun 67

SCOTT ARMSTRONG

17 The home of furs and Ferraris, glitter and glamour, the place where movie stars can be spotted in palm-fringed cafés and where limousines are as frequent as *Rocky* sequels.
On idealized concept of Hollywood, *Christian Science Monitor* 19 May 86

CECIL BEATON

18 I can't afford a whole new set of enemies.
When asked why he didn't go into films, quoted by Hugo Vickers *Cecil Beaton* Little, Brown 85

PAUL V BECKLEY

1 *The Entertainer* . . . has set itself to scratching the dandruff out of the mane of life.
NY *Herald Tribune* 4 Oct 60

ROBERT BRUSTEIN

2 Olivier's idea of introspection was to hood his eyes, dentalize his consonants and let the camera circle his blondined head like a sparrow looking for a place to deposit its droppings.
On Laurence Olivier as Hamlet in a 1948 film, *New Republic* 3 Nov 86

VINCENT CANBY

3 Through the magic of motion pictures, someone who's never left Peoria knows the softness of a Paris spring, the color of a Nile sunset, the sorts of vegetation one will find along the upper Amazon and that Big Ben has not yet gone digital.
"A Reminder of Innocence Lost" *ib* 18 May 80

4 [His acting] remains forever fixed in a time that never dates.
On Cary Grant, *ib* 1 Dec 86

5 [It is] guaranteed to put all teeth on edge, including George Washington's, wherever they might be.
On film production of Helene Hanff's *84 Charing Cross Road*, *ib* 13 Feb 87

CHARLES CHAMPLIN

6 The wrong man at the studio saw the test and hired him. The right man had rejected him, but was fired before it made any difference.
On Robert Preston's debut in films, Boston *Globe* 23 Mar 87

JEAN COCTEAU

7 He has the manner of a giant with the look of a child, a lazy activeness, a mad wisdom, a solitude encompassing the world.
On Orson Welles, quoted in NY *Times* 11 Oct 85

ALISTAIR COOKE

8 Hollywood grew to be the most flourishing factory of popular mythology since the Greeks.
America Knopf 73

RICHARD CORLISS

9 Hollywood was born schizophrenic. For 75 years it has been both a town and a state of mind, an industry and an art form.
"Backing into the Future" *Time* 3 Feb 86

10 Today . . . is a time of turbulence and stagnation, of threat and promise from a competitor: the magic, omnivorous videocassette recorder (VCR). In other words, it is business as usual.
ib

ALICE DEMORÉE

11 Mediocrity shuffles after banality in an unending process.
On the French cinema, BBC Radio 20 Aug 68

DAVID DENBY

12 The action comes at us through a buzz of nattering remarks.
On the film *Heartburn*, *New York* 4 Aug 86

DAVID ELLIOTT

13 It's time to put out an All Points Bulletin on Sylvester Stallone. Not for artistic crimes . . . but for so grossly abusing his license to pander.
On *Over the Top*, San Diego *Union* 17 Feb 87

DIANA GEDDES

14 With her unmistakable pout and jutting breasts . . . Brigitte Bardot was more than just a goddess. For a war-weary generation she came to personify a new, liberated, sunsoaked, carefree France.
"Bardot at 50" London *Times* 28 Sep 84

WOLCOTT GIBBS

15 It is my indignant opinion that 90 percent of the moving pictures exhibited in America are so vulgar, witless and dull that it is preposterous to write about them in any publication not intended to be read while chewing gum.
Quoted by John Robert Colombo *Popcorn in Paradise* Holt, Rinehart & Winston 80

SHEILAH GRAHAM

16 No one has a closest friend in Hollywood.
The Rest of the Story Coward-McCann 64

CHARLIE HAAS

17 From the German verb *tinzelle*—literally, "to book a turkey into 1,200 theaters and make one's money before word of mouth hits."
On Hollywood's nickname Tinseltown, *People* 9 Feb 87

LEARNED HAND

18 A self-made man may prefer a self-made name.
Granting court permission for Samuel Goldfish

to change his name to Samuel Goldwyn, quoted by Bosley Crowther *The Lion's Share* Dutton 57

C DAVID HEYMANN

1 In the 1930s . . . people went [to see films] not just to be entertained or to escape the dreariness of their workaday lives but to gain an education, to see the world, to learn table manners and interior decoration, how to dress, kiss, to laugh and cry, how to react to tragedy and happiness, how to be brave, evil and good.
Poor Little Rich Girl Lyle Stuart 84

2 Hollywood was a silver-nitrate finishing school for a whole generation . . . with a faculty that included Lillian Gish, Douglas Fairbanks, Mary Pickford, John Gilbert, Pola Negri, Gloria Swanson, Clara Bow, Lon Chaney, Charlie Chaplin and Rudolf Valentino.
ib

CLIVE JAMES

3 As far as talent goes, Marilyn Monroe was so minimally gifted as to be almost unemployable, and anyone who holds to the opinion that she was a great natural comic identifies himself immediately as a dunce.
Commentary Oct 73

4 She was good at playing abstract confusion in the same way that a midget is good at being short.
On Marilyn Monroe, PBS TV 18 Jan 79

PAULINE KAEL

5 *Citizen Kane* is perhaps the one American talking picture that seems as fresh now as the day it opened. It may seem even fresher.
"Raising Kane" in *The Citizen Kane Book* Bantam 71

6 This movie is a toupee made up to look like honest baldness.
On *Nothing in Common, New Yorker* 8 Sep 86

FLETCHER KNEBEL

7 Hollywood, to hear some writers tell it, is the place where they take an author's steak tartare and make cheeseburger out of it. . . . Upon seeing the film, they say, the author promptly cuts his throat, bleeding to death in a pool of money.
On how *Seven Days in May*, a novel he coauthored, was made into a motion picture, *Look* 19 Nov 63

JACK KROLL

8 Wrap up the 20th century; Fred Astaire is gone.
On death of Fred Astaire, *Newsweek* 6 Jul 87

RICHARD LACAYO

9 He was the embodiment of big-city scrappiness, a mean-streets survivor who got ahead on a good grin, good moves and better hustle.
On James Cagney, *Time* 14 Apr 86

OSCAR LEVANT

10 Strip away the phony tinsel of Hollywood and you'll find the real tinsel underneath.
Quoted in Nat Shapiro ed *Whatever It Is, I'm Against It* Simon & Schuster 84

MELVIN MADDOCKS

11 Cary Grant, born Archie Leach, was a poor boy who could barely spell *posh*. That's acting for you—or maybe Hollywood.
Christian Science Monitor 3 Dec 86

WILLIAM MANCHESTER

12 Actors who have tried to play Churchill and MacArthur have failed abysmally because each of those men was a great actor playing himself.
Book-of-the-Month Club News Jun 83

MARGRETHE II, Queen of Denmark

13 [He is] the Pied Piper to the children of the world.
On knighting Danny Kaye in 1983, recalled on his death, *US News & World Report* 16 Mar 87

EDWARD MARSH

14 How I dislike "Technicolor," which suffuses everything with stale mustard.
Ambrosia and Small Beer Harcourt, Brace & Winston 65

NEW YORKER

15 Newman delivered his lines with the emotional fervor of a [railroad] conductor announcing local stops.
1954 review of Paul Newman's first film role as a Roman slave in *The Silver Chalice*, recalled by Newman in NY *Times* 28 Sep 86

NEW YORK TIMES

16 Cary Grant was not supposed to die. [He] was supposed to stick around, our perpetual touchstone of charm and elegance and romance and youth.
Editorial 2 Dec 86

FREDERIC RAPHAEL

1 Hollywood was not a geographic location; it was a Fate Worse Than The *Reader's Digest*.

On how young writers felt about writing screenplays, "A Writer Stalks the Hollywood Myth" NY *Times* 6 Jan 85

2 We all knew that unspeakable things happened to talent once it had crossed the Rockies. ... The Warner Brothers' commissary, and similar places where they eat writers along with the caesar salad.

ib

HARRY REASONER

3 Bond smoked like Peter Lorre, drank like Humphrey Bogart, ate like Sydney Greenstreet, used up girls like Errol Flynn ... then went to a steam bath and came out looking like Clark Gable.

On Ian Fleming's character James Bond in numerous films, NY *Journal-American* 13 Aug 64

REX REED

4 It's hate at first sight.

On Goldie Hawn's role as a football coach in *Wildcats*, Palm Beach *Daily News* 6 Apr 86

5 I don't think she ever remembered giving me the interview, but she sure remembered reading it.

On May 1967 *Esquire* profile of Ava Gardner, quoted in *US* 19 May 86

RICHARD SCHICKEL

6 A great novel is concerned primarily with the interior lives of its characters as they respond to the inconvenient narratives that fate imposes on them. Movie adaptations of these monumental fictions often fail because they become mere exercises in interior decoration.

"The Adaptation as Antique Show" *Time* 15 Oct 84

7 This is a soul under perpetual migraine attack.

On Vanessa Redgrave as Olive in *The Bostonians, ib*

GENE SHALIT

8 Some films could only have been cast in one way: Screen tests were given and the losers got the parts.

NBC TV 18 May 71

CLANCY SIGAL

9 Too many freeways, too much sun, too much abnormality taken normally, too many pink stucco houses and pink stucco consciences.

On Hollywood, *Going Away* Houghton Mifflin 62

JOHN SIMON

10 Miss Garland's figure resembles the giant-economy-size tube of toothpaste in girls' bathrooms: Squeezed intemperately at all points, it acquires a shape that defies definition by the most resourceful solid geometrician.

On Judy Garland, *ib*

IGOR STRAVINSKY

11 Film music should have the same relationship to the film drama that somebody's piano playing in my living room has on the book I am reading.

Recalled on his death 6 Apr 71

TIME MAGAZINE

12 A British comedienne whose appearance suggests an overstuffed electric chair.

On Margaret Rutherford in *Murder, She Says*, 2 Feb 62

13 Her writhing stare could reduce a rabid dog to foaming jelly.

On Margaret Rutherford in *Mrs John Bull, Ltd*, 24 May 63

KENNETH TYNAN

14 What, when drunk, one sees in other women, one sees in Garbo sober.

Recalled on his death 26 Jul 80

15 The vengeful hag is played by Ingrid Bergman, which is like casting Eleanor Roosevelt as Lizzie Borden.

On *The Visit, ib*

16 Pearl is a disease of oysters. Levant is a disease of Hollywood.

On Oscar Levant, quoted in news summaries 31 Dec 84

FOOD & DRINK

Chefs & Restaurateurs

JAMES BEARD

17 I believe that if ever I had to practice cannibalism, I might manage if there were enough tarragon around.

Recalled on his death 23 Jan 85

18 I don't like gourmet cooking or "this" cooking or "that" cooking. I like *good* cooking.

Quoted in *Newsweek* 4 Feb 85

VICTOR J ("TRADER VIC") BERGERON

19 The real, native South Seas food is lousy. You can't eat it.

Newsweek 21 Apr 58

LYNNE BIEN, co-owner, Pie in the Sky restaurant, NYC

1 People are getting tired of going out to expensive restaurants and spending lots of money for seven pea pods and a two-inch steak.
NY *Times* 3 Oct 84

2 Oh, that curdles my soul.
On adding mace and nutmeg to a recipe for apple pie, *ib* 24 Sep 86

ALICE MAY BROCK

3 Tomatoes and oregano make it Italian; wine and tarragon make it French. Sour cream makes it Russian; lemon and cinnamon make it Greek. Soy sauce makes it Chinese; garlic makes it good.
Alice's Restaurant Cookbook Random House 69

GIULIANO BUGIALLI

4 There are only two questions to ask about food. Is it good? And is it authentic? We are open [to] new ideas, but not if it means destroying our history. And food is history.
NY *Times* 9 May 84

ROBERT FARRAR CAPON, priest-chef

5 Give us this day our daily taste. Restore to us soups that spoons will not sink in and sauces which are never the same twice. Raise up among us stews with more gravy than we have bread to blot it with ... Give us pasta with a hundred fillings.
People 13 Oct 75

6 At the root of many a woman's failure to become a great cook lies her failure to develop a workmanlike regard for knives.
News summaries 31 Dec 76

JULIA CHILD

7 Nobody thinks it's silly to invest two hours' work in two minutes' enjoyment; but if cooking is evanescent, well, so is the ballet.
NBC TV 1 Dec 66

8 In department stores, so much kitchen equipment is bought indiscriminately by people who just come in for men's underwear.
ib 12 Dec 73

9 Life itself is the proper binge.
Time 7 Jan 80

10 I was 32 when I started cooking; up until then, I just ate.
Quoted by Lynn Gilbert and Gaylen Moore *Particular Passions* Crown 81

11 In France, cooking is a serious art form and a national sport.
NY *Times* 26 Nov 86

ALEXANDRE DUMAINE

12 The French peasant cuisine is at the basis of the culinary art. By this I mean it is composed of honest elements that *la grande cuisine* only embellishes.
Recalled on his death 23 Apr 74

PHILIPPE GAERTNER, chef, Aux Armes de France restaurant, Ammerschwihr, France

13 I'm taking only my toque blanche and my savoir-faire.
Comment on his departure for NYC as one of the 22 French chefs chosen to cook during Statue of Liberty's centennial celebration, NY *Times* 14 May 86

OSCAR GIZELT, food and beverage manager, Delmonico's restaurant, NYC

14 Fish should smell like the tide. Once they smell like fish, it's too late.
Vogue 15 Apr 64

OTTO GOEBEL, chef to Saudi Arabian royal family

15 We had too much camel in the fridge, so I tried some ways to preserve it.
To Le Club des Chefs des Chefs, NY *Times* 29 Aug 86

STANLEY KRAMER, chef, Grand Central Terminal's Oyster Bar restaurant, NYC

16 George knows everything about every fish that comes in here—where they came from, what they were doing before they were caught, who their mothers and fathers were.
On assistant manager George Morfogen, in charge of purchasing $24,000 worth of fresh seafood a week, *Manhattan Inc* Sep 84

WARNER LEROY, founder, Maxwell's Plum restaurant, NYC

17 A restaurant is a fantasy—a kind of living fantasy in which diners are the most important members of the cast.
NY *Times* 9 Jul 76

ERNEST MATTHEW MICKLER

18 Simmer til you can't stand it any more, then take it off the fire and dive in.
White Trash Cooking Jargon Society 86, quoted by Edwin McDowell NY *Times* 22 Sep 86

JEFF SMITH, minister-chef

1 Please understand the reason why Chinese vegetables taste so good. It is simple. The Chinese do not cook them, they just threaten them!

The Frugal Gourmet Cooks with Wine Morrow 86

2 I prefer the Chinese method of eating. . . . You can do anything at the table except arm wrestle.

Boston *Globe* 11 Jan 87

3 I don't go for the nouvelle approach—serving a rabbit rump with coffee extract sauce and a slice of kiwi fruit.

ib

4 The way I feel about it is: Beat me or feed me, but don't tease me. It's toy food; who needs it? Serve it to toy people.

ib

RENÉ VEAUX, chef, Lasserre restaurant, Paris

5 One person cooking at home cannot pay attention to too many things. If a woman makes three dishes, she will get nervous on the first, the second will suffer and the third will be a disaster.

Quoted by Michael Demarest "Tips from the Toques" *Time* 19 Dec 77

6 A few years ago it was considered chic to serve Beef Wellington; fortunately, like Napoleon, it met its Waterloo.

On fads in cooking, *ib*

7 The feminist movement has helped open minds and kitchens to the notion that men can be at home on the range.

ib

DONALD BRUCE WHITE

8 Catering is the cottage industry of New York. All a caterer needs is a Cuisinart, some pots and pans and a couple of food magazines to start out. They get jobs, though they don't necessarily get repeats.

NY *Times* 28 Nov 84

Manufacturers, Merchants & Promoters

GEORGES AUER

9 Suppose we had tried selective breeding of frogs and found we were developing the head instead of the legs? But a snail is just a walking intestine.

On why he and his partners chose to go into the snail-farming business, *Fortune* 7 Apr 80

BRUCE R BYE, Director of Brand Management, Durkee Famous Foods

10 You can tell how long a couple has been married by whether they are on their first, second or third bottle of Tabasco.

On average shelf life of a hot sauce measured out in dashes and drops, NY *Times* 29 Jun 86

TERRENCE CONWAY, President, John T Handy Co

11 The best thing is not to do anything interesting.

Suggesting sautéing soft-shell crabs in clarified butter, *Christian Science Monitor* 8 May 85

BILL DEMMOND, Vice President, Inland Seafood Corp

12 If it swims, it's edible.

Time 18 Feb 85

E THOMAS HUGHES, founder, Potato Museum, Washington DC

13 We're serious but not solemn about potatoes here. The potato has lots of eyes, but no mouth. That's where I come in.

Christian Science Monitor 7 Jul 86

PETER MORRELL, vintner

14 I edit out the bad stuff and deliver the good stuff. Seventy-five percent of all wine is awful.

Quoted in "Wine Wars" *Manhattan Inc* Jul 85

PHILIPPE DE ROTHSCHILD

15 Excellent wine generates enthusiasm. And whatever you do with enthusiasm is generally successful.

W 9 May 80

WILLIAM SOKOLIN, vintner

16 What is the definition of a good wine? It should start and end with a smile.

Advertisement in NY *Times* 15 Dec 84

M TAITTINGER, French champagne vintner

17 You put your left index finger on your eye and your right index finger on the cheese . . . if they sort of feel the same, the cheese is ready.

On how to test the ripeness of a Camembert cheese, *This Week* 10 Jul 66

ALAIN DE VOGUE, French vintner

18 Can you imagine opening a bottle of champagne with a bottle opener. I can't. It would eliminate half the fun.

On movement to substitute bottle caps for corks, *National Observer* 1 Jul 63

JOSHUA WESSON, wine consultant

1 I didn't know which way I was going to die—run through, conked or poisoned.
> On approach of a man with a sword, a gnarled stick and a silver goblet during ceremony in which he became a knight in the prestigious wine society La Commanderies des Côtes du Rhône, NY *Times* 1 Feb 87

Observers & Critics

JONATHAN AITKEN

2 If you find an Australian indoors, it's a fair bet that he will have a glass in his hand.
> *Land of Fortune* Secker & Warburg 71

KINGSLEY AMIS

3 I sometimes feel that more lousy dishes are presented under the banner of pâté than any other.
> *London Illustrated News* May 86

4 I want a dish to taste good, rather than to have been seethed in pig's milk and served wrapped in a rhubarb leaf with grated thistle root.
> *ib*

SUSAN HELLER ANDERSON and DAVID W DUNLAP

5 There is nothing as American as a French chef from the Bronx.
> NY *Times* 14 Jan 85

ANONYMOUS

6 Protect your bagels, put lox on them.
> Sign at Bagel Connection, New Haven CT, quoted by Ron Alexander *ib* 5 Feb 86

7 Waitresses who are tipped don't spill.
> Sign in diner, quoted by Melvin Maddocks "Early Risers Get Their Reward" *Christian Science Monitor* 15 Aug 86

8 This has got to be the most expensive food ever laminated.
> On lunch or dinner for two from $80 to $100 at Manhattan's Casual Quilted Giraffe restaurant, quoted by Bryan Miller NY *Times* 15 Aug 86

BROOKS ATKINSON

9 The cocktail party . . . is a device either for getting rid of social obligations hurriedly en masse or for making overtures toward more serious social relationships, as in the etiquette of whoring.
> *Once around the Sun* Harcourt, Brace 51

W H AUDEN

10 Murder is commoner among cooks than among members of any other profession.
> *Forewords and Afterwords* Random House 73

JACQUES BAEYENS, French consul general in NYC

11 Soufflé is more important than you think. If men ate soufflé before meetings, life could be much different.
> NY *Journal-American* 7 May 58

RUSSELL BAKER

12 Goat cheese . . . produced a bizarre eating era when sensible people insisted that this miserable cheese produced by these miserable creatures reared on miserable hardscrabble earth was actually superior to the magnificent creamy cheeses of the noblest dairy animals bred in the richest green valleys of the earth.
> NY *Times* 27 Nov 85

MARY CATHERINE BATESON

13 Human beings do not eat nutrients, they eat food.
> *With a Daughter's Eye* Morrow 84

LUDWIG BEMELMANS

14 The true gourmet, like the true artist, is one of the unhappiest creatures existent. His trouble comes from so seldom finding what he constantly seeks: perfection.
> Recalled on his death 1 Oct 62

15 Caviar is to dining what a sable coat is to a girl in evening dress.
> *ib*

AMANDA BENNETT

16 Cantonese will eat anything in the sky but airplanes, anything in the sea but submarines and anything with four legs but the table.
> *Wall Street Journal* 4 Oct 83

WILLIAM SAMUEL BENWELL

17 The soft extractive note of an aged cork being withdrawn has the true sound of a man opening his heart.
> *Journey to Wine in Victoria* Melbourne 76

SUE BERKMAN

18 There has always been a food processor in the kitchen. But once upon a time she was usually called the missus, or Mom.
> "Everything but the Kitchen Sink" *Esquire* Sep 84

ALAN BRIEN

1 New York waiters, probably the surliest in the Western world ... are better images of their city than that journalistic favorite—the taxi driver.
Quoted in *Saturday Review* 5 Feb 66

2 The majority of them give the impression of being men who have been drafted into the job during a period of martial law and are only waiting for the end of the emergency to get back to a really congenial occupation such as slum demolition or debt collecting.
ib

D W BROGAN

3 Man does not live by bread alone, even presliced bread.
On decline of US baking industry, *Forbes* 1 Mar 64

MARIAN BURROS

4 Today's restaurant is theater on a grand scale.
"Celebrities Take on New Roles as Restaurateurs" *ib* 28 May 86

5 If Broadway shows charge preview prices while the cast is in dress rehearsal, why should restaurants charge full price when their dining room and kitchen staffs are still practicing?
"Practical Prices for Practice Food" *ib* 27 Sep 86

6 Someone is putting brandy in your bonbons, Grand Marnier in your breakfast jam, Kahlua in your ice cream, Scotch in your mustard and Wild Turkey in your cake.
"Alcohol, the Ultimate Additive" *ib* 20 Dec 86

7 Americans may be drinking fewer alcoholic beverages, but they are certainly eating more of them than ever before. Wittingly or un.
ib

RICHARD BURTON

8 If you drink it straight down, you can feel it going into each individual intestine.
On raicilla, 180-proof distillate of the maguey plant, *Time* 8 Nov 63

TRUMAN CAPOTE

9 I can see every monster as they come in.
On lunching at Manhattan's La Côte Basque restaurant, *New York* 29 Oct 84

DAVID CECIL

10 You must be careful about giving any drink whatsoever to a bore. A lit-up bore is the worst in the world.
Quote 17 Jan 65

CENTURY CLUB OF NEW YORK

11 Members who never sit idly at the Long Table or loiter fecklessly at the Bar are missing the best features the Club has to offer. . . . savoring the pleasures of the commercially worthless discourse that is there in such plentiful supply.
Announcement from the House Committee, *Century Customs: The Spirit and the Letter* 85

12 Finally, a rule that isn't. A member may introduce himself to his bar or table neighbors at lunch but ancient and perhaps inexorable custom seems to render such politesse extraneous. You can, but you need not.
ib

JEAN MICHEL CHAPEREAU

13 We were taken to a fast-food café where our order was fed into a computer. Our hamburger, made from the flesh of chemically impregnated cattle, had been broiled over counterfeit charcoal, placed between slices of artificially flavored cardboard and served to us by recycled juvenile delinquents.
Un Hiver Américain, quoted in news summaries 31 Dec 75

WINSTON CHURCHILL

14 My wife and I tried two or three times in the last 40 years to have breakfast together, but it was so disagreeable we had to stop.
Letter to an American friend, news summaries 4 Dec 50

15 I have taken more out of alcohol than alcohol has taken out of me.
Quoted in *By Quentin Reynolds* McGraw-Hill 63

CRAIG CLAIBORNE

16 Give me a platter of choice finnan haddie, freshly cooked in its bath of water and milk, add melted butter, a slice or two of hot toast, a pot of steaming Darjeeling tea, and you may tell the butler to dispense with the caviar, truffles and nightingales' tongues.
NY *Times* 31 Dec 77

ELEANOR CLARK

17 If you don't love life you can't enjoy an oyster; there is a shock of freshness to it and intimations of the ages of man, some piercing intuition of the sea and all its weeds and breezes. [They] shiver you for a split second.
The Oysters of Locmariaquer Pantheon 64

251

ALISON COOK

1 People are getting really baroque with their perversions.

On new popularity of fajitas, including some with meat marinated in Coca-Cola and Dr Pepper instead of lime juice, NY *Times* 4 Aug 84

ALISTAIR COOKE

2 Las Vegas is Everyman's cut-rate Babylon. Not far away there is, or was, a roadside lunch counter and over it a sign proclaiming in three words that a Roman emperor's orgy is now a democratic institution. ... "Topless Pizza Lunch."

America Knopf 73

JOHN CORRY

3 One of the glories of New York is its ethnic food, and only McDonald's and Burger King equalize us all.

NY *Times* 10 Mar 75

BARBARA COSTIKYAN

4 In the childhood memories of every good cook, there's a large kitchen, a warm stove, a simmering pot and a mom.

"Holiday Entertaining" *New York* 22 Oct 84

CAROL CUTLER

5 A pâté is nothing more than a French meat loaf that's had a couple of cocktails.

Pâté, The New Main Course for the 80s Rawson 83, quoted in *Time* 21 Nov 83

WILLIAM DENTON

6 Food is to eat, not to frame and hang on the wall.

On nouvelle cuisine, quoted by William E Geist NY *Times* 28 Mar 87

ELSIE DE WOLFE (Lady Mendl)

7 No, I don't take soup. You can't build a meal on a lake.

Quoted by Jane S Smith and Diana Vreeland *Elsie de Wolfe: A Life in the High Style* Atheneum 82

PHIL DONAHUE

8 Miss Child is never bashful with butter.

On Julia Child, NBC TV 18 Nov 85

JACK DOUGLAS

9 I personally prefer a nice frozen TV Dinner at home, mainly because it's so little trouble. All you have to do is have another drink while you're throwing it in the garbage.

Never Trust a Naked Bus Driver Dutton 60

ELEANOR EARLY

10 Alcohol removes inhibitions—like that scared little mouse who got drunk and shook his whiskers and shouted: "Now bring on that damn cat!"

News summaries 30 Jan 50

NORA EPHRON

11 Whenever I get married, I start buying *Gourmet* magazine.

News summaries 31 Dec 83

FLORENCE FABRICANT

12 Peanut butter [is] the pâté of childhood.

"An Enduring American Passion" NY *Times* 21 May 86

CLIFTON FADIMAN

13 Cheese—milk's leap toward immortality.

Any Number Can Play World 57

14 To take wine into our mouths is to savor a droplet of the river of human history.

Comment included in a collection of food and wine memorabilia displayed at Hallmark Gallery, NY *Times* 8 Mar 67

WILLIAM FERRIS, Director, University of Mississippi Center for the Study of Southern Culture

15 The Moon Pie is a bedrock of the country store and rural tradition. It is more than a snack. It is a cultural artifact.

NY *Times* 30 Apr 86

MALCOLM S FORBES

16 Their steaks are often good, but the lobsters—with claws the size of Arnold Schwarzenegger's forearms—are as glazed and tough as most of the customers.

On Manhattan's Palm restaurant, *Forbes* 28 Apr 80

17 The Palm is a joint for sadists to entertain masochists.

On crowded conditions at the restaurant, *ib*

GENE FOWLER

18 He has a profound respect for old age. Especially when it's bottled.

On W C Field's fondness for aged bourbon, quoted in *Parade* 7 Apr 68

BEATRICE AND IRA HENRY FREEMAN

1 The bagel [is] an unsweetened doughnut with rigor mortis.

"About Bagels" NY *Times* 22 May 60

ALICE FURLAND

2 If rich food can kill, people live dangerously here.

On Alsatian restaurants, NY *Times* 14 May 86

WILLIAM E GEIST

3 Grown men have been seen fleeing after reading the menu posted outside.

On the opening of Petrossian, a new "caviar restaurant," NY *Times* 17 Nov 84

4 They used to have a fish on the menu ... that was smoked, grilled *and* peppered ... They did everything to this fish but pistol-whip it and dress it in Bermuda shorts.

On Manhattan's One Fifth restaurant, *ib* 28 Mar 87

LEWIS GRIZZARD

5 The only way that I could figure they could improve upon Coca-Cola, one of life's most delightful elixirs, which studies prove will heal the sick and occasionally raise the dead, is to put rum or bourbon in it.

On Coca-Cola's announcement that it was changing its secret formula after 99 years, quoted in NY *Times* 26 Apr 85

ARTHUR E GROSSER, Professor of Chemistry, McGill University

6 When we decode a cookbook, every one of us is a practicing chemist. Cooking is really the oldest, most basic application of physical and chemical forces to natural materials.

NY *Times* 29 May 84

JOHN GUNTHER

7 All happiness depends on a leisurely breakfast.

Newsweek 14 Apr 59

JOAN GUSSOW, Assistant Professor of Nutrition and Education, Teachers College, Columbia University

8 As for butter versus margarine, I trust cows more than chemists.

NY *Times* 16 Apr 86

RICHARD GUTMAN

9 The diner is everybody's kitchen.

On renewed popularity of roadside diners, *Smithsonian* Nov 86

PHILLIP W HABERMAN JR

10 A gourmet is just a glutton with brains.

"How to Be a Calorie Chiseler" *Vogue* 15 Jan 61

DANIEL HALPERN

11 Light the candles and pour the red wine into your glass. Before you begin to eat, raise your glass in honor of yourself. The company is the best you'll ever have.

"How to Eat Alone" *Esquire* May 80

S I HAYAKAWA, US Senator

12 So I will say it with relish. Give me a hamburger but hold the lawsuit.

Address to the Senate on legal debate over which fast-food chain makes the biggest hamburger, NY *Times* 6 Oct 82

DUNCAN HINES

13 I've run more risk eating my way across the country than in all my driving.

Adventures in Good Eating 56

14 More people will die from hit-or-miss eating than from hit-and-run driving.

ib

15 We have to get away from the "bolt it and beat it" idea of eating.

ib

ALFRED HITCHCOCK

16 I'm frightened of eggs, worse than frightened, they revolt me. That white round thing without any holes ... have you ever seen anything more revolting than an egg yolk breaking and spilling its yellow liquid? Blood is jolly, red. But egg yolk is yellow, revolting. I've never tasted it.

News summaries 31 Dec 63

STANLEY HUNT, nutritionist, Greater London Council

17 You're going out on a dangerous limb, making healthy sausages.

On introduction of leaner sausages, *Wall Street Journal* 12 Feb 85

NANCY HARMON JENKINS

18 Italian wine was something rough and red that came in a straw-covered flask ... with a candle stuck in its neck, [the empty bottle] was an unmistakable badge of sophomore sophistication.

On Italian wine in the 1960s, NY *Times* 6 Aug 86

POPE JOHN XXIII

1 When I eat alone I feel like a seminarian being punished. . . . I tried it for one week and I was not comfortable. Then I searched through Sacred Scripture for something saying I had to eat alone. I found nothing, so I gave it up and it's much better now.

> On breaking the papal precedent of dining alone, recalled on his death 3 Jun 63

HUGH JOHNSON

2 [They] face each other across the road . . . like mad old duchesses in party clothes.

> On vineyards of southwestern France, NY *Times* 2 Mar 86

MARILYN KAYTOR

3 Condiments are like old friends—highly thought of, but often taken for granted.

> "Condiments: The Tastemakers" *Look* 29 Jan 63

HANK KETCHAM

4 No more turkey, but I'd like some more of the bread it ate.

> Lines for his cartoon *Dennis the Menace,* quoted by Marian Burros "At Thanksgiving, Trimmings Steal the Limelight" NY *Times* 20 Nov 85

ALAN KING

5 As life's pleasures go, food is second only to sex. Except for salami and eggs. Now that's better than sex, but only if the salami is thickly sliced.

> Quoted by Mimi Sheraton NY *Times* 28 Oct 81

EDWARD KOCH, Mayor of NYC

6 If they don't want to pay for it, they can stop drinking it.

> On charging diplomatic missions for using city water, NY *Times* 21 Jan 80

7 The best way to lose weight is to close your mouth—something very difficult for a politician. Or watch your food—just watch it, don't eat it.

> *People* 10 May 82

JEANINE LARMOTH

8 Marmalade in the morning has the same effect on taste buds that a cold shower has on the body.

> *Town & Country* Feb 86

JOE E LEWIS

9 Whenever someone asks me if I want water with my Scotch, I say I'm thirsty, not dirty.

> Quoted by Alan King and Mimi Sheraton *Is Salami and Eggs Better than Sex?* Little, Brown 85

A J LIEBLING

10 An Englishman teaching an American about food is like the blind leading the one-eyed.

> Quoted by Alistair Cooke *Masterpiece Theater* PBS TV 20 Oct 74

PATRICIA LINDEN

11 Popcorn [is] the sentimental good-time Charlie of American foods.

> "Popcorn!" *Town & Country* May 84

12 It's the national addiction: warmth on chilly winter nights, innocence on Saturday afternoons, the essence of hearth, home and blissful abandon.

> *ib*

EDMUND G LOVE

13 When I was a small boy, my father told me never to recommend a church or a woman to anyone. And I have found it wise never to recommend a restaurant either. Something always goes wrong with the cheese soufflé.

> On eating his way through 5,000 NYC restaurants in alphabetical order, *Saturday Evening Post* 23 May 64

SOMERSET MAUGHAM

14 To eat well in England, you should have a breakfast three times a day.

> Recalled on his death 16 Dec 65

ELSA MAXWELL

15 Serve the dinner backward, do anything—but for goodness sake, do something weird.

> On entertaining, quoted in NY *Herald Tribune* 2 Nov 63

DAVID MICHAELIS

16 Under barrel-vaulted ceilings and among the vibrations of trains, in a spot 12.6 miles from the Atlantic Ocean, 28 feet above sea level and 22 feet below 42nd Street, at the epicenter of a metropolis that annually devours $1.5 billion worth of seafood, the most in the nation—stands Grand Central Terminal's celebrated seafood restaurant, the Oyster Bar.

> "Ode to the Oyster Bar" *Manhattan Inc* Sep 84

17 New York's Fulton Street is the Vatican City of fish markets.

> *ib*

BRYAN MILLER

18 The qualities of an exceptional cook are akin

to those of a successful tightrope walker: an abiding passion for the task, courage to go out on a limb and an impeccable sense of balance.
"What Makes a Great Cook Great?" NY *Times* 23 Feb 83

1 The moist, flavorful meat is concealed under a thick slab of crisp fat that would make a cardiologist blanch.
On Pig Heaven, a Manhattan restaurant specializing in pork dishes, *ib* 28 Sep 84

2 I know a viscous butter sauce when I eat one, and that was one indeed!
Responding to protests by Charles Masson, owner of Manhattan's La Grenouille, after an unfavorable review of the restaurant, *ib* 25 Mar 85

3 At lunchtime the place is jumping, while at night ... the dining rooms could have been rented out for chess tournaments.
On Manhattan's René Pujol restaurant, *ib* 26 Sep 86

4 Square meals, not adventurous ones, are what you should seek.
ib

FRANÇOIS MINOT, Editor, *Guide Michelin*

5 Anybody can make you enjoy the first bite of a dish, but only a real chef can make you enjoy the last.
Quoted in NY *Times* 19 Jul 64

ROBERT MORLEY

6 If people take the trouble to cook, you should take the trouble to eat.
On why he opposes dieting, WNYW TV 3 Nov 78

JACQUELINE KENNEDY ONASSIS

7 You are about to have your first experience with a Greek lunch. I will kill you if you pretend to like it.
On welcoming decorator Billy Baldwin to the island of Skorpios, quoted by Peter Evans *Ari* Summit 86

RICHARD OWEN

8 The relationship between a Russian and a bottle of vodka is almost mystical.
On Soviet efforts to decrease drinking, London *Times* 17 May 85

CLEMENTINE PADDLEFORD

9 Beer is the Danish national drink, and the Danish national weakness is another beer.
NY *Herald Tribune* 20 Jun 64

LOUIS PARRISH

10 If you can organize your kitchen, you can organize your life.
Cooking as Therapy Arbor House 75

PRINCE PHILIP, Duke of Edinburgh

11 I never see any home cooking. All I get is fancy stuff.
News summaries 5 Feb 55

ANTHONY POOLE

12 Dinner ... possessed only two dramatic features—the wine was a farce and the food a tragedy.
Interview 3 Mar 53

FRANK J PRIAL

13 Bordeaux calls to mind a distinguished figure in a frock coat. ... He enters his moderate enthusiasms in a leather pocketbook, observing the progress of beauty across his palate like moves in a game of chess.
"Days of Wine and Prose" NY *Times* 8 Jul 79

14 A peculiar subgenre of the English language ... has flowered wildly in recent years, like some pulpy jungle plant. It's called winespeak.
"Words, Words, Words" *ib* 1 Mar 87

JONATHAN PROBBER

15 The legume family is so talented, that if its members were humans, they would be the Leakeys, the Buckleys or perhaps the Osmonds.
"Nature's Bountiful Bean" NY *Times* 8 Oct 86

FREDERIC RAPHAEL

16 The food alone is adequate deterrent, unless you're very heavily into two-scoop tuna or best leather pastrami.
On Warner Brothers Studio commissary, "A Writer Stalks the Hollywood Myth" NY *Times* 5 Jan 85

TOM ROBBINS

17 McDonald's is a reductive kitchen for a classless culture that hasn't time to dally on its way to the next rainbow's end.
Esquire Dec 83

DONALD ROGERS

18 Few things are more revolting than the spectacle of a normally reasonable father and husband gowned in one of those hot, massive

255

aprons inscribed with disgustingly corny legends, presiding over a noisome brazier as he destroys huge hunks of good meat and fills the neighborhood with greasy, acrid smoke: a Boy Scout with five o'clock shadow.

"Cookout's Got to Go" NY *Herald Tribune* 21 Jul 61

ANDY ROONEY

1 The biggest seller is cookbooks and the second is diet books—how not to eat what you've just learned how to cook.

CBS TV 9 Aug 82

WILLIAM SAFIRE

2 In the lexicon of lip-smacking, an *epicure* is fastidious in his choice and enjoyment of food, just a soupçon more expert than a *gastronome;* a *gourmet* is a connoisseur of the exotic, taste buds attuned to the calibrations of deliciousness, who savors the masterly techniques of great chefs; a *gourmand* is a hearty bon vivant who enjoys food without truffles and flourishes; a *glutton* overindulges greedily, the word rooted in the Latin for "one who devours."

"The Post-Holiday Strip" NY *Times* 6 Jan 85

3 After eating, an *epicure* gives a thin smile of satisfaction; a *gastronome,* burping into his napkin, praises the food in a magazine; a *gourmet,* repressing his burp, criticizes the food in the same magazine; a *gourmand* belches happily and tells everybody where he ate; a *glutton* embraces the white porcelain altar, or, more plainly, he barfs.

ib

ELSA SCHIAPARELLI

4 A good cook is like a sorceress who dispenses happiness.

Shocking Life Dutton 54

FRANK SCHOONMAKER

5 The more specific the name, the better the wine.

Frank Schoonmaker's Encyclopedia of Wine Hastings House 65

DAVID SCHWARTZ

6 For two decades, the name of the author, Duncan Hines, was etched on the biting edge of the American appetite. ... the best known and most purposeful vagabond.

"He Made Gastronomes out of Motorists" *Smithsonian* Nov 84

LAWRENCE CARDINAL SHEHAN, Archbishop of Baltimore

7 I am ready to defend the right of the tasty crab, the luscious oyster, the noble rockfish and the incomparable terrapin to continue their part in the penitential practice of Friday.

Expressing his hope that Friday abstinence would remain a tradition even though it was rarely a hardship for Marylanders, NY *Times* 16 Jan 66

ISRAEL SHENKER

8 Savor sufficient to lure the wispiest ghost into corpulence.

On food at Scotland's Culzean Castle, NY *Times* 4 Jul 82

9 Another assault by massed calories.

ib

MIMI SHERATON

10 If it is true, as used to be said, that oversalting means the cook is in love, at least one cook at Le Cirque must be head over heels.

On a Manhattan restaurant, NY *Times* 26 Aug 77

11 Before long it will be the animals who do the dieting so that the ultimate consumer does not have to.

On leaner beef with less fat and fewer calories, *Time* 19 May 86

STRATFORD P SHERMAN

12 Brie with the rind sliced off is among the most essential tokens of yuppiedom.

Fortune 18 Mar 85

HERMANN SMITH-JOHANNSON, 103-year-old cross-country skier

13 The secret to a long life is to stay busy, get plenty of exercise and don't drink too much. Then again, don't drink too little.

NY *Times* 20 Mar 79

RAYMOND SOKOLOV

14 Manhattan is a narrow island off the coast of New Jersey devoted to the pursuit of lunch.

"Design for Lunching" *Wall Street Journal* 20 Jun 84

CONSTANTINE STACKELBERG

15 What do [I] eat an hors d'oeuvre for? Because I have a drink, and then I have to have blotting paper in my tummy.

Washington Post 3 Aug 86

JOHN STEINBECK

1 So in our pride we ordered for breakfast an omelet, toast and coffee and what has just arrived is a tomato salad with onions, a dish of pickles, a big slice of watermelon and two bottles of cream soda.
On traveling in the USSR, recalled on his death 20 Dec 68

JANE AND MICHAEL STERN

2 The slices are piled high on rye and each is beet red, lean except for a sultry halo of fat, edged with black pepper—profound pastrami, firm and muscular.
On the main dish at a Queens delicatessen, NY *Daily News* 10 Nov 85

3 If it swims and it's Jewish, the Town Sturgeon Shop has it.
ib

MARK STEVENS

4 They serve you your importance.
On dining at a celebrity restaurant, *Summer in the City* Random House 84, quoted in *Time* 21 May 84

VIRGIL THOMSON

5 I said to my friends that if I was going to starve, I might as well starve where the food is good.
On life in Paris as a young man, PBS TV 23 Nov 86

JAMES THURBER

6 It's a naive domestic Burgundy without any breeding, but I think you'll be amused by its presumption.
Cartoon caption from his 1943 collection *Men, Women and Dogs,* recalled on his death 2 Nov 61

TIME MAGAZINE

7 The kind of crunchy novelty snack that children and their dentists dream about.
On introduction of the Choco Taco in Philadelphia, 29 Apr 85

ALICE B TOKLAS

8 What is sauce for the goose may be sauce for the gander but is not necessarily sauce for the chicken, the duck, the turkey or the guinea hen.
The Alice B Toklas Cookbook Harper & Row 54

9 The carp was dead, killed, assassinated, murdered in the first, second and third degree. Limp, I fell into a chair, with my hands still unwashed reached for a cigarette, lighted it and waited for the police to come and take me into custody.
Recalled on her death 7 Mar 67

ABIGAIL TRILLIN, age four

10 My tongue is smiling.
On finishing a dish of chocolate ice cream, quoted by her father Calvin Trillin *Alice, Let's Eat* Random House 78

CALVIN TRILLIN

11 I never eat in a restaurant that's over a hundred feet off the ground and won't stand still.
Interview 29 Dec 79

12 Even today, well-brought-up English girls are taught by their mothers to boil all veggies for at least a month and a half, just in case one of the dinner guests turns up without his teeth.
Third Helpings Houghton Mifflin 83

13 Given the clientele, the restaurants on Capri might resemble those fancy Northern Italian places on the East Side of Manhattan where the captain has taken bilingual sneering lessons from the maitre d' at the French joint down the street and the waiter, whose father was born in Palermo, would deny under torture that tomato sauce has ever touched his lips.
ib

14 When it comes to Chinese food I have always operated under the policy that the less known about the preparation the better. ... A wise diner who is invited to visit the kitchen replies by saying, as politely as possible, that he has a pressing engagement elsewhere.
ib

KENNETH TURAN

15 A book does not make bad jokes, drink too much or eat more than you can afford to pay for.
On reading a book while dining out, NY *Times* 13 Apr 83

LAWRENCE VAN GELDER

16 The mere fact of an undiscovered restaurant, in a city where gourmands travel in ravening packs, creates an excitement unrelated to the quality of the cuisine.
NY *Times* 25 Apr 79

HARRIET VAN HORNE

1 Cooking is like love. It should be entered into with abandon or not at all.
   Vogue 15 Oct 56

DIANA VREELAND

2 Poor, darling fellow—he *died* of food. He was killed by the dinner table.
   On Christian Dior, *Country Life* 15 May 86

W MAGAZINE

3 Dining at Chatfield's is like kissing your kid sister—it's just not worth the effort.
   On a Manhattan bistro, 10 Apr 81

ALICE WALKER

4 Tea to the English is really a picnic indoors.
   The Color Purple Simon & Schuster 82

NINA E WARREN

5 I let Earl go with me to a delicatessen just once. We never could afford it again.
   On shopping with her husband Chief Justice Earl Warren, recalled on his death 9 Jul 74

ALEC WAUGH

6 I am prepared to believe that a dry martini slightly impairs the palate, but think what it does for the soul.
   In Praise of Wine and Certain Noble Spirits Sloane 59

RICHARD WEST

7 It's a place people would go to even if the cook had just died of smallpox in the kitchen.
   On Manhattan's "21" Club, "The Power of 21" *New York* 5 Oct 82

HILMA WOLITZER

8 The waitress intoned the specialties of the day, "Chicken Cordon Bleu, Sole Amandine, Veal Marsala." She might have been a train conductor in a foreign country, calling out the strange names of the stations.
   Hearts Farrar, Straus & Giroux 80

HERMAN WOUK

9 This is an excellent martini—sort of tastes like it isn't there at all, just a cold cloud.
   The Winds of War ABC TV 10 Sep 86

LITERATURE
Writers & Editors

RICHARD BACH

10 A professional writer is an amateur who didn't quit.
   A Gift of Wings Delacorte 74

SAMUEL BECKETT

11 I write about myself with the same pencil and in the same exercise book as about him. It is no longer I, but another whose life is just beginning.
   On being taken over by a fictional character, quoted by Hugh Kenner NY *Times* 13 Apr 86

HILAIRE BELLOC

12 When I am dead
   I hope it may be said
   "His sins were scarlet,
   But his books were read."
   Quoted by A N Wilson *Hilaire Belloc* Atheneum 84

SAUL BELLOW

13 A novel is balanced between a few true impressions and the multitude of false ones that make up most of what we call life.
   Accepting Nobel Prize 12 Dec 76

14 I discovered that rejections are not altogether a bad thing. They teach a writer to rely on his own judgment and to say in his heart of hearts, "To hell with you."
   NY *Times* 21 Jul 85

LUDWIG BEMELMANS

15 I don't keep any copy of my books around.... they would embarass me. When I finish writing my books, I kick them in the belly, and have done with them.
   NY *Herald Tribune* 15 Dec 57

DANIEL J BOORSTIN, Librarian of Congress

16 I write to discover what I think. After all, the bars aren't open that early.
   On why he writes at home from 6:30 to 8:30 AM, *Wall Street Journal* 31 Dec 85

CATHERINE DRINKER BOWEN

17 Writing, I think, is not apart from living. Writing is a kind of double living The writer experiences everything twice. Once in reality and once in that mirror which waits always before or behind.
   Atlantic Dec 57

1 Will the reader turn the page?
>Note posted in her study, quoted in *MD* Jul 81

RAY BRADBURY

2 [My stories] run up and bite me on the leg—I respond by writing down everything that goes on during the bite. When I finish, the idea lets go and runs off.
>"Drunk and in Charge of a Bicycle," introduction to *The Stories of Ray Bradbury* Knopf 80

JOHN BRAINE

3 Being a writer in a library is rather like being a eunuch in a harem.
>NY *Times* 7 Oct 62

MAEVE BRENNAN, alter ego of the Long-Winded Lady in *New Yorker* "Talk of the Town" column

4 The fewer writers you know the better, and if you're working on anything, don't tell them.
>*Time* 1 Jul 74

JAMES M CAIN

5 I write of the wish that comes true—for some reason, a terrifying concept.
>Recalled on his death 27 Oct 77

HORTENSE CALISHER

6 The words! I collected them in all shapes and sizes and hung them like bangles in my mind.
>*Extreme Magic* Little, Brown 64

ALBERT CAMUS

7 A guilty conscience needs to confess. A work of art is a confession.
>*Notebooks 1935-42* Knopf 63

TRUMAN CAPOTE

8 I got this idea of doing a really serious big work—it would be precisely like a novel, with a single difference: Every word of it would be true from beginning to end.
>On *In Cold Blood* Random House 66, which he called "in my mind, a nonfiction novel," *Saturday Review* 22 Jan 66

BARBARA CARTLAND

9 A historical romance is the only kind of book where chastity really counts.
>To Romantic Novelists Assn of England, *Queen* 30 Jan 62

JOHN CHEEVER

10 The novel remains for me one of the few forms where we can record man's complexity and the strength and decency of his longings. Where we can describe, step by step, minute by minute, our not altogether unpleasant struggle to put ourselves into a viable and devout relationship to our beloved and mistaken world.
>Accepting National Book Award, *The Writer* Sep 58

11 Art is the triumph over chaos.
>*The Stories of John Cheever* Knopf 78

12 I can't write without a reader. It's precisely like a kiss—you can't do it alone.
>*Christian Science Monitor* 24 Oct 79

AGATHA CHRISTIE

13 I specialize in murders of quiet, domestic interest.
>*Life* 14 May 56

WINSTON CHURCHILL

14 I do hope you are right.
>Accepting Nobel Prize for Literature, news summaries 31 Dec 53

15 The short words are best, and the old words are the best of all.
>Quoted by Alistair Cooke *America* Knopf 73

MARCHETTE CHUTE

16 I've never signed a contract, so never have a deadline. A deadline's an unnerving thing. I just finish a book, and if the publisher doesn't like it, that's his privilege.
>NY *Times* 18 Oct 53

TOM CLANCY

17 I've made up stuff that's turned out to be real, that's the spooky part.
>On his books of international intrigue, NY *Times* 27 Jul 86

COLETTE

18 Sit down and put down everything that comes into your head and then you're a writer. But an author is one who can judge his own stuff's worth, without pity, and destroy most of it.
>*Casual Change* Morrow 64

IVY COMPTON-BURNETT

19 At a certain point my novels set. They set just as hard as that jam jar. And then I know they are finished.
>Quoted by Joyce Cary *Art and Reality* Harper & Row 58

CYRIL CONNOLLY

1 Literature is the art of writing something that will be read twice.
Quote 12 Sep 65

2 The true function of a writer is to produce a masterpiece and ... no other task is of any consequence.
Quoted in review of books reissued after his death, *Newsweek* 19 Mar 84

PAT CONROY

3 My mother, Southern to the bone, once told me, "All Southern literature can be summed up in these words: 'On the night the hogs ate Willie, Mama died when she heard what Daddy did to Sister.'" She raised me up to be a Southern writer, but it wasn't easy.
Book-of-the-Month Club News Dec 86

PATRICK DENNIS

4 I always start writing with a clean piece of paper and a dirty mind.
Vogue 15 Feb 56

JOAN DIDION

5 Call me the author.
Democracy Simon & Schuster 84

E L DOCTOROW

6 Writing is an exploration. You start from nothing and learn as you go.
NY *Times* 20 Oct 85

JOHN DOS PASSOS

7 If there is a special Hell for writers it would be in the forced contemplation of their own works.
NY *Times* 25 Oct 59

8 A satirist is a man whose flesh creeps so at the ugly and the savage and the incongruous aspects of society that he has to express them as brutally and nakedly as possible in order to get relief.
Occasions and Protests Regnery 64

DAPHNE DU MAURIER

9 All autobiography is self-indulgent.
Myself When Young Doubleday 77

JOHN GREGORY DUNNE

10 Writing is manual labor of the mind: a job, like laying pipe.
Esquire Oct 86

11 I started all over again on page 1, circling the 262 pages like a vulture looking for live flesh to scavenge.
On resuming work on *The Red, White and Blue,* ib

WILL AND ARIEL DURANT

12 A book is like a quarrel: One word leads to another, and may erupt in blood or print, irrevocably.
A Dual Autobiography Simon & Schuster 77

LAWRENCE DURRELL

13 It takes a lot of energy and a lot of neurosis to write a novel. ... If you were really sensible, you'd do something else.
Washington *Post* 29 May 86

UMBERTO ECO

14 A book is a fragile creature, it suffers the wear of time, it fears rodents, the elements and clumsy hands. ... so the librarian protects the books not only against mankind but also against nature and devotes his life to this war with the forces of oblivion.
On librarians of the year 1327, *The Name of the Rose* Warner 84

LEON EDEL

15 Any biographer must of necessity become a pilgrim ... a peripatetic, obsessed literary pilgrim, a traveler with four eyes.
NY *Times* 21 Jan 73

WILLIAM FAULKNER

16 Everything goes by the board: honor, pride, decency ... to get the book written.
Quoted in Malcolm Cowley ed *Writers at Work* Viking 58

17 If a writer has to rob his mother, he will not hesitate: The "Ode on a Grecian Urn" is worth any number of old ladies.
ib

18 The aim of every artist is to arrest motion, which is life, by artificial means.
ib

19 A writer is congenitally unable to tell the truth and that is why we call what he writes fiction.
Recalled on his death 6 Jul 62

20 A writer must teach himself that the basest of all things is to be afraid.
ib

21 It wasn't until the Nobel Prize that they really

thawed out. They couldn't understand my books, but they could understand $30,000.

On reviewers, quoted in *National Observer* 3 Feb 64

EDNA FERBER

1 Life can't ever really defeat a writer who is in love with writing, for life itself is a writer's lover until death—fascinating, cruel, lavish, warm, cold, treacherous, constant.

Recalled on her death 16 Apr 68

2 Your idea of bliss is to wake up on a Monday morning knowing you haven't a single engagement for the entire week. You are cradled in a white paper cocoon tied up with typewriter ribbon.

On uninterrupted writing, *ib*

THOMAS FLEMING

3 Actors yearn for the perfect director, athletes for the perfect coach, priests for the perfect pope, presidents for the perfect historian. Writers hunger for the perfect reviewer.

"The War between Writers and Reviewers" NY *Times* 6 Jan 85

E M FORSTER

4 Yes, oh dear, yes, the novel tells a story.

Aspects of the Novel Harcourt, Brace 54

5 It is my fate and perhaps my temperament to sign agreements with fools.

Asserting that "booksellers are dishonest and publishers largely morons," quoted in Mary Lago and P N Furbank eds *Selected Letters of E M Forster 1921-70* Belknap Press/Harvard 84

GENE FOWLER

6 Sometimes I think [my writing] sounds like I walked out of the room and left the typewriter running.

Newsweek 1 Nov 54

PAULA FOX

7 A lie hides the truth. A story tries to find it.

A Servant's Tale North Point 84, quoted in NY *Times* 18 Nov 84

MAX FRISCH

8 The difference between an author and a horse is that the horse doesn't understand the horse dealer's language.

Quoted by Siegfried Unseld *The Author and His Publisher* University of Chicago 80

GABRIEL GARCÍA MÁRQUEZ

9 One of the things which makes me happier today is that I will never be a Nobel Prize candidate again.

On winning Nobel Prize, London *Times* 22 Oct 82

CAMPBELL GEESLIN

10 I then go miserably enough to the typewriter and I edit with tiny little pen scribbles until you can't read it anymore. And *then,* I put it into a word processor.

On editing his longhand drafts written on yellow legal pads, quoted by Eleanor Blau "The Long and Short of It: Yellow Pads Are Thriving" NY *Times* 4 Nov 86

THEODOR GEISEL ("Dr Seuss")

11 You can get help from teachers, but you are going to have to learn a lot by yourself, sitting alone in a room.

On becoming a writer, NY *Times* 21 May 86

ANDRÉ GIDE

12 Art begins with resistance—at the point where resistance is overcome. No human masterpiece has ever been created without great labor.

Recalled on his death 19 Feb 51

BRENDAN GILL

13 I will try to cram these paragraphs full of facts and give them a weight and shape no greater than that of a cloud of blue butterflies.

Here at the New Yorker Random House 75

RUMER GODDEN

14 For a dyed-in-the-wool author, nothing is as dead as a book once it is written. .... She is rather like a cat whose kittens have grown up.

NY *Times* 1 Dec 63

15 If books were Persian carpets, one would not look only at the outer side. .... because it is the stitch that makes a carpet wear, gives it its life and bloom.

Book-of-the-Month Club News Sep 69

16 The stitch of a book is its words.

ib

DORIS KEARNS GOODWIN

17 The past is not simply the past, but a prism through which the subject filters his own changing self-image.

On the shifting quality of Lyndon B Johnson's

memories as he neared the end of his life, quoted in Marc Patcher ed *Telling Lives: The Biographer's Art* New Republic Books 79

NADINE GORDIMER

1 The creative act is not pure. History evidences it. Sociology extracts it. The writer loses Eden, writes to be read and comes to realize that he is answerable.

Paper quoted in Sterling McMurrin ed *The Tanner Lectures on Human Values* University of Utah 85

GRAHAM GREENE

2 My two fingers on a typewriter have never connected with my brain. My hand on a pen does. A fountain pen, of course. Ball-point pens are only good for filling out forms on a plane.

International Herald Tribune 7 Oct 77

3 A major character has to come somehow out of the unconscious.

NY *Times* 9 Oct 85

4 The moment comes when a character does or says something you hadn't thought about. At that moment he's alive and you leave it to him.

ib

A B GUTHRIE JR

5 If you are inclined to leave your character solitary for any considerable length of time, better question yourself. Fiction is association, not withdrawal.

The Blue Hen's Chick McGraw-Hill 65

6 Fiction is love and hate and agreement and conflict and common adventure, not lonely musings on have-beens and might-have-beens.

ib

SHIRLEY HAZZARD

7 It's a nervous work. The state that you need to write is the state that others are paying large sums to get rid of.

NY *Times* 25 Mar 80

ROBERT HEINLEIN

8 They didn't want it good, they wanted it Wednesday.

On writing science fiction for pulp magazines, NY *Times* 24 Aug 80

LILLIAN HELLMAN

9 What a word is truth. Slippery, tricky, unreliable. I tried in these books to tell the truth.

"On Reading Again" in *Three: An Unfinished Woman, Pentimento, Scoundrel Time* Little, Brown 79

ERNEST HEMINGWAY

10 The most essential gift for a good writer is a built-in, shockproof shit detector. This is the writer's radar and all great writers have had it.

Paris Review Spring 58

11 All good books have one thing in common— they are truer than if they had really happened.

Quoted by A E Hotchner *Papa Hemingway* Random House 66

12 When I have an idea, I turn down the flame, as if it were a little alcohol stove, as low as it will go. Then it explodes and that is my idea.

Quoted by James Mellow *Charmed Circle: Gertrude Stein & Co* Praeger 74

13 If you have a success you have it for the wrong reasons. If you become popular it is always because of the worst aspects of your work.

Quoted by Morley Callaghan *That Summer in Paris* Penguin 79

14 It's none of their business that you have to learn how to write. Let them think you were born that way.

On loss of a suitcase containing work that would have enabled critics to trace his first two years as a writer, quoted by Arnold Samuelson *With Hemingway* Random House 84

JOHN HERSEY

15 Journalism allows its readers to witness history; fiction gives its readers an opportunity to live it.

Time 13 Mar 50

FANNIE HURST

16 Any writer worth the name is always getting into one thing or getting out of another thing.

NY *Mirror* 28 Aug 56

ALDOUS HUXLEY

17 A bad book is as much of a labor to write as a good one, it comes as sincerely from the author's soul.

Newsweek 2 Jan 56

CHARLES JACKSON

18 [The writer] must essentially draw from life as he sees it, lives it, overhears it or steals it, and the truer the writer, perhaps the bigger the blackguard. He lives by biting the hand that feeds him.

Recalled on his death 21 Sep 68

TOM JENKS

1 Editing Hemingway was like wrestling with a god.
> On turning 1,500 pages of manuscript into the 247-page posthumous novel *The Garden of Eden* Scribner's 86, quoted in *Time* 26 May 86

PAMELA HANSFORD JOHNSON

2 I have always wanted to write in such a way that will make people think, "Why, I've always thought that but never found the words for it."
> Recalled on her death, NY *Times* 20 Jun 81

GARSON KANIN

3 There are thousands of causes for stress, and one antidote to stress is self-expression. That's what happens to me every day. My thoughts get off my chest, down my sleeves and onto my pad.
> *Publishers Weekly* 23 Jan 78

ELIA KAZAN

4 The writer, when he is also an artist, is someone who admits what others don't dare reveal.
> NY *Times* 3 Dec 79

NIKOS KAZANTZAKIS

5 My entire soul is a cry, and all my work is a commentary on that cry.
> *Report to Greco* Simon & Schuster 65

ALFRED KAZIN

6 When a writer talks about his work, he's talking about a love affair.
> San Francisco *Examiner & Chronicle* 16 Jul 78

7 One writes to make a home for oneself, on paper, in time and in others' minds.
> Quoted in Marc Patcher ed *Telling Lives: The Biographer's Art* New Republic Books 79

CLARENCE B KELLAND

8 I get up in the morning, torture a typewriter until it screams, then stop.
> On how he wrote an estimated 10 million words in 61 years, recalled on his death, NY *Herald Tribune* 20 Feb 64

WILLIAM KENNEDY

9 There's only a short walk from the hallelujah to the hoot.
> On the similarity between good writing and poor writing, CBS TV 28 Jul 85

JACK KEROUAC

10 It is not my fault that certain so-called bohemian elements have found in my writings something to hang their peculiar beatnik theories on.
> NY *Journal-American* 8 Dec 60

STEPHEN KING

11 [I work until] beer o'clock.
> On his 9 to 5 writing day, *Time* 6 Oct 86

12 [French is] the language that turns dirt into romance.
> *ib*

EDWARD KOCH, Mayor of NYC

13 I know many writers who first dictate passages, then polish what they have dictated. I speak, then I polish—occasionally I do windows.
> On his best-selling book *Politics*, NY *Times* 26 Feb 86

MARGARET LAURENCE

14 When I say "work" I only mean writing. Everything else is just odd jobs.
> Quoted in Donald Cameron ed *Conversations with Canadian Novelists* Macmillan 73

JOHN LE CARRÉ

15 Writing is like walking in a deserted street. Out of the dust in the street you make a mud pie.
> *Time* 1 May 64

MADELEINE L'ENGLE

16 A book comes and says, "Write me." My job is to try to serve it to the best of my ability, which is never good enough, but all I can do is listen to it, do what it tells me and collaborate.
> "Collaborating with Inspiration" *Anglican Digest* Pentecost 83

ELMORE LEONARD

17 If it sounds like writing, I rewrite it.
> *Newsweek* 22 Apr 85

18 I leave out the parts that people skip.
> When asked about popularity of his detective novels, quoted by William Zinsser *A Family of Readers* Book-of-the-Month Club 86

DORIS LESSING

19 In the writing process, the more a story cooks, the better.
> NY *Times* 22 Apr 84

NORMAN MAILER

1 When I read it, I don't wince, which is all I ever ask for a book I write.
> On publication of his first mystery, *Tough Guys Don't Dance* Random House 84, NY *Times* 8 Jun 84

BERNARD MALAMUD

2 Those who write about life, reflect about life. . . . you see in others who you are.
> *Dublin's Lives* Farrar, Straus & Giroux 79

3 It was all those biographies in me yelling, "We want out. We want to tell you what we've done to you."
> On how *Dublin's Lives* resulted from a lifetime of reading biographies, *W* 16 Feb 79

4 With me, it's story, story, story.
> On the most important element of his writing, *ib*

5 The idea is to get the pencil moving quickly.
> On the task of beginning, *ib*

6 Once you've got some words looking back at you, you can take two or three—or throw them away and look for others.
> *ib*

THOMAS MANN

7 A writer is somebody for whom writing is more difficult than it is for other people.
> Recalled on his death 12 Aug 55

SOMERSET MAUGHAM

8 Have common sense and . . . stick to the point.
> On writing, quoted by Ted Morgan *Maugham* Simon & Schuster 80

9 Writing is the supreme solace.
> *ib*

ANDRÉ MAUROIS

10 Style is the hallmark of a temperament stamped upon the material at hand.
> *The Art of Writing* Dutton 60

11 Writing is a difficult trade which must be learned slowly by reading great authors; by trying at the outset to imitate them; by daring then to be original; by destroying one's first productions.
> NY *Journal-American* 31 Jul 63

12 There are deserts in every life, and the desert must be depicted if we are to give a fair and complete idea of the country.
> On the biographer's task, recalled on his death 9 Oct 67

MARY McCARTHY

13 I am putting real plums into an imaginary cake.
> On *The Group,* her 1963 novel about eight 1933 Vassar alumnae, NY *Herald Tribune* 5 Jan 64

14 To be disesteemed by people you don't have much respect for is not the worst fate.
> On reviewers, quoted by Samuel G Freedman NY *Times* 27 Aug 84

CARSON McCULLERS

15 I live with the people I create and it has always made my essential loneliness less keen.
> Preface to *The Square Root of Wonderful* Houghton Mifflin 58

THOMAS MERTON

16 There was this shadow, this double, this writer who had followed me into the cloister. . . . He rides my shoulders . . . I cannot lose him.
> *Elected Silence* Hollis & Carter 69

17 An author in a Trappist monastery is like a duck in a chicken coop. And he would give anything in the world to be a chicken instead of a duck.
> Quoted by Monica Furlong *Merton* Harper & Row 80

GRACE METALIOUS

18 Even Tom Sawyer had a girlfriend and to talk about adults without talking about their sex drives is like talking about a window without glass.
> Defending *Peyton Place*, NY *Mirror* 6 Feb 58

JAMES A MICHENER

19 Russia, France, Germany and China. They revere their writers. America is still a frontier country that almost shudders at the idea of creative expression.
> "A Spelunker in the Caves of History" *Modern Maturity* Aug 85

20 The arrogance of the artist is a very profound thing, and it fortifies you.
> Quoted by Caryn James "The Michener Phenomenon" NY *Times* 8 Sep 85

21 The really great writers are people like Emily Brontë who sit in a room and write out of their limited experience and unlimited imagination.
> *ib*

TED MORGAN

22 A writer is always going to betray somebody.

If you're going to be honest with your subject, you can't be genteel.

On writing biographies, quoted in *Publishers Weekly* 11 Oct 85

WILLIE MORRIS

1 When a writer knows home in his heart, his heart must remain subtly apart from it. He must always be a stranger to the place he loves, and its people.

"Coming on Back" *Life* Jun 81

VLADIMIR NABOKOV

2 Here lies the sense of literary creation: to portray ordinary objects as they will be reflected in kindly mirrors of future times. . . . To find in objects around us the fragrant tenderness that only posterity will discern when every trifle of our everyday life will become exquisite and festive in its own right.

Details of a Sunset McGraw-Hill 76

KATHLEEN NORRIS

3 Get a girl in trouble, then get her out again.

Describing her formula for 81 "relentlessly wholesome" novels, *Time* 28 Jan 66

JOYCE CAROL OATES

4 If you are a writer you locate yourself behind a wall of silence and no matter what you are doing, driving a car or walking or doing housework . . . you can still be writing, because you have that space.

NY *Times* 27 Jul 80

EDNA O'BRIEN

5 I am obsessive, also I am industrious. Besides, the time when you are most alive and most aware is in childhood and one is trying to recapture that heightened awareness.

NY *Times* 18 Nov 84

6 My hand does the work and I don't have to think; in fact, were I to think, it would stop the flow. It's like a dam in the brain that bursts.

ib

7 Writing is like carrying a fetus.

Quoted in George Plimpton ed *Writers at Work* Viking 86

FLANNERY O'CONNOR

8 When a book leaves your hands, it belongs to God. He may use it to save a few souls or to try a few others, but I think that for the writer to worry is to take over God's business.

The Habit of Being Farrar, Straus & Giroux 79

9 I don't deserve any credit for turning the other cheek as my tongue is always in it.

ib

JOHN O'HARA

10 They say great themes make great novels. . . . but what these young writers don't understand is that there is no greater theme than men and women.

On publication of his 35th book, NY *Times* 13 Nov 67

11 An artist is his own fault.

Introduction to stories by F Scott Fitzgerald, recalled on O'Hara's death 11 Apr 70

12 Much as I like owning a Rolls-Royce, I could do without it. What I could not do without is a typewriter, a supply of yellow second sheets and the time to put them to good use.

Introduction to *And Other Stories* Random House 68, quoted in *National Observer* 20 Apr 70

JOHN OSBORNE

13 Asking a working writer what he thinks about critics is like asking a lamppost what it feels about dogs.

Time 31 Oct 77

BORIS PASTERNAK

14 Immensely grateful, touched, proud, astonished, abashed.

Telegram accepting Nobel Prize, NY *Mirror* 26 Oct 58

15 In view of the meaning given to this honor in the community to which I belong, I should abstain from the undeserved prize that has been awarded to me. Do not meet my voluntary refusal with ill will.

Telegram reversing his acceptance of Nobel Prize after criticism by Soviets, NY *Times* 30 Oct 58

16 They don't ask much of you. They only want you to hate the things you love and to love the things you despise.

On Soviet bureaucrats, *Life* 13 Jun 60

WALKER PERCY

17 [Tuberculosis was] the best disease I ever had. If I hadn't had it, I might be a second-rate shrink practicing in Birmingham, at best.

On convalescence that permitted him to read voraciously and turned his interest from psychiatry to writing, quoted by Malcolm Jones "Moralist of the South" NY *Times* 22 Mar 87

JAYNE ANNE PHILLIPS

1 If the first novel has been successful, the writer buys a serious, writerly object that bespeaks investment and confidence—a word processor, a new bookshelf, reams of white paper.... In any case, a new and bigger wastebasket.

On writing a second novel, NY *Times* 17 Mar 85

KATHERINE ANNE PORTER

2 I finished the thing; but I think I sprained my soul.

On completing *Ship of Fools*, her 1962 novel, *McCalls's* Aug 65

J B PRIESTLEY

3 Most writers enjoy two periods of happiness— when a glorious idea comes to mind and, secondly, when a last page has been written and you haven't had time to know how much better it ought to be.

International Herald Tribune 3 Jan 78

4 Much of writing might be described as mental pregnancy with successive difficult deliveries.
ib

V S PRITCHETT

5 I am under the spell of language, which has ruled me since I was 10.

"Looking Back at 80" NY *Times* 14 Dec 80

MORDECAI RICHLER

6 Coming from Canada, being a writer and Jewish as well, I have impeccable paranoia credentials.

"It's a Plot" *Playboy* May 75

FRANÇOISE SAGAN

7 Life has confirmed for me the thoughts and impressions I had when I was 18, as if it was all intuition.

W 17 May 74

8 There are moments when you feel trapped, ill at ease. A year later the same feeling can turn out to be the theme of a book.
ib

J D SALINGER

9 A confessional passage has probably never been written that didn't stink a little bit of the writer's pride in having given up his pride.
The Catcher in the Rye Little, Brown 51

10 [It's] like saying she's a beautiful girl, except for her face.

On an editor who praised a story while rejecting it, quoted in NY *Times* 30 Jan 87

CARL SANDBURG

11 I was up day and night with Lincoln for years. I couldn't have picked a better companion.

On his biography of Abraham Lincoln, NY *Times* 6 Jan 64

WILLIAM SANSOM

12 A writer lives, at best, in a state of astonishment.

Blue Skies, Brown Studies Hogarth 61

JEAN PAUL SARTRE

13 A writer who takes political, social or literary positions must act only with the means that are his. These means are the written words.

Refusing Nobel Prize, NY *Times* 22 Oct 64

RICHARD SELZER

14 I don't dawdle. I'm a surgeon. I make an incision, do what needs to be done and sew up the wound. There is a beginning, a middle and an end.

On rewriting, NY *Times* 28 Sep 79

MAURICE SENDAK

15 You cannot write for children ... They're much too complicated. You can only write books that are of interest to them.

Boston *Globe* 4 Jan 87

ROD SERLING

16 Every writer is a frustrated actor who recites his lines in the hidden auditorium of his skull.

Vogue 1 Apr 57

WILFRID SHEED

17 Every writer is a writer of the generation before.

On his parents, NY *Times* 10 Nov 85

CLAUDE SIMON

18 For me, the big chore is always the same: how to begin a sentence, how to continue it, how to complete it.

On writing his Nobel acceptance speech, *ib*

ISAAC BASHEVIS SINGER

19 I don't invent characters because the Almightly has already invented millions. ... Just like experts at fingerprints do not create fingerprints but learn how to read them.

NY *Times* 26 Nov 78

20 When I was a little boy, they called me a liar,

but now that I am grown up, they call me a writer.
Time 18 Jul 83

OSBERT SITWELL

1 It is music to my ears. I have always said that if I were a rich man, I would employ a professional praiser.
On hearing his books read aloud, NBC TV 2 Jan 55

ALEXANDER SOLZHENITSYN

2 For a country to have a great writer is like having a second government. That is why no regime has ever loved great writers, only minor ones.
The First Circle Bantam 76

SUSAN SONTAG

3 Volume depends precisely on the writer's having been able to sit in a room every day, year after year, alone.
"When Writers Talk among Themselves" NY *Times* 5 Jan 86

4 The writer is either a practicing recluse or a delinquent, guilt-ridden one; or both. Usually both.
ib

JOHN STEINBECK

5 Writers are a little below clowns and a little above trained seals.
Quote 18 Jun 61

6 In utter loneliness a writer tries to explain the inexplicable.
In diary used to warm up for his daily stint of writing, NY *Times* 2 Jun 69

GLORIA STEINEM

7 Writing is the only thing that, when I do it, I don't feel I should be doing something else.
Publishers Weekly 12 Aug 83

WILLIAM STRUNK JR

8 Vigorous writing is concise. A sentence should contain no unnecessary words, a paragraph no unnecessary sentences, for the same reason that a drawing should have no unnecessary lines and a machine no unnecessary parts.
In *Elements of Style* 3rd ed, revised by E B White, Macmillan 79

WILLIAM STYRON

9 The good writing of any age has always been the product of *someone's* neurosis.
NY *Times* 27 Oct 63

GLORIA SWANSON

10 I've given my memoirs far more thought than any of my marriages. You can't divorce a book.
NY *Times* 10 Mar 79

PAUL THEROUX

11 Fiction gives us a second chance that life denies us.
NY *Times* 28 Jul 76

VIRGIL THOMSON

12 Let your mind alone, and see what happens.
On writing, *Christian Science Monitor* 12 Feb 85

JAMES THURBER

13 With 60 staring me in the face, I have developed inflammation of the sentence structure and a definite hardening of the paragraphs.
NY *Post* 30 Jun 55

J R R TOLKIEN

14 I am told that I talk in shorthand and then smudge it.
Acknowledging critics who said his writing was difficult to understand, NY *Times* 3 Mar 57

ARNOLD TOYNBEE

15 I don't believe a committee can write a book. ... It can, oh, govern a country, perhaps, but I don't believe it can write a book.
NBC TV 17 Apr 55

P L TRAVERS

16 A writer is, after all, only half his book. The other half is the reader and from the reader the writer learns.
NY *Times* 2 Jul 78

LIONEL TRILLING

17 Immature artists imitate. Mature artists steal.
Esquire Sep 62

BARBARA TUCHMAN

18 Books are the carriers of civilization. Without books, history is silent, literature dumb, science crippled, thought and speculation at a standstill.
Authors' League Bulletin Nov 79

19 Books are humanity in print.
ib

20 Nothing sickens me more than the closed door of a library.
On raising funds for NY Public Library, *New Yorker* 21 Apr 86

1 For me, the card catalog has been a companion all my working life. To leave it is like leaving the house one was brought up in.

> Informal talk to library staff when 8,000 oak drawers were replaced with 800 black-bound dictionary catalogs, *ib*

LOUIS UNTERMEYER

2 Write out of love, write out of instinct, write out of reason. But always for money.

> NY *Times* 30 Sep 75

JOHN UPDIKE

3 I would especially like to recourt the Muse of poetry, who ran off with the mailman four years ago, and drops me only a scribbled postcard from time to time.

> On completing a long novel, NY *Times* 7 Apr 68

MARIO VARGAS LLOSA

4 If you are killed because you are a writer, that's the maximum expression of respect, you know.

> *Time* 5 Nov 84

GORE VIDAL

5 The greatest pleasure when I started making money was not buying cars or yachts but finding myself able to have as many freshly typed drafts as possible.

> Interviewed on 30th anniversary of his 1st book, NY *Times* 24 Feb 76

6 I am an obsessive rewriter, doing one draft and then another and another, usually five. In a way, I have nothing to say, but a great deal to add.

> *ib*

7 I don't want anything. I don't want a job. I don't want to be respectable. I don't want prizes. I turned down the National Institute of Arts and Letters when I was elected to it in 1976 on the grounds that I already belonged to the Diners Club.

> Quoted in *Wall Street Journal* 3 Jul 84

ROBERT PENN WARREN

8 I've been to a lot of places and done a lot of things, but writing was always first. It's a kind of pain I can't do without.

> *National Observer* 12 Mar 77

EUDORA WELTY

9 Writing a story or a novel is one way of discovering *sequence* in experience, of stumbling upon cause and effect in the happenings of a writer's own life.

> *One Writer's Beginnings* Harper & Row 84

REBECCA WEST

10 Just how difficult it is to write biography can be reckoned by anybody who sits down and considers just how many people know the real truth about his or her love affairs.

> "The Art of Skepticism" *Vogue* Nov 52

11 [Writing] has nothing to do with communication between person and person, only with communication between different parts of a person's mind.

> *ib*

E B WHITE

12 Oh, I never look under the hood.

> When asked for the sources of his short stories, NY *Times* 30 Aug 79

T H WHITE

13 I class myself as a manual laborer.

> Letter to his publisher, recalled on his death, NY *Herald Tribune* 18 Jan 64

THEODORE H WHITE

14 I, alas, must present myself somewhat ignominiously as a chef in a busy kitchen. Somewhere a novel is bubbling on a back burner, an old attempt at history may come out of the freezer.

> NY *Times* 19 Jul 79

THORNTON WILDER

15 I would love to be the poet laureate of Coney Island.

> On his ultimate ambition, NY *Journal-American* 11 Nov 55

TENNESSEE WILLIAMS

16 When I stop [working] the rest of the day is posthumous. I'm only really alive when I'm writing.

> Pittsburgh *Press* 30 May 60

WILLIAM CARLOS WILLIAMS

17 I think all writing is a disease. You can't stop it.

> *Newsweek* 7 Jan 57

EDMUND WILSON

18 I am not quite a poet but I am something of the kind.

> Note in his boyhood journal, quoted by David Castronovo *Edmund Wilson* Ungar 84

P G Wodehouse

1 I just sit at a typewriter and curse a bit.
On his writing technique, *Collier's* 31 Aug 56

Herman Wouk

2 I regard the writing of humor as a supreme artistic challenge.
Book-of-the-Month Club News May 85

Richard Wright

3 I would hurl words into the darkness and wait for an echo. If an echo sounded, no matter how faintly, I would send other words to tell, to march, to fight.
American Hunger Harper & Row 77

Marguerite Yourcenar

4 Leaving behind books is even more beautiful—there are far too many children.
On having no children, NY *Times* 5 May 80

5 I have never seasoned a truth with the sauce of a lie in order to digest it more easily.
ib

William Zinsser

6 I almost always urge people to write in the first person. . . . Writing is an act of ego and you might as well admit it.
On Writing Well Harper & Row 76

Poets

Diane Ackerman

7 I don't want to get to the end of my life and find that I lived just the length of it. I want to have lived the width of it as well.
At age 37, looking back on two volumes of published poetry plus experiences as a teacher, cowhand and pilot, *Newsweek* 22 Sep 86

John Ashbery

8 I don't look on poetry as closed works. I feel they're going on all the time in my head and I occasionally snip off a length.
London *Times* 23 Aug 84

W H Auden

9 Before people complain of the obscurity of modern poetry, they should first examine their consciences and ask themselves with how many people and on how many occasions they have genuinely and profoundly shared some experience with another.
Newsweek 17 Mar 58

10 A poet is, before anything else, a person who is passionately in love with language.
NY *Times* 9 Oct 60

11 It's a sad fact about our culture that a poet can earn much more money writing or talking about his art than he can by practicing it.
The Dyer's Hand Random House 68

12 A poet is a professional maker of verbal objects.
Newsweek 29 Jan 68

13 Art is our chief means of breaking bread with the dead.
NY *Times* 7 Aug 71

John Betjeman

14 I don't think I am any good. If I thought I was any good, I wouldn't be.
People 2 Jul 84

Maxwell Bodenheim

15 Poetry is the impish attempt to paint the color of the wind.
Quoted in Ben Hecht's 1958 play *Winkelberg*

Joseph Brodsky

16 A language . . . is a more ancient and inevitable thing than any state.
NY *Times* 1 Oct 72

17 For a writer only one form of patriotism exists: his attitude toward language.
ib

18 Bad literature . . . is a form of treason.
ib

19 Poetry is rather an approach to things, to life, than it is typographical production.
ib

20 Who included me among the ranks of the human race?
Response when asked at a 1964 trial, "Who included you among the ranks of the poets?" quoted in *ib*

21 Man is what he reads.
Quoted by Thomas D'Evelyn *Christian Science Monitor* 21 May 86

John Ciardi

22 Poetry lies its way to the truth.
Saturday Review 28 Apr 62

23 You don't have to suffer to be a poet. Adolescence is enough suffering for anyone.
Simmons Review Fall 62

JEAN COCTEAU

1 The poet never asks for admiration; he wants to be believed.
Newsweek 7 Apr 58

J V CUNNINGHAM

2 I like the trivial, vulgar and exalted.
On light verse, quoted by Thomas D'Evelyn *Christian Science Monitor* 26 Nov 86

T S ELIOT

3 Poetry is not a turning loose of emotion, but an escape from emotion; it is not the expression of personality, but an escape from personality.
Recalled on his death 4 Jan 65

4 The Nobel is a ticket to one's own funeral. No one has ever done anything after he got it.
On winning Nobel Prize in 1948, *ib*

PAUL ENGLE

5 All poetry is an ordered voice, one which tries to tell you about a vision in the unvisionary language of farm, city and love.
Life 28 May 56

6 Poetry is ordinary language raised to the *N*th power. Poetry is boned with ideas, nerved and blooded with emotions, all held together by the delicate, tough skin of words.
NY *Times* 17 Feb 57

7 Verse is not written, it is bled;
Out of the poet's abstract head.
Words drip the poem on the page;
Out of his grief, delight and rage.
A Woman Unashamed and Other Poems Random House 65

ROBERT FROST

8 I have never started a poem yet whose end I knew. Writing a poem is discovering.
NY *Times* 7 Nov 55

9 You can be a little ungrammatical if you come from the right part of the country.
Atlantic Jan 62

10 I alone of English writers have consciously set myself to make music out of what I may call the sound of sense.
Quoted by Margaret Bartlett Anderson *Robert Frost and John Bartlett* Holt, Rinehart & Winston 63

11 The ear is the only true writer and the only true reader.
ib

12 A poem ... begins as a lump in the throat, a sense of wrong, a homesickness, a lovesickness.
Quoted in *The Letters of Robert Frost to Louis Untermeyer* Holt, Rinehart & Winston 63

13 I would have written of me on my stone: I had a lover's quarrel with the world.
Recalled on his death 29 Jan 63

14 Poetry is a way of taking life by the throat.
Vogue 15 Mar 63

15 Humor is the most engaging cowardice.
On wit as a form of evasiveness, quoted in L R Thompson ed *Selected Letters of Robert Frost* Holt, Rinehart & Winston 64

16 A poet never takes notes. You never take notes in a love affair.
Quoted in Edward Connery Lathem ed *Interviews with Robert Frost* Holt, Rinehart & Winston 66

CHRISTOPHER FRY

17 [Poetry] has the virtue of being able to say twice as much as prose in half the time, and the drawback, if you do not give it your full attention, of seeming to say half as much in twice the time.
Time 3 Apr 50

PHYLLIS GOTLIEB

18 You don't go after poetry, you take what comes. Maybe the gods do it through me but I certainly do a hell of a lot of the work.
Quoted by Merle Shain *Chatelaine* Oct 72

ROBERT GRAVES

19 Prose books are the show dogs I breed and sell to support my cat.
On writing novels to support his love of writing poetry, NY *Times* 13 Jul 58

20 Poetry is no more a narcotic than a stimulant; it is a universal bittersweet mixture for all possible household emergencies and its action varies accordingly as it is taken in a wineglass or a tablespoon, inhaled, gargled or rubbed on the chest by hard fingers covered with rings.
ib 9 Oct 60

21 There's no money in poetry, but then there's no poetry in money either.
Quoted by Huw Wheldon *Monitor* Macdonald 62

PHILIP LARKIN

22 I can't understand these chaps who go round

American universities explaining how they write poems: It's like going round explaining how you sleep with your wife.

> Quoted by John Updike "Writers on Themselves" NY *Times* 17 Aug 86

C DAY LEWIS

1 No good poem, however confessional it may be, is just a self-expression. Who on earth would claim that the pearl *expresses* the oyster?

> "The Poet on His Work" *Christian Science Monitor* 24 May 66

ARCHIBALD MACLEISH

2 Journalism is concerned with events, poetry with feelings. Journalism is concerned with the look of the world, poetry with the feel of the world.

> "The Poet and the Press" *Atlantic* Mar 59

3 Journalism wishes to tell what it is that has happened everywhere as though the same things had happened for every man. Poetry wishes to say what it is like for any man to be himself in the presence of a particular occurrence as though only he were alone there.

> *ib*

4 To separate journalism and poetry, therefore—history and poetry—to set them up at opposite ends of the world of discourse, is to separate seeing from the feel of seeing, emotion from the acting of emotion, knowledge from the realization of knowledge.

> *ib*

5 A real writer learns from earlier writers the way a boy learns from an apple orchard—by stealing what he has a taste for and can carry off.

> *A Continuing Journey, Essays and Addresses* Houghton Mifflin 68

JACQUES MARITAIN

6 Poetry proceeds from the totality of man, sense, imagination, intellect, love, desire, instinct, blood and spirit together.

> Quoted in Robert Fitzgerald ed *Enlarging the Change: The Princeton Seminars in Literary Criticism 1949-51* Northeastern University 85

7 The poet knows himself only on the condition that things resound in him, and that in him, at a single awakening, they and he come forth together out of sleep.

> *ib*

JOHN MASEFIELD

8 In the power and splendor of the universe, inspiration waits for the millions to come. Man has only to strive for it. Poems greater than the *Iliad,* plays greater than *Macbeth,* stories more engaging than *Don Quixote* await their seeker and finder.

> NY *Times* 1 Jun 58

JAMES MERRILL

9 He puts his right hand lightly on the cup, I put my left, leaving the right free to transcribe, and away we go. We get, oh, 500 to 600 words an hour. Better than gasoline.

> On deriving material for three volumes of poetry from Ouija-board sessions with a friend, quoted in George Plimpton ed *Writers at Work* Viking 84

MARIANNE MOORE

10 Any writer overwhelmingly honest about pleasing himself is almost sure to please others.

> *Vogue* 15 Aug 63

11 In a poem the excitement has to maintain itself. I am governed by the pull of the sentence as the pull of a fabric is governed by gravity.

> Quoted by Louis Untermeyer "Five Famous Poetesses" *Ladies' Home Journal* May 64

SALVATORE QUASIMODO

12 Poetry is the revelation of a feeling that the poet believes to be interior and personal [but] which the reader recognizes as his own.

> NY *Times* 14 May 60

CARL SANDBURG

13 I'll die propped up in bed trying to do a poem about America.

> On plans for his 79th birthday, news summaries 6 Jan 57

JAROSLAV SEIFERT

14 If an ordinary person is silent, it may be a tactical maneuver. If a writer is silent, he is lying.

> On winning Nobel Prize 14 years after organizing resistance to Communist takeover of Prague, *Time* 22 Oct 84

EDITH SITWELL

15 Poetry is the deification of reality.

> *Life* 4 Jan 63

16 I am an unpopular electric eel in a pool of catfish.

> *ib*

1 The poet is a brother speaking to a brother of "a moment of their other lives"—a moment that had been buried beneath the dust of the busy world.
> Recalled on her death 9 Dec 64

STEPHEN SPENDER

2 Great poetry is always written by somebody straining to go beyond what he can do.
> NY *Times* 26 Mar 61

WALLACE STEVENS

3 Accuracy of observation is the equivalent of accuracy of thinking.
> *Opus Posthumous* Knopf 57

4 Money is a kind of poetry.
> *Harper's* Oct 85

5 Most people read [poetry] listening for echoes because the echoes are familiar to them. They wade through it the way a boy wades through water, feeling with his toes for the bottom: The echoes are the bottom.
> Quoted in Beverly Coyle and Alan Filreis eds *Secretaries of the Moon: The Letters of Wallace Stevens and José Rodríguez Feo* Duke University 86

DYLAN THOMAS

6 I hold a beast, an angel and a madman in me, and my enquiry is as to their working, and my problem is their subjugation and victory, downthrow and upheaval, and my effort is their self-expression.
> Quoted by Constantine FitzGibbon *The Life of Dylan Thomas* Little, Brown 65

7 A born writer is born scrofulous; his career is an accident dictated by physical or circumstantial disabilities.
> Quoted in Paul Ferris ed *The Collected Letters of Dylan Thomas* Macmillan 86

8 I went on all over the States, ranting poems to enthusiastic audiences that, the week before, had been equally enthusiastic about lectures on Railway Development or the Modern Turkish Essay.
> *ib*

LOUIS UNTERMEYER

9 Every poet knows the pun is Pierian, that it springs from the same soil as the Muse. . . . a matching and shifting of vowels and consonants, an adroit assonance sometimes derided as jackassonance.
> *Bygones* Harcourt, Brace & World 65

JOHN UPDIKE

10 There's a crystallization that goes on in a poem which the young man can bring off, but which the middle-aged man can't.
> Quoted by Michiko Kakutani "When Writers Turn to Brave New Forms" NY *Times* 24 Mar 86

ROBERT PENN WARREN

11 The poem . . . is a little myth of man's capacity of making life meaningful. And in the end, the poem is not a thing we see—it is, rather, a light by which we may see—and what we see is life.
> *Saturday Review* 22 Mar 58

12 The urge to write poetry is like having an itch. When the itch becomes annoying enough, you scratch it.
> NY *Times* 16 Dec 69

13 How do poems grow? They grow out of your life.
> "Poetry Is a Kind of Unconscious Autobiography" *ib* 12 May 85

14 What is a poem but a hazardous attempt at self-understanding? It is the deepest part of autobiography.
> *ib*

RICHARD WILBUR

15 It is true that the poet does not directly address his neighbors; but he does address a great congress of persons who dwell at the back of his mind, a congress of all those who have taught him and whom he has admired; they constitute his ideal audience and his better self.
> Accepting National Book Award, NY *Herald Tribune* 24 Mar 57

16 To this congress the poet speaks not of peculiar and personal things, but of what in himself is most common, most anonymous, most fundamental, most true of all men.
> *ib*

WILLIAM CARLOS WILLIAMS

17 Nothing whips my blood like verse.
> Quoted in John Thirlwall ed *The Selected Letters of William Carlos Williams* Astor-Honor 57

YEVGENY YEVTUSHENKO

18 A poet's autobiography is his poetry. Anything else can be only a footnote.
> NY *Times* 3 Nov 63

19 Poetry is like a bird, it ignores all frontiers.
> *Quote* 2 Jul 67

1 In Russia all tyrants believe poets to be their worst enemies.

> *A Precocious Autobiography* Dutton 63, quoted by Robert Conquest "The Politics of Poetry" NY *Times* 30 Sep 73

Observers & Critics

LORD ALTRINCHAM (John Edward Poynder Grigg)

2 Autobiography is now as common as adultery, and hardly less reprehensible.

> London *Sunday Times* 28 Feb 62

EDWARD ASWELL

3 Studying the mass of his manuscript was something like excavating the site of ancient Troy. One came upon evidences of entire civilizations buried and forgotten at different levels.

> On editing Thomas Wolfe's writings into the posthumous novels *The Web and the Rock* and *You Can't Go Home Again,* quoted in NY *Times* 10 Sep 84

JAMES ATLAS

4 A penumbra of somber dignity has descended over his reputation.

> On Edmund Wilson, in review of David Castronovo's *Edmund Wilson* Ungar 84, NY *Times* 28 Jul 85

5 To read Wilson ... is to be instructed and amused in the highest sense—that is, to be educated.

> *ib*

LOUIS AUCHINCLOSS

6 Perfection irritates as well as it attracts, in fiction as in life.

> *Pioneers & Caretakers: A Study of 9 American Women Novelists* University of Minnesota 65

7 A neurotic can perfectly well be a literary genius, but his greatest danger is always that he will not recognize when he is dull.

> *ib*

W H AUDEN

8 A real book is not one that's read, but one that reads us.

> Recalled on his death 28 Sep 73

PAUL BAILEY

9 It is one of the ironies of biographical art that some details are more relevant than others, and many details have no relevance at all.

> On Donald Spoto's *The Kindness of Strangers:*

The Life of Tennessee Williams Little, Brown 85, *Country Life* 18 Jul 85

RUSSELL BAKER

10 Americans like fat books and thin women.

> Quoted in James Charlton comp *The Writer's Quotation Book* Pushcart Press 80

MARTHA BAYLES

11 If we are told of some four-volume epic. ... we're apt to say "How interesting," but we never will read it unless we have both legs in traction.

> In review of *The Jewel in the Crown*, PBS television serial based on *The Raj Quartet* by Paul Scott, *Wall Street Journal* 17 Dec 84

LAURENCE BERGREEN

12 He was not fit for marriage, only for work. A major writer, he conceded, required major torment.

> *James Agee* Dutton 84

ROGER BERTHOUD

13 Biographers, like actors, have to think their way into other people's minds and allow their own to be partially invaded by their subject's.

> Interview with Peter Ackroyd after Ackroyd had completed lives of Oscar Wilde and T S Eliot and had named his cat Dickens to mark the start of work on a biography of Charles Dickens, "A Writer Who Achieves His Goals" *Illustrated London News* Apr 86

JIM BISHOP

14 A good writer is not, per se, a good book critic. No more so than a good drunk is automatically a good bartender.

> NY *Journal-American* 26 Nov 57

HAROLD BLOOM

15 What matters in literature in the end is surely the idiosyncratic, the individual, the flavor or the color of a particular human suffering.

> *Newsweek* 18 Aug 86

16 [In the finest critics] one hears the full cry of the human. They tell one why it matters to read.

> *ib*

17 I have never believed that the critic is the rival of the poet, but I do believe that criticism is a genre of literature or it does not exist.

> *ib*

CATHERINE DRINKER BOWEN

1 In writing biography, fact and fiction shouldn't be mixed. And if they are, the fiction parts should be printed in red ink, the fact parts in black ink.
Publishers Weekly 24 Mar 58

PIERS BRENDON

2 To make a criticism is a bit like complaining about the shape of the Pyramids.
On Martin Gilbert's *Winston S Churchill* Houghton Mifflin 83, London *Times* 30 Jun 83

JOSEPH BRODSKY

3 Twentieth-century Russian literature has produced nothing special except perhaps one novel and two stories by Andrei Platonov, who ended his days sweeping streets.
NY *Times* 1 Oct 72

4 [Robert] Frost's triumph was not being at John Kennedy's inauguration ceremony, but the day when he put the last period on "West-Running Brook."
ib

ANITA BROOKNER

5 It is my contention that Aesop was writing for the tortoise market. . . . hares have no time to read.
Quoted by Rushworth M Kidder *Christian Science Monitor* 1 Mar 85

CLEANTH BROOKS

6 The cunning old codger knows that no emphasis often constitutes the most powerful emphasis of all.
On Robert Frost, *Christian Science Monitor* 13 May 85

ANATOLE BROYARD

7 It is one of the paradoxes of American literature that our writers are forever looking back with love and nostalgia at lives they couldn't wait to leave.
On Curtis Harnack's *We Have All Gone Away* Doubleday 73, NY *Times* 16 Mar 73

8 Ruefulness is one of the classical tones of American fiction. . . . It fosters a native, deglamorized form of anxiety.
On authors and characters who "reflect ruefully," *ib* 17 Jan 81

9 Aphorisms are bad for novels. They stick in the reader's teeth.
On Barbara Grizzuti Harrison's *Foreign Bodies* Doubleday 84, *ib* 6 Jun 84

10 To be misunderstood can be the writer's punishment for having disturbed the reader's peace. The greater the disturbance, the greater the possibility of misunderstanding.
On Terry Garrity's *The Story of "J"* Morrow 84, *ib* 18 Jul 84

11 If a book is really good, it deserves to be read again, and if it's great, it should be read at least three times.
"Rereading and Other Excesses" *ib* 3 Mar 85

12 The more I like a book, the more reluctant I am to turn the page. Lovers, even book lovers, tend to cling. No one-night stands or "reads" for them.
"Confessions of a Page-Stayer, Staller, Stopper" *ib* 1 Sep 85

MARY CABLE

13 The best biographies leave their readers with a sense of having all but entered into a second life and of having come to know another human being in some ways better than he knew himself.
On Louise Hall Tharp's *Saint-Gaudens and the Gilded Era* Little, Brown 69, NY *Times* 9 Nov 69

VINCENT CANBY

14 Good fiction reveals feeling, refines events, locates importance and, though its methods are as mysterious as they are varied, intensifies the experience of living our own lives.
NY *Times* 3 Feb 80

15 Hack fiction exploits curiosity without really satisfying it or making connections between it and anything else in the world.
ib

TRUMAN CAPOTE

16 That's not writing, that's typing.
On the work of Jack Kerouac, quoted by Myrick Land *The Fine Art of Literary Mayhem* Holt, Rinehart & Winston 63

JOHN CAREY

17 If you are unhealthily addicted to reading about murder trials, this book may cure you.
On Diana Trilling's *Mrs Harris: The Death of the Scarsdale Diet Doctor* Harcourt Brace Jovanovich 81, London *Sunday Times* 9 May 82

HUMPHREY CARPENTER

18 Autobiography is probably the most respectable form of lying.
NY *Times* 7 Feb 82

RAYMOND CARVER

1 Isak Dinesen said that she wrote a little every day, without hope and without despair. I like that.

Quoted in George Plimpton ed *Writers at Work* Viking 86

BENNETT CERF

2 There have been too many [books] in which some young man is looking forward, backward or sideways in anger. Or in which some Southern youth is being chased through the magnolia bushes by his aunt. She catches him on page 28 with horrid results.

News summaries 9 Jun 58

CHICAGO SUN-TIMES

3 Enough to give trash a bad name.

On Andrew Greeley's *The Cardinal Sins* Warner 81, with a character reportedly based on John Cardinal Cody, recalled on Cody's death 25 Apr 82

CAROLYN CHUTE

4 He uses a lot of big words, and his sentences run from here back to the airport.

On William Faulkner, NY *Times* 30 Jun 85

GREGORY CLARK

5 You'll never get anywhere with all those damned little short sentences.

To fellow Toronto *Star* newspapermen Ernest Hemingway in the 1920s, quoted in Robert Thomas Allen ed *A Treasury of Canadian Humor* McClelland & Stewart 67

WALTER CLEMONS

6 Rebecca was a busy liar in her distinguished old age, reinventing her past for gullible biographers.

On Rebecca West, *Newsweek* 28 May 84

JEAN COCTEAU

7 That pile of paper on his left side went on living like the watch on a dead soldier's wrist.

On visiting the deathbed of Marcel Proust, quoted by Edmund White "Cocteau: The Great Enchanter" *Vogue* May 84

ARTHUR A COHEN

8 Russia is a conspicious murderer of her poets and ennobler of their poems.

On Joseph Brodsky's *Selected Poems* Harper & Row 73, NY *Times* 30 Dec 73

JOHN COLVILLE

9 He fertilizes a phrase or a line of poetry for weeks and then gives birth to it in a speech.

On Winston Churchill, *The Fringes of Power* Norton 85

CYRIL CONNOLLY

10 Vulgarity is the garlic in the salad of life.

Quoted by Joseph Epstein *The Middle of My Tether* Norton 83

GEOFFREY COTTRELL

11 In America only the successful writer is important, in France all writers are important, in England no writer is important and in Australia you have to explain what a writer is.

NY *Journal-American* 22 Sep 61

NORMAN COUSINS

12 A book is like a piece of rope; it takes on meaning only in connection with the things it holds together.

Saturday Review 15 Apr 78

MALCOLM COWLEY

13 Authors are sometimes like tomcats: They distrust all the other toms but they are kind to kittens.

Introduction to *Writers at Work* Viking 58

14 It would have been the equivalent of Jackson Pollock's attempts to copy the Sistine Chapel.

On a manuscript John Cheever had submitted that seemed obviously based on a Hemingway story, quoted by Susan Cheever *Home before Dark* Houghton Mifflin 84

FREDERICK CREWS

15 "Little magazines" are, for the most part, the mayflies of the literary world.

Skeptical Engagements Oxford 87, quoted in NY *Times* 15 Mar 87

16 Ephemerality is the little magazine's generic fate; by promptly dying it gives proof that it remained loyal to its first program.

ib

JAMES DICKEY

17 [She was] the Judy Garland of American poetry.

On Sylvia Plath, quoted in George Plimpton ed *Writers at Work* Viking 81

RONALD DUNCAN

18 I was lecturing to a group of English teachers

about Dante. Suddenly one of them got up—English teachers, mind you—and said, "What is Dante?" "Well, Madam," I replied, "It is a kind of detergent."

London *Sunday Times* 14 Sep 80

GEORGE P ELLIOTT

1 A novel is not just a work of art: It is somehow a work of life as well.

A Piece of Lettuce Random House 64

NORA EPHRON

2 It shines like a rhinestone in a trash can.

On Jacqueline Susann's *The Love Machine* Simon & Schuster 69, NY *Times* 11 Mar 69

CLIFTON FADIMAN

3 The adjective is the banana peel of the parts of speech.

Reader's Digest Sep 56

MARK FEENEY

4 Once the implicit aim of biography was to *uplift* . . . now it is to *unveil*.

"Profitable Lives" Boston *Globe* 25 Jan 87

JAMES FENTON

5 When Mr Ackroyd says that in the 18th century, stranglers bit off the noses of their victims, I feel that he probably knows what he is talking about. I just wish he hadn't told me.

On Peter Ackroyd's *Hawksmoor* Hamish Hamilton 85, London *Times* 26 Sep 85

JOHN KENNETH GALBRAITH

6 We have escapist fiction, so why not escapist biography?

On W A Swanberg's *Whitney Father, Whitney Heiress* Scribner's 80, NY *Times* 27 Jul 80

MARILYN GARDNER

7 The gift of the family novelist is to turn the cleaning of a closet into an inventory of love and loss—to scan a poem from a shopping list.

On Anne Tyler's *The Accidental Tourist* Knopf 85, *Christian Science Monitor* 4 Oct 85

WILLIAM H GASS

8 [For the speedy reader] paragraphs become a country the eye flies over looking for landmarks, reference points, airports, restrooms, passages of sex.

Habitations of the Word Simon & Schuster 85, quoted by Frank Kermode "Adornment and Fantastication" NY *Times* 10 Mar 85

9 The speeding reader guts a book the way the skillful clean fish. The gills are gone, the tail, the scales, the fins; then the fillet slides away swifly as though fed to a seal.

ib

10 Only the slow reader . . . will notice the odd crowd of images—flier, butcher, seal—which have gathered to comment on the aims and activities of the speeding reader, perhaps like gossips at a wedding.

ib

11 If you believed yourself to be a writer of . . . eminence, you are now assured of being over the hill—not a sturdy mountain flower but a little wilted lily of the valley.

Contending that "the Pulitzer Prize in fiction takes dead aim at mediocrity and almost never misses," *ib* 5 May 85

BRENDAN GILL

12 Parody is homage gone sour.

Here at the New Yorker Random House 75

REN GLASSER

13 He shows her through a magnifying glass which he holds in a velvet glove.

On Patrick O'Higgins's biography of Helena Rubinstein, *Madame* Viking 71, NY *Times* 22 Aug 71

HERBERT GOLD

14 He carried his childhood like a hurt warm bird held to his middle-aged breast.

On Sherwood Anderson, *The Age of Happy Problems* Dial 62

WALTER GOODMAN

15 He uses anecdotes for the same reason other people climb mountains—they are there.

On Robert Sam Anson, in review of *Exile: The Unquiet Oblivion of Richard M Nixon* Simon & Schuster 84, NY *Times* 28 Jun 84

ROBERT GRAVES

16 A remarkable thing about Shakespeare is that he is really very good in spite of all the people who say he is very good.

Recalled on his death 7 Dec 85

PAUL GRAY

17 [It] even looks exactly like a real book, with pages and print and dust jacket and everything. This disguise is extremely clever, considering the contents: the longest lounge act never performed in the history of the Catskills.

On Joseph Heller's *God Knows* Knopf 84, *ib* 24 Sep 84

1 People joked that Forster became more renowned with every book he did not write.
> On E M Forster, *ib* 31 Dec 84

JOHN GROSS

2 He has managed to capture the particular aura
that made even the poet's more mundane activities—of which there were many—
fascinatingly boring, so to speak, rather than
merely boringly boring.
> On Peter Ackroyd's *T S Eliot* Simon & Schuster
> 84, NY *Times* 7 Nov 84

3 The cliché is a hackneyed idiom that hopes
that it can still palm itself off as a fresh response.
> On Eric Partridge's *A Dictionary of Catch
> Phrases*, revised by Paul Beale, Stein & Day 85,
> *ib* 2 Jan 87

PHILIP GUEDALLA

4 Biography, like big game hunting, is one of the
recognized forms of sport, and it is [as] unfair
as only sport can be.
> Quoted by Robin Maugham "The Art of Biogra-
> phy" *MD* Mar 80

5 Autobiography is an unrivaled vehicle for telling the truth about other people.
> Quoted by Hugh Leonard NY *Times* 23 Nov 80

MEL GUSSOW

6 On her pages sacred cows become blustering
pachyderms.
> On Anita Loos's *Kiss Hollywood Good-bye* Vi-
> king 74, NY *Times* 31 Aug 74

THEODOR HAECKER

7 One of the most arrogant undertakings, to my
mind, is to write the biography of a man which
pretends to go beyond external facts and gives
the inmost motives. One of the most menda-
cious is autobiography.
> *Journal in the Night* Pantheon 50

JOHN HEILPERN

8 He left the self-conscious literary demimonde
of New York for the quiet infidelities of New
England.
> On John Updike, London *Observer* 25 Mar 79

ERNEST HEMINGWAY

9 All modern American literature comes from
one book by Mark Twain called *Huckleberry
Finn*.
> Quoted in NY *Times* 9 Dec 84

DONAL HENAHAN

10 Next to the writer of real estate advertisements, the autobiographer is the most suspect
of prose artists.
> NY *Times* 11 Feb 77

GEORGE V HIGGINS

11 Writing is the only trade I know of in which
sniveling confessions of extreme incompetence are taken as credentials probative of
powers to astound the multitude.
> *Harper's* Sep 84

12 The received image of a writer is that of an un-
productive sensitive who suffers from the va-
pors, is enslaved by his gonads, falls victim to
romantic swoons and passes out at deadlines.
> *ib*

DAVID HOLAHAN

13 Your piece stinks. We fed it to the turtle.
> Envisioning the ultimate, honest rejection by an
> editor, "Dining on Cardboard Au Gratin: A
> Free-lancer's Lament" *Christian Science Moni-
> tor* 13 Feb 85

A E HOUSMAN

14 Great literature should do some good to the
reader: must quicken his perception though
dull, and sharpen his discrimination though
blunt, and mellow the rawness of his personal
opinions.
> Quoted in report on Great Books discussion
> groups, NY *Times* 28 Feb 85

PHILIP HOWARD

15 Ted Hughes has been appointed poet laureate
to succeed Sir John Betjeman, which is a bit
like appointing a grim young crow to replace
a cuddly old teddy bear.
> London *Times* 20 Dec 84

16 He brings a gust of acrid provincial air to the
ancient office. He is an angry young prophet
rather than a smooth courtier. His verse is an-
gular, savage, robust and very good.
> *ib*

IRVING HOWE

17 The cruelest thing anyone can do to *Portnoy's
Complaint* is to read it twice.
> On Philip Roth's novel, quoted by Thomas
> Fleming "The War between Writers and Re-
> viewers" NY *Times* 6 Jan 85

RANDALL JARRELL

1 He thinks that Schiller and St Paul were just two *Partisan Review* editors.

> On Delmore Schwartz, quoted in Mary Jarrell ed *Randall Jarrell's Letters* Houghton Mifflin 85

HORACE JUDSON

2 At his best he penerated the magnolia curtain of Southern illusions to the secret springs of motive and action. He said, in effect, "This is the way it feels to be Southern"—something the North needs to know and the South may even need to be reminded of.

> On William Faulkner, *Time* 17 Jul 64

MICHIKO KAKUTANI

3 Glossy, efficient prose, garnished with a pinch of irony and a dab of melodrama.

> On Louis Auchincloss's *The Book Class* Houghton Mifflin 84, NY *Times* 26 Jul 84

T E KALEM

4 The English language brings out the best in the Irish. They court it like a beautiful woman. They make it bray with donkey laughter. They hurl it at the sky like a paint pot full of rainbows, and then make it chant a dirge for man's fate and man's follies that is as mournful as misty spring rain crying over the fallow earth.

> On Brendan Behan's 1958 play *Borstal Boy*, quoted in a *Time* advertisement, NY *Times* 17 Mar 79

5 Rarely has a people paid the lavish compliment and taken the subtle revenge of turning its oppressor's speech into sorcery.

> *ib*

STEFAN KANFER

6 The catalogue of miseries seems to cry out for commercial spots and a station break: the stuff of noonday soap opera.

> On Susan Kenney's *In Another Country* Viking 84, *Time* 11 Jun 84

7 Kenney . . . knows two essential truths about melodrama: First that it is most powerful when combined with irony and understatement; and second that it is a salient feature of modern life.

> *ib*

JOHN F KENNEDY, 35th US President

8 When power leads man toward arrogance, poetry reminds him of his limitations. When power narrows the area of man's concern, poetry reminds him of the richness and diversity of existence. When power corrupts, poetry cleanses.

> Last major public address, at dedication of Robert Frost Library, Amherst College, 26 Oct 63

RHODA KOENIG

9 Characters drop into whorehouses, have a little sex between paragraphs and leave without advancing the plot.

> On Gore Vidal's *Lincoln* Random House 84, *New York* 18 Jun 84

JOHN LAHR

10 His life was one long extravaganza, like living inside a Fabergé egg.

> On Noel Coward, "Politics of Charm" *Harper's* Oct 82

F R LEAVIS

11 He doesn't know what he means, and doesn't know he doesn't know.

> *Two Cultures? The Significance of C P Snow* Pantheon 63

CHRISTOPHER LEHMANN-HAUPT

12 Rice Krispies happens to be one of my favorite junk foods, just as I regard Michener as superior among junk writers.

> On James A Michener, in review of *Chesapeake* Random House 78, *International Herald Tribune* 8 Aug 78

13 One misses the hiss of acid.

> On Gore Vidal's *Lincoln* Random House 84, NY *Times* 30 May 84

14 We breathe, we think, we conceive of our lives as narratives.

> On Peter Brooks's *Reading for the Plot* Knopf 84, *ib* 11 Jul 84

15 What they have in common is that if the reviewer did not already possess them, he would long for them most greedily.

> On coffee-table books, *ib* 28 Nov 84

JOSEPH LELYVELD

16 His laughter, which was never far below the surface of his conversation, now sparkled like a splash of water in sunlight.

> From interview with V S Pritchett at age 85, NY *Times* 16 Dec 85

JOHN LEONARD

17 He seems to have . . . gone to his icebox, pulled out all the cold obsessions, mixed them in a bowl, beat too lightly and baked too long.

> On Gore Vidal's *Two Sisters* Little, Brown 70, NY *Times* 7 Jul 70

1 Aspiring to a soufflé, he achieves a pancake at which the reader saws without much appetite.
ib

2 There are too many ironies in the fire.
ib

3 His memoir is a splendid artichoke of anecdotes, in which not merely the heart and leaves but the thistles as well are edible.
On Brendan Gill's *Here at the New Yorker* Random House 75, *ib* 16 Feb 75

4 Books fall from Garry Wills like leaves from a maple tree in a sort of permanent October.
ib 15 Jul 79

5 [As] the Silks ... walk around the Establishment and poke it with a stick ... flocks of multicolored anecdotes rise into the air on flapping wings, and, occasionally, a bee stings.
On Leonard and Mark Silk's *The American Establishment* Basic 80, *ib* 15 Sep 80

6 A lollipop speaking baby talk.
On Suzanne Massie's *Land of the Firebird: The Beauty of Old Russia* Simon & Schuster 80, *ib* 8 Oct 80

Dwight Macdonald

7 The dominant rhetoric is academese relieved by flashes of cliché.
On NY *Times Book Review*, a criticism to which Sunday Editor Lester Markel replied, "Good people think I'm great, bad people think I'm a bastard," *Newsweek* 14 Sep 64

Melvin Maddocks

8 It is one test of a fully developed writer that he reminds us of no one but himself.
On Anthony Powell's *What's Become of Waring* Little, Brown 63, *Christian Science Monitor* 2 May 63

9 Writing is the most demanding of callings, more harrowing than a warrior's, more lonely than a whaling captain's—that, in essence, is the modern writer's message.
Christian Science Monitor 10 Apr 85

10 To choose art means to turn one's back on the world, or at least on certain of its distractions.
ib

Groucho Marx

11 From the moment I picked your book up until I laid it down I was convulsed with laughter. Someday I intend reading it.
On S J Perelman's 1929 book *Dawn Ginsbergh's Revenge*, quoted in *Life* 9 Feb 62

Somerset Maugham

12 The crown of literature is poetry.
Saturday Review 20 July 57

13 The writer of prose can only step aside when the poet passes.
ib

14 It is unsafe to take your reader for more of a fool than he is.
Selected Prefaces and Introductions Doubleday 63

André Maurois

15 *Lost Illusion* is the undisclosed title of every novel.
The Art of Writing Dutton 60

16 In literature as in love, we are astonished at what is chosen by others.
NY *Times* 14 Apr 63

Mary McCarthy

17 Every word she writes is a lie, including *and* and *the*.
On Lillian Hellman, a 1979 televised comment that resulted in a libel suit unresolved at the time of Hellman's death, recalled on opening of the play *Lillian*, NY *Times* 12 Jan 86

David McCord

18 Metaphorically these essays move as a quiet but observant coast-guard cutter among the rocks and islands up and down the littoral of our life.
On J B Priestley's *Essays of Five Decades* Little, Brown 68, NY *Times* 27 Oct 68

Cathleen McGuigan

19 Don't think of ... Diana Vreeland's memoir as a book; it's more like a lunch. A bit of soufflé, a glass of champagne, some green grapes—light, bubbly and slightly tart—all served up by an egocentric but inventive hostess.
On *DV* Knopf 84, *Newsweek* 25 Jun 84

H L Mencken

20 There are some people who read too much: the bibliobibuli.
Minority Report: H L Mencken's Notebooks Knopf 56

Suzy Menkes

21 This is a book lined with hard facts and stitched up with strong opinions.
On *McDowell's Directory of 20th-Century Fashion*, London *Times* 11 Dec 84

TED MORGAN

1 He saw them bearing not frankincense and myrrh but wormwood and hemlock.
> On Somerset Maugham's regard for biographers, *Maugham* Simon & Schuster 80

2 The Sitwells were less a family than a literary cartel with a gift for self-propagation.
> *ib*

3 He seemed embalmed in hatred.
> On Maugham's last years, *ib*

MALCOLM MUGGERIDGE

4 [Evelyn Waugh] was an antique in search of a period, a snob in search of a class.
> Quoted in Ian Hunter ed *Things Past: A Malcolm Muggeridge Anthology* Morrow 79

GLORIA NAYLOR

5 One should be able to return to the first sentence of a novel and find the resonances of the entire work.
> NY *Times* 2 June 85

JACK NEWFIELD

6 Koch has committed egocide with this book.
> On Edward Koch's *Mayor* Simon & Schuster 84, quoted in *People* 9 Apr 84

NEWSWEEK

7 The hotelkeeper's daughter is a nymphomaniac, the cab driver's wife is a prostitute, the druggist and the newspaper editor are rivals in lechery and the corresponding secretary of the WCTU is a dope addict. Just folks, one and all.
> On Day Keene and Dwight Vincent's *Chautauqua* Putnam 59, 29 Feb 60

8 Dipping into Marianne Moore is like trying potluck at Cartier's.
> 27 Nov 61

NEW YORK TIMES

9 A New Yorker looks to Neil Simon for cheering-up, Sigmund Freud for shocks of recognition and Sir Thomas More for Utopia.
> Editorial on books most frequently stolen from NY Public Library, "New Yorkers, by the Book" 4 Oct 86

10 The best way to read [a poem] is off the top of your head, and out of the corner of your eye.
> "Noted with Pleasure" 15 Mar 87

JOYCE CAROL OATES

11 When people say there is too much violence in [my books], what they are saying is there is too much reality in life.
> NY *Times* 27 Jul 80

JOHN O'HARA

12 So who's perfect? ... Washington had false teeth. Franklin was nearsighted. Mussolini had syphilis. Unpleasant things have been said about Walt Whitman and Oscar Wilde. Tchaikovsky had his problems, too. And Lincoln was constipated.
> Replying to criticism, *Carte Blanche* Fall 65

13 Little old ladies of both sexes. Why do I let them bother me?
> On reviewers, quoted by Thomas Fleming "The War Between Writers and Reviewers" NY *Times* 6 Jan 85

JACK PAAR

14 One gets the impression that this is how Ernest Hemingway would have written had he gone to Vassar.
> On Mary McCarthy's novel about Vassar's Class of '33, *The Group* Harcourt, Brace & World 63, quoted in *Look* 25 Feb 64

CHARLES POORE

15 An essayist is a lucky person who has found a way to discourse without being interrupted.
> NY *Times* 31 May 62

16 Satire is the most aggressive form of flattery.
> On Gilbert Highet's *The Anatomy of Satire* Princeton 62, *ib* 29 Sep 62

CHRISTOPHER PORTERFIELD

17 The case against interviews with writers is historic: They exploit personalities, expose their subjects in verbal undress, without their styles hitched up, and they traffic in anecdotes and gossip.
> On George Plimpton ed's *Writers at Work* Viking 84, *Time* 10 Sep 84

EZRA POUND

18 A dirty book worth reading.
> On Henry Miller's 1934 book *Tropic of Cancer*, recalled on Miller's death 7 Jun 80

PETER S PRESCOTT

19 Two things a novelist can do with a hat: Talk through it or pull a rabbit from it.
> On Muriel Spark's *The Only Problem* Putnam 84, *ib* 2 Jul 84

V S Pritchett

1 Detective stories are the art-for-art's sake of yawning Philistinism.
Books in General Harcourt, Brace 53

2 I swallow Dickens whole and put up with the indigestion.
Quoted by Richard Locke "In Praise of V S Pritchett" NY *Times* 29 Jun 80

3 A company of actors inside one suit, each twitting the others.
On T S Eliot, quoted by Peter Ackroyd *T S Eliot* Simon & Schuster 84

4 The wrongs of childhood and upbringing have made a large and obsessional contribution to autobiography and the novel. [But] such wrongs are a static capital unless invested in matters far beyond the sense of personal injury.
On Anthony West's *H G Wells* Random House 84, *New Yorker* 30 Jul 84

5 It is less the business of the novelist to tell us what happened than to show how it happened.
A Man of Letters Random House 86

6 [He was] the autodidact of the jails.
On Jean Genet, recalled on Genet's death, NY *Times* 16 Apr 86

Jonathan Raban

7 Good travel books are novels at heart.
Quoted by Christopher Lehmann-Haupt NY *Times* 26 Jan 87

J D Reed

8 After 18 chapters of crudités and quiche, one longs for some meat and potatoes.
On Mark Stevens's *Summer in the City* Random House 84, *Time* 21 May 84

Christopher Rick

9 A cliché begins as heartfelt and then its heart sinks.
Quoted by Anatole Broyard NY *Times* 20 Oct 83

Edward Sachs

10 Never underestimate an editor's intelligence and never overestimate a publisher's morality.
Publishers Weekly 6 Jul 84

Webster Schott

11 For all the "I's," he is a man of many masks.
On W H Auden, *Christian Science Monitor* 26 Aug 65

Delmore Schwartz

12 I should like you to consider this letter as a resignation; I want to resign as one of your most studious and faithful admirers.
Condemning Ezra Pound's anti-Semitism, quoted by James Atlas *Delmore Schwartz* Farrar, Straus & Giroux 77

Gene Shalit

13 Her books were put down by most critics but readers would not put down her books.
Eulogy for Jacqueline Susann, whose sales were greater at the time of her death than those of any other novelist, *Today* NBC TV 24 Sep 74

Vincent Sheean

14 I have always thought that the surest proof of talent is its condescension to genius.
On George Jean Nathan's tolerance of Sinclair Lewis, *Dorothy and Red* Houghton Mifflin 63

Wilfrid Sheed

15 Mr Michener, as timeless as a stack of *National Geographic*s, is the ultimate Summer Writer. Just as one goes back to the cottage in Maine, so one goes back to one's Michener.
On James A Michener, NY *Times* 6 Jul 80

Israel Shenker

16 From bar mitzvah on, [S J Perelman] had dreamed of being a Jewish Robert Louis Stevenson.
Coat of Many Colors Doubleday 85, quoted by Hugh Nissenson NY *Times* 17 Mar 85

Richard F Shepard

17 Queens, as yet unheard from in the world of New York letters, has found its bard.
On Jimmy Breslin, in review of *Table Money* Ticknor & Fields 86, NY *Times* 8 May 86

R F Sheppard

18 If one merely could name-drop most of the titles listed, he could be a social success; if one really read them all, he might be unbearable.
"Good Reading: A Helpful Guide for Serious Readers" NY *Times* 20 Feb 63

R Z Sheppard

19 The short story is like an old friend who calls whenever he is in town. We are happy to hear from it; we casually fan the embers of past intimacies, and buy it lunch.
On Ted Solotaroff ed's *The Best American Short Stories 1978* Houghton Mifflin 78, *ib* 9 Apr 79

1 His reserve of disdain appears endless. He could no sooner shut it off than a vampire could forgo his nightcap.

On Gore Vidal, *ib* 13 Jun 83

2 An able practitioner of glitz lit.

On Erich Segal, *ib* 13 May 85

FRANK SINATRA

3 Hell hath no fury like a hustler with a literary agent.

On Judith Exner's *My Story* Grove 77, quoted in *US* 16 Dec 85

ISAAC BASHEVIS SINGER

4 We write not only for children but also for their parents. They, too, are serious children.

Stories for Children Farrar, Straus & Giroux 85

EDITH SITWELL

5 A great many people now reading and writing would be better employed keeping rabbits.

Recalled on her death 9 Dec 64

ROBERT SKIDELSKY

6 [It is] voyeurism embellished with footnotes.

On modern biography writing, quoted by Mark Feeney "Profitable Lives" Boston *Globe* 25 Jan 87

JOHN SKOW

7 Nothing is more pleasurable than to sit in the shade, sip gin and contemplate other people's adulteries, and while the wormy apple of marriage still lives, the novel will not die.

On Alison Lurie's *The War between the Tates* Random House 74, *Time* 29 Jul 74

STEPHEN SPENDER

8 There is a certain justice in criticism. The critic is like a midwife—a tyrannical midwife.

Lecturing at Brooklyn College, NY *Times* 20 Nov 84

FRANCIS STEEGMULLER

9 I'm told that when Auden died, they found his Oxford [English Dictionary] all but clawed to pieces. That is the way a poet and his dictionary should come out.

NY *Times* 26 Mar 80

JOHN STEINBECK

10 Syntax, my lad. It has been restored to the highest place in the republic.

When asked his reaction to John F Kennedy's inaugural address, quoted by *Atlantic* Nov 69

GLORIA STEINEM

11 For the reader who has put away comic books, but isn't yet ready for editorials in the *Daily News*.

On Jacqueline Susann's first novel, *Valley of the Dolls,* quoted in review of Susann's last book, NY *Times* 11 Jul 76

JEAN STROUSE

12 Book critics are a weird journalistic subspecies: We may pull all-nighters, but they tend to take place at home, where page 648 leads inexorably to page 649.

In review of Osborn Elliott's *The World of Oz* Viking 80, *Newsweek* 12 May 80

DOROTHY THOMPSON

13 What was once Sinclair Lewis is buried in no ground. Even in life he was fully alive only in his writing. He lives in public libraries from Maine to California, in worn copies in the bookshelves of women from small towns who, in their girlhood, imagined themselves as Carol Kennicotts, and of medical men who, as youths, were inspired by Martin Arrowsmith.

"The Boy From Sauk Center" *Atlantic* Nov 60

14 He is an ineradicable part of American cultural history in the 1920s and 1930s, and no one seeking to recapture and record the habits, frames of mind, social movements, speech, aspirations, admirations, radicalism, reactions, crusades and Gargantuan absurdities of the American demos during those 20 years will be able to do without him.

ib

TIME MAGAZINE

15 Two of the most difficult tasks a writer can undertake, to write the truth about himself and about his mother.

On Frank O'Connor's *An Only Child* Knopf 61, 31 Mar 61

16 Sex is too often not only Topic A, but also Topic B and C as well.

On John O'Hara's novels, 7 Jun 63

17 She writes in ink as green as Irish grass—or vitriol.

On Edna O'Brien, 16 May 67

18 Some men kiss and do not tell; they are called gentlemen. Some men tell but do not kiss; they are called liars. Some men kiss and tell; they are called best-seller writers.

On Roger Vadim's *Bardot, Deneuve, Fonda* Simon & Schuster 85, *ib*

LIONEL TRILLING

1 Youth is a time when we find the books we give up but do not get over.
NY *Times* 6 Mar 66

SIEGFRIED UNSELD

2 One of the signs of Napoleon's greatness is the fact that he once had a publisher shot.
The Author and His Publisher University of Chicago 80, quoted by Herbert Mitgang NY *Times* 27 Jul 80

LOUIS UNTERMEYER

3 She has something to say about what life is like—which is all we ask of poetry.
On Phyllis McGinley, *Time* 18 Jun 65

JOHN UPDIKE

4 The refusal to rest content, the willingness to risk excess on behalf of one's obsessions, is what distinguishes artists from entertainers, and what makes some artists adventurers on behalf of us all.
On J D Salinger, *Christian Science Monitor* 26 Aug 65

5 The inner spaces that a good story lets us enter are the old apartments of religion.
Introduction to *The Best American Short Stories 1984* Houghton Mifflin 84, quoted by Anatole Broyard NY *Times* 11 Nov 84

6 A narrative is like a room on whose walls a number of false doors have been painted; while within the narrative, we have many apparent choices of exit, but when the author leads us to one particular door, we know it is the right one because it opens.
ib

7 Her sentences march under a harsh sun that bleaches color from them but bestows a peculiar, invigorating, Pascalian clarity.
On Muriel Spark's *The Only Problem* Putnam 84, *New Yorker* 23 Jul 84

8 [He had a] sensation of anxiety and shame, a sensitivity acute beyond usefulness, as if the nervous system, flayed of its old hide of social usage, must record every touch of pain.
On Franz Kafka, quoted in report on Great Books discussion groups, NY *Times* 28 Feb 85

9 But for a few phrases from his letters and an odd line or two of his verse, the poet walks gagged through his own biography.
On Peter Ackroyd's *T S Eliot* Simon & Schuster 84, in which the Eliot estate forbade quotation

from Eliot's books and letters, *New Yorker* 25 Mar 85

10 He skates saucily over great tracts of confessed ignorance.
On T S Matthews's biography of Eliot, *Great Tom* Harper & Row 74, *ib*

RICHARD USBORNE

11 There are only two kinds of Wodehouse readers, those who adore him and those who have never read him.
Quoted on centenary of P G Wodehouse's birth, *International Herald Tribune* 10 Oct 81

VANITY FAIR

12 Her acidic bons mots were the olives of the martini age.
On Dorothy Parker, Jun 86

GORE VIDAL

13 What is in question is a kind of book reviewing which seems to be more and more popular: the loose putting down of opinions as though they were facts, and the treating of facts as though they were opinions.
Taking issue with Dudley Fitt's review of his novel *Julian* Little, Brown 64, NY *Times* 5 Jul 64

14 Many writers who choose to be active in the world lose not virtue but time, and that stillness without which literature cannot be made.
Réalités Aug 66

15 This is not at all bad, except as prose.
On Herman Wouk's *The Winds of War* Little, Brown 71, quoted in *Time* 21 May 84

JOHN VINOCUR

16 Graham looks up ... It is a still look, and it shuts the door gently on the subject.
"The Soul-Searching Continues for Graham Greene" NY *Times* 3 Mar 85

EVELYN WAUGH

17 I think to be oversensitive about clichés is like being oversensitive about table manners.
Quoted in Donat Gallagher ed *A Little Order: A Selection from His Journalism* Little, Brown 81

18 Professional reviewers read so many bad books in the course of duty that they get an unhealthy craving for arresting phrases.
ib

E B WHITE

19 Thurber did not write the way a surgeon oper-

ates, he wrote the way a child skips rope, the way a mouse waltzes.

> Tribute to James Thurber, *New Yorker* 11 Nov 61

1 She would write 8 or 10 words, then draw her gun and shoot them down.

> On his wife Katharine S White, *Onward and Upward in the Garden* Farrar, Straus & Giroux 79

THORNTON WILDER

2 Literature is the orchestration of platitudes.

> *Time* 12 Jan 53

TENNESSEE WILLIAMS

3 [He is] a sweetly vicious old lady.

> On Truman Capote, *People* 11 Mar 85

EDMUND WILSON

4 The cruelest thing that has happened to Lincoln since he was shot by Booth was to fall into the hands of Carl Sandburg.

> *Time* 26 Jun 72

HERMAN WOUK

5 We are in the black theater of nonexistence. In an eye blink the curtain is up, the stage ablaze, for the vast drama of ourselves.

> On Genesis I as his favorite opening passage, NY *Times* 2 Jun 85

MUSIC & DANCE

Artists & Entertainers

FRED ASTAIRE

6 Dancing is a sweat job.

> Recalled on his death 22 Jun 87

JOAN BAEZ

7 Good morning, children of the 80s. This is your Woodstock, and it's long overdue.

> Opening Philadelphia Live Aid concert for African famine relief, NY *Times* 16 Jul 85

ROBERT BAKER

8 After you've designed and placed an organ as well as you possibly can, some well-meaning lady is able to ruin the whole thing by donating memorial carpeting.

> On modern organ building, *New Yorker* 23 Dec 61

GEORGE BALANCHINE

9 First comes the sweat. Then comes the beau-

ty—if you're very lucky and have said your prayers.

> Quoted by Bernard Taper *Balanchine* Harper & Row 63

10 God creates, I do not create. I assemble and I steal everywhere to do it—from what I see, from what the dancers can do, from what others do.

> NY *Times* 16 Dec 63

11 Most ballet teachers in the United States are terrible. If they were in medicine, everyone would be poisoned.

> *Newsweek* 4 May 64

12 In my ballets, woman is first. Men are consorts. God made men to sing the praises of women. They are not equal to men: They are better.

> *Time* 15 Sep 80

MIKHAIL BARYSHNIKOV

13 The essence of all art is to have pleasure in giving pleasure.

> *Time* 19 May 75

14 No dancer can watch Fred Astaire and not know that we all should have been in another business.

> Recalled on Astaire's death, *Newsweek* 6 Jul 87

THOMAS BEECHAM

15 Most of them sound like they live on seaweed.

> On sopranos, *Newsweek* 30 Apr 56

16 Movie music is noise. . . . even more painful than my sciatica.

> *Time* 24 Feb 58

17 No operatic star has yet died soon enough for me.

> Quoted on *Who Said That?* BBC TV 22 Aug 58

18 The English may not like music, but they absolutely love the noise it makes.

> NY *Herald Tribune* 9 Mar 61

LEONARD BERNSTEIN

19 Music . . . can name the unnamable and communicate the unknowable.

> *The Unanswered Question* Harvard 76

20 I'm not interested in having an orchestra sound like *itself.* I want it to sound like the composer.

> Quoted by Will Crutchfield "Orchestras in the Age of Jet-Set Sound" NY *Times* 6 Jan 85

E Power Biggs

1 The wonderful old paaah and chaah became just plain aaah.

On introduction of electric organs, *Newsweek* 21 Mar 77

Lois Bootsin

2 One day I'm a prostitute and the next day I'm a nun. Where else could you get instant conversion like that?

On work as supernumerary at Metropolitan Opera, NY *Times* 19 Nov 84

Nadia Boulanger

3 I've been a woman for a little over 50 years and have gotten over my initial astonishment. As for conducting an orchestra, that's a job where I don't think sex plays much part.

On becoming first woman to conduct Boston Symphony Orchestra, recalled on her death, *International Herald Tribune* 23 Oct 79

Pierre Boulez

4 The aim of music is not to express feelings but to express music. It is not a vessel into which the composer distills his soul drop by drop, but a labyrinth with no beginning and no end, full of new paths to discover, where mystery remains eternal.

Réalités Aug 65

Benjamin Britten

5 Composing is like driving down a foggy road toward a house. Slowly you see more details of the house—the color of the slates and bricks, the shape of the windows. The notes are the bricks and the mortar of the house.

Life 7 Aug 64

6 The old idea . . . of a composer suddenly having a terrific idea and sitting up all night to write it is nonsense. Nighttime is for sleeping.

ib

Grace Bumbry

7 I've gone from reluctance to acceptance to gung ho.

On singing title role in Metropolitan Opera's 1985 production of *Porgy and Bess*, NY *Times* 5 Feb 85

Sammy Cahn

8 The popular song is America's greatest ambassador.

NY *Times* 17 Apr 84

Maria Callas

9 I cannot switch my voice. My voice is not like an elevator going up and down.

After being fired by Rudolf Bing for refusing to sing 3 performances of *Traviata* during a 26-performance contract, quoted by Arianna Stassinopoulos *Maria Callas* Ballantine 81

10 When my enemies stop hissing, I shall know I'm slipping.

ib

11 I would like to be Maria, but there is La Callas who demands that I carry myself with her dignity.

ib

Elliot T Carter

12 My compositions deserve the medal, not me.

On receiving MacDowell Medal, NY *Times* 22 Aug 83

Pablo Casals

13 The cello is like a beautiful woman who has not grown older, but younger with time, more slender, more supple, more graceful.

Time 29 Apr 57

14 I am perhaps the oldest musician in the world. I am an old man but in many senses a very young man. And this is what I want you to be, young, young all your life, and to say things to the world that are true.

At a concert the summer before his death at age 96, NY *Times* 23 Oct 73

Gower Champion

15 I use dancing to embellish, extend or enlarge upon an existing emotion.

Recalled on his death 25 Aug 80

Van Cliburn

16 I'm not a success, I'm a sensation.

After winning International Tchaikovsky Piano Competition in Moscow, news summaries 31 Dec 58

17 An artist can be truly evaluated only after he is dead.

NY *Times* 9 Jun 85

Eddie Condon

18 Someday we may have as many followers as the harpsichord.

After financial failures of his early jazz guitar concerts, quoted in NY *Times* 17 May 64

AARON COPLAND

1 Don't ever let him near a microphone.

On Leonard Bernstein's tactlessness, quoted by Joan Peyser *Publishers Weekly* 5 Jun 87

AGNES DE MILLE

2 A good education is usually harmful to a dancer. A good calf is better than a good head.

News summaries 1 Feb 54

3 The practice mirror is to be used for the correction of faults, not for a love affair, and the figure you watch should not become your dearest friend.

"To a Young Dancer" *Atlantic* Dec 60

4 Modern dancers give a sinister portent about our times.

On teenage dance fads, NY *Times* 10 Jun 63

HOWARD DIETZ

5 Composers shouldn't think too much—it interferes with their plagiarism.

News summaries 31 Dec 74

BOB DYLAN

6 Chaos is a friend of mine.

Defining his musical style in the mid 1960s, quoted in *Newsweek* 9 Dec 85

DUKE ELLINGTON

7 Playing "bop" is like playing Scrabble with all the vowels missing.

Look 10 Aug 54

8 It's like an act of murder; you play with intent to commit something.

On jazz, NY *Herald Tribune* 9 Jul 61

9 Now I can say loudly and openly what I have been saying to myself on my knees.

When asked to compose sacred music, recalled on his death 24 May 74

10 Fate is being kind to me. Fate doesn't want me to be too famous too young.

On being passed over for Pulitzer Prize in 1965, quoted in *Christian Science Monitor* 24 Dec 86

ARTHUR FIEDLER

11 It's nice to eat a good hunk of beef but you want a light dessert, too.

On Boston Pops Orchestra, recalled on his death 10 Jul 79

MARGOT FONTEYN

12 Life offstage has sometimes been a wilderness of unpredictables in an unchoreographed world.

Margot Fonteyn: Autobiography Knopf 76

13 Great artists are people who find the way to be themselves in their art. Any sort of pretension induces mediocrity in art and life alike.

ib

IRA GERSHWIN

14 A song without music is a lot like H_2 without the O.

Connoisseur Feb 86

BENNY GOODMAN

15 If a guy's got it, let him give it. I'm selling music, not prejudice.

On including blacks in his orchestra, *Saturday Evening Post* 18 Dec 54

GLENN GOULD

16 The G-minor Symphony consists of eight remarkable measures . . . surrounded by a half-hour of banality.

On Mozart, quoted in Tim Page ed *The Glenn Gould Reader* Knopf 84

17 A record is a concert without halls and a museum whose curator is the owner.

Paraphrasing André Malraux, quoted in *Christian Science Monitor* 2 Aug 85

MARTHA GRAHAM

18 Dance is the hidden language of the soul of the body.

NY *Times* 31 Mar 85

OSCAR HAMMERSTEIN II

19 I hand him a lyric and get out of his way.

On partnership with Richard Rodgers, news summaries 12 May 55

JASCHA HEIFETZ

20 I occasionally play works by contemporary composers and for two reasons. First to discourage the composer from writing any more and secondly to remind myself how much I appreciate Beethoven.

Life 28 Jul 61

21 If I don't practice one day, I know it; two days, the critics know it; three days, the public knows it.

San Francisco *Examiner & Chronicle* 18 Apr 71

MARGARET HILLIS, choral director, Chicago Symphony Orchestra

1 There's only one woman I know of who could never be a symphony conductor, and that's the Venus de Milo.
NY *Times* 13 Jun 79

VLADIMIR HOROWITZ

2 My future is in my past and my past is my present. I must now make the present my future.
On resuming concert career after 12-year retirement, NY *Times* 17 Mar 65

3 Perfection itself is imperfection.
Defending false notes, *Newsweek* 17 May 65

4 I am a general. My soldiers are the keys and I have to command them.
NY *Times* 8 Jan 78

5 My face is my passport.
To Soviet official on visit to USSR, *Time* 28 Apr 86

GELSEY KIRKLAND

6 I danced with passion to spite the music.
On dancing title role in *The Firebird*, from her autobiography *Dancing on My Grave* Doubleday 86, quoted in *Vogue* Oct 86

ANDRÉ KOSTELANETZ

7 One of the greatest sounds of them all—and to me it is a sound—is utter, complete silence.
NY *Journal)American* 8 Feb 55

8 The conductor has the advantage of not seeing the audience.
Recalled on his death 13 Jan 80

FRITZ KREISLER

9 Genius is an overused word. The world has known only about a half dozen geniuses. . . . I got only fairly near.
News summaries 2 Feb 55

WANDA LANDOWSKA

10 I never practice; I always play.
Time 1 Dec 52

LOTTE LEHMANN

11 You have always given me more than I gave to you. . . . You were the wings on which I soared.
To farewell concert audience, *Life* 5 Mar 51

12 I had hoped you would protest, but please don't argue.
Announcing her retirement, recalled on her death 26 Aug 76

JOHN LENNON

13 We're more popular than Jesus Christ now.
Quoted in *Time* 12 Aug 66

14 I don't know which will go first—rock 'n' roll or Christianity.
ib

ALAN JAY LERNER

15 You're an egghead with two yolks.
On youthful self-confidence, recalled on his death 14 Jun 86

JAMES LEVINE

16 We do not seem to be finding . . . tomorrow's Toscas.
On shortage of great operatic voices, NY *Times* 23 Sep 79

LIBERACE

17 You can have either the Resurrection or you can have Liberace. But you can't have both.
On billing with Easter show at Radio City Music Hall, *New York* 15 Sep 86

JOSÉ LIMÓN

18 Dancers aren't pompous; they're too tired.
NY *Times* 31 Jul 66

FREDERICK LOEWE

19 It won't be long before we'll be writing together again. I just hope they have a decent piano up there.
Letter read at Alan Jay Lerner's memorial service, *Time* 21 Jul 86

GUY LOMBARDO

20 The sweetest music this side of heaven.
Slogan for Guy Lombardo and his Royal Canadians, recalled on his death 5 Nov 77

GEORGE LONDON

21 It was like a Japanese ball player being invited to play first base for the Yankees.
On being first American to sing *Boris Godunov* in the USSR, *Time* 26 Sep 60

MARCEL MARCEAU

22 Music conveys moods and images. Even in opera, where plots deal with the structure of destiny, it's music, not words, that provides power.
US News & World Report 23 Feb 87

23 Music and silence . . . combine strongly be-

cause music is done with silence, and silence is full of music.
ib

1 In silence and movement you can show the reflection of people.
ib

2 To communicate through silence is a link between the thoughts of man.
ib

IGOR MARKEVITCH

3 Baton technique is to a conductor what fingers are to a pianist.
Recalled on his death, *Time* 21 Mar 83

ZUBIN MEHTA

4 Although I am flexible and ready to take advice, I can't carry an umbrella of thoughts over my head that would distract me and affect my music making.
On why he doesn't read reviews, *New York* 14 Jan 85

LAURITZ MELCHIOR

5 Regard your voice as capital in the bank. . . . Sing on your interest and your voice will last.
News summaries 1 Apr 56

GIAN CARLO MENOTTI

6 Not an audience but a habit.
On patrons of the Metropolitan Opera, *Time* 1 May 50

7 Melody is a form of remembrance. . . . It must have a quality of inevitability in our ears.
ib

8 Any subject is good for opera if the composer feels it so intently he must sing it out.
ib

YEHUDI MENUHIN

9 The violinist is that peculiarly human phenomenon distilled to a rare potency—half tiger, half poet.
The Compleat Violinist Summit 86

ROBERT MERRILL

10 If you think you've hit a false note, sing loud. When in doubt, sing loud.
Saturday Evening Post 26 Oct 57

11 I felt I was painting with a Popsicle.
On singing *La Bohème* in English, NY *Times* 30 Dec 75

MITCH MILLER

12 Keep it simple, keep it sexy, keep it sad.
On popular music, *Time* 23 Feb 50

DIMITRI MITROPOULOS

13 I never use a score when conducting my orchestra. . . . Does a lion tamer enter a cage with a book on how to tame a lion?
News summaries 22 Jan 51

RUDOLF NUREYEV

14 A pas de deux is a dialogue of love. How can there be conversation if one partner is dumb?
On expanding role of danseur, *Newsweek* 19 Apr 65

EUGENE ORMANDY

15 I'm one of the boys, no better than the last second violinist. . . . I'm just the lucky one to be standing in the center, telling them how to play.
NY *Times* 4 May 80

ITZHAK PERLMAN

16 You see, our fingers are circumcised . . . which gives them very good dexterity, particularly in the pinky.
On observation that many world-class violinists are Jewish, *60 Minutes* CBS TV 21 Dec 80

BERNADETTE PETERS

17 Singing lessons are like body building for your larynx.
NY *Times* 20 Sep 85

COLE PORTER

18 My sole inspiration is a telephone call from a producer.
News summaries 28 Feb 55

MENAHEM PRESSLER

19 There is a greater sense of brilliance when a trio plays, just because of the sheer volume that they can create and still be equals.
On playing the piano in Beaux Arts Trio, NY *Times* 18 Nov 84

DORY PREVIN

20 If I can say something honest about my feelings and thoughts and problems as a minority of one, then won't it be meaningful to all the other individual minorities of one?
On writing ballads, NY *Times* 16 Jan 72

LEONTYNE PRICE

1 It was the first operatic mountain I climbed, and the view from it was astounding, exhilarating, stupefying.

On her 1961 Metropolitan Opera debut, *NY Times* 31 Dec 84

2 I prefer to leave standing up, like a well-mannered guest at a party.

On her retirement from opera, *Newsweek* 14 Jan 85

3 It makes me feel just wonderful to have this black god standing behind me.

On singing with Simon Estes in *Aida, ib*

NED ROREM

4 Composition is notation of distortion of what composers think they've heard before. Masterpieces are marvelous misquotations.

The Paris Diary of Ned Rorem Braziller 66

5 If music could be translated into human speech, it would no longer need to exist.

Music from Inside Out Braziller 67

6 [Musical] themes are people, the notes are people's actions.

The Final Diary Holt, Rinehart & Winston 74

7 It isn't evil that's running the earth, but mediocrity. The crime is not that Nero played while Rome burned, but that he played badly.

ib

8 To see itself through, music must have idea or magic. ... Music with neither dies young though rich.

Pure Contraption Holt, Rinehart & Winston 74

9 Music is the sole art which evokes nostalgia for the future.

Edition Peters Contemporary Music Catalogue 75

10 No artist wants to be "understood." If he's "understood," he feels superficial. What an artist wants is not to be misunderstood.

W 10 Oct 80

11 To have a large audience is not obscene. To want one is.

ib

12 Art means to dare—and to have been right.

ib

DIANA ROSS

13 We is terrific.

Motto of The Supremes, quoted by Mary Wilson *Dreamgirl* St Martin's 86

MSTISLAV ROSTROPOVICH

14 [It is my] wooden wife.

On his Stradivarius, *Wall Street Journal* 23 Feb 87

ARTUR RUBINSTEIN

15 Sometimes when I sit down to practice and there is no one else in the room, I have to stifle an impulse to ring for the elevator man and offer him money to come in and hear me.

Holiday May 63

16 Composing a concert is like composing a menu. ... If you start with light pieces and play a 45-minute sonata after the interlude, it's like starting dinner with hors d'oeuvres and dessert and finishing with a Châteaubriand and vegetables.

Time 9 Apr 79

17 The first movement represented the struggles of my youth, the following andante the beginning of a more serious aspect of my talent, a scherzo represented well the unexpected success and the finale turned out to be a wonderfully moving end.

On final concert in London's Wigmore Hall, where he had given his first recital, *My Many Years* Knopf 80

ARTUR SCHNABEL

18 The notes I handle no better than many pianists. But the pauses between the notes—ah, that is where the art resides!

Chicago *Daily News* 11 Jun 58

ARNOLD SCHÖNBERG

19 There is still a lot of good music waiting to be written in C major.

News summaries 31 Dec 51

ANDRÉS SEGOVIA

20 Sometimes one is without the pleasure of playing. But when the silence of the audience is perfect, we recover that.

Christian Science Monitor 18 Mar 60

21 Among God's creatures two, the dog and the guitar, have taken all the sizes and all the shapes, in order not to be separated from the man.

NY Times 16 Feb 64

22 The guitar is a small orchestra. It is polyphonic. Every string is a different color, a different voice.

Christian Science Monitor 5 Aug 86

1 The piano is a monster that screams when you touch its teeth.

> Quoted by Eugenia Zukerman *Sunday Morning* CBS TV 7 Jun 87

TED SHAWN

2 Dance is the only art of which we ourselves are the stuff of which it is made.

> *Time* 25 Jul 55

DIMITRI SHOSTAKOVICH

3 A creative artist works on his next composition because he was not satisfied with his previous one.

> NY *Times* 25 Oct 59

BEVERLY SILLS

4 My voice had a long, nonstop career. It deserves to be put to bed with quiet and dignity, not yanked out every once in a while to see if it can still do what it used to do. It can't.

> On refusal to sing after her retirement from opera, *Time* 18 Jul 83

5 So long as it doesn't get to the point where you don't remember whose opera you're listening to, I'm willing to experiment.

> On set design at NYC Opera, quoted in *Newsweek* 8 Oct 84

6 I lived through the garbage. I might as well dine on the caviar.

> Answering speculation that NYC Opera's success would lead to her resignation as director, NY *Times* 15 Oct 84

7 Art is the signature of civilizations.

> NBC TV 4 May 85

LEONARD SLATKIN

8 I use my hands like a sculptor, to mold and shape the sound I want, to clarify.

> Quoted by Tim Page "An American Conductor Succeeds at Home" NY *Times* 20 May 84

9 How could a New Yorker possibly take something called the Hollywood String Quartet seriously?

> *ib*

BRUCE SPRINGSTEEN

10 This music is forever for me. It's the stage thing, that rush moment that you live for. It never lasts, but that's what you live for.

> *Time* 27 Oct 75

11 Music was my way of keeping people from looking through and around me. I wanted the heavies to know I was around.

> On writing his own music, *ib*

12 Born in the USA.

> Title of 1984 song and concert tour

ISAAC STERN

13 Playing a concerto with Zubin is like being surrounded by a well-loved, cashmere-lined silk glove.

> On Zubin Mehta, *New York* 14 Jan 85

14 Everywhere in the world, music enhances a hall, with one exception: Carnegie Hall enhances the music.

> As president of Carnegie Hall, quoted in NY *Times* 17 May 85

LEOPOLD STOKOWSKI

15 On matters of intonation and technicalities I am more than a martinet—I am a martinetissimo.

> Recalled on his death 13 Sep 77

IGOR STRAVINSKY

16 To listen is an effort, and just to hear is no merit. A duck hears also.

> News summaries 24 Jun 57

17 The real composer thinks about his work the whole time; he is not always conscious of this, but he is aware of it later when he suddenly knows what he will do.

> *Saturday Review* 9 Nov 57

18 My music is best understood by children and animals.

> London *Sunday Observer* 8 Oct 61

19 Harpists spend 90 percent of their lives tuning their harps and 10 percent playing out of tune.

> Recalled on his death 6 Apr 71

GEORGE SZELL

20 Conductors must give unmistakable and suggestive signals to the orchestra—not choreography to the audience.

> *Newsweek* 28 Jan 63

LOUISE TALMA

21 Too many composers become involved in intellectual speculation which seems to matter more to them than the sound that comes out of all this speculation.

> NY *Times* 19 Oct 86

VIRGIL THOMSON

22 I thought of myself as a species of knight errant attacking dragons single-handedly and rescuing musical virtue in distress.

> On role as critic, quoted in NY *Times* 22 Nov 81

1 I never learned to verbalize an abstract musical concept. No thank you. The whole point of being a serious musician is to avoid verbalization whenever you can.
Christian Science Monitor 12 Feb 85

2 You explain how it went, and as far as you can figure out how it got that way.
On role as critic, *ib*

3 I don't have to worry ... No matter what they do to it, it works.
On his 1947 opera *The Mother of Us All, ib*

4 I don't care what [other critics] say, I only hope to be played.
On being asked which of his compositions would endure, *ib*

5 Musicians ... own music because music owns them.
Commencement address at New England Conservatory of Music 18 May 86

6 I've never known a musician who regretted being one. Whatever deceptions life may have in store for you, music itself is not going to let you down.
ib

7 I let her alone and when she got that finished she left me alone. We trusted each other.
On collaborating with Gertrude Stein on *Four Saints in Three Acts*, NY *Times* 9 Nov 86

8 I don't go around regretting things that don't happen.
On infrequency with which the Thomson-Stein opera has been produced, *ib*

9 I seem to write an opera about every 20 years; if you live long enough you can write four operas. I finished my third in 1970.
Interview at age 90, PBS TV 23 Nov 86

ARTURO TOSCANINI

10 God tells me how the music should sound, but *you* stand in the way.
To a trumpet player, NY *Times* 11 Apr 54

11 After I die I shall return to earth as the doorkeeper of a bordello and I won't let a one of you in.
To an orchestra that displeased him, recalled on his death 16 Jan 57

12 Assassins!
After rehearsing an orchestra, *ib*

13 To some it is Napoleon, to some it is a philosophical struggle, to me it is allegro con brio.
On Beethoven's Eroica, recalled on the opening

of Toscanini archive at NY Public Library, NY *Times* 5 Apr 87

RICHARD TUCKER

14 To sing it right, Franco, you have to be Jewish.
To Franco Corelli when asked to explain his success with Puccini, quoted by Ethan Mordden *Opera Anecdotes* Oxford 85

ALAIN VAËS

15 You translate paint to fabric, somebody gets into it and the ballet begins.
On designing costumes, *Christian Science Monitor* 21 Jul 86

RALPH VAUGHAN WILLIAMS

16 I don't know whether I like it, but it is what I meant.
On his *London* Symphony, quoted by Adrian Boult BBC Radio 1 Aug 65

FRED WARING

17 Be on your toes tonight—or I'll be on yours tomorrow.
To his chorus, recalled on his death 29 Jul 84

LEONARD WARREN

18 Tenors are noble, pure and heroic and get the soprano, if she has not tragically expired before the final curtain. But baritones are born villains in opera. Always the heavy and never the hero—that's me.
NY *World-Telegram & Sun* 13 Mar 57

ETHEL WATERS

19 We are all gifted. That is our inheritance.
On black singers, CBS TV 8 Jan 54

LAWRENCE WELK

20 If they can't hum it after we play it, it's not for us.
On music performed on his long-running television program, *Saturday Evening Post* Mar 80

21 It's the first time I ever got a standing ovation in the sky.
After giving autographs on a flight from Florida to California, *ib*

Producers, Directors & Managers

RUDOLF BING

22 The opera always loses money. That's as it should be. Opera has no business making money.
NY *Times* 15 Nov 59

1 I prefer to remember the happy things over 10 years, the things that went well. Let me see, what did go well?

After a decade as manager of Metropolitan Opera, NY *Herald Tribune* 9 Oct 60

2 I will not enter into a public feud with Madame Callas, since I am well aware that she has considerably greater competence and experience at that kind of thing than I have.

Quoted in Cleveland Amory and Earl Blackwell eds *Celebrity Register* Harper & Row 63

3 I don't want them to come in with a white tie, and I don't want them to come in a black tie. But I do want them to come in a tie.

On standees, NY *Times* 16 Feb 64

4 Expressions of disapproval are on a level of vulgarity that cannot be tolerated. The way to express disapproval is to do without applause.

NY *Herald Tribune* 9 Apr 64

5 It is becoming increasingly difficult to obtain the services of first-class conductors. . . . They are sick and tired of dealing with singers, as I am.

ib

6 I never for a moment believed they would perform at 10 o'clock in the morning. It's hard enough getting them to perform at 8 at night.

Apologizing to World's Fair audience for singers who overslept, NY *Times* 5 May 64

7 I am perfectly happy to believe that nobody likes us but the public.

Replying to newspaper criticism of Metropolitan Opera, *Texaco Theater of the Air* 17 Apr 65

8 We are similar to a museum. My function is to present old masterpieces in modern frames.

Time 8 Oct 65

9 There are two sighs of relief every night in the life of an opera manager. The first comes when the curtain goes up . . . The second sigh of relief comes when the final curtain goes down without any disaster, and one realizes, gratefully, that the miracle has happened again.

New Yorker 17 Sep 66

10 She will sing only if her husband conducts, so I accept the old Viennese saying that if you want the meat, you have to take the bones.

On Joan Sutherland, *5,000 Nights at the Opera* Doubleday 72

11 Miss Renata Tebaldi was always sweet and very firm. . . . she had dimples of iron.

ib

12 We want an ensemble of stars, not comets.

On continuity among performers, *National Observer* 29 Apr 72

13 How nice the human voice is when it isn't singing.

Newsweek 1 May 72

14 They have a disease of the throat.

On singers, *ib*

15 If that is not enough, will you please politely indicate that she can go to hell.

November 21, 1957, letter to Metropolitan Opera's Italian representative on prolonged financial negotiations with Maria Callas, quoted in "A Century of Offstage Life at the Metropolitan Opera" NY *Times* 25 Sep 83

GOERAN GENTELE

16 Opera is an 18th- and 19th-century art that must find a 20th-century audience.

On becoming general manager of Metropolitan Opera, NY *Times* 12 Sep 71

17 There are so many tensions involved in any creative activity . . . so when there is a catastrophe you never indicate that you think the end of the world has come. You examine it and say, "Well, this is a fine new catastrophe. Now, what else is important today?"

ib

LORD HAREWOOD (George Henry Hubert Lascelles)

18 There is an old proverb much in evidence now at the [National Opera]: If you want the flowers in your garden to be glorious and to smell good, you must risk an occasional stink.

On retiring, "A Lifetime of Undaunted Passion" London *Times* 20 Jun 85

JOAN INGPEN

19 I really love them but, of course, they tend to be more highly strung than actors because everything depends on those two little vocal cords and their life is a perpetual worry.

On booking opera singers, NY *Times* 23 Sep 79

LINCOLN KIRSTEIN

20 In liberal democracy and anxious anarchy, the traditional classic dance, compact of aristocratic authority and absolute freedom in a necessity of order, has never been so promising as an independent expression as it is today.

Classic Ballet, with Muriel Stuart, Knopf 52

21 A repertory, a patrimony of ballets, tended as

carefully as the collection of 600-year-old bonsai in Tokyo's Imperial Palace conservatory, is not replaced; it is preserved, maintained, refreshed to give rebirth by grafting and seedlings.
>On NYC Ballet, NY *Times* 17 Mar 83

1 I've always had the idea ... that we were conducting a military operation. It always seemed to me to be in a state of emergency.
>*New Yorker* 15 Dec 86

JOSHUA LOGAN

2 His music was direct from his heart and brain in the purest form possible.
>On Richard Rodgers, NY *Times* 17 Mar 85

3 Music has a poetry of its own, and that poetry is called melody.
>*ib*

ROUBEN MAMOULIAN

4 Critics complained it wasn't opera, it wasn't a musical. You give someone something delicious to eat and they complain because they have no name for it.
>Recalling his direction of the 1935 production of *Porgy and Bess*, NY *Times* 3 Feb 85

ANDRÉ MERTENS

5 Singers' husbands! Find me stones heavy enough to place around their necks and drown them all!
>*Time* 1 Aug 60

6 Somewhere in the brain of every prima donna there is a deep craving for security and comfort, linked with a fear of old age. This causes her to pick a man who is prepared to act as a permanent wet nurse.
>*ib*

SEYMOUR ROSEN

7 One of the biggest problems today is the era of the guest conductor, and the music director who isn't.
>Quoted by Will Crutchfield "Orchestras in the Age of Jet-Set Sound" NY *Times* 6 Jan 85

Observers & Critics

CHRISTOPHER ANDREAE

8 To the sound itself ... the conductor adds the italics and punctuation of gesture, of strained arms, of startling tautness of the shoulders, of brisk nod, of hands flung apart in some wild appeal to the universe.
>"Maestro" *Christian Science Monitor* 18 Dec 85

W H AUDEN

9 No good opera plot can be sensible, for people do not sing when they are feeling sensible.
>*Time* 29 Dec 61

10 [Music] can be made anywhere, is invisible and does not smell.
>From 1951 poem "In Praise of Limestone," quoted in Kent Hieatt and William Clark eds *College Anthology of British and American Poetry* Allyn & Bacon 72

CLIVE BARNES

11 One of the few things in dance to match the Royal Ballet's curtain calls is the Royal Ballet's dancing.
>"The Art of Acknowledgment" NY *Times* 10 Jun 66

KARL BARTH

12 Whether the angels play only Bach praising God, I am not quite sure. I am sure, however, that *en famille* they play Mozart.
>Recalled on his death 9 Dec 68

JACQUES BARZUN

13 The piano is the social instrument par excellence. ... drawing-room furniture, a sign of bourgeois prosperity, the most massive of the devices by which the young are tortured in the name of education and the grown-up in the name of entertainment.
>Preface to Arthur Loesser *Men, Women and Pianos* Simon & Schuster 54

14 Music is intended and designed for sentient beings that have hopes and purposes and emotions.
>Introduction to Joan Peyser *The New Music* Delacorte 71

WILLIAM F BUCKLEY JR

15 The Beatles are not merely awful. ... They are so unbelievably horrible, so appallingly unmusical, so dogmatically insensitive to the magic of the art, that they qualify as crowned heads of antimusic.
>News summaries 8 Sep 64

PERCY CATER

16 It is no part of the functions of orchestral hall managers to tell me when I should cough. Anybody who wants to collect British seat money in the British winter must put up with the British cough.
>On "coughing instructions" inserted in programs

at London's Royal Festival Hall, *Newsweek* 18 Feb 63

JAY COCKS

1 He is a glorified gutter rat from a dying New Jersey town who walks with an easy swagger that is part residual stage presence, part boardwalk braggadocio.
On Bruce Springsteen, *Time* 27 Oct 75

JEAN COCTEAU

2 The ear disapproves but tolerates certain musical pieces; transfer them into the domain of our nose, and we will be forced to flee.
Recalled on his death 11 Oct 63

ALISTAIR COOKE

3 Cocktail music is accepted as audible wallpaper.
"The Innocent American" *Holiday* Jul 62

JOHN CORRY

4 His words and music weren't just joined; they were inseparably married.
On Cole Porter, NY *Times* 29 Jul 87

PETER DE VRIES

5 The tuba is certainly the most intestinal of instruments, the very lower bowel of music.
The Glory of the Hummingbird Little, Brown 74

RABBI CHAIM DRIZIN

6 Song is the pen of the soul.
At funeral for tenor Jan Peerce, NY *Times* 18 Dec 84

CHET FLIPPO

7 [The star] had to be from humble beginnings, just like the audience.
On country music singers, NY *Times* 6 Sep 85

E M FORSTER

8 This opera is my *Nunc Dimittis*, in that it dismisses me peacefully and convinces me I have achieved.
On *Billy Budd*, in letter to collaborator Benjamin Britten, quoted in Mary Lago and P N Furbank eds *Selected Letters of E M Forster 1921-70* Belknap Press/Harvard 84

GEROLD FRANK

9 You heard a leaf fall, she heard a house crash.
On Judy Garland, NBC TV 9 Jul 75

SAMUEL G FREEDMAN

10 His song "King of the Road" remains one of the anthems of the asphalt.
On Roger Miller, NY *Times* 21 Apr 85

FORD FRICK, baseball commissioner

11 I'd hate this to get out but I really like opera.
News summaries 8 Feb 54

WILLIAM E GEIST

12 Kristin Brown looks as though she could have been mailed first-class to New York for about a dollar and a half.
On 13-year-old ballerina from Dunwoody GA, NY *Times* 17 Jul 85

DONAL HENAHAN

13 Real folk music long ago went to Nashville and left no known survivors.
NY *Times* 8 May 77

14 It might be argued that genuine spontaneity is not really possible or desirable so long as printed scores of great works exist. .... All modern musicians are, for better or worse, prisoners of Gutenberg.
"Whatever Happened to Spontaneity in Performance?" *ib* 13 May 84

15 [Rubinstein was] a fountain from which music spouted, not a recitalist.
On Artur Rubinstein, *ib*

16 The irrepressible spirit that made his playing seem like good conversation . . . is the Rubinstein legacy for pianists, if they can pick up their heads from the keyboard long enough to claim it.
ib

17 In her most taxing aria, "O patria mia," there were powerful reminders of the Price that we remember best and want to remember, a Price beyond pearls.
Reviewing Leontyne Price's farewell performance in *Aida*, *ib* 4 Jan 85

18 The human brain can soften as a result of incessant listening to music with an intent to commit prose.
On reviewing, "When Inspired Awfulness Becomes Interesting" *ib* 31 Aug 86

19 The more disastrous the mishaps the simpler the reviewing task.
ib

20 Perhaps no hall of comparable size anywhere has served so nobly as a spawning ground for

young talent and, it must be said, as a grave-yard for the hopes of the mediocre.

> On renovated Weill Recital Hall in Carnegie Hall, *ib* 6 Jan 87

1 [It] will never be mistaken for a high school gymnasium or a meeting room in a Midwestern motel.

> *ib*

JON LANDAU

2 I saw rock 'n' roll future and its name is Bruce Springsteen.

> Quoted by Dave Marsh *Glory Days* Pantheon 87

PHILIP LARKIN

3 The chromatic scale is what you use to give the effect of drinking a quinine martini and having an enema simultaneously.

> *Required Writing* Farrar, Straus & Giroux 84, quoted in *Newsweek* 25 Jun 84

GODDARD LIEBERSON

4 Show me an orchestra that likes its conductor and I'll show you a lousy conductor.

> Quoted by Herbet Kupferberg *Those Fabulous Philadelphians* Scribner's 69

RUSSELL LYNES

5 [Ragtime] was a fanfare for the 20th century.

> *The Lively Audience* Harper & Row 85, quoted in *Christian Science Monitor* 18 Nov 85

MELVIN MADDOCKS

6 Giving jazz the Congressional seal of approval is a little like making Huck Finn an honorary Boy Scout.

> On resolution to designate jazz as a US national treasure, *Christian Science Monitor* 24 Dec 86

KENNETH MILLER

7 The piano's world encompasses glass-nerved virtuosi and stomping barrel-housers in fedoras; it is a world of pasture and storm, of perfumed smoke, of liquid mathematics.

> "How to Buy a Piano "*Esquire* Apr 86

8 No other acoustic instrument can match the piano's expressive range, and no electric instrument can match its mystery.

> *ib*

9 [The piano is] able to communicate the subtlest universal truths by means of wood, metal and vibrating air.

> *ib*

HENRY MITCHELL

10 The choirs left the main tune and soared two octaves past heaven in a descant to rattle the bones and surge the heart.

> On dedication of nave of Washington DC's National Cathedral, Washington *Post* 9 Jul 76

RALPH NOVAK

11 Her voice sounded like an eagle being goosed.

> On Yoko Ono in television documentary *John and Yoko, People* 2 Dec 85

WALTER NURENA

12 The ballet people are champagne drinkers. They are a younger, more exciting crowd than the opera people.

> On tending bar at Lincoln Center, NY *Times* 23 Nov 84

13 With each ballet we know what to expect. A pas de deux brings out a lot of excitement. And a lot of champagne.

> *ib*

VANCE PACKARD

14 Rock 'n' roll might best be summed up as monotony tinged with hysteria.

> Testimony to Senate Subcommittee on Interstate Commerce, news summaries 31 Dec 58

TONY PALMER

15 Wagner *was* a monster. He was anti-Semitic on Mondays and vegetarian on Tuesdays. On Wednesday he was in favor of annexing Newfoundland, Thursday he wanted to sink Venice and Friday he wanted to blow up the pope.

> On directing a nine-hour biographical film about Richard Wagner, *TV Guide* 18 Oct 86

JOAN PEYSER

16 Musicians, even more than writers or artists, tend to be deified, and the institutions that surround them like to preserve that.

> On why there are few unauthorized biographies of living musical figures, *Publishers Weekly* 5 Jun 87

HENRY PLEASANTS

17 [She] could hold a note as long as the Chase National Bank.

> On Ethel Merman, *The Great American Popular Singers* Simon & Schuster 85, quoted in NY *Times* 16 Feb 85

18 One small town boy, born at the right time, in the right place, in the right environment and

under the right circumstances [represented the convergence] of all the musical currents of America's subculture: black and white gospel, country and western and rhythm and blues.

On Elvis Presley, *ib*

TOM PRIDEAUX

1 It wasn't a man singing a song. It was a man singing his autobiography.

On Irving Berlin singing "There's No Business Like Show Business," *Life* 3 May 63

DUNCAN PURNEY

2 I can see fiddling around with a banjo, but how do you banjo around with a fiddle?

Musical Notes WQXR Radio 16 May 84

ALAN RICH

3 No composer in history . . . has been so widely jazzed up, watered down, electrified and otherwise transmogrified, debated and admired as this German provincial.

On Johann Sebastian Bach, *Newsweek* 24 Dec 84

4 From the first, critics had no difficulty recognizing his talents: 10 omnipotent fingers at the command of a musical intelligence that made light of the most fearful musical challenges.

On Glenn Gould, *ib* 28 Jan 85

HAROLD C SCHONBERG

5 When Callas carried a grudge, she planted it, nursed it, fostered it, watered it and watched it grow to sequoia size.

On Maria Callas, *The Glorious Ones* Times Books 85, quoted in NY *Times* 21 Aug 85

ANITA T SULLIVAN

6 A piano is full of suppressed desires, recalcitrance, inhibition, conflict.

The Seventh Dragon Metamorphous Press 85, quoted in NY *Times* 24 Aug 86

BERNARD TAPER

7 Balanchine has trained his cat to perform brilliant *jetés* and *tours en l'air*; he says that at last he has a body worth choreographing for.

Balanchine Harper & Row 63

VARIETY

8 It will be gone by June.

1955 statement on rock 'n' roll, quoted by Christopher Cerf and Victor Navasky *The Experts Speak* Pantheon 84

REBECCA WEST

9 Great music is in a sense serene; it is certain of the values it asserts.

This Real Night Viking 85, quoted in *Time* 25 Mar 85

PRESS
Reporters & Editors

JOSEPH W ALSOP JR

10 The plain truth is that the reporter's trade is for young men. Your feet, which do the legwork, are nine times more important than your head, which fits the facts into a coherent pattern.

On retiring at age 64, *Newsweek* 7 Oct 74

JACK ANDERSON

11 I don't like to hurt people, I really don't like it at all. But in order to get a red light at the intersection, you sometimes have to have an accident.

Newsweek 3 Mar 72

BEN BAGDIKIAN

12 Trying to be a first-rate reporter on the average American newspaper is like trying to play Bach's St Matthew Passion on a ukulele: The instrument is too crude for the work, for the audience and for the performer.

Quoted by Melvin Maddocks *Christian Science Monitor* 23 Jan 85

CARL BERNSTEIN and BOB WOODWARD

13 From then on, any Watergate story would carry both names. [Our] colleagues melded the two into one and gleefully named [our] byline Woodstein.

On joint byline for Washington *Post* coverage of Watergate, *All the President's Men* Simon & Schuster 74

THEODORE M BERNSTEIN

14 If writing must be a precise form of communication, it should be treated like a precision instrument. It should be sharpened, and it should not be used carelessly.

On ideal writing and editing at the NY *Times*, recalled on his death 27 Jun 79

15 I favor *whom*'s doom except after a preposition.

Ending some years of ambivalence on the use of *who* and *whom*, *ib*

JIM BISHOP

1 A newspaper is lumber made malleable. It is ink made into words and pictures. It is conceived, born, grows up and dies of old age in a day.
Quill Oct 63

ERMA BOMBECK

2 I was too old for a paper route, too young for Social Security and too tired for an affair.
On beginning her humor column, *Time* 2 Jul 84

JOHN BORRELL

3 Covering Africa is 80 percent logistics and 20 percent reporting.
Time 29 Aug 83

JIMMY BRESLIN

4 A job on a newspaper is a special thing. Every day you take something that you found out about, and you put it down and in a matter of hours it becomes a product. Not just a product like a can or something. It is a personal product that people, a lot of people, take the time to sit down and read.
On closing of NY *Mirror*, NY *Herald Tribune* 17 Oct 63

HELEN GURLEY BROWN, Editor in Chief, *Cosmopolitan*

5 I care. I care a lot. I think of *Cosmopolitan* all day, and I run scared. So it's a combination of fright, caring and anxiety.
To Amer Magazine Conference, NY *Times* 25 Oct 84

WILLIAM BUCHANAN

6 The general outlook is not that the person has died but that the person has lived.
On writing obituaries for the Boston *Globe*, quoted in Northwestern University *Byline* Winter 82

HODDING CARTER III

7 I put a premium on responsibility. Too much of the television thing consists of the unseen hand with the up-front mouth, and the news magazine's separating the reporter and writer scares me. When you are clearly accountable, it breeds more rigorous reporting.
Quoted in report of libel suits against *Time* and CBS, NY *Times* 31 Jan 85

TURNER CATLEDGE

8 Hell, that's what the news is—an emergency. Why, we look at this as pretty much routine.
On sinking of *Andrea Doria*, covered in NY *Times*'s final edition seven hours after first reports of the accident, *ib* 6 Aug 56

RAY CAVE

9 A quote is a personal possession and you have no right to change it.
To journalism alumni of Northwestern University 29 May 85

JOHN CIARDI

10 The reader deserves an honest opinion. If he doesn't deserve it, give it to him anyhow.
"The Reviewer's Duty to Damn" *Saturday Review* 16 Feb 57

BOB CONSIDINE

11 Call it vanity, call it arrogant presumption, call it what you wish, but I would grope for the nearest open grave if I had no newspaper to work for, no need to search for and sometimes find the winged word that just fits, no keen wonder over what each unfolding day may bring.
It's All News to Me Meredith Press 67

CLIFTON DANIEL

12 Write about society as news and ... treat it like sociology.
1963 assignment for Charlotte Curtis, recalled on her death, NY *Times* 17 Apr 87

HEDLEY DONOVAN, Editor in Chief, Time Inc

13 The music, the news, is provided out there by Carter and Sadat and Begin and Reggie Jackson and others, who perhaps are the equivalent of Brahms and Bach and Beethoven. The editor doesn't make the news ... but he does interpret it and shape it, as the conductor does. ... Above all, he selects what's going to be on the program, which is one hell of a power.
Quoted by his successor Henry Anatole Grunwald, address to Amer Society of Magazine Editors, *SMW Newsletter* 9 Dec 84

OSBORN ELLIOTT

14 Journalistic hours are odd and long and often tense, and newsmen seek each other out as natural allies in a world that is so much part of them, but which they visit so randomly.
The World of Oz Viking 80

15 There is another reason journalists like to drink and eat together: they simply cannot think of better company.
ib

JANET FLANNER ("Genêt")

1 I act as a sponge. I soak it up and squeeze it out in ink every two weeks.

> On her "Letter from Paris" published in the *New Yorker* over a 50-year period, recalled on her death 7 Nov 78

2 I keep going over a sentence. I nag it, gnaw it, pat and flatter it.

> *ib*

GENE FOWLER

3 News is history shot on the wing. The huntsmen from the Fourth Estate seek to bag only the peacock or the eagle of the swifting day.

> *Skyline* Viking 61

JAMES P GANNON, Editor, Des Moines *Register*

4 Every good newspaper is muckraking to some degree. It's part of our job. Where there's muck, we ought to rake it.

> NY *Times* 10 Apr 85

JOHN GATES

5 The first thing I am going to do is to rejoin the American people and find out what Americans are thinking about.

> On resigning after a decade as editor of the *Daily Worker* and 27 years as a Communist Party member, *Editor & Publisher* 18 Jan 58

WOLCOTT GIBBS

6 Our writers are full of clichés just as old barns are full of bats. There is obviously no rule about this, except that anything that you suspect of being a cliché undoubtedly is one and had better be removed.

> "Theory and Practice of Editing *New Yorker* Articles," quoted by James Thurber *The Years with Ross* Atlantic-Little, Brown 59

WILLIAM E GILES

7 Surprise, the stuff that news is made of.

> *National Observer* 19 Oct 64

BRENDAN GILL

8 It is in the nature of the *New Yorker* to be as topical as possible, on a level that is often small in scale and playful in intention.

> *Here at the New Yorker* Random House 75

9 The guns of the big events rumble through our pages, but the tiny firecrackers are constantly hissing and popping there as well; it appears that much of my life as a journalist has been devoted to sedulously setting off firecrackers.

> *ib*

ROBERT A GOTTLIEB

10 I don't have lunches, dinners, go to plays or movies. I don't meditate, escalate, deviate or have affairs. So I have plenty of time.

> On succeeding William Shawn as editor of the *New Yorker*, NY *Times* 13 Jan 87

REBECCA GREER

11 My chief responsibilities have been described as soliciting and procuring. The illegal variety would be easier. And it certainly would be more profitable.

> On her job as articles editor of *Woman's Day*, address to Society of Magazine Writers 12 Nov 70

WILLIAM H GRIMES, Editor, *Wall Street Journal*

12 We are not much interested in labels but if we were to choose one, we would say we are radical. Just as radical as the Christian doctrine.

> "A Newspaper's Philosophy," recalled by his successor Vermont Royster on the paper's 75th anniversary, *Wall Street Journal* 8 Jul 64

13 We have friends but they have not been made by silence or pussyfooting. If we have enemies, we do not placate them.

> *ib*

HENRY ANATOLE GRUNWALD, Editor in Chief, Time Inc

14 Journalism can never be silent: that is its greatest virtue and its greatest fault. It must speak, and speak immediately, while the echoes of wonder, the claims of triumph and the signs of horror are still in the air.

> Introduction to *Time* magazine's 60th anniversary issue, Fall 83

15 Libel actions, when we look at them in perspective, are an ornament of a civilized society. They have replaced, after all, at least in most cases, a resort to weapons in defense of a reputation.

> Chet Huntley Memorial Lecture at NY University, NY *Times* 16 Nov 84

JOHN GUNTHER

16 It's the equivalent of putting on the brakes suddenly while driving uphill.

> On writing magazine articles to pay the travel expenses engendered by writing books, *Saturday Review* 13 Dec 62

17 What interested me was not news, but appraisal. What I sought was to grasp the flavor of a man, his texture, his impact, what he stood

for, what he believed in, what made him what he was and what color he gave to the fabric of his time.

On figures profiled in *Procession* Harper & Row 65

PETE HAMILL

1 The best newspapermen I know are those most thrilled by the daily pump of city room excitements; they long fondly for a "good murder"; they pray that assassinations, wars, catastrophes break on their editions.

NY *Times* 11 Nov 84

SYDNEY J HARRIS

2 Every morning I take out my bankbook, stare at it, shudder—and turn quickly to my typewriter.

On incentive as a journalist, quoted by Rosamund Essex *Church Times* 30 Dec 83

FRED M HECHINGER

3 I narrow-mindedly outlawed the word *unique*. Practically every press release contains it. Practically nothing ever is.

On resigning as education editor, NY *Herald Tribune* 5 Aug 56

BEN HECHT

4 We looked on the hopheads, crooks and gunsels and on their bawdy ladies as members of a family among whom we were privileged to move.... There was no caste system, moral or social, in our manners.

On crime reporting in Chicago, *Charlie* Harper 57

5 Chicago is a sort of journalistic Yellowstone Park, offering haven to a last herd of fantastic bravos.

On hard-drinking, cynical, exuberantly emotional breed of newspapermen described in his play *The Front Page*, written with Charles MacArthur, recalled on Hecht's death 18 Apr 64

HUGH HEFNER, Editor, *Playboy*

6 The interesting thing is how one guy, through living out his own fantasies, is living out the fantasies of so many other people.

On 25th anniversary of the magazine, *Newsweek* 1 Jan 79

ANTHONY HOLDEN

7 If you have an anecdote from one source, you file it away. If you hear it again, it may be true. Then the more times you hear it the less likely it is to be true.

International Herald Tribune 9 Jun 79

JENKIN LLOYD JONES, Editor, Tulsa *Tribune*

8 Let there be a fresh breeze of new honesty, new idealism, new integrity. ... You have typewriters, presses and a huge audience. How about raising hell?

To Inland Daily Press Assn, *US News & World Report* 28 May 62

WILLIAM F KERBY, Executive Editor, *Wall Street Journal*

9 News work is highly addictive. It is the cocaine of crafts.

A Proud Profession: Memoirs of a Reporter, Editor and Publisher Dow Jones-Irwin 81

JACK C LANDAU

10 If [newsmen] violate their promises of confidentiality, they may never again be able to operate effectively, except to cover news which is offered by government handout or is a matter of public record.

Testifying before House subcommittee as a member of the Reporters Committee for Freedom of the Press, LA *Herald-Examiner* 19 Feb 73

11 Consider what kind of nation we would be ... if hundreds of scandals involving state and local government still lay locked in the mouths of citizens.

ib

JOSEPH LELYVELD

12 If I have lived by any maxim as a reporter, it was that every person is an expert on the circumstances of his life.

On returning to South Africa, which he had first covered in the 1960s, *Move Your Shadow: South Africa, Black and White* Times Books 85

WALTER LIPPMANN

13 A long life in journalism convinced me many presidents ago that there should be a large air space between a journalist and the head of a state.

Farewell to colleagues, quoted in NY *Times* 26 May 67

DAVID LOW, British editorial cartoonist

14 Here lies a nuisance dedicated to sanity.

Self-epitaph recalled on his death 19 Sep 63

15 I have learned from experience that, in the bluff and counterbluff of world politics, to draw a hostile war lord as a horrible monster is to play his game. What he doesn't like is being shown as a silly ass.

ib

ROBERT MANNING, former Editor, *Atlantic*

1 Newspapermen, as journalists used to be called, have long been charged with the sin of cynicism. . . . a characterization that many of us encourage to deflect attention from our far more widespread flaw, incorrigible sentimentalism.

NY *Times* 12 Jun 82

T S MATTHEWS

2 This is Choctaw, now try it in English.

Marginal note asking for a rewrite, quoted by Henry Anatole Grunwald, address to Amer Society of Magazine Editors, *SMW Newsletter* 9 Dec 84

AILEEN MEHLE ("Suzy Knickerbocker")

3 Socialites kid each other, their way of life, their friends; and I kid the whole setup.

On her role as society columnist for the Hearst newspapers, *Time* 24 Sep 65

4 What I do is kick them in the pants with a diamond-buckled shoe.

NY *Times* 14 May 67

MALCOLM MUGGERIDGE

5 Good taste and humor are a contradiction in terms, like a chaste whore.

Defending his editorship of *Punch*, quoted in *Time* 14 Sep 53

6 It was a somber place, haunted by old jokes and lost laughter. Life, as I discovered, holds no more wretched occupation than trying to make the English laugh.

On *Punch* offices, *The Most of Malcolm Muggeridge* Simon & Schuster 66

NEW YORKER

7 The business ownership of the *New Yorker* may change hands, but the idea of the *New Yorker*—the tradition of the *New Yorker*, the spirit of the *New Yorker*—has never been owned by anyone and never will be owned by anyone.

"Talk of the Town" statement after sale of magazine to Newhouse family, 22 Apr 85

GERT NIERS, Executive Editor, *Aufbau*

8 Every obituary we put in, we know that's a reader we're losing.

On readership of Manhattan German-language newspaper, NY *Times* 16 Nov 84

DOROTHY PARKER

9 Somebody was using the pencil.

On why she missed a *New Yorker* deadline, quoted by James Thurber *The Years with Ross* Atlantic-Little, Brown 59

WESTBROOK PEGLER

10 My hates have always occupied my mind much more actively and have given greater spiritual satisfactions than my friendships.

Quoted by Oliver Pilat *Pegler* Beacon 63

11 I am a member of the rabble in good standing.

ib

WILLIAM REES-MOGG, Editor, London *Times*

12 Information, free from interest or prejudice, free from the vanity of the writer or the influence of a government, is as necessary to the human mind as pure air and water to the human body.

Christian Science Monitor 22 Sep 70

ALASTAIR REID

13 In reporting with some accuracy, at times we have to go much further than the strictly factual. Facts are part of the perceived whole.

On why he made up characters, rearranged events and invented dialogue in search of "a larger reality" for a nonfiction *New Yorker* article, *Wall Street Journal* 18 Jun 84

ROGER ROSENBLATT

14 The news on an ordinary day [is] a strange assembly that swoops down on one's life like cousins from Oslo one has never seen before, will never see again, and who, between planes, thought they would call to say hello.

"The News: Living in the Present Tense" *Time* 12 Dec 83

A M ROSENTHAL, Executive Editor, NY *Times*

15 It has been our policy not to use obscenities in the paper. It's a harmless little eccentricity of ours.

On not quoting presidential candidate Jimmy Carter's "vulgarism for sexual relations," *Time* 4 Oct 76

16 Other papers have added water to the soup, but we've added vegetables.

On new feature coverage that substantially increased the *Times*'s income and circulation, *ib* 15 Aug 77

17 If you don't have a sensation of apprehension when you set out to find a story and a swagger when you sit down to write it, you are in the wrong business.

On stepping down as executive editor, "Learning on the Job" NY *Times* 14 Dec 86

1 It was an interesting experience being metropolitan editor of the *Times*, in precisely the same way as being simmered in a saucepan for a few years is terribly interesting.
ib

HAROLD ROSS, Editor, *New Yorker*

2 Editing is the same as quarreling with writers—same thing exactly.
On the magazine's 25th anniversary, *Time* 6 Mar 50

3 The *New Yorker* . . . hopes to reflect metropolitan life and affairs of the day, to be gay, humorous, satirical, but to be more than a jester . . . It is not edited for the old lady in Dubuque.
Recalled on his death 5 Dec 51

4 There will be a personal-mention column —a jotting down in the small-town newspaper style of the comings, goings and doings in the village of New York.
1924 prospectus for *New Yorker*, recalled by James Thurber, *The Years with Ross* Atlantic-Little, Brown 59

5 This will contain some josh and some news value.
ib

WILLIAM SAFIRE

6 A reader should be able to identify a column without its byline or funny little picture on top—purely by look or feel, or its turgidity ratio.
Quoted by Robert H Yoakum *Vanity Fair* Sep 84

7 Create your own constituency of the infuriated.
Formula for writing a column, *ib*

8 The most successful column is one that causes the reader to throw down the paper in a peak of fit.
ib

ROBERT SHAND, Managing Editor, NY *Daily News*

9 The real appeal of the *News*, I think, is that it lights up the narrow routine of millions of lives with gleams from the great outside. Its readers thrill with secondhand emotions they will never know, they shudder from crimes they will never commit, they quiver with courage that shall never be theirs.
Recalled on his death 25 Nov 66

10 We believe that motive is more interesting than murder. We think that consequences are more important than commission. We consider that what people think and feel is often more significant than what they do.
ib

WILLIAM SHAWN, Editor, *New Yorker*

11 We do not permit composites. . . . We do not create conversations.
Memo following a reporter's admission of having made up characters and conversations in a nonfiction article, NY *Times* 3 Jul 84

12 The *New Yorker* has devoted itself for 59 years not only to facts and literal accuracy but to truth. And truth begins, journalistically, with the facts.
ib

LIZ SMITH

13 Gossip is just news running ahead of itself in a red satin dress.
Dallas *Times-Herald* 3 Aug 78

MERRIMAN SMITH

14 The relationship between a reporter and a president is exactly the same as that between a pitcher and a batter. . . . They both are trying to keep each other away.
NBC TV 2 Aug 61

RED SMITH

15 I like to get where the cabbage is cooking and catch the scents.
On departure to cover California baseball games played by the Giants and Dodgers, *Newsweek* 21 Apr 58

16 The natural habitat of the tongue is the left cheek.
On covering sports, quoted by Richard Kluger *The Paper: The Life and Death of the New York Herald Tribune* Knopf 86

JAMES B STEWART

17 A newspaper reporter is related to a telephone as a musician is related to a piano.
On difficulty of reporting from India, lay sermon, St Michael's Church, NYC, 14 Apr 85

HERBERT BAYARD SWOPE, Editor, NY *World*

18 The first duty of a newspaper is to be accurate. If it be accurate, it follows that it is fair.
Letter to NY *Herald Tribune* 16 Mar 58

19 The secret of a successful newspaper is to take one story each day and bang the hell out of it. Give the public what it wants to have and part

of what it ought to have whether it wants it or not.

> Recalled on his death 20 Jun 58

1 Don't forget that the only two things people read in a story are the first and last sentences. Give them blood in the eye on the first one.

> *ib*

FREDERICK TAYLOR, Executive Editor, *Wall Street Journal*

2 It's easier to make a reporter into an economist than an economist into a reporter.

> On the policy of his newspaper, quoted by Stephen Hess *Christian Science Monitor* 7 May 85

PETER UTLEY

3 An obituary should be an exercise in contemporary history, not a funeral oration.

> On writing candid obituaries for the London *Times*, NY *Times* 15 Mar 87

4 We never search for scandal, but we use it if it cries out to excess.

> *ib*

5 You never ring up the potential corpse because, you know, they'll be greatly upset.

> *ib*

JOHN WALCOTT

6 You never stop, except occasionally to put a fork in your mouth.

> On breakfast and lunch with government sources as "information meals" vital for covering Washington DC, NY *Times* 30 Apr 85

THEODORE H WHITE

7 When a reporter sits down at the typewriter, he's nobody's friend.

> *Newsweek* 23 Oct 72

8 I'd get into a room and disappear into the woodwork. Now the rooms are so crowded with reporters getting behind-the-scenes stories that nobody can get behind-the-scenes stories.

> On his method of reporting, recalled on his death 15 May 86

ALDEN WHITMAN

9 Death, the cliché assures us, is the great leveler; but it obviously levels some a great deal more than others.

> Introduction to *The Obituary Book* Stein & Day 71

10 That's what an obit is supposed to be—a pic-

ture, a snapshot. It's not a full-length biography, it's not a portrait. It's a quick picture.

> *W* 18 Jul 80

WILLIAM WHITWORTH, Editor, *Atlantic*

11 All "little" magazines have the luxury of thinking the reader is the same person as their editors.

> *Christian Science Monitor* 31 Jul 85

WALTER WINCHELL

12 Today's gossip is tomorrow's headline.

> Quoted by Liz Smith Dallas *Times-Herald* 3 Aug 78

Publishers & Management

ANONYMOUS

13 Our professionals miscalculated on every major point. ... Always their approach was "Give 'em nothing—and do it retroactively."

> Spokesperson for NY Publishers' Assn commenting on four-month newspaper strike, quoted in NY *Times* 1 Apr 63

FRANK H BARTHOLOMEW, President, United Press

14 The handout and the spokesman threaten our diligence, our ingenuity, our skepticism, our zeal. For zealots we must be. Not for a cause. For facts and for truth—and all of the truth.

> Address at University of Washington 21 Feb 58

15 Like the newspapers dependent upon us for news, ours will be a business organization, collecting and distributing one of the world's most perishable products, *news*.

> Announcing merger of United Press and International News Service, NY *Times* 25 May 58

LORD BEAVERBROOK (William Maxwell Aitken)

16 I suppose I will go on selling newspapers until at last will come the late night final.

> On 75th birthday, news summaries 7 Jun 54

OTTO BETTMANN, Director, Bettmann Archive

17 He outsells Jesus!

> On requests for pictures of Sigmund Freud, *Time* 23 Mar 81

LOREN GHIGLIONE, Publisher, Southbridge MA *News*

18 Ignorance, inertia and indifference are alive and well in America's newspapers. Minority still equals inferiority in the minds of many American editors and publishers.

> On need for more nonwhites in high-level management positions, NY *Times* 11 Mar 87

KATHARINE GRAHAM, Publisher, Washington *Post*

1 If we had failed to pursue the facts as far as they led, we would have denied the public any knowledge of an unprecedented scheme of political surveillance and sabotage.

> On Watergate coverage, Washington *Post* 3 Mar 73

PHILIP L GRAHAM, Publisher, Washington *Post*

2 I am insatiably curious about the state of our world. I revel in the recitation of the daily and weekly grist of journalism. . . . So let us drudge on about our inescapably impossible task of providing every week a first rough draft of a history that will never be completed about a world we can never understand.

> Addressing his editors and correspondents, recalled on his death 3 Aug 63

HARRY J GRANT, Publisher, Milwaukee *Journal*

3 It takes a long time to educate a community and it can't be done by spellbinders, money-bags, hypnotizers or magicians . . . or Aladdin's lamp. Character is what matters on a paper.

> *Time* 1 Feb 54

4 We're not a loved paper. But we're a respected one.

> *ib*

WILLIAM RANDOLPH HEARST JR

5 I don't have the umbilical cord Pop had with each paper.

> On closing of NY *Mirror*, founded by his father, NY *Times* 16 Oct 63

CHRISTIE HEFNER, President, Playboy Enterprises

6 She no longer has a staple in her navel.

> On the traditional nude centerfold after new binding techniques were developed for the magazine, NBC TV 28 Aug 85

ANDREW HEISKELL, former Chairman, Time Inc

7 A publication depends on a great idea, not there being a market out there. . . . You start with an idea rather than trying to get an idea which goes with that market.

> *New York* 3 Mar 86

ROY W HOWARD, Chairman, Scripps-Howard Newspapers

8 No date on the calendar is as important as tomorrow.

> Creed for newspaper personnel, recalled on his death, *Time* 27 Nov 64

JAMES A LINEN, Publisher, *Time* magazine

9 Moving a magazine is like ordering 100,000 gallons of alphabet soup, to go. Last week, in Manhattan, it went.

> On move to new headquarters, *Time* 21 Mar 60

HENRY R LUCE

10 To see, and to show, is the mission now undertaken by *Life*.

> Prospectus for *Life* magazine, quoted in *Saturday Evening Post* 16 Jan 65

11 Publishing is a business, but journalism never was and is not essentially a business. Nor is it a profession.

> Recalled on his death 28 Feb 67

12 Journalism is the art of collecting varying kinds of information (commonly called "news") which a few people possess and of transmitting it to a much larger number of people who are supposed to desire to share it.

> *ib*

13 There are men who can write poetry, and there are men who can read balance sheets. The men who can read balance sheets cannot write.

> On recruiting a staff for *Fortune* magazine, *ib*

14 Show me a man who claims he is objective and I'll show you a man with illusions.

> Quoted in NY *Times* 1 Mar 67

15 I became a journalist to come as close as possible to the heart of the world.

> Quoted in *Esquire* Dec 83

16 I am all for titillating trivialities. I am all for the epic touch. I could almost say that everything in *Time* should be either titillating or epic or starkly, supercurtly factual.

> *ib*

17 *Time* should make enemies and *Life* should make friends.

> Quoted by Charles Whittingham, publisher of *Life*, on the magazine's 50th anniversary, *Live at Five* WNBC TV 3 Nov 86

RUPERT MURDOCK, newspaper magnate

18 I think a newspaper should be provocative, stir 'em up, but you can't do that on television. It's just not on.

> Declaring that he did not plan any television tabloids, *Business Week* 20 May 85

ALLEN NEUHARTH, founder, *USA Today*

19 We look like television in print.

> NBC TV 19 Nov 85

ELEANOR MEDILL ("CISSY") PATTERSON, Publisher, Washington *Times-Herald*

1 The trouble with me is that I am a vindictive old shanty-Irish bitch.
Time 13 Sep 54

LORD ROTHERMERE (Harold Sydney Harmsworth), Chairman, London *Daily Mail*

2 I buy wood pulp, process it and sell it at a profit.
Quoted by David Frost and Antony Jay *The English* Stein & Day 68

ARTHUR HAYS SULZBERGER, Publisher, NY *Times*

3 We tell the public which way the cat is jumping. The public will take care of the cat.
On impartial news reporting, *Time* 8 May 50

ARTHUR OCHS SULZBERGER, Publisher, NY *Times*

4 More than print and ink, a newspaper is a collection of fierce individualists who somehow manage to perform the astounding daily miracle of merging their own personalities under the discipline of the deadline and retain the flavor of their own minds in print.
Introduction to A M Rosenthal *Thirty-eight Witnesses* McGraw-Hill 64

5 In dread fear of sentimentality, another thing true is not said—that for its staff the paper is a source of pride and, I do believe, an object of affection and—yes, love.
ib

6 Anybody who claims to read the entire paper every day is either the world's fastest reader or the world's biggest liar.
Quoted in *Time* 15 Aug 77

7 Journalism's ultimate purpose [is] to inform the reader, to bring him each day a letter from home and never to permit the serving of special interests.
NY *Times* 28 Apr 83

8 The Defense Department's plan to ban newspaper reporters from [pool coverage of] military operations is incredible. It reveals the administration to be out of touch with journalism, reality and the First Amendment.
ib 11 Oct 84

LILA ACHESON WALLACE

9 I knew right away that it was a gorgeous idea.
On her husband's proposal for *Reader's Digest*, quoted in *Time* 13 Apr 81

JOHN HAY WHITNEY, Publisher, NY *Herald Tribune*

10 To be fair is not enough any more. We must be ferociously fair.
Address at Colby College, Waterville ME, *Time* 20 Nov 64

11 The role we can play every day, if we try, is to take the whole experience of every day and shape it to involve American man. It is our job to interest him in his community and to give his ideas the excitement they should have.
ib

CHARLES A WHITTINGHAM, Publisher, *Life* magazine

12 [It was] America's scrapbook.
On 50th anniversary of *Life* magazine, *Live at Five* WNBC TV 3 Nov 86

WILL WOODWARD, General Manager, Dubuque *Telegraph-Herald*

13 When I listen to people here who say that of course something was put in the paper because I ordered it in, it scares the hell out of me. That tells me what those people would do if they were in my place.
Quoted in "The Little Old Daily of Dubuque" NY *Times* 3 Feb 74

Observers & Critics

SPIRO T AGNEW, US Vice President

14 In the United States today, we have more than our share of the nattering nabobs of negativism.
Address at San Diego 11 Sep 70

15 [They have formed their own 4-H club—the] hopeless, hysterical hypochondriacs of history.
ib

SHANA ALEXANDER

16 At Gatling-gun tempo ... word-perfect the first time out. . . . the journalistic equivalent of a high-wire front somersault without a net.
On fellow *Life* reporter Tommy Thompson meeting a deadline, *Nutcracker* Doubleday 85

PRINCESS ANNE

17 *You* are a pest, by the very nature of that camera in your hand.
To a photographer, quoted by John Pearson *The Selling of the Royal Family* Simon & Schuster 86

ANONYMOUS

18 Reporters are like alligators. You don't have to

love them, you don't necessarily have to like them. But you do have to feed them.

> White House source, on plans for frequent press briefings during Tokyo economic summit meeting, quoted in *US News & World Report* 5 May 86

CORAZON C AQUINO, President of the Philippines

1 You, the foreign media, have been the companion of my people in its long and painful journey to freedom.

> To 400 guests at *Time*'s Distinguished Speakers Program, *Time* 29 Sep 86

2 The media's power is frail. Without the people's support, it can be shut off with the ease of turning a light switch.

> *ib*

RUSSELL BAKER

3 Live by publicity, you'll probably die by publicity.

> On President Ronald Reagan's changing image after news of Iranian arms sales, NY *Times* 3 Dec 86

THOMAS BARR

4 The press's job [is] to dig . . . to pick at things that may not be pleasant or comfortable for the people involved, to try to get as much of the story as possible into the hands of the public so that the public can make decisions about how we want to run our lives.

> Summation for Time Inc in libel suit brought by Ariel Sharon, former Israeli defense minister, *Time* 21 Jan 85

BRUCE BARTON JR

5 Rumor, that most efficient of press agents.

> On behind-the-scenes talk in Manhattan art galleries, *Time* 24 Nov 61

CELÂL BAYAR, President of Turkey

6 Photographers are the only dictators in America.

> On US visit, news summaries 1 Feb 54

JIM BISHOP

7 The morning after a death, we learned an avalanche of goodies about the renowned, some of which persuaded the reader that he should have cultivated the deceased in life.

> On NY *Times* obituary writer Alden Whitman, Shrewsbury NJ *Daily Register* 11 Jun 80

8 He dropped pejoratives like subliminal seasoning.

> *ib*

HUGO L BLACK, Associate Justice, US Supreme Court

9 The Founding Fathers gave the free press the protection it must have [to] bare the secrets of government and inform the people.

> On publication of the Pentagon Papers, NY *Times* 30 Jun 71

DANIEL J BOORSTIN

10 The celebrity is a person who is known for his well-knownness.

> *The Image* Atheneum 61

ARNAUD DE BORCHGRAVE

11 *Newsweek* is a perpetual French Revolution. They keep eliminating their best people.

> Quoted in *Manhattan Inc* Oct 84

JIMMY BRESLIN

12 Anything to the *Daily News* should be kept to two paragraphs, the first of which was to contain a personal insult to the paper or to the subject of an antilabor story. A letter to the *Times* newspaper should begin with a mention of the offending article, a factual presentation and not a personal insult [since] the editors were so ego-ridden that they needed to be told that even their obvious misdeeds were intellectually sound.

> On letters to the editor, *Table Money* Ticknor & Fields 86

KINGMAN BREWSTER, President, Yale

13 It won't make for a quiet life but it will make for an interesting paper . . . vastly more significant because it is doing something only a daily paper can do.

> Urging newspaper editors to indulge creativity of young reporters, NY *Times* 30 Oct 64

14 While the spoken word can travel faster, you can't take it home in your hand. Only the written word can be absorbed wholly at the convenience of the reader.

> *ib*

15 The newspaper fits the reader's program while the listener must fit the broadcaster's program.

> *ib*

PATRICK J BUCHANAN, White House director of communications

16 Saying the Washington *Post* is just a newspaper is like saying Rasputin was just a country priest.

> On *Post* coverage of Watergate and arms sales to Iran, CNN TV 9 Dec 86

WILLIAM F BUCKLEY JR

1 He invented the news magazine. He invested [it] with an interpretation ... Tell what happened, tell it well, tell it concisely, but with attention to the belletristic imperative.

"The *Life* and *Time* of Henry Luce" *Esquire* Dec 83

2 Relate it to what *should* happen; fuse it into the long morality play that began, really, in the Garden of Eden.

ib

JAY CARR

3 One of the things that will keep *The Front Page* burning bright as long as newspapers are alive is the myth that newspapermen are breezy and raffish. What other play has for so long fed the self-image of journalists?

Reviewing Broadway revival of Ben Hecht and Charles MacArthur's 58-year-old play, Boston *Globe* 4 Dec 86

4 They were fast-moving opportunists encased in cynicism and proud of it.

On Chicago reporters, *ib*

5 [Walter Burns is] the archetypal managing editor—ruthless, self-righteous, manipulative, downright maniacal if it means an exclusive, especially one that it can congratulate itself for on its own front page.

ib

FERN SCHUMER CHAPMAN

6 A big-city newsroom can be a snake pit. The politics put Mayor Daley's machine to shame, the competition proves beyond a doubt Darwin's theory of survival of the fittest and the hierarchy of editors is more complicated than the Vatican's.

Wall Street Journal 26 Feb 85

FRANCIS X CLINES

7 Death's sting has a new meaning now that the *Times* of London is including candid descriptions of human peccadilloes in its obituaries.

NY *Times* 15 Mar 87

8 It is "lifestyle" journalism the way Chaucer first invented it, and the *Times*, onto a good thing, is uninhibitedly publishing articles on the passing of a cuckolded poet, a rock promoter strangely addicted to collecting orangutans and an Italian writer striving "to avoid becoming a bore."

ib

9 Peter Utley, the newspaper's obituary editor ... cheerfully checked with Primrose Palmer, his assistant, on the day's soul traffic. The late archbishop from New Zealand sounded promising, it was agreed, but then again it was lunch time, and who knew what had been happening in some now-ending life.

ib

CHARLES W COLSON, White House aide

10 The first 20 stories written about a public figure set the tone for the next 2,000 and it is almost impossible to reverse it.

NY *Times* 7 Jul 74

TIMOTHY CROUSE

11 A lightweight, by definition, is a man who cannot assert his authority over the national press, cannot manipulate reporters, cannot finesse questions, prevent leaks or command a professional public relations operation.

On covering presidential candidates, *The Boys on the Bus* Random House 72

JERRY DELLA FEMINA

12 A lot of its readers are of an age where they forget to cancel.

On wide circulation of *Reader's Digest*, quoted by *Newsweek* 12 Jan 87

EVERETTE E DENNIS, Executive Director, Gannet Center for Media Studies, Columbia University

13 Broadcasters are storytellers, newspapers are fact-gatherers and organizers of information and news magazines are kind of a hybrid of both.

NY *Times* 31 Jan 85

THOMAS D'EVELYN

14 [Russell] Baker writes columns as a poet writes light verse—with tongue in cheek and a steady hand.

Christian Science Monitor 26 Nov 86

MARLENE DIETRICH

15 They want you to bring out your intestines.

On interviewers, *People* 3 Sep 84

ERVIN S DUGGAN

16 The bad boy tweaking the nose of the Establishment [with] the countenance of a Jewish leprechaun.

On Art Buchwald, *Washingtonian* Jan 85

DWIGHT D EISENHOWER, 34th US President

1 I don't attempt to be a poker player before this crowd.

> To press conference 30 Apr 58

2 Well, when you come down to it, I don't see that a reporter could do much to a president, do you?

> At his last and most candid press conference, quoted in NY *Times* 9 Aug 64

GEOFFREY FISHER, Archbishop of Canterbury

3 Some of the press who speak loudly about the freedom of the press are themselves the enemies of freedom. Countless people dare not say a thing because they know it will be picked up and made a song of by the press. That limits freedom.

> *Look* 17 Mar 59

FELIX FRANKFURTER, Associate Justice, US Supreme Court

4 Freedom of the press is not an end in itself but a means to the end of [achieving] a free society.

> NY *Times* 28 Nov 54

FRED W FRIENDLY, Columbia School of Journalism

5 A composite is a euphemism for a lie. It's disorderly. It's dishonest and it's not journalism.

> On *New Yorker* writer who admitted he made up characters, rearranged events and invented dialogue for nonfiction article, news summaries 19 Jun 84

PHIL GAILEY

6 If Washington were a circus, as some like to think it is, the Washington *Post* would be the ringmaster.

> NY *Times* 26 Jun 84

WOLCOTT GIBBS

7 Backward ran sentences until reeled the mind.

> In *New Yorker* parody on sentence structure of *Time*, recalled on his death 16 Aug 58

8 Where it all will end, knows God.

> *ib*

9 He wrote about nothing that didn't carry either his name or his initials—sometimes his pieces were signed at both ends.

> On Ralph Ingersoll, editor of *PM*, quoted by Roy Hoopes *Ralph Ingersoll* Atheneum 85

BRENDAN GILL

10 Questioning a comma, he will shake his head and say in his soft voice that he realizes perfectly well what a lot of time and thought have gone into the comma and that in the ordinary course of events he would be the first to say that the comma was precisely the form of punctuation that he would have been most happy to encounter at that very place in the sentence, but isn't there the possibility—oh, only the remotest one, to be sure, and yet perhaps worth considering for a moment in the light of the care already bestowed on the construction—that the sentence could be made to read infinitesimally more clearly if, say, instead of a comma a semicolon were to be inserted at just that point?

> On editor William Shawn, *Here at the New Yorker* Random House 75

NEIL E GOLDSCHMIDT, US Secretary of Transportation

11 Editorial writers ... enter after battle and shoot the wounded.

> *Wall Street Journal* 5 May 80

BARRY M GOLDWATER, US Senator

12 I won't say that the papers misquote me, but I sometimes wonder where Christianity would be today if some of those reporters had been Matthew, Mark, Luke and John.

> In first speech after accepting Republican presidential nomination, NY *Times* 11 Aug 64

PAUL GRAY

13 The image of the reporter as a nicotine-stained Quixote, slugging back Scotch while skewering city hall with an exposé ripped out of a typewriter on the crack of deadline, persists despite munificent evidence to the contrary.

> In review of Richard Kluger's *The Paper: The Life and Death of the New York Herald Tribune* Knopf 86, *Time* 27 Oct 86

14 In the end, the *Tribune* lost touch with the world it was supposed to reach; it mattered passionately, but almost exclusively, to those who worked for it.

> *ib*

BOB GREENE

15 The meat-and-potatoes work of world journalism is performed by the wire service reporters.

> NY *Daily News* 5 May 85

307

THOMAS GRIFFITH

1 Editors may think of themselves as dignified headwaiters in a well-run restaurant but more often [they] operate a snack bar . . . and expect you to be grateful that at least they got the food to the table warm.

How True: A Skeptic's Guide to Believing the News Atlantic-Little, Brown 74

2 Journalism constructs momentarily arrested equilibriums and gives disorder an implied order. That is already two steps from reality.

ib

3 Anderson's muckraking is one of debatable ends constantly used to justify questionable works.

On Jack Anderson, "Muckraking Is Sometimes Sordid Work" *Time* 23 Jul 79

4 To the public, the press is not David among Goliaths; it has become one of the Goliaths, Big Media, a combination of powerful television networks, large magazine groups and newspaper chains that are near-monopolies.

"Credibility at Stake" *ib* 11 Mar 84

MURRAY I GURFEIN, Judge, US Court of Appeals, 2nd Circuit

5 A cantankerous press, an obstinate press, a ubiquitous press, must be suffered by those in authority in order to preserve . . . the right of the people to know.

1971 ruling affirming the NY *Times*'s right to publish the Pentagon Papers, recalled on his death 16 Dec 79

JAMES C HAGERTY, former White House press secretary

6 If you lose your temper at a newspaper columnist, he'll get rich or famous or both.

NY *Times* 17 Mar 68

WILLIAM A HENRY III

7 Any departure from fact is the first step on a slippery slope toward unbelievability.

On *New Yorker* reporter who admitted creating dialogue and composite characters for a nonfiction article, *Time* 2 Jul 84

HENRY HILLMAN, President, Hillman Co

8 A whale is harpooned only when it spouts.

On why he avoids interviews, *Fortune* 31 May 82

LEE ISRAEL

9 Hatchet murders were the house speciality of the *Journal*, whose front page was a virtual abattoir of murder most foul.

On crime reporting in NY newspaper, *Kilgallen* Delacorte 79

HUGH NEWELL JACOBSEN

10 The permanent power brokers of this city are the columnists.

On Washington DC, NY *Times* 31 May 84

LYNDON B JOHNSON, 36th US President

11 The fact that a man is a newspaper reporter is evidence of some flaw of character.

Quoted in *People* 2 Feb 87

JACQUELINE KENNEDY

12 Whenever I was upset by something in the papers, [Jack] always told me to be more tolerant, like a horse flicking away flies in the summer.

Quoted by Ralph G Martin *A Hero for Our Time* Macmillan 83

13 [I want] minimum information given with maximum politeness.

Instructions to press secretary Pamela Turnure, *ib*

JOHN F KENNEDY, 35th US President

14 I am reading it more and enjoying it less.

On his treatment by the press, quoted by Pierre Salinger *With Kennedy* Doubleday 66

WALTER KERR

15 Seymour Peck's editorial hand ranged far, wide and deep, touching lightly but expertly . . . He seemed less an editor of any sort than the very best sort of guardian angel.

Tribute to *Times* drama editor, NY *Times* 5 Jan 85

16 He wove a great web of knowledge, linking everything together, and sat modestly at a switchboard at the center, eager to help.

ib

NIKITA S KHRUSHCHEV, Soviet Premier

17 They pay little attention to what we say and prefer to read tea leaves.

On interpretation of Soviet attitudes by members of the press, 5 Jul 55

18 The press is our chief ideological weapon.

NY *Times* 29 Sep 57

LANE KIRKLAND, President, AFL-CIO

19 My pappy told me never to bet my bladder against a brewery or get into an argument with people who buy ink by the barrel.

On labor reporting, *Fortune* 23 Dec 85

RICHARD KLUGER

1 Every time a newspaper dies, even a bad one, the country moves a little closer to authoritarianism; when a great one goes, like the New York *Herald Tribune*, history itself is denied a devoted witness.

> *The Paper: The Life and Death of the New York Herald Tribune* Knopf 86

EDWARD KOCH, Mayor of NYC

2 The most guileful amongst the reporters ... are those who appear friendly and smile and seem to be supportive. They are the ones who will seek to gut you on every occasion.

> NY *Times* 18 Jan 84

ARTHUR KROCK

3 Every president after Jefferson has professed agreement with Jefferson's concept that the freedom of the American press to print its versions of the facts, background and likely consequences of human events was a constitutional principle permanently reserved from any form of interference by government. Consequently Jefferson denounced ... either direct or indirect attempts by government to do what in current parlance has become known as "management of the news."

> "Mr. Kennedy's Management of the News" *Fortune* Mar 63

LEWIS H LAPHAM

4 [He was] as uncommunicative as a vending machine.

> On White House press secretary George E Reedy, *Saturday Evening Post* 11 Sep 65

G GORDON LIDDY

5 The press is like the peculiar uncle you keep in the attic—just one of those unfortunate things.

> Quoted in *Newsweek* 12 Jan 87

A J LIEBLING

6 People everywhere confuse what they read in newspapers with news.

> "A Talkative Something or Other" *New Yorker* 7 Apr 56

7 I take a grave view of the press. It is the weak slat under the bed of democracy.

> Quoted by Melvin Maddocks *Christian Science Monitor* 23 Jan 85

8 Freedom of the press is guaranteed only to those who own one.

> Quoted by Richard Kluger *The Paper: The Life and Death of the New York Herald Tribune* Knopf 86

WALTER LIPPMANN

9 The senator might remember that the Evangelists had a more inspiring subject.

> On Barry M Goldwater's speculation about how he might have fared at the hands of Matthew, Mark, Luke and John rather than the press, news summaries 13 Aug 64

ALICE ROOSEVELT LONGWORTH

10 Dorothy is the only woman in history who has had her menopause in public and made it pay.

> On writing style of columnist Dorothy Thompson, quoted by Vincent Sheean *Dorothy and Red* Houghton Mifflin 63

CURTIS D MACDOUGALL, Professor Emeritus of Journalism, Northwestern University

11 A good reporter cannot afford to be cynical; a good reporter cannot afford to be skeptical.

> Recalled on his death 10 Nov 85

MELVIN MADDOCKS

12 Nothing is more idealistic than a journalist on the defensive.

> "How Journalists Regard Their Field" *Christian Science Monitor* 23 Jan 85

13 Journalists do not like to report on uncertainties. They would almost rather be wrong than ambiguous.

> *ib*

YAKOV MALIK, Soviet diplomat

14 It's like vodka without breakfast.

> On being photographed but not interviewed, NY *Times* 13 Feb 69

DAVID MARGOLICK

15 The *Review*'s labyrinthine editing process ... does to the written word what the Cuisinart does to broccoli.

> On *Harvard Law Review*, NY *Times* 24 Sep 84

EDWIN MCDOWELL

16 There are serpents in that journalistic Eden.

> On the *New Yorker*'s policy of holding articles for several years before either publishing them or rejecting them, NY *Times* 26 Jan 87

ROBERT G MENZIES, Prime Minister of Australia

17 You don't have a democracy. It's a photocracy.

> On Washington news photographers, news summaries 6 Nov 54

ARTHUR MILLER

1 A good newspaper, I suppose, is a nation talking to itself.
London *Observer* 26 Nov 61

FERDINAND MOUNT

2 One of the unsung freedoms that go with a free press is the freedom not to read it.
London *Daily Telegraph* 22 May 86

BETTY SOUTHARD MURPHY, National Labor Relations Board

3 The broad spectrum of knowledge, the ability to probe into the meaning of an event and the ability to write clearly and concisely in newspaper style are the essence of professionalism.
Dissenting opinion to board's ruling that journalists cannot be defined as professionals under federal law because their bargaining units also represent such employees as messengers and restaurant workers, NY *Times* 6 Apr 76

EDWARD R MURROW

4 Most of us probably feel we couldn't be free without newspapers, and that is the real reason we want the newspapers to be free.
NY *Herald Tribune* 12 Mar 58

EDMUND S MUSKIE, US Secretary of State

5 Looking at yourself through the media is like looking at one of those rippled mirrors in an amusement park.
Newsweek 26 May 80

NEW YORKER

6 It's a strange phenomenon of journalistic life today that the greatest potential "story" of our time—the self-extermination of mankind in a nuclear holocaust—is one that, by its very nature, can never be written.
21 Nov 83

NEW YORKER STAFF COMMITTEE

7 It is our strange and powerfully held conviction that only an editor who has been a longstanding member of the staff will have a reasonable chance of assuring our continuity, cohesion and independence.
Protest by 154 writers, cartoonists and editors against publisher's appointment of Robert A Gottlieb, Editor in Chief of Knopf, to succeed William Shawn as editor, NY *Times* 15 Jan 87

NEW YORK TIMES

8 Its history is the history of the newspaper and we owe it much, even—since it invented both the editorial and the editorial "we"—our voice.
On 200th anniversary of the London *Times*, 11 Jul 85

9 England would have been worse if governed without its tyranny.
ib

10 Those who live by secrecy can also perish by it.
Editorial on Soviet suppression of news about nuclear accident at Chernobyl, "Mayday! and May Day" 1 May 86

11 Secrecy is a disease and Chernobyl is its symptom, a threat both to the Soviet Union and its neighbors.
ib

12 The chance to work with William Shawn was like being asked to dance with Fred Astaire.
On retirement of veteran *New Yorker* editor, 18 Jan 87

RICHARD M NIXON, 37th US President

13 You won't have Nixon to kick around anymore, because, gentlemen, this is my last press conference.
After his defeat in California gubernatorial election, 7 Nov 62

14 The American people are entitled to see the president and to hear his views directly, and not to see him only through the press.
Press conference 10 Dec 70

15 Don't get the impression that you arouse my anger. You see, one can only be angry with those he respects.
To the press during Watergate investigation 26 Oct 73

16 If I talked about Watergate, I was described as struggling to free myself from the morass. If I did not talk about Watergate, I was accused of being out of touch with reality.
On press coverage, *RN: Memoirs of Richard Nixon* Grosset & Dunlap 78

17 Watergate had become the center of the media's universe, and during the remaining year of my presidency the media tried to force everything else to revolve around it.
ib

18 One thing, Ron, old boy. We won't have to have any more press conferences, and we won't even have to tell them that either!
To White House press secretary Ronald L

Ziegler two days before resigning the presidency, *ib*

1 People in the media say they must look . . . at the president with a microscope. Now, I don't mind a microscope, but boy, when they use a proctoscope, that's going too far.
NBC TV 8 Apr 84

2 I've never canceled a subscription to a newspaper because of bad cartoons or editorials. If that were the case, I wouldn't have any newspapers or magazines to read.
ib

3 As far as I am concerned now, I have no enemies in the press whatsoever.
To Amer Society of Newspaper Editors, *Time* 21 May 84

JOHN PEARSON

4 Given the chance, most people easily become voyeurs of royalty.
The Selling of the Royal Family Simon & Schuster 86

PRINCE PHILIP, Duke of Edinburgh

5 You must sometimes stretch out your neck but not actually give them the ax.
On what he called "dontopedology" in dealing with the press, quoted by Elizabeth Longford *The Queen: The Life of Elizabeth II* Knopf 83

JODY POWELL, White House press secretary

6 If I had my way, I'd ask the f---ing Ayatollah to keep 50 reporters . . . Then you people who have all the answers could figure how to get them out.
On the media during Iranian hostage crisis, quoted in *Newsweek* 2 Apr 84

ABE RASKIN

7 Of all the institutions in our inordinately complacent society, none is so addicted as the press to self-righteousness, self-satisfaction and self-congratulation.
Quoted by Melvin Maddocks *Christian Science Monitor* 23 Jan 85

WILLIAM RAUCH, NYC press secretary

8 Never trust a reporter who has a nice smile.
NY *Times* 18 Jan 84

RONALD REAGAN, 40th US President

9 Now we shall get on with our first attempt at Reagan roulette.
At his only press conference where questions were chosen by lottery 6 Mar 81

10 The District of Columbia is one gigantic ear.
Time 23 Nov 81

11 I was going to have an opening statement, but I decided I wanted a lot of attention so I decided to wait and "leak" it.
On first anniversary of his presidency 19 Jan 82

12 Just remember my best side is my right side—my *far* right side.
To White House News Photographers Assn 18 May 83

13 I like photographers—you don't ask questions.
ib

14 I like your motto: One picture is worth 1,000 denials.
ib

HARRY REASONER, CBS News

15 Week after week their lead stories on [Watergate] have been more in the style of pejorative pamphleteering than objective journalism, and since they are highly visible and normally highly respected organs of our craft, they embarrass and discredit us all.
On *Time* and *Newsweek*, quoted by Richard M Nixon *RN: Memoirs of Richard Nixon* Grosset & Dunlap 78

J D REED

16 From Puget Sound to Pennsylvania Avenue, typewriters clack at kitchen tables and computer screens glow in closets.
On writers who seek to duplicate columnist Erma Bombeck's success, "And on Other Home Fronts" *Time* 2 Jul 84

17 Who cares if the roast burns or the dog sheds on the couch? . . . Such trifles must wait their turn behind dreams of hitting it big.
ib

RICHARD REEVES

18 The White House Press Room [is] an adult day-care center built over what used to be the swimming pool where Lyndon Johnson skinny-dipped.
In review of John Herbers's *No Thank You, Mr President* Norton 76, NY *Times* 21 Mar 76

JAMES RESTON

19 Somehow—I don't know why—peace seems to have a better chance in the [New York] *Times*.
New Leader 7 Jan 63

1 People are always dying in the *Times* who don't seem to die in other papers, and they die at greater length and maybe even with a little more grace.
ib

2 How do I know what to think if I can't read what I write?
On NYC newspaper strike, *ib*

3 Like officials in Washington, we suffer from Afghanistanism. If it's far away, it's news, but if it's close at home, it's sociology.
To Columbia University convocation, *Wall Street Journal* 27 May 63

DOROTHY RIDINGS, President, League of Women Voters

4 We do not expect journalists to be political eunuchs.
On respect for personal opinions of questioners selected for presidential campaign debates, *Time* 22 Oct 84

CHALMERS M ROBERTS

5 The trouble with daily journalism is that you get so involved with "Who hit John?" that you never really know why John had his chin out in the first place.
Newsweek 6 Jan 58

CARL T ROWAN JR, US Ambassador to Finland

6 There aren't any embarrassing questions—just embarrassing answers.
On press conferences, *New Yorker* 7 Dec 63

7 My advice to any diplomat who wants to have a good press is to have two or three kids and a dog.
ib

RENE SAGUISAG

8 [The word] *media* is the plural for *mediocre*.
On press coverage of Philippines President Corazon C Aquino's administration, NY *Times* 22 Jan 87

9 Every day when I read the papers, I find out that I did or said or thought things that I did not do, say or think.
ib

ANTHONY SAMPSON

10 In America, journalism is apt to be regarded as an extension of history: in Britain, as an extension of conversation.
The Anatomy of Britain Harper & Row 62

DAVID SANFORD

11 Certain people seem to die in the *Times* more than others do. Doctors, for instance; obits give the impression that physicians die in droves.
On NY *Times* obituaries, *Wall Street Journal* 29 Aug 85

SERGE SCHMEMANN

12 The art of reading between the lines is as old as manipulated information.
On distortion of news, NY *Times* 10 Nov 85

DANIEL SCHORR, CBS News

13 There was a vacuum in investigation, and the press began to try men in the most effective court in the country.
On Watergate investigations, quoted by Richard M Nixon *RN: Memoirs of Richard Nixon* Grosset & Dunlap 78

R Z SHEPPARD

14 [Ken] Kesey practices what has come to be known as gonzo journalism. The reporter, often intoxicated, fails to get the story but delivers instead a stylishly bizarre account that mocks conventional journalism.
Time 8 Sep 86

GEORGE P SHULTZ, US Secretary of State

15 If there are ways in which we can make Qaddafi nervous, why shouldn't we? . . . That is not deceiving you, but just using your predictable tendencies to report things that we try to keep secret.
On Libya, NY *Times* 3 Oct 86

16 The higher the classification [of secrecy], the quicker you will report it.
ib

HUGH SIDEY

17 The legions of reporters who cover politics don't want to quit the clash and thunder of electoral combat for the dry duty of analyzing the federal budget. As a consequence, we have created the perpetual presidential campaign.
Time 5 Nov 84

FRANK SINATRA

18 All day long, they lie in the sun, and when the sun goes down, they lie some more.
On Hollywood reporters, *US* 16 Dec 85

ISAAC BASHEVIS SINGER

1 If Moses had been paid newspaper rates for the Ten Commandments, he might have written the Two Thousand Commandments.
NY *Times* 30 Jun 85

JOHN SKOW

2 In journalistic terms, syndication is equivalent to ascending to heaven on a pillar of cloud.
On Erma Bombeck, "Erma in Bomburbia" *Time* 2 Jul 84

RED SMITH

3 My best girl is dead.
On August 15, 1966, closing of NY *Herald Tribune*, quoted by Richard Kluger *The Paper: The Life and Death of the New York Herald Tribune* Knopf 86

FRANKLIN BLISS SNYDER, President, Northwestern University

4 The greatest privilege in our society is to be a purveyor of news.
1949 commencement address at Medill School of Journalism, recalled on his death 11 May 58

LARRY SPEAKES, White House press spokesman

5 You don't tell us how to stage the news and we don't tell you how to cover it.
Sign on his desk, quoted by Steven Weisman "The President and the Press" NY *Times* 14 Oct 84

6 Those who talk don't know what is going on and those who know what is going on won't talk.
On news blackout at Geneva summit meeting, *ib* 20 Nov 85

7 Being a press secretary [is like] learning to type: You're hunting and pecking for a while and then you find yourself doing the touch system and don't realize it. You're speaking for the president without ever having to go to him.
ib 10 Oct 86

8 I would dodge, not lie, in the national interest.
ib

9 This job has probably got the most screwing-up potential in the world.
On retiring, ABC TV 31 Jan 87

LADY DIANA SPENCER

10 I know it's just a job they have to do, but sometimes I do wish they wouldn't.
On photographers who followed her during her engagement to Prince Charles, NY *Times* 25 Feb 81

RONALD STEEL

11 [There is a] curious relationship between a candidate and the reporters who cover him. It can be affected by small things like a competent press staff, enough seats, sandwiches and briefings and the ability to understand deadlines.
NY *Times* 5 Aug 84

ADLAI E STEVENSON

12 An editor is one who separates the wheat from the chaff and prints the chaff.
Quoted in Bill Adler comp *The Stevenson Wit* Doubleday 66

GAY TALESE

13 Most journalists are restless voyeurs who see the warts on the world, the imperfections in people and places. . . . gloom is their game, the spectacle their passion, normality their nemesis.
The Kingdom and the Power World 69

14 News, if unreported, has no impact. It might as well have not happened at all.
ib

FRANCISCO S TATAD

15 If you want unverified gossip passed on as truth, it is there. If you want a person's private fault reported as public fact, it is there, too. If you want the most inconsequential nonsense blown up into an earthshaking event, you will find no shortage of it.
On press coverage of Philippines President Corazon C Aquino's administration, quoted in NY *Times* 22 Jan 87

MARGARET THATCHER, Prime Minister of Great Britain

16 [Democratic nations] must try to find ways to starve the terrorist and the hijacker of the oxygen of publicity on which they depend.
Calling for ban on headlines that offer publicity for political causes, to London meeting of Amer Bar Assn 15 Jul 85

17 Ought we not to ask the media to agree among themselves a voluntary code of conduct, under which they would not say or show anything which could assist the terrorists' morale or their cause while the hijack lasted.
ib

ROGER THÉROND, Editor in Chief, *Paris-Match*

1 Look, it is our *Dallas*, our serial, and they are our Kennedys, and we didn't invent any of it. The scenario is beyond belief.

On covering Monaco's royal family, NY *Times* 28 Aug 84

2 The public has invested in this story. It participates, it judges, it condemns, it pities. It's a second life for a lot of people.
ib

VIRGIL THOMSON

3 Reviewing music or reviewing anything is a writing job. It's nice if you are experienced in the field you are writing about, but writing is what you are doing.

On role of the critic, *Christian Science Monitor* 12 Feb 85

JAMES THURBER

4 No other editor has ever been lost and saved so often in the course of a working week. When his heart leaped up, it leaped a long way, because it started from so far down, and its commutings over the years from the depths to the heights made Ross a specialist in appreciation.

On *New Yorker* editor Harold Ross, *The Years with Ross* Atlantic-Little, Brown 59

5 The story of Harold Ross, the *New Yorker* and me is a mere footnote to the story of our time, and we might as well face the truth that to researchers of the future, poking about among the ruins of time, we shall all be tiny glitters. But then, so are diamonds.

Quoted in Helen Thurber and Edward Weeks eds *Selected Letters of James Thurber* Atlantic-Little, Brown 81

TIME MAGAZINE

6 Her friends stand by her: When she prematurely published the claim that a certain actress was pregnant, the actress's husband hastened to prove her correct.

On Hollywood columnist Louella Parsons, 24 Nov 61

MARTIN TOLCHIN

7 The stakeout [is] the lowest form of journalism and a boring penance for . . . journalistic sins.

On reporters' vigil outside closed Senate Intelligence Committee hearings about Iran arms sales, NY *Times* 20 Dec 86

HARRY S TRUMAN, 33rd US President

8 To hell with them. When history is written they will be the sons of bitches—not I.

On criticism by what he called the "sabotage press," quoted by Margaret Truman *Bess W Truman* Macmillan 86

MARGARET TRUMAN

9 Mother . . . considered a press conference on a par with a visit to a cage of cobras.
Bess W Truman Macmillan 86

JOHN UPDIKE

10 [We] hope . . . the "real" person behind the words will be revealed as ignominiously as a shapeless snail without its shapely shell.

On "consumeristic appetite for interviews," NY *Times* 17 Aug 86

UPPER & LOWER CASE MAGAZINE

11 Regardless of the devices that are conjured up by the technicians, designers have the last word with the words.
Jun 80

12 The job to entice, surprise, engage, entertain, inform, persuade—in short, communicate with readers—has been the burden of the artist from Day 1.
ib

13 Every age has had its specialists. When smoke signals were the medium, there were surely some Indians a little more nimble with their blankets . . . in the jungles, some drummers had a better beat . . . in the medieval cloisters, almost any brother could grind the pigment, but only a few penned the manuscripts.
ib

PETER USTINOV

14 Her virtue was that she said what she thought, her vice that what she thought didn't amount to much.

On Hollywood columnist Hedda Hopper, quoted by Herbert R Mayes *The Magazine Maze* Doubleday 80

JOHN VINOCUR

15 The public relations warriors fought and lost Monte Carlo's Battle of the Magazine Covers.

On Monaco's attempt to curb unfavorable publicity about its royal family, NY *Times* 28 Aug 84

JAMES G WATT, US Secretary of Interior

16 They kill good trees to put out bad newspapers.
Newsweek 8 Mar 82

THEODORE H WHITE

1 Those 40 or 50 national correspondents who had followed Kennedy since the beginning of his electoral exertions into the November days had become more than a press corps—they had become his friends and, some of them, his most devoted admirers.
The Making of the President 1960 Atheneum 61

2 When the bus or the plane rolled or flew through the night, they sang songs of their own composition about Mr Nixon and the Republicans in chorus with the Kennedy staff and felt that they, too, were marching like soldiers of the Lord to the New Frontier.
ib

RADIO & TELEVISION

Personalities

FRED ALLEN

3 Ed Sullivan will be around as long as someone else has talent.
On 10th anniversary of Sullivan's Sunday night variety show, *TV Guide* 21 Jun 58

STEVE ALLEN

4 Is it larger than a bread box?
Favorite question for guests on the panel show *What's My Line* CBS TV 2 Feb 50 to 3 Sep 67

JIMMY BRESLIN

5 ABC Television Network: Your services, such as they are, will no longer be required as of 12/20/86.
Page 1 advertisement that he intended to quit as host of his short-lived late-night program, NY *Times* 24 Nov 86

DAVID BRINKLEY and CHET HUNTLEY

6 Good night, Chet.
Good night, David.
Sign-off lines on *Huntley-Brinkley Report* NBC TV 29 Oct 56 to 30 Jul 70

TOM BROKAW, NBC News

7 It's all storytelling, you know. That's what journalism is all about.
Northwestern University *Byline* Spring 82

CAROL BURNETT

8 I liked myself better when I wasn't me.
On her high-school drama classes, *One More Time* Random House 86, quoted by Andrea Carla Michaels *Wall Street Journal* 28 Sep 86

JOHNNY CARSON

9 We're more effective than birth control pills.
On late-night television programs, *Time* 19 May 67

JOHN CHANCELLOR, NBC News

10 Other administrations have had a love-hate relationship with the press. The Nixon administration has a hate-hate relationship.
Quoted by Osborn Elliott *The World of Oz* Viking 80

WALTER CRONKITE, CBS News

11 And that's the way it is, March 6, 1981.
Sign-off line on his last night as anchor

12 Everything is being compressed into tiny tablets. You take a little pill of news every day—23 minutes—and that's supposed to be enough.
On superficiality of television news, *Newsweek* 5 Dec 83

13 Television [is] a high-impact medium. It does some things no other force can do—transmitting electronic pictures through the air. Still, as an explored, comprehensive medium, it is not a substitute for print.
NY *Times* 18 Jul 84

14 The great sadness of my life is that I never achieved the hour newscast, which would not have been twice as good as the half-hour newscast, but many times as good.
ib

PHIL DONAHUE

15 In order to keep this feather in the air—and that's what it is—my people have to *stay on fire* creatively.
On moving his long-running interview show from Chicago to New York, *60 Minutes* CBS TV 24 Feb 85

16 I see all those Solomons out there, I can't wait to hear your wisdom.
Hosting program on adoption, NBC TV 9 Jan 86

SAM DONALDSON, ABC News

17 News conferences are the only chance the American public has to see Ronald Reagan use his mind.
NY *Times* 27 Sep 86

18 The questions don't do the damage. Only the answers do.
On presidential press conferences, *Hold On, Mr President!* Random House 87

1 Call me a braggart, call me arrogant. People at ABC (and elsewhere) have called me worse. But when you need the job done on deadline, you'll call me.
  ib

JIMMY DURANTE

2 Good night, Mrs Calabash, wherever you are!
  Sign-off line referring to nickname of his late wife, recalled on his death, *Time* 11 Feb 80

LINDA ELLERBEE

3 When the anchorman is wearing a colonel's uniform, it tells you something.
  On countries where "good" news is presented regularly on television, *"And So It Goes"* Putnam 86

4 The new national campfire—radio.
  Our World: The Year 1938 ABC TV 30 Oct 86

AVA GARDNER

5 For the loot, honey, for the loot.
  On why she came out of retirement to appear on a prime time soap opera, *People* 10 Jun 85

JACKIE GLEASON

6 I only made $200 a week and I had to buy my own bullets.
  On his early film career, recalled on his death, NY *Times* 26 Jun 87

7 How sweet it is!
  Stock phrase used in his television programs, *ib*

8 One of these days, Alice. Pow! Right in the kisser!
  Line from his 1950s series *The Honeymooners*, quoted in *People* 13 Jul 87

MAX HEADROOM (Matt Frewer)

9 I think it was Shakespeare who once said:
  "Blipverts may come
  And blipverts may go
  But the laziness upon which they breed is with us
    always."
  Actually, that's quite good; perhaps it was me who
    said it.
  As computer-generated television character, quoted in *Newsweek* 20 Apr 87

GARRISON KEILLOR

10 I want to resume the life of a shy person.
  On retiring after 13 years as the host of his radio show *Prairie Home Companion,* quoted in *US News & World Report* 2 Mar 87

TED KOPPEL, ABC News

11 I have the necessary lack of tact.
  On interviewing guests on *Nightline*, quoted by Nancy Collins "The Smartest Man on TV" *New York* 13 Aug 84

12 Emotions get in the way [but] they don't pay me to start crying at the loss of 269 lives. They pay me to put some perspective on the situation.
  ib

13 In the days of Caesar, kings had fools and jesters. Now network presidents have anchormen.
  People 17 Dec 84

14 I think we're glazing eyes all across America.
  Interrupting a long-winded guest, *Nightline* ABC TV 13 Feb 87

GROUCHO MARX

15 I read in the newspapers they are going to have 30 minutes of intellectual stuff on television every Monday from 7:30 to 8. . . . to educate America. They couldn't educate America if they started at 6:30.
  Boston *Globe* 22 Jan 60

CLAYTON MOORE

16 I will continue wearing the white hat and black mask until I ride up into the big ranch in the sky.
  On his costume as the Lone Ranger, *Time* 4 Feb 85

BILL MOYERS

17 A journalist is basically a chronicler, not an interpreter of events. Where else in society do you have the license to eavesdrop on so many different conversations as you have in journalism? Where else can you delve into the life of our times? I consider myself a fortunate man to have a forum for my curiosity.
  Channel Maker 29 Feb 79

18 The printed page conveys information and commitment, and requires active involvement. Television conveys emotion and experience, and it's very limited in what it can do logically. It's an existential experience—there and then gone.
  NY *Times* 3 Jan 82

19 A producer is a saboteur who tries to infiltrate the passivity of viewers and to create impressions that are lasting.
  ib

1 I own and operate a ferocious ego.
ib

EDWARD R MURROW, CBS News

2 Don't be deluded into believing that the titular heads of the networks control what appears on their networks. They all have better taste.
To convention of radio and television news directors, Chicago, news summaries 15 Oct 58

3 We cannot make good news out of bad practice.
Reply as director of US Information Agency to Senate critics who wanted him to ignore racial strife in order to project a better image abroad, recalled on his death, *Life* 7 May 65

4 The speed of communications is wondrous to behold. It is also true that speed can multiply the distribution of information that we know to be untrue.
On receiving 1964 Family of Man Award, quoted by Alexander Kendrick *Prime Time* Little, Brown 69

5 [A] satellite has no conscience.
ib

6 The newest computer can merely compound, at speed, the oldest problem in the relations between human beings, and in the end the communicator will be confronted with the old problem, of what to say and how to say it.
ib

7 If we were to do the Second Coming of Christ in color for a full hour, there would be a considerable number of stations which would decline to carry it on the grounds that a Western or a quiz show would be more profitable.
ib

8 Good night, and good luck.
Sign-off line, quoted by A M Sperber *Murrow* Freundlich 86

JACK PAAR

9 Statistics show that many people watch our show from the bedroom. . . . and people you ask into your bedroom have to be more interesting than those you ask into your living room. I kid you not!
As host of NBC TV's *Tonight Show*, NY *Herald Tribune* 22 Apr 58

ROBERT PIERPOINT, CBS News

10 Most people are not worth interviewing if they are not known to the public, and . . . once known, they often don't want to be interviewed.
Time 27 Dec 82

DAN RATHER, CBS News

11 They know where the levers of power are.
On White House officials who criticized CBS News coverage, NY *Times* 14 Nov 83

12 The mine field doesn't have any end. You think, "If I could just get through it to the other side . . . But there's no getting through it."
On job of CBS president Howard Stringer, quoted by Peter J Boyer "CBS News in Search of Itself," *ib* 28 Dec 86

13 Every time Howard puts his foot down he runs the risk of stepping on something that will maim him, if not destroy him.
ib

14 News is a business, but it is also a public trust.
ib 10 Mar 87

15 Anyone who says network news cannot be profitable doesn't know what he is talking about. But anyone who says it must *always* make money is misguided and irresponsible.
ib

ANDY ROONEY

16 It's not so much that I write well—I just don't write badly very often, and that passes for good on television.
On his essays for CBS TV's *60 Minutes, Time* 11 Jul 69

17 I've had 30 bosses at CBS. I've outlived them all.
On his disagreements with network management, Boston *Globe* 8 Apr 87

MORLEY SAFER, CBS News

18 BBC Radio is not so much an art or industry as it is a way of life . . . a mirror that reflects . . . the eccentricities, the looniness that make Britons slightly different from other humans.
60 Minutes CBS TV 15 Sep 85

19 The BBC is a perfect example of uncontrolled growth, [occupying] old churches and manor houses, the old Langham Hotel where Sherlock Holmes once met Moriarty and where this correspondent once shared an office with an 8-foot bathtub.
ib

20 [The] BBC was known as Auntie—suggesting someone prudish and Victorian—and that she still is on some days. On others she's a champagne-soaked floozie, her skirts in disarray, her mind in the gutter, and the mixture can be quite wonderful.
ib

1 BBC Radio is a never-never land of broadcasting, a safe haven from commercial considerations, a honey pot for every scholar and every hare-brained nut to stick a finger into.
ib

2 It's back to the future.
On new management at CBS, quoted in *US* 3 Nov 86

DANIEL SCHORR, CBS News

3 All news is an exaggeration of life.
Newsweek 11 Jul 83

RED SKELTON

4 His death was the first time that Ed Wynn ever made anyone sad.
Time 1 Jul 66

MIKE WALLACE, CBS News

5 I determined that if I was to carve out a piece of reportorial territory for myself . . . it would be [doing] the hard interview, irreverent if necessary, the façade-piercing interview.
NY *Daily News* 14 Oct 84

WALTER WINCHELL

6 Good evening Mr and Mrs America, from border to border and coast to coast and all the ships at sea. Let's go to press.
Opening for Sunday evening newscasts, recalled on his death 20 Feb 72

Writers, Producers & Directors

ROONE ARLEDGE, President, ABC News

7 They're indispensable. They're the glue that holds a newscast together.
On anchors, *US News & World Report* 20 Nov 78

JAMES T AUBREY, President, CBS

8 If I had my way we'd have some guy come on at 11 AM and say, "The following six men made horses' asses of themselves at the Republican Convention," and then he'd give the six names and that would be it.
Quoted by David Halberstam *The Powers That Be* Knopf 79

DON BRESNAHAN

9 I am always apologizing for it, criticizing it, defending it, praising it, damning it, loving it and hating it . . . that glamorous enfant terrible of journalism, television news.
On producing documentaries, *Newsweek* 19 Apr 82

10 We are guilty of giving you too little because we are desperately afraid that you don't really want any more.
ib

BARRY DILLER, Chief of Programming, ABC

11 The American public tunes in every night hoping to see two people screwing. Obviously, we can't give them that . . . but let's always keep it in mind.
Quoted in *Newsweek* 20 May 85

REUVEN FRANK, President, NBC News

12 The printed press does not show the reporter asking the question. What is peculiar to television is that the intrusiveness is part of the story.
Time 12 Dec 83

ROBERT FRASER, Chief, British Independent Television Authority

13 Television should be kept in its proper place—beside us, before us, but never between us and the larger life.
Look 18 Feb 58

STEVE FRIEDMAN, Producer, NBC *Today* Show

14 It's *The Mourning Show*. Is it true that the theme song is going to be "Taps"?
On new format for rival CBS *Morning Program*, NY *Times* 4 Jan 87

LAWRENCE GROSSMAN, President, NBC News

15 You wait for a gem in an endless sea of blah.
On television coverage of political conventions, NY *Times* 20 Jul 84

DON HEWITT, CBS TV producer

16 Let's give the conventions back to the politicians. . . . If we think there's any news, we can tack it on afterward as commentary. But the conventions should be their show, not ours.
Quoted by Theodore H White *Time* 19 Nov 84

17 Confrontation is not a dirty word. . . . Sometimes it's the best kind of journalism as long you don't confront people just for the sake of a confrontation.
Minute by Minute Random House 85

18 He can thread a needle with a well-turned phrase.
On Morley Safer, *ib*

ALFRED HITCHCOCK

19 [Television is] like the invention of indoor

plumbing. It didn't change people's habits. It just kept them inside the house.

NY *Journal-American* 25 Aug 65

1 One of television's great contributions is that it brought murder back into the home, where it belongs.

National Observer 15 Aug 66

ARTHUR MILLER

2 In the theater, while you recognized that you were looking at a house, it was a house in quotation marks. On screen, the quotation marks tend to be blotted out by the camera.

On television production of *Death of a Salesman*, NY *Times* 15 Sep 85

3 The problem was to sustain at any cost the feeling you had in the theater that you were watching a real person, yes, but an intense condensation of his experience, not simply a realistic series of episodes.

ib

4 It isn't easy to do in the theater, but it's twice as hard in film.

ib

GLORIA MONTY

5 Some people call it a rape. *We* call it a seduction.

On controversial 1981 story line for the soap opera *General Hospital*, quoted in *US* 13 Jul 87

TONY PALMER

6 I think my greatest single achievement . . . took place on a Tuesday in March, when, with much bribery and corruption, I got them to clear the Grand Canal. . . . *That* was truly Wagnerian.

On re-creating Richard Wagner's funeral cortège in Venice for *Wagner*, multipart PBS TV presentation, *TV Guide* 18 Oct 86

C WREDE PETERSMEYER, Chairman, Corinthian Broadcasting Corp

7 The size of television's footprint is as long and as wide as the country itself. . . . measured by the allegiance of audiences and advertisers.

"Born of the Vitality of Advertising" *Printers' Ink* 20 Mar 64

8 This sight, sound and motion medium has made mass salesmanship an indispensable facet of mass production and mass employment.

ib

FRANK PIERSON

9 After all, what was *Medea*? Just another child custody case.

On lack of originality in television plots, NY *Times* 23 Mar 62

JOHN B SIAS, President, ABC

10 We're going to run that program come rain, blood or horse manure.

On controversial miniseries *Amerika*, about a peaceful Soviet takeover of the US, NY *Times* 28 Jan 87

HENRY SIEGEL, Chairman, LBS Communications

11 I don't think anybody in our business is creative. What we do is copy something better than the next person.

NY *Times* 5 Sep 85

FRANK STANTON, President, CBS

12 [It is] ominous [because] it is made upon the journalism of a medium licensed by the government of which he is a high-ranking officer.

On Vice President Spiro T Agnew's attack on the power of network news divisions, quoted in NY *Times* 14 Nov 83

ALAN WAGNER, Vice President, CBS

13 I'm afraid we felt the wrong end of the elephant first.

On failure of pioneering nighttime drama series *Beacon Hill*, NY *Times* 28 Oct 75

CHRISTY WELKER, Vice President, ABC

14 There has to be a strong love story. That gives the audience an easily identifiable, emotional umbilical cord.

On her "biovid" *Napoleon and Josephine*, quoted in *Newsweek* 20 May 85

Observers & Critics

ROBERT McC ADAMS, Secretary, Smithsonian Institution

15 Television probably has become the most evocative, widely observed signpost we have.

On adding television memorabilia to the museum's collection, *Smithsonian* Jul 85

RICHARD P ADLER, Institute of the Future, Palo Alto CA

16 *All* television is children's television.

Quoted by Jonathan Rowe "Modern Advertising: The Hidden Persuasion" *Christian Science Monitor* 29 Jan 87

SPIRO T AGNEW, US Vice President

1 A tiny and closed fraternity of privileged men, elected by no one, and enjoying a monopoly sanctioned and licensed by government.
> On network news divisions, nationally televised address 13 Nov 69

WOODY ALLEN

2 The whole country was tied together by radio. We all experienced the same heroes and comedians and singers. They were giants.
> On *Radio Days*, his film about the 1940s, NY *Times* 25 Jan 87

BURNETT ANDERSON

3 Sports broadcasters are the only reporters . . . who describe past events in the future tense.
> Quoted by William Safire NY *Times* 6 Nov 83

ANONYMOUS

4 You'll never have a nervous breakdown, but you sure are a carrier.
> To CBS's Fred W Friendly, quoted in *Newsweek* 27 Mar 72

5 [He is] the gynecologist of the airways.
> On Phil Donahue, known for provoking frank discussions on his program, quoted by Mike Wallace *60 Minutes* CBS TV 24 Feb 85

6 Daddy, Daddy, there's the man who lives in our TV.
> Child who spotted Florida Governor Bob Graham at a rally during Graham's US Senate campaign, quoted in Boston *Globe* 21 Nov 86

R W APPLE JR

7 The sense of national catastrophe is inevitably heightened in a television age, when the whole country participates in it.
> On explosion of Challenger space shuttle, NY *Times* 29 Jan 86

8 A first hint of the power of the electronic media to bring disaster directly into living rooms came with the radio broadcast of the explosion of the zeppelin *Hindenburg* in 1937; but that was as nothing compared with the pictures . . . of the space shuttle exploding, disintegrating and etching chaotic, sickening contrails against the blue sky.
> *ib*

W H AUDEN

9 What the mass media offer is not popular art, but entertainment which is intended to be consumed like food, forgotten and replaced by a new dish.
> *The Dyer's Hand* Random House 68

CLIVE BARNES

10 Television is the first truly democratic culture—the first culture available to everyone and entirely governed by what the people want. The most terrifying thing is what people do want.
> NY *Times* 30 Dec 69

MARTHA BAYLES

11 If we think of [television] programming as an all-American menu, then the detective show is definitely the hamburger.
> "What Makes a Formula Work?" *Wall Street Journal* 22 Oct 84

KENNETH BILBY

12 [He] had come to view [television] as a force of nearly preternatural dimensions, life-transforming in its impact.
> *The General: David Sarnoff and the Rise of the Communications Industry* Harper & Row 86, quoted by Charles Fountain *Christian Science Monitor* 10 Dec 86

MICHAEL BOBICK

13 You get these small-town feuds because people don't have cablevision. You don't have anything else to do.
> On warring factions in Pine Hill NY, NY *Times* 20 Nov 84

DANIEL J BOORSTIN, Librarian of Congress

14 Nothing is really real unless it happens on television.
> NY *Times* 19 Feb 78

JOHN MASON BROWN

15 Some television programs are so much chewing gum for the eyes.
> Recalled on his death 16 Mar 69

LES BROWN

16 Unlike productions in the other arts, all television shows are born to destroy two other shows.
> *Harper's* Mar 85

17 When a show fails to destroy the competition—and it can fail while attracting 20 million viewers—it is itself destroyed.
> *ib*

ART BUCHWALD

18 Every time you think television has hit its lowest ebb, a new . . . program comes along to

make you wonder where you thought the ebb was.

Have I Ever Lied to You? Putnam 68

WARREN E BURGER, Chief Justice, US Supreme Court

1 It is not possible to arrange for any broadcast of any Supreme Court proceeding, but when you get the Cabinet meetings on the air, call me.

Reply to Mutual Broadcasting System's request for live radio coverage, quoted in *International Herald Tribune* 24 Mar 86

VINCENT CANBY

2 When Uncle Bob (or Ted or Ray) promised to send a shooting star over the house to mark a young listener's birthday, the young listener, who had hung out the window for an hour without seeing the star, questioned not Uncle Bob (or Ted or Ray), but his own eyesight.

On the Golden Age of radio, NY *Times* 30 Jan 87

3 Radio wasn't outside our lives. It coincided with—and helped to shape—our childhood and adolescence. As we slogged toward maturity, it also grew up and turned into television, leaving behind, like dead skin, transistorized talk-radio and nonstop music shows.

ib

HUGH CASSON, President, Royal Academy of Art

4 Strangers often come up to me and say, "I saw you on television." To them it's a sort of confirmation that I exist.

Architectural Digest Dec 85

FRANCIS X CLINES

5 Delegates crane their gaze at overhead screens. The producers, using fast-cutting close-up shots, have added the narcissistic touch of allowing delegates to watch themselves watch themselves at a convention of people watching them.

On televised proceedings of Democratic National Convention in San Francisco, NY *Times* 18 Jul 84

6 Britain's gnawing hunger for retrospection is of Proustian proportions; historical confections of past glory are always being sugared up and nibbled at somewhere in the land.

On 50th anniversary of BBC's first telecast, *ib* 9 Nov 86

7 The grand institution, at once hoary and ethe-real, that some call Auntie and others call the Beeb, and that most, it seems, must call controversial.

ib

8 The wine and special video samplings of five decades of funny, nostalgic programs—Benny Hill so young and foolish, Elizabeth so young and regal, Joan Collins so young and vampy—had a number of the mass pack of TV writers chuckling or at least struck glassy-eyed by mortal identity with the grainy ghosts of TV past.

ib

9 The earnest weatherman is even more hilarious than in America because his forecasts of change are even more unchanging, and his wondrous maps are always pocked with countless rain cloud symbols that seem permanently rooted across the beloved isle.

ib

10 Thus does the Beeb ease the English into another gray familiar day, another half-century of magic mystic rays.

ib

THAD COCHRANE, US Senator

11 The camera is a natural attraction for a politician. And if a camera is here, we're going to be here. And we're going to say something, even if we have nothing to say.

On allowing televised coverage of Senate floor debates, NY *Times* 16 Sep 85

JOHN CONDRY, Department of Human Development, Cornell University

12 Advertising causes conflicts at exactly the most vulnerable age for children to be in conflict with parents.

Quoted by Jonathan Rowe "Modern Advertising: The Subtle Persuasion" *Christian Science Monitor* 29 Jan 87

JOHN CROSBY

13 He is forced to be literate about the illiterate, witty about the witless and coherent about the incoherent.

On role of a television critic, news summaries 20 Mar 55

CHARLES DE GAULLE, President of France

14 I might have had trouble saving France in 1946—I didn't have television then.

Newsweek 19 Aug 63

ROBERT DUVALL

1 They have a tourniquet on the brain.
On producers of some soap operas, *Live at Five* WNBC TV 24 Sep 86

T S ELIOT

2 It is a medium of entertainment which permits millions of people to listen to the same joke at the same time, and yet remain lonesome.
On television, NY *Post* 22 Sep 63

ELIZABETH II, Queen of England

3 It's inevitable that I should seem a rather remote figure to many of you—a successor to the kings and queens of history; someone whose face may be familiar in newspapers and films but who never touches your personal lives. But now, at least for a few minutes, I welcome you to the peace of my own home.
First televised Christmas address 25 Dec 57

EDWARD ROBB ELLIS

4 The world is going mad at an accelerating rate and television is the Typhoid Mary of this madness.
NY *Times* 25 Feb 81

HENRY FAIRLIE

5 There is a middlebrow snobbery in America that praises everything on public television and disdains everything on the commercial networks as a blight.
On US reaction to television presentation of Evelyn Waugh's *Brideshead Revisited,* London *Times* 1 Feb 82

FRED W FRIENDLY

6 Television makes so much at its worst that it can't afford to do its best.
After becoming professor of broadcast journalism at Columbia University, *US News & World Report* 12 Jun 67

7 Television was supposed to be a national park. [Instead] it has become a money machine. . . . It's a commodity now, just like pork bellies.
Quoted by Rushworth M Kidder "Videoculture" *Christian Science Monitor* 10 Jun 85

GEORGE GERBNER, Dean, Annenberg School of Communications, University of Pennsylvania

8 The product is the delivery of the largest number of people at the least cost.
On television programmers, *Christian Science Monitor* 10 Jun 85

DAVID GERGEN, White House director of communications

9 Ronald Reagan is clearly to television what Franklin Roosevelt was to radio.
Newsweek 18 Apr 83

PETER GOLDMAN

10 A debate before 70 million people is in fact a distorting glass, a fun-house mirror in which wrinkles look like canyons and hesitation like an attack of amnesia.
On debate between presidential candidates Ronald Reagan and Walter F Mondale, *Newsweek* special election issue Nov/Dec 84

SAMUEL GOLDWYN

11 Why should people go out and pay money to see bad films when they can stay at home and see bad television for nothing?
Recalled on his death 31 Jan 74

JACK GOULD

12 It's like being called up in the draft. The peculiar joy of hemorrhaging without bleeding starts when the evil little red light glows on the monstrous camera.
On telecasting his columns during a prolonged newspaper strike, *Time* 15 Feb 63

13 There is something supremely reassuring about television; the worst is always yet to come.
NY *Times* 3 Nov 66

THOMAS GRIFFITH

14 Journalism as theater [is what] TV news is.
On coverage of return of Iranian-held hostages, *Time* 9 Feb 81

15 Just to be seen strolling to or from a helicopter on the White House lawn, shouting an evasive answer to Sam Donaldson, must seem to the Reagans not quite satisfactory enough of a 7 PM presence, and this inane scene certainly galls the press.
On White House move to supply "appropriate soapboxes and visual backdrops" for the president, "Making News and Non-News" *ib* 1 Sep 86

SUE HALPERN

16 The resident kvetch of *60 Minutes*. . . . an unabashed fogy.
On Andy Rooney, NY *Times* 7 Oct 84

ALAN HAMILTON

17 In the opulence of its set, its cast was remark-

ably adept . . . and it was richly endowed with character actors able, indeed anxious, to play cameo roles.

> On initial telecasts from House of Lords, "Cast of the Lords' TV Show in Sparkling Form" London *Times* 24 Jan 85

1 Its plot is loose and tortuous and will take some time for its stars to emerge.
> *ib*

2 There is, as yet, no Beast and definitely no Bitch.
> *ib*

GARY HART, US Senator

3 You can get awful famous in this country in seven days.
> On television coverage of his presidential campaign, NY *Times* 7 Oct 84

BEN HECHT

4 Television excites me because it seems to be the last stamping ground of poetry, the last place where I hear women's hair rhapsodically described, women's faces acclaimed in odelike language.
> NY *Herald Tribune* 26 May 58

CARRIE HEETER, Director, Communications Technology Laboratory, Michigan State University

5 They don't watch programs anymore; they watch pieces of programs.
> On viewers' tendency to change channels, NY *Times* 9 Oct 85

HOWELL HEFLIN, US Senator

6 I see a little better grooming. Some might even be trying a little powder.
> On first day of televised Senate proceedings, NY *Times* 2 May 86

NICHOLAS JOHNSON, Federal Communications Commission

7 All television is educational television. The only question is what is it teaching?
> *Life* 10 Sep 71

8 A viewer who skips the advertising is the moral equivalent of a shoplifter.
> To Amer Magazine Conference, NY *Times* 25 Oct 84

E J KAHN

9 Looking at *60 Minutes,* in full or in part, has roughly the impact on Hewitt that standing at the edge of an unruffled pool had on Narcissus.
> On CBS TV producer Don Hewitt, *New Yorker* 19 Jul 82

ALEXANDER KENDRICK

10 He believed that . . . there had to be a message to start with, that in the beginning was the Word. Otherwise, he said, "all you have is a lot of wires and lights in a box."
> *Prime Time: The Life of Edward R Murrow* Little, Brown 69

CHARLES KRAUTHAMMER

11 In the old days one merely gawked at these unfortunates. Donahue's genius is to get them to talk.
> On guests of Phil Donahue's talk show, *Cutting Edges: Making Sense of the 80s* Random House 85, quoted in NY *Times* 12 Nov 85

LOUIS KRONENBERGER

12 For tens of millions of people [television] has become habit-forming, brain-softening, taste-degrading.
> *The Cart and the Horse* Knopf 64

13 Privacy was in sufficient danger before TV appeared, and TV has given it its death blow.
> *ib*

CHRISTOPHER LEHMANN-HAUPT

14 There is no medical proof that television causes brain damage—at least from over five feet away. In fact, TV is probably the least physically harmful of all the narcotics known to man.
> NY *Times* 24 Sep 69

JOHN LEONARD

15 The British Broadcasting Corporation, like the British tabloids, adores aristocrats. Their houses are big and their servants are cute and, when they aren't eating immense amounts of overcooked food, they stand around on their broad, rolled lawns like croquet hoops waiting for history to pop through the holes in their heads.
> "Television: Costumes without Drama" *New York* 30 Apr 84

LEE LOEVINGER, Federal Communications Commission

16 Television is the literature of the illiterate, the culture of the lowbrow, the wealth of the poor, the privilege of the underprivileged, the exclusive club of the excluded masses.
> To New Jersey Broadcasters Assn, *National Observer* 17 Oct 66

17 Television is a golden goose that lays scram-

bled eggs; and it is futile and probably fatal to beat it for not laying caviar. Anyway, more people like scrambled eggs than caviar.
ib

1 Television is simply automated daydreaming.
Vogue Jun 67

LONDON TIMES

2 The BBC will wear a brisk morning face.
On plans for first venture into early morning television, 12 Apr 82

ALBERT A MARKS JR, Chief Executive Officer, Miss America Pageant

3 He really did put Vaseline on his teeth, you know that?
On long-time host Bert Parks, quoted in *US* 20 Oct 86

MARSHALL McLUHAN

4 The medium is the message.
Assessing the impact of television, *Understanding Media* McGraw-Hill 64

JOHN McNULTY, Vice President of Public Relations, General Motors Corp

5 They'll leave anything incompatible with their view on the cutting-room floor. *60 Minutes* is to journalism what *Charley's Aunt* is to criminology.
Quoted by Walter Guzzardi Jr "How Much Should Companies Talk?" *Fortune* 4 Mar 85

MARGARET MEAD

6 Thanks to television, for the first time the young are seeing history made before it is censored by their elders.
Recalled on her death 15 Nov 78

NEWTON N MINOW, Federal Communications Commission

7 You will observe a vast wasteland.
On television, to National Assn of Broadcasters, NY *Times* 10 May 61

8 When television is good, nothing is better. When it's bad, nothing is worse.
Recalled on 25th anniversary of his "vast wasteland" speech, *Nightline* ABC TV 9 May 86

WALTER F MONDALE

9 Modern politics today requires a mastery of television. I've never really warmed up to television and, in fairness to television, it's never warmed up to me.
After losing presidential election, NY *Times* 8 Nov 84

10 By instinct and tradition, I don't like the thing. I like to look someone in the eye.
On television, *Newsweek* 19 Nov 84

SAM MOORE

11 It came from nowhere, blazed up like a brush fire, pulled us together at the bottom of the Depression, held us together through a war, galloped up to the brink of television and fell over dead.
On radio, *Life* 13 Nov 64

12 Radio invented a new kind of drama called soap opera, a form of serial in which the main rule was, "Don't let anything happen!"—because if something happened on a Wednesday and you were at the dentist, on Thursday you wouldn't know what the hell was going on and you'd get mad and switch soap operas, and soap, too.
ib

13 Radio tried everything, and it all worked. It invented a new kind of singer whose voice wasn't even loud enough to carry across a hotel bedroom, and Americans, as it turned out, would rather hear these "crooners" than any big-bellied tenor who ever shook an opera house chandelier.
ib

NEW YORK TIMES

14 His fans eat it up, along with their toast and morning coffee.
On 25th anniversary of John Gambling's radio show, 20 Oct 84

15 Radio let people see things with their own ears.
Editorial, 30 Jan 86

16 Once upon a time—from 1974 to 1977, to be precise—Sunday night went like this: After you washed the dishes and put the kids to bed and made sure you had enough cigarettes (lots of us were smoking then, remember?) and maybe poured yourself a little something, you sat down in front of the television set and thought of England.
On return of PBS series *Upstairs, Downstairs*, 15 Mar 87

17 There is now a good reason to live through March.
ib

RICHARD M NIXON, 37th US President

18 I knew if I continued to look around . . . it

would be difficult for me to contain my own emotions. So I turned away from the red eyes of the crowd and looked only at the red eye of the camera, talking to all the nation.

On his departure from the White House, *RN: Memoirs of Richard Nixon* Grosset & Dunlap 78

1 In the television age, the key distinction is between the candidate who can speak poetry and the one who can only speak prose.

After 1984 presidential campaign between Ronald Reagan and Walter F Mondale, *New York* 19 Nov 84

MARTIN F NOLAN

2 [Television executives] are afraid to advertise condoms that could save lives, but do not blush about telecasting a National Geographic special on President Reagan's pelvic plumbing.

Boston *Globe* 9 Feb 87

3 If the Barons of Bad Taste known as network executives believe in chastity as an anti-AIDS measure, it doesn't show on the soaps, night or day.

ib

JOHN J O'CONNOR

4 [They are] the video equivalent of junk food.

On miniseries, NY *Times* 16 Nov 78

5 Silly sitcoms are designed to attract juveniles of all ages.

News summaries 31 Dec 79

TERRENCE O'FLAHERTY

6 No wonder the audiences for the late-night talk shows are growing. Who can get to sleep after hearing the 11 PM news?

Reader's Digest Nov 72

MIKE PETERS

7 What do you want to watch tonight? The president's enlarged prostate on 2, his benign polyp on 4 or a colonoscopy on 5?

Cartoon caption on obsessive coverage of President Ronald Reagan's health, *Newsweek* 12 Jan 87

IVER PETERSON

8 Eighty channels in the sky, offering a glimpse of anything from sunrise prayers to soft-core pornography.

On satellite dishes used to pick up programs without charge, NY *Times* 15 Jan 86

RONALD REAGAN, 40th US President

9 I usually never walk by a microphone.

On abiding love of broadcasting, NY *Times* 31 Mar 85

NELSON A ROCKEFELLER, Governor of NY

10 Others looked at radio and saw a gadget; his genius lay in his capacity to look at the same thing ... but to see far more.

On David Sarnoff, *Newsweek* 27 Dec 71

11 [To] David Sarnoff, the word *visionary* meant a capacity to see into tomorrow and make it work.

ib

CARL SANDBURG

12 The impact of television on our culture is ... indescribable. There's a certain sense in which it is nearly as important as the invention of printing.

News summaries 30 Dec 55

ARTHUR M SCHLESINGER JR

13 [Television] has spread the habit of instant reaction and stimulated the hope of instant results.

Newsweek 6 Jul 70

MARTIN SCHRAM

14 Television ... often cannot cover the passing of the torch without fanning the flames in the process.

New York 26 Mar 84

MURRAY SCHUMACH

15 Television is the bland leading the bland.

The Face on the Cutting Room Floor Morrow 64

HUGH SIDEY

16 [Kennedy] did not have to run the risk of having his ideas and his words shortened and adulterated by a correspondent. This was the television era, not only in campaigning, but in holding the presidency.

John F Kennedy, President Atheneum 63

17 [He is] television's sultan of splutter.

On ABC News correspondent Sam Donaldson, *Time* 30 Sep 85

A M SPERBER

18 Little figures on a little screen showed newsreel footage, talked about the war with maps and pointers, unable to compete as yet with radio.

On television coverage of the Korean War in the 1950s, *Murrow* Freundlich 86

1 [He had] a cheekiness bordering at times on nail-file abrasive.

On producer Fred W Friendly, *ib*

RONALD STEEL

2 Television has made places look alike, and it has transformed the way we see. A whole generation of Americans, maybe two, has grown up looking at the world through a lens.

"Life in the Last 50 Years" *Esquire* Jun 83

3 Television has changed how we choose our leaders. It elected Ronald Reagan and a host of Kennedy-look-alike congressmen with blow-dried hair and gleaming teeth. It destroyed Senator Joe McCarthy by showing him in action and it created Jerry Falwell.

ib

JAMES THURBER

4 The chill Miss Trent has her men frustrated to a point at which a mortal male would smack her little mouth, so smooth, so firm, so free of nicotine, alcohol and emotion.

On soap opera heroine Helen Trent, recalled on his death 2 Nov 61

TIME MAGAZINE

5 Political conventions are the intramural Olympics of television.

On Republican National Convention in San Francisco, to which the networks sent 1,825 employees to cover the activities of 1,308 delegates, 24 Jul 64

6 Most of its investigative pieces are playlets in which a Lone Ranger journalist corners a villain, not with a gun but with an interview.

On CBS TV's *60 Minutes*, 12 Dec 83

JOHN UPDIKE

7 I secretly understood: the primitive appeal of the hearth. Television is—its irresistible charm—a fire.

On child doing homework near the family's television set, *Roger's Version* Knopf 86, quoted in NY *Times* 31 Aug 86

HARRIET VAN HORNE

8 There are days when any electrical appliance in the house, including the vacuum cleaner, seems to offer more entertainment possibilities than the [television] set.

NY *World-Telegram & Sun* 7 Jun 57

9 One who roams the channels after dark, searching for buried treasure.

On her role as television critic, *ib* 27 Feb 58

10 The time of the rack and the screws is come. Summer television has set in with its usual severity. And the small screen, where late the sweet birds sang, is now awash with repeats, reruns, rejects, replacements and reversions to the primitive.

"Time to Buy a Polo Mallet" *ib* 2 Jun 58

11 Rarely in broadcasting history has so much been riding on the whimsical flick of a few thousand wrists.

"The Battle for TV's Midnight Millions" *Look* 11 Jul 67

GORE VIDAL

12 Television is now so desperately hungry for material that they're scraping the top of the barrel.

News summaries 20 Jul 55

TOM WALTERS

13 You own anything which comes down in your yard, and you have a right to use it.

On selling satellite dishes, *Time* 16 Sep 85

ANDY WARHOL

14 When I got my first television set, I stopped caring so much about having close relationships.

Recalled on his death, *Newsweek* 9 Mar 87

HARRY F WATERS

15 He was both [television's] first celebrity and its most persistent conscience.

On Edward R Murrow, *Newsweek* 23 Jun 86

HENRY A WAXMAN, US Congressman

16 The routine promotion of condoms through advertising has been stopped by networks who are so hypocritically priggish that they refuse to describe disease control as they promote disease transmission.

US News & World Report 23 Feb 87

ORSON WELLES

17 I hate television. I hate it as much as peanuts. But I can't stop eating peanuts.

NY *Herald Tribune* 12 Oct 56

WILLIAM C WESTMORELAND

18 Television is an instrument which can paralyze this country.

On Vietnam as the first war ever reported without censorship, *Time* 5 Apr 82

1 I was participating in my own lynching, but the problem was I didn't know what I was being lynched for.

> On being interviewed by Mike Wallace for *CBS Reports: The Uncounted Enemy: A Vietnam Deception*, which prompted Westmoreland to sue CBS for $120 million, NY *Times* 20 Nov 84

E B White

2 [Television] should be our Lyceum, our Chautauqua, our Minsky's and our Camelot.

> Quoted by Alexander Kendrick *Prime Time* Little, Brown 69

3 It should restate and clarify the social dilemma and the political pickle. Once in a while it does, and you get a quick glimpse of its potential.

> *ib*

Theodore H White

4 With electricity we were wired into a new world, for electricity brought the radio, a "crystal set" [and] with enough ingenuity, one could tickle the crystal with a cat's whisker and pick up anything.

> *In Search of History: A Personal Adventure* Harper & Row 78

5 He who is created by television can be destroyed by television.

> *Television and the Presidency* WOR TV 24 Jun 84

George F Will

6 They seem to have a license to lie.

> On docudramas, programs that blend reality and entertainment, quoted by Victor Lasky *Reader's Digest* Apr 86

Walter Winchell

7 The only ones who like Milton Berle are his mother—and the public.

> Recalled by Berle in address at Museum of Broadcasting dinner honoring him as Mr Television, NY *Times* 16 Apr 85

Lois Wyse

8 You don't laugh with me;
I don't laugh with you.
All the wit comes pouring out of the tube.
And we laugh at it together.
The more we avoid talking
the more passive the relationship becomes.
Television permits us to walk through life
with minor speaking parts.
And the more we fail to speak,
the more difficult speaking becomes.

> *Lovetalk* Doubleday 73

Linda Yglestas

9 Nostrils flaring, every muscle in his face working overtime while his right index finger beat his point into the table. . . . That smirking half-smile of righteousness that lands its blow with the coolness of Carrara marble.

> On Mike Wallace, NY *Sunday News* 14 Oct 84

Vladimir Zworykin

10 The technique is wonderful. I didn't even dream it would be so good. But I would never let my children come close to the thing.

> Comments of developer of television, interviewed on his 92nd birthday, news summaries 31 Dec 81

SPORTS
Athletes & Players

Henry ("Hank") Aaron, NY Yankees

11 Didn't come up here to read. Came up here to hit.

> To Casey Stengel, who had told him to hold the bat in such a way that he could see its trademark, quoted by Bob Uecker and Mickey Herskowitz *Catcher in the Wry* Putnam 82

Muhammad Ali, prizefighter

12 I'm not the greatest; I'm the double greatest. Not only do I knock 'em out, I pick the round.

> As US 1960 Olympic gold medalist in boxing, NY *Times* 9 Dec 62

13 I'll be floating like a butterfly and stinging like a bee.

> Before defeating Sonny Liston for world heavyweight championship, NY *Herald Tribune* 26 Feb 64

14 I'll beat him so bad he'll need a shoehorn to put his hat on.

> On fight with Floyd Patterson, quoted in NY *Times* 21 Nov 65

15 It's just a job. Grass grows, birds fly, waves pound the sand. I beat people up.

> NY *Times* 6 Apr 77

16 When you can whip any man in the world, you never know peace.

> On beginning treatment for Parkinson's syndrome, *Newsweek* 1 Oct 84

17 Superman don't need no seat belt.

> Comment to flight attendant, who replied, "Superman don't need no airplane, either," quoted by Clifton Fadiman comp *The Little, Brown Book of Anecdotes* Little, Brown 85

1 I'm the best. I just haven't played yet.
> On his golf game, *ib*

ANONYMOUS

2 When he says "Sit down!" I don't even look for a chair.
> Green Bay Packers player on coach Vince Lombardi, recalled on Lombardi's death 3 Sep 70

JOHN BACHAR, rock climber

3 Soloing is serious business, because you can be seriously dead.
> On climbing sheer rock faces alone without mechanical aid, *Newsweek* 1 Oct 84

YOGI BERRA, NY Yankees catcher

4 So I'm ugly. So what? I never saw anyone hit with his face.
> Quoted in Bert Sugar comp *The Book of Sports Quotes* Quick Fox 79

JIM BURT, NY Giants nose tackle

5 I was a dirt-bag. Now I'm an All-Pro.
> On winning first NFC championship since 1956, quoted by Eric Pooley "True Blue: From Giants to Supermen" *New York* 26 Jan 87

ROGER CLEMENS, Boston Red Sox pitcher

6 I was pitching on all adrenaline . . . and challenging them. I was throwing the ball right down the heart of the plate.
> On breaking record by striking out 20 batters in a 9-inning game, NY *Times* 1 May 86

DENNIS CONNER, yachtsman

7 Design has taken the place of what sailing used to be.
> After 1983 loss of America's Cup to Australia, recalled before he regained the cup, *Time* 9 Feb 87

8 It basically was an art before. We're just starting to scratch it into a science.
> On yacht racing, after regaining America's Cup, *ib* 16 Feb 87

JIMMY CONNORS, tennis player

9 People don't seem to understand that it's a damn war out there.
> Quoted by Thomas Tutko and William Bruns *Winning Is Everything and Other American Myths* Macmillan 76

TOM COURTNEY, US 1956 Olympic gold medalist, track

10 My head was exploding, my stomach ripping, and even the tips of my fingers ached. The only thing I could think was, "If I live, I will never run again!"
> *Life* Summer 1984

JACK DEMPSEY, prizefighter

11 Honey, I forgot to duck.
> Comment to his wife after losing 1926 fight to Gene Tunney, recalled on his death 31 May 83.

12 Tell him he can have my title, but I want it back in the morning.
> On a drunk who challenged him, *ib*

JOE DIMAGGIO, NY Yankees outfielder

13 A ball player's got to be kept hungry to become a big leaguer. That's why no boy from a rich family ever made the big leagues.
> NY *Times* 30 Apr 61

EL CORDOBÉS (MANUEL BENÍTEZ PÉREZ), Spanish matador

14 Where is the university for courage? . . . The university for courage is to do what you believe in!
> Quoted by Larry Collins and Dominique Lapierre *Or I'll Dress You in Mourning* New American Library 70

ROGER ERICKSON, NY Yankees pitcher

15 I don't want to be in your future. It's frustrating enough being in your present.
> On retiring after being demoted to the Yankees' farm team, *Sports Illustrated* 2 May 83

CHRIS EVERT LLOYD, tennis player

16 If you can react the same way to winning and losing, that's a big accomplishment. That quality is important because it stays with you the rest of your life, and there's going to be a life after tennis that's a lot longer than your tennis life.
> Quoted by William Safire and Leonard Safir *Good Advice* Times Books 82

BOBBY FISCHER, chess player

17 I like the moment when I break a man's ego.
> *Newsweek* 31 Jul 72

JOE FRAZIER, prizefighter

18 I want to hit him, step away and watch him hurt. I want his heart.
> Before losing 1975 fight to Muhammad Ali, *Newsweek* 29 Sep 75

FRANK GIFFORD, NY Giants halfback

1 Pro football is like nuclear warfare. There are no winners, only survivors.
Sports Illustrated 4 Jul 60

HAROLD ("RED") GRANGE, Chicago Bears halfback

2 If you can't explain it, how can you take credit for it?
On his extraordinary ability to elude tacklers, news summaries 31 Dec 51

FRANCO HARRIS, Seattle Seahawks fullback

3 After 12 years, the old butterflies came back. Well, I guess at my age you call them moths.
On playing for a new team, *Sports Illustrated* 1 Oct 84

BOBBY JONES, golfer

4 You might as well praise a man for not robbing a bank.
On penalizing himself one stroke that cost him a national championship, quoted by Alistair Cooke *America* Knopf 73

5 I will tell you privately it's not going to get better, it's going to get worse all the time, but don't fret. Remember, we "play the ball where it lies," and now let's not talk about this, ever again.
On being stricken by a rare disease in his mid 40s, *ib*

HENRY JORDAN, Green Bay Packers right tackle

6 He's fair. He treats us all the same—like dogs.
On Vince Lombardi, recalled on Lombardi's death 3 Sep 70

MICHAEL JORDAN, Chicago Bulls basketball player

7 The game is my wife. It demands loyalty and responsibility, and it gives me back fulfillment and peace.
Quoted by Pete Axthelm *Newsweek* 5 Jan 87

8 My body could stand the crutches but my mind couldn't stand the sideline.
On broken foot bone that caused him to miss 64 games in 1985-86 season, *ib*

JOE KAPP, former Minnesota Vikings quarterback

9 Is it normal to wake up in the morning in a sweat because you can't wait to beat another human's guts out?
News summaries 31 Dec 79

BILLIE JEAN KING, tennis player

10 Tennis is a perfect combination of violent action taking place in an atmosphere of total tranquillity.
Billie Jean Harper & Row 74

SANDY KOUFAX, Los Angeles Dodgers pitcher

11 Pitching is . . . the art of instilling fear.
Quoted by Robert Hood *The Gashouse Gang* Morrow 76

VERNON LAW, Pittsburgh Pirates pitcher

12 Experience is a hard teacher because she gives the test first, the lesson afterward.
"How to Be a Winner" *This Week* 14 Aug 60

13 Some people are so busy learning the tricks of the trade that they never learn the trade.
ib

SUGAR RAY LEONARD, prizefighter

14 I figure it's like something that has to be, before Marvin and me can be content with ourselves. There is a burning desire in me now.
On challenge to fight middleweight champion Marvin Hagler, *Sports Illustrated* 8 Sep 86

BEN LEXCEN, Australian yachtsman

15 We don't have any sailors in Australia, we have rowers.
On US victory at America's Cup races, NY *Times* 3 Feb 87

GENE LITTLER, golfer

16 Golf is not a game of great shots. It's a game of the most misses. The people who win make the smallest mistakes.
News summaries 22 Mar 69

BOBBY LOCKE, golfer

17 You drive for show but putt for dough.
Recalled on his death 9 Mar 87

ROGER MARSHALL, mountain climber

18 Having seen all the Sherpas who are mutilated, the Sherpanis who are without husbands, I would never employ a Sherpa.
On not using Sherpa porters for his ascent of Mt Everest, NY *Times* 10 Aug 86

JOHN McENROE, tennis player

19 You are the pits of the world! Vultures! Trash!
To the umpire, spectators and reporters at Wimbledon, quoted in *Time* 28 Dec 81

20 I'll let the racket do the talking.
On defending his title as Wimbledon champion, London *Times* 26 Jun 84

1 This taught me a lesson, but I'm not sure what it is.

On losing to Tim Mayotte in the Ebel US Indoor Championships, NY *Times* 9 Feb 87

MICHAEL McGUIRE, adventurer

2 I like to collect experiences the way other people like to collect coins and stamps.

On hiking across the polar ice cap, *Christian Science Monitor* 26 Feb 85

FRANK MUNDUS

3 This is it. There are no world records after this.

On fellow fisherman Donnie Braddick's landing of a 17-foot, 3,450-pound great white shark, believed to be the largest ever caught with rod and reel, *Sports Illustrated* 18 Aug 86

JOE NAMATH, NY Jets quarterback

4 Till I was 13, I thought my name was "Shut Up."

I Can't Wait until Tomorrow Random House 69

5 When we won the league championship, all the married guys on the club had to thank their wives for putting up with all the stress and strain all season. I had to thank all the single broads in New York.

News summaries 31 Dec 79

MARTINA NAVRATILOVA, tennis player

6 I hope, when I stop, people will think that somehow I mattered.

International Herald Tribune 22 Jul 86

7 I just try to concentrate on concentrating.

On strategy for winning the US Open, quoted in *US* 20 Oct 86

JACK NICKLAUS, golfer

8 It's hard not to play golf that's up to Jack Nicklaus standards when you *are* Jack Nicklaus.

On winning his 70th PGA tournament, WINS Radio 28 May 84

TENZING NORGAY, Sherpa guide

9 If I know I make this much trouble, I never climb Everest.

On trying to secure a passport, news summaries 29 Mar 54

BRIAN ORSER, ice skater

10 It's not who does the most tricks, but the total package.

On refusal to perform a quadruple jump in his free-skating program at the world figure skating championships, NY *Times* 12 Mar 87

DON OTT, Athletes in Action basketball player

11 You might say they did unto us as we did unto others.

On loss to UCLA, *Sports Illustrated* 24 Jan 83

JESSE OWENS, US 1936 Olympic gold medalist, track and field

12 Another old friend gone!

On learning that his last remaining world record had been broken, news summaries 31 Dec 60

WILLIAM ("REFRIGERATOR") PERRY, Chicago Bears defensive tackle

13 Even when I was little, I was big.

On his weight, quoted in *Life* Jan 86

14 Some people call me the Kitchen, some call me the Dining Room—and some call me the Cafeteria!

NBC TV 23 Sep 86

GARY PLAYER, golfer

15 Golf asks something of a man. It makes one loathe mediocrity. It seems to say, "If you are going to keep company with me, don't embarrass me."

Christian Science Monitor 24 Jun 65

SUGAR RAY ROBINSON, prizefighter

16 My business is hurting people.

Comment to NY State Boxing Commission, news summaries 23 May 62

JOHN ROSKELLEY, mountain climber

17 You've got to know when to turn around.

On those who have failed to duplicate the feat of two men who climbed Mt Everest without bottled oxygen in 1975, NY *Times* 10 Aug 86

ARNOLD SCHWARZENEGGER, body builder

18 I just use my muscles as a conversation piece, like someone walking a cheetah down 42nd Street.

News summaries 31 Dec 79

WILLIE SHOEMAKER, jockey

19 If Jack Nicklaus can win the Masters at 46, I can win the Kentucky Derby at 54.

Quoted by *Life* Jan 87

LEON SPINKS, prizefighter

20 I know a lot of people think I'm dumb. Well, at least I ain't no educated fool.

LA *Times* 28 Jun 78

Yun Lou, Chinese 1984 Olympic gymnast

1 Suit too big. Grabbed pants instead of pommel.
>On scoring low in pommel horse competition, news summaries 30 Jul 84

Coaches, Officials & Owners

Alex Agase, University of Michigan, assistant football coach

2 If you really want to advise me, do it on Saturday afternoon between 1 and 4 o'clock. And you've got 25 seconds to do it, between plays. Not on Monday. I know the right thing to do on Monday.
>Quoted by Thomas J Peters and Nancy K Austin "A Passion for Excellence" *Fortune* 13 May 85

Yogi Berra, professional baseball manager

3 What difference does the uniform make? You don't hit with it.
>On becoming coach of the Houston Astros, NY *Times* 8 May 86

4 It ain't over till it's over.
>As 1973 manager of NY Mets in National League pennant race, quoted by William Safire *ib* 15 Feb 87

Terry Brennan, University of Notre Dame football coach

5 If you're old and you lose, they say you're outmoded. If you're young and you lose, they say you're green. So don't lose.
>*Life* 25 Mar 57

Dave Bristol, Cincinnati Reds manager

6 Boys, baseball is a game where you gotta have fun. You do that by winning.
>On becoming manager, *Time* 26 May 67

Avery Brundage, President, International Olympic Committee

7 Sport must be amateur or it is not sport. Sports played professionally are entertainment.
>*This Week* 14 Jan 68

Bobby Clarke, Philadelphia Flyers manager

8 I've discovered that the less I say, the more rumors I start.
>*Sports Illustrated* 15 Jul 84

Dave Currey, University of Cincinnati football coach

9 We don't have any refrigerators. We have a few potbelly stoves, but they're on the coaching staff.
>Referring to Chicago Bears player William "Refrigerator" Perry, *Sports Illustrated* 2 Dec 85

Marvin Davis, Oakland Athletics owner

10 As men get older, the toys get more expensive.
>On purchase of team for a rumored $12 million, news summaries 31 Dec 79

Leo Durocher, NY Giants manager

11 You don't save a pitcher for tomorrow. Tomorrow it may rain.
>NY *Times* 16 May 65

12 There are only five things you can do in baseball—run, throw, catch, hit and hit with power.
>*Time* 16 Jul 73

13 Nice guys finish last.
>1946 remark as manager of Brooklyn Dodgers, quoted in Eric Partridge *A Dictionary of Catch Phrases*, edited by Paul Beale, Stein & Day 86

Al Forman, National League umpire

14 I occasionally get birthday cards from fans. But it's often the same message: They hope it's my last.
>*Time* 25 Aug 61

Tom Gorman, National League umpire

15 It's a strange business, all jeers and no cheers.
>Recalled on his death, NY *Times* 17 Aug 86

George Halas, professional football coach

16 When they boo you, you know they mean *you*.
>On San Francisco, his "favorite booing city," recalled on his death 31 Oct 83

Lou Holtz, University of Arkansas football coach

17 The man who complains about the way the ball bounces is likely the one who dropped it.
>LA *Times* 13 Dec 78

Frank Leahy, former University of Notre Dame football coach

18 Egotism is the anesthetic that dulls the pain of stupidity.
>*Look* 10 Jan 55

Vince Lombardi, professional football coach

19 A game that requires the constant conjuring of animosity.
>On football, NY *Times* 10 Dec 67

1 Winning isn't everything, it's the only thing.
Recalled on his death 3 Sep 70

2 Some people try to find things in this game that don't exist but football is only two things—blocking and tackling.
ib

3 A school without football is in danger of deteriorating into a medieval study hall.
ib

BILL PARCELLS, NY Giants coach

4 I *like* linebackers. I *collect* 'em. You can't have too many good ones.
Quoted by Eric Pooley "True Blue: From Giants to Supermen" *New York* 26 Jan 87

RUSS PERRY, ski resort owner

5 It's a gold mine. We can see the green falling.
On a heavy snowfall, NY *Times* 7 Dec 81

RICHARD W POUND, International Olympic Committee

6 Watching Carl Lewis run against his countrymen is little short of boring. But put him, as an American, in a race against the rest of the world, and suddenly everything changes.
"Sport Is a Point of Contact for a Shrinking World" NY *Times* 29 Jun 86

7 Even baseball instinctively recognized that the "World Series" is better than simply a national championship.
ib

LOU SCHULTZ, trainer of Alaskan Huskies

8 First you learn a new language, profanity; and second you learn not to discipline your dogs when you're mad, and that's most of the time when you're training dogs.
NY *Times* 15 Mar 80

9 "No" is something you use a lot, and when you start using it you have a whip in your hands.
ib

10 A good snow machine will cost $2,000 and last four to five years. With dogs, you've got regenerative powers. Snow machines don't have pups.
ib

WILLIAM E SIMON, President, US Olympic Committee

11 Explaining something sensible to Lord Killanin is akin to explaining something to a cauliflower. The advantage of the cauliflower is that if all else fails, you can always cover it with melted cheese and eat it.
On former president of International Olympic Committee, NY *Times* 29 Jul 84

CASEY STENGEL, professional baseball manager

12 The team has come along slow but fast.
On NY Mets, NY *Times* 6 Oct 69

13 There comes a time in every man's life and I've had many of them.
Recalled on his death 29 Sep 75

14 Managing is getting paid for home runs someone else runs.
ib

15 Sure I played, did you think I was born at the age of 70 sitting in a dugout trying to manage guys like you?
At age 72 when asked by Mickey Mantle if he had ever played ball, *ib*

16 I was not successful as a ball player, as it was a game of skill.
ib

BARRY SWITZER, University of Oklahoma football coach

17 It was like a heart transplant. We tried to implant college in him but his head rejected it.
On player who dropped out of school, *Sports Illustrated* 12 Nov 73

GEORGE THOMA, grounds keeper

18 Grass grows by inches but it's killed by feet.
On care of Kansas City football field, NBC TV 21 Jan 87

MIKE TRAINER, boxing manager

19 [Sugar] Ray Leonard is the kind of guy who's always looking at the edge of the cliff, fascinated as to how close he can get to it. He hasn't gotten to the edge yet.
Sports Illustrated 8 Sep 86

PETER UEBERROTH, baseball commissioner

20 The integrity of the game is everything.
Urging players to submit to drug tests, NY *Times* 12 May 85

21 Other sports play once a week ... but this sport is with us every day.
ib 9 Aug 85

22 Baseball is a public trust. Players turn over, owners turn over and certain commissioners turn over. But baseball goes on.
ib

1 A cloud hangs over baseball. It's a cloud called drugs and it's permeated our game.
ib 25 Sep 85

ED VARGO, Supervisor of Umpires, National League

2 You're expected to be perfect the day you start, and then improve.
Wall Street Journal 8 Apr 85

BILL VEECK, Chicago White Sox owner

3 The most beautiful thing in the world is a ballpark filled with people.
Recalled on his death, NY *Times* 4 Jan 86

DOUG WEAVER, former Kansas State University football coach

4 I'm glad it happened in front of the library. I've always emphasized scholarship.
On being hanged in effigy, *Sports Illustrated* 9 Jun 86

Observers & Critics

JOEY ADAMS

5 If you break 100, watch your golf. If you break 80, watch your business.
News summaries 31 Dec 82

DAVE ANDERSON

6 The perfect going-away gift for a college student-athlete. A dictionary.
NY *Times* 20 May 86

7 In the America's Cup, you can't go to your backup quarterback. You can't juggle your batting order. . . . You can't fire the manager either, although Iain Murray might not be safe if George Steinbrenner were the principal owner of the *Kookaburra III*.
On *Kookaburra III*'s loss to the US yacht *Stars & Stripes*, *ib* 3 Feb 87

8 Dennis Conner is Pete Rose in deck shoes.
On skipper of *Stars & Stripes*, *ib* 5 Feb 87

JACQUES BARZUN

9 Whoever wants to know the heart and mind of America had better learn baseball, the rules and realities of the game—and do it by watching first some high-school or small-town teams.
Quoted in NY *Times* 31 May 81

DICK BEDDOES

10 The sportswriting confraternity is burdened with hacks who make tin-can gods out of cast-iron jerks.
Quoted in John Robert Colombo ed *Colombo's Concise Canadian Quotations* Hurtig 76

IRA BERKOW

11 If millionaires and corporations want to spend their money trying to drown one another in the Indian Ocean—the movers and shakers are still millionaires and corporations at that level, and the rest of them are glorified galley slaves—then who am I to try to stop them.
On America's Cup races, NY *Times* 10 Feb 87

ERMA BOMBECK

12 If a man watches three football games in a row, he should be declared legally dead.
Quoted by Phil Donahue, NBC TV 22 May 86

JOSEPH F BOYLE, President, Amer Medical Assn

13 It seems to us an extraordinarily incongruous thing that we have a sport in which two people are literally paid to get into a ring and try to beat one another to death, or at least beat them into a state of senselessness which will then leave them permanently brain-damaged.
On resolution calling for abolition of boxing, NY *Times* 6 Dec 84

RICHARD BRAUTIGAN

14 The sun was like a huge 50-cent piece that someone had poured kerosene on and then had lit with a match, and said, "Here, hold this while I go get a newspaper," and put the coin in my hand, but never came back.
Trout Fishing in America Delta 69

TOM BROKAW

15 I'm honored that you invited me, especially when for $10,000 and a new convertible you could have had the top running-back prospect at SMU.
As master of ceremonies for NCAA's honors luncheon, *Sports Illustrated* 27 Jan 86

HEYWOOD HALE BROUN

16 Sweat is the cologne of accomplishment.
On rodeos, CBS TV 21 Jul 73

NELSON BRYANT

17 A stream is music and motion: smooth glides, fast, turbulent riffles and deep pools, each posing a special challenge.
"Plumbing the Subtle Joys of Trout Ponds" NY *Times* 28 May 84

1 At some moment in September when there is an intimation of fall—perhaps a certain slant of light across the browning meadow in the hush of a late afternoon when the wind from the sea has suddenly died—I think of the fiercely independent ruffed grouse, a game bird without peer.

> "Grouse Hunting Has Its Ritual" *ib* 27 Sep 84

TOM CALLAHAN

2 [He] was blessed to have forgotten his binoculars.

> On veteran horse trainer Charlie Whittingham when his horse Ferdinand won the Kentucky Derby, *Time* 12 May 86

JIMMY CANNON

3 A sportswriter is entombed in a prolonged boyhood.

> Quoted in Jerome Holtzman ed *No Cheering in the Press Box* Holt 74

JOHN CHEEVER

4 All literary men are Red Sox fans—to be a Yankee fan in a literate society is to endanger your life.

> Quoted in *Newsweek* 20 Oct 86

MARSHALL S COGAN

5 I couldn't buy the Red Sox. They're both in the entertainment business.

> On why he bought the "21" Club in NYC, *NY Times* 15 Feb 87

BUD COLLINS

6 Is the quick and stoic stepper ... going to spawn a secondary event—a maternithon for expectant mothers?

> On Joan Benoit's decision to run in the Boston Marathon while pregnant, Boston *Globe* 27 Mar 87

7 Benoit should get one adult first prize ($41,000 and a Mercedes sedan) if she wins, plus one child's portion ($20,500 and a stroller).

> *ib*

ALISTAIR COOKE

8 Golf is an open exhibition of overweening ambition, courage deflated by stupidity, skill soured by a whiff of arrogance.

> Quoted in Bob Chieger and Pat Sullivan eds *Inside Golf* Atheneum 85

9 These humiliations are the essence of the game.

> *ib*

HOWARD COSELL

10 Sports is the toy department of human life.

> News summaries 31 Dec 77

JOHN CROSBY

11 If they hit the ball out, they'd say "Sorry." If they hit it in but too hot for me to handle, they'd say "Sorry." If it was too well hit, they were sorry; too badly hit, they were sorry.

> On playing tennis in England, NY *Herald Tribune* 4 Nov 63

MARIO CUOMO, Governor of NY

12 It was anticipating self-defense.

> On why he once hit a catcher in the face mask while playing minor league baseball, CBS TV 30 Dec 84

FRANK DEFORD

13 It almost seemed as if the Statue of Liberty had gone on tour, turning in her torch for a Yonex racket.

> On Martina Navratilova's return to her native Czechoslovakia to lead the US team to victory in the Federation Cup tournament, "Yes, You Can Go Home Again" *Sports Illustrated* 4 Aug 86

DENNIS DIAZ

14 I fished a lot, dove a lot, boated a lot—and made Johnny Walker Red about a quarter of a million dollars richer.

> On why he started breeding horses, including 1985 Kentucky Derby winner Spend a Buck, two years after his retirement at age 38, *People* 20 May 85

PHIL DONAHUE

15 It's like threading a needle while walking on a water bed.

> On detecting drug use by athletes, NBC TV 23 Mar 87

EDWARD, Duke of Windsor

16 I like going there for golf. America's one vast golf course these days.

> Recalled on his death 28 May 72

DWIGHT D EISENHOWER, 34th US President

17 A lot more people beat me now.

> On how his golf game had fared since he left the White House, recalled on his death 28 Mar 69

BILL EMERSON

18 A bicycle does get you there and more ... And there is always the thin edge of danger to keep

you alert and comfortably apprehensive. Dogs become dogs again and snap at your raincoat; potholes become personal. And getting there is all the fun.

On bicycling, *Saturday Evening Post* 29 Jul 67

WILLIAM FAULKNER

1 There is something about jumping a horse over a fence, something that makes you feel good. Perhaps it's the risk, the gamble. In any event it's a thing I need.

National Observer 3 Feb 64

JAMES FIXX

2 The qualities and capacities that are important in running—such factors as will power, the ability to apply effort during extreme fatigue and the acceptance of pain—have a radiating power that subtly influences one's life.

The Complete Book of Running Random House 77, recalled on his death, *Newsweek* 30 Jul 84

3 [Eventually the] hoopla will die down [and people will] run the same way we brush our teeth—every day, without a fuss.

ib

JOE FLAHERTY

4 When the Dodgers left, it was not only a loss of a team, it was the disruption of a social pattern. . . . a total destruction of a culture.

Quoted by Peter Golenbock *Bums: An Oral History of the Brooklyn Dodgers* Putnam 84

ASHRITA FURMAN

5 Everything is in slow motion down there and silent. It could replace psychotherapy.

On aqua pogo, NY *Times* 22 Mar 86

PAUL GALLICO

6 If there is any larceny in a man, golf will bring it out.

NY *Times* 6 Mar 77

WILLIAM E GEIST

7 The crack of a bat sounded amplified in cavernous Yankee Stadium, sprinkled lightly with fans on a cool September evening.

"At Yankee Stadium, a Wistful September Song" NY *Times* 22 Sep 84

CLARA GERMANI

8 Their tails are high and tongues awag—the twin banners of sled dog contentment.

On Alaskan Huskies in thousand-mile sled dog

race following the Klondike gold rush trail, *Christian Science Monitor* 29 Jan 85

RICHARD GILMAN

9 Being a sports fan is a complex matter, in part irrational . . . but not unworthy . . . a relief from the seriousness of the real world, with its unending pressures and often grave obligations.

"The Wounded Giant Regains His Dignity" NY *Times* 25 Jan 87

10 There's an appreciation, not unlike that for dancers or tightrope walkers, of the body undergoing tests and coming through them by courage and technique; a desire for "clean" results.

ib

11 The Giants will always represent New York [in] the sort of in-your-face move that being in the Super Bowl presents to the way the rest of the country mostly thinks of us: huge, cold, rich, conceited, *unnatural*, deserving therefore of all our misfortunes.

ib

LUIS GONZÁLEZ SEARA

12 Some violent spectacle is normal in most countries.

On bullfighting as compared to boxing in the US and fox hunting in Great Britain, NY *Times* 17 Sep 85

HANK GREENBERG

13 The Pied Piper . . . enjoyed people enjoying themselves. He was colorblind and race-blind and religion-blind.

On Bill Veeck, owner of Chicago White Sox, NY *Times* 4 Jan 86

MAURICE GRIMAUD, Prefect of Paris Police

14 Not to open the hunting season on the pretext that there is no game would be as if one gave up celebrating Christmas because there was not enough snow to go by sleigh to midnight Mass.

NY *Times* 3 Oct 68

SANFORD HANSELL, bowling center manager

15 The bowling alley is the poor man's country club.

NY *Times* 11 May 75

THEODORE M HESBURGH, President, Notre Dame

16 The fundamental difference between intercol-

legiate and professional athletics is that in college the players are supposed to be students first and foremost. This does not mean that they should all be Phi Beta Kappas or physics majors, but neither should they be subnormal students majoring in Ping-Pong.
Sports Illustrated 27 Sep 54

HERBERT HOOVER, 31st US President

1 Fishing is much more than fish. . . . It is the great occasion when we may return to the fine simplicity of our forefathers.
Recalled on his 90th birthday, NY *Times* 9 Aug 64

2 All men are equal before fish.
ib

BOB HOPE

3 If you watch a game, it's fun. If you play it, it's recreation. If you work at it, it's golf.
Reader's Digest Oct 58

STANLEY KUBRICK

4 You sit at the board and suddenly your heart leaps. Your hand trembles to pick up the piece and move it. But what chess teaches you is that you must sit there calmly and think about whether it's really a good idea and whether there are other, better ideas.
Newsweek 26 May 80

CHARLES KURALT

5 If there are bleachers in heaven and a warm sun, that's where you'll find Bill Veeck.
On owner of Chicago White Sox, *Sunday Morning* CBS TV 27 Dec 86

JACK LEMMON

6 If you think it's hard to meet new people, try picking up the wrong golf ball.
Sports Illustrated 9 Dec 85

JOHN LEONARD

7 Baseball happens to be a game of cumulative tension but football, basketball and hockey are played with hand grenades and machine guns.
NY *Times* 2 Nov 75

OREN LYONS JR, adviser to chiefs of the Onondaga Nation

8 When you talk about lacrosse, you talk about the lifeblood of the Six Nations. The game is ingrained into our culture and our system and our lives.
NY *Times* 15 Jun 86

9 There are two times of the year that stir the blood. In the fall, for the hunt, and now for lacrosse.
ib

10 When you look at where team sports are going, the National Football League is turning into organized warfare.
ib

CHARLES BLAIR MACDONALD, golf course architect

11 The object of a bunker or trap is not only to punish a physical mistake, to punish lack of control, but also to punish pride and egotism.
Quoted in Bob Chieger and Pat Sullivan eds *Inside Golf* Atheneum 85

MELVIN MADDOCKS

12 Watching baseball under the lights is like observing dogs indoors, at a pedigree show. In both instances, the environment is too controlled to suit the species.
"Baseball—The Difference between Night and Day" *Christian Science Monitor* 3 Apr 85

DEAN MARTIN

13 If you drink, don't drive. Don't even putt.
News summaries 31 Dec 79

JOHN ALLAN MAY

14 The king and queen of games [hold] court.
On tennis, "100th Wimbledon: Masterpiece Tennis Theater" *Christian Science Monitor* 23 Jun 86

GORDON McLENDON, sportscaster

15 What harm is there in making 100,000 people happy on a hot summer afternoon?
On "fictionalizing" baseball games, recalled on his death, *Sports Illustrated* 29 Sep 86

H L MENCKEN

16 I hate all sports as rabidly as a person who likes sports hates common sense.
Recalled on his death 29 Jan 56

JAMIE MURPHY

17 Chess, like mathematics and music, is a nursery for child prodigies.
On Budapest's chess-playing Polgar sisters, *Time* 21 Apr 86

NEW JERSEY STATE COMMISSION OF INVESTIGATION

18 No truly viable social or economic benefits can be derived from such legal savagery.
On boxing, NY *Times* 12 Dec 85

JOYCE CAROL OATES

1 To be knocked out doesn't mean what it seems. A boxer does not have to get up.
Quoted by George Vecsey NY *Times* 4 Mar 87

2 [Boxing is] a celebration of the lost religion of masculinity all the more trenchant for its being lost.
On Boxing Doubleday 87, quoted in *Newsweek* 9 Mar 87

3 [The] third man in the ring makes boxing possible.
On introduction of referees in late 19th century, *ib*

DAN PARKER

4 The reason the Yankees never lay an egg is because they don't operate on chicken feed.
Sports Illustrated 7 Apr 58

LESTER B PEARSON, Prime Minister of Canada

5 This fastest of all games has become almost as much of a national symbol as the maple leaf or the beaver.
On hockey, quoted in John Robert Colombo ed *Colombo's Canadian Quotations* Hurtig 74

6 Most young Canadians ... are born with skates on their feet rather than with silver spoons in their mouths.
ib

GEORGE PLIMPTON

7 The smaller the ball used in the sport, the better the book.
Theory on why books about football don't sell as well as those about baseball, tennis or golf, NY *Times* 25 Sep 86

MARTIN QUIGLEY

8 The story of the curve ball is the story of the game itself. Some would say of life itself.
The Curve Ball in American Baseball History Algonquin 84

STEVE RATINETZ

9 I only save decent fights. ... I can't be bothered with every two-minute penalty.
On his videotape collection of 120 hours of televised hockey fights, NY *Times* 2 Feb 86

HARRY REASONER

10 Statistics are to baseball what a flaky crust is to Mom's apple pie.
60 Minutes CBS TV 20 Oct 85

JIM ROBBINS

11 Throughout the city, the talk now is of the kill or of the near kill. Some of it may even be true.
On Helena MT during hunting season, NY *Times* 17 Nov 84

SYBIL ROBINSON

12 Many manufacturers are competing for your foot.
On production of running shoes, news summaries 30 Jun 86

JOHN D ROCKEFELLER

13 Golf courses are the best place to observe ministers, but none of them are above cheating a bit.
Quoted by William Manchester *A Rockefeller Family Portrait* Little, Brown 59

WILLIAM SAFIRE

14 The perfect Christmas gift for a sportscaster, as all fans of sports clichés know, is a scoreless tie.
NY *Times* 6 Nov 83

HAROLD SEGALL

15 Golf is not just exercise; it is an adventure, a romance. .... a Shakespeare play in which disaster and comedy are intertwined [and] you have to live with the consequences of each action.
"Golf Is a Funny Game; Tennis Not So" NY *Times* 15 Jun 86

SUE SIMMONS

16 The cup that went down under has now come up again.
On regaining America's Cup after 1983 loss to Australia, NBC TV 9 Feb 87

RED SMITH

17 He had splendid conformation—broad shoulders, white hair and erect carriage—and was beautifully turned out in an ensemble of rich brown. One was inclined to hope he would, in the end, award first prize to himself.
On a judge at a dog show, *Newsweek* 21 Apr 58

TED SOLOTAROFF

18 A professional football team warms up grimly and disparately, like an army on maneuvers: the ground troops here, the tanks there, the artillery and air force over there.
NY *Times* 11 Jun 72

RAY SONS

1 The best use of fat since the invention of bacon.
> On Chicago Bears rookie William "Refrigerator" Perry, *Time* 30 Dec 85

JOHN STEINBECK

2 Sectional football games have the glory and the despair of war, and when a Texas team takes the field against a foreign state, it is an army with banners.
> *Travels with Charlie* Viking 62, quoted in NY *Times* 5 Mar 87

GEORGE STEINER

3 Chess may be the deepest, least exhaustible of pastimes, but it is nothing more. As for a chess genius, he is a human being who focuses vast, little-understood mental gifts and labors on an ultimately trivial human enterprise.
> *Fields of Force* Viking 74

PHIL STONE

4 He looks like he's just been told there's no cannelloni in the world.
> On LA Dodgers manager Tommy Lasorda's dejection after a loss to the San Fancisco Giants, *Sports Illustrated* 12 May 86

E M SWIFT

5 A traveling traffic jam of one-night stands.
> On the 23-day Tour de France bicycle race, "An American Takes Paris" *Sports Illustrated* 4 Aug 86

DALE TALLON

6 I wouldn't say it's cold, but every year Winnipeg's athlete of the year is an ice fisherman.
> On covering hockey game between Chicago Blackhawks and Winnipeg Jets, *Sports Illustrated* 22 Dec 86

PATRICK THOMPSON

7 He rides in the game like heavy cavalry getting into position for the assault. ... trots about, keenly watchful, biding his time, a master of tactics and strategy.
> On polo style of Winston Churchill, quoted by William Manchester *The Last Lion* Little, Brown 83

TIME MAGAZINE

8 Ideally, the umpire should combine the integrity of a Supreme Court justice, the physical agility of an acrobat, the endurance of Job and the imperturbability of Buddha.
> "The Villains in Blue" 25 Aug 61

TED TURNER

9 Sports is like a war without the killing.
> *60 Minutes* CBS TV 24 Jul 77

UNITED STATES DEPARTMENT OF COMMERCE

10 Baseball, like cricket, is an elegant and leisurely summer game during which tension builds up slowly.
> Travel information booklet prepared for British tourists, quoted in NY *Times* 9 Aug 79

UNITED STATES INFORMATION AGENCY

11 Americans are achievers. They are obsessed with records of achievement in sports and they keep business achievement charts on their office walls and sports awards displayed in their homes.
> Booklet for foreign students, quoted in NY *Times* 15 Apr 85

GEORGE VECSEY

12 For about 15 minutes, Doug Flutie was the toast of New York—not just the toast but the challah and the pita and the croissants, too.
> On the day financier Donald J Trump signed Flutie to play for the New Jersey Generals, NY *Times* 28 Sep 86

JOHNNY WALKER

13 The players on the Maryland football team all made straight As. Their Bs were a little crooked.
> *Sports Illustrated* 23 Dec 85

EARL WARREN, former Chief Justice, US Supreme Court

14 I always turn to the sports page first. ... They record people's accomplishments; the front page, nothing but man's failure.
> Quoted by Marabel Morgan *Total Joy* Revell 76

GEORGE F WILL

15 It is committee meetings, called huddles, separated by outbursts of violence.
> On football, *Newsweek* 6 Sep 76

16 Scholars concede but cannot explain the amazing chemistry of Cub fans' loyalty. But their unique steadfastness through thin and thin has something to do with the team's Franciscan simplicity.
> On the Chicago Cubs, *ib* 27 Jun 77

THEATER
Actors & Actresses

TALLULAH BANKHEAD

1 Nobody can be exactly like me. Sometimes even I have trouble doing it.
News summaries 1 Jan 51

2 If you really want to help the American theater, don't be an actress, dahling. Be an audience.
ib 31 Dec 52

ETHEL BARRYMORE

3 I never let them cough. They wouldn't dare.
On control of audiences during dramatic moments, NY *Post* 7 Jun 56

INGRID BERGMAN

4 I have had my different husbands, my families. I am fond of them all and I visit them all. But deep inside me there is the feeling that I belong to show business.
Interview after opening in a Broadway play, NY *Times* 20 Apr 75

SHIRLEY BOOTH

5 Actors should be overheard, not listened to, and the audience is 50 percent of the performance.
News summaries 13 Dec 54

YUL BRYNNER

6 I am just a nice, clean-cut Mongolian boy.
Self-description, NY *Post* 24 Sep 56

7 When I am dead and buried, on my tombstone I would like to have it written, "I have arrived." Because when you feel that you have arrived, you are dead.
ib 30 Sep 56

BETTE DAVIS

8 You can't say I didn't fall for you.
To the audience after fainting on stage during Broadway opening of *Two's Company*, quoted by B D Hyman *My Mother's Keeper* Morrow 85

ALBERT FINNEY

9 To be a character who feels a deep emotion, one must go into the memory's vault and mix in a sad memory from one's own life.
International Herald Tribune 29 Mar 85

LYNN FONTANNE

10 I lied to everybody. I lie very well, being an actress, naturally.
On refusal to reveal her true age, even to her husband Alfred Lunt, NY *Times* 24 Apr 78

11 We can be bought, but we can't be bored.
On offers from Hollywood, interview on Milwaukee's WMVS TV, aired in NYC 22 Jun 80

JUDY GARLAND

12 You are never so *alone* as when you are ill on stage. The most nightmarish feeling in the world is suddenly to feel like throwing up in front of four thousand people.
Life 2 Jun 61

JOHN GIELGUD

13 Your English style will no doubt put all the other gentlemen to bed. I speak figuratively, of course.
On Cecil Beaton's decision to act in a production of *Lady Windermere's Fan*, quoted by Hugo Vickers *Cecil Beaton* Little, Brown 85

ALEC GUINNESS

14 An actor is totally vulnerable. . . . his total personality is exposed to critical judgment—his intellect, his bearing, his diction, his whole appearance. In short, his ego.
NY *Times* 17 May 64

KENNETH HAIGH

15 You need three things in the theater—the play, the actors and the audience, and each must give something.
Theatre Arts Jul 58

CEDRIC HARDWICKE

16 Actors must practice restraint, else think what might happen in a love scene.
NY *Herald Tribune* 7 Aug 64

REX HARRISON

17 Whatever it is that makes a person charming, it needs to remain a mystery ... once the charmer is aware of a mannerism or characteristic that others find charming, it ceases to be a mannerism and becomes an affectation. And good Lord, there is nothing less charming than affectations!
LA *Herald-Examiner* 24 Jun 78

HELEN HAYES

18 An actress's life is so transitory—suddenly you're a building.
On Broadway theater named in her honor, news summaries 9 Nov 55

KATHARINE HEPBURN

1 Drive on. We'll sweep up the blood later!

> To her chauffeur, on fans at a London theater, quoted by Anne Edwards *A Remarkable Woman* Morrow 85

JOSEPHINE HULL

2 Playing Shakespeare is so tiring. You never get a chance to sit down unless you're a king.

> *Time* 16 Nov 53

JACK LEMMON

3 I won't quit until I get run over by a truck, a producer or a critic.

> On returning to the stage, *Newsweek* 5 May 86

MARCEL MARCEAU

4 I have designed my style pantomimes as white ink drawings on black backgrounds, so that man's destiny appears as a thread lost in an endless labyrinth. . . . I have tried to shed some gleams of light on the shadow of man startled by his anguish.

> *Wall Street Journal* 19 Nov 65

LAURENCE OLIVIER

5 When you're a young man, Macbeth is a character part. When you're older, it's a straight part.

> On playing Macbeth at age 30 and age 48, *Theatre Arts* May 58

6 I don't know what is better than the work that is given to the actor—to teach the human heart the knowledge of itself.

> *Look* 27 Jan 70

7 I'm rather bored by the subject—meaning me. It's a sort of a yoke, but at times you know, a yoke is a kind of comfort. And it's always there.

> Interviewed at age 72, NY *Times* 27 Feb 80

8 I'd like [people] to remember me for a diligent . . . expert workman. . . . I think a poet is a workman. I think Shakespeare was a workman. And God's a workman. I don't think there's anything better than a workman.

> *Christian Science Monitor* 16 Jun 80

9 The office of drama is to exercise, possibly to exhaust, human emotions. The purpose of comedy is to tickle those emotions into an expression of light relief; of tragedy, to wound them and bring the relief of tears. Disgust and terror are the other points of the compass.

> *Confessions of an Actor* Simon & Schuster 82

10 There is a spirit in us . . . that makes our brass to blare and our cymbals crash—all, of course, supported by the practicalities of trained lung power, throat, heart, guts.

> *ib*

11 I believe in the theater; I believe in it as the first glamorizer of thought. It restores dramatic dynamics and their relations to life size.

> First address in House of Lords, 1971, *ib*

12 I believe that in a great city, or even in a small city or a village, a great theater is the outward and visible sign of an inward and probable culture.

> *ib*

13 It's just like a nursery game of make-believe.

> On the theater, *60 Minutes* CBS TV 2 Jan 83

14 Surely we have always acted; it is an instinct inherent in all of us. Some of us are better at it than others, but we all do it.

> "Olivier on Acting" NY *Times* 26 Oct 86

15 We have all, at one time or another, been performers, and many of us still are—politicians, playboys, cardinals and kings.

> *ib*

16 We ape, we mimic, we mock. We act.

> *ib*

17 The actor should be able to create the universe in the palm of his hand.

> *ib*

18 I often think that could we creep behind the actor's eyes, we would find an attic of forgotten toys and a copy of the Domesday Book.

> *ib*

19 Lead the audience by the nose to the thought.

> *ib*

20 I should be soaring away with my head tilted slightly toward the gods, feeding on the caviar of Shakespeare. . . . An actor must act.

> On resentment at his forced retirement from the stage after he was fired by Britain's National Theater, *On Acting* Simon & Schuster 86, quoted by Robert Brustein *New Republic* 3 Nov 86

21 My stage successes have provided me with the greatest moments outside myself, my film successes the best moments, professionally, within myself.

> *ib*

22 If he was lost for a moment, he would dive straight back into its honey.

> On belief that John Gielgud was infatuated with his own voice, *ib*

RALPH RICHARDSON

1 You've got to perform in a role hundreds of times. In keeping it fresh one can become a large, madly humming, demented refrigerator.
Time 21 Aug 78

2 I know he's a boring old scoutmaster on the face of it, but being that it's Shakespeare, he's the exaltation of all scoutmasters. He's the cold-bath king, and you have to glory in it.
To Laurence Olivier on title role in *Henry V*, quoted by Olivier *Confessions of an Actor* Simon & Schuster 82

3 Actors are the jockeys of literature. Others supply the horses, the plays, and we simply make them run.
Recalled on his death 10 Oct 83

4 Acting is merely the art of keeping a large group of people from coughing.
Quoted in *Time* 24 Oct 83

CYRIL RITCHARD

5 Two thousand dear ladies. All very careful and diplomatic with one another. Ever so sweet and catty, you know. I can hear that sweet-and-catty sound through the curtain while the house lights are still on. They all applaud with their gloves on, never too hard or too much. They're busier watching each other than the show.
On matinee audiences, *Holiday* Sep 60

JASON ROBARDS

6 Acting is make-believe. . . . If you make believe well enough, [audiences] make believe, too.
On being honored at Library of Congress dinner, NY *Times* 23 Jul 85

BARBRA STREISAND

7 What does it mean when people applaud? . . . Should I give 'em money? Say thank you? Lift my dress? The *lack* of applause—that I can respond to.
Life 22 May 64

8 They're called "angels" because they're in heaven until the reviews come out.
On financial backers, *Playbill* Oct 69

LAURETTE TAYLOR

9 I sometimes forget a face, but I *never* forget a back.
On meeting a man who had walked out during a performance, quoted in Clifton Fadiman comp

The Little, Brown Book of Anecdotes Little, Brown 85

SYBIL THORNDIKE

10 It's only people who are hysterical who can play hysterical parts.
On Noel Coward's stage roles, quoted by John Lahr "The Politics of Charm" *Harper's* Oct 82

PETER USTINOV

11 Critics search for ages for the wrong word, which, to give them credit, they eventually find.
BBC Radio Feb 52

12 By increasing the size of the keyhole, today's playwrights are in danger of doing away with the door.
Christian Science Monitor 14 Nov 62

13 Playwrights are like men who have been dining for a month in an Indian restaurant. After eating curry night after night, they deny the existence of asparagus.
ib

ED WYNN

14 A comedian is not a man who says funny things. A comedian is one who says things funny.
Recalled on his death, *Time* 1 Jul 66

Playwrights, Producers & Directors

MARCEL ACHARD

15 The career of a writer is comparable to that of a woman of easy virtue. You write first for pleasure, later for the pleasure of others and finally for money.
Quote 3 Jul 66

EDWARD ALBEE

16 One must let the play happen to one; one must let the mind loose to respond as it will, to receive impressions, to sense rather than know, to gather rather than immediately understand.
On his play *Tiny Alice*, quoted in *National Observer* 5 Apr 65

17 Good writers define reality; bad ones merely restate it. A good writer turns fact into truth; a bad writer will, more often than not, accomplish the opposite.
Saturday Review 4 May 66

18 A play is fiction—and fiction is fact distilled into truth.
NY *Times* 18 Sep 66

1 What people really want in the theater is fantasy involvement and not reality involvement.
Quote 4 Jun 67

JEAN ANOUILH

2 Talent is like a faucet, while it is open, one must write.
NY *Times* 2 Oct 60

3 Inspiration is a farce that poets have invented to give themselves importance.
ib

EMANUEL AZENBERG

4 This is an industry that doesn't have the common cold. . . . It has cholera.
Quoted by Samuel G Freedman "The Last of the Red-Hot Producers" NY *Times* 2 Jun 85

5 Will the theater disappear? No. Is it healthy? Also no.
ib

CECIL BEATON

6 Be daring, be different, be impractical; be anything that will assert integrity of purpose and imaginative vision against the play-it-safers, the creatures of the commonplace, the slaves of the ordinary. Routines have their purposes, but the merely routine is the hidden enemy of high art.
Advice to theatrical designers, "The Secret of How to Startle" *Theatre Arts* May 57

7 I have the *worst* ear for criticism; even when I have created a stage set I like, I *always* hear the woman in the back of the dress circle who says she doesn't like blue.
BBC TV 18 Feb 62

SAMUEL BECKETT

8 [James] Joyce was a synthesizer, trying to bring in as much as he could. I am an analyzer, trying to leave out as much as I can.
Quoted by Mel Gussow "Beckett at 75—An Appraisal" NY *Times* 19 Apr 81

9 My characters have nothing. I'm working with impotence, ignorance. . . . that whole zone of being that has always been set aside by artists as something unusable—something by definition incompatible with art.
London *Times* 10 Apr 86

BRENDAN BEHAN

10 Ninety-seven saint days a year wouldn't affect the theater, but two Yom Kippurs would ruin it.
Recalled on his death, NY *Post* 22 Mar 64

11 Critics are like eunuchs in a harem. They're there every night, they see it done every night, they see how it should be done every night, but they can't do it themselves.
Quoted by Gyles Brandreth *Great Theatrical Disasters* St Martin's 83

ALLAN CARR

12 It's *Charley's Aunt* and *The Odd Couple* rolled into one.
On his production of *La Cage aux Folles*, interview with Merv Griffin WNYW TV 15 Nov 84

JEAN COCTEAU

13 Commissions suit me. They set limits. Jean Marais dared me to write a play in which he would not speak in the first act, would weep for joy in the second and in the last would fall backward down a flight of stairs.
On *The Eagle Has Two Heads,* quoted in *Vogue* May 83

NOEL COWARD

14 *Private Lives* was described variously as "tenuous, thin, brittle, gossamer, iridescent and delightfully daring," all of which connoted to the public mind cocktails, evening dress, repartee and irreverent allusions to copulation, thereby causing a gratifying number of respectable people to queue up at the box office.
Recalled on his death 26 Mar 73

15 If you must have motivation, think of your paycheck on Friday.
Advice to actors, *ib*

16 Consider the public. . . . Never fear it nor despise it. Coax it, charm it, interest it, stimulate it, shock it now and then if you must, make it laugh, make it cry, but above all . . . never, never, never bore the living hell out of it.
Advice to playwrights, *ib*

17 Work is much more fun than fun.
ib

18 Someday I suspect, when Jesus has definitely got me for a sunbeam, my works may be adequately assessed.
Quoted by Cole Lesley *Remembered Laughter* Knopf 76

EDWARD GORDON CRAIG

19 That is what the title of artist means: one who perceives more than his fellows, and who records more than he has seen.
On the Art of the Theater Theatre Arts Books 57

BILL C DAVIS

1 Audiences cry in the theater when people make a hard choice—for life.
> On his plays *Mass Appeal* and *End Zone*, NY *Times* 30 Dec 84

HOWARD DIETZ

2 A day away from Tallulah is like a month in the country.
> On Tallulah Bankhead, news summaries 31 Dec 68

JOSEPH J DIOGUARDI

3 You can't kiss an oil well.
> On his investment in a play, NY *Times* 17 Aug 83

JAMES DUFF

4 I realized there was something I didn't quite like in myself that I didn't want to hear about.
> On expressing his feelings about the Vietnam War in *Home Front*, NY *Times* 30 Dec 84

T S ELIOT

5 My greatest trouble is getting the curtain up and down.
> On writing plays, *Time* 6 Mar 50

ZELDA FICHANDLER, Director, Arena Stage, Washington DC

6 There is a hunger to see the human presence acted out. As long as that need remains, people will find a way to do theater.
> *Christian Science Monitor* 5 Jun 86

CHRISTOPHER FRY

7 In my plays I want to look at life—at the commonplace of existence—as if we had just turned a corner and run into it for the first time.
> *Time* 20 Nov 50

8 In tragedy every moment is eternity; in comedy, eternity is a moment.
> *ib*

JOHN GOODWIN, Producer, National Theater, London

9 Theater people work by instinct. . . . I've never known a really calculated artistic decision.
> *Christian Science Monitor* 11 Feb 85

PETER HALL

10 Whoever becomes the head of the National Theater finds himself in a position like that of Nelson's Column—pigeons dump on you because you're there.
> On directing Britain's National Theater, W 6 Apr 84

TERRY HANDS, Director, Royal Shakespeare Company

11 Our contention has always been that Shakespeare is our greatest living author. If he can survive a season on Broadway, he must be.
> On production of *Much Ado about Nothing*, NY *Times* 6 Jan 85

12 My real pleasure is that 4 times a week 1,800 people are standing up and shouting on Broadway for an author who died hundreds of years ago.
> *ib*

MOSS HART

13 Charity in the theater begins and ends with those who have a play opening within a week of one's own.
> *Act One* Random House 59

BEN HECHT

14 I have written a raucous valentine to a poet's dream and agony.
> On *Winkelberg*, 1958 play based on life of his friend Maxwell Bodenheim, recalled on Hecht's death 18 Apr 64

LILLIAN HELLMAN

15 If you believe, as the Greeks did, that man is at the mercy of the gods, then you write tragedy. The end is inevitable from the beginning. But if you believe that man can solve his own problems and is at nobody's mercy, then you will probably write melodrama.
> Answering critics' complaints that her plots were melodramatic, recalled on her death 30 Jun 84

16 Tallulah was sitting in a group of people, giving the monologue she always thought was conversation.
> On Tallulah Bankhead, quoted in portrayal of Hellman by Zoe Caldwell, *Time* 27 Jan 86

SOL HUROK

17 When people don't want to come, nothing will stop them.
> On his philosophy as a producer, NY *Times* 25 Feb 69

18 The sky's the limit if you have a roof over your head.
> *ib*

1 If I would be in this business for business, I wouldn't be in this business.
ib 28 Aug 70

2 If they're not temperamental, I don't want them. It's in the nature of a great artist to be that way.
ib 6 Mar 74

WILLIAM INGE

3 Theater is, of course, a reflection of life. Maybe we have to improve life before we can hope to improve theater.
Saturday Review 22 Feb 64

GEORGE S KAUFMAN

4 They're not understudies, they're overstudies.
On substitute actors who overplay their roles, recalled on his death 2 Jun 61

5 Satire is what closes on Saturday night.
Quoted by Howard Teichmann *George S Kaufman* Atheneum 72

6 I understand your new play is full of single entendres.
Remark to Howard Dietz about his play *Between the Devil, ib*

ALAN JAY LERNER

7 We used to say that inside Cecil Beaton there was another Cecil Beaton sending out lots of little Cecils into the world. One did the sets, another did the costumes. A third took the photographs. Another put the sketches in an exhibition, then into magazines, then in a book.
Quoted by Hugo Vickers *Cecil Beaton* Little, Brown 85

CARSON McCULLERS

8 The theme is the theme of humiliation, which is the square root of sin, as opposed to the freedom from humiliation, and love, which is the square root of wonderful.
On her play *The Square Root of Wonderful*, NY *Herald Tribune* 27 Oct 57

ARTHUR MILLER

9 I know that my works are a credit to this nation and I dare say they will endure longer than the McCarran Act.
On being refused a passport for supposed disloyalty, NY *Herald Tribune* 31 Mar 54

10 A play is made by sensing how the forces in life simulate ignorance—you set free the concealed irony, the deadly joke.
Harper's Nov 60

11 The best of our theater is standing on tiptoe, striving to see over the shoulders of father and mother. The worst is exploiting and wallowing in the self-pity of adolescence and obsessive keyhole sexuality. The way out, as the poet says, is always *through*.
On *After the Fall*, quoted in *National Observer* 20 Jan 64

12 I think now that the great thing is not so much the formulation of an answer for myself, for the theater, or the play—but rather the most accurate possible statement of the problem.
ib

13 The job is to ask questions—it always was—and to ask them as inexorably as I can. And to face the absence of precise answers with a certain humility.
ib

14 Certainly the most diverse, if minor, pastime of literary life is the game of Find the Author.
Reply to charges that his former wife Marilyn Monroe was portrayed in *After the Fall*, quoted in *Life* 7 Feb 64

15 The number of elements that have to go into a hit would break a computer down. ... the right season for that play, the right historical moment, the right tonality.
On Broadway revival of *Death of a Salesman*, NY *Times* 9 May 84

16 The theater is so endlessly fascinating because it's so accidental. It's so much like life.
ib

17 I understand [Willy Loman's] longing for immortality ... Willy's writing his name in a cake of ice on a hot day, but he wishes he were writing in stone.
ib

18 If I see an ending, I can work backward.
ib 9 Feb 86

19 A playwright lives in an occupied country. ... And if you can't live that way you don't stay.
ib

20 Well, all the plays that I was trying to write ... were plays that would grab an audience by the throat and not release them, rather than presenting an emotion which you could observe and walk away from.
ib

JONATHAN MILLER

21 Being a doctor has taught me a lot about directing. ... You're doing the same thing:

You're reconstructing the manifold of behavior to the point where an audience says, yes, that's exactly like people I know.

Christian Science Monitor 1 May 86

MIKE NICHOLS

1 Opening night . . . you will find a sizable number of people with severe respiratory infections who have, it appears, defied their doctors, torn aside oxygen tents, evaded the floor nurses at various hospitals and courageously made their way to the theater to enjoy the play—the Discreet Choker and the Straight Cougher.

"Let's Hear It for (Cough) Opening Nights" NY *Times* 2 Oct 77

EDNA O'BRIEN

2 Writers really live in the mind and in hotels of the soul.

Interviewed when she brought her play *Virginia* to the US, *Vogue* Apr 85

SEAN O'CASEY

3 The hallway of every man's life is paced with pictures; pictures gay and pictures gloomy, all useful, for if we be wise, we can learn from them a richer and braver way to live.

On *Pictures in the Hallway*, NY *Times* 16 Sep 56

SEÁN O'FAOLÁIN

4 I have learned in my 30-odd years of serious writing only one sure lesson: Stories, like whiskey, must be allowed to mature in the cask.

Atlantic Dec 56

JOHN OSBORNE

5 The British public has always had an unerring taste for ungifted amateurs.

Speaking as one of the Angry Young Men of the London theater, BBC TV 18 Feb 58

HOWARD OTWAY, theater owner

6 If you have a hit, the best thing that can happen to you is having a bigger hit open next door.

Explaining that pleased playgoers tend to seek yet another evening of entertainment, NY *Times* 14 Mar 86

J B PRIESTLEY

7 I'm in the business of providing people with secondary satisfactions. It wouldn't have done me much good if they had all written their own plays, would it?

Interviewed at age 89, *Illustrated London News* Sep 84

TERENCE RATTIGAN

8 A playwright must be his own audience. A novelist may lose his readers for a few pages; a playwright never dares lose his audience for a minute.

NY *Journal-American* 29 Oct 56

WILLIAM SAROYAN

9 One of us is obviously mistaken.

To British critic who had panned his latest play, NY *Mirror* 10 Jun 60

10 The role of art is to make a world which can be inhabited.

Recalled at his Broadway memorial service, NY *Times* 31 Oct 83

GEORGE BERNARD SHAW

11 Why, except as a means of livelihood, a man should desire to act on the stage when he has the whole world to act in, is not clear to me.

Recalled on his death 2 Nov 50

12 General consultant to mankind.

Self-description, *ib*

13 The utmost I can bear for myself in my best days is that I was one of the hundred best playwrights in the world, which is hardly a supreme distinction.

Letter to W D Chase, president of US Shaw Society, *ib*

14 A drama critic is a man who leaves no turn unstoned.

Quoted in NY *Times* 5 Nov 50

15 Go on writing plays, my boy, One of these days one of these London producers will go into his office and say to his secretary, "Is there a play from Shaw this morning?" and when she says, "No," he will say, "Well, then we'll have to start on the rubbish." And that's your chance, my boy.

Advice to a young playwright, quoted by William Douglas Home *ib* 7 Oct 56

16 Am reserving two tickets for you for my première. Come and bring a friend—if you have one.

Wire inviting Winston Churchill to opening night of *Pygmalion*; Churchill wired back, "Impossible to be present for the first performance. Will attend the second—if there is one," quoted by William Manchester *The Last Lion* Little, Brown 83

NEIL SIMON

17 You must realize that honorary degrees are

given generally to people whose SAT scores were too low to get them into schools the regular way. As a matter of fact, it was my SAT scores that led me into my present vocation in life, comedy.

> On receiving an honorary degree, NY *Times* 4 Jun 84

1 Everyone thinks they can write a play; you just write down what happened to you. But the art of it is drawing from all the moments of your life.

> *ib* 24 Mar 85

2 I felt like writing about a time when I was probably, and I think all of us are, the happiest in our lives—before the obligations start in.

> On his play *Brighton Beach Memoirs, ib* 25 Jan 87

WOLE SOYINKA

3 [It] takes a jaundiced view of the much-vaunted glorious past of Africa. And I suppose since then I've been doing nothing but the danse macabre in this political jungle of ours.

> On his play *A Dance of the Forests,* recalled on winning Nobel Prize, NY *Times* 17 Oct 86

ROGER L STEVENS, Chairman, Kennedy Center for the Performing Arts, Washington DC

4 A quarter of the time I have big hits, a quarter of the time artistic successes, a quarter of the time the critics were crazy and a quarter of the time I was crazy.

> Quoted in NY *Times* 7 Oct 85

TOM STOPPARD

5 Skill without imagination is craftsmanship and gives us many useful objects such as wickerwork picnic baskets. Imagination without skill gives us modern art.

> News summaries 31 Dec 72

JAMES THURBER

6 We are a nation that has always gone in for the loud laugh, the wow, the belly laugh and the dozen other labels for the roll-'em-in-the-aisles gagerissimo. This is the kind of laugh that delights actors, directors and producers, but dismays writers of comedy because it is the laugh that often dies in the lobby.

> "The Quality of Mirth" NY *Times* 21 Feb 60

7 The appreciative smile, the chuckle, the soundless mirth, so important to the success of comedy, cannot be understood unless one sits among the audience and feels the warmth created by the quality of laughter that the audience takes home with it.

> *ib*

GORE VIDAL

8 A talent for drama is not a talent for writing, but is an ability to articulate human relationships.

> NY *Times* 17 Jun 56

9 The theater needs continual reminders that there is nothing more debasing than the work of those who do well what is not worth doing at all.

> *Newsweek* 25 Mar 68

10 Each writer is born with a repertory company in his head. Shakespeare has perhaps 20 players, and Tennessee Williams has about 5, and Samuel Beckett one—and maybe a clone of that one. I have 10 or so, and that's a lot. As you get older, you become more skillful at casting them.

> Dallas *Times-Herald* 18 Jun 78

11 Some writers take to drink, others take to audiences.

> NY *Times* 12 Mar 81

DAVID WATSON, director, Sharon CT summer playhouse

12 It's for that little bit of Judy Garland and Mickey Rooney in all of us.

> On summer stock, NY *Times* 18 Jun 84

THORNTON WILDER

13 Many plays—certainly mine—are like blank checks. The actors and directors put their own signatures on them.

> NY *Mirror* 13 Jul 56

14 A dramatist is one who believes that the pure event, an action involving human beings, is more arresting than any comment that can be made upon it.

> Quoted in Malcolm Cowley ed *Writers at Work* Viking 58

15 On the stage it is always *now*; the personages are standing on that razor edge, between the past and the future, which is the essential character of conscious being; the words are rising to their lips in immediate spontaneity . . . The theater is supremely fitted to say: "Behold! These things are."

> *ib*

16 I am not interested in the ephemeral—such subjects as the adulteries of dentists. I am in-

terested in those things that repeat and repeat and repeat in the lives of the millions.
NY *Times* 6 Nov 61

TENNESSEE WILLIAMS

1 My own creed as a playwright is fairly close to that expressed by the painter in Shaw's play *The Doctor's Dilemma*, "I believe in Michelangelo, Velásquez and Rembrandt; in the might of design, the mystery of color, the redemption of all things by beauty everlasting and the message of art that has made these hands blessed. Amen."
Afterword to his 1953 play *Camino Real*

2 Some mystery should be left in the revelation of character in a play, just as a great deal of mystery is always left in the revelation of character in life, even in one's own character to himself.
Stage directions for *Cat on a Hot Tin Roof* New Directions 55

3 If the writing is honest it cannot be separated from the man who wrote it.
Preface to William Inge *The Dark at the Top of the Stairs* Random House 58

4 I have found it easier to identify with the characters who verge upon hysteria, who were frightened of life, who were desperate to reach out to another person. But these seemingly fragile people are the strong people really.
NY *Times* 18 Mar 65

5 Most of the confidence which I appear to feel, especially when influenced by noon wine, is only a pretense.
"I Am Widely Regarded as the Ghost of a Writer" *ib* 8 May 77

6 Maybe they weren't punks at all, but New York drama critics.
On being mugged in Key West FL, *People* 7 May 79

7 This country of endured but unendurable pain.
On the emotional environment of his characters, whether they live in New Orleans, St Louis or abroad, NY *Times* 18 May 86

P G WODEHOUSE

8 Has anybody ever seen a dramatic critic in the daytime? Of course not. They come out after dark, up to no good.
NY *Mirror* 27 May 55

Observers & Critics

BROOKS ATKINSON

9 It seems not to have been written. It is the quintessence of life. It is the basic truth.
On Tennessee Williams's *Cat on a Hot Tin Roof*, NY *Times* 25 Mar 55

10 Good plays drive bad playgoers crazy.
Theatre Arts Aug 56

11 In the 1920s dramatists attacked their subjects as if the inequities could be resolved. Some of the traditional optimism of America lurked behind most of the early plays. But not now. There is no conviction now that the problem will be solved.
The Lively Years Association Press 73

12 Ethel Waters, the flaming tower of dusky regality, who knows how to make a song stand on tiptoe.
Recalled on her death 1 Sep 77

13 There is no joy so great as that of reporting that a good play has come to town.
Recalled on his death 13 Jan 84

PHYLLIS BATTELLE

14 A reporter discovers, in the course of many years of interviewing celebrities, that most actors are more attractive behind a spotlight than over a spot of tea.
NY *Journal-American* 30 Apr 61

ERIC BENTLEY

15 A play has two authors, the playwright and the actor.
NY State Theater Program Jun 66

JOHN MASON BROWN

16 Among the Round Tablers [at the Algonquin Hotel],Sherwood stood out like a grandfather's clock. The tick of his talk was measured, his words seeming to be spaced by minutes, but when he chimed he struck gaily.
The Worlds of Robert E. Sherwood Harper and Row 65

17 The more one has seen of the good, the more one asks for the better.
"More Than 1,001 First Nights" *Saturday Review* 29 Aug 65

18 The critic is a man who prefers the indolence of opinion to the trials of action.
Town & Country May 66

ANATOLE BROYARD

1 There is something about seeing *real people* on a stage that makes a bad play more intimately, more personally offensive than any other art form.

> NY*Times* 6 Feb 76

VINCENT CANBY

2 Miss Dietrich is not so much a performer as a one-woman environment.

> On Marlene Dietrich's first Broadway appearance, NY *Times* 10 Oct 67

JAY CARR

3 [*The Front Page*] is still full of peppy banter as it sends its seedy knights after cheap scoops.

> On Broadway revival of Ben Hecht and Charles MacArthur's 58-year-old play, Boston *Globe* 4 Dec 86

MARC CHAGALL

4 I adore the theater and I am a painter. I think the two are made for a marriage of love. I will give all my soul to prove this once more.

> On painting new ceiling for the Paris Opéra, *Newsweek* 14 Oct 63

JOHN CHAPMAN

5 It is three and a half hours long, four characters wide and a cesspool deep.

> On Edward Albee's *Who's Afraid of Virginia Woolf?* NY *Daily News* 15 Oct 62

HAROLD CLURMAN

6 From the holocausts of the day he lights his own flaming torch. It illuminates what we are, what we have wrought, what we must renounce.

> On Jean Genet, recalled on Genet's death, NY *Times* 16 Apr 86

JEAN COCTEAU

7 There are too many souls of wood not to love those wooden characters who do indeed have a soul.

> On marionettes, NY *Times* 15 Feb 87

RICHARD CORLISS

8 By dint of dogged charisma, Brynner has identified himself with a role more than any other actor since Bela Lugosi hung up his fangs.

> On Yul Brynner's performance as the king of Siam in a revival of a role he first played in 1951, *Time* 21 Jan 85

9 Mausoleum air and anguished pauses: If this production were a poem, it would be mostly white space.

> On Max Stafford-Clark's direction of Michael Hastings's *Tom and Viv, ib* 25 Feb 85

10 [Michael Hastings] has composed a dirge to incompatibility, which, because it raises expectations only to defeat them, leaves a taste of exhumed ashes.

> *ib*

ROBERTSON DAVIES

11 The drama may be called that part of theatrical art which lends itself most readily to intellectual discussion: what is left is theater.

> *A Voice in the Attic* Knopf 60

MAUREEN DOWD

12 They have been painting the barn red and white . . ... chasing skunks from the stage, clearing bird nests from the spotlights, scraping mildew from costumes and very gingerly, in the manner of city slickers, shooing snakes out of the yard.

> On managers of summer theaters, NY *Times* 18 Jun 84

13 It is empty and dark now, with green paint covering the windows, and a jagged hole where the orchestra once played, and cats roaming after rats, and plaster everywhere. But the imagination dances back 70 years to scenes of Fanny Brice introducing "Secondhand Rose" and Eddie Cantor mugging his way through "Makin' Whoopee" and Will Rogers cracking wise.

> On Manhattan's New Amsterdam Theater, *ib* 2 Aug 84

HELEN DUDAR

14 She saw *Death of a Salesman* from the balcony. From the evidence of her essay, it was close enough.

> On Mimi Kramer, who lost her theater press pass because of her acerbic criticism. *Wall Street Journal* 9 Jul 84

RICHARD EDER

15 A prettiness mummified by years of chalk dust.

> On Estelle Parson's portrayal of a schoolteacher in *Miss Margarida's Way*, NY *Times* 1 Aug 77

16 This sentimental comedy by the Soviet playwright Aleksei Arbuzov is said to have had a great success in its own country. So do fringed lamp shades.

> On *Do You Turn Somersaults? ib* 10 Jan 78

ANNE EDWARDS

1 She represented the distilled essence of the battle between the sexes.

On Katharine Hepburn in her early Broadway performances. *A Remarkable Woman* Morrow 85

T S ELIOT

2 I must say Bernard Shaw is greatly improved by music.

On being asked by Rex Harrison for his opinion of the opening night performance of *My Fair Lady,* recalled by Robert Giroux NY *Times* 21 Dec 84

SAMUEL G FREEDMAN

3 When St Genesius, the patron saint of actors, refused to act in a Roman play that ridiculed Christianity, the legend goes, the producers executed him. It reminds some people of Broadway today.

NY *Times* 29 Dec 83

WILLIAM E GEIST

4 George, a camel, stepped on the foot of a Rockette; six sheep came off the elevator as three kings bearing gifts got on; human Christmas trees bumped into eight maids-a-milking at the water cooler and an elf came down with the flu.

On the day "pandemonium paid a visit backstage" at opening of Radio City Music Hall's Christmas spectacular. NY *Times* 29 Nov 86

5 Scrooge pushed past Mary number 1 and Joseph number 2 in the wings without so much as an "excuse me". Typical.

ib

BRENDAN GILL

6 If it were better, it wouldn't be as good.

On *Butterflies Are Free* by Leonard Gersche, *New Yorker* 1 Nov 69

7 Of . . . plays by authors of high reputation and of the most serious dramaturgic intentions. [*The Iceman Cometh*] is *the* most boring play ever written. [But] immediately after *The Iceman Cometh,* O'Neill sat down and wrote "Long Day's Journey Into Night". It is easily the greatest play written in English in my lifetime.

On Eugene O'Neill's plays, *ib* 7 Oct 85

STANLEY GREEN

8 They were not merely quipsters and storytell-ers, nor were they only song and dance entertainers. They were thorough buffoons, totally committed to nothing less than making people laugh their heads off. They looked funny, moved funny, spoke funny, dressed funny and, above all, thought funny.

The Great Clowns of Broadway Oxford 84, quoted in *Christian Science Monitor* 20 Dec 84

9 They didn't portray comic characters, they *were* comic characters.

ib

MEL GUSSOW

10 Though the clown is often deadpan, he is a connoisseur of laughter.

On Avner Eisenberg in his one-man show *Avner the Eccentric,* NY *Times* 21 Sep 84

11 Genet was . . . an actor in the play of his life, putting on masks, rearranging facts to suit his purpose and clouding himself in mystique.

On Jean Genet, *ib* 16 Apr 86

DASHIELL HAMMETT

12 The truth is you don't like the theater except the times when you're in a room by yourself putting the play on paper.

To Lillian Hellman, recalled on her death 30 Jun 84

JOHN HARVEY

13 Inevitably, a dramatist writes one play, his director interprets another, the actors perform a third and the public sees a fourth and an altogether different one.

Preface to *Anouilh, A Study in Theatrics* Yale 64

WILLIAM A HENRY III

14 A poet laureate of adolescent sexuality and middle-age longing.

On William Inge, *Time* 23 Jul 83

15 The title refers to the wife's calling for a lost puppy, yet it is clear that hers is in truth a *cri de cœur* for the unassuageable pain of growing old before she has even grown up.

On Inge's *Come Back, Little Sheba, ib*

16 Inge did not transform his characters: They end where they began. But he understood them. In their interplay was genuine life, often blunted but ever resilient.

ib

17 What you get is first-draft Neil Simon.

On interviewing the playwright, noted for producing many drafts of his plays, *ib* 15 Dec 86

DAVID RICHARD JONES

1 Starting with its title, everything about this play is designed to crack the spectator on the jaw, then douse him with ice-cold water, then force him to assess intelligently what has happened to him, then give him a kick ... then bring him to his senses again.

> On Peter Brook's production of Peter Weiss's *Marat/Sade*, quoted by Robert Brustein NY *Times* 27 Jul 86

T E KALEM

2 He sometimes ran a purple ribbon through his typewriter and gushed where he should have dammed.

> On Tennessee Williams, *Time* 7 Mar 83

WALTER KERR

3 Wherever it came from, the musical came with its hair mussed and with an innocent, indolent, irreverent look on its bright, bland face.

> On musical comedy, NY *Herald Tribune* 1 Sep 63

4 Reviewers ... must normally function as huff-and-puff artists blowing laggard theatergoers stageward.

> 1975 statement quoted in NY *Times* 30 Sep 83

DENA KLEIMAN

5 A virtually uninterrupted duet of seduction, an exquisitely choreographed collage of tickling, kneeling, lounging, smoking, reading, sliding, leaping, posing, massaging, pushing, shaking, pulling, bouncing, tugging, stretching, crawling, limping, yanking, waving—not to mention singing as well.

> On *Me and My Girl*, "A Pas de Deux of Flirting and Fun" NY *Times* 18 Aug 86

JOHN DAVID KLEIN

6 I saw this show under adverse circumstances—my seat was facing the stage.

> On *Three Guys Naked from the Waist Down*, WNET TV 5 Feb 85

STEWART KLEIN

7 I have seen stronger plots than this in a cemetery.

> On *Break a Leg*, WNYW TV 29 Apr 79

JAN KOTT

8 When I met Genet I could not conceive of him as the author of his plays. He looks like a terrified baby.

> On Jean Genet, NY *Times* 2 Feb 85

PIA LINDSTROM

9 *Tom and Viv* is a literary whodunit and a medical what-did-it.

> On Michael Hastings's *Tom and Viv*, about T S Eliot and the illness of his first wife, NBC TV 6 Feb 85

ANITA LOOS

10 Tallulah never bored anyone, and I consider that humanitarianism of a very high order indeed.

> Eulogy for Tallulah Bankhead, NY *Times* 17 Dec 68

DONALD MALCOLM

11 [It is] a genuine delight to those amiable qualities that thrive best when the critical sense is out to lunch.

> On *Little Mary Sunshine* in an off-Broadway production, *New Yorker* 28 Nov 59

JAMES McCOURT

12 A kind of cross between Helen Traubel and Martha Raye ... an uncanny amalgam of Joan Sutherland and Phyllis Diller.

> On Anna Russell, NY *Times* 15 Dec 85

ROBERT D McFADDEN

13 Tall, bald, and pouch-eyed, with a velvet voice, a droll wit and the face of a cunning bloodhound ... a performer who made audiences twitter and roar with subtle ease.

> On Alastair Sim, NY *Times* 21 Aug 76

JOHN McPHEE

14 A tympanic resonance, so rich and overpowering that it could give an air of verse to a recipe for stewed hare.

> On Richard Burton, recalled on Burton's death 5 Aug 84

TED MORGAN

15 A round ball of a man with protruding lower lip and seal-colored eyes, [he] spun like a top from continent to continent, jabbing a pudgy forefinger at everything that stood in his way.

> On Charles Frohman, developer of the "star system," "*Maugham* Simon & Schuster 80

16 It is less artificial than his other comedies. The epigrams do not seem to have been added on like candied cherries on a cake.

> On Somerset Maugham's 1921 play *The Circle*, *ib*

SHERIDAN MORLEY

1 There is something remarkably and peculiarly English about the passion for sitting on damp seats watching open-air drama . . . only the English have mastered the art of being truly uncomfortable while facing up to culture.

London *Times* 18 Jun 83

2 Her education was erratic, though she learned to add by counting the nightly box-office takings.

On Helen Hayes, *ib* 19 Dec 84

GEORGE JEAN NATHAN

3 [It is] bosh sprinkled with mystic cologne.

On T S Eliot's *The Cocktail Party*, quoted in Charles Angoff ed *The World of George Jean Nathan* Knopf 52

4 So long as there is one pretty girl left on the stage, the professional undertakers may hold up their burial of the theater.

Theatre Arts Jul 58

NEW YORKER

5 [It is] a comedy that verges on autohagiography, the hero being the author.

Review of Neil Simon's *Biloxi Blues*, 28 Oct 85

BENEDICT NIGHTINGALE

6 [William Inge]handles symbolism rather like an Olympic weight lifter, raising it with agonizing care, brandishing it with a tiny grunt of triumph, then dropping it with a terrible clang.

On Broadway revival of *Come Back, Little Sheba*, NY *Times* 29 Jul 84

GEORGES POMPIDOU, PRESIDENT OF FRANCE

7 He imitated me so well that I couldn't stand myself any longer.

On impersonation by satirist Thierry Le Luron, recalled on Le Luron's death, NY *Times* 14 Nov 86

FRANK RICH

8 As synthetic and padded as the transvestites' cleavage.

On *La Cage aux Folles*, NY *Times* 22 Aug 83

9 The actor doesn't merely command the stage, he seems to own it by divine right.

On Richard Burton's revival of *Camelot* role he created in 1960, recalled on Burton's death, *ib* 6 Aug 84

10 Yul Brynner's performance in *The King and I* . . . can no longer be regarded as a feat of acting or even endurance. After 30-odd years . . . Mr Brynner is, quite simply, The King.

On opening night of Brynner's farewell engagement in the title role he created in 1951, *ib* 8 Jan 85

11 There's something endearingly crackpot about this play—it speaks to us from the century's boom time, when our culture, like the author, was at once naive and inordinately ambitious.

On revival of Eugene O'Neill's *Strange Interlude*, *ib* 22 Feb 85

12 The playwright starts off angry, soon becomes furious and then skyrockets into sheer rage.

On Larry Kramer's *The Normal Heart*, about AIDS, *ib* 22 Apr 85

13 Lillian Hellman brought out the knee-jerk in almost everyone.

ib 13 Nov 86

14 A confusing jamboree of piercing noise, routine roller-skating, misogyny and Orwellian special effects, *Starlight Express* is the perfect gift for the kid who has everything except parents.

ib 16 Mar 87

ELEANOR ROOSEVELT

15 An excellent play . . . but I have no feeling of reality about it. It had no more to do with me than the man in the moon.

On *Sunrise at Campobello*, about her family in the 1920s, *Theatre Arts* Apr 58

RICHARD SCHICKEL

16 Memory is the personal journalism of the soul.

On Harold Pinter's plays, *Time* 23 Jan 84

RICHARD SEVERO

17 [Monty] Woolley reduced the nurse in *The Man Who Came to Dinner* to the potency of a pound of wet Kleenex. It was probably the best thing that had happened to the art of the insult since the Medicis stopped talking in the 16th century.

NY *Herald Tribune* 7 May 63

JOEL SIEGEL

18 His Texas accent doesn't come closer than Perth Amboy.

On Carroll O'Connor in *Home Front*, WNYW TV 2 Jan 85

JOHN SIMON

19 Diana Rigg is built like a brick mausoleum with insufficient flying buttresses.

On nude scene in *Abelard and Heloise*, New York 15 May 70

1 Like springs, adaptations can only go downhill.

On Broadway production of *Singin' in the Rain*, *ib* 15 Jul 85

MERVYN STOCKWOOD, BISHOP OF SOUTHWARK, ENGLAND

2 As boring as a boarding school on bath night.

On nudity in *Oh! Calcutta*, London *Sunday Times* 2 Nov 80

DAN SULLIVAN

3 She presents no beauty but the memory of beauty, sustained by cosmetics, clever lighting, good health and will power ... At times she seems to join the audience in watching the image she is creating, and she winks a little as if to say: not bad.

On Broadway appearance by Marlene Dietrich, NY *Times* 4 Oct 68

TIME MAGAZINE

4 While tragedy moves from sanity toward madness, comedy moves from madness toward sanity. In his pride, the tragic hero overreaches human limits and dies. In his folly, the comic hero ludicrously pounds his head against those limits, is brought to his senses and lives.

22 Jan 65

5 The measuring out of life in tepid teacups.

On contemporary English drama, 26 Mar 65

6 Man, as they see him, is a creature trapped between two voids, prenatal and posthumous, on a shrinking spit of sand he calls time.

On European dramatists such as Beckett, Ionesco, Genet, Pinter and Osborne, "The Modern Theater, or the World as a Metaphor of Dread" 8 Jul 66

KENNETH TYNAN

7 A good many inconveniences attend playgoing in any large city, but the greatest of them is usually the play itself.

NY *Herald Tribune* 17 Feb 57

8 The sheer complexity of writing a play always had dazzled me. In an effort to understand it, I became a critic.

NY *Mirror* 6 Jun 63

9 No theater could sanely flourish until there was an umbilical connection between what was happening on the stage and what was happening in the world.

Recalled on his death 26 Jul 80

E B WHITE

10 The critic leaves at curtain fall
To find, in starting to review it,
He scarcely saw the play at all
For starting to review it.

NY *Times* 19 Sep 65

Index by Sources

Index by Subjects and Key Lines

monarchy of, 195:20
National Theater, 343:10
Oxford, 169:4
Parliament of, 19:18, 195:17
party system in, 34:8
people of, 164:12, 183:16, 205:8, 284:18, 300:6,
    317:18, 345:5, 351:1
prime minister of, 18:13, 46:8, 49:17, 52:18
Profumo Affair in, 10:8, 52:18
Royal Ballet, 293:11
royal family of, 22:11, 236:6, 239:2, 311:4, 313:10
royal yacht, 160:2
Stonehenge, 168:14
telephone booths, 165:3
television in, 321:10
tennis in, 334:11
theater in, 352:5
unemployment in, 10:12
in United Nations, 54:1–3, 54:5, 55:16, 59:15
upper class in, 177:1
and World War II, 2:19–20, 3:1
See also British Broadcasting Corporation; British
    Commonwealth; London, England; Scotland
"greatest week in the history of the world," 12:3
"great Satan," 9:10
Great Society, 7:7, 40:10
Great Train Robbery, 94:8
Greece, 54:15
    food of, 255:7
    Parthenon in, 226:10
Greeley, Andrew, 275:3
Greene, Graham, 283:16
greenmail, 120:14
Greenstreet, Sydney, 247:3
greeting cards, 151:7
Grenada, 46:13
grief, 175:4, 179:14, 182:13, 204:19
Grissom, Virgil I, 151:7
Gromyko, Andrei A, 55:6
"group therapy for the world," 56:1
grudges, 296:5
"grumbling is the death of love," 184:9
grunts, 66:12
Gucci, 165:18
guilty conscience, 259:7
guitar, 289:21–22
    jazz, 285:18
Gulf of Tonkin, 7:8
gunpowder, 214:9
guns, 4:20, 23:16
    controls on, 16:11
"guns are neat little things," 96:11
gymnastics, 331:1
"gynecologist of the airways," 320:5

habits, 197:1
Hagler, Marvin, 329:14
hair, 85:10, 101:3, 141:7, 141:14, 237:3
    dressing, 241:7
    gray, 202:18
    style, 236:9

Haiti, 4:15–17, 28:1
"half tiger, half poet," 288:9
Hamptons, Long Island, 225:3
hand, 40:4
"handbag economist," 27:3
handicapped, rights of, 82:8–9, 87:11
hangover, 193:18
Hanson, John K, 112:6
happiness, 116:6, 145:10, 195:8, 203:21, 210:12,
    213:9, 214:17, 217:13, 253:7
    in marriage, 236:5
    pursuit of, 2:14
    secret of, 217:2
"hardening of the paragraphs," 267:13
"hardest unpaid job in the world," 24:10
Harding, Warren G, 201:2
"harmless little eccentricity of ours," 300:15
harp, 290:19
harpsichord, 285:18
Harris, Jean, 75:4–5
Hart, Gary, 42:1, 52:11
Harvard Law Review, 309:15
Harvard University, 8:3, 31:4, 116:9, 121:15, 122:17,
    127:11, 127:13, 132:7, 132:12–13, 133:6, 135:5
Hastings, Michael, 348:9–10, 350:9
hate, 186:1, 204:2, 210:20, 300:10
hats
    men's, 237:5
    of Queen Elizabeth II, 236:6
"have you no sense of decency, sir, at long last?"
    51:16
Hawkins, Paula, 45:9
hawks and doves, 19:11, 20:9
Hawn, Goldie, 247:4
Hayes, Helen, 351:2
headaches, migraine, 138:11
health, 103:14, 109:12, 118:1, 141:11, 142:9, 187:9
    See also medical care
heart, 142:2, 340:6
    artificial, 138:9–10, 142:16, 144:2
    broken, 183:12–13, 218:20, 221:16
    disease, 139:9
    surgery, 140:12
    transplants, 136:14, 141:3
"he is a national hero," 17:2
Helen Trent, soap opera, 326:4
Helga. See Testorf, Helga
helicopters, 163:8
"he likes to go around bombing," 62:16
hell, 190:4, 218:6
Heller, Joseph, 276:17
"hell is other people," 217:16
Hellman, Lillian, 279:17, 349:12, 351:13
"help and support of the woman I love," 184:14
Hemingway, Ernest, 263:1, 275:5
"he outsells Jesus!" 302:17
Hepburn, Katharine, 242:20, 244:16, 349:1
"here I don't go again," 36:10
heroes, 174:5, 206:3, 208:14, 217:5
    war, 198:4
"he spoke of love and the Supreme Court," 183:14
heterosexuality, 97:6, 145:2

terrorists, 2:11, 16:8, 313:16–17, 37:11, 47:9, 58:2,
        65:13, 164:3
    Arab, 38:12
    in Berlin, 16:17
    dealing with, 57:11
    in Middle East, 51:12
    negotiations with, 23:9
    Palestinian, 14:18
Testorf, Helga, 233:1
Texas, 46:1
    football teams in, 338:2
    Houston, 166:9
    legislature, 30:6
    University of, 95:16
thankfulness, 191:13
"thank God it's Monday," 177:4
Tharp, Louise Hall, 274:13
Thatcher, Margaret, 27:3, 32:4, 34:4, 34:14–15, 39:1,
        39:12, 46:11, 47:12, 48:14–15
"that's not writing, that's typing," 274:16
"that's the way it is," 315:11
"that was the order of the day," 61:6
theater, 339:1–352:10
    actors and actresses, 240:14
    adaptations, 352:1
    audience, 339:2, 339:3, 339:15, 342:16, 343:1,
        344:21, 345:1, 346:7, 346:11, 347:10
    Broadway shows, 251:5
    buildings, 226:1
    costume design, 236:12, 291:15
    critics, 341:11, 342:11, 343:15, 345:9, 345:14,
        346:4, 347:6, 347:8, 350:4, 352:10
    designers, 342:6
    directors, 341:15–347:8
    financial backers, 341:8, 343:3
    matinee audience, 341:5
    Me and My Girl, 350:5
    musical, 289:6, 350:3
    Normal Heart, The, 351:12
    Oh! Calcutta, 352:2
    open-air, 351:1
    Pictures in the Hallway, 345:3
    plots, 350:7
    Private Lives, 342:14
    producers, 288:18, 341:15–347:8
    Strange Interlude, 351:11
    summer stock, 346:12, 348:12
    Sunrise at Campobello, 351:15
    Three Guys Naked from the Waist Down, 350:6
    Tiny Alice, 341:16
    tragedy, 343:8, 343:15, 352:4
theft and thieves, 92:12–13, 93:3, 93:14–17, 94:5–6,
        94:8, 95:15, 96:16–17, 98:9, 99:16, 101:6–7,
        102:4, 103:2–3
    of towels, 159:12
theology, 187:9
"theory of relatives," 244:13
"there, but for the grace of God, goes God," 244:2
"these proceedings are closed," 63:12
"they can gas me, but I am famous," 101:15
"thin, tinny 'arf,' " 52:15
thirties, 200:10

Thompson, Dorothy, 309:10
Thompson, Tommy, 304:16
Three Guys Naked from the Waist Down, 350:6
Thurber, James, 283:19
tiaras, 163:13
"ticket to one's own funeral," 270:4
Tiffany glass, 165:18
"tightrope over the abyss," 21:8
time, 150:1, 204:1, 221:12
Time magazine, 303:16–17, 311:15
    libel suit against, 78:12, 305:4
"time of scoundrels," 34:7
"tin-can architecture in a tin-horn culture," 227:7
Tiny Alice, 341:16
"tiny and enclosed fraternity of privileged men,"
        320:1
toastmaster, 202:3
tobacco industry, 142:10
    See also smoking
"to be loose with grammar," 123:3
"today's gossip is tomorrow's headline," 302:12
tomorrow, 216:11, 303:8
Tonkin, Gulf of, 7:8
"too old for a paper route . . . too tired for an affair,"
        297:2
"toothpaste is out of the tube," 33:14
topless restaurants, 252:2
"torch has been passed," 8:6
"torture a typewriter until it screams," 263:8
"tossed its cap over the wall of space," 155:5
totalitarian regimes, 7:14
toupee, 193:17
tour, escorted, 160:10
    Thomas Cook, 163:4
tourists, American
    in Great Britain, 165:4
    See also travel
towns, small, 174:8, 221:15
    deteriorating, 225:2
"toy food . . . serve it to toy people," 249:4
track, 328:10, 330:12, 332:6
trade
    with Canada, 11:16
    deficit, 29:14
tradition, 214:1
traffic, automobile, 149:11
tragedy, 209:6, 219:9, 343:8, 343:15, 352:4
    in drama. See theater
trains. See railroad
traitor, 34:7
tranquilizers, 148:5
"Tranquillity base here," 152:2
transsexualism, 141:12
Trappist monks, 190:11, 264:16–17
travel, 159:11–170:2
    by air, 160:6, 161:7, 163:11, 163:3
    in America, 160:4, 160:12
    armchair, 163:16
    by automobile, 180:4
    books, 281:7
    by bus, 160:2
    in China, 161:3